S0-ACC-739

Time Out

Miami

Orlando & South Florida

Penguin Books

PENGUIN BOOKS

Published by the Penguin Group
Penguin Books Ltd, 27 Wrights Lane, London W8 5TZ, England
Penguin Books USA Inc., 375 Hudson Street, New York, New York 10014, USA
Penguin Books Australia Ltd, Ringwood, Victoria, Australia
Penguin Books Canada Ltd, 10 Alcorn Avenue, Toronto, Ontario, Canada M4V 3B2
Penguin Books (NZ) Ltd, 182-190 Wairau Road, Auckland 10, New Zealand

Penguin Books Ltd, Registered Offices: Harmondsworth, Middlesex, England

First published 1997
10 9 8 7 6 5 4 3 2 1

Copyright © Time Out Group Ltd, 1997
All rights reserved

Colour reprographics by Precise Litho, 34-35 Great Sutton Street, London EC1
Mono reprographics, printed and bound by William Clowes Ltd, Beccles, Suffolk NR34 9QE

Except in the United States of America, this book is sold subject to the condition that it shall not, by way of trade or
otherwise, be lent, re-sold, hired out, or otherwise circulated without the publisher's prior consent in any form of binding
or cover other than that in which it is published and without a similar condition including this condition being imposed
on the subsequent purchaser.

Edited and designed by

Time Out Magazine Limited
Universal House
251 Tottenham Court Road
London W1P 0AB
Tel: 0171 813 3000
Fax: 0171 813 6001
E-mail guides@timeout.co.uk
http://www.timeout.co.uk

Editorial

Managing Editor Peter Fiennes
Editor Ruth Jarvis
Consultant Editor Eugene Patron
Orlando Consultant Richard J Grula
Copy Editor Cath Phillips
Listings Editor Nina Korman
Indexer Jackie Brind

Design

Art Director Warren Beeby
Associate Art Director John Oakey
Art Editor Paul Tansley
Designer Mandy Martin
Design assistant Wayne Davies
Picture Editor Catherine Hardcastle
Picture Researcher Michaela Freeman

Advertising

Group Advertisement Director Lesley Gill
Sales Director Mark Phillips
Advertisment Sales (Florida) JCI New York

Administration

Publisher Tony Elliott
Managing Director Mike Hardwick
Financial Director Kevin Ellis
Marketing Director Gillian Auld
Production Manager Mark Lamond
Accountant Catherine Bowen

Features in this guide were written and researched by:

Introduction Alexander Stuart. **Essential Information** Ruth Jarvis, Matthew Duersten (*Habla usted Spanglish?* Nina Korman). **Getting Around** Bonnie Brower (*Electric Avenue* Ruth Jarvis). **Miami by Season** Nina Korman. **Sightseeing** Gretchen Schmidt (*If you've only got two days...* Ruth Jarvis). **Accommodation** Nina Korman. **Orientation** Eugene Patron, Ruth Jarvis. **The Beaches** Laura Kelly. **Downtown** Timothy Schmand. **Coral Gables** Nina Korman. **Coconut Grove** Nina Korman. **Little Havana** Judy Cantor. **Little Haiti & the Design District** Leslie Casimir. **History** Tony Thompson. **Miami Today** Timothy Schmand (*Miami Crime* Emily Compston, *Miami by Numbers* Ruth Jarvis). **Latin Miami** Eduardo Aparicio. **Architecture** Eugene Patron. **Restaurants & Cafés** Lesley Abravanel. **Bars** Todd Anthony. **Shopping & Services** Cyn Zarco. **Clubs** Lesley Abravanel (sex clubs Todd Anthony). **Film** Todd Anthony. **Museums & Galleries** Judy Cantor. **Media** Tony Thompson. **Music** Todd Anthony (Classical; Rock, Roots & Jazz), Judy Cantor (Latin). **Sport & Fitness** Todd Anthony. **Theatre & Dance** Pamela Gordon. **Gay & Lesbian** Eugene Patron. **Business** Tony Thompson (*Getting online* Ruth Jarvis). **Children** Pamela Gordon. **Survival** Tony Thompson (*Gator life, Working the cruise liners* Eugene Patron). **Getting Started** Bonnie Brower (*Fantasy islands* Eugene Patron). **The Everglades** Eugene Patron. **Fort Lauderdale & Palm Beach** Mark Agnew. **The Florida Keys** Emily Compston. **Orlando & Walt Disney World** Richard J Grula. **The Gulf Coast** David J Wilson. **Cuba** Keith Richards. **Further Reading** Ruth Jarvis, Eugene Patron.

The editors would like to thank the following:

Michael Aller at the City of Miami Beach Tourism Liaison, Billie at STA Travel, Hilary Bower, Doug DeWitt at the Avalon, Katy O'Dowd, Dilip at Kingsbury Electronics, Katy Harris, Phil Harriss, Mimi Korman, José Lima at the Greater Miami & the Beaches Convention & Visitors Bureau, Orlando/Orange County Convention & Visitors Bureau, Ben McAlister, Julian Prokaza at *What PC?*, Caro Taverne, Andrew Tuck.

Maps by JS Graphics, Hill View Cottage, 17 Beadles Lane, Old Oxted, Surrey RH8 9JG.

Photography by **Charlie Varley** except for: page 170 courtesy of the **George Adams Gallery**/New York; 93 **Eduardo Aparicio**; 187 **Allsport**; 78, 80, 81, 83, 85, 87, 96, 199, 261 **Corbis**; 23, 63 **Greater Miami CVB**; 89 **Arthur Harvey/Frank Spooner Pictures**; 267 **Katinka Herbert**; 82 **Historical Museum of Southern Florida**; 143 **Ed Marshall**; 252, 255 **©Disney/Image Bank**. Pictures on pages 55, 162, 163, 167, 171, 191, were supplied by the featured establishments.

The Walt Disney Company is the owner of the registered trademarks of Walt Disney World® Resort and its constituent attractions. Other attraction names in the guide may also be the property of their registered trademark owners.

© Copyright Time Out Group Ltd
All rights reserved

Contents

About the Guide

This is the first edition of the *Time Out Guide to Miami, Orlando & South Florida*, the latest in Time Out's expanding series of city guides. It has been compiled by a team of resident experts who have brought to it the same inside knowledge and attention to detail that Time Out's magazines in London and New York have built their reputations on.

The bulk of the book is devoted to Miami, but there is a substantial section on Orlando and other South and Central Florida destinations. The first chapter, Essential Information, is relevant to the whole area. It is followed by a comprehensive Miami section, then the Beyond Miami chapters.

DETAIL DESCRIPTION

We have tried to make this book as useful as possible. Addresses, telephone numbers, transport details, opening times, admission prices and credit card details are all included in our listings, and many of our chapters are divided according to area, so you don't have to look too far for somewhere local to go. Colour maps at the back of the book cover all the major South and Central Florida destinations; the Miami maps have the exact locations of restaurants, hotels and attractions marked. To help those not familiar with the city to locate the places we've listed, we always give an area name, even if the postal address is technically just 'Miami'. Conversely, for anywhere you might want to write to, we have given the full postal address including zip code.

TALKING TELEPHONE NUMBERS

All Miami phone numbers are prefaced by 305. Orlando's code is 407. Within the area you need only dial the seven-figure local number; if you're calling from outside, you need to preface it with 1, followed by the area code. To call the US from abroad, dial the international code, then 1 for the US, followed by the area code and the number. Note that you can now dial most – but not all – 1-800 numbers from outside the US. Calls will be charged at the usual international rates.

CREDIT CARDS

The following abbreviations have been used for credit cards: **AmEx**: American Express; **DC**: Diners' Club; **Disc**: Discover; **JCB**: Japanese credit cards; **MC**: Mastercard; **V**: Visa.

Virtually all shops, restaurants, attractions and gas stations will accept US dollar travellers cheques issued by a major financial institution, such as American Express.

PRICES

The prices we've given should be treated as guidelines, not gospel. Seasonal variations and inflation can cause prices to change rapidly. Note that prices marked in shops do not include sales tax, currently 6.5 per cent. If prices vary wildly from those we've quoted, ask if there's a good reason. If not, go elsewhere. Then please write and let us know.

CHECKED & CORRECT

All listings information and other factual details have been thoroughly checked. However, inevitably businesses open and close, change their hours, relocate or alter their service in some other way. Clubs, hotels, restaurants and bars in Miami's South Beach are particularly volatile. We strongly recommend that you phone ahead before setting out on a visit. While every effort and care has been made to ensure the accuracy of the information contained in this guide, the publishers cannot accept responsibility for any errors it may contain.

RIGHT TO REPLY

It should be stressed that all the information we give is impartial. No organisation has been included in this guide because it has advertised in any of *Time Out*'s publications, and all opinions given are wholly independent.

We hope you enjoy the *Time Out Guide to Miami, Orlando & South Florida*, but we'd also like to know if you don't. We welcome tips from readers – feedback on current entries and suggestions for new ones. There's a reader's reply card for your comments at the back of the book.

> There's an on-line version of this guide, as well as weekly events listings for Miami and other international cities, at:
> http://www.timeout.co.uk

Introduction

The palm trees are caught in a blood-red apocalypse. The sun sets, I smile at the inflatable *Baywatch* babe at my side and aim my rented convertible across the MacArthur Causeway towards mainland Miami's too-hip island neighbour, Miami Beach – aka South Beach/The Beach/SoBe/Twinkle Town.

I'm following in the smouldering tyre tracks of Sly & Sharon in *The Specialist*, but it might equally be Pacino in *Scarface* or those Versace dicks in *Miami Vice*, because South Florida is a place where fact merges with fiction. A place where there really is a police car 50 feet above the ground, sticking out of the wall of Miami's Police Museum as if it had just smashed through from some celluloid chase. Where the highest elevation in former swampland really is Space Mountain at Walt Disney World (followed by Mount Trashmore, a landfill dump). And where, on South Beach's Ocean Drive, far from the theme parks, your waiter may resemble Donald Duck in drag – and that's a conservative look by Miami standards.

Pretty well anything and everything is not only imaginable but achievable in South Florida. If you want to rollerblade in just a thong bikini, that's fine (South Beach is one of the few beaches in the US where you can sunbathe topless). If you want to strip completely naked, save for a little decorative body paint, and dance like a maniac through the streets of Key West, book your tickets for the annual, gay-oriented Fantasy Fest. Should you simply wish to get down till 5am any night of the week, just check out any one of Miami Beach's clubs (I'd recommend Liquid or Groove Jet). Chances are you'll wind up shimmying next to some ridiculously toned and tuned fashion model of any sex.

If your tastes are a little quieter, you can head out to the Everglades, where aside from alligators the only trouble you might run into is the occasional newly arrived Russian mafia mobster attempting to smuggle cocaine in a former Soviet submarine. Still relatively unspoiled despite the diversion of too much water by agriculture and the sugar industry, the Everglades National Park does offer more peaceable pursuits, including airboat rides, nature walks through mangrove swamps and a wide variety of non-Soviet wildlife, but try to time your visit to avoid deep summer's mosquito hell or the intense tropical rainstorms which authentically replicate the experience of standing under an industrial-strength shower, fully clothed.

Water is South Florida's greatest asset. It's surrounded by it, and the ocean is a reliably stunning turquoise/blue. While locals find October-to-April surf temperatures a little brisk, the water is still probably warmer than Skegness in August. From July to September (when the air is so humid you feel like you're underwater already), the Atlantic on the east coast and the Gulf of Mexico on the west provide saltwater at blissful bathtime temperatures, and sailboats, scuba diving and jet-skis are available at only moderately extortionate rental rates.

Ethnically, South Florida is one of the United States' most fascinating destinations. While the Keys offer a chilled-out Caribbean pace and Orlando just a hint of the Deep South (both in terms of congeniality and a slightly white-bread mentality), Miami is often more like the Third World than part of the USA. With the city's only major newspaper, the *Miami Herald*, publishing English and Spanish editions, Spanish is the first language in some areas, due to a large, predominantly Cuban population – though the ethnic mix includes plenty of other Latin Americans, Haitians, Canadians and Europeans. The city often seems like a switching point, where people come to change tracks before moving on, which makes for a diverse and interestingly dodgy population, whose reasons for being here may range from refuge and regeneration to some elaborate new banking scam. Since Miami's history is one of shady land deals and vacationing hoods, it's only fitting that your glitzy meal at Michael Caine's Miami Beach restaurant, for instance, might put you alongside a former henchman of Baby Doc Duvalier, the newly paroled president of a bankrupt savings and loan – or Harry Palmer himself. Not a lot of people know that.

On a darker note, since the much-reported tourist killings of the early 1990s, perhaps the wrong accent has been placed on violence in Miami. Certainly it exists, but it's confined largely to two poor African-American neighbourhoods, Liberty City and Overtown, and it is the people who live there who suffer its consequences the most. After seven years in Miami, I have never even witnessed a serious fight in a club, let alone on the streets, and the only time I saw a gun drawn was when I went riding with a cop in Liberty City in the wake of the tourist attacks.

There are perhaps places on this earth with more theatres, museums and art galleries than South Florida. Barcelona may have finer architecture (though South Beach's deco district is striking enough); Australia may have more pristine beaches; London may currently offer more of a buzz. But for sheer undiluted warm-weather hedonism, South Florida takes the cake. And if you know where to look (try Weeki Wachee Spring, near Tampa), it's got mermaids, too.

● Alexander Stuart is the author of *Life on Mars: Gangsters, Runaways, Exiles, Drag Queens and Other Aliens in Florida* (Black Swan, £6.99).

A POLISHED LITTLE JEWEL
IN THE HEART OF PALM BEACH

The Chesterfield Hotel... an intimate 4-star
boutique hotel, registered as one of Palm Beach's
historical sites, located two blocks from
Worth Avenue and the Atlantic Ocean.

- Exquisitely appointed Guest Rooms and Suites
- Heated Outdoor Pool and Jacuzzi
- Traditional English Tea served in the Library
- Private Cigar Club "Churchill's"
- Private Meeting and Banquet Rooms
- Award Winning Leopard Lounge and Restaurant
- Evening Entertainment Nightly

The
Chesterfield
Hotel

363 Cocoanut Row · Palm Beach, Florida 33480
(561) 659-5800 · 1-800-243-7871

I-95 and Turnpike: Exit West Palm Beach/Okeechobee Blvd.
East over the Royal Park Bridge. Right at the 1st traffic light.

Essential Information

Florida facts and figures: a research resource for planning and profiting from your stay.

Local mailbox art.

For more practical information, *see chapter* **Survival**. For information on the abbreviations used in this guide, *see page vi* **About the Guide**.

Attitude

Its hot weather, short, improvisational history and reliance on the tourist industry combine to make South and Central Florida generally informal and friendly (though all bets are off on the highways). Dress is generally casual, except in a few particularly upmarket restaurants. Miami's South Beach is probably the only place where you will come across surly attitudes: waiting staff there can be positively uncivil.

Disabled

See chapter **Survival**.

Electricity/appliances

Rather than the 220-240V, 50-cycle AC used in Europe, Miami and the United States use a 110-120V, 60-cycle AC voltage. Except for dual-voltage, flat-pin plug shavers, you will need to run any appliances you bring with you via an adaptor, available at airport shops. Bear in mind that most US videos and TVs use a different frequency from those in Europe: you will not be able to play back footage during your trip. However, you can buy and use blank tapes.

Immigration & customs

The sheer volume of air traffic to Florida guarantees long queues at Immigration. At Miami International Airport the wait averages about half an hour, and can be considerably longer in high season or when several planes arrive together. At least the staff are relatively friendly. Whatever you do, make sure you've filled in the right forms – you should have been given two by your flight attendant, one for Immigration, one for Customs – or you'll risk another long wait in line. If you come through Miami in transit from overseas, you still have to pick up your luggage, go through Immigration and then check in again. The queues move slightly faster at Fort Lauderdale and Orlando's airports.

Current US customs regulations allow foreign visitors to import the following, duty-free: 200 cigarettes or 50 cigars (not Cuban; over-18s only), or 2kg of smoking tobacco; one litre (1.05 US quart) of wine or spirits (over-21s only); and up to $100 in gifts ($400 for returning Americans). You can take up to $10,000 in cash, travellers cheques or endorsed bank drafts in or out of the country tax-free. Anything above that you must declare, or you risk forfeiting the lot. (It happens.) You must also declare any foodstuffs or plants you may have and if your shoes are considered too mucky (ie full of micro-organisms) they may be taken away. For more information contact the **US Customs Service** at MIA (1-305 526 7472).

Insurance

Baggage, trip-cancellation, and medical insurance should be taken care of before you even get on the plane from your starting point. The US is renowned for its superb healthcare facilities; the catch is that the cost will most likely put you back in the hospital. The majority of medical centres require that you give details of your insurance company and your policy number if you require treatment. For further information, *see chapter* **Survival**.

Language

Miami is virtually a bi-lingual city, and you will hear Spanish spoken almost everywhere. In Latin areas such as Little Havana and Hiahleah, it is the lingua franca. You can certainly get by with just English, especially in the major tourist areas, but you will be missing out on the flavour of the city. If you've ever picked up any kind of holiday Spanish, dust off that phrasebook now and at least learn to say please and thank-you. The only places you're really likely to need it, though, are small mom-and-pop style businesses in Little Havana where no English is spoken. Speakers of European Spanish will find the Latin American version perfectly understandable. One phrasebook we'd recommend if you're planning on securing your own Latin lover is *Hot Spanish for Guys and Girls* and its gay equivalent *Hot Spanish for Guys and Guys*. Out of Miami, English will be all you'll need. For Spanish vocabulary, *see chapter* **Survival**.

Money & costs

You can pitch at your own cost level on a visit to Florida. There are certain inescapable high charges (entry to Orlando's attractions and hotel accommodation on Miami's South Beach, not ruinous but slightly over the odds, especially in high season), but restaurants and lodging generally span all the price ranges and a bouyant tourism market ensures healthy competition. Goods in shops are often cheaper than they would be in London or New York. Florida sales tax is currently six or seven per cent, depending on the county. If you're coming from abroad, you will probably get a better deal on foreign exchange in your home country, so stock up with (dollar) travellers cheques of a well-known brand. Once you arrive, the best exchange deals can usually be found either at the airport or at **Barnett Bank**, which has branches in most cities (and lots in Miami). Call 1-800 553 9026 for your nearest.

Currency

The United States' monetary system is decimal based: the US dollar ($) is divisible into 100 cents (c). Coin denominations are the penny (1c; Abraham Lincoln on the only copper-coloured coin); the nickel (5c; Thomas Jefferson); dime (10c; Franklin Delano Roosevelt); quarter (25c; George Washington); and the less common half-dollar (50c; John F Kennedy). Notes (bills), all the same size, come in $1 (George Washington); $5 (Abraham Lincoln); $10 (Alexander Hamilton); $20 (Andrew Jackson); $50 (Ulysses S Grant); and $100 (Benjamin Franklin) denominations.

Travellers cheques

Unless you're in the sticks, you can cash travellers cheques pretty much everywhere – hotels, restaurants, shops and gas stations will all take them happily, and give you change in currency. (It's not usually a problem to make a $5 purchase in order to get $95 cash, but some places do have a minimum purchase requirement, so you should ask first.) You will need to show your passport or other picture ID. If you need to buy travellers cheques in Florida, many commercial banks sell them for 1-3% of the face value.

Banks

Bank hours are usually 9am-4pm Monday to Friday, and sometimes 7pm on Thursdays, with drive-in windows open until 6pm. Larger branches open on Saturday mornings. Two of the bigger Florida banks are **Barnett** (*see above*) and **Sun Trust** (1-800 808 5057 for branches), most of whose locations offer the full range of international services, including cable transfers, foreign drafts on overseas banks and import/export financing. They can also raise cash on a credit card.

Bureaux de change

Bureaux de change are less common in the US than in Europe, but you will find them in tourist areas and larger cities. They generally charge higher commission and offer lower rates than the banks. To find your nearest **American Express** travel services office, call 1-800 528 4800. There are five in the Miami area, in Downtown (330 Biscayne Boulevard), Bal Harbour, Coral Gables, Miami International Airport and Homestead. Orlando branches are at 2 West Church Street, Suite No.1, Downtown Orlando (1-407 843 0004) and Epcot Center, Main Entrance, West Gate, Lake Buena Vista (1-407 827 7500). **Thomas Cook** has locations in Miami, Fort Lauderdale and Orlando: for details, call 1-800 287 7362. Independent bureaux abound in tourist areas such as Miami's South Beach, including **Chequepoint** (1-305 538 5348; open 9am-9pm Mon-Fri; 9am-6pm Sat, Sun) at 865 Collins Avenue, on Ninth Street.

ATMs

Automated Teller Machines are the most convenient way for visitors to top up their funds, now that national/international networks such as **Cirrus** and **Plus** allow you to withdraw money from your usual account from any machine that bears the appropriate symbol. You'll find them all over: in (and outside) banks, car parks, shopping malls, supermarkets and convenience stores. Call 1-800 424 7787 to locate your nearest Cirrus machine, 1-800 843 7587 for the nearest Plus. Withdrawals are free if you have an account at that bank, and sometimes at another US bank, but otherwise carry a variable fee, often with a minimum charge (sometimes this information is displayed) – meaning it can be cheaper to make one larger withdrawal than several small ones. Check with your bank before you go. You can also withdraw cash from ATMs on your credit card, though you will incur interest. If you use your (US) ATM card to make a purchase in a supermarket, you can often get cash too.

Follow the usual safety procedures when using an ATM. Don't let anyone see your PIN, take somebody with you and use a safe, well-lit location with people around.

Credit cards

The two major credit cards accepted just about everywhere in the United States are **MasterCard** (1-800 826 2181) and **Visa** (1-800 336 8472). **American Express** (1-800 528 4800) is also prominent at higher-end places. Other, less ubiquitous cards are Discover (1-800 347 2683), Carte Blanche, JCB and Diners Club (1-800 234 6377). You will find it inconvenient at best and impossible at worst to get by without a credit card (you almost always need one to rent a car), but you will also find some smaller shops and restaurants, notably in Miami's Little Havana, which require cash.

Cash crisis

If you lose or have your credit cards stolen, call the numbers given above. To report lost or stolen travellers cheques call 1-800 221 7282 for American Express, 1-800 223 7373 for Thomas Cook/MasterCard and 1-800 227 6811 for Visa. If you haven't kept a separate note of the numbers of your cheques, they may not be able to help as quickly as you might like. In a real emergency, you can get friends or family to send money from abroad via agencies such as **Western Union**. Call 1-800 325 6000 to find your nearest branch, and remind yourself not to wince when you hear how high the commission is.

Nuisances

Although Miami itself has an effective control programme which ensure that mosquitoes are rarely a pest, be prepared to be eaten alive the moment you pass the city limits. The Everglades and other woody areas are the worst affected, so buy an insect repellent you like the smell of, and use it. Mosquitoes are most active after long wet periods and least active along the beach where the cool sea breeze acts as an effective natural deterrent. Summer, from about May to October, is the peak season, and the public radio station, WLRN (91.3 FM), runs bulletins on mossie activity. Mosquitoes in Florida do not carry malaria but like those of sandflies, fire ants, sea-lice and no-see-ums (near-invisble flies that come out at dusk on beaches and by lakes) their bites can be painful and itchy. You should also be prepared for the occasional sighting of larger than average cockroaches, even in the better hotels, and their winged relations, palmetto bugs, both unpleasant but harmless.

The Florida sun is fierce, and should be avoided at its height until you are acclimatised. Protect yourself and your children throughout the day with a high-factor sun cream, a hat and good sunglasses both on the beach and when stuck in queues for Orlando's attractions. For swimming and beach hazards, *see chapter* **Sightseeing**.

Opening times

Office hours in Florida are usually 9am-5pm, give or take half an hour. Shop hours vary considerably according to location: businesses in malls and other pedestrian areas are often open until 9pm or later, Sundays included. Some Miami clubs and restaurants take a breather after the weekend, with the occasional restaurant closing on Sunday and Monday, and a handful of clubs dark on Monday and Tuesday. Some museums are closed on Mondays. Orlando's service economy guarantees that its shops, attractions andrestaurants have generous opening hours. Theme parks are usually open seven days a week, but their hours vary with the season (some outdoor attractions close at dusk unless there is evening entertainment). Big parks open at 8am or earlier and Disney is open until midnight during high season. Non-commercial attractions such as public museums stay closed on Sundays and sometimes Saturdays too, but otherwise, if you want to do it, it'll probably be open.

Post offices

Post offices are usually open from about 8.30am to 5-5.30pm Monday to Friday and until 1.30-2pm on Saturdays. You can sometimes use lobby services (stamp vending machines and scales) after hours. US mailboxes are red, white and blue with the US Mail bald eagle logo on the front and side. Pull the handle down and put your post (no packages) in the slot. There is usually a schedule of pick-ups inside the lid.

Some office shops offer mailing services. Hours are longer and queues shorter, but you do pay a premium for the

convenience. You can buy stamps from machines in hotels and shops, but again, you may pay a supplement. Supermarkets are the only place outside post offices where stamps are (usually) sold at face value. In our experience, delivery times from Florida to Europe are quite erratic – letters can take anything between five days and three weeks. If you want a guaranteed fast service, send letters World Post Priority from a post office. To Europe they take three to five days and cost $3.75 (small) or $6.95 (large). Miami post offices are listed in **Survival**; the Miami Beach branch is pictured above. Orlando's Downtown branch is at 46 E Robinson Street, open 7am-5pm Mon-Fri; 9am-noon Sat; there's also a 24-hour, seven-day-a-week office at the airport. For general postal information and locations, check the front of a local phone book, or dial **1-800 725 2161**.

Safety

Florida got itself a horrible reputation for tourist crime, murder included, in the early to mid 1990s. Sometimes tourists were targeted, sometimes they were simply in the way of the Big Kahuna of all crime waves that the state was experiencing. Visitor figures took a dive and, swift to protect the goose that laid about £20 billion worth of golden eggs a year, the authorities moved with alacrity to introduce anti-crime measures. Tourist areas are now heavily, and visibly, policed, and precautions have been taken to reduce car crime: signage has been improved, rental cars are no longer marked out with rental plates, and renters are required to provide adequate maps and directions. These measures have had the desired result: tourist crime has been falling fast. There was an 87 per cent fall in tourist robbery from 1995 to 1996 in Dade County, Miami's home authority, the second dramatic decrease running, and as we go to press it's been some time since a tourist was killed.

General crime figures too are going down. Since 1990 murders in Dade County have fallen by 25%, robbery 33%. It's still Florida's most crime-ridden county, however – and although Florida is no longer the murder capital of the US, it does still have the highest recorded rate of violent crime. The UK Foreign Office is still issuing safety advice.

Central Park SUMMERSTAGE *'97

Brought to you by

MILLER BREWING COMPANY

Supported by

New York City's favorite FREE music, dance, and spoken word festival. Every summer.

The Radisson Empire Hotel in NYC is pleased
to offer special weekend packages for SummerStage
visitors. Package includes discount hotel, VIP passes
to concerts, souvenirs, dinner or lunch for two at the
Hard Rock Cafe, passes to local clubs and more.

**Call 800-333-3333 (US and Canada only)
or 212-265-7400 for details.**

Visit us in NYC

Radisson
E·M·P·I·R·E

Pick up a copy of TIME OUT NEW YORK when you
arrive this summer for a complete schedule of Central Park
SummerStage events.
Call the CPSS hotline at 212-360-2777 or check out our website at
www.SummerStage.org for calendar details.

Central Park SummerStage is a project of the City Parks Foundation in cooperation
with the City of New York/Parks and Recreation

The bottom line is that although paranoia is unjustified, you do need to be careful – don't leave your street smarts at home. In well-touristed areas such as Miami's South Beach and Orlando's Attrations Area there will be a high police presence and, barring random occurences, such as Gianni Versace's shooting, you should be fine, but elsewhere the usual urban crime thrives and you could run into trouble quite easily by crossing an invisible line that only locals are wise to. Play it safe. We've tried to give safety information for all the areas we discuss, but if in doubt, stay out.

Safety tips

● The universal emergency number for police, ambulance, fire and coastguard is **911**. No money is required for 911 calls from public phones. If you dial 911 on Walt Disney property, you will be connected to a Disney emergency operator.

● If your hotel has a safe, keep your valuables there. If you do carry them with you, do so discreetly and don't flash large amounts of cash around. Don't leave anything you want to keep on the beach while you swim.

● Keep a note of your travellers cheque and credit card numbers separately. It's a good idea to leave a note of these with someone at home, along with any other information you might need in an emergency, such as your insurers' contact number and passport number.

● Keep all credit card slips, including receipts from credit sales at gas stations, and don't let anyone overhear your card number. If your hotel asked for an imprint when you checked in, insist it is destroyed when you leave.

● Don't let anyone into your hotel room who you don't know. Call the front desk if you need to check that someone is a member of staff.

● Sudden distractions or jostling may be diversions for a pickpocket.

● If somebody threatens you and demands money/goods, quietly give them what you have. Then go straight to the nearest phone or police station to report the crime. Make sure you get a reference number for any crime you report – you will need it for your insurance claim.

Driving

● Never set off on a journey without knowing exactly where you are going and how to get there. Any restaurant or hotel will give you driving directions if you call in advance. It's better to make yourself a written note of directions than try to use a map en route.

● If you get lost, stay calm. If you're on the freeway, wait until you see a gas station or restaurant where you can ask directions signed at an exit. If not, keep going until you hit a sign to somewhere you recognise or see a well-lit, reputable-looking business with other people around. If people can't give you directions, phone your destination, your hotel or, as a last resort, the Convention & Vistors Bureau (*see above* **Visitor Information**). Alternatively, consider renting a cellular phone. They're often available from car rental counters in addition to specialist shops (*see chapter* **Business**).

● Keep the car doors locked and the windows up, and don't open either for anyone. Never stop in a deserted area, especially at night. If someone bumps into you from behind, indicate that they follow you to a gas station or other well-lit, populated area.

● Don't take naps in roadside rest areas.

● If you arrive at night, consider getting a taxi from the airport and collecting your rental car the following day.

● Try and avoid leaving luggage in the car. If you have to, then lock it out of sight in the boot.

● Do not rely on Miami's 'sun signs' that are supposed to guide you to tourist destinations. They sometimes disappear just when you most need them.

● When you return to your car, check that no-one is in it, and, if you are in a parking lot, that no-one is lurking.

● If you break down, use your judgement about whether to leave the car and phone for help. The AAA recommends you wait until a police car passes and flag it down. If someone

offers to help, roll down your window and ask them to call your rental company's emergency number. Emergency phones are provided on freeways. If you have a mobile phone, dial *FHP for the highway patrol.

Telephones

There is just one code in Miami: **305**, which extends all the way south to Key West. The code for Orlando is **407**, Broward County including Fort Lauderdale is **954** and Palm Beach County **561**. Numbers prefaced by (1) **800** are free, though if you dial them from your hotel you will incur a flat fee (usually 50¢-$1). You can dial most (but not all) 1-800 numbers from outside the United States, but they will be charged at usual international rates.

For local calls within your area code, pick up the phone and dial the number. For local calls outside your area code or national long-distance calls, dial 1 + [area code] + [the number]. Note that although Key West shares the 305 code with Miami, you still need to prefix it with 1. For local enquiries, call 411; for national long-distance enquiries, dial 1 + [area code] + 555 1212 (if you don't know the area code, dial 0 for the operator). For international calls, dial 011 followed by the country code (UK 44; New Zealand 64; Australia 61, Germany 49; Japan 81 – see the phone book for others) and the number (drop the first zero of UK numbers). For collect (reverse charge) calls, dial the operator on 0. **For police, fire, or medical emergencies, dial 911.**

In hotels, you may have to dial an 0 or 9 before all these numbers to get a line. You will also pay a surcharge – ask how much at your hotel, as using a phonecard, credit card or payphone (*see below*) can work out significantly cheaper, especially on long-distance/international calls.

To use a public phone, pick up the receiver, listen for a dialling tone and feed it change. Operator and directory calls are free. Local calls cost 25¢ (some are 20¢), with the cost increasing with the distance (a recorded voice will tell you to feed in more quarters). Make sure you have plenty of change as pay phones only take nickels, dimes and quarters. It's nigh on impossible to make international calls this way, but you can use your MasterCard with **AT&T** (1-800 225 5288) or **MCI** (1-800 950 5555) or buy phonecards ($4-$50) from large stores like Thrifty and Payless Drug, which give you a fixed amount of time anywhere in the US – or less time internationally. Shop around for different brands. Unicall, for example, offers 54 minutes talk time to the UK for $20.

Phone bureaux, ranks of booths offering metered or card-managed phone time, are common, especially in immigrant areas. **MiniPost Office Express** at 1059 Collins Avenue, Suite 101 (538 7414) offers calls to the UK at $1.40 for the first minute, 61¢ thereafter, $1.79/75¢ to Germany and 25¢ per minute in the US. You can also send faxes.

If you encounter voicemail, note that the 'pound' key is the one marked # and the 'star' key *.

Time

Florida operates on **Eastern Standard Time**, which is five hours behind Greenwich Mean Time (London), one hour ahead of Central Time (Chicago), two hours ahead of Mountain Time (Denver) and three hours ahead of Pacific Standard Time (the west coast). Clocks go forward by an hour on the last Sunday in April, and back again on the last Sunday in October.

Tipping

Aim to tip at about 15 per cent in restaurants, but first check that the bill doesn't already include service. Hand over $1 for a round of drinks, more for a long order, or run a tab and tip at the end. Other tip amounts are:

Taxi driver	10-15 per cent plus $1 per bag
Cloakroom attendant	$1
Doorman (for calling a cab)	$1
Valet parker	nothing if the service carries a charge. Otherwise $1
Shoeshine	$1-2
Hotel maid	$1-$2 per night of stay

Tourist information

Visitor guides, including lists of accommodation, brochures and maps are available free of charge from the following tourist offices:

Greater Miami Convention & Visitors Bureau

701 Brickell Avenue, Suite 2700, at SE Seventh Street, Downtown Miami, FL 33131 (1-305 539 3063/539 3113 fax). Bus 24, 48, B/Metromover Eighth Street. **Open** 8.30am-5pm Mon-Fri.

Miami Beach Chamber of Commerce

1920 Meridian Avenue, at Dade Boulevard, Miami Beach, FL 33140 (1-305 672 1270/538 4336 fax). Bus A, G, K, L, R. **Open** 9am-6pm Mon-Fri; 10am-4pm Sat, Sun.

Art Deco Welcome Center

Miami Design Preservation League, Ocean Front Auditorium, 1001 Ocean Drive at 10th Street, Miami Beach, FL 33139 (1-305 672 2014). Bus C, H, K, W. **Open** 11am-6pm Mon-Wed; 11am-11pm Thur-Sun. Leaflets, maps, merchandise, friendly service and bike and walking tours of the Deco District.

Official Visitors Center of the Orlando Convention & Visitors Bureau

8723 I-Drive, Suite 101, Orlando, FL 32819 (1-407 363 5871). **Open** 8am-7pm daily for tickets; 8am-8pm daily for information.

Florida Tourism

PO Box 1100, Tallahassee, FL 32302 (1-904 487 1462). 2701 Le Jeune Road, Suite 406, Coral Gables, FL 33134 (1-305 442 6926). ABC Florida, PO Box 35, Abingdon, Oxfordshire, United Kingdom, OX14 4SF.
Florida Tourism has an extremely useful holiday pack containing a vacation guide, maps and other information. It's free to US addresses from the US offices and costs £2 (cheques to ABC Florida) within Britain from the UK branch.

When to go

Miami's **average** minimum and maximum temperatures run up to from 59-75°F (15-24°C) in January to 77-89°F (25-32°C) in July and August. Winter air is warm, dry and pleasant, though you'll need a sweater in the evening, and the sea is still warm enough to swim in, especially for those used to chillier waters. Summer gets very hot and unpleasantly humid during the day, and sultry in the evening, with mornings and late afternoon the best time for going to the beach for a dip in Jacuzzi-warm sea. June to November is hurricane season: winds are high and storms rush in during the afternoon. Most are brief but sometimes tropical rains set in. Weather watchers will find the dramatic display of clouds and lightning, with the possiblity of a stray tornado, intoxicating. For more information on hurricanes, *see chapter* **Survival**.

The Season – when South Beach is at the peak of its cycle – goes from the end of November to May. This is when accommodation and car rental prices shoot up and most major events and photo shoots are scheduled.

November/December and late April/early May are good times to visit – the weather's usually good but prices haven't hit their peak, though given South Beach's apparently unshakeable popularity the off-season has become a relative term.

Orlando generally has warm, sunny days and mild nights. Humidity can be high due to a lack of ocean breezes. During the rainy season (June to September), expect temperatures in the mid-90°Fs (early 30°s centigrade) and heavy rainfall lasting about an hour each afternoon. Thunder, lightning and heavy winds are common during these storms, so drive with caution. From January to March, the weather is fine with highs in the mid-70°Fs and lows in the upper 40°Fs. However, freezes also occur during these months as do weeklong rain patterns. Orlando is occasionally subject to hurricanes in season, but they're usually much weaker inland than when they hit the beaches.

For phone forecasts, dial 511 followed by 4400 for Florida, 4020 for Miami, 4374 for Orlando and 4998 for hurricanes.

Habla usted Spanglish?

Those who suppose that a visit to Miami requires them to memorise a Spanish phrase book, think again. Just mix and mangle assorted Spanish phrases with English and you'll be understood – recognised as one of the privileged few who have mastered the unique Miami hybrid language of Spanglish, which consists of transliterations that have somehow come to be universally understood by all Miamians.

La Saguesera (noun), pronounced 'Sow-wes-erah': Derived from the 'southwest area' of town, encompassing Little Havana, of course. The place where you are most likely to use these words.

El mol or **el chopping** (nouns): A direct translation of the mall or the shopping center.

Pulover; blue yeen (nouns): A pullover T-shirt and blue jeans, two pieces of clothing you might buy at el mol.

Tensen (noun): Before the popularity of malls, the five-and-ten-cent store was the place to shop. Hence this word.

Champu (noun): Shampoo, an item commonly found at the tensen.

Lonchar (verb), pronounced 'lone-shar': The act of eating lunch.

Sangueiche (noun), pronounced 'saang-weech': A sandwich.

Bistec (noun), pronounced 'bee-stay': from beef steak; usually arrives covered by a mountain of french fries.

Fooboll, **baskeybol**, **beisbol** (nouns): Football, basketball and baseball, the latter being the favourite of the Cuban.

Miami Basics

Getting Around

Stay in South Beach and stay on foot; tackle the mainland and take on Miami's tangled transport options. Your choice – here's how to make it.

Let's face it, it's a lot easier to get to Miami, Gateway to the Americas, than to get around it. Dade County, home to the Miami urban sprawl, is a vast geographic area, characterised by myriad confusing, non-uniform street grids; a terribly inadequate public transportation system; more than two dozen separate cities, including Miami, Miami Beach and Coral Gables, each with scores of separate neighbourhoods; an ever-expanding suburban sprawl; and a polyglot driver population renowned for its ignorance and/or indifference to road rules and etiquette. But don't despair, it can be done.

On paper, Miami's street grid is logical. The city is divided into four quadrants – NW, NE, SE and SW – with point zero located in Downtown Miami at Flagler Street (the north-south divide) and Miami Avenue (the east-west divide). But there are so many quirks that it's not easy to get around, by foot or car, without a good street map. The map given to you by your car rental company is inadequate for most purposes: you're better off buying one or – just as good, since none of the commercial maps are particularly brilliant – picking up one of the abundant free maps available from hotels and visitor information centres. Of these, we found the one produced by Gabelli US most useful. The maps in the back of this book focus on the areas tourists are most likely to visit, and aim to cater for people exploring by public transport and on foot. Drivers will need to complement them with a route map.

By contrast, Miami Beach is a long, narrow island that is relatively easy to master. Streets that run east-west between the ocean and the bay are

numbered, starting with First Street at the southernmost tip of the island, and go north sequentially (with a few named streets thrown in). Avenues run north-south and are named, not numbered. Each of the three main areas of Miami Beach – South Beach, Mid-Beach and North Beach (not to be confused with the city of North Miami Beach on the mainland) – is compact enough to navigate easily and cheaply by foot, bike, rollerblade, bus or taxi. Travel between the areas is also relatively simple.

If you're staying on Miami Beach, you not only don't need a car, you're better off without one. Parking is a nightmare: hard to find and very expensive. You can always rent a car for day trips, and the new electric buses (*see box*) will make short hops a doddle. If you're staying on the mainland, in Downtown Miami, Coral Gables or elsewhere in Dade, you probably will need a car.

To & from the airport

Miami International Airport (MIA)
Information 876 7000.

By shuttle
MIA is northwest of Downtown Miami. Unless you're planning to rent a car, the easiest and cheapest way to get from the airport is the **SuperShuttle**, a shared-ride van service. You'll find dispatchers waiting on the kerb wherever you exit on the lower level of the arrivals building. Fares are $14 to South Beach; $11 to Coral Gables; $14 to Coconut Grove. You can arrange for the SuperShuttle to take you back to MIA by calling 871 2000 24 hours in advance.

By taxi
You'll find taxis waiting outside MIA's arrival terminals. There is a $22 flat rate to South Beach – be sure to ask for it. The fare to Coral Gables is about $15; to Coconut Grove $20, both without tip.

By bus
You can take a Metro Dade bus from MIA to different destinations in Miami, but they're infrequent and a hassle if you've got luggage. Buses stop outside the lower level of the arrivals building at concourse E. For Miami Beach, catch the J bus; it goes to 41st Street (aka Arthur Godfrey Road) and then turns north on Collins Avenue, ending at 72nd Street. If you're going to South Beach, you'll have to change to the C or H bus at 41st Street. If you arrive at night, forget using the bus – they don't run often enough.

By car
The Triangle, the area of MIA containing over two dozen car rental agencies, is an incredibly confusing place, where many

MIA, *the US's second busiest airport.*

tourists get lost. Make sure you receive good, detailed directions from your rental agent, and review them while looking at a map before starting out. The Miami-Dade Police Department recently launched a programme (the Triangle Enforcement Unit) to help tourists, with police cars patrolling the area 24 hours a day, seven days a week. Note that there are several gas stations along Le Jeune Road (NW 42nd Avenue) for pre-return refills. *See map* **p290.**

Fort Lauderdale-Hollywood International Airport

Information 1-954 359 1200.

From Fort Lauderdale airport you have several options on how to make the 30-mile trip to Miami. The best is to rent a car at the airport and drive south on I-95 or the Florida Turnpike. Alternatively, take a shuttle bus from the lower level at the eastern end of Terminals 1 and 3 to the airport's Tri-Rail station and then take a commuter train south to Miami. Note, however, that the Tri-Rail schedule is very limited, running hourly or every two hours during the week, less frequently at the weekend. There is also a shared-ride van service, **Bahama Link**, which will take you to your hotel in Miami or Miami Beach ($39 for 1-2 people to South Beach; $49 for 1-2 to Coconut Grove or Coral Gables; $10 per person groups of 10). Book 24 hours in advance on 1-800 854 2182.

When you return to Fort Lauderdale airport from Miami, there is another, cheaper option: you can book the **Miami SuperShuttle** (871 2000) 24 hours in advance for $22 from South Beach, $31 from Coconut Grove and Coral Gables. Unfortunately, it doesn't pick up from the airport.

Public transport

Information

Miami's public transportation system is run by **Metro-Dade Transit**. For information on Metrobus, Metrorail and Metromover routes and schedules, call **638 6700** (6am-10pm Mon-Fri; 9am-5pm Sat, Sun). The operators will help you plan your trip from point A to point B, including all connections. Call **654 6586** if you want bus schedules and a transit map sent by mail, or visit the Transit Information Booth at Government Center station in Downtown Miami.

Buses

Metrobuses are the heart of public transport in Miami, and, in tourist areas, are generally clean, air-conditioned, safe and relatively comfortable, except for rush hours, when they are mobbed. They crisscross Dade County, spanning enormous distances and exposing riders to Miami's amazing cultural, ethnic and age diversity. The main disadvantages are that the buses travel highly congested routes, make frequent stops, don't always go to or near your destination, often break down, and, above all, rarely run on schedule.

Express buses cover routes at somewhat faster paces from North and South Dade to Metrorail stations and elsewhere (including a new South Dade Busway from Dadeland to Cutler Ridge), but the routes are limited and follow the same congested roads as cars. Bus frequency varies enormously by route, time and day of week: they may run as often as every 10 or 15 minutes or only every 45 minutes. When you use buses to travel long distances, leave yourself lots of time, go off-hours, take a patience pill and try to enjoy the scenery, both human and environmental.

Fares & bus stops

A one-way bus fare is $1.25; children up to 42in tall travel free. Express buses cost $1.50. Transfers cost an additional 25¢; you must ask and pay for a transfer when you get on the bus. You'll need the exact fare, but the machines take silver, crisp dollar bills and tokens. Bus stops are marked by a rectangular white sign with a blue and green metal marker bearing the specific bus route(s), often by a yellow kerb stripe, and sometimes by benches and/or bus shelters. It can get really hot waiting for the bus, so carry a hat.

Tokens, passes & permits

For frequent bus use, it pays to buy tokens from designated stores or Metro-Dade Transit. A roll contains 10 tokens and costs $10, saving you $2.50 and the hassle of needing exact change. Tokens are also valid on the Metrorail but don't use them on the Metromover, which costs only 25¢. If you're in Miami for a few weeks and plan to do major schlepping on buses, Metrorail or Metromover, consider buying a monthly Metropass for $60 ($30 for seniors and people with disabilities), which gives you unlimited travel on all three. You can buy tokens and passes from Metro-Dade Transit at Government Center station in Downtown Miami, and tokens only from stores throughout Miami and on Miami Beach; call Metro-Dade Transit for your nearest outlet.

Trains

There are three train lines in Miami Dade – Metromover, Metrorail and Tri-Rail – which most tourists (and natives) rarely, if ever, use. However, they have their purposes.

Metromover

This is Miami's high-tech Toonerville Trolley, an elevated, electric monorail that runs a 4½ mile loop around Downtown Miami daily from 6am to midnight, costs only 25¢ and offers fabulous views of Biscayne Bay and the city. Clean, cool and comfortable when it's working (it can be temperamental), it

What's in a name?

One of the biggest headaches for drivers in Miami-Dade is the frequent use of multiple names – or changes in the names – for major arteries, not all of which are marked on maps or directional signs. The result is major confusion, unless you master the following name changes and aliases:

● SR 112, also known as the Airport Expressway, becomes I-195, aka the Julia Tuttle Causeway, at I-95 heading east to Miami Beach.
● SR 836, also known as the Dolphin Expressway, becomes I-395, aka the MacArthur Causeway and A1A, east of I-95, heading to Miami Beach.
● SR 826 is also called the Palmetto Expressway.
● US 1, also known as Federal Highway, is called Brickell Avenue in Downtown Miami south of the Miami River; South Dixie Highway when it passes the Rickenbacker Causeway; and Biscayne Boulevard as it wends its way from Flagler Street in Downtown Miami all the way north to the Broward County line.
● A1A is the overall name for the oceanfront route that runs north up Miami Beach, through Sunny Isles, Hollywood and into Fort Lauderdale. At different points along the way it is known as Ocean Drive, Collins Avenue and many other names.
● SR 874, which runs between the Florida Turnpike and SR 826, is also known as the Don Shula Expressway.

Time Out

Film Guide

Edited by John Pym

Annually updated, the *Time Out* Film Guide is a comprehensive A-Z of films from every area of world cinema and has stronger international coverage than any other film guide.

Each entry includes full details of director, cast, running time, release date and reviews from the *Time Out* magazine critics. There are also indexes covering films by country, genre, subject, director and actor. So if you want to get the lowdown on a film, pick up the latest edition of the *Time Out* Film Guide - available in a bookshop near you.

'Without doubt, the "bible" for film buffs.'
British Film and TV Academy News

runs from the Omni Center to Brickell Avenue via stops including Bayside and Government Center. A transfer to Metrorail costs $1 or a token. The best way to use it may be to ride it at sunset just for the view (*see chapter* **Downtown**).

Metrorail

A 21-mile elevated train system that runs north-south from Hialeah to Dadeland, with stops approximately every mile, Metrorail is Miami's very expensive and very under-used rapid transit system. Like Metrobus, a trip costs $1.25, plus 25¢ for a transfer to/from a bus; transferring to Metromover is free. If you're in Downtown Miami, don't have a car and want to go to Vizcaya, Coconut Grove or the University of Miami, it's a pleasant way to travel, with trains running about every 20 minutes until midnight. The Metrorail connects to Tri-Rail, the Gulf Coast's inter-city commuter system (*see chapter* **Getting Started**).

Taxis & limos

Taxi meters start at $1.10 and click away at $1.75 per mile, plus waiting time charges. For short distances, they're affordable; for long distances, they can cost a small fortune. Some approximate fares (without tips or traffic) from South Beach are: $20 to Miracle Mile in Coral Gables; $23 to CocoWalk in Coconut Grove; $25 to Key Biscayne; $15 to Bayside in Downtown Miami. Cabs are usually radio-dispatched, although on the Beach and in Downtown Miami you can find them at kerbside stations and major hotels or probably flag one down by waving wildly. Restaurants and hotels routinely call cabs for patrons. Many fleets have old, decrepit vehicles, and many drivers speak little or no English. Some generally reliable companies (with easy-to-remember phone numbers) are **Eights Cab** (888 8888); Beach-based **Central Cab** (532 5555); **Best Taxi Service** (444 4444) and **Flamingo Taxi** (759 8100).

Limos are a dime a dozen in some areas, especially South Beach, where they're the size of small ocean liners. Hiring rates start at $35 per hour for a Lincoln Town Car and escalate to $65-$75 per hour for a 10-passenger stretch limo.

Virtually all companies require a three-hour minimum rental time, and many tack on a 20% 'gratuity'. There are nine pages of limo services listed in the current Miami Yellow Pages, so ask your hotel to recommend one. If you want to be queen or king for a day, consider hiring a vintage Rolls Royce limo with a fully liveried chauffeur from $75 to $175 per hour plus 20% gratuity from Vintage Limos on 444 7657.

Driving

Miamians regard driving as their birthright. But because such a large segment of the population was neither born nor raised here, many residents drive without knowledge of local traffic rules. So, despite the geographic sprawl and lack of good public transport, we don't advise driving here unless you are a Type A personality. In addition to the usual big-city problems, you'll encounter some unique Miami driving migraines, including local drivers who change lanes without signalling, stop suddenly at the top of on-ramps and merging lanes and routinely ignore stop signs and red lights; elderly drivers who proceed at a snail's pace but won't yield; major arteries that change names frequently (*see box* **What's in a name?**); and notoriously inadequate road signage, including the cheery, ubiquitous orange sun signs, developed to help tourists get safely to the major tourist

To & from South Beach

As lovely and lively as SoBe is, you might start getting island fever if you don't occasionally venture off-island. Unfortunately, the expense of taxis and the lack of efficient public transport might make you hesitate to try. Don't despair: here are some prime escape routes.

To Downtown

Both the C Metrobus on Washington Avenue and the S on Collins Avenue south to 17th Street and then on Alton Road will take you from South Beach to Downtown Miami (Bayside or Flagler Street) for $1.25 in about 25-35 minutes. From there, you can walk around Downtown or take the Metromover or Metrorail. Or call the Water Taxi and turn the trip Downtown into a great expedition via Biscayne Bay.

To Coconut Grove, Vizcaya or Coral Gables

Take a Metrobus (as above) to the last stop on Flagler Street in Downtown Miami, walk two blocks north to the Metrorail station at Government Center on NW First Street and hop a southbound Metrorail train. It only takes

15-20 minutes, and costs a 25¢ transfer if you buy one on the bus. Vizcaya Museum & Gardens is virtually next to the eponymous station; central Coconut Grove is a 10-minute walk (or a ride on the 27 bus, though they're only every half an hour) from Coconut Grove station. For Coral Gables, get off at Douglas Road. Most points of interest are a five- to ten-minute walk away, or you could get the 37 bus to Miracle Mile or the 72 to the Biltmore – a short ride but possibly a long wait. Alternatively, there are usually taxis outside the station.

To Key Biscayne

Take a Metrobus (as above) to the last stop on Flagler Street, find the corner of SW First Street and First Avenue (it's right there) and wait 30-40 minutes for the B Metrobus, which will take you down Crandon Boulevard on Key Biscayne past Crandon Park Beach to Grape Tree Drive.

To Little Havana (Calle Ocho)

Take a Metrobus (as above) to the junction of Miami Avenue and Flagler Street, one stop before the last stop downtown. Walk across both streets to mid-block and find the marker for bus 8. Take the 8 to 36th Avenue and Eighth Street, near the Versailles Restaurant, the heart of Little Havana.

destinations, but which seem to appear and disappear at random. They're handy pointers, but don't rely on them.

Other potentially lethal driving dangers for which Miami became notorious in the early 1990s, such as carjackings, have subsided to normal (for the US) levels, although you still don't want to get lost in certain neighbourhoods. Two last points: during rush hours, only vehicles carrying one or more passengers in addition to the driver can travel in lanes marked 'HOV' (High Occupancy Vehicle); and Florida law allows you to turn right on a red light if the road is clear.

If at all possible, avoid driving during rush hours: 7-9am, 4-6pm weekdays, to and from Downtown Miami, for work traffic, and Friday and Saturday evenings for party traffic to and from the Beach and Coconut Grove. Always map and know your route in advance, paying particular attention to your junction numbers and any changes in route names. Consider renting a cellphone (by the hour, day or week) if you'll be driving a lot. Some rental agents have phone hire desks – and even vending machines – in their offices. As well as enabling you to call for help if necessary (by mid-1997, you should be able to call 311 for non-emergency police assistance), it will help you blend into the scenery as a native, not a tourist, since virtually every local uses a cellphone while driving (thereby creating yet another Miami driving hazard).

Parking

Parking in Downtown Miami or on Miami Beach is an ordeal, and an expensive one to boot. Invariably, you will have to use meters, parking lots (many of which have meters), garages or valet parking. For meters, you'll need tons of quarters, and for garages and valet services, tons of money, period.

Car rental

There are many rental companies, national and local, to choose from as long as you have a major credit card and are over 25 years old. (Some local car rental agencies will rent to people without credit cards if they are over 25, produce a licence and a round-trip air ticket and pay a deposit of several hundred dollars, or to persons aged 21-25 if they have a major credit card; one such company is Andre, on 871 1837.)

Rental rates range wildly, depending on company and time of year. Do some comparative shopping by calling several national companies on their 1-800 numbers before your trip, making sure to ask about any discounts (for example, as a member of the AAA – British AA members also qualify – or the AARP, the American Association of Retired Persons). Booking via web site can net you extra incentives. Also research fly-drive deals and rentals through your travel agent. These often offer the best value, particularly if you're coming from outside the US; otherwise, reserve a car at the best price you've found; you can always cancel with no penalty.

Remember that the prices companies quote you do not include state sales tax or either collision damage or liability insurance. If your home policy or credit card doesn't cover you, bite your lip and stump up the extra – even though it may almost double the rental bill. Finally, unless you're going to Miami in the middle of summer, consider spending the extra bucks for a convertible: there are few things you can experience legally in public as sensuous as driving over a causeway to Miami Beach with the wind blowing through your hair and the sight and smell of the turquoise bay.

National car rental companies

Alamo 1-800 327-9633/http://www.freeways.com
Avis 1-800 831-2847/http://www.avis.com
Budget 1-800 527-0700/http://www.budgetrentacar.com
Dollar 1-800 800-4000/http://www.dollarcar.com
Enterprise 1-800 325-8007/http://www.pickenterprise.com
Hertz 1-800 654-3131/http://www.hertz.com
National 1-800 227 7368/http://www.nationalcar.com
Thrifty 1-800 367-2277/http://www.thrifty.com
Value 1-800 468-2583/http://www.go-value.com

Local car rental companies

If you want to rent a car for a day or two in the middle of your stay, you don't have to make the inconvenient and expensive trip to MIA – there are local rental companies that will, for no extra cost, either deliver and pick up your rental car at your hotel or pick up and deliver you to their office. Those that offer competitive rates ($29.99-$34.95 per day for a midsize car) include **Marlin's International Auto Rental** (636 4107); **Al's Rent-A-Car** (887 4226); and, on Miami Beach, **Inter American Car Rental** (534 1100). Many local and national companies have offices on the Beach. Those in South Beach include **Arena** (672 9890); **Avis** (538 4441) and **Budget** (871 3053).

Bikes & rollerblades

If you're spending time on South Beach, definitely consider exploring or cruising by bicycle and/or rollerblades (aka inline skates). There are plenty of places to rent both, plus safety equipment, on Washington Avenue and Lincoln Road. They're a lot cheaper and more mobile than renting a car and you'll fit right into the local scene.

Water transport

Although the wonderful **Water Taxi** no longer provides scheduled trips between Miami Beach and Downtown Miami (Bayside), you can still book passage on it by calling 1-954 467 6677. A one-way trip across Biscayne Bay to or from Miami Beach costs $7 per person; the round-trip is $12. For $15, you can buy an all-day pass that will not only provide round-trip transportation between the Beach and Miami, but also take you up the Miami River, a fascinating trip.

Electric avenue

By September 1997 a new electric bus service should be on line in South Beach. If, that is, all goes according to plan, which precedent suggests it might not – the launch date has already been put back several times. The service will be free, frequent (every six to eight minutes) and tailored to South Beach's style: the 22-seater buses will be late-running, neon-festooned and artist-designed. The route goes along 17th Street from Alton Road, down Washington Avenue, west along Fifth Street to Lenox Avenue and back in the other direction, and times of operation are from 8am to 2am Mondays to Wednesdays and until 4am the rest of the week. The scheme's main aim is to encourage mainlanders to abandon their cars further away from the honeypot areas, alleviating traffic and parking problems, but it should also be of great benefit to visitors – South Beach is walkable, but less so in the summer sun, or with one too many cocktails inside you. A small, free, electric tram already runs east-west on the Lincoln Road pedestrian mall.

Miami by Season

Join in the street parties, music festivals and arts extravaganzas as Miami makes the most of its sunny weather and multicultural mix.

One of the most common reasons people give for leaving Miami is: 'I want to be in a place that has four seasons'. Miami, it seems, is a place notoriously without seasons. Actually, this is a myth. Weather-wise, Miami has two: Summer and Not Summer. From May to September, it is usually hot, sticky and rainy. From about October to April, it is sunny and hot, sometimes getting a bit cool and dry. Hence, activity-wise, Miami also has two seasons: Off Season and the Season. Guess which comes when?

In a land of mostly sunny days, the summer is a time of sometimes unbearably steamy temperatures, record-high humidity and almost-daily torrential rainfalls. Although the rain brings welcome relief from the heat, it is still the time when those who can go north. Why risk sustaining third-degree burns from the car seat or, worse, getting fried by lightning during a sudden squall? (Florida is the lightning-strike capital of the US.) Those who do stay in town spend their days trying to beat the heat by guzzling gallons of water and ducking from one air-conditioned building into another. In the summer, Miami is the tropics – without the breeze.

Around Hallowe'en things slowly change. Leaves rustle on the pavement as the wind picks up a bit. People start reappearing outdoors for reasons other than just walking from car to house to office. Plenty of December days can be spent comfortably lounging on the beach. And the few times it does get chilly (for natives, this counts as in the 50°Fs), it is rarely a protracted arctic blast but usually a temporary cold snap, never lasting longer than a week or two.

In the past, the Season used to begin officially after Thanksgiving. But in recent years, perhaps due to Miami's increasingly hip reputation as a vacation destination, things have changed. The Season is now starting earlier and earlier, as soon as late October. The majority of festivals occur in the fall and winter. During these months, almost every immigrant group pays tribute to itself publicly – sometimes more than once. Nearly every suburb throws its own art fair. And movies, books, music, food and sports all get to have their moment in and out of the sun.

National holidays

New Year's Day (1 Jan); Martin Luther King Jr Day (3rd Mon in Jan); President's Day (3rd Mon in Feb); Memorial Day (last Mon in May); Independence Day (4 July); Labor Day (1st Mon in Sept); Columbus Day (2nd Mon in Oct); Election Day (1st Tue in Nov); Veteran's Day (11 Nov); Thanksgiving Day (4th Thur in Nov); Christmas Day (25 Dec).

Spring

Asian Arts Festival

Information 247 5727. Fruit & Spice Park, 24801 SW 187th Avenue, at SW 256th Street, Homestead. **Date** first weekend in Mar.

South Florida's thousands of Asian immigrants (over 20 different ethnic groups) get together in this annual two-day fest, which features art, crafts, food, performances, exhibitions and activities for children.

Carnaval Miami/Calle Ocho

Information 644 8888. Throughout Dade County. **Date** begins first Sat in Mar.

The highlight of this nine-day event showcasing Miami's Latin community is Calle Ocho: Open House, the world's largest street party, held on the final Sunday, which attracts over one million attendees. The road is sealed off to traffic and taken over by a mass of revellers. Other activities include Carnaval Night in the Orange Bowl, featuring major Latin stars, and the Paseo parade along Flagler Street. If you're here at the right time, don't miss it.

Miami Grand Prix

Information 230 5200. Homestead Motorsports Complex, One Speedway Boulevard, at SW 328th Street & 137th Avenue, Homestead. **Date** first weekend in Mar.

An audience of more than 50,000 watches enrapt as world-class Indy car drivers spin around the South Florida Indy track during a weekend of driving at unreal speeds for unreal amounts of money.

Italian Renaissance Festival

Information 250 9133. Vizcaya Museum & Gardens, 3251 S Miami Avenue, at 32nd Road, Coconut Grove. **Date** third weekend in Mar.

Miami's landmark home plays host to 'Florida's Official Renaissance Festival'. The atmosphere of a fifteenth-century marketplace is recreated with merchants, crafts and food vendors. Dressed in period costumes, jugglers, jesters, madrigal groups, strolling minstrels and troubadours provide entertainment. Don't miss the Living Chess Tournament or the International Flag Throwers from Asti, Italy.

The Lipton Championships

Information 446 2200. International Tennis Center, 6800 Crandon Boulevard, Key Biscayne. **Date** late Mar.

Ten days of non-stop tennis. Nearly 100 top-rated professional racquet-wielders descend on Key Biscayne and compete for millions of dollars. Cool breezes notwithstanding, the temperature on the 26 courts sometimes reaches sauna-like proportions of over 100°F, making the event a true test of endurance, and not just for the players.

Dade Heritage Days

Information 358 9572. Throughout Dade County. **Date** begins first week in April.

A six-week celebration of the people, places and structures that make up Dade County's varied historic neighbourhoods. Activities include walking and bicycle tours, lectures, films, demonstrations and historical re-enactments.

The Female Impersonators Pageant.

Merrick Festival
Information 447 9299. Ponce Circle Park, Ponce de Leon Boulevard, at Sevilla Avenue, Coral Gables. **Date** second weekend in April.
Named after Coral Gables' founder, this performing arts festival features dance recitals, art exhibits, continuous concerts, theatre performances and photography competitions for amateurs and professionals. Tastings from the area's exceptional restaurants are also provided.

Miss National for Female Impersonators Pageant
Information 535 1400. Venue varies. **Date** April.
The national final of one of the US's premier high-gloss she-men parades, open to transvestites and pre-op transsexuals. Expect class to count as the contestants compete in cabaret, evening gown and question-and-answer events. Feminine, rather than drag, is the watchword here.

Arabian Knights Festival
Information 688 4611. Opa-Locka City Hall, 777 Sharazad Boulevard, off Ali Baba Avenue, Opa-Locka. **Date** first weekend in May.
Created in 1926 by Glenn Curtiss, the city of Opa-Locka, known as the 'Baghdad of the South', possesses the largest collection of Moorish-inspired architecture in the US. For over 70 years, an annual weekend-long party has celebrated the neighbourhood's heritage. People don Arab attire for a Fantasy Parade led by a celebrity grand marshal, enjoy carnival rides, take tours of the historic neighbourhood and buy food and crafts while enjoying musical acts.

Taste of the Beach
Information 672 1270. South Pointe Park, 1 Washington Avenue, South Beach. **Date** first weekend in May.
Miami Beach's hottest chefs haul out their best recipes for a weekend of tastings to benefit charity.

Subtropics Music Festival
Information 758 6676. Various venues around Dade County. **Date** begins mid-May.
Dance, film, video and radio are a few of the art forms that are highlighted in this 15-day new music festival.

Coconut Grove Bed Race
Information 624 3714. Peacock Park, 2820 McFarlane Road, at S Bayshore Drive, Coconut Grove. **Date** third Sun in May.
Now in its 19th year, an event like this could only occur in wacky Coconut Grove. Souped-up aerodynamic beds mounted on wheels are raced down Bayshore Drive by teams composed of perfectly respectable business people, clubs and other organisations. All proceeds go to benefit a charity for people with neuromuscular diseases. After the race, rock acts provide entertainment.

The Great Sunrise Balloon Race & Festival
Information 275 3317. Golf course at Homestead Air Reserve Station, SW 268th Street & 127th Avenue, Homestead. **Date** Memorial Day Weekend.
Dozens of multicoloured hot-air balloons ascend and several fearless skydivers descend in this two-day celebration. Meanwhile, on the ground, participants sample ethnic foods, listen to music and check out art and crafts stalls.

Miami/Bahamas Goombay Festival
Information 372 9966. Downtown Coconut Grove. **Date** first weekend in June.
Join artisans, Junkanoo parades and the Royal Bahamian Police Marching Band as they pay tribute to Coconut Grove's original Bahamian roots. Don't miss the conch fritters, among the best of the authentic Caribbean food on offer.

Summer

Annual America's Birthday Bash
Information 358 7550. AT&T Amphitheater, Bayfront Park, 401 Biscayne Boulevard, Downtown. **Date** 4 July.
The largest Independence Day party in Florida. Three stages host rock and Latin musicians, and there's also an ethnic food court, kids' activities, a laser light show and, of course, a fabulous fireworks display.

Miami Reggae Festival
Information 891 2944. AT&T Amphitheater, Bayfront Park, 401 Biscayne Boulevard, Downtown. **Date** first weekend in Aug.
Miami's Caribbean influences are underscored with performances from local, national and international musicians at this annual two-day event.

Autumn

Hispanic Heritage Festival
Information 541 5023. Various venues around Dade County. **Date** 1-31 Oct.
A month-long commemoration of Columbus' discovery of America, including a historical re-enactment of the event, the internationally televised Miss Hispanidad pageant and a cultural showcase, Festival of the Americas.

Columbus Day Regatta
Information 573 9592. Biscayne Bay. **Date** Columbus Day weekend.
More a giant floating party for some participants than a serious boat race, this two-day event sees vessels of all kinds making their way down Biscayne Bay to the Keys. The flotilla makes a pretty majestic sight.

West Indian Carnival Extravaganza

Information 1-954 435 4845. Miami-Dade Community College, North Campus, 11380 NW 27th Avenue, at NW 119th Street, North Dade. **Date** Columbus Day weekend.
Events evoke the pulse of the islands with music, costumes, crafts and entertainment.

South Miami Arts Festival

Information 661 1621. Along SW 72nd Street, between SW 57th Avenue & US 1, South Miami. **Date** first weekend in Nov.
Established for over 25 years, this is a juried competition where regional and national artists exhibit and sell.

Miami Book Fair International

Information 237 3258. Miami-Dade Community College, Wolfson Campus, 300 NE Second Avenue, at Third Street, Downtown. **Date** begins second Sun in Nov.
One of the biggest literary events in the country, this 10-day extravaganza features appearances by authors of local, national and international standing, over 300 exhibitors' and publishers' booths and activities for children and food lovers.

Banyan Arts & Crafts Festival

Information 444 7270. Downtown Coconut Grove. **Date** third weekend in Nov.
Some 160 artists display and peddle their work at this smaller alternative to the Coconut Grove Arts Festival (*see below*).

Winter

Orange Bowl Festival & Big Orange New Year's Eve Celebration

Information 371 4600. Throughout Dade County. **Date** mid Dec-mid Jan.
Numerous amateur and professional sporting events run through the month, culminating in the massive New Year's Eve Orange Bowl Parade and the New Year's Day football game played by nationally ranked college teams.

Miccosukee Indian Arts Festival

Information 223 8380 ext 346. Miccosukee Indian Village, SW Eighth Street, at SW 177th Avenue, West Dade. **Date** 26 Dec-2 Jan.
Native Americans from all over the US, South and Central America participate in this showcase of their culture at this Indian village, 25 miles west of Miami. Art, crafts, dance, music and song.

King Mango Strut

Information 445 1865. Downtown Coconut Grove. **Date** last Sun in Dec.
Inaugurated in 1982, this ultimate take-off of the Orange Bowl Parade specialises in spoofing local and national events and characters. No one is sacred. Marchers have included the 'Bobbitt Brigade', composed of women wielding butcher knives, and in 1994 a white Bronco led the festivities in honour of OJ Simpson.

Three Kings Day Parade

Information 447 1140. SW Eighth Street, from Fourth to 27th Avenues, Little Havana. **Date** Sun nearest 6 Jan.
This annual parade, thrown by a local Spanish-language radio station, honours the arrival of the three kings with marching bands, Latin music, floats, food – and live camels. A Cuban tradition held on Little Havana's main drag.

Art Deco Weekend

Information 672 2014. Along Ocean Drive, between Fifth & 15th Streets, South Beach. **Date** second weekend in Jan.
South Beach's Ocean Drive, the centre of Miami Beach's splendid National Historic Art Deco District, comes more alive than usual with booths of artwork, memorabilia, collectibles and food. Period automobiles and entertainment from big bands help transport you back in time.

Taste of the Grove

Information 444 7270. Peacock Park, 2820 McFarlane Road, at S Bayshore Drive, Coconut Grove. **Date** third weekend in Jan.
Two days of food, music and fun as Coconut Grove's chefs offer samples from their restaurants and music acts perform.

Miami Film Festival

Information 377 3456. Gusman Center for the Performing Arts, 174 E Flagler Street, at Second Avenue, Downtown. **Date** begins first Fri in Feb.
Ten days of ecstasy for the cineaste. World and US premieres of international and domestic films plus screenings of big-budget movies and more esoteric fare. Also seminars with producers, directors and stars – and plenty of parties.

Coconut Grove Arts Festival

Information 447 0401. Downtown Coconut Grove. **Date** President's Day Weekend.
Close to a million people visit this event (dubbed the number one fine arts festival in the US), which shows the work of over 300 artists. With outdoor concerts and ethnic food.

Bang, bang: Happy New Year!

Watching the ball drop in Times Square has become a New Year's Eve ritual for New Yorkers and TV watchers everywhere. In Miami, around midnight on 31 December, you can watch two things drop: the Big Orange in Downtown, a giant illuminated sphere launched from the top of the Hotel Inter-Continental – and people ducking flying bullets. For some celebrants it has become a tradition to step outside, shoot guns in the air and ring in the New Year with a hail of bullets. Unfortunately, people sometimes get hurt. In Hialeah, where the practice is more prevalent than in the City of Miami, a grand-mother standing inside her house was killed by random gunfire in 1993. In the Liberty City neighbourhood, a policeman sitting in his patrol car was also a victim of a stray bullet in 1996.

Some attribute the tradition to immigrants who refuse to forsake their customs, illegal or not, when they get to this country. Others blame the gunplay on irresponsible people who think that they're having fun. Whatever the cause, the best advice that police can give to a New Year's reveller in South Florida is: when midnight rolls around, if you are outside, get inside. And if you live in Hialeah? Duck.

Reality.

find your place at

Liquid New York - Fall 1997

LIQUID NIGHTCLUB • 1439 Washington Ave.
THE LOUNGE • 1437 Washington Ave. • South Beach
Tel: 305 532.9154 • VIP Table Reservations: 305 532.8899
Fax: 305 532.9980 • email: liquid@thenet.net
visit our website at : http://www.liquidnightclub.com

Photos:Victor Magide / Makeup Artist: Jessie Correa / Stylist: Holly Hadesty

Sightseeing

Tropical gardens, palm-lined beaches, exotic animals and views to die for: Miami's attractions will give you a natural high. Oh, and there's some nice art deco, too...

Areas

For more information on these areas, and others, *see* **By Neighbourhood**.

Miami Beach

It's hard to believe that only a decade or so ago, much of Miami Beach was rundown, with a significant population of elderly retirees sitting in front of shabby deco buildings and Cuban refugees seeking cheap shelter. Well, things change. Thanks to its rediscovery by a few fashion photographers and the diligent efforts of preservationists and civic supporters, Miami Beach has not only regained its hotspot resort status, it's ready to drown in its own fabulousness. From the supermodels to the influx of trendy New Yorkers and Europeans here for the nightlife that begins after a disco nap and ends at sunrise, the current crowd in Miami Beach, along with its ambience, is beautiful and hip.

South Beach is the epicentre. Covering more than a square mile in area, this living architectural archive features more than 900 buildings in the art deco, streamline moderne and Spanish Mediterranean revival styles, from Sixth to 23rd Streets. Ocean Drive – so cool a popular fashion magazine is named after it – is its main promenade, with pastel-coloured hotels on one side and glorious beach on the other. The quieter Collins Avenue is the site of landmark hotels including the Marlin and Delano. Washington Avenue, a block west, is the main drag for restaurants, shops and clubs. Lincoln Road, a pedestrian promenade recently freshened by a $16 million overhaul, is the arts centre, home of the New World Symphony's Lincoln Theatre, the Miami City Ballet and countless art galleries. Espanola Way is a charming street inspired by old Spain. The whole South Beach area is appealingly walkable and as safe as any city gets.

At Mid-Beach (from Dade Boulevard north to 62nd Street), the skyline shoots skyward in the form of elaborate 1950s hotels like the Eden Roc and Fontainebleau, where gala showgirl extravaganzas are the expected entertainment. Though style gurus may be on the lookout for the next trendy destination, Miami Beach isn't falling from favour anytime soon. Its natural assets – beautiful beach, offbeat architecture, warm climate – are big hits with the fashion and movie industries as well as tourists. It's easy to want to return here.

Downtown Miami

Downtown Miami has been largely abandoned by locals for the suburbs and turned over to visitors and the lawyer/banker types who work here. As a result, its heart is a combination of shiny high-rises and cluttered discount stores targeting Brazilian and other South American shoppers. The 55-storey First Union Financial Center (200 S Biscayne Boulevard, at SE Second Street), the tallest structure south of Atlanta, dominates the skyline, but the older buildings deliver charm, among them the Freedom Tower on Biscayne Boulevard (at NE Seventh Street), gateway for Cuban refugees arriving in Miami in the 1960s; and the Gusman Center for the Performing Arts (174 E Flagler Street, at NE Second Avenue), a fabulous 1920s theatre for concerts, plays and the Miami Film Festival. Royal palm-lined

Hanging out on Miami Beach's Ocean Drive.

Biscayne Boulevard, site of the Orange Bowl Parade, is Miami's grand avenue. Bayside, the tourist marketplace, is on the water here; just to the south are the John F Kennedy Memorial and the Challenger Space Shuttle Memorial.

Coral Gables

Behind the stately Old Spanish facade of Coral Gables, the 'City Beautiful', there's money – and lots of it. This thriving suburb is the base for more than 140 multinational corporations, whose dealings are often conducted in no-nonsense business hotels such as the Hyatt Regency and Omni Colonnade or the concentration of swanky restaurants and cafés downtown. As one of the first planned communities in the 1920s, when it was dreamed up by its creator, George Merrick, Coral Gables is justifiably proud of its history and architectural heritage – its beautifully maintained tree-lined streets and plazas, ornate Mediterranean entrances and fountains, and carefully preserved landmarks such as the Venetian Pool (*see below* **Attractions**), the Merrick House (907 Coral Way, between Toledo Street & Granada Boulevard) and the Biltmore Hotel (1200 Anastasia Avenue, at Granada Boulevard), a magnificent structure with an awesome swimming pool, the largest hotel pool in the continental US.

Coconut Grove

No matter how developers try to homogenise Coconut Grove with bland commercial buildings and manufactured charm, they can't overpower the irrepressible artist/hippy spirit that still lingers in this village of friendly eccentrics. Street artists still peddle their wares and independent shops and restaurants such as the Maya Hatcha (3058 Grand Avenue, at Fuller Street) or the Taurus (3540 Main Highway, between Charles & Franklin Avenues), still easily outshine the slick but ubiquitous Gaps or Planet Hollywoods. The Grove also has in its favour a legitimate sense of history as a former hangout for pirates, Bahamian settlers and prominent Northerners. For a glimpse into Coconut Grove pioneer life, visit the Barnacle State Historic Site, the 1891 home of settler Commodore Ralph Middleton Munroe, and stop by Plymouth Congregational Church for an example of coral rock architecture (for details, *see chapter* **Architecture**).

Little Havana

Calle Ocho (SW Eighth Street) is the main drag of this neighbourhood west of Brickell Avenue. Its roots may have sprung from the Cuban exiles who came here in the 1950s and 1960s, worked hard, and prospered, but today Little Havana is home to nearly as many Nicaraguans, Hondurans, Guatemalans and Puerto Ricans as Cubans, making this a true Hispanic melting pot. The best way to experience La Saguesera (Spanglish for 'South-west area') is on foot, taking in its vivid sights, smells, sounds and flavours: old men playing dominoes at Domino Park; hand-rolled cigar factories; botanicas offering herbal cures and potions; rhythmic salsa music; eye-opening Cuban coffee.

Attractions

Bayside Marketplace

Biscayne Boulevard & NE Fourth Street, Downtown (577 3344). Bus 3, 16, 48, 95, C/Metromover College/Bayside.
Nearly every major city has its touristy marketplace full of shops, kiosks and entertainment – and Bayside is Miami's. Located north of Bayfront Park opposite the Port of Miami, it is home to the requisite Hard Rock Café, chains such as The Gap and Victoria's Secret and a food court where you can sample churros (Spanish doughnut strips), cajun grill and teriyaki, and wash them down with something from Let's Make A Daiquiri. Daily live music creates a festive air, and if you're feeling really touristy, go to the marina, where you can ride in a gondola, take a sightseeing cruise or board one of the garish neon-lighted disco boats that cruise the bay blaring salsa music.

Coral Castle

28655 S Dixie Highway, at SW 286th Street, Homestead (248 6344). Metrorail Dadeland North then bus 38.
Open 9am-6pm daily. **Admission** $7.75 adults; $6.50 senior citizens; $5 7-12s; free under-7s with paid adult. **No credit cards.**
Hand-built by a 97lb man over a 30-year span, Coral Castle is as baffling as it is offbeat. However did this slight fellow manage to move the tons of coral rock (oolite, a native limestone) required to create this furnished castle, a tribute to the fiancée who jilted him in his native Latvia? His obsession is chronicled in fittingly bizarre fashion: as you tour the castle, there is a recorded narrative delivered with first-person drama in a heavy faux-Latvian accent. Weird, but amusing.

Metrozoo

12400 SW 152nd Street, at SW 124th Avenue, South Dade (251 0400). Metrorail Dadeland North then Zoobus.
Open 9.30am-5.30pm daily; ticket booth closes at 4pm. **Admission** $8 adults; $4 3-12s; free under-3s. **Credit** AmEx, MC, V.
If you like zoos, you should know that Metrozoo is considered one of the best, with more than 900 wild animals in a completely cageless environment. But be warned: it's a 45-minute drive from Downtown Miami or Miami Beach, and in the summer it's beastly hot. The open-air environments reproduce native habitats, such as the Bengal tiger exhibit, which has a replica of the Angkor Wat temple facade, and the Asian River Life display, where clouded leopards and giant monitor lizards appear and disappear in a mist of waterfalls and exotic sound effects. In the children's petting area, kids can visit tame animals and take an elephant ride. There are also regular wildlife shows scheduled and an excellent monorail tour.

Miami Seaquarium

4400 Rickenbacker Causeway, Virginia Key (361 5705). Bus B. **Open** 9.30am-6pm daily; ticket booth closes at 4.30pm. **Admission** $19.95 adults; $14.95 3-9s; free under-3s. **Credit** AmEx, MC, V.
If you've been to Sea World in Orlando, this venerable marine life attraction may not impress you. The windows of the Reef Tank are cloudy, the passageways shabby. But the killer whale, dolphin and sea lion shows presented by their youthful trainers are lively, and the manatee presentation offers a close look at these huge, docile sea creatures found in South Florida waters. During the summer, on Friday and Saturday nights, take advantage of Summer Nights, whereby for a special admission you can enjoy the shows plus live music and entertainment without the oppressive daytime heat.

Miccosukee Indian Village

SW Eighth Street, at SW 177th Avenue, West Dade (223 8380). No public transport. **Open** 9am-5pm daily. **Admission** $5 adults; $4 senior citizens; $3.50 5-12s; free under-4s. **No credit cards.**
Miccosukee tribal craftsmen exhibit patchwork and basketry and wrestle alligators in this lukewarm attraction, 25 miles west of Miami. If you've come this far, your best bet is to skip the village and instead take a ride in an airboat (small, flat-bottomed boats with huge propellers mounted on the back) for an action-filled view of the Everglades. You can arrange a ride ($7) across the street from the village.

Monkey Jungle

14805 SW 216th Street, at SW 147th Avenue, South Dade (235 1611). No public transport. **Open** 9.30am-5pm daily; ticket booth closes at 4pm. **Admission** $11.50 adults; $9.50 senior citizens; $6 4-12s; free under-4s. **Credit** AmEx, DC, Disc, MC, V.
Immediately after Hurricane Andrew ravaged South Dade in 1992, it was rumoured that bands of AIDS-infected monkeys from this attraction were on the loose, terrorising everyone in their sight. (Another popular rumour was that the government was hiding the corpses of hundreds of hurricane victims in this area – utterly untrue, but widely believed to this day). Well, the diseased animals were someone else's research monkeys: Monkey Jungle's territorial monkeys stayed put, this unique attraction was rebuilt, and you can once again observe all sorts of primates in a lush tropical jungle – they run free, while the visitors are 'caged'. Much of the Amazonian jungle scenery has been restored to stunning effect, and this remains a singular attraction.

Parrot Jungle & Gardens

11000 SW 57th Avenue, at SW 111th Street, South Dade (666-7834). Metrorail South Miami then bus 57. **Open** 9.30am-6pm; ticket booth closes at 5pm. **Admission** $12.95 adults; $8.95 senior citizens; $8.95 3-10s; free under-3s. **Credit** AmEx, MC, V.
You can have your picture taken with colourful macaws perched on your shoulder as a corny souvenir, but what you'll really come away with after a visit to Parrot Jungle and Gardens is a sense of South Florida's subtropical beauty and awesome flora and fauna. This longtime tourist attraction, located smack dab in the middle of prime residential property 11 miles south-west of Miami, is a dense jungle of exotic palms, orchids and bromeliads, with fantastically coloured parrots, flamingos and entertaining wildlife shows such as Creatures in the Mist, a rainforest exhibit that cools visitors down with an actual cloud of mist. Have breakfast at the Parrot Café (open daily at 8am) and you'll beat the heat when the park opens at 9.30am. Parrot Jungle and Gardens plans to move to Watson Island, off the MacArthur Causeway, in 1999.

Spanish Monastery

16711 W Dixie Highway, at NE 167th Street, North Miami Beach (945 1461). Bus 3, V. **Open** 10am-4pm Mon-Sat; noon-4pm Sun. **Admission** $4.50 adults; $2.50 senior citizens; $1 under-12s. **No credit cards.**
What bills itself as the oldest building in the western hemisphere (we have our doubts) sits unassumingly in North Miami Beach. The Monastery of St Bernard de Clairvaux

was originally built in Segovia, Spain, in around 1133 and was occupied by Cistercian monks for nearly 700 years. In 1925, newspaper magnate William Randolph Hearst purchased the buildings for his California estates and had them dismantled stone by stone. But the shipment was quarantined in Brooklyn, Hearst suffered financial woes and the crates sat in a warehouse for 26 years before they were purchased, moved to North Miami Beach and reassembled as an attraction and place of worship. The monastery is off the beaten track, but if you're a fan of romanesque architecture, it's worth a visit.

Venetian Pool

2701 DeSoto Boulevard, at Toledo Street, Coral Gables (460 5356). Bus 24, 72. **Open** 11am-5.30pm Tue-Fri; 10am-4.30pm Sat, Sun. **Admission** $5 adults; $4 13-17s; $2 3-12s; under-3s not allowed in pool. **No credit cards.**
This quirky attraction is well worth a visit. Once a quarry, the Venetian Pool was built in the 1920s as an exotic locale for swimming and entertainment, with gondolas, movie stars such as Esther Williams and Johnny Weismuller of *Tarzan* fame and orchestras serenading poolside dancers. Nowadays, you might catch the filming of Spanish-language dance shows. With its vine-covered loggias, cascading waterfalls, rock caves and sand beach, it's a delightful place to spend an afternoon sunbathing.

Vizcaya Museum & Gardens

3251 S Miami Ave, at 32nd Road, Coconut Grove (250 9133). Bus 48/Metrorail Vizcaya. **Open** *house* 9.30am-5pm, *gardens* 9.30am-5.30pm, daily; ticket booth closes at 4.30pm. **Admission** $10 adults; $5 6-12s; free under-6s. **Credit** AmEx, MC, V.
The favoured site for lavish galas and elegant weddings, Vizcaya is an Italian Renaissance-style villa and formal gardens built in 1916 as the winter residence of industrialist James Deering. Its 34 rooms are filled with antiques, art and tapestries from the fifteenth to nineteenth centuries, and the grounds are magnificent, with more than 10 acres of Italian gardens, statues and fountains, perched perfectly on Biscayne Bay, with views of the skyline and Key Biscayne. Fittingly, the Italian Renaissance Festival is held here every March (*see chapter* **By Season**). There's an excellent café for lunch and you can linger in the gardens till 5.30pm.

Beaches

South Florida's beaches are consistently ranked among the best in the nation. Atlantic waters are generally clean, safe and pleasantly warm, there are plenty of lifeguard stands and most beaches have restrooms, showers, snack stands and watersport equipment rental. Umbrellas and lounge chairs are available at many beaches; if you don't see an attendant, just claim an empty chair and they'll show up sooner or later to collect the fee, usually a few dollars. Topless sunbathing is permitted in Miami Beach, and there is a totally nude beach at Haulover Park.

Beach safety tips

● South Florida's sun is subtropical and you can get burned even on overcast days. Respect it. Use a sunscreen with a sun protection factor (SPF) of at least 15 (30 for children), year round, and take a hat.
● Swim in guarded areas only, avoiding stretches where surfers are active. Lifeguards post warning flags and signs by their stations. 'No swimming' (red) means just that. 'Caution' (yellow) means hazardous conditions, such as riptides, so your best bet is to ask the lifeguard just what

Best beaches for...

… **nude sunbathing**: Haulover Beach
… **children**: Crandon Park
… **watersports**: Hobie Beach
… **scenic setting**: Matheson Hammock
… **gay beach**: 12th Street Beach
… **straight pick-up**: any beach on South Beach
… **volleyball**: Lummus Park
… **surfing**: South Pointe Park

dangers exist. Green flags, a new addition to Miami Beach sign language, mean it's safe to swim.
● Rip currents, aka riptides, result in drownings every year. These strong currents occur on days with strong onshore winds and can carry even the most experienced swimmer out to sea. Take the warning flags seriously. If it happens to you, don't panic. Save your energy and aim to swim parallel to the shore until you are out of the rip's hold, then turn to swim towards shore.
● Watch out for Portuguese men-of-war, jellyfish-like sea creatures that look like blue bubbles floating on the water or washed up amid seaweed. Their long tentacles have layers of cells that pack a nasty sting and occasionally cause allergic reactions. If you get stung, head for the lifeguard, who will treat the stings with vinegar and meat tenderiser. You'll smart for a few hours, but that's usually all.
● Sea lice, or immature men-of-war, are more annoying than dangerous. They attach to your swimming costume and cause itching rather than stinging. To relieve the itching, shower with soap and water and make sure to wash under your bathing suit.
● Although there are many species of shark in South Florida waters, they are really not a concern for beach-users. Beach Patrol Captain Vincent Andreano says no one has ever been bitten by a shark on Miami Beach. If lifeguards see sharks close in, they may ask swimmers to get out of the water, but this rarely happens.

Miami Beach & northwards

Beaches within the City of Miami Beach are open every day. There are public parking lots and metered street parking, but by 10am the lots are full, so you may have to resort to public transport or a taxi. You can't miss the fabulous painted lifeguard stands. The Beach Patrol watches over 21 locations from South Pointe Park north to 83rd Street, with beautiful deco headquarters at 1001 Ocean Drive, at 10th Street (673 7714). There's a 1½ mile boardwalk from 21st to 46th Streets.

Most of the following beaches (listed from south to north) have restrooms, showers and a boardwalk or promenade; many have snack bars and special areas for children.

South Pointe Park *1 Washington Avenue, at the southernmost tip of South Beach*
Surfers enjoy this beach, part of a 17-acre park with picnic areas, tot lot, fishing pier and a marked vita course, a fitness circuit with equipment and instructions. Also great views of cruise ships – and people giving friends aboard a send-off – as they ply the Port of Miami.

YOU'RE IN
MIAMI NOW
BUT WHEN IN
NEW YORK CITY

**CHECK OUT HOTEL 31
MOVING COOL INTO
MID-TOWN**

**CALL FOR OUR BROCHURE:
120 E 31 ST STREET
NYC 10016
TEL: 212-685-3060
FAX: 212-532-1232**

15% discount for Time Out readers

http://www.timeout.co.uk

**Amsterdam, Barcelona,
Berlin, Boston, Brussels,
Budapest, Chicago,
Edinburgh, Glasgow, London,
Madrid, Miami, New York,
Paris, Philadelphia, Prague,
Rome, San Francisco, Sydney,
Tokyo & Washington DC.**

* Credit card transfers available in the US, UK and Ireland.

Blown all your bucks? No problem. Western Union can send you money in minutes. Phone someone at home who can deposit* the amount you need at their nearest Western Union office. Then collect it, in cash, from your nearest Western Union Office. There are over 21,000 locations across the US. Many open 24 hours a day. For more details all free 1 800 325 6000.

WESTERN UNION | MONEY TRANSFER

The fastest way to send money worldwide.

Lummus Park Beach *Ocean Drive, between Fifth & 15th Streets*
Beach volleyball, palm trees and thatched chickee huts. There's a gay beach at 12th Street.

21st-35th Street Beach *Collins Avenue*
Small beaches with a boardwalk and a snack bar.

53rd-63rd Street Beach *Collins Avenue*
Pleasant beaches between high-rises.

North Shore Open Space Park *Collins Avenue, between 79th & 86th Streets*
Wooden boardwalks, pavilions, barbecue grills, vita course.

Surfside *Collins Avenue, between 88th & 96th Streets*
Lifeguard station at 93rd Street in front of the Surfside Community Center. Limited facilities.

Bal Harbour Beach *Collins Avenue, at 96th Street*
Small beach with a vita course.

Haulover Park Beach *10800 Collins Avenue, north of Bal Harbour (944 3040)*
Nestled between the Intracoastal Waterway and the Atlantic Ocean, Haulover Beach is a 1½ mile stretch of sand and surf with something for everyone: white sand shores, open ocean surf, shaded picnic facilities, landscaped sand dunes and concession stands. The southern end of the beach is popular with families; moving north, there's a nude beach, followed by a gay nude beach, with nude volleyball for players of any sexual preference. Across the street is a marina, restaurant, tennis courts and nine-hole family golf course.

Sunny Isles *Collins Avenue, between 163rd & 192nd Streets*
Two miles of public beaches and surrounding souvenir shops and hotels offer a kitschy sampling of resort Florida. Popular with Canadian snowbirds.

Key Biscayne & Virgina Key

Beaches both north and south of the Rickenbacker Causeway, which leads to Key Biscayne, are user-friendly, with a focus on watersports. (Note that at the time of writing Virginia Key Beach had been closed indefinitely due to lack of funding.) The following beaches are listed from north to south:

Hobie Beach *Virginia Key*
Windsurfing, jet-ski, sailboat and sailboard rentals. On the beaches after the big bridge, the warm bay waters are a natural for families with children and dogs. Inline skaters and bike riders start here, taking the bike path towards Key Biscayne or back over the bridge.

Crandon Park *4000 Crandon Boulevard (361 5421)*
Once home to Indian tribes, soldiers and pirates, then a huge coconut plantation, Crandon Park's three-mile beach is consistently named one of the top 10 in the nation. On any sunny weekend, you'll see Dade County's multi-ethnic make-up as local families spend the day grilling chorizos, ribs or burgers while listening to merengue or hip-hop. Crandon offers pristine sand, calm shallow water, a winding boardwalk, concession stands and convenient parking. There are no waves or undertow here, making this a good family beach.

Bill Baggs Cape Florida State Recreation Area *1200 S Crandon Boulevard (361 5811)*
Another nationally ranked beach, Cape Florida offers 410 acres of beautiful beaches, bicycle trails, fishing and picnic areas, even history – the lighthouse, recently restored to its 1825 condition, is the oldest structure in Dade County and has exhibits depicting early island life. Get seafood at the beachfront Lighthouse Café.

South Miami

Matheson Hammock Park Beach *9610 Old Cutler Road, between SW 93rd & 101st Streets (665 5475)*
This scenic park has an unusual feature – a man-made atoll pool which is flushed naturally by the tidal action of adja-cent Biscayne Bay. The tranquil beach is popular with families because of its warm, safe waters and tropical hardwood forest surroundings. There's also an excellent restaurant housed in a historic coral rock building.

Miami by water

Water Taxi

The Water Taxi (1-954 467 6677) operates like a taxi: call them and they'll pick you up (and deliver you) at one of about 10 points along the water in Downtown Miami and South Beach. The boats are 26ft Oldports seating 27 people. It's not the most practical means of transport, but it's a big buzz and the views are great. Operating hours are usually 10am-midnight daily; fares are $7 one-way, $12 round trip and $15 for an all-day pass.

Boat tours

Many short sightseeing boat tours depart from Bayside Marketplace. Ninety-minute cruises aboard the yacht **Celebration** (373 7001) and the **Island Queen** (379 5119) tour waterfront estates along Millionaires Row, the private islands of Miami Beach and the cruise ships at the Port of Miami. The **Miami Queen**, a Mississippi River-style paddlewheeler (448 5866), makes a one-hour jaunt that goes past Fisher Island. The **Heritage of Miami** (442 9697), a 85-footer, two-masted passenger schooner offers sightseeing tours of Biscayne Bay at 1.30pm, 4pm, and 6.30pm daily from September to June ($12 adults, $7 children). Soft drinks and snacks are available on board, or bring your own provisions.

Watersports

The Miami area is a natural mecca for watersports, from admiring fish as they swim among coral to catching and stuffing them; from sailing the tranquil seas to tearing them up on a jet-ski. The biggest concentration of rental outlets for jet-skis, windsurfers, sailboat and kayaks is on Virginia Key (on the way to Key Biscayne). For full details *see chapter* Sport & Fitness.

Outdoors

Bill Baggs Cape Florida State Park

1200 S Crandon Boulevard, Key Biscayne (361 5811). Bus B. **Open** 8am-sundown daily. **Admission** per vehicle $2 (1 person); $4 (2-8 people); on foot $1.
Great beaches and watersports, including shoreline fishing, scuba diving and snorkelling, make this a family favourite, and a wooden walkway makes it pushchair friendly. Visit the newly restored Cape Florida lighthouse and museum and eat lunch at the Lighthouse Café (*see above* **Beaches**).

The opulent **Vizcaya** (see page 21).

Biscayne National Underwater Park

9700 SW 328th Street, at SW 97th Avenue, Homestead (230 7275/230 1100). No public transport. **Open** 8am-5.30pm daily. **Admission** free to park; *scuba diving* $35 (excluding equipment); *snorkelling* $27.95 (including equipment); *glass-bottom boat tour* $19.95 adults; $17.95 senior citizens; $9.95 under-12s.

Coral reefs are one of the major resources protected in the park, 95% of which is underwater. Mangrove shorelines, lush seagrass beds and barrier islands are part of the fascinating marine wilderness, which can be explored on glass-bottom boats, via snorkelling/scuba or rented canoe. Scuba divers must be certified. A new visitor centre, replacing the facility destroyed by Hurricane Andrew, has exhibits, an auditorium and a museum.

Fairchild Tropical Garden

10901 Old Cutler Road, at SW 101st Street, Coral Gables (667 1651). Bus 65. **Open** 9.30am-4.30pm daily. **Admission** $8 adults; free under-13s. **Credit** AmEx, Disc, MC, V.

One of South Florida's most underpromoted natural treasures, Fairchild Tropical Garden is 83 acres of tropical and subtropical beauty: extraordinary palms, lush bromeliads and orchids, flowering trees, shrubs and vines. Wander winding paths alongside lakes and lily pools, or take the tram ride for a relaxing tour. The conservatory, Windows on the Tropics, features fragile and rare rainforest plants. The Rainforest Café is open on weekends (11am-3pm), and there's a delightful bookstore. Much of the garden was torn up by Hurricane Andrew in 1992, but thanks to hours of work by volunteers and the remarkable restorative powers of Mother Nature in the subtropics, Fairchild is greener and lusher than ever. One of the hurricane's legacies is a small plot called Andrew's Garden, which features an uprooted (but still growing) oak tree and other foliage left intact after the storm.

Fruit & Spice Park

24801 SW 187th Avenue, at SW 256th Street, Homestead (247 5727). No public transport. **Open** 10am-5pm daily. **Admission** $2 adults; 50¢ under-12s; *guided tours* $1.50 adults; $1 under-12s.

The only garden of its kind in the US, this 30-acre park, 35 miles south of Miami, exhibits more than 500 varieties of fruits, vegetables, spices, herbs, nuts and exotic edibles. An old schoolhouse and coral rock building show South Florida pioneer life, and the charming gift shop sells spices, jams and jellies, unusual seeds and aromatic teas, and cookbooks on tropical fruits and vegetables. The park is also the site of the Redland Natural Arts Festival in January and the Asian Arts Festival in March (*see chapter* **By Season**).

Holocaust Memorial

1933-1945 Meridian Avenue, at Dade Boulevard, Miami Beach (538 1663). Bus A, G, K, R, W. **Open** 9am-9pm daily. **Admission** free.

Sculptor and architect Kenneth Triester's vivid conception of the six million Jewish lives lost in the Holocaust, this 42ft bronze sculpture is surrounded by haunting images of the death camps.

Oleta River State Recreation Area

3400 NE 163rd Street, between Biscayne Boulevard & Collins Avenue, Sunny Isles (919 1846). Bus E, H, V. **Open** 8am-sundown daily. **Admission** per vehicle $3.25 (up to 8 people); on foot $1; free under-8s.

This 854-acre park contains an 80-acre lagoon and a mangrove-lined island. There's plenty of wildlife, including raccoons, fiddler crabs, land crabs, bald eagles, hawks, pelicans, ibis, egrets and manatees. You can swim, fish, canoe, bicycle, jog, hike or rent a paddleboat here. Greynolds Park abuts the Oleta to the north and takes in much of the watery areas. You can rent kayaks on Collins Avenue before Haulover Beach Park.

Viewpoints

An overview of Downtown

Take Metrorail to Government Center station and then jump on the Metromover, an automated elevated monorail that makes a Downtown loop with a north leg near the Omni International Mall and a south leg down Brickell Avenue. Look for the gold-domed roof of Central Baptist Church, Freedom Tower and a nice aerial view of Bayfront Park. On the south leg, you'll go high over the Miami River and into the Brickell area, home to international banks and high-rises. For a more detailed Metromover tour, *see chapter* **Downtown**.

Best city skyline views

Miami's many causeways guarantee stunning waterfront views. Good for the Downtown skyline is the MacArthur, which links the southern tip of Miami Beach with the mainland, also giving views of the Port of Miami and its cruise ships and various of the Biscayne Bay islands. The Rickenbacker Causeway bridge, joining the mainland to Virginia Key, soars high over the bay: from the top, you'll see the glorious city skyline and the port to the north, and the grounds of waterfront estates, including Vizcaya, to the south. If you want to see more than flashing past in a car allows, go for a jog or a bike ride, ideally at sunset, or drive over the bridge to the Rusty Pelican, a restaurant that juts out into the bay. Incidentally, Miami's skyline is rated one of the best-lit, with 40 permanently illuminated Downtown buildings. The colours of the NationsBank tower change frequently to represent sports team colours and celebrate holidays and other events.

South Beach

Because regulations limit the height of buildings in the Deco District, there are few buildings tall enough to furnish a bird's-eye view. Best is Decoplage Condos at 100 Lincoln Road, two blocks in from the seafront; ask the concierge nicely and you'll be allowed to scoot up to the 27th floor for a great view of Ocean Drive. Otherwise try your luck at the taller hotels. We were allowed up to the penthouse floor of the Delano after a drink in the bar (no great hardship). The mens' room at the Rooftop Lounge in the Howard Johnson Hotel (4000 Alton Road) has a picture window guaranteed to take your mind off the job in hand. If you're swimming, don't forget to turn back to land to get a layered view of sand, lifeguard huts, palms and the deco skyline.

Cruise flash

Don't have the time or money for a long ocean cruise? Hop on one of several day cruises that depart from the Port of Miami and the Miami Beach Marina. Las Vegas-style shows, live entertainment and meals are part of the deal, but gambling is the main focus as these ships head out to international waters so that passengers can play the casinos. **Discovery Cruise Lines** (Port of Miami; 1-800 937 4477) offers short cruises to nowhere and one-day cruises that stop at Freeport, Bahamas, for a few hours. **Europa SeaKruz** (Miami Beach Marina; 538 8300) operates short gambling cruises daily.

Best picnic spot

Head to the seaplane base at Watson Island, at the mainland end of the MacArthur Causeway, pick up sandwiches and beers at the convenience store, and sit back and watch the world around you: the Downtown skyline looming to the west, PanAm's retro-looking seaplanes taking off from Government Cut on their way to Bimini and the Bahamas, and Cruise Ship Alley at the Port of Miami across the way. Cruise line company Carnival's newest ship, the Destiny, is the largest cruise liner in the world, with a capacity of 3,400, and looks pretty awesome even from a distance. Friday afternoons at around 4pm is a good time to watch the big ships head out to sea.

Arts & museums

See also chapter **Museums & Galleries**.

Lincoln Road

The freshly refurbished Lincoln Road pedestrian mall in South Beach is home to five major cultural institutions: the New World Symphony at the Lincoln Theatre, the South Florida Art Center, the Miami City Ballet (which rehearses before your eyes at 905 Lincoln Road), Colony Theater (a dance and performing arts venue) and the Area Stage, as well as a clutch of galleries. The Alliance Cinema, with the freshest programming in town, is also here.

If you've only got two days...

...but want to cram as much as possible into your visit to Miami, try this itinerary.

Day one

5.30am Watch the sun rise over the ocean from the South Beach sand (avoiding last night's couples getting their own romantic kicks). Stroll around the Deco District while the sun is still flat and the eyeshadow colours intense.

7am Breakfast at the News Café, not so much for the food as the vibe: this is South Beach ground zero. Watch as the models dash out of the hotels around you for their early morning (great light) shoots.

8am Head out along the Tamiami Trail for a drive to the Everglades, before the sun gets too pumped up. Rent a bike and ride the 13-mile paved route around Shark Valley, then take an airboat tour and see it all the easy way.

12.30pm Head back to town. When the Tamiami Trail becomes SW Eighth Street and enters Little Havana, stop to buy cigars and fuel up on Cuban coffee from a stand.

1.30pm Get lunch at Joe's Stone Crab, back on South Beach. But don't wait in line for a table: go to Joe's shop and take your claws (and Key lime pie) out into South Pointe Park for a picnic.

2.30pm Rent some skates from one of the beach concessions and cruise north along the beachfront until the path runs out. Come back along Ocean Drive at least half competently and everyone will assume you're a local.

3.30pm The sun should be low enough for beach neophytes to take to the sand without frying, so pick a stretch of South Beach where the human scenery pleases you and chill out.

5.30pm Amble back to your hotel and put some serious time in (and maybe a nap) preparing for a night out.

8pm Stroll over to Lincoln Road to take dinner where the locals go. Check out the chunky Cuban platefuls at the Lincoln Road Café, then

have a coffee or a digestif at the pavement café of your choice.

11pm Non-ravers head for bed; for the rest, the party starts here. Pick out a bar from our listings: we suggest starting at 821 Lincoln Road, where the crowd is mixed in every way and the atmosphere hip and easygoing. Thus warmed up, hit a nightclub proper: Bash, mixed and celebrity-connected (Mick Hucknall and Sean Penn are co-owners) would be a classic South Beach choice.

3am Lower your weary body onto a velour barstool at the Deuce Bar, the quintessential late-night bar – tack, attitude and all. Then fuel up with a burrito from Benny's, opposite.

Day two

10.30am Put sunglasses on; stumble out of room; get a serious breakfast at the Eleventh Street diner. Then take a water taxi to Downtown and hop onto the Metromover train for a bird's-eye circular tour – for a mere 25¢.

1.30pm Take lunch at Big Fish by the Miami River: great view, great food and a 20ft high stiletto out front.

3pm More relaxation: take your choice between a visit to the Venetian Pools in Coral Gables, the grand-daddy of all exotic swimming pools, or a drive to quietly beautiful Crandon Beach on Key Biscayne. On your way back, stop at the Rusty Pelican for a drink or two: it's the perfect place to watch sunset.

8.30pm A quiet meal is probably all you'll be able to cope with by now. Avoid the frenzy of Ocean Drive and retire to the brightly coloured but deeply relaxing Tap Tap for a taste of Haitian cuisine.

(Note: timings are approximate.)

Exclusive **Star Island**, *the Estefans' home.*

Metro-Dade Cultural Center
101 W Flagler Street, at NW First Avenue, Downtown (375 1700). Bus 3, 16, 95, C, S/Metrorail & Metromover Government Center. **Open** Opening times, admission and credit card details vary according to facility.
Part of a huge cultural complex, containing the Historical Museum of Southern Florida and the Miami Art Museum, which hosts touring shows as well as its own exhibitions, with special emphasis on the art of the western hemisphere from 1940 to the present.

The Wolfsonian
1001 Washington Avenue, at 10th Street, South Beach (531 1001). Bus C, H, K, W. **Open** 11am-6pm Tue, Wed, Fri, Sat; 11am-9pm Thur; noon-5pm Sun. **Admission** $5 adults; $3.50 students, senior citizens; free under-6s; free or by donation 6-9pm Thur. **Credit** AmEx, MC, V.
An intriguing cultural institution with a vast collection of American and European art and design from 1885-1945, all amassed by the eccentric Micky Wolfson Jr. Free admission on Thursday evenings.

Gallery walks
Every month, galleries, studios, shops and restaurants hold co-ordinated open houses that feature exhibition openings, receptions and special events.

Lincoln Road
Second Saturday of the month, 6-10pm (674 8278).

Downtown Coral Gables
First Friday of the month, 7-10pm (445 5125).

Design District (between NE 37th-41st Streets & North Miami-NE Second Avenues)
Second Friday of the month, 6-10pm.

Rich & famous
Historically, Miami and Miami Beach have been the sites of winter residences of the rich and famous, but in the past decade celebs are not only staying here, they're setting up businesses. In Miami Beach, one of the most visible celebrity mansions is that of Italian fashion designer Gianni Versace, who took the former Casa Casuarina, a 1930s Mediterranean revival estate at Ocean Drive and 12th Street, and restored it to legendary opulence (though it is said he is in residence for only a few days a year). In Coconut Grove, Madonna and Sylvester Stallone are currently neighbours, with waterfront estates on Brickell Avenue and SE 32nd Road, north of the entrance to Vizcaya. Sly's house is the first on the right; Madonna's is a few doors down and has tall stands of royal palms looming behind the gates.

Star Island, off the MacArthur Causeway, is home to pop singer Gloria Estefan. Tennis star Jim Courier and talkshow host Oprah Winfrey have places at Fisher Island at the tip of South Beach. Latin crooner Julio Iglesias and golf legend Ray Floyd are longtime residents of the exclusive Indian Creek Village near Surfside. Celeb-owned restaurants include Lario's on the Beach (the Estefans) and South Beach Brasserie (Michael Caine). Supermodel sightings are common in South Beach, Coconut Grove and Coral Gables, where fashion shoots run non-stop; if you see a huge mobile home parked in the street, you can be sure models and crews are nearby. The free weekly business paper *Miami Today* lists all film, TV and photo shoots underway in town.

Scenic drives
Vizcaya south to Homestead (about 28 miles)
Start in front of Vizcaya Museum & Gardens (S Miami Avenue, at 32nd Road) and head south down S Bayshore Drive past elegant homes on a bluff. As you approach Coconut Grove, on your left you'll see picturesque boats bobbing in the bay and the charming City Hall building at Dinner Key, site of a seaplane base and terminal for Pan American World Airways in the 1930s. The road becomes Main Highway and twists around the lively heart of the Grove, turning into scenic Ingraham Highway.

Turn left at Le Jeune Road and you'll find yourself at Cocoplum Circle (note the big shoes sculpture, a gift from Coral Gables' sister city of Cartagena, Colombia). Follow banyan tree-lined Old Cutler Road south past Matheson Hammock Park and Fairchild Tropical Garden. Continue on Old Cutler all the way down through Cutler Ridge (the bare native pine trees are evidence of Hurricane Andrew's wrath). At SW 216th Street, pick up US 1 south and continue about nine miles south to Homestead's Cauley Square, a quaint village of shops and a tea room.

Downtown's illuminated skyline (top) and Deco mecca Ocean Drive.

VIRGIN MEGASTORE

HEADING NORTH WITH A SONG IN YOUR HEART?

WHILE YOU'RE VISITING ORLANDO

BE SURE TO STOP BY

VIRGIN MEGASTORE AND TAKE HOME

A SAMPLE OF OUR HUGE SELECTION

OF MUSIC, MOVIES, MULTIMEDIA

AND MUCH, MUCH MORE.

MEGASTORE
Downtown Disney
MUSIC · MOVIES · MULTIMEDIA · MORE

DOWNTOWN DISNEY AT DISNEYWORLD

VIRGIN MEGASTORE

South Beach north to Golden Beach (about 18 miles)

You can't go wrong with a drive up Collins Avenue on Miami Beach, from its southernmost origin at First Street to the Dade County line. As you travel, the art deco hotels of South Beach switch to the 1950s glitz of the Fontainebleau in Mid-Beach, followed by small-town Surfside and the unabashed wealth of Bal Harbour before hitting Sunny Isles kitsch. You'll pass the elegant homes of Golden Beach before the condo canyons begin again.

Miami International Airport to South Beach (about 10 miles)

If you arrive at Miami airport, this is the most direct route to South Beach, so you're likely to take it whatever your means of transport. No hardship – it's a great introduction to Miami, giving views of Downtown Miami, Biscayne Bay and Miami Beach.

From MIA, take the Dolphin Expressway (aka SR 836) heading east. About four miles after you get on the expressway, there's a toll plaza, after which the expressway rises and the Orange Bowl stadium, once a much-used venue for pro football games and rock concerts, now relegated to college football, is immediately visible on your right, with the high-rises of Downtown looming to the south. Follow the signs to the beaches via I-395 (MacArthur Causeway). Just before the causeway rises over the water, you'll see the Miami Herald building and Plaza Venetia/Omni on your left, the Freedom Tower to your right. You'll pass Watson Island and its seaplanes on the right; Palm, Hibiscus and Star Islands on the left; and the huge cruise ships of the Port of Miami on the right. The causeway rises again as it turns east to South Beach, providing a lovely view of luxury island homes on your left and spiffy yachts and sport fishing boats at the Miami Beach Marina to the right.

Coral Gables (about 20 miles)

The very picturesque city of Coral Gables offers a 20-mile self-guided automobile tour that takes about two hours. Visitors can pick up a detailed free map at Coral Gables City Hall (Le Jeune Road and Miracle Mile) – a good idea because this is a confusing area: Coral Gables' streets are named not numbered and wind about canals and suchlike. You'll follow a scenic route that includes the historic Biltmore Hotel, the Venetian Pool, the Chinese, French and Dutch South African residential villages, Fairchild Tropical Garden and various stately and historic homes.

Strictly for the birds

Forget what you saw on the opening sequence of *Miami Vice*: the city isn't really populated by photogenic squadrons of wild flamingos. You'll have to go to **Hialeah Park Racetrack**, **Parrot Jungle & Gardens** or **Metrozoo**, or look for the plastic variety in a tacky souvenir shop. Hialeah's flamingos, the only reproducing colony in North America, number more than 800; their wings are not clipped but they remain at the park year-round. However, there are many other exotic winged creatures in the skies overhead. Just look up and you may see:

● Huge turkey vultures, with wingspans of eight to ten feet, circling over Downtown buildings. These migratory birds arrive in October and stay until the end of March.

● Brilliantly coloured macaws flying down Grand Avenue in Coconut Grove, usually in pairs, recognisable by their long tails and raucous squawking.

● Squadrons of pelicans flying low over Collins Avenue, Miami Beach, moving in such precise formation that, inexplicably, you begin humming 'The Ride of the Valkyries'.

For serious bird enthusiasts, the **Tropical Audubon Society** offers field trips to some of the best rare bird sites in South Florida; call 666 5111 for details. It also runs a hotline giving tips on what can be seen where (667 7337). **Greynolds Park Rookery** (662 4124) in north-east Dade is one of the few roosting and nesting areas for wading bird species in Dade County, with bird walks and owl prowls available. You can get a close-up look at pelicans for

free at **Pelican Harbor Seabird Rescue Station** (Pelican Harbor, north side of 79th Street Causeway, North Bay Village; 751 9840). This non-profit-making operation takes in injured birds and cares for them until they can be released; sometimes the injuries, usually from fish hooks or fishing line, are so severe that the pelicans stay for good.

THREE TONS OF KILLER POWER!

55 degree showers daily
with killer whale Lolita~top predator of the seas

Visit Miami's premier attraction~home of *Lolita* the killer whale and TV superstar *Flipper*. Enjoy great shows and dozens of marine life exhibits. Come spend a fun-filled day at Miami Seaquarium,® just ten minutes from downtown and the port of Miami. **For more information, call (305) 361-5705.**

Miami Seaquarium®

4400 Rickenbacker Causeway Miami, FL 33149

© 1997 Miami Seaquarium

Tours

See also chapter **Architecture**.

South Beach tours

The **Miami Design Preservation League** organises various tours of the Deco District. Walking tours ($10) are offered twice weekly, on Thursdays at 6.30pm and Saturdays at 10.30am; meet at the Art Deco Welcome Center at 1001 Ocean Drive, at 10th Street. For $5 you can also hire audio equipment for a self-guided tour (11am-4pm daily); more info on these and other tours on 672 2014. MDPL also offers two-hour bicycle tours on the first and third Sundays of the month for $15 ($5 for bike rental, $10 tour fee). Meet by 10.30am at the Miami Beach Bike Center at 601 Fifth Street; you must book in advance on 674 0150.

Dr Paul George Historical Tours

Local historian Dr Paul George is well known for his walking, boat and Metrorail tours of Greater Miami, including the Downtown/Miami River Walking Tour, the Many Faces of Little Havana Walking Tour and the Metrorail Tour of Greater Miami, a comprehensive tour of multicultural Dade County. History buffs will enjoy his Miami River Boat Tour which takes you to sites of a Tequesta Indian village and early trading posts. Tours cost $15-$25 and average 2½hrs; call 375 1625 for a current schedule.

Tours of the Biltmore Hotel

Get an up-close look at the magnificent Biltmore Hotel in Coral Gables (1200 Anastasia Avenue, at Granada Boulevard), which is listed on the National Register of Historic Places. Free tours take place on Sundays at 12.30pm, 1.30pm and 2.30pm. Call the hotel on 445 1926 for more details.

South Beach's principal means of transport.

Tours for nature lovers

Naturalist tours, including marine wading tours off Key Biscayne, canoe trips through Coral Gables waterways and a Key Biscayne sunset canoe trip, are offered by **Metro-Dade Parks & Recreation Department**. Walks and wading tours take one to three hours and cost $3 per person; canoe trips last up to 10 hours and cost $20-$30 per person. Call 662 4124 for more information.

Flights & helicopter rides

Scenic Flight (1-800 771 3910), operating out of Tamiami airport and Opa-Locka airport, offers daily flights (8am-8pm) in planes holding three passengers. A 30-minute flight to Miami Beach costs $35 per person and a 50-minute flight over Biscayne Bay is $55 per person; booking is essential. **Dean International** (282 3058) also operates out of Tamiami airport: $95 will get a 45-minute tour of Miami Beach, Downtown and Coral Gables for three people. **Dade Helicopter Tours** (374 3737) at Watson Island offers daily tours lasting from 10 to 30 minutes for $55-$149 per person. Depending on which option you choose, your helicopter flight will take you over South Beach, the Port of Miami, Coconut Grove and up to Bal Harbour.

Moon over Miami

One of Miami's greatest treasures is its spectacular moonrises. You'll be struck breathless by the sight of the impossibly large full moon rising from the ocean until it is a huge, glowing beacon illuminating the entire beach. If you are here during a full moon (check the weather page of the *Miami Herald* for phases of the moon or just keep an eye on the sky), take advantage of these special full moon events.

● The **Miami Sailing Club** (858 1130) hosts Full Moon Cruises on the 65ft Malu Kai out of the Dinner Key Marina in Coconut Grove; the $50 price includes beer, wine, soft drinks, food and a front-row seat for a glorious natural event.

● The **Barnacle Historical Site** in Coconut Grove (3485 Main Highway, at Charles Avenue; 448 9445) sponsors musical moonlight events every month (except July and August).

● Moonlight Garden Tours at **Vizcaya Museum & Gardens** (3251 South Miami Avenue; 250 9133). If Vizcaya is splendid by day, imagine how much more enchanting it is by the light of the full moon. Call for the dates and to make reservations.

● **Fairchild Tropical Garden** Moonlight Events (10901 Old Cutler Road; 667 1651). If one of their moonlight events coincides with your visit, go: it's a unique opportunity to enjoy this lush garden illuminated by moonglow on a silent tram.

● Every full moon at **World Resources Café** (719 Lincoln Road, between Euclid & Meridian Avenues; 534 9095) you'll hear drumming from Haitian, African and Peruvian bands, among others – often leading to an impromptu drumming circle and dancing.

How to get from Peoria to Pretoria.

 AND **1 800 CALL ATT**® GETS YOU FROM
THE U.S. TO THE WORLD.

It's all within your reach.

Accommodation

Miami Beach's art deco hotels are an attraction in their own right, but if you'd rather stay off the scene, pick from kitsch and rich with lots between.

*Sybarism at its chicest at the **Delano**, page 34.*

Miami is a city known for its diversity. Ethnic is one thing, but accommodation is another. In this city, there are probably more places and types of places to stay than there are ethnic groups. How happy you end up will invariably depend on your choice of area. If you're a sun-worshipper, you'll certainly not favour a downtown room, no matter how low the rate. And if you're a quiet type, you won't want to be stationed right in the middle of things on South Beach. So choose carefully.

PRICES & SERVICES

Rates for rooms vary wildly throughout the year. The most expensive time is November to the end of April, and those are the rates quoted here. If you come to town in summer, expect them to be reduced by as much as 40 per cent.

During the season, a budget hotel will cost you about $70-$120 (less off South Beach); a moderate hotel $120-$175; and a first-class hotel from $175 up into the thousands (for a penthouse suite).

Location is a major factor. A hotel on the beach with a room facing the water will cost you a lot more than one near the airport facing the highway.

It's always worth trying to get lower rates. Often there are weekend package deals, and hotels that cater to business travellers reduce their rates then, too. All sorts of discounts – to Automobile Association members and senior citizens, for example – may be available, but you will not be told about them unless you ask. Also ask about taxes, which range from 10 to 15 per cent, depending on where you are staying.

Something you can pretty much count on having in every hotel room is air-conditioning – otherwise hotels would have to close down during the sweltering summers. Television and telephones are usually standard too, except in some guest houses and the youth hostels.

A law passed in 1990 made disabled access to public buildings compulsory. In Miami most hotels comply but in South Beach, where the majority were built in the 1930s, many do not – yet. They have been given a grace period to make the necessary alterations. Meanwhile, wheelchair access is not necessarily impossible, so call ahead to check.

Among the complaints about South Beach is the conspicuous lack of a good convention-sized hotel other than the 40-year-old Fontainebleau. That need is finally going to be met in 1998 by the Loews corporation, though statistics suggest that the new venue won't solve all the problems. Also a nuisance is the horrendous parking situation. If you have the option of valet parking at your hotel, take it. Rates are for the day, so for one price you can come and go as often as you please. This will save you having to ply your meter with quarters every few hours. Alternatively, forget about wheels for a while. You won't need them if you're planning to spend most of your time on South Beach.

A final caveat: if you're staying at a hotel in the historic Art Deco District, don't expect luxurious amenities and rooms the size of the Ritz, unless, of course, it's been renovated. Most of the hotels here were constructed in the 1930s for a middle-class clientele seeking relief from the poor economic times which they had just endured. These are diminutive, human-scale buildings and the rooms and bathrooms often follow suit.

The South Beach hotels we have listed can only be a selection of the hundreds there. For a wider choice, look in the Greater Miami Convention & Visitors Bureau's Visitors Guide (*see chapter* **Essential Information**) or contact the **Greater Miami & the Beaches Hotel Association** (531 3553/1-800 733 6426), which acts as a booking agency. Short-term rental agencies include **Florida SunBreak** (1-800 786 2732) and **IDP Reservations** (1-954 434 8611/1-800 434 8611).

Due to open just too late for review in this chapter is the **National**, at 1677 Collins Avenue, South Beach (532 2311), the latest fashionable deco restoration, destined to shoot straight into the A list.

The Beaches

South Beach

First-class

Casa Grande Suite Hotel

834 Ocean Drive, between Eighth & Ninth Streets, Miami Beach, FL 33139 (reservations 1-800 688 7678/front desk 672 7003/fax 673 3669). Bus C, H, K, W. **Rates** all suites: studio $230; one bedroom $265; two-three bedroom $450-$1,125. **Credit** AmEx, Disc, MC, V.

One of the holdings in music-mogul-turned-hotel-proprietor Chris Blackwell's resort empire, Island Outpost. The Outpost 'village' on South Beach includes six hotels located within walking distance of each other. All offer superb amenities. These include entertainment centres, generously stocked minibars, on-account payment at all the chain's restaurants and bars and a 10 per cent discount in the Island Trading Company Store, which features the exotic fabrics and items used to decorate the rooms. This hotel is one of Island's

pricier South Beach destinations. In a building made up mostly of condominiums, 33 stark suites have ocean vistas. All contain weighty carved teak and mahogany furnishings, which sit on sisal floors. Indonesian batik fabrics and antiques, fresh flowers and brightly coloured tiled bathrooms lend cheer to the otherwise austere atmosphere.
Hotel services *Babysitting. Bar. Car park (valet; $14). Conference facilities. Laundry service. Multi-lingual staff. Restaurant. Sports/fitness facilities (access to nearby health club).*
Room services *Coffeemaker. Stereo with CD player. Fully equipped kitchenettes. Minibar. Refrigerator. Voicemail. VCR.*

The Delano

1685 Collins Avenue, between 16th & 17th Streets, Miami Beach, FL 33139 (reservations 1-800 555 5001/front desk 672 2000/fax 532 0099). Bus C, G, H, L. **Rates** single $200-$300; double $400-$550; suites $600-$1,500. **Credit** AmEx, Disc, MC, V.

Studio 54 partner-turned-wildly-successful-hotelier Ian Schrager recently added this trendy hostelry to his chain. A completely renovated 1947 structure capped by a fluted spire, set squarely on the beach, The Delano (pronounced Dell-uh-no) has received more publicity than some movie stars. Early on, the over-exposure attracted such teeming crowds of plebeians traipsing through the lobby to see and be seen that the staff were forced to bar entry to all but registered guests. Blinding white is the hotel's trademark. It covers the building's exterior (except for the blue door that the restaurant is named after), is the colour of the staff's uniforms and, not counting the Granny Smith apple replaced daily, it is the predominant palette in the pristine rooms. A bit sterile? Sometimes, but just look out of the window and you'll be assaulted by the vibrant South Florida colourscape. The lobby is fantasyland à la Philippe Starck. Think cathedral ceilings, massive chalky columns, dark wood-panelled walls and floors and gauzy ivory curtains. Conversation nooks are delineated by groupings of oversize and whimsical furniture, some antique, others in shocking colours, punctuated by gilt candelabra. Two bars cater to people-watchers and create different moods: one resembles an airy country-house kitchen; the other, dimly lit by Venetian-style chandeliers, a sophisticated antique lounge. The open-plan Blue Door restaurant shares the back of the lobby and extends out to the patio, where a few feet away the prized and very expensive two-storey bungalows surround a palm-lined pool.
Hotel services *Babysitting. Three bars. Business services (faxing, photocopying, courier). Car park (valet; $12). Conference facilities. Laundry service. Multi-lingual staff. No-smoking rooms. Two restaurants. Sports/fitness facilities (gym, rooftop spa). Swimming pool.*
Room services *Stereo with CD player. Minibar. Refrigerator. VCR on request. Voicemail.*

Fisher Island Club

One Fisher Island Drive, Fisher Island, FL 33109 (reservations 1-800 537 3708/front desk 535 6020/fax 535 6003). Bus C, K, S, F/M. **Rates** $385-$1,295. **Credit** AmEx, DC, MC, V.

This 216-acre private island is home to some of the world's wealthiest (Oprah Winfrey, Jim Courier). Think *Lifestyles of the Rich and Famous* meets *Fantasy Island* – people here have Rolls Royce golf carts. This is the big time. Accessible only by ferry (by water or air, as Islanders say), Fisher Island is the epitome of unbridled elegance, complete with endangered bird sanctuary, championship golf course, 18 tennis courts, a renowned spa and security so tight it rivals that of the Secret Service – which is why world leaders including

The Tides *(page 39), the high point of Ocean Drive – literally.*

All Castles On The Beach Are Not Made Of Sand.

Miami's most renowned landmark hotel is situated in the midst of 20 lush tropical acres. The Fontainebleau Hilton Resort & Towers sets the pace and pulse of Miami Beach. Experience the energy. Enjoy spacious guest rooms, sweeping terraces and breathtaking views. A rejuvenating beachside spa, 10 fabulous restaurants and a half-acre lagoon-size pool with cascading waterfall will entice you. Music and dancing await you at Club Tropigala's exciting international floor show. We invite you to come discover the crown jewel of Miami Beach.

Fontainebleau Hilton

RESORT AND TOWERS

4441 Collins Avenue • Miami Beach, FL 33140
305-538-2000 • Fax 305-674-4607
For reservations, call Hilton Direct at 1-800-321-3232 or the
Fontainebleau Hilton Resort and Towers at 1-800-548-8886.

President Bill Clinton stay here when they're in town. Luxurious accommodation is available in a variety of villas and cottages, surrounding the grand William K Vanderbilt Mansion, which serves as a clubhouse. Unlike Gilligan's Island, this one is completely self-contained, with fine restaurants, bars and a disco. Beach club and pools provide doting service. The only drawback is the depression you'll experience on the day you leave. As they say, you get what you pay for.
Hotel services *Four bars. Business services (secretarial). Conference facilities. Garden. Helipad. Five restaurants. Sea plane ramp. Sports/fitness facilities: golf course, two marinas, spa, tennis courts). Swimming pools.*
Room services *Kitchenettes in suites. VCR. Wet bars. Whirlpool.*

Hotel Impala

1228 Collins Avenue, between 12th & 13th Streets, Miami Beach, FL 33139 (reservations 1-800 646 7252/front desk 673 2021/fax 673 5984). Bus C, H, K, W. **Rates** single $189; double $199; suite $269-$369. **Credit** AmEx, DC, MC, V.
A respite from the craziness of Ocean Drive, this tiny European-style hotel exudes Mediterranean villa charm. A sunburst mosaic floor and lazy twirling ceiling fans greet you in the lobby. Rooms are done in an earthy colour palette, accented by sisal floors, custom-made wrought iron work, imported cotton linens, wood furniture, cane chairs and lots of plants. Bathrooms mix materials like stainless steel and coral rock. The superb Spiga restaurant is worth several visits. As private as you can get on South Beach, the Impala has been a hideaway for numerous celebrities (such as Antonio Banderas and Melanie Griffith), whose indentities the management would never divulge, of course.
Hotel services *Car park (valet; $15). Disabled: access; rooms. Laundry service. Multi- lingual staff. No-smoking rooms. Restaurant. Sports/fitness facilities (access to health club).*
Room services *Stereo with CD player. Fax/modem hook-ups. Hair dryers on request. VCR. Voicemail.*

Marlin

1200 Collins Avenue, at 12th Street, Miami Beach, FL 33139 (reservations 1-800 688 7678/front desk 673 8770/fax 673 9609). Bus C, H, K. **Rates** all suites: studio $260; one bedroom $290-$400. **Credit** AmEx, DC, Disc, MC, V.
The first South Beach property in the Island Outpost hotel chain, the Marlin is considered the forerunner of Collins Avenue's fashionable renovations. Caribbean-inspired interiors are designed by Barbara Hulanicki of Biba fame. Built in 1939 by architect L Murray Dixon (proficient in the streamline style), the hotel exhibits typical touches: an ocean-liner-like porch hemmed in by a decorative metal railing; rounded corners; a roof topped by a trylon and lined in indigo neon; and a white and indigo facade with a trio of bas-reliefs. Each of the 12 suites has a personality of its own, such as the baby pink Barbie room or the art-filled African room. Internationally famous musicians (Aerosmith, U2, Nine Inch Nails) favour the hotel for its funky décor and the renowned 72-channel South Beach Studios on the premises, where many top-selling albums have been mixed. Ordinary guests need not feel common; they too can reach the top – by trekking up to the rooftop bar.
Hotel services *Two bars. Business services (cellphones, computers, data ports, fax). Car park (valet; $14). Multi-lingual staff. No-smoking rooms. Recording studio. Sports/fitness facilities (affiliation with local health club). Video rental.*
Room services *Hair dryer. Minibar. Radio. Kitchenette. Safe. Stereo with CD player. VCR. Voicemail.*

Raleigh

1775 Collins Avenue, between 17th & 18th Streets, Miami Beach, FL 33139 (reservations 1-800 848 1775/front desk 534 6300/fax 538 8140). Bus C, G, L, H. **Rates** single $219; double $249-$279. **Credit** AmEx, DC, MC, V.
An old stand-by, the Raleigh was one of the first of the larger art deco hotels to get a renovation in the early days of the

The **Kent** *(page 43): nice place, nice price.*

Water covers 2/3 of the world.

We cover the rest.

150 countries.

5,400 locations.

2,000 at airports.

500,000 cars.

18,000 staff.

Wherever you are going the world, whether it's f business or pleasure, yo can rely on an unbeatab combination of price an service from Hertz.

To find out more, or make a reservation simply visit your loc Travel Agency or ca Hertz direct on:

0990 90 60 90

The World's #1 Car Rental Company

Hertz rents and leases Fords and other fine cars.

*Could this be South Beach's cheapest room? The clean and credible **Clay Hotel** (page 45).*

Miami Beach renaissance. Built in 1940, it's since had a very '90s update. Rooms contain all the modern conveniences: among them three-line phones and fax/data ports. Sleek furniture is perfect for the sleek clientele of fashion industry types. Tranquil and elegant, the lobby sports polished wood details and original terrazzo floors. Visit the intimate bar and sip a martini, reputed to be the best in town. Hang out under the palms by the scalloped swimming pool and model-watch, or have a meal in the first-rate restaurant, less trendy than its counterparts these days, but still worth a visit.
Hotel services *Two bars. Car park (valet; $14). Two restaurants. Sports/fitness facilities (health club). Swimming pool.*
Room services *Stereo with CD player. Fax/modem hookups. Voicemail. VCR.*

The Tides

1220 Ocean Drive, between 12th & 13th Streets, Miami Beach, FL 33139 (reservations 1-800 688 7678). Bus C, H, K, W. **Rates** all suites: standard to penthouse $175-$1,100. **Credit** AmEx, DC, Disc, MC, V.
Another L Murray Dixon design (built in 1936), the Tides features porthole windows, abundant stainless steel and frosted glass, bringing to mind a luxurious land-locked cruise ship. Destined to become the next South Beach must-stay, it is the sixth and most opulent property in the Island Outpost Chain. The hotel boasts 45 suites, all facing the ocean. The penthouses on the ninth and tenth floors are the highest points on Ocean Drive, and naturally offer stunning ocean, beach and skyline views. A rooftop gym and a variety of restaurants are just a few of the amenities that surpass those in its sister facilities.
Hotel services *Babysitting on request. Bar. Car park (valet; $14). Conference facilities. Laundry service. Multilingual staff. Two restaurants. Sports/fitness facilities (fitness centre). Swimming pool.*
Room services *Coffeemaker. Stereo.*

Mid-range

The Albion

1650 James Avenue, at Lincoln Road, Miami Beach, FL 33139 (reservations 1-888 665 0008/front desk 913 1000/fax 674 0507). Bus C, G, H, K, S. **Rates** single $150-$195; double $195-$205; suite $375-$700. **Credit** AmEx, MC, V.
This pristine nautical edifice, built in 1939 by the firm of Polevitsky & Russell, is distinguished by its wraparound windows and the divided turret that proudly exhibits its name. Conveniently located a few blocks from the convention centre, theatres, shops, restaurants and clubs, not to mention the beach, it's owned by the Rubell family, relatives of the late Steve Rubell of Studio 54 fame. There's no disco here, though. Just an understated, elegant building renovated by Ecuadorean architect Carlos Zapata. Tranquil tones dominate. Rooms may overlook a garden or the ocean. If you're too inhibited to go out to the beach, bask in the sun by the pool area's white sand-drenched deck.
Hotel services *Bar. Business services (fax, photocopying). Car park (valet; $15). Disabled: access; rooms. Limo service to airport. Sports/fitness facilities (fitness centre). Swimming pool.*
Room services *Stereo with CD player. Fax/modem hook-ups. Minibar. Refrigerator. Voicemail.*

Hotel Astor

956 Washington Avenue, at 10th Street, Miami Beach, FL 33139 (reservations 1-800 270 4981/front desk 531 8081/fax 531 3193). Bus C, H, K, W. **Rates** single $135-$195; double $135-$195; suite $250-$550. **Credit** AmEx, DC, Disc, MC, V.
Low-key luxury prevails in this 1936 streamline hotel, tastefully renovated down to the last detail. The restful, intimate lobby is decorated in sand, willow green and soft lights.

The best hotels for...

...eating exotic animals

The Alexander Hotel (*Mid-Beach: First-class*), where Dominique's restaurant offers diamond back rattlesnake salad and alligator scaloppini.

...feeling stupid

The Delano (*South Beach: First-class*), whose Philippe Starck sinks in the lobby bathrooms appear devoid of fixtures, leaving you gaping dumbly at your reflection. Get angry, stomp your feet and you'll discover that the water flow is controlled by a foot pedal hidden underneath the vanity unit.

...getting lost

The Fontainebleau Hilton (*Mid-Beach: First-class*), which has over 1,000 rooms and employees, miles of labyrinthine corridors and a basement shopping arcade on its 20-acre site. Rumour has it that some of the original 1950s guests have yet to check out.

...hiding from your fans

Hotel Impala (*South Beach: First-class*), with only 17 rooms and a staff so discreet that even truth serum wouldn't get them to talk. For all we know, Elvis could be a resident here.

...going psycho

The Pelican (*South Beach: Mid-range*): a few days here will finally get you that prescription for Prozac you've always wanted. If the incessant noise from Ocean Drive doesn't send you over the edge, the sense-assaulting décor is bound to do the trick (pictured below).

...pretending you're at the beach

The Albion Hotel (*South Beach: Mid-range*), whose pool is bordered by a sand-covered sundeck. Do a few days of preliminary tanning here before hitting the beach proper and natives will think you're one of them.

...recording a hit album

The Marlin (*South Beach: First-class*), home to 72-track South Beach Studios. If U2 aren't busy mixing their latest, maybe you could reserve a couple of hours to lay down a few tracks.

...spotting celebs

The Delano (*South Beach: First-class*): High-profile celebrities and supermodels (Calvin Klein, Johnny Depp, Kate Moss, Cindy Crawford) who say they want privacy but really don't all stay here. How can they possibly blend into the surroundings when everything around them is white?

...stealing a car

The Dezerland Surfside Beach Hotel (*North Beach: Mid-range*). If you can distract the staff long enough to back a tow truck into this automobile wonderland, you might end up the proud owner of a vintage Thunderbird or Chevy. (Joke.)

...time travelling

The Indian Creek Hotel (*South Beach: Mid-range*), an object lesson in the difference between a renovation and a restoration. Curvy furniture, original terrazzo floors, a vintage steamer trunk and authentic frosted glass chandeliers all make you feel distinctly 1930s.

Miami River Inn *(page 48): a little bit of New England in Downtown Miami.*

Comfy overstuffed chairs and blond wood furniture rest on the original polished terrazzo floors. Beautifully appointed rooms resemble 1920s ocean liner interiors and are adorned in muted colours with French-milled furniture. Marble covers the bathroom walls, floors and counters. Double-insulated windows drown out the SoBe noise. Outside is as carefully re-done as inside. A small lap pool, adjoined by a diminutive whirlpool, is fed by a wall of water sculpture. The Astor Place Bar & Grill offers superlative New American cuisine and provides the room service.
Hotel services *Babysitting on request. Business services at front desk. Two bars. Car park (valet; $14). Disabled: access; rooms. Laundry service. Multi-lingual staff. Restaurant. Sports/fitness facilities (health club affiliation). Swimming pool.*
Room services *Stereo with CD player Hair dryer. Minibar. Refrigerator. Safe. Voicemail.*

Avalon Hotel
700 Ocean Drive, at Seventh Street, Miami Beach, FL 33139 (reservations 1-800 933 3306/front desk 538 0133/534 0258). Bus C, H, K, W. **Rates** *single $120; double $140; suite $170-$190.* **Credit** *AmEx, DC, MC, V.*
The streamline-styled architecture of this classic deco hotel is more interesting than the actual rooms, which are simply small and tidy, but that makes it no less popular among those looking for a clean, friendly and functional place to stay in a prime location. A lobby and patio restaurant named A Fish Called Avalon is always packed, featuring a pleasant crowd of locals and tourists. The buffet breakfast is served here.
Hotel services *Bar. Business services (photocopying, fax, Federal Express). Car park (valet; $14). Complimentary continental breakfast. Disabled: access; rooms. Restaurant.*
Room services *Cable radio. Refrigerator in most rooms. Safe. VCR.*

Cardozo Hotel
1300 Ocean Drive, at 13th Street, Miami Beach, FL 33139 (reservations 1-800 782 6500/front desk 535 6500/fax 532 3563). Bus C, H, K, W. **Rates** *single/double $130-$145; suite $210-$385.* **Credit** *AmEx, MC, V.*

A celluloid favourite, the Gloria Estefan-owned Cardozo made its film debut in the 1959 Sinatra film *A Hole in the Head* and has since been featured in the Robin Williams' 1996 drag-extravaganza *Birdcage.* Henry Hohauser (perhaps the King of Streamline; his architectural firm built over 300 buildings in the Miami area) created this structure in 1939. Look for the rust-coloured keystone on the facade, veranda, columns and balustrade and you'll know you're there. Besides its colourfully renovated, photogenic exterior, this hotel's interior is Dali meets deco, with whimsical modern designs, hand-crafted wrought-iron furniture and 56 recently refurbished rooms featuring hardwood floors. The festive Allioli restaurant, located in the lobby and on the outdoor patio, is one of South Beach's most popular. A nice touch is the welcome daiquiri at check-in.
Hotel services *Bar. Business centre (fax). Car park (valet; $14). Conference facilities.*
Room services *Stereo with CD player. Minibar. Safe.*

Century
140 Ocean Drive, between First & Second Streets, Miami Beach, FL 33139 (reservations/front desk 674 8855/fax 538 5733). Bus H, W. **Rates** *single $125-$215; double $140-$230; suite $215-$290.* **Credit** *AmEx, DC, MC, V.*
Catering to a fashionable and fashion industry crowd, this 1939 Henry Hohauser gem sports a simple white, mint green and grey colour scheme. From the low porch wall poked with holes and the 'eyebrows' over the windows to the racing stripes and discs clinging to the facade and ziggurat-like trylon on the roof, this hotel screams streamline. The Century was due for a refit as we went to press, so there's no saying whether it will retain its post-modern tropical interiors.
Hotel services *Bar. Car park (self; free). Garden. Multi-lingual staff. Restaurant.*
Room services *Hair dryers. Fax/modem hook ups in some rooms. VCR.*

The Clevelander
1020 Ocean Drive, between 10th & 11th Streets, Miami Beach, FL 33139 (reservations/front desk 531 3485/fax 534 4707). Bus C, H, K. **Rates** *all rooms $90.* **Credit** *AmEx, DC, MC, V.*

The Biltmore Hotel

The background for many fashion shoots and beer commercials, the Clevelander is probably better known for its poolside glass-block and neon bar than as a place to stay. But if you're a college student down in SoBe for spring break, don't plan to spend much time in your room at night (it'll be neat but not without noise) and don't mind curt service, it could be a fun place to stay.

Hotel services *Bar. Sports/fitness facilities (fitness centre). Swimming pool.*
Room services *Radio.*

Edison Hotel

960 Ocean Drive, at 10th Street, Miami Beach, FL 33139 (reservations/front desk 531 2744/fax 672 4153). Bus C, H, K, W. **Rates** standard $75; oceanfront $95. **Credit** AmEx, MC, V.

Another Henry Hohauser masterpiece, this is one of Ocean Drive's largest. It boasts a Mediterranean Revival motif through its five storeys. Rooms are rather simple, though those facing the ocean are slightly more enticing. A large outdoor bar/patio and illuminated pool compensate for the interior's lack of appeal. Most recently, the Edison leased its restaurant space to the sports-minded All Star Café themerie (slated to open summer 1997), which is sure to attract a lively, sporty clientele.

Hotel services *Bar. Business services (fax). Car park (valet; $14). Disabled: access; rooms. Restaurant. Swimming pool.*
Room services *Radio.*

The Greenview Hotel

1651 Washington Avenue, between Lincoln Road & 17th Street, Miami Beach, FL 33139 (reservations/front desk 531 6588/fax 531 4580) Bus A, C, F/M, G, S. **Rates** single $125-$150; double $125-$150; suite $200-$250. **Credit** AmEx, MC, V.

Another stunning renovation of a small Henry Hohauser-designed hotel by the Rubell family. Eyebrow windows, a curved-edged facade, geometric railings and gurgling floor-level fountains mark the serene yellow and white exterior. The 1939 structure has been redone by Parisian designer Chahan Minassian, who has lent a dramatic yet spare touch. Tranquil tones dominate the minimal rooms, which combine hand-made, clean-lined furniture with 20th-century design classics. Although the prevailing vibe is both urban and urbane, the friendly staff counteract any coldness.

Hotel services *Business services (courier service, express mail, fax). Car park (self). Laundry service. Multi-lingual staff. No-smoking rooms.*
Room services *Hair dryer. Voicemail. VCR offered in some rooms.*

Hotel Leon

841 Collins Avenue, between Eighth & Ninth Streets, Miami Beach, FL 33139 (reservations/front desk 673 3767/fax 673 5866). Bus C, H, K. **Rates** single $125; double $165; suite $215-375. **Credit** AmEx, MC, V.

With the exception of the outer facade, a mix of more present and less past is what you get from many hotels on South Beach. The Leon, however, unlike some of its restored brethren, retained many of its 1929 details in its 1996 renovation, including much original of the woodwork in the cosy rooms as well as (yes!) fireplaces. Overall, a quaint, well-placed respite for the weary.

Hotel services *Bar. Business centre. Car park (self; free). Conference facilities. Garden. Laundry service. Multi-lingual staff. Two restaurants. Sports/fitness facilities (affiliation with nearby gym).*
Room services *Stereo. VCR on request.*

The stately **Biltmore** *(page 48).*

Hotel Leslie

1244 Ocean Drive, at 12th Street, Miami Beach, FL 33139 (reservations 1-800 688 7678/front desk 534 2138/fax 531 5543). Bus C, H, K, W. **Rates** single/double $145-$180; suite $275-$300. **Credit** AmEx, DC, Disc, MC, V.

The sun always shines at this brilliantly hued yellow and white Ocean Drive hotel, which Island Records founder and hotelier Chris Blackwell recently added to his collection. It features state-of-the-art amenities, including in-room compact disc players on which, of course, to play one of Island's many records. All guest rooms also feature ethnicky interior accents from the Blackwell-owned Island Trading Company Store. Favoured by the fashion industry.

Hotel services *Business services (cellphone, computers). Car park (valet; $14). Disabled: access; rooms. Laundry service. Multi-lingual staff. No-smoking rooms. Restaurant. Sports/fitness facilities (access to local health club). Video rental.*
Room services *Stereo with CD player. Minibar. Safe. VCR. Voicemail.*

Indian Creek Hotel

2727 Indian Creek Drive, between 27th & 28th Streets, Miami Beach, FL 33139 (reservations/front desk 531 2727/fax 531 5651). Bus C, G, F/M, H, L. **Rates** single/double $120; suite $200. **Credit** AmEx, DC, MC, V.

A few blocks north of the Art Deco District, facing the Indian Creek waterway and one block from the beach, this cosy, painstakingly restored hotel is fast becoming known as a must-stay. Pueblo deco is the reigning style here. The funky lobby transports you back to 1936 with its clean-lined vintage furniture, immense planters, deco-style chandeliers and comfy oversized chairs upholstered in splashy tropical prints. Rooms are equally pleasant, featuring amenities such as a writing desk. Spotless, serviceable bathrooms sport pastel-coloured tiles. The Pan Coast restaurant serves outstanding cuisine in its tiny dining room or al fresco in the lushly landscaped gardens. The warm, efficient staff make guests feel as if they never left home.

Hotel services *Business services (fax, photocopier, modem). Conference facilities. Garden. Laundry service. Multi-lingual staff. No-smoking rooms. Restaurant. Sports/fitness facilities (exercise rooms). Swimming pool.*
Room services *Hair dryers on request. Refrigerators in suites.*

Kent

1131 Collins Avenue, between 11th & 12th Streets, Miami Beach, FL 33139 (reservations 1-800 688 7678/front desk 531 6771/fax 531 0720). Bus C, H, K. **Rates** single $120; double $155; suite $255. **Credit** AmEx, DC, Disc, MC, V.

Another new addition to the Island Outpost empire, the less expensive, more expansive Kent is a wonderful choice for the budget-conscious young traveller. Fear not, though: it still contains many of the amenities found in the chain's other hotels. The lobby is a frequent site for fashion shoots. Rooms are unpretentiously done in the trademark world-chic Outpost style. The one thing the hotel does not provide: binoculars for peeping into designer Gianni Versace's adjoining mansion. For that you are on your own.

Hotel services *Babysitting. Bar. Car park (valet; $14). Disabled: access; rooms. Garden. Laundry service. Multi-lingual staff. No-smoking rooms. Restaurant. Sports/fitness facilities (access to local health club). Video rental.*
Room services *Stereo with CD player. Minibar. Safe. VCR. Voicemail.*

Ocean Front

1230-1238 Ocean Drive, between 11th & 12th Streets, Miami Beach, FL 33139 (reservations/front desk 672 2579/fax 672 7665). Bus C, H, K, W. **Rates** all suites: $165-$450. **Credit** AmEx, DC, JCB, MC, V.

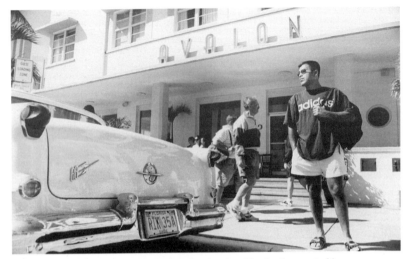

Classic streamline design – and the hotel's nice, too. **The Avalon**, *page 41.*

A peaceful bit of France on hectic Ocean Drive, this hotel is composed of two buildings which have been thoroughly renovated to become splendid digs. A refreshing change from the endless stream of streamline, these structures have a decidedly Mediterranean bent. Corners are angular. Roofs are covered in terracotta-coloured barrel tiles. French doors and arches signal entrances. Period furniture and shades of beige, burgundy and blue highlight the understated rooms, many of which face Ocean Drive but are sound-proofed to guarantee a good night's rest. Marble tiles surround the spacious bathrooms. Les Deux Fontaines, the hotel's restaurant serving Mediterranean French cuisine on the charming patio, is a preferred spot for Euro and Europhile crowds.

Hotel services *Bar. Car park (valet; $14). Conference facilities. Disabled: access; rooms. Laundry services. Multi-lingual staff. Two restaurants. Sports/fitness facilities (access to local health club).*
Room services *Hairdryer. Stereo with CD player. Minibar. Refrigerator. Safe. Whirlpools in some rooms. VCR.*

Park Central Hotel

640 Ocean Drive, between Sixth & Seventh Streets, Miami Beach, FL 33139 (reservations 1-800 727 5236/front desk 538 1611/fax 534 7520). Bus C, H, K, W. **Rates** *single $130-$175; suites $225-$275.* **Credit** AmEx, DC, MC, V.

Tony Goldman, the man responsible for the South Beach and now the Wall Street renaissance, renovated this 1937 art deco Henry Hohauser hotel, taking its old deco glory and infusing it with sleek, modern touches, such as octagonal etched glass windows. Mahogany pieces from the Phillipines furnish the 75 rooms. The lobby bar is a bit of a scene, attracting a crowd as chic as its interior. The restaurant is constantly changing hands but remains crowded.

Hotel services *Bar. Business services (secretarial and others). Car park (valet; $14). Conference facilities. Disabled: access; rooms. Garden. Laundry service. Restaurant. Sports/fitness facilities (exercise room). Swimming pool.*
Room services *Fax/modem hook-ups. Refrigerator. Voicemail.*

Pelican

826 Ocean Drive, between Eighth & Ninth Streets, Miami Beach, FL 33139 (reservations 1-800 773 5422/front desk 673 3373/fax 673 3255). Bus C, H, K, W. **Rates** standard $160-$180; suites $280. **Credit** AmEx, DC, MC, V.

Owned by the Diesel jeans company, the Pelican is the perfect place for Ocean Drive. The frenetic, energetic décor emulates the environs: loud! But, nevertheless, inventive. Swedish designer Magnus Erhland was given free reign to run amok and create any atmosphere he wanted. Instead of just one, he created many. The rooms, 26 in all, each possess distinct identities and names. You might find yourself put up in 'Me Tarzan, You Vain' or 'Best Whorehouse' if staff feel you fit the profile. Splashy psychedelic shades and fabulous 1950s and '60s furniture make some rooms reminiscent of the sets from *Barbarella.*

Hotel services *Bar. Car park (valet; $14). Disabled: access; rooms. Multi-lingual staff. Restaurant.*
Room services *Stereo with CD player. Minibar. Refrigerator. Safe. VCR. Voicemail.*

Budget

Beachcomber Hotel

1340 Collins Avenue, between 13th & 14th Streets, Miami Beach, FL 33139 (reservations/front desk 531 3755/fax 673 8609) Bus C, H, K, W. **Rates** single $70; double $85; suite $95-$135. **Credit** AmEx, DC, Disc, MC, V.

This small hotel is a bright ray of sunshine on what can be a dismal stretch of Collins Avenue. The Beachcomber's immaculate white exterior houses an inviting porch and a sunny lobby, where a bargain breakfast buffet is served every morning. There are few luxuries here: no pool, minibar or laundry facilities, but the beach is a block away, bars can be found in every direction and there's a 24-hour laundromat just around the corner. Rooms are small, functional and well-scrubbed. The staff are friendly. And the popular Sushi Rock Café directly across the street serves some of the freshest fish on the beach.

Hotel services *Bar. Car park (self; $6). Multi-lingual staff. Restaurant.*
Room services *Refrigerator.*

San Juan Hotel

1680 Collins Avenue, between 16th & 17th Streets, Miami Beach, FL 33139 (reservations 1-800 468 1688/front desk 538 7531/fax 532 5704). Bus C, G, H, L. **Rates** All rooms double: $55-$59. **Credit** AmEx, DC, Disc, MC, V.

Want a vacation at the ultra-trendy Delano but can't afford the steep prices? Spend your sleeping hours across the street at the ultra-budget San Juan. While the facilities are not exactly brand new, there are some conveniences: all of the utilitarian rooms are doubles and contain a microwave oven and refrigerator. Waking hours can be whiled away hanging out at the Delano. Work out at their gym (day membership available), try to sneak onto a chaise lounge in the pool area or stake out a place at one of the bars and nurse a few drinks all day or night. No-one will suspect that you're not actually staying there. When the day is done, slink back to your room and sleep on the cheap.

Hotel services *Car park (self; $5). Laundromat.*
Room services *Kitchenette in some rooms. Microwave oven. Refrigerator.*

Park Washington Hotel

1020 Washington Avenue, between 10th & 11th Streets, Miami Beach, FL 33139 (reservations/front desk 532 1930/fax 672 6706). Bus C, H, K, W. **Rates** single $79; double $89; suite $89-$129. **Credit** AmEx, MC, V.

A block-long compound opposite the Astor Hotel is bordered by an undulating low wall and dense, towering foliage. Hidden behind are two small hotels – the Park Washington and its sister hotel the Kenmore. The tranquil, pleasant surroundings hold a few other surprises – a flourishing garden and a small swimming pool. Vivid tropical décor prevails, with cool pastels and rattan furniture in the lobby; jarring brights and solid wood furniture in rooms. Although not yet brought into the 1990s design-wise, the rooms are perfectly serviceable – refrigerators in each and reasonable prices ensure this. Bathrooms seem to have original tiling, but fixtures look recently fitted and are clean. Coffee and danish are served free in the lobby each morning. All round, a great deal in a great location.

Hotel services *Car park (self $4). Garden. Multi-lingual Staff. Swimming pool.*
Room services *Refrigerator.*

Guest houses & youth hostels

South Beach's desirability rating hoiks even humble hotels up a price bracket or two, so you can find yourself paying moderate rates for facilities that anywhere else would be considered budget. But it does have a couple of good hostels, both of which have private rooms, and a number of guest houses, where rates aren't ruinous and the atmosphere is personal and friendly.

Brigham Gardens Guest House

1411 Collins Avenue, between 14th &15th Streets, South Beach, FL 33139 (reservations/front desk 531 1331/fax 538 9898). Bus C, H, K, W. **Rates** single $75; double $100-$105; suite $115-$125. **Credit** AmEx, MC, V.

This quaint 1934 retreat in the heart of the hustle and bustle has a secluded feel, thanks to the garden with its gurgling fountain and luxuriant flora. Birds of all kinds like to roost here, as do guests, who enjoy the reasonable rates, complimentary breakfast and neat rooms, the larger of which come with fully equipped kitchens.

Hotel services *Car park (self). Laundromat. Sports/fitness facilities (access to local health club).*
Room services *Coffeemaker. Microwave oven. Kitchenettes in most rooms. Refrigerator.*

Clay Hotel & International Hostelling

1438 Washington Avenue, between 14th Street & Espanola Way, Miami Beach, FL 33139 (reservations 1-800 379 2529/front desk 534 2988). Bus C, H, K, W. **Rates** dorm $12; hotel room $38-$55. **Credit** JCB, MC, V.

This Mediterranean-style building looks small from the outside but holds a whole world of adventurous nomads who know how to get good travel deals. If you don't mind the vaguely dorm-like facilities you can be one of these people. The Clay is both a hotel and hostel, so other as well as single-sex dorm-style rooms, there are some private rooms, too. All are clean, plain and brightly decorated. Some have their own bathrooms; others have connecting bathrooms. The building is steeped in history. Once the home of Al Capone's gambling syndicate and the place where the rumba dance craze originated, the Clay was more recently a backdrop for many episodes of *Miami Vice*. You don't need YHA membership to stay here, and it only knocks a dollar off the dorm rate.

Hotel services *Dining room. Fully equipped kitchen. Lockers. Refrigerators and phones in hotel rooms. TV on request in hotel rooms. TV room.*

Mermaid Guest House

909 Collins Avenue, between Ninth & 10th Streets, Miami Beach, FL 33139 (reservations/front desk 538 5324). Bus C, H, K, W. **Rates** single $95; double $105. **Credit** AmEx, MC, V.

Another charming hideaway, screened behind lush vegetation. A young European and South American crowd predominates among the guests. A relaxed Caribbean mood prevails and is reflected in the friendly service and spice-bright décor of the neat, colourful rooms. A basic breakfast (included) is served in the fairy-lit garden courtyard.

Hotel services *Airport shuttle service. Bar.*
Room services *Radio. Refrigerator on request. TV on request. Telephone.*

Miami Beach International Travellers Hostel

236 Ninth Street, at Washington Avenue, Miami Beach, FL 33139 (reservations 1-800 978 6787/front desk 534 0268). Bus C, H, K, W. **Rates** $14-$43. **Credit** MC, V.

A convivial atmosphere reigns at this family-run facility, which features utilitarian rooms for three, some with bunk beds, and private rooms. On top of its good location and low cost, another plus is the private bathrooms.

Hotel services *Bar. Car park (self). Disabled: access; rooms. Kitchen. Laundromat. Lockers. No-smoking rooms. Restaurant. TV room.*

Villa Paradiso Guest House

1415 Collins Avenue, between 14th &15th Streets, Miami Beach, FL 33139 (reservations/front desk 532 0616/fax 667 0074). Bus C, H, K, W. **Rates** single/double $99; suite $125-$145. **Credit** AmEx, DC, MC, V.

When you encounter places like this, you wonder why people ever choose to stay in a hotel. A hospitable host runs this house, which has rooms ranged around a sun-dappled courtyard. The newly renovated quarters have hardwood floors, ceiling fans, antique furniture and French doors.

Hotel services *Laundromat. Multi-lingual staff.*
Room services *Kitchens in all rooms. Telephone.*

Mid-Beach

First-class

The Alexander All-Suite Luxury Hotel

5225 Collins Avenue, between 52nd & 53rd Streets, Miami Beach, FL 33140 (reservations 1-800 327 6121/front desk 865 6500/fax 864 8525). Bus C, G, H, L, S. **Rates** all suites: one bedroom $310-$540; two bedroom $450-$975. **Credit** AmEx, DC, MC, V.

The name says it all. This apartment-hotel comprises one-and two-bedroom suites with living rooms, fully equipped kitchens, two bathrooms and a balcony. The room décor is understated yet definitely luxurious, as are the public areas of the hotel, which has a sweeping curved stairway and is peppered with antiques, paintings and sculptures. The gardens are tropically sumptuous with a vigorous waterfall and lavish flora. The Alexander also boasts the gourmet Dominique's, where you can dine on rattlesnake or alligator if you're feeling brave enough.

Hotel services *Babysitting. Two bars. Business centre. Conference facilities. Car park (valet; $10). Disabled: access; rooms. Laundry service. Two restaurants. Sports/fitness facilities (bicycle rental, small health club, sauna, four whirlpools). Two swimming pools.*
Room services *Hair dryer. Kitchenettes in some suites. Radio. Refrigerator. Fax/modem hook-ups in some suites. Voicemail. VCR on request.*

Eden Roc Hotel

4525 Collins Avenue, between 45th & 46th Streets, Miami Beach, FL 33140 (reservations 1-800 327 8337/front desk 531 0000/fax 531 6955). Bus C, G, H, L. **Rates** single $195-$350; double $205-$365; suites $290-$1,500. **Credit** AmEx, DC, Disc, MC, V.

One of the immense Miami Beach hotels built during the 1950s, the Eden Roc, even after a recent renovation, still sports the flamboyant look of the past. Splashy technicolour rules in the vast lobby and the ample rooms, which are trimmed in aqua, acid green, purple and white. During the Beach's heyday in the 1960s, all the greats – including Frank Sinatra, Dean Martin and Sammy Davis, Jr – stayed and performed here. And just a few years ago, Madonna writhed on the bed in the penthouse posing for the cover shoot of her Bedtime Stories LP.

Hotel services *Babysitting on request. Beauty salon. Business services (secretarial). Conference facilities. Car park (valet; $9). Laundry service. Three restaurants. Sports/fitness facilities (health spa, racquetball, squash and basketball courts). Two swimming pools.*
Room services *Fax/modem hook-ups. Hair dryer. Radio. Safe. VCR on request. Voicemail.*

Fontainebleau Hilton and Resort Towers

4441 Collins Avenue, between 44th & 45th Streets, Miami Beach, FL 33140 (reservations 1-800 445 8667/front desk 538 2000/fax 531 9274). Bus C, G, L, H. **Rates** single $290-$350; double $315-$375; suite $410-$700. **Credit** AmEx, DC, Disc, JCB, MC, V.

When you see the trompe l'oeil mural on the building's side beckoning you to drive right into the lush Babylon-like gardens and pool, you know you have arrived at the Disneyworld of Miami Beach hotels. This is a veritable city unto itself, stretching out over 20 acres, with over 1,000 employees and room for triple that amount of guests. Another gargantuan 1950s mega-resort, the Fontainebleau was built in garish Hollywood style by architect Morris Lapidus (*see chapter* **Architecture**), who for many years was vilified but whose reputation has recently been resuscitated. A vast, nay, grandiose lobby, large rooms and enough activity to keep anyone busy 24 hours a day allows the hotel to succeed in attracting both conventioneers (in spades) and well-off families.

Hotel services *Babysitting on request. Four bars. Beauty salon. Business services (many: call for details). Car park (valet; $10). Conference facilities. Disabled: access; rooms. Laundry service. No-smoking rooms. Twelve restaurants. Sports/fitness facilities (bicycle rental, health spa, sauna, seven tennis courts, three whirlpools, water-sports equipment rental). Two swimming pools.*
Room services *Coffeemakers in some rooms. Fax/modem hook-ups. Minibars in some rooms. Refrigerators in some rooms. Safes in some rooms.*

Budget

Howard Johnson Hotel-Bayshore

4000 Alton Road, at 40th Street, Miami Beach, FL 33140 (reservations 1-800 532 4411/front desk 532 4411/fax 534 6540). Bus C, F/M, J, R, T. **Rates** single $71; double $91; suite $101. **Credit** AmEx, DC, Disc, MC, V.

Another find for those who want to visit South Beach but don't want to stay where they play. This 140-room hotel is located just off the I-95, 15 minutes from the airport. Plunked on the edge of a quiet mid-Miami Beach neighbourhood, its rooms are decorated in chain-style chic: non-descript modern furniture, earth tones on the walls, splashy prints on the curtains and bedspreads. An unusual bonus: balconies. On nights when you don't fancy hitting South Beach, in-house entertainment can be had in the hotel's roof-top lounge. Its western orientation and floor-to-ceiling windows provide unbeatable, breathtaking sunset views of Downtown Miami.

Hotel services *Airport shuttle service. Bar. Business services (fax, photocopying). Car park (self; free). Valet laundry service. Restaurant. Swimming pool.*
Room services *Fax/modem hookups. Radio.*

North Beach
Mid-range

Dezerland Surfside Beach Hotel

8701 Collins Avenue, at 87th Street, Miami Beach, FL 33154 (reservations1-800 331 9346/front desk 865 6661/fax 866 2630). Bus H, K, S, T. **Rates** single/double $80-$115. **Credit** AmEx, Disc, MC, V.

A vintage car-lover's paradise. Walk into the lobby and you'll think you've stumbled into a scene from American Grafitti. Automobiles from the 1950s are everywhere – a Cadillac at the front door, a Thunderbird in the lobby and various immaculate models on each floor. The automotive theme covers the walls and even stretches to the tidy rooms, which are named after classic models, and to the restaurant, where you can dine in booths fashioned from car interiors.

Hotel services *Babysitting on request. Bar. Car park (self; free). Laundromat. No-smoking rooms. Restaurant. Sports/fitness facilities (access to local health club, water sports equipment rentals, whirlpool). Swimming pool.*
Room services *Kitchenettes in some rooms. Radio. Voicemail.*

Surfside to Golden Beach
First-class

Sea View

9909 Collins Avenue, between 99th & 100th Streets, Bal Harbour, FL 33154 (reservations1-800 447 1010/front desk 868 4441/fax 868 1898). Bus K, H, S, T. **Rates** single $185; double $255; suite $475. **Credit** AmEx, DC, MC, V.

Directly on the beach in sleepy, ritzy Bal Harbour, the Sea View attracts a conservative clientele and celebrities doing the hermit thing (recently Bob Dylan): people who want to be on the beach, but not on South Beach. The lobby, an understated mix of antique and contemporary furniture, is done in pastel colours; the commodious and refined rooms face the ocean or Biscayne Bay. The beach is out of the back door and the upscale Bal Harbour shops are out of the front door.

Hotel services *Two bars. Car park (valet; $4). Conference facilities. Laundry service. No-smoking rooms. Three restaurants. Sports/fitness facilities (health club). Swimming pool.*
Room services *Hair dryer. Kitchenettes in some rooms. Refrigerator.*

Mid-range

Bay Harbor Inn

9660 East Bay Harbor Drive, between Kane Concourse & 97th Street, Bay Harbor Islands, FL 33154 (reservations/front desk 868 4141/fax 868 4141). Bus G, H, K, V. **Rates** single $90-$126; double $112-$126; suite $150-$235. **Credit** AmEx, DC, MC, V.

A combination of two modest buildings across the street from each other, one modern, one traditional. The modern building has a pool at the back and faces the Intercoastal Waterway where it has a yacht, *The Celeste*, where patrons dine on their complimentary breakfast. The traditional structure has neither, but houses the popular and consistently good steak and seafood restaurant, the Palm. Rooms are comfortably appointed with modern and traditional wood furnishings and many are reserved a year in advance by a clientele that returns every season. Not surprising, since the inn is located in a quiet neighbourhood, close to the upscale Bal Harbour shops and a few blocks from the beach.
Hotel services *Bar. Business services (fax, secretarial). Car park (free). Conference room. Garden. Two restaurants. Swimming pool.*
Room services *Refrigerator on request.*

Budget Suez Oceanfront Resort

18215 Collins Avenue, at 182nd Street, Sunny Isles, FL 33160 (reservations 1-800 327 5278/front desk 932 0661/fax 937 0058). Bus K, S, V. **Rates** $70-$108. **Credit** AmEx, MC, V.

A touch of Egypt on the beach. You know you've arrived when you spot the model camel and the sphinx on the front lawn. But don't worry: your room will in no way resemble a tomb. This family-owned and run facility is a classic of kitsch. Going strong for over 30 years, it provides utilitarian rooms, well-cared for grounds and a restaurant.
Hotel services *Bar. Car park (self; free). Disabled: access; rooms. Laundromat. Multi-lingual staff. No-smoking rooms. Restaurant. Sports/fitness facilities (exercise room, sauna, tennis court). Two swimming pools.*
Room services *Kitchenette in some rooms. Refrigerator.*

Key Biscayne

First-class

Sonesta Beach Resort

350 Ocean Drive, at East & East Heather Drives, Key Biscayne, FL 33149 (reservations 1-800 766 3782/front desk 361 2021/fax 361 2082). Bus B. **Rates** all doubles: island view/bay view $245-$285; ocean view $295-$350. **Credit** AmEx, DC, Disc, JCB, MC, V.

Ravaged by Hurricane Andrew in 1992, this secluded resort has been thoroughly renovated and is now the outdoor type's idea of heaven. Set on 10 acres overlooking the ocean, the grounds include nine tennis courts, a swimming pool and access to a championship golf course. All sorts of aquatic sports can be indulged in: fishing, sailing, snorkelling, kayaking, windsurfing, wave-running, and aqua biking. All the sunny, Caribbean-inspired modern rooms have private balconies facing the sea. For the reclusive rich, there are three-bedroom, two-bath villas (four-ten night minimum) with their own fully equipped kitchen, swimming pool and daily maid service for anywhere from $800-$1,200 per night.
Hotel services *Babysitting. Five bars. Business services (secretarial). Car park (valet; $13, self; free). Conference facilities. Disabled: access; rooms. Laundry service. No-smoking rooms. Seven restaurants. Sports/fitness facilities (aerobic classes, bicycle rental, exercise room, jogging track, sauna, 9 tennis courts, steamroom, whirlpool). Video rental.*
Room services *Fax/modem hook-ups. Minibar. Safes. VCR rental.*

Mid-range

Silver Sands Oceanfront Motel

301 Ocean Drive, at East Drive, Key Biscayne, FL 33149 (reservations/front desk 361 5441/fax 361 5477). **Bus** B. **Rates** mini-suites $149-$179; cottages $275. **Credit** AmEx, DC, MC, V.

Dwarfed by its next-door neighbour, the sprawling Sonesta, this pleasant one-storey motel is a is a smart buy if you don't have the dollars or the desire for a full-scale resort. Also completely rebuilt since Hurricane Andrew, it's plunked right on the beach. A tropical theme pervades in the spotless rooms. Mini-suites have two double beds; cottages can accommodate up to two adults and four children. If you want to upgrade yourself temporarily, pop over to the Sonesta and posh it out at one of the seven restaurants there.
Hotel services *Babysitting. Car park (self; free). Laundromat. Sports/fitness facilities (bicycle rentals, access to tennis courts and water sports). Swimming pool.*
Room services *Coffeemaker. Microwave ovens. Refrigerator. VCR.*

The Mainland

Downtown

First-class

Hotel Inter-Continental Miami

100 Chopin Plaza, at Biscayne Boulevard, Miami, FL 33131 (reservations 1-800 332 4246/front desk 577 1000/fax 577 0384). Bus S, 3, 16, 48. **Rates** double $209-$289; suite $329-$450. **Credit** AmEx, DC, MC, V.

What looks like a cross between a skyscraper and a mausoleum is actually Downtown Miami's finest convention-sized hotel with over 600 rooms. Constructed from honey-coloured marble, the Inter-Continental is lightened by a five-storey lobby which has a bright skylight, casual wicker furniture, copious plants and a huge Henry Moore sculpture. Decorated in sombre shades of beige and grey, rooms are well-appointed and many have views of the bay. This is the place to stay downtown.
Hotel services *Babysitting on request. Bar. Beauty salon. Business services (secretarial, fax, etc.). Car park (valet; $11). Conference facilities. Disabled: access; rooms. Laundry service. Multi-lingual staff. No-smoking rooms. Three restaurants. Sports/fitness facilities (access to nearby health club, jogging track). Swimming pool.*
Room services *Stereo with CD player. Kitchenettes in some rooms. Minibar. Refrigerator. VCR. Voicemail.*

Mid-range

Everglades Hotel

244 Biscayne Boulevard, at Third Street, Miami, FL 33136 (reservations 1-800 327 5700/front desk 379 5461/fax 577 8445). Bus S, 3, 16, 48. **Rates** double $89; suite $115. **Credit** AmEx, Disc, MC, V.

A Biscayne Boulevard relic, this hotel has been around for what seems forever and in many ways it shows. The lobby as well as the rooms are a bit shabby and could use some refurbishing. Cheap rates and the convenient downtown location are what keep people coming back.
Hotel services *Babysitting on request. Bar. Business services (secretarial). Car park (valet; $7). Conference facilities. Disabled: access; rooms. Laundry service. Restaurant. Sports/fitness facilities (access to local health club). Swimming pool.*
Room services *Radios in some rooms. Refrigerators on request.*

Miami River Inn

118 SW South River Drive, at SW Fourth Avenue,
Miami, FL 33130 (reservations/front desk 325 0045/fax
325 9227). Bus 8. **Rates** double $89-$109. **Credit**
AmEx, DC, Disc, MC, V.

A historic bed-and-breakfast close to imposing Downtown
Miami? Yes, believe it or not. The compound is made up of
five restored clapboard buildings built between 1906 and
1910 that look as if they were transported south from New
England. Rooms are gracious and traditionally furnished
with wood-plank floors, brass beds, cheery flowered wall-
paper, wicker chairs and wood panelling. Bathrooms are
tidy. A nice change from lofty, impersonal big-city hotels,
but in the middle of a rather seedy neighbourhood.

Hotel services *Breakfast included in room rate. Car*
park (self; free). Conference facilities. Disabled: access;
rooms. Garden. Laundromat. Multi-lingual staff. No-
smoking rooms. Sports/fitness facilities (access to nearby
YMCA, whirlpool). Swimming pool.

Coral Gables

First-class

Biltmore

1200 Anastasia Avenue, at Granada Boulevard, Coral
Gables, FL 33134 (reservations 1-800 228 300/front
desk 445 1926/fax 448 9976). Bus 52, 56, 72. **Rates**
single $239-$259; double $259-$279; suite $379-$1,950.
Credit AmEx, DC, Disc, JCB, MC, V.

Old-world elegance with a touch of Seville, Spain. This
majestic monument to the Gables of the boom times sports
a 300-foot bell tower, modelled after the Giralda Bell Tower
of the Cathedral of Seville, and the largest pool in the world,
at 17,000 square feet. Built in 1926 by the same architects
(Shultze & Weaver) who designed the Waldorf-Astoria in
New York City, the Biltmore flourished as a hotel and country club for many years. Used by the US government as a
veterans' hospital during World War II, it was neglected for

Survival of the kitschest

During the 1960s and well into the 1980s, Sunny
Isles's hotel row was a capital of kitsch. A visit
here guaranteed a low-budget Las Vegas-style
atmosphere – without the gambling. There was
the **Marco Polo Hotel**, a vision from *The
Arabian Nights*, decorated as an ersatz Taj Mahal
and topped off with minarets (now the Radisson
Aventura Beach Resort on 932 2233, renovated
but still recognisable); the **Thunderbird** (still
there; 931 7700), a paeon to Indian tribes with its
proud bird motif; and **The Budget Suez** (*listed
under* **Mid-Beach**), Miami Beach's tribute to
Egypt, still standing proud behind its model
camels and sphinx. Looking at them now, it is
hard to believe these were once hip places to hang
out. Yes, hip, like South Beach. More than just a

feast for the eyes in fantasy décor, these hotels
provided a feast for the ears – they swung! Top-
quality entertainment was provided by world-
class performers – Sammy Davis, Jr., Vic Damone
– who put on shows in the hotels' lounges. Alas,
the glory days were short-lived. Soon other
venues gained in popularity, and this part of
Miami Beach started to decline. The entertainers
exited and the hotels fell on hard times. Yet mirac-
ulously many of them survived. The vibe in
Sunny Isles of the 1990s is different now. Some
hotels have been incorporated into chains; others
are still family-run and retain their campiness. A
good deal of them, however, have evolved into
'resorts', appealing more to families and foreign
tourists than to citizens of the cocktail nation.

decades afterwards, eventually closing altogether. Ghosts of wounded soldiers were said to wander the halls. The hotel re-opened in 1986, after a $50 million renovation, but tough financial times persisted until the hotel joined the Westin chain in 1992. The lobby has an intricate hand-painted vaulted ceiling and French and Spanish furniture. Marble floors, oriental rugs, 25-foot columns, over-sized arches and blue and white porcelain planters add to the splendour. The rooms are furnished with period reproductions. The Biltmore retains its reputation as an elegant wedding location. Its sumptuous Sunday brunch is also popular.

Hotel services *Babysitting. Three bars. Conference facilities. Disabled: access, rooms. Beauty salon. Laundry service. No-smoking rooms. Three restaurants. Sports/fitness facilities (15,000 sq ft spa, ten tennis courts, 18-hole golf course). Swimming pool. Shuttle to airport.*
Room services *Coffeemaker on request. Fax/modem hook-ups. Hair dryer. Kitchenette in presidential suite. Refrigerator on request. Safe. VCR on request. Voicemail.*

Mid-range

Hotel Place St Michel

162 Alcazar Avenue, at Ponce de Leon Boulevard, Coral Gables, FL 33134 (reservations 1-800 848 4683/front desk 444 1666/fax 529 0074). Bus 56, 73. **Rates** single $165; double $165; suite $200. **Credit** AmEx, MC, V.
Tiny European-style gem in the heart of Coral Gables. Fresh flowers and fans adorn the cosy lobby. The distinctive rooms have wood floors, dark-panelled walls, antique furniture and a fruit basket. Room rates include continental breakfast. The exceptional Restaurant St Michel is downstairs.
Hotel services *Bar. Car park ($7; self). Fax. Laundry service. No-smoking rooms. Restaurant.*
Room services *Hair dryer. Radio.*

Omni Colonnade Hotel

180 Aragon Avenue, at Miracle Mile, Coral Gables, FL 33134 (reservations 1-800 843 6664/front desk 441 2600/fax 445 3929). Bus 24, 40, 72. **Rates** single $145-$225; double $145-$225; suite $275-$699. **Credit** AmEx, DC, Disc, MC, V.
Once the offices of Coral Gables' founder, George Merrick, this building later housed the Florida National Bank for almost 40 years. In the mid-1980s it was renovated to become an ultra-elegant hotel, catering mainly to a business clientele. The immense entrance is a two-storey rotunda with two corinthian columns, decorated with hand-blown crystal chandeliers and a fountain in the centre of the inlaid marble floor. Rooms are equally plush with marble vanity tops, brass fixtures and rich mahogany furniture. Pampering is key: champagne is served on arrival and complimentary coffee and newspaper are part of your wake-up call.
Hotel services *Babysitting. Bar. Car park (valet; $10, self; $9). Conference centres. Disabled: access; rooms. Laundry service. No-smoking rooms. Two restaurants. Fitness facilities (rooftop fitness centre, Jacuzzi). Swimming pool.*
Room services *Fax. Hair dryer. Minibar. Refrigerator. Radio. Voicemail. VCR on request.*

Budget

Hotel ChateauBleau

1111 Ponce de Leon Boulevard, at Antilla Avenue, Coral Gables, FL 33134 (reservations & front desk 448 2634/fax 448 2017). Bus J, 42. **Rates** single $69; double $69; suite $79. **Credit** AmEx, DC, MC, V.
A small, serviceable hotel – good value for its location and the comforts provided – conveniently placed for the Gables' shopping and dining districts. Rooms are spacious and neat.

Hotel services *Bar. Car park (self; free). Laundromat. No-smoking rooms. Restaurant. Safe. Swimming pool.*
Room services *Kitchenette in suite. Radio in some rooms. Refrigerator in suite and on request.*

Coconut Grove

First-class

Grand Bay

2669 South Bayshore Drive, at 27th Avenue, Coconut Grove, FL 33133 (reservations 1-800 327 2788/front desk 858 9600/fax 858 1532). Bus 48. **Rates** single $295; double $295; suite $350-$1,200. **Credit** AmEx, DC, MC, V.
Pull up to the ziggurat-like structure and an enormous red tubular sculpture by former Condé Nast editorial-director Alexander Lieberman greets you in the driveway. This top-line luxury hotel is the choice of many celebrities, some of whom have proven finicky guests. Years ago the management redecorated the presidential suite to Michael Jackson's specifications. The quietly elegant lobby is decorated with beige tones, marble floors and striking flower arrangements. Classical music wafts in the air. Enjoy a flute of champagne while you check in at the antique desk and then retreat to your well-appointed room, which has a terrace where you can sit, relax and take in the partial bay views. Dine at the stellar Grand Café, long one of Miami's finest restaurants.
Hotel services *Babysitting. Two bars. Beauty salon. Business centre (faxes and computers). Car park (valet; $13). Conference facilities. Disabled: access; rooms. Laundry service. No-smoking rooms. Restaurant. Sports/fitness facilities (Jacuzzi, sauna, 24-hour health club, personal trainers on call). Heated swimming pool.*
Room services *Stereo with CD player. Fax/modem hook-ups. Hair dryer. Minibar. Refrigerator. Safe. VCR. Video rental delivery to room. Voicemail.*

Mayfair

3000 Florida Avenue, at Virginia Street, Coconut Grove, FL 33133 (reservations 1-800 433 4555/front desk 441 0000/fax 447 9173). Bus 48, 42. **Rates** all suites: $249-$550. **Credit** AmEx, DC, Disc, MC, V.
Located in the Gaudi-esque Streets of Mayfair mall, this all-suite hotel is nevertheless intimate. Although rooms are

Hotel chains

The following chains have branches in Dade County:

First-class

Hilton 1-800 445 8667; **Hyatt** 1-800 236 1234; **Sheraton** 1-800 325 3535; **Westin** 1-800 228 3000.

Mid-range

Holiday Inn 1-800 327 5476; **Howard Johnson** 1-800 446 4656; **Marriott** 1-800 228 9290; **Radisson** 1-800 333 3333.

Budget

Best Western 1-800 528 1234; **Comfort Inn** 1-800 228 5150; **Days Inn** 1-800 325 2525; **Quality Inn** 1-800 228 5151; **Ramada Inn** 1-800 272 6232; **Travelodge** 1-800 255 3050.

arranged around an atrium, once inside you'll feel cloistered from the mayhem of Coconut Grove. Art nouveau details – dark wood, decorative glass lamps and furniture reminiscent of Frank Lloyd Wright designs – enhance the cave-like lobby. Rooms are individually designed and feature private terraces, most of which have a Japanese spa tub or a Roman tub. Guests are greeted with a glass of champagne.
Hotel services *Bar. Babysitting. Business centre. Conference facilities. Car park (valet; $14, self; $6). Disabled: access; rooms. Two restaurants. Laundry service. Massage service. No-smoking rooms. Rooftop swimming pool. Sauna. Twice daily maid service.* **Room services** *Fax/modem hook-ups. Hair dryer. Minibar. Radio. Refrigerator. Safe. VCR.*

Mid-range

Doubletree Hotel at Coconut Grove
2649 South Bayshore Drive, at Darwin Street, Coconut Grove, FL 33133 (reservations 1-800 222 8733/front desk 858 2500/fax 858 5776). Bus 48, 42. **Rates** single $169; double $179; suite $209. **Credit** AmEx, DC, Disc, MC, V.
Formerly the Coconut Grove Hotel, this facility was subsumed by the business traveller-focused Doubletree chain and has been renovated to the tune of $1 million. Rooms are bright and cheery. Higher floors overlook the boats at Dinner Key Marina and Biscayne Bay. The hotel is within comfortable walking distance of the Grove's shops, restaurants and attractions. An extra perk at check-in: not champagne, but chocolate chip cookies.
Hotel services *On-call babysitting. Business services (fax). Two bars. Car park (valet; $9). Conference facilities. Disabled: access; rooms. Laundry service. Massage service. No-smoking rooms. Restaurant. Sports/fitness facilities (two tennis courts). Swimming pool. Twice-daily maid service on request.* **Room services** *Hair dryer. Radio. Refrigerators (some rooms). Safe. Voicemail.*

North Bay Village
Budget

Best Western on the Bay Inn & Marina
1819 NE 79th Street Causeway, North Bay Village, FL 33141 (reservations 1-800 528 1234/front desk 865 7100/fax 868 3483). Bus L. **Rates** single $79; double $84; suite $99. **Credit** AmEx, DC, MC, V.
Conveniently located halfway between Downtown Miami and Miami Beach in sedate North Bay Village, this hotel is a newly renovated bargain. Rooms are spic and span and feature a happy islands-inspired décor. Some are equipped with kitchenettes. For the relaxed, lcoal-style vibe, arrive on a boat and dock at the popular, laid-back Shuckers, home of beach volleyball, raw and alcohol bars and, at times, live reggae.
Hotel services *Two bars. Car park (self; free). Disabled: access; rooms. No-smoking rooms. Restaurant. Swimming pool.* **Room services** *Kitchenette in some rooms. Refrigerator.*

North Dade
First-class

Turnberry Isle Resort & Club
19999 West Country Club Drive, between Aventura Boulevard & NE 197th Street, Aventura, FL 33180 (reservations 1-800 327 7028/front desk 932 6200/fax 933 6560). Bus E, S, 3. **Rates** resort $375-$405; yacht club $295-$335. **Credit** AmEx, DC, MC, V.

A mammoth resort covering 300 acres, and one of the few hotels in South Florida with its own helipad. Turnberry offers enough choices to make your head spin and keep you constantly occupied during your visit. Mediterranean-style buildings offer five different accommodation options. Golf lovers can choose the Country Club Hotel, adjacent to one of the property's two golf courses. Sea enthusiasts can decide on either the Yacht Club on the Intercoastal Waterway or the more modest Marina Hotel. Wherever you end up, you are guaranteed an exceptional room: light, airy, luxurious, decorated in earth tones and with unparalleled amenities, especially for the sporty type.
Hotel services *Babysitting on request. Five bars. Business services (secretarial). Car park (valet; $8, self; free). Conference facilities. Disabled: access; rooms. Laundry service. No-smoking rooms. Six restaurants. Sports/fitness facilities (two golf courses, health club, jogging track, racquetball courts, sauna, spa, steam room, 24 tennis courts, water sport equipment rentals). Four swimming pools. Video rental.* **Room services** *Stereo with CD player. Fax/modem hook-ups. Hair dryer. Minibar. Refrigerator. Safe. Voicemail. VCR.*

South Dade
First-class

Doral Golf Resort & Spa
4400 NW 87th Avenue, at NW 41st Street, Miami, FL 33178 (reservations 1-800 713 6725/front desk 592 2000/fax 594 4682). Bus 36, 87. **Rates** double $175-$370; suite $315-$945; spa suite $350-$1,280. **Credit** AmEx, DC, Disc, JCB, MC, V.
Located in a curious spot – four miles west of Miami International Airport – this 2,400-acre facility is Dade's largest and most luxurious resort: nirvana for the sportsman or the sybarite. Seven golf courses – one known as the Blue Monster – and 15 tennis courts, as well as a health club, keep the athlete occupied whose idea of fun is more passive. Eight separate lodges of three and four storeys provide over 600 rooms. Lobbies are stately; rooms are spacious, many overlooking a golf course or garden.
Hotel services *Babysitting on request. Three bars. Beauty salon. Business services (secretarial). Car park (valet; $9, self; free). Conference facilities. Disabled: access; rooms. Garden. Laundry service. Four restaurants. Sports/fitness facilities (bicycle rental, seven golf courses, health club, jogging track, sauna, spa, 15 tennis courts, whirlpool). Four swimming pools.* **Room services** *Stereo with CD player. Hairdryer. Minibar. Refrigerator. VCR. Voicemail.*

Budget

Dominican Retreat House
7275 SW 124th Street, between 72nd & 73rd Avenues, South Dade, FL 33156 (238 2711). Bus 57 (weekdays only). **No credit cards.**
For those stressed out, this oasis of tranquillity is something to shout about – except that loud noises and even talking are discouraged. Run by a congregation within the Dominican order of the Catholic Church, the Retreat House stresses spiritual and twelve step-programmes and has plain rooms on ten acres of lush grounds with library, chapel and dinning room. It shouldn't be considered simply as an alternative to a hotel – staff prefer visitors to have been on retreats before. There are organised programmes scheduled for most weekends ($100 approx with meals); other stays can be arranged on an individual basis (about $45 a night). A weekend here would make an interesting break-within-a-break.

Miami by Neighbourhood

Orientation

You'll probably stick to South Beach and other well-visited areas, but there's a hell of a lot more of Miami. Here's how to make sense of the urban sprawl.

There's so much more to Miami than meets the eye – especially when you look at a map. The metropolitan area that sprawls across 1,945 square miles of **Dade County** comprises 29 separately governed cities, surrounded by a nebulous spread of county-administered neighbourhoods known somewhat ominously as Unincorporated Dade. Thus several of the areas that comprise the Miami of popular imagination, including the Cities of Miami Beach and Coral Gables, are technically not part of Miami at all – the City of Miami, although Dade's urban core, accounts for only 15% of the county's population. And for all the skyscrapers in Downtown Miami, bucolic Coral Gables to the south-west is an economic powerhouse in its own right, home to the offices of more than 140 multinational corporations. In fact, the City of Miami has the unflattering distinction of being one of the poorest cities in the US, with urban decay and poverty clearly visible in Overtown and Liberty City.

If the overall geography seems complicated, don't expect things to get any more coherent within the City of Miami itself. The Downtown business district extending along Biscayne Boulevard (US 1), north from the Miami river to the Omni mall, and south along Brickell Avenue from the river to 15th Road, is a good three miles from the administrative and entertainment centre in Coconut Grove to the south. And many Cubans, Nicaraguans and other Spanish-speaking people think of SW Eighth Street in the neighbourhood of Little Havana (to the immediate south and west of Downtown) as the city's centre when it comes to shopping, banking and entertainment.

So far, so confusing – but don't be alarmed. The governmental boundaries make little difference to the visitor, except in following the street numbering system (*see below*), and most of the areas of interest are found in a relatively self-contained area, south and west of Downtown and over the causeways on Miami Beach.

THE PALMETTO EXPRESSWAY

The core areas of metropolitan Dade County hug the coast, framed by the Palmetto Expressway (SR 826) to the west and north. Starting at the south-western corner, the Palmetto goes north from **Kendall**, a community that grew up around a shopping centre, Dadeland Mall, and is now a

sprawling community of moderately priced homes and townhouses. It then passes to the west of the graciously conceived City of **Coral Gables** before coming up to the west of the airport – forced into the core of the urban area by the unstable swampland to the west. Next to the east is the quiet City of **Miami Springs**, notable for a sprinkling of buildings designed in Pueblo Indian style, followed by **Hialeah**, Dade's second largest city, where Spanish is the first language. Bordered by the Miami Canal to the south and Le Jeune Road to the east, Hialeah is less a city than miles of endless strip malls and fast-food outlets, plus the beleaguered but beautiful racetrack with its breeding colony of flamingoes.

The Palmetto swings east through 90° at Miami Lakes, the fiefdom of legendary Dolphins coach Don Shula – among the homes lining a dozen-odd man-made lakes is the Don Shula Hotel, Steak House and Golf Course – then continues east past **Opa-Locka**. Though a poor community, Opa-Locka is rich in architectural fantasy, with the city hall and many homes inspired by the minarets and domes of Middle Eastern design. The Expressway becomes 163rd Street after the junction with I-95, but is still known as Route 826 all the way east to the ocean at Sunny Isles. On its way it passes through **North Miami Beach** (no relation to Miami Beach proper), where it's lined by long strips of shops, including some good ethnic Asian, Italian and Middle Eastern markets. A little way north up the coast in the far north-east corner of the county is the newly incorporated city of **Aventura**, whose hallmarks are pricey condominiums and numerous golf courses.

THE COASTAL STRIP

I-95 and **US 1** (which merge a few miles south of Downtown) are the principal north-south arteries on the coastal side. US 1 (Biscayne Boulevard as the northern stretch is called) was the original highway leading south from Boston; the growth of Miami can be traced in the progression of neighbourhoods north from **Downtown** to the county line. Urban pioneers are beginning to refurbish the charming but rundown 1920s and 1930s homes in the neighbourhoods of **Buena Vista**, **Bell Mead** and **Morningside**, just north of Downtown. Also in this area is the burgeoning **Design District**, touted as the next South Beach (but with a long way to go), and continuing north is **Little Haiti**, one of the earliest areas of settlement, now one of the most derelict. Areas west of I-95 include some of Miami's poorer neighbourhoods, such as **Brownsville** and **Liberty City**.

More suburban homes begin to appear between I-95 and Biscayne Boulevard in the quiet residential neighbourhoods of **Miami Shores** and **North Miami**. 125th Street in North Miami is home to the new and innovative Museum of Contemporary Art, some good local shops and restaurants and Greenwich Studios, Miami's largest indoor film lot. Further north, you reach North Miami Beach and the Palmetto Expressway.

SOUTH FROM DOWNTOWN

I-95 ends just south of Downtown and merges into US 1. Once past **Coconut Grove** to the east of US 1 and **Coral Gables**, it can seem as if all the traffic is heading to Dadeland Mall in Kendall (*see above*). The homes are older and grounds more lush in **Cutler** and **Cutler Ridge** to the south and east. Finally, the urban sprawl starts to let up as the road heads towards the farms of **Homestead**, **Florida City** and the **Redlands**.

ACROSS THE BAY

Miami Beach, a couple of miles offshore across Biscayne Bay, has been called the 'Billion Dollar Sandbar', a fitting description for a piece of prime real estate built out of mangrove swamps. The City of **Miami Beach** occupies the southern half of the offshore spur, with the **Deco District** at its tip (between Fifth Street and Dade Boulevard). The largely upscale neighbourhoods of **Surfside**, **Bal Harbour**, **Sunny Isles** and **Golden Beach** occupy the northern end.

If it weren't for the causeways built across the bay, there would be no Miami Beach. The main access from Miami International Airport and the City of Miami is across the **MacArthur Causeway** (SR 395) to South Beach or the **Julia Tuttle Causeway** (I-195) to Mid-Beach. The **JF Kennedy Causeway** (SR 934) links 79th Street in the City of Miami with 71st Street in Miami Beach, via the small island city of North Bay Village. For the privilege of visiting the ritzy shops and flashy condominiums of Bal Harbour (per square mile, the most pricey real estate in Dade County), you'll have to pay a 50¢ toll to travel across the **Broad Causeway**.

Likewise, to enjoy one of the best views of the City of Miami, you'll have to cough up a dollar to pay the one-way toll on the **Rickenbacker Causeway**, which takes you from just south of Downtown Miami first to the public beaches on **Virginia Key** and then to **Key Biscayne**. Along with some top-end but characterless resort hotels

and condos, Key Biscayne has perhaps the best beaches in all of Dade County in Crandon Park and a landmark lighthouse in Bill Baggs State Recreation Area at the island's tip.

STREET NUMBERING

With the notable exceptions of the cities of Miami Beach and Hialeah, it is **Flagler Street** in Downtown Miami that is the dividing line between north and south for addresses in Dade County. Likewise, and again with the notable exceptions of Miami Beach and Hialeah, **Miami Avenue** is the east-west divide for numbered streets and avenues in Dade County: from 15th Road in the south (the southern end of Downtown), north to the Dade County line. Navigation is made easier by the fact that street numbers usually correspond with cross streets: thus 2410 SW 22nd Street will be between 24th and 25th Avenues.

South of 15th Road there is no street or avenue to serve as an east-west marker. Still, that hasn't stopped many streets and avenues in Coral Gables, Kendall and other cities in south Dade County from being marked as 'SW', for south of Flagler Street – and west of some notional highway.

Luckily, on Miami Beach and beach cities to the north (Surfside, Bal Harbour, Sunny Isles and Golden Beach), as well as Key Biscayne, no-one tried to be so cute with street addresses. Except for a handful of streets in Miami Beach which stop and start again on either side of a canal or golf course and are preceded by 'East' or 'West', numbered streets and avenues in these cities never take a prefix. Be careful, however, of street names that end with 'Dr', for Drive: many of these loop around in more than one direction and are often preceded with North, South, East or West to indicate which section of the drive a house or business is in. Still, you can find some solace in the fact that these streets generally are never more than a mile or two in length, so you can't get that lost.

Miami Beach's street numbering by and large adheres to the 'corresponding cross street' formula: thus 1140 Ocean Drive will be somewhere between 11th and 12th Streets. This makes finding your way between addresses pretty straightforward, though in South Beach the north-south roads are named rather than numbered.

OUR AREAS

In the Miami by Neighbourhood section, we have focused on areas that are of most interest to the visitor: **The Beaches** (Miami Beach and Key Biscayne), **Downtown**, **Coral Gables**, **Coconut Grove**, **Little Havana** and the **Design District/Little Haiti**. We have followed a similar breakdown in listings chapters when breaking entries down into area categories. For a **map** of the Miami urban area, see page 279.

The Beaches

Tourist-brochure Miami: palm trees, white sand, art deco and beautiful people – plus locals with attitude.

'Life's a Beach' proclaimed the bumper sticker on the back of a cherry-red convertible Mustang cruising down Ocean Drive. Indeed. The sticker articulates the prevailing philosophy of the islands of Miami Beach and Key Biscayne. Both were augmented with muck and sludge from the bottom of Biscayne Bay when prescient pioneers in the early 1900s foresaw the value and allure of beach, beach, and more beach. Miami Beach, a city of 92,000 residents that is three miles from Miami but light years away in attitude and glamour, is still called the Billion Dollar Sandbar. On that oft-photographed sandbar sits a cluster of beachside communities that stretch from the forbiddingly wealthy and insulated Golden Beach on the northern end to the hedonistic carnival and tourist mecca of South Beach on the southern terminus. Key Biscayne and its neighbouring island of Virginia Key are affluent, poky residential communities that lure visitors with what else? Beaches.

Islands & causeways

Four causeways span the three miles of Biscayne Bay between Miami and Miami Beach, plus two further north, providing the sort of vistas that give Miami its Chamber of Commerce moniker, the Magic City. Approaching Miami from the Beach, pleasure boats dot the bay, cruise ships huddle at the port and hulking skyscrapers cluster in the distance, their lights shimmering at night.

The **Rickenbacker** (SW 26th Road on the Miami side) is the southernmost causeway, linking Miami to suburban Key Biscayne and Virginia Key. The **MacArthur Causeway** (I-395), the busiest, crosses just north of Downtown Miami, spilling three lanes of traffic into South Beach's Fifth Street. On Friday and Saturday nights it can be bumper-to-bumper traffic with suburban clubgoers making the weekend pilgrimage across the bay. As the MacArthur spans the bay, it provides access to **Watson Island**, a scruffy island one mile east of Downtown, slated to become the new home of Parrot Jungle. Watson has a marina, helicopter rides, a Japanese garden and waterside park benches ideal for ogling the behemoth cruise ships docked across the Government Cut channel at the **Port of Miami**, located on Dodge and Lummus Islands, working-class islands in a bay full of wealthy, residential ones. Three small bridges lace off the MacArthur's north side toward a trio of exclusive residential islands: **Palm**, the former home of Al Capone; **Hibiscus**, former home of author Damon Runyon; and **Star**, former home of *Miami Vice*'s Don Johnson and current residence of Gloria Estefan.

Before the final stretch of the MacArthur spans over the bay onto Miami Beach, you'll see the ferry dock for **Fisher Island**, a well-manicured private island clustered with Spanish Mediterranean-style condominiums, visible just across the channel. Originally the southernmost tip of Miami Beach, Fisher was created in 1905 when Government Cut was dredged to improve access to the port. Less than a mile north is the **Venetian Causeway** (the first to be built), a slow, two-lane street that stretches from the northern edge of the art deco district to Downtown Miami. The causeway bisects a half dozen residential islands (Dilido, Rivo Alto, Belle Isle, San Marino and Biscayne Isle) and is a popular cycling and jogging trail. In Miami, the **Julia Tuttle Causeway** feeds directly into I-95, the freeway that is South Florida's Main Street. On the beach side, the Tuttle becomes 41st Street, the commercial hub of Mid-Beach. At the 'Welcome To Miami Beach' sign at the foot of 41st Street, a dozen palm trees wear neon necklaces that pierce the night in vibrant colours. Further north, the **JFK Causeway** and **Broad Causeway** provide further links to the mainland.

Miami Beach

South Beach

South Beach prompts hyperbole. It is the epicentre of all that is hip and happening in Miami. Rollerbladers glide down Ocean Drive wearing thongs and muscle shirts. Whimsical, pastel-hued art deco buildings line the streets, laid out on a rectilinear grid. Fashion models, suntanned geriatrics, Eurovisitors, artists, celebs, hipsters and a sprinkling of regular folk stroll past sidewalk cafés, art galleries, designer boutiques, bars and clubs. And then there's the ocean, the palm trees, the backdrop of impossibly blue skies and sunshine. A low-key sort of chic and a hint of seediness keep the place from running away with its own fabulousness.

Ten years ago much of the area was in decline; the recent high-octane renaissance has garnered worldwide press and draws thousands of tourists to the southern tip of Miami Beach, especially from

November through May. SoBe (it's OK to use the abbreviation in writing, but it's a bit naff in speech) remains a favourite of fashion photographers, who helped spawn international interest in the area. They still flock, especially during winter. They bring their entourages and cull from the top-name modelling agencies that have opened South Beach offices, drawing upon the exotic, multicultural talent pool. Locals have become almost blasé about the incredible number of leggy and hunky beauties strolling the streets, portfolios in hand.

SOUTH OF FIFTH STREET

Falling outside the preservation area, this lower swathe of South Beach is in the thick of development that many believe will derail its intimate feel. The 26-storey **South Pointe Towers**, grossly out of scale with the neighbourhood, is

Vice or virtue?

It was the 1980s and, according to the uber-stylish TV drama *Miami Vice*, the city was awash in guns, drugs, babes, pastels and a seductive sort of lawlessness. Okay, it is true that in the first half of that decade, Miami's crime stats led the nation by a couple of lengths, race riots dominated local news, an elaborate cocaine smuggling ring was discovered at the airport and *Time* magazine dubbed the place 'Paradise Lost'. But for five years of prime-time television, *Vice* used the worst about Miami and made it look its best.

Vice, a weekly cop show, premiered in the US in 1984 and by the following year was showcasing the city's charms in 136 countries worldwide. Chamber of Commerce types initially fretted about its over-the-top body count and heavy crime content, but soon recognised it as a promotional dream tool. The show was, in effect, an ad campaign, increasing international curiosity, boosting tourism and upping the city's sex appeal. Locally, *Vice* jump-started the film industry, injecting thousands of dollars into the economy, and gave Miami a dash of Hollywood glamour in the midst of all its mayhem.

Lush cinematography was the programme's forte. Beguiling sequences of images unfolding against a Top 40 soundtrack crafted a prime-time love poem to Miami – and particularly South Beach. Some credit the show with helping feed a fever that would soon propel SoBe to its position at the top of the international hip parade. The show's stars, Philip Michael Thomas and Don Johnson, detectives Crockett and Tubbs, forged a look for men that remains in the South Florida fashion primer: slouchy linen suits over T-shirts, sockless feet in expensive Italian shoes and a rugged two-day stubble.

Long-time South Beach residents speak of the *Vice* days almost nostalgically, if for nothing else than the absurdities the show prompted. Some tourists forgot television's tenuous relationship with reality and arrived in Miami expecting every resident to be packing heat, driving a Ferrari and to witness flocks of drug

Don Johnson, the smooth one.

dealers gunned down on the street every day. The richest irony came when the governor of Florida gave Don Johnson an award for helping promote Miami's image. The show was all style and scant substance, but seeing Miami on TV made people all over the world fall in love with the place, including the people who lived here.

In 1996, the Fox network confected a new guns, babes and cops show shot on South Beach and starring a couple of crimefighters. It was called *Lawless*, and publicity material promised that the show was a *Miami Vice* for the 1990s. Apparently not. *Lawless* was cancelled after its first episode. However, rumours still rumble about a possible reunion for Crockett and Tubbs.

Baywatch, South Beach style, at the 10th Street lifeguard stand.

now dwarfed by neighbouring, controversial, 50-storey condominium towers built by Thomas Kramer, a flamboyant developer and the nemesis of local preservationists. Smaller-scale condos and refurbished deco apartment buildings, many occupied by retirees, fill most of the area making this a more sedate (read: quiet) neighbourhood than the Deco District, but you'll find four of SoBe's best restaurants here: the critically acclaimed **Nemo** (100 Collins Avenue), **Savannah** (437 Washington Avenue), where the gorgeous and gregarious dine on upscale Southern food, the attitudinous **China Grill** (404 Washington Avenue) and **Joe's Stone Crab** (220 Biscayne Street), for years, the only reason to venture south of Fifth. Known worldwide for its succulent crab claws and key lime pie, the restaurant is a local institution. If hunger outruns patience (queues are notoriously long and no reservations are taken), **Joe's Take Away** next door has the same menu to go.

For a cheaper bill and a dress code that leans toward sandy feet and T-shirts over wet bathing suits, duck into **Big Pink** (157 Collins Avenue) for diner food. Clubgoers may want to find their way to **Amnesia** (136 Collins Avenue), a cavernous open-air dance club lined with bleacher seats for viewing the undulating masses. The best respite for urban madness is **South Pointe Park**, a verdant park on the very tip of Miami Beach; it's surrounded by the Atlantic Ocean and Government Cut channel, the aquatic highway for cruise ships, of which it furnishes a great view.

THE DECO DISTRICT

A compact area easily navigable on foot and safe to walk day and night, the Deco District officially stretches north-south from Fifth Street to Dade Boulevard and from the Atlantic Ocean to Biscayne Bay. Three north-south streets are home to the highest concentration of clubs, bars, restaurants and shops: Ocean Drive, Collins Avenue and Washington Avenue. More than 800 buildings in the fanciful art deco style give the district its name. The **Miami Design Preservation League** (MDPL) (1001 Washington Avenue) distributes free maps, savvy information and conducts chatty, 90-minute, $5 walking tours of the district for those who desire a detailed orientation.

The 10-block strip of **Ocean Drive** from Fifth to 14th Streets is the area's epicentre and an adequate sampler of the architecture. On the eastern side of the street, the dunes and sports courts of **Lummus Park** front the Atlantic Ocean and the white sandy beaches that cost millions to refurbish after erosion binges. Six funky, campy, lifeguard stands decorate the beach. A mod antenna spikes the one at 10th Street, 12th Street's resembles a purple mobile home and the one at 14th Street sports a circular roof crowned with Astroturf. Back on terra firma, terrace bars and sidewalk cafés spill patrons from the patios of the classic deco hotels on the street's western side. One of the district's most memorable views is in the evening, neck deep in the Atlantic, from where you can ogle the flesh parade and watch cars cruise the strip under the radioactive glow of the neon signs.

Ocean Drive is one sidewalk café after another. Let whim guide you or bank on the perennially popular spot for noshing, people-watching, and gazing at the ocean – the **News Café**, a buzzing café at the corner of Eighth Street and Ocean Drive, where tables are sardined with trendies 24 hours a day. During the annual Art Deco Weekend festival (held the second weekend in January), Ocean is closed to traffic and transforms into a street fair, antiques market and outdoor concert.

Collins Avenue is one block west of Ocean, with a blend of deco apartment buildings, hotel cafés and high-end retail boutiques such as Nicole Miller and Armani Exchange A/X. In the midst of the retail gloss is **Puerta Sagua** (700 Collins Avenue), a Cuban restaurant where a full meal will arrive on a plate larger than Wales and cost less than $7. Inside it's usually a lively mix of old-time Cubanos, hip-hop kids, budget-minded backpackers and artists downing cups of café cubano.

Further on is the gorgeous **Marlin Hotel** (No.1200); if you can't afford the room rates, at least have a drink at Shabeen, a lobby bar that screams tropics with hyper-funky furniture splashed with high-voltage Caribbean colour. Above 14th Street, apartment buildings give way to hotels. Two worth a visit are the white-themed **Delano Hotel** (No.1685) and the **Raleigh Hotel** (No.1775). Both have had millions poured into renovation and bespeak class, style and grandeur.

One block west is **Washington Avenue**, the SoBe street that has retained a bit of raffish charm amid its hyper-hipness. Cuban mercados, fruit stands and dusty beauty parlours intersperse with one-of-a-kind boutiques selling retro houseware, faddish clubgear and $500 sunglasses. Retail's the thing here. For those who can't get enough of that architecture stuff, the **Miami Beach Post Office** (No.1300) deviates from the art deco norm with its depression moderne style that includes a rotunda

Those we have loved

In a city that is little more than 100 years old, history can be a fuzzy concept and preservation an even more foreign idea. Until the 1980s, the prevailing philosophy was that old buildings should be torn down and replaced with something newer, higher, glitzier. History, schmistory, many said.

Before a preservation movement took root in South Beach in the late 1970s, the area lost some gems, including the Fifth Street Gym, where a young Muhammad Ali trained; the Senator Hotel, which was bulldozed into a parking lot; and the Amsterdam Palace, a bohemian Ocean Drive apartment building that was purchased by Gianni Versace and turned into Villa Causina, one of his residences. (Versace also bought the adjoining Revere Hotel and ploughed it down to give himself room for a swimming pool.)

Barbara Baer Capitman was the tirelessly tenacious woman credited with pricking the consciences of Miami Beach and beginning the slow process of educating residents about the rich art deco, streamline moderne and Spanish Mediterranean revival treasures between First and 23rd Streets. In 1976, Capitman founded the Miami Design Preservation League (MDPL), an organisation whose first meeting drew only six participants. By 1979, the MDPL had won its fight to place more than 900 South Beach buildings on the National Register of Historic Places. The Deco District was born, making it the only collection of 20th-century architecture included on the Register. But Beach politicians appeared

something less than impressed. It took seven more years before a local preservation district was created with legal clout to enforce guidelines and punish offenders.

Historic preservation is still in its infancy in South Beach and as property values soar and opportunities for profit increase, preservationists and developers engage in frequent battle. Locals fear the character and scale of South Beach may be forsaken for the lure of the almighty dollar. Some contend the developers are winning the war. One of the most reviled local developers is the flamboyant Thomas Kramer, a favourite of local gossip columnists for his personal and professional antics. He first outraged locals with the construction of South Pointe, a high-rise on the south tip of the Beach that was resoundingly out of context with the intimate scale of the area. His latest venture is six 50-storey towers next door to South Pointe, a development a local environmental lawyer calls 'instant visual blight'.

Another hotly debated project involves the pedestrian Lincoln Road Mall. South Beach has only one cinema, and that shows primarily art films. City commissioners have okayed a project that will raze a block of buildings on the western end of the mall and build a dozen movie theatres, along with chain stores à la Gap and Banana Republic. Some locals see the invasion of the chains as the beginning of the end for South Beach's funky flavour. Others call it the inevitable march of progress.

with exquisite acoustics. The quiet glamour of a hotel bar in a scrupulously restored art deco hotel is another way to soak up the style. The **Astor Bar & Grill** (No.956) in the Astor Hotel bears investigation for its intimate vibe and sexy interior. An undervisited institution, but one that boggles the mind with its eclectic exhibits is the **Wolfsonian Foundation** (1001 Washington Avenue). Local millionaire Mickey Wolfson has turned a storage space into an impeccably restored museum displaying twentieth-century decorative art objects from his massive private collection.

One east-west street worth noting is **Espanola Way**, a block-long cluster of Spanish Mediterranean buildings ornamented with awnings and balconies. Espanola sits between Washington and Drexel Avenues and interrupts the numerical sequence between 14th and 15th Streets. Originally designed as an artists' colony, it retains its bohemian flavour. Art galleries, boutiques and cafés are at street level while artists' lofts fill the upper storeys. The **Clay Hotel & International Hostel** on the corner of Washington draws an international crowd.

LINCOLN ROAD MALL

The LRM, local shorthand for the Lincoln Road Mall, had its heyday in the 1950s, when it was designed by reigning architectural iconmeister Morris Lapidus and dubbed the Fifth Avenue of the South. In the past five years, this popular and refurbished pedestrian mall has re-emerged as a South Beach gathering spot, especially for locals who tire of the crowds, volume and preening of Ocean Drive. Gussied up in 1997 with a $16 million facelift, the mall sits between 16th and 17th Streets and stretches from the Atlantic to Alton Road. Sidewalk cafés, clubs, boutiques, restaurants, cultural venues, artists' studios and galleries line the mall, which pedestrians share with dogwalkers, street musicians, rollerbladers, joggers and bicyclists. The LRM has free outdoor concerts, hosts a fruit and vegetable market on Sunday mornings and an antique market on Saturdays and synchronises its galleries into a **Gallery Night** on the second Saturday of the month.

Other cultural venues on Lincoln include the **Colony Theater** (No.1040), a deco gem that hosts theatre, dance and music performances, and the **Lincoln Theater** (No.540), home of the New World Symphony, at the mall's eastern end . Plate-glass windows fronting the studios of the **Miami City Ballet** (No.905) allow passers-by to watch rehearsals in progress. **Books & Books** (No.933) hosts author readings, and its Russian Bear Café coffee bar is peopled with earnest bibliophiles. Next door, at the edgily hip **Alliance Cinema** (No.927) only art films make it to the screen. **Artcenter south florida** (No.810), a consortium of local and immigrant artists, leans toward the

Streetlife (and wildlife) on Lincoln Road Mall.

provocative and the multicultural. Affiliated galleries are signalled by a yellow awning.

Dozens of restaurants have doubled their dining rooms by setting up sidewalk tables. The **Van Dyke Café** (1641 Jefferson Avenue, at Lincoln Road) bustles 24 hours a day with a see-and-be-seen clientele. **Da Leo Trattoria Toscana** (819 Lincoln Road) recreates the conviviality of a neighbourhood Tuscan restaurant and **World Resources** (No.719) looks like the dinner stop for the cast of a Benetton ad. The outdoor tables arc around a fountain, and the café hosts ethnic music most nights of the week.

On the drawing board as of mid-1997 is the controversial addition of a dozen movie theatres at the western end of the LRM. Some contend that it will ruin the atmosphere of the mall, now characterised by funky, locally owned stores.

ALTON ROAD & AROUND

Less funky and polished than the other shopping and commercial areas of SoBe, Alton Road is its western commercial artery. In a residential area, it is frequented mostly by locals. Cheap furniture stores, auto-repair shops, delis and mercados selling Cuban goods line the street, although corporate America is beginning to arrive in the form of fast-food joints and chain retail stores (Dunkin Donuts, McDonald's, Blockbuster Video and Domino's Pizza). For a dose of true local flavour

(and some cheap goods), duck into **SoBe Thrifty** (1435 Alton Road), where the area's drag queens comb crowded rails for frocks and props. If you want to pack some nosh for a day at the beach, the **Epicure** market (No.1656) has a choice selection of pricey fine foods and produce. A block away, **Biga** bakery (No.1710) is where to duck for a scone, a baguette and a cup of espresso.

Mid-Beach (Dade Boulevard to 62th Street)

In the 1950s, the kitschly oversized hotels that sit shoulder to shoulder on mid Miami Beach (or Mid-Beach) defined the vacation in Miami Beach. Grande dames like the **Fontainebleau** (with its trompe l'oeil mural) and the **Eden Roc** went all out for a large and campy interpretation of glamour. These days the icons seem ironic and benign, and cater now to conventioneers and Latin American visitors instead of starlets and movie moguls.

The hotels get larger, the crowds get older, and the pace gets slower as you head north out of South Beach. West of Collins Avenue, Mid-Beach is a mix of golf courses and upper-class residential, with sprawling estates fronting **Indian Creek**, a narrow waterway west of Collins Avenue where yachts bob and the University of

The shifting sands

The wide, white carpet of sand that makes South Beach so photogenic needs a bit of help now and then to keep in shape. The surf and wind erode Miami Beach's shoreline, a persistent problem aggravated by human bumbling. Here in Beachville, remedies are costly, but essential, since the beach is the undisputed top lure for tourists. To fatten them up, millions have been spent in the past 15 years, mostly to rectify uneducated decisions that disrespected nature's business.

In 1925, a channel was created and dredged at Haulover Cut, a waterway in North Beach wedged between Bal Harbour and Sunny Isles. The tidal flow of sand was severely interrupted. Compound-ing this, as hotel and condos were built on the shoreline, bulldozers flattened the sand dunes nature uses as erosion buffers. Sea walls were built to protect the buildings, causing more interference with wave patterns. In 1982, the beaches from Bal Harbour all the way down to South Beach were just thin strips of sand with little territory for sunbathers and beachcombers. Hotel owners began to fear property loss as their backyard swimming pools threatened to float out to sea.

Experts confabbed and devised first aid in three steps. An offshore sandbar was created to encourage larger waves to break farther away and lose their punch. A hurricane dune was erected, and sand was dredged and piped in from the ocean floor to widen a 10-mile stretch of beach. Unfortunately for the image-makers, this sand was an unsightly brown, so in some areas (including South Beach) a second layer of powdery white sand has been added as beach idyll set dressing.

The Army Corps of Engineers completed the job in 1982 and returned in 1997 for its second major shore-up. (There have been 15 dredge projects in Dade and Broward counties in the past 25 years.) This time the $6.5 million project drew the ire of local conservationists, who charged that coral reefs are destroyed every time a hopper dredge – it's been called an 'ocean-going vacuum cleaner' – dips its neck below the waterline. This most recent project piped in millions of gallons of sand between 36th and 46th Streets in Mid-Beach, a stretch thick with high-rise hotels and condominiums. Further north, some stretches of sand remain threadbare.

Miami rowing club practices at dawn. Unless ogling grand homes intrigues (try old-money La Gorce and Pine Tree Drives on the west side of the creek for mixed imitation architecture lurking behind imposing gates), Collins is the only street of any consequence and it becomes more soulless in the 50s and 60s as unremarkable beige buildings tower over both sides of the street, turning it into a condo canyon.

Ten blocks of beach behind the big hotels (36th to 46th Streets) underwent a $7 million facelift in 1997 to counteract erosion and give the sun-worshippers more real estate for their beach chairs. A public beach just north of the Eden Roc has ample parking. A wooden boardwalk popular with joggers, elderly couples and orthodox Jewish families runs behind the hotels, allowing you to peer into beachfront bars and restaurants.

North Beach

North Beach is local slang; you won't find the appellation on any official cartography. Extending north of the condo canyon, this middle-class residential area stretches roughly from 65th Street to 86th Street. The two smatterings of commercial activity are on 71st Street, where the JFK Causeway spans the bay, and Collins Avenue, where slightly seedy restaurants, cafés and shops intersperse with hotels that cater to budget-minded South Americans. Not as chic as South Beach nor as residential as Mid-Beach, North Beach has a few hidden charms, including the **MoJazz Café** (928 71st Street). The best jazz house in the county, it's a dark and smoky club with a menu of Vietnamese food. The **bandshell** on 74th Street and Collins Avenue is the kind of photo background that telegraphs the sun and fun of Miami Beach. Painted buttermint yellow and aqua, its rounded forms and art deco details telegraph wordlessly that you aren't in Kansas anymore.

Surfside to Golden Beach

The seven-mile strip of beachfront land north of North Beach up to the Broward County line consists of four distinct, if not terribly interesting communities – Surfside, Bal Harbour, Sunny Isles and Golden Beach. French Canadians, sedate South Americans, families and vacationers who travel in budget-minded packs frequent the middle-class communities of Surfside and Sunny Isles. Bal Harbour and Golden Beach are like rich cousins: wealthier, stuffy villages with real estate worthy of *Lifestyles of the Rich and Famous*.

Proceeding north from North Beach on a two-block, seedy, commercial slice of Collins Avenue is **North Shore Park**, the southern border of **Surfside**. The park is a lovely and underutilised stretch of pristine beach lined with sea grape trees, sand dunes, a boardwalk, a vita exercise course

and amenities such as changing rooms, picnic tables and barbecue pits. Surfside's commercial street, **Harding Avenue**, runs just west of Collins and offers a slightly tarnished group of shops, restaurants and cheesy souvenir stores. Surfside is a small city, less than a mile square, clotted with two- and three-storey apartment buildings, with little to entice or interest visitors.

You don't need to see a city limits sign to know you're in **Bal Harbour**, the elegant burg just north of Surfside. The landscape sports an expensive topiary manicure, luxury cars ply the streets, chauffeurs in caps keep the motor idling and the AC on while madam shops, and there's a distinct whiff of money in the air. **Bal Harbour Shops** (9700 Collins Avenue) is an oppressively top-end mall whose concession list reads like a who's who of haute couture. Security guards in faux colonial uniforms and Styrofoam pith helmets prowl the parking lots in golf carts. A handful of large and lacklustre chain hotels court convention business on the oceanfront across Collins Avenue. On 96th Street, the city's commercial artery, the commercial space leans toward cosmetic surgeons, fine food stores and stuffy art galleries. In Bal Harbour crime is low (the local police are notoriously zealous at dispensing speeding tickets), real estate prices are high and the median age is at least 30 years older than on the southern half of the sandbar. TV newsman David Brinkley winters here and former president George Bush has been snapped sunning himself at one of the button-down high-rises on Collins.

Haulover Beach Park, just north of Bal Harbour, scores big points as one the area's most scenic stretches of beachfront, offering unimpeded views that span the southern sweep of Miami Beach. Worth a drive, the beach is fringed with dense vegetation that blocks out the visual pollution of nearby high-rises. Known primarily as a nude beach, Haulover also has a 1,100ft pier enabling good fishing, picnic tables, concession stands and a kayak rental outfitter for jaunts into the nearby Oleta River, a pristine waterway that wends westward through a state park.

Beyond Haulover Beach Park lies **Sunny Isles Beach**, where architectural kitsch and older tourists prevail. Two miles of beachfront hotels (and some of the patrons) look untouched since the 1950s. Campy, musclebound sheiks stand sentinel at the **Sahara** (18335 Collins Avenue) and, four blocks up, wenches hoist crescent moons to decorate the **Blue Mist Hotel** (No.19111). One of the few redeeming features of Sunny Isles is Wolfie Cohen's **Rascal House** (No.17190), a bustling restaurant/deli serving favourite Jewish dishes, which has earned the distinction of landmark status. Waitresses wear nametags and call you honey, and patrons kvetch in Yiddish. The food is rib sticking, and the sociology lesson offers an insight into one of Miami Beach's dominant ethnic groups.

Private oceanfront homes are a rarity in Miami Beach. The wealthy enclave of **Golden Beach**, the northernmost community on the beach side of Dade County, boasts two miles of palatial estates constructed on the ocean's edge and shielded from public view by elaborate fortifications. Beaches here are for residents only.

Key Biscayne

The Rickenbacker Causeway arcs onto the two sleepy and physically striking islands of **Key Biscayne** and its silent partner, **Virginia Key**. The Key, as locals call Key Biscayne, is the northernmost island in the Florida Keys. Its life as an exclusive resort began in the early 1900s when sea captain William Commodore dredged the bay, zealously planted tropical foliage and built yacht basins for his monied pals. Locals feared the worst – the invasion of riff-raff – in the late 1940s when flamboyant flying ace Eddie Rickenbacker opened the toll bridge, and indeed construction went into a bit of a frenzy when the condos that cluster on the western end of the island were built. Still, the Key remained an unknown, affluent burg until its most famous resident – impeached US president Richard Nixon – bought a home here in the 1970s.

Nixon may have helped push up real estate prices and put the Key on the map, but the mendacious prez did little to make the island more lively. With little nightlife, shopping or culture, the lures for visitors are purely natural – beaches, two waterfront parks, a cycling path and screamingly photographable views of Miami. The few lacklustre hotels are mainly used by vacationing families.

Just over the bridge on Virginia Key are **Hobie Beach**, **Windsurfer Beach** and **Jet Ski Beach**, named, aptly enough, for the watersports popular here. Rental stands for windsurfers, kayaks,

sailboats and jet-skis dot the white-sand shoreline. The azure water of Biscayne Bay forms a wide, relatively shallow pan serviced by steady winds. On the northern side of the causeway as it hits Virginia Key sits the **Rusty Pelican**, a seafood house with a corny nautical motif, average fare and stunning Miami views, particularly at sunset. For funkier surroundings, duck into **Bayside Hut Restaurant** (3501 Rickenbacker Causeway), next to the Rickenbacker Marina and the Miami Marine Stadium, an antiquated waterfront concert venue. Patrons sit outside beneath a chickee hut in shorts and T-shirts and nibble on the restaurant's signature fish dip and fresh seafood. Further down on the casual scale and higher on the scenic meter is **Jimbo's**, a slice of genuine Floridiana. The salty dive is a wooden shack-cum-menuless-restaurant tucked into Virginia Key's mangroves at the edge of Biscayne Bay. Fishermen play bocce ball. Locals in the know buy tins of beer from a cooler and smoked fish. A cluster of electric-coloured facades form a faux Caribbean street once used as a backdrop for the TV series *Flipper*.

Crossing to Key Biscayne, the causeway is renamed Crandon Boulevard, the main thoroughfare. The prime attractions are **Crandon Park** on the east and **Bill Baggs State Recreation Area**, the 400-acre park at the tip of the island. Palm trees line Crandon and shallow waters, barbecues and picnic tables make it a family favourite. Another good swimming beach is Bill Baggs. The shoreline is tufted with dunes and boardwalks lead to the **Cape Florida Lighthouse**, built in about 1820. In the distance, where Biscayne Bay and the Atlantic converge, half a dozen houses sit in the water on wooden legs like oversized grasshoppers. Stiltsville was built in the 1940s by fishermen who wanted to circumvent property taxes; recent laws forbid repairs and the fate of the unusual village has been left to the vagaries of nature.

Downtown

There's more to Miami's business centre than gleaming skyscrapers: you'll find museums, parks and stunning views of Biscayne Bay from the elevated railway.

In 1911, 15 years after the founding of Miami, public relations wizard and mayor EG 'Ev' Sewell encouraged the locals to dress in light coloured suits and straw hats to reinforce the young city's tropical and exotic image. Today, no-one needs encouragement. Downtown has become that tropical and, on its own terms, exotic location – the. meeting place of Miami's diverse population and the commercial heart of south Florida.

Downtown is a 28-block area running south from NE 15th Street to SE 14th Street, bordered by I-95 to the west and Biscayne Bay to the east. It includes the Central Business District and the Brickell and Omni areas. The string that ties these distinct neighbourhoods together is the Metromover, an elevated rail system (*see box page 65* **Let the train take the strain**). Downtown is best visited from Monday to Friday, 10am to 5pm, since the neighbourhood pulls down its shutters after dark, and is less interesting over the weekend, with the exception of the commercial stretch of Flagler Street and the tourist-oriented Bayside Marketplace.

Central Business District

Miami's Central Business District (CBD) is bounded on the south by the Miami River, on the north by Fifth Street, on the west by I-95 and on the east by Biscayne Bay. Few people live in the CBD, though it is crowded during weekdays with workers, shoppers and tourists.

Government Center

The western edge of the CBD was redeveloped in the late 1970s and 1980s in an attempt to revitalise the area. Government offices and Metrorail/Metromover's main station occupy the monolithic **Metro-Dade Government Center** (111 NW First Street). Its strange, spaceship-like appendage, is the County Commission Chambers, the legislative headquarters for Dade County. Immediately west of the chambers is Claes Oldenburg's 'Dropped Bowl with Scattered Slices and Peels', a huge, whimsical, sculptural fountain depicting orange peels scattered around a broken bowl; the fountain is often broken, too.

Miami's historic African-American neighbourhood, **Overtown**, is located north and west of

West Flagler's iconic billboard.

Government Center, across NW Fifth Street. Ravaged in the 1960s by the construction of I-95, this once vibrant neighbourhood (known in its early days as 'Coloredtown') is potentially dangerous and is not recommended as a destination, even during daylight hours.

Across NW First Street from Government Center is the **Metro-Dade Cultural Center** (101 W Flagler Street), built by architect Philip Johnson in the neo-Mediterranean style. This Italian fortress is home to the **Miami-Dade Public Library**, the **Historical Museum of Southern Florida** and the **Miami Art Museum (MAM)**. The centre is not one of Johnson's most successful works; the sloping covered ramp and fountain on the Flagler Street side are the building's most pleasing details. The large central plaza hosts occasional free performances.

Seeing orange: Claes Oldenburg's whimsical sculpture at Government Center.

Flagler Street

Downtown's main commercial drag, Flagler Street, is a narrow two-lane street that runs east-west through the CBD. At the western end stands the ziggurat-capped, neo-classical **Dade County Courthouse** (73 W Flagler Street), dating from 1925. On the building's west side, above the garage entrance, a small granite step at the base of the windows is a reminder of Miami's segregationist past. Blacks were not allowed to stand inside the courthouse with whites, so they paid their property taxes through a small window above the step (replaced during aeent renovation).

Across Flagler Street, on the eastern wall of 66 W Flagler, is another relic of Miami's past – a large billboard advertising **Coppertone** suntan lotion. Before concerns over the ozone layer and skin cancer, Coppertone's little girl and her dog served as icons of South Florida sun and fun. Local preservationists rescued the sign from a building slated for demolition and installed it at its present site.

The **Latin House Restaurant** (8 W Flagler Street) serves traditional Miami-Cuban food. Stop at the outside window and order a Cuban coffee for a quick caffeine jolt. A few steps from Latin House lies the intersection of Miami Avenue and Flagler Streets – Miami, ground zero – the point from which all the city's streets are numbered.

Across Miami Avenue is **Burdines** department store (22 E Flagler Street). The Burdines family opened their first shop in Miami in 1898. This streamline moderne building, built in 1936, was once the upmarket chain's flagship store; now you can find Burdines in every suburban mall. East of Miami Avenue is the **Seybold Arcade** (33 E Flagler Street; the arcade runs through the block to First Street), home of Miami's jewellery trade. The shop windows display jewellery ranging from posh to gaudy.

Further down Flagler is Abel Holtz Boulevard (aka Second Avenue). Mr Holtz, a prominent local banker, lied to a grand jury and spent some time in a federal penitentiary in the mid 1990s. The corner is anchored by the **Gusman Center for the Performing Arts** (174 E Flagler Street) and the **Alfred I Dupont Building** (No.169). The Gusman Center, built as the Olympia Theater in 1925, was the first air-conditioned building in Miami. Its interior resembles an Italianate garden, complete with stars blinking in a night sky. It's currently used for concerts and films (it's a venue for screenings in the Miami Film Festival). Built in 1936 in the Depression moderne style, the Alfred I Dupont Building's elaborate wrought ironwork and ceiling murals on the second floor are worth a trip up the escalator.

Further east on Flagler Street, between Second Avenue and Biscayne Boulevard, is a stretch of hyper-gaudy electronics, camera and shoe shops catering mainly for Latin American visitors. Music blares from speakers, flashy displays fill the windows, employees stand before the shops distributing discount coupons. It's cold, calculated capitalism. Buy today. You're gone tomorrow. Did we discuss refund policies? It's also good fun, with a bustling, carnivalesque atmosphere and high score on the kitsch-ometer.

South-east CBD & the Miami River

South of Flagler Street and east of Miami Avenue contains two remnants of the economic extravagance of the 1980s. The **NationsBank Building** (200 SE First Avenue) is an IM Pei-designed structure whose curved and mirrored exterior is a playful addition to Miami's skyline. It was built by the Centrust Corporation, whose president felt flush enough to install gold urinals in his private restroom. The business went down the pan, the urinals removed and the president is currently serving time in a federal penitentiary. At night the building is lit with colours that vary according to the season. The **First Union Financial Center** (200 S Biscayne Boulevard), built by another now-defunct bank, is the tallest building south of Atlanta and towers over a palm-planted, covered plaza, one of the most striking public spaces in Downtown.

The **Miami River** served as an important artery in the cocaine trade of the late 1970s and early 1980s and is still heavily trafficked by freighters from throughout the Caribbean. The best approach to the river is through the open-air restaurant, **Bijan's on the River** (64 SE Fourth Street), next to the Riverwalk Metromover station. To your left, as you face the river, is the **Brickell Avenue Bridge**. The column rising from the bridge supports a sculpture of a Tequesta family (the once-local Native Americans). In true Miami fashion, as local dignitaries were cutting the ribbon on the new bridge in 1996, federal drug agents were swarming over a freighter loaded with drugs as it passed beneath.

Bayside Marketplace/Bayfront Park

Biscayne Boulevard separates Bayfront Park and Bayside Marketplace from the commercial district. Brazilian landscape architect Roberto Burle Marx designed the boulevard's colourful, patterned brick pavement. Constructed on dredged land in 1926, and redesigned in 1987 by Isamu Noguchi, **Bayfront Park** (301 N Biscayne Boulevard) hosts community and ethnic festivals large and small. The walkway at its eastern edge provides a great view of Biscayne Bay and the Port of Miami. The double helix memorial rising in the south-east corner (also designed by Noguchi) commemorates the Space Shuttle Challenger disaster.

Bayside Marketplace (401 N Biscayne Boulevard) is an open-air tourist mall and the most visited destination in Dade County. Housing shops from the ubiquitous to the unique, it's home to Miami's Hard Rock Café and a perfect place (if you can cope with the terribly tasteful commercialism) to enjoy frozen rum drinks, catch a boat tour of the Bay or grab a snack at the food court. Within the small plaza on Biscayne Boulevard between Bayfront Park and Bayside Marketplace is the **JFK Torch of Friendship**, which has plaques decorated with the national symbols of

Brickell Avenue Bridge's crowning column.

Caribbean and South and Central American countries – and a blank space where Cuba should be. The plaza is used for solemn commemorations and occasionally angry demonstrations.

Miami Dade Community College

The ebb and flow of students at the Miami Dade Community College (MDCC) Wolfson Campus (300 NE Second Avenue) makes it one of the liveliest spots in the CBD. Non-students are welcome, too. Check out Building 1's soaring atrium, Escher-like escalators and the **Centre Gallery** (on the third floor), one of Miami's most interesting contemporary art venues. Across NE Second Avenue from Building 1 is **Brittle Star Park**. The multicoloured starfish sculpture was installed by Landmind, a local environmental arts group. The red, grey and yellow building on the north side of NE Fourth Street is MDCC's Building 3; its fifth-floor terrace provides an excellent view of Biscayne Bay and beyond.

West of MDCC's Building 1 is the federal courthouse and prison complex. The coral rock building is Miami's old federal courthouse and post office, built in the 1930s; the new courthouse (99 NE Fourth Street) opened in the 1990s. The malevolent grey building adjacent is a federal prison. The small pastel-coloured buildings, called the Chaille Block, tucked incongruously against the prison's west side, date from the 1900s.

Let the train take the strain

At only 25¢ per passenger, Miami's Metromover is by far the best amusement park ride for the money in Florida. This elevated system of computer-operated, driverless trains offers a bird's-eye view of Downtown – the good, the bad and the yet to be developed. The system is divided between an inner and outer loop. The inner loop circles the Central Business District; the outer loop traverses a 28-block stretch from Brickell Avenue in the south to Omni in the north. Operational glitches occasionally interrupt service. If you feel lost, stay in the train to Government Center station (all trains go there eventually) and ask directions. It will take you about 50 minutes to ride the whole system.

Information and maps are available at Government Center station (111 NW First Street). *See also chapter* **Getting Around**.

Tour 1: north to Omni

This tour takes you from the Central Business District north to School Board station; though much redevelopment is occurring, this is a risky area and not recommended for walking.

Change to the School Board train at College/Bayside station. As the system leaves the CBD, the **Freedom Tower** (600 Biscayne Boulevard) is on the right. This copy of Seville's Giralda Tower was built in the 1920s by the now-defunct *Miami News*; it was renamed the Freedom Tower after its use as a processing centre for Cuban refugees in the early 1960s. It's currently empty.

Miami's **Greyhound bus station** (700 Biscayne Boulevard) is on the right, just past the Freedom Tower station. If you arrive in Miami by bus, take great care in this neighbourhood. The area immediately beneath the tracks from the Freedom Tower to Eleventh Street station is home to pawnshops, cheap hotels, parking lots and homeless people.

The large, round, pink building on the left is the **Miami Arena** (701 Arena Boulevard). Opened in 1988, this 15,000-seat arena is home to the region's professional ice-hockey and basketball teams and site of numerous large concerts. The hockey team will move north to Broward County in 1998/99, and the basketball team threatened to leave, too, if a new bayfront arena wasn't built. The question of building an arena for a private company on public land sparked a heated debate, settled by a public vote to go ahead in 1996. The site slated for the construction of the new 14-storey, 19,000-seat arena, scheduled to open in 1999, is on your right. Designed by famed local firm Arquitectonica, the new building, according to drawings, rises from the ground as if caught in a whirlwind.

Just north of the new arena site is **Bicentennial Park**. Originally developed in the 1970s it has become a refuge for homeless people and is now being converted to cruise ship terminals and retail shops.

As the track parallels I-395, just past the Bicentennial Park station on your right is a spectacular view of the **Port of Miami**, the largest cruise port in the world. On your left, after the tracks cross the interstate, is the future site of the Cesar Pelli-designed Performing Arts Center of Greater Miami. This much talked-about project will comprise

tiered, glass-fronted buildings covering two city blocks and containing an opera/ballet house and concert hall – but at press time no-one had yet stuck a shovel in the ground.

On the right, the large, modern, wall-like structure is the home of the *Miami Herald* and *El Nuevo Herald*, the region's largest daily newspapers. The **Omni International Mall**, a shopping mall and hotel complex, is on the right as the track curves west. The system ends at the School Board station, which is in a dicey neighbourhood. Remain on the train and ride back the way you came.

Tour 2: south to Brickell

This tour heads south from the CBD to the Financial District station and runs parallel to **Brickell Avenue**. Once the site of wealthy mansions, Brickell developed in the 1970s and 1980s as a centre for financial and commercial enterprises focusing on Latin America and the Caribbean. South of SE 14th Street (where the Metromover line ends) commercial high-rises give way to luxury apartments and condominiums.

Change to the Financial District train at Third Street station. As the train exits Riverwalk station, note the excellent views of Miami River upstream and down. Between Tenth Street and Brickell stations the tracks pass over a shrinking collection of tiny wood-frame houses, remnants of Miami's first suburb. The eastern edge of Little Havana is on the right side of the tracks at Brickell station.

As the train exits Brickell station, luxury condos rise in front of you. As the tracks curve east, office buildings tower up on the left. Remain on the train at Financial District station for the return trip

Coral Gables

Wealthy, charming and obsessively proud of its architectural heritage, the Gables aims to live up to its nickname of the City Beautiful.

Gracious, quiet, genteel Coral Gables, the 'City Beautiful', was virtually invented in 1921 by George Merrick, who named it after the colour of the tiles on his family home's gabled rooftop. Son of a prominent citrus farmer, Merrick returned to Miami from college in 1911 following his father's death and found his burgeoning hometown in disarray, growing 'like topsey'. So he corralled his artist-uncle Denman Fink and landscape architect Frank Button and created one of the first planned cities in the US, inspired by sixteenth-century Spain and Italy.

Coral Gables is an expansive 12 square mile area bordered by SW 37th Avenue (aka Douglas Road) to the east, SW 57th Avenue (Red Road) to the west, SW Eighth Street to the north and SW 72nd Street to the south, extending down east of Old Cutler Road to Biscayne Bay.

It was incorporated as a city in 1925. Merrick fuelled a building boom, investing $100 million of his own money, including $5 million on advertising alone. He created a city of European charm, consisting of fountains, plazas, arched entrance gateways, churches, parks, canals and tree-lined streets with names like Segovia, Giralda and Valencia. Ideal for the Florida climate, the Mediterranean-style architecture was used for both residential and commercial buildings. Native materials and stucco were utilised to give the grand structures a deliberately weathered look.

Following the 1926 hurricane, the boom went bust and Merrick lost his holdings. In 1928, the Coral Gables Commission removed him from the town council. A resurgence occurred after World War II and the Gables became more 'modern' than Mediterranean. Downtown business district buildings were either demolished or disguised.

These days, however, Coral Gables is a haven for preservation. Strict ordinances protect the remaining historic structures and promote construction and restoration of the area's distinctive architecture. An upscale, pedestrian-friendly, neighbourhood has evolved. Tranquil residential areas co-exist with a thriving downtown. With a crime rate that has dropped steadily since 1995 and draconian zoning laws that ensure a quiet and immaculate environment, the Gables has an unmistakable appeal. Houses, many valued at $200,000 and above, predominate. Apartments are

not as plentiful but also in demand, pushing rents to almost $1,000 per month for a one-bedroom flat.

The civic zeal for preserving Coral Gables' bucolic character can, however, border on the anal. A hefty list of official 'dos' and 'don'ts' applies to everything from replacing window panes to how many guests can park their cars in front of a home for a dinner party without the host having to rent an off-duty police officer to supervise parking.

Conversely, if Coral Gables facades are notably restrained, its residents are not. Monthly gallery nights find everyone decked out in glitzy designer wear with eyes focused more on bustlines than brush strokes. And local gossip has it that the area's abundance of romantic restaurants do not pay the rent from couples celebrating spousal fidelity. Affairs of the heart are well represented at intimate corner tables, which may explain why a number of the top divorce lawyers in the Miami area call Coral Gables home.

Downtown Coral Gables considers itself the 'corporate capital of the Americas', perhaps rightfully so, for it is home to 32 banks and the Latin American or regional HQ of over 140 multinational corporations. The business centre is **Alhambra Circle**; not, in fact, a circle at all but a wide street lined with tall buildings holding acres of office space.

The Gables is also known for two other types of business: restaurants and art galleries. Restaurants proliferate in the area around the intersection of Miracle Mile and the very walkable **Ponce de Leon Boulevard**, which is also home to a conglomeration of art galleries (*see chapter* **Museums & Galleries**).

Three of the best

Coral Gables is home to three of Miami's landmark attractions. Listed on the National Register of Historic Places, the Mediterranean-style **Biltmore Hotel** (1200 Anastasia Avenue, at Columbus Boulevard) is a must-see. Built in 1926, everything about the 18-storey Biltmore is huge: the swimming pool (the largest hotel pool in the continental US); the 315ft-high tower, modelled after the Giralda bell tower of Seville Cathedral; the 45ft-high painted ceilings in the lobby; the two 18-hole golf courses on adjacent land. Al Capone used to have a suite here and it hosted the 1994 Summit of the Americas, Clinton's historic conflab with 34 Latin American and Caribbean heads of state. Free guided tours are held on Sundays.

For natural wonders, visit the 83-acre **Fairchild Tropical Garden** (10901 Old Cutler Road), at the southern edge of Coral Gables by Biscayne Bay. Named in honour of distinguished botanist Dr David Fairchild, it is an Edenic haven of tropical and subtropical trees, plants, lakes and pools and has a café, bookshop and conservatory.

And don't miss the **Venetian Pool**, at 2701 DeSoto Boulevard, about two blocks south of Coral Way. A former rock quarry, turned in 1924 into a freshwater pool in the style of a Venetian lagoon, this is home to the coolest apartment in Miami, that of the lifeguard who inhabits one of the towers.

For more information on all these places, *see* *chapter* **Sightseeing**.

Business district

To see some of Coral Gables' oldest buildings, walk through its business district. Start at the **City Hall** (405 Biltmore Way). Exemplifying the Spanish Renaissance style, this stately edifice is listed on the National Register of Historic Places. Encircled by 12 columns and topped off by a three-tiered clock tower, it is made of local oolitic limestone, also known as coral rock. Two blocks north-east is the John M Stabile Building, now the home of **Books & Books**, Miami's premier independent bookstore (296 Aragon Avenue). Built in 1924, it was one of the area's first commercial structures. Diminutive, with a red barrel-tiled roof characteristic of the Mediterranean revival style, it originally housed an ornamental block shop.

Across the street is the **Fire House and Police Station** (285 Aragon Avenue); now containing offices, this building is also on the National Register. Combining simple Depression-era architecture with Mediterranean revival accents, it was constructed of coral rock by the Works Progress Administration (WPA) in 1939. Walk one block west and one block north and you'll come upon the **Dream Theatre/Consolidated Bank** (2308 Ponce de Leon Boulevard). Originally an outdoor silent movie theatre built in 1926 to emulate a Spanish bullring, it now houses the offices of Consolidated Bank. Details remain, including the tower where the film projector once stood.

Cross Alhambra Circle and you will come to the tiny **Hotel Place St Michel** (162 Alcazar Avenue). An office in 1926, it was soon converted into the Hotel Seville, which in the 1960s sported dropped ceilings, fluorescent lighting and Danish modern furniture. In 1979, it became the ultra-quaint Place St Michel, extensively renovated and featuring European antiques, Spanish tile and arched ceilings. Two blocks north is the ultimate

arch-lover's dream, **Coral Gables Elementary School** (105 Minorca Avenue). Built between 1923-1925, this exquisite school is graced by arcaded loggias and expansive courtyards. About six blocks south is the **Omni Colonnade Hotel** (133-169 Coral Way), originally built in 1925 to house George Merrick's offices. A mixture of Spanish colonial and baroque architecture, this massive landmark features two-storey columns, ornate embellishments and a 75ft high rotunda.

Coral Way

Coral Way (SW 24th Street) is the major east-west street through the Gables. The section that runs through the central business district is known as **Miracle Mile** from 37th to 42nd Avenues. A one-time bustling shopping zone, full of neighbourhood boutiques, retail traffic has slowed over the years but it is now making a comeback, with chains such as Barnes & Noble, Starbucks and the Old Navy Clothing Co moving in.

Some of the Gables' most interesting residences lie on the western part of Coral Way, shaded by massive banyan trees. These include:

Pape House (900 Coral Way), 1926. A Mediterranean revival architectural showplace, with arched openings, exposed coral rock, French doors and a walled garden.
Poinciana Place (937 Coral Way), 1916. Pre-dating the Mediterranean structures, this house, one of the Gables' earliest, was built by George Merrick for his wife, Eunice Peacock.
Coral Gables House (907 Coral Way), 1900-1906. Designed by George Merrick's mother, Althea, this is *the* house. Built of oolitic limestone and Dade County pine, it is New England à la Florida. The architecture has many Florida adaptations, such as cross-ventilation and concrete columns.
Doc Dammers' House (1141 Coral Way), 1924. Constructed by Merrick for Edward 'Doc' Dammers, the city's first mayor and Merrick's major huckster when it came to selling Gables real estate.
Casa Azul (1254 Coral Way), 1924. The 'blue house' is so named in honour of its blue glazed-tile roof. The home of architect H George Fink, Merrick's cousin, who designed many Gables buildings between 1921 and 1928.

Outdoor architecture

The design of the outdoors was just as important as the design of the indoors for the planners of Coral Gables. Among the essentials are entrance gateways, plazas and fountains.

Entrances

Ringing the city's boundaries, fortress-like gateways for foot or automobile traffic are further tribute to Old Spain. Eight entrances were planned but only four were completed: The Douglas, Country Club Prado, Granada and Commercial.

Douglas Entrance (SW 37th Avenue & Eighth Street). Also known as La Puerta del Sol, this cost almost $1 million to construct in 1927 and projected a deliberately insular urban feel, reflecting the Spanish walled-in towns from which it took inspiration. Located in the city's north-east

*The **Country Club Prado entrance** epitomises the grace of the Gables.*

corner, closest to the City of Miami. A tower, arches and gateways made up a walled-in mini-city containing shops, meeting rooms and apartments. Although it was never finished, it remains an imposing reminder of Merrick's plans. It is now on the National Register of Historic Places. Construction respectful of its architecture has added many offices, making it a successful example of adaptive re-use.

Country Club Prado Entrance (Country Club Prado & SW Eighth Street). Located in the north-west, this entrance was completed in the same year as the Douglas Entrance and at similar cost, but is more bucolic and open. A city block in length, it has 20 elliptically arranged columns topped with vine-covered trellises. In the centre is a Spanish-style fountain, surrounded by a reflecting pool. Concrete, brick and stucco as well as extensive landscaping are reminiscent of a formal Italian garden. Many Miami brides have posed here for wedding portraits.

Plazas & fountains

There are also 14 exquisite, European-styled resting places-cum-traffic circles in Coral Gables. Many feature pillars, fountains, reflecting pools, pergolas, wrought iron, rough-hewn coral rock, lush landscaping and dramatic night lighting.

Granada Plaza (Granada Boulevard & Alhambra Circle). Walls and pillars made up of rough-cut rock, stucco and brick plus vine-laden pergolas complement matching pools placed at opposite ends of this plaza. Take a break on the one of the concrete benches.

DeSoto Plaza and Fountain (Sevilla Avenue, Granada & DeSoto Boulevards). Three roads meet at a stepped fountain built of rough-cut rock. A column encircled by wrought-iron light fixtures rises majestically from the circular pool and a steady stream of water gurgles from four sculptured faces. DeSoto is particularly striking at night when illuminated.

Ponce De Leon Plaza (Coral Way & Granada Boulevard). Built in 1921 on the site of George Merrick's first land sale and bordering on what was then his residence, this was the first of all the plazas and entrances in the Gables. Fountains and pergolas decorate the area that encircles the intersection.

International villages

When George Merrick decided to add some diversity to the Gables' predominantly Mediterranean feel, he did it architecturally, of course. His eclecticism can be witnessed in the area's seven ' international villages':

Chinese (Riviera Drive, Menendez, Castania, San Sovino Avenues & Maggiore Street). Eight houses with Oriental details trimmed in bright colours. Look for the 'good luck' animal figures on the rooftops.

Colonial (Santa Maria Street). White mansions built in the Georgian style. Lots of pillars, porticoes and verandahs.

Dutch South African(Le Jeune Road, Riviera Drive & Maya Avenue). Five houses modelled on the farmhouses of wealthy Dutch colonists. Look for the distinctive scrollwork, walled gardens, turned chimneys and high-pitched roofs.

French City (10000 block of Hardee Road). Inspired by the French Assembly members' Versailles residences, these elegant, eighteenth century-style townhomes are recognisable by the elegant mouldings that decorate them and the four-foot high walls that surround them.

French Country (500 block of Hardee Road). Large homes built to resemble country farmhouses and eighteenth-century chateaux.

French Normandy (Le Jeune Road & Viscaya Avenue). Eleven townhouses modelled after the French Normandy structures of fifteenth-century English and French towns.

Italian (Monserrate Street, Altara Avenue & Palmarito Street). Hard to find since they blend in so well with other Gables structures. Five houses reminiscent of seventeenth-century Italian villas, with walled gardens and stepped entrances facing the street.

Coconut Grove

The Grove was home to Miami's original pioneers, and retains an independent spirit and bohemian reputation.

Before there was Miami, there was Coconut Grove. On the shores of Biscayne Bay, south of Downtown, bordered by the South Dixie Highway (US 1), the Rickenbacker Causeway and the Coral Gables Waterway, this neighbourhood has been as singular as its independent, ornery settlers. First came Bahamian seafarers and a handful of pioneer families. Later, and more significant, were the Peacocks and the Munroes, who began the transformation of Coconut Grove from little more than tropical jungle into a distinct community.

Commodore Ralph Munroe, visiting from New England, met Brits Isabella and Charles Peacock, whose brother John had leased a house in the area. Camping out at the Fort Dallas settlement at the mouth of the Miami River, Munroe assured the Peacocks that if they built an inn, he would keep their rooms filled by spreading the word up north about the new paradise of South Florida.

In 1873, the Peacocks found a waterfront parcel of land in an area that had been dubbed 'Cocoanut Grove' by a doctor who had opened the first post office there. The doctor and the post office didn't stay around for long, but the Peacocks did. In 1883, they completed Bay View House – later expanded and renamed the Peacock Inn – and Munroe made good on his word. During one of his frequent visits, he reopened the post office, dropping the letter 'a' from its name.

Quirky Coconut Grove began to flower. In 1888, Munroe moved there permanently and a community of environmentalists, sea enthusiasts, writers and intellectuals, attracted by the warm weather and lush natural beauty, soon followed. The Peacock Inn flourished as a centre of activity. Many black families from the Bahamas migrated here to work at the Inn and Miami's earliest black settlement was founded in the Grove.

Early on, Coconut Grove gained a reputation, which it partly maintains to this day, as a place of tolerance. Straitlaced and eccentric, intellectual and uneducated, rich and poor, black and white: all try to co-exist harmoniously. An esprit de corps has always reigned – whether people are living in mansions, treehouses or underground bomb shelters (look for the turret on Hibiscus Street). A unifying preoccupation has been the fight against exploitation by outsiders, whether the government or dastardly developers trying to turn this verdant eden into a giant outdoor theme-park-cum-mall. In 1919, Groveites incorporated, hoping to defend themselves from annexation by the quickly growing City of Miami. Those halcyon days lasted six years before the Grove was gobbled up.

In the 1960s, Coconut Grove was the centre of the counterculture in Miami. Since then, Groveites have tried to secede from the City of Miami at least three times, almost succeeding in 1991. While the Grove of the 1990s has undergone numerous changes, to the great consternation of its longtime residents, it retains an essential charm and tranquillity that no amount of development will displace. However, to the day-tripping visitor, this may not be immediately evident – this is a living, working community, with all the attendant symptoms of traffic, an apparent lack of cohesion and an element of the seedy.

For details of the huge Coconut Grove Arts Festival in February and other annual neighbourhood celebrations, *see chapter* **By Season**.

South Miami Avenue

To explore Coconut Grove, begin south of US 1 at S Miami Avenue; you'll need to drive this section. Head south (with the bay on your left) and after about five blocks, turn left onto SE 32nd Road and left again onto Brickell Avenue. This last vestige of residential bayfront property is part of what was once known as Millionaires' Row. Now it is home to millionaire celebrities **Madonna** (3029 Brickell Avenue) and **Sylvester Stallone** (100 SE 32nd Road). Back on S Miami Avenue, about half a block south, is **Vizcaya**, built in 1916 by James Deering, heir to the International Harvester farm machinery fortune. No expense was spared on this Italian Renaissance-style villa and its extensive gardens, both open to the public.

Continue on S Miami Avenue, which turns into S Bayshore Drive. A large oolitic limestone formation on your right signals the **Silver Bluff** area (1600-2100 blocks), containing architecturally interesting homes that were built between 1918 and 1925. Just down the street, two yacht clubs appear on the left: the **Coral Reef Yacht Club** (at number 2484) and the very exclusive **Biscayne Bay Yacht Club** (No.2540). The former is housed in a Mediterranean-style mansion built in 1923. The latter, Dade County's oldest social institution, founded by Ralph Munroe in

1887, is in a 1932 bungalow designed by prominent Miami architect Walter DeGarmo.

Don't miss the old Pan American seaplane base and terminal (3500 Pan American Drive), the nation's busiest during World War II when it was used as a US naval base. It has been home to **Miami City Hall** for over 40 years. While you're there, check out the boats docked at **Dinner Key** marina, the city's largest. Look just past the docks towards Biscayne Bay and you'll see still more boats at anchor, part of a controversial community known as 'The Anchorage', which the City of Miami has been trying to get rid of for years, without success.

Continue south on S Bayshore Drive until you reach the curve and climb a slight hill, the start of McFarlane Avenue. On the left, facing the water, is **Peacock Park**, the original site of Bay View

The Black Grove

In the late 1880s, Coconut Grove was a wilderness covered with vast amounts of tropical foliage and infested with ravenous mosquitoes. Those immigrants accustomed to the icy climes of New England learned how to cope in such a hot and hostile environment from the black Bahamians who began trickling in when the Peacock Inn needed more labourers. First was Miss Mariah Brown from Upper Boque, Eleuthra, then a few more, and soon a community was formed.

The area's first black settlement emerged on what is now Charles Avenue – named after the son of landowner Joseph Frow. The avenue became the centre of the 'Black Grove', thanks to Ebenezer Woodbury Frank Stirrup, a Bahamian who made good in Florida. A large landholder, Stirrup built over 100 homes, which he sold and rented very inexpensively to black families. So many churches also existed on Charles Avenue that it was originally dubbed 'Evangelist Street'. Other structures that added life to the district were a library for the Colored Literary Society and the Old Fellows Hall, a popular meeting place, both no longer standing.

Today's Black Grove is increasingly impoverished and divided, unlike in the 1920s and 1930s when it was a prosperous, tight-knit community with 80 per cent home-ownership. Now centred on Grand Avenue, the struggling community consists of more renters than homeowners. The Grove's Bahamian roots are celebrated annually, during the Miami/Bahamas Goombay Festival in June; for more information, *see chapter* **By Season**.

House which was torn down in 1926. In the 1960s, hippies hung out here, getting stoned and playing frisbee. Now a new generation is carrying the torch by doing the same – albeit only at weekends. Just across the street is the **Coconut Grove Public Library** (2875 McFarlane Road), the grounds of which contain the oldest marked grave in Dade County, that of Ralph Munroe's first wife, Eva.

Downtown Coconut Grove

Continue along MacFarlane Road and you will reach the intersection with Main Highway and Grand Avenue. You are now in the heart of downtown Coconut Grove. Overflowing with shops, offices and restaurants, it is one of the most pedestrian-friendly areas in Miami. Grand Avenue runs east to west: here you'll find tons of shopping and thus tons of tourists: between Mary and Virginia Streets is the **Streets of Mayfair**, once a veritable fortress of a shopping mall, now rehabbed to be more pedestrian-friendly. At Virginia Street stands **CocoWalk**, the giant, very successful open-air mall that helped revitalise the Grove in the early 1990s. Two blocks down Virginia Street at Day Avenue is the **Hare Krishna Temple**, the Grove's best-kept free-meal secret. If you don't mind a little dancing and chanting, come in around dinner time and the Krishnas will feed you a hearty vegetarian meal, gratis.

You can escape the throng of tourists by heading west on Grand Avenue – but don't walk too far inland beyond McDonald Street (aka SW 32nd Avenue), where things can get a bit dangerous. Instead, head south on vegetation-lined Main Highway. About two blocks down, hidden away behind a thicket of plants and trees, is the **Barnacle State Historic Site**, the tiny oasis built by pioneer Ralph Munroe. Don't miss it: it's open to the public and highly recommended to gain a feeling for the Grove of yore.

Back on Main Highway is the **Coconut Grove Playhouse** (at 3500). Built as a movie house in the 1920s, the Spanish-style building was converted into a theatre in the 1950s. Samuel Beckett's *Waiting for Godot* premiered here in 1956; nowadays, it hosts mainly Broadway-wannabe productions, often starring B-list TV stars. About two blocks south, on Devon Road, is the 1917 Mission-style **Plymouth Congregational Church** and Dade County's first public schoolhouse. Built in 1887 out of lumber salvaged from shipwrecks, the schoolhouse was originally located across from the Peacock Inn and used as a Sunday school. It was restored and moved to its present site in 1970.

Back on Main Highway, **Bryan Memorial Church** (at number 3713), built in the 1920s as a memorial to orator, politician, salesman and attorney William Jennings Bryan, is an unusual Byzantine-style building. Nearby is **El Jardin** at Carollton School; constructed in 1917, it is the

Madonna's modest little waterside pad.

earliest-known complete Mediterranean revival structure left in Miami. Continue on Main Highway and you will reach the end of Coconut Grove at the **Kampong** (4013 Douglas Road). This was home in the 1870s to Charles Peacock's brother John, and later to Dr David Fairchild, founder of the famous Fairchild Tropical Garden, who planted a huge variety of exotic plants here. One of only two tropical plant research sites in the country, it is a stunning place, with an Indonesian-inspired house set by a lagoon, and is occasionally open to the public; call 445 8076 for more details.

Little Havana

Cuban coffee, santeria sacrifices and the strains of salsa: welcome to Little Havana, Latin America's Miami HQ.

When Cubans began to arrive in Miami in great numbers in the early 1960s, fleeing from the newly formed revolutionary government of Fidel Castro, Miami was not the multicultural metropolis it is today. The Cuban exiles found themselves in a provincial Southern US city that was not particularly welcoming to non-English speakers. So the industrious Cubans set about creating their own community: they set up small businesses in a neighbourhood west of Downtown Miami, where they built houses that reminded them of the ones they had left behind in Cuba. The area became known as Little Havana.

Today, most of the Cuban families who settled here as part of that original wave have moved on to ritzier neighbourhoods, and Little Havana remains the first place of settlement for recently arrived immigrants. These days, they tend to be Cuban 'balseros' who came to Miami on home-made rafts in the early 1990s and families from Nicaragua, El Salvador and the Dominican Republic. English is still rarely spoken.

Little Havana's main drag is listed on city maps as SW Eighth Street, but everyone calls it by its Spanish name, Calle Ocho. The heart of Little Havana is between 12th and 27th Avenues, with commercial activity centred on or just off Calle Ocho. The rest of the neighbourhood is residential, with an eclectic conglomeration of stucco bunga-lows and larger Spanish-style houses shaded by fruit trees, which do resemble homes in Havana. Recently, some of the grander residences have been split into apartments to accommodate the area's lower-income Latin American immigrants.

Walk these quiet streets surrounding Calle Ocho, and you're liable to see the kind of door-to-door salesmen that would seem more at home in a small Latin American town then a big US city – an open-sided truck packed with yuca (cassava), malanga (a potato-like tuber), mangos, papayas and other tropical tubers and fruits, a man selling snowcones from a cart loaded with bottles of brightly coloured syrups, a hand-painted ice-cream truck or a silver aluminum-sided van selling

*Cops make a coffee stop at **Exquisito Restaurant**.*

coffee and sandwiches. These small touches are what give Little Havana its unique flavour and make it an interesting place to visit.

However, for an area considered a tourist attraction, Little Havana is not all that accommodating to outsiders. Don't expect it to be as picturesque as San Francisco's Chinatown or New York's Little Italy: when you arrive in the centre of the Cuban district you might not even realise you're there. Rather than a quaint enclave of Cuban culture, Little Havana is pretty seedy and considered a high-crime area after dark. There have been some vain attempts to revitalise the neighbourhood to make it more tourist-friendly, but Calle Ocho is still basically a strip of discount furniture stores, cheque-cashing outlets, pawnshops and low-rent bars, peppered with Cuban restaurants, cigar shops and record stores. It's a neighbourhood in service of its residents: salsa music blasts from open windows all day long and old men gather on the pavements, drinking coffee and arguing endlessly about Cuban politics.

Spanish is definitely the official language of Little Havana, but staff in most establishments do speak a few words of English. If not, be patient, use sign language or try your high-school Spanish. They will try to make themselves understood; they are used to encountering English speakers. After all, although it may not look like it, Little Havana is part of the United States.

If you're here at the beginning of March, you might hit the **Calle Ocho Festival**, billed as the largest street festival in the US, when hundreds of thousands jam the narrow width of Calle Ocho; it's great fun but not for the claustrophobic. For more details of this and other Little Havana celebrations, *see chapter* **By Season**. For more information on Miami's past and present relationship with Cuba, *see chapters* **History** *and* **Latin Miami**.

Calle Ocho

The best way to start a visit to Little Havana is with a good cigar. At **El Credito Cigars** (1106 SW Eighth Street) the air is dense and musty with the smell of fresh tobacco leaves. Rows of employees, most of whom learned the trade in Cuba, sit at small tables rolling cigars. You can't buy Cuban cigars in the US but *Cigar Aficionado* magazine has rated El Credito's La Gloria Cubana, which are made with tobacco grown in the Dominican Republic from seeds taken from Cuban soil, as the top brand in the US. Order a box, a bundle or a single smoke from the glass counter while you watch the rollers at work.

Walk up Calle Ocho to **Memorial Boulevard**, at the corner of 13th Avenue, where an eternal flame burns in memory of the 94 Cuban exiles who died in the foiled Bay of Pigs invasion of Cuba in 1961. Other monuments on this shaded

Game on at **Domino Park**.

street include a statue of José Marti, writer, philosopher and leader of Cuba's independence struggle against Spain, and a bronze map of Cuba. A huge ceiba tree, a tree considered sacred by African religions, stands in the centre of the block. Practitioners of the syncretic Afro-Cuban religion santeria often leave ritual sacrifices to their deities at this spot; look out for candles, chicken bones or cloth bundles scattered among the tree's enormous roots. Be careful not to touch or step on any of these offerings: it's said to bring bad luck and is certainly disrespectful.

More artefacts of Afro-Cuban religion can be found in Little Havana's many botanicas – religious pharmacies that sell all kinds of roots and powders, statuary and candles for home shrines, coloured beads, and books on santeria. There is usually a priest or priestess in residence who does tarot readings or tells fortunes by throwing cowrie shells. Many Miamians consult regularly with these 'santeros', as the advisers are known (for more information, *see chapter* **Shopping**). Botanicas can be found every few blocks on Calle Ocho; try **Botanica Negra Francisca** (1323 SW Eighth Street). Outsiders will be tolerated in botanicas but not particularly welcomed; remember that this is someone else's religion, not an attraction designed for tourists.

A few blocks up the street, you will find elderly men engaged in a popular secular Cuban pastime – dominos. At Calle Ocho and SW 15th Avenue is Maximo Gomez Park, better known as **Domino Park**, an outdoor social club for senior citizens. There are some masterful players here, and the place really gets going after lunch, when the clacking of the black and white tiles can be heard all the way down the block.

You could stop for a bite at **Exquisito Restaurant** (1510 SW Eighth Street), a favourite among local Cubans, for palomilla (flank) steak or fried chicken and rice and beans. There are Cuban restaurants all along the strip. **Versailles** (at number 3555), a Cuban kitsch palace decorated with mirrors and chandeliers, is packed out on Sundays with large, noisy Cuban American families. Other residents of the neighbourhood are represented by restaurants offering varied Latin American cuisine. **Taquerias el Mejicano**, a really authentic Mexican lunch counter, has two locations, at 521 and 1961 SW Eighth Street, while **Guayacan** (at 1933) serves exceptional Nicaraguan food. At Dominican restaurant **El Padrinito** (No. 3494), sweet coconut milk sauces and heavy portions of rice and beans accompany fish bursting with flavour. For more eating places in Little Havana, *see chapter* **Restaurants & Cafés**.

Calle Ocho is, understandably, the best place to buy Latin music in Miami, and arguably the premier spot in the US for recordings from Latin America and Spain, including rumba, salsa, Latin jazz, merengue, cumbia, tango, Spanish-language rock and much more. At **Casino Records** (1208 SW Eighth Street), CDs are organised by country, with the biggest bins reserved for music from Cuba. Re-issues of recordings made in pre-revolutionary Cuba and new music fresh from the island are both stocked. The selection is huge; ask the bilingual salespeople for advice. **Do-Re-Mi Music Center** (No.1829) has every kind of Cuban music, including a fine selection of rare European and Japanese imports of 1940s and '50s Cuban jazz bands. Ask owner Rolando Rivero for help; he's an expert on Cuban orchestras past and present.

Upper Calle Ocho

In the centre of Little Havana, SW Eighth Street is a one-way street, heading east; at SW 27th Avenue, traffic starts going in both directions. So if you're driving west, take SW Seventh Avenue and turn left onto SW 27th Avenue before taking a right to join Calle Ocho.

Heading west at night, you'll see the coloured lights and heart-shaped neon signs of tryst motels, such as El Nido ('The Nest') and the Miami Executive (heart-shaped Jacuzzis, too). These motels are a Calle Ocho phenomenon, where married people take their lovers. Stop for some Southern-style ribs or chicken at **Uncle Tom's Barbecue** (3988 SW Eighth Street), an old cookshack next to a recently built shopping mall. Or pick up a dozen doughnuts at the **Velvet Creme** shop at 33rd Avenue. Baked fresh on the premises every hour, this Southern US chain's hot doughnuts are widely considered to be the best in the country. (Cops take note.)

For a stylish souvenir of Miami, head for **La Casa de las Guayaberas** (5840 SW Eighth Street). Guayaberas, elegant Cuban smock shirts, are almost a uniform for Miami men in the summer, when most offices allow male employees to wear them instead of shirts and ties. The store stocks the traditional white linen model as well as inexpensive cotton and polyester versions in a variety of colours. Prices range from a $15 cheapie to $275 for a custom-made shirt.

In addition to restaurants, Little Havana offers some unique entertainment options. For live Cuban music, head to **Café Nostalgia** (2212 SW Eight Street), an atmospheric and very popular club with a superb house band. **Teatro Bellas Artes** (at 2173) features a drag show, Midnight Follies, every Saturday at midnight. A favourite among Latin American tourists, it features a cast of gorgeous cross-dressers lip-synching to hits by Latin singing stars from Celia Cruz to Selena. For other Cuban music spots, *see chapter* **Music**.

The quintessential Cuban-American entertainment is at **Teatro Trail** (3713 SW Eighth Street) where impersonator Armando Roblan plays a remarkably authentic Castro in a series of dramatic comedies that reflect current events in Cuba. The show turns surreal when Roblan walks on stage, and the audience of exiles boos and shouts insults.

A word of caution: you can walk where you will through Calle Ocho and its environs during the day, but this is not a place to wander aimlessly at night. There is little danger in heading out to a restaurant, theatre or club, but you should use your street smarts. Waving cash around and wearing expensive jewellery while conversing loudly in English is not a great idea, and you should take care to park in a well-lighted spot.

Café Cubano

Almost every block of Calle Ocho has at least one cafeteria, where syrupy Cuban espresso is served at window counters that open onto the street. Miami Cubans brew their coffee strong, with sugar mixed in with the grinds – the result is already cloyingly sweet but most drinkers add more sugar to their cup. This jolting combination of caffeine and sugar fuels Miamians through the working day and long into the night.

If you simply ask for coffee, or *café*, you'll probably get a *colada*. Sweet and dark, this is a mini espresso served in a thimble-sized plastic cup. For a milder version with a splash of milk, ask for a *cortadito*, which essentially means a small coffee cut with milk (derived from the verb 'cortar', to cut). *Café con leche*, about two parts milk and one part coffee, is served at breakfast and makes for a soothing afternoon pick-me-up. Many Cuban restaurants also keep a pot of drip coffee brewing. Cubans call this *café americano* and tend to dismiss it as a sissy drink that, to their taste, is as weak as water.

Little Haiti & the Design District

Miami's Caribbean enclave, plus the new pretender to SoBe's crown.

Miami's Little Haiti neighbourhood, home to thousands of recently arrived Haitian immigrants, was once the centre of the commercial life that thrived in the late 1890s from the bustling trade on Biscayne Bay and the Little River. But the only signs left of those glory days are the shabby wood frame houses – now packed with immigrant tenants – and the old, now-abandoned post office on NE 62nd Street and Second Avenue. Although the sign on the post office is faded and illegible, this neighbourhood was once known as Lemon City, for the citrus groves and strawberry fields that decorated this north-east corridor.

These days, residents call it 'Ti Ayiti' (creole for Little Haiti), and dozens of struggling mom-and-pop record stores, botanicas, money-wiring centres, churches and restaurants line the main artery, NE Second Avenue between 47th and 85th Streets. You can reach Little Haiti from I-95, exiting at 62nd or 79th Street and heading east – don't go west or you'll end up in Liberty City, a notorious ghetto.

Economically, Little Haiti is poor, a situation exacerbated by illegal trash dumpings and an increasing number of crack houses and homeless people. Many of the area's inhabitants have to work two menial jobs to support one household in Miami and one back home in Haiti. At night, the community schools' classrooms are filled with immigrants learning to speak and write English.

Haitians started to move to this area back in the late 1970s, when thousands fled the dictatorship of Francois 'Papa Doc' Duvalier and, later, his son, Jean-Claude, known as 'Baby Doc'. A mass exodus occurred during the early 1980s, when thousands of desperate Haitians packed rickety wooden boats to make the journey to this promised land. Hundreds never made it to Miami alive. Those who did are going to school, working and planting roots here – building the American dream. It is not known how many Haitians live in the neighbourhood, but city officials put the figure at over 30,000.

The 1960s live on at **Ray's Farm** (see page 76).

Crime and youth gangs are a rising concern, so walking around with valuables is not suggested and it's best not to visit after dark. But by day Little Haiti is a rough jewel – rich in colour, food, and spirit. Bright murals that depict Caribbean landscapes and political issues decorate shop storefront walls. On the corner of First Avenue and 54th Street, a portrait of former Haitian president Jean-Bertrand Aristide next to a conga that represents liberty graces a corner wall. And a painting of a kneeling Haitian man pleading to the Statue of Liberty to allow him to emigrate sums up the work the **Haitian Refugee Center** (119 NE 54th Street) was doing in providing free legal help to Haitians seeking political asylum.

Foods from the homeland abound here. The smell of fried pork, plantains, seafood and rice, stewing in garlic and thyme, lingers in the air at all hours. Although service is slow and the dining rooms are cramped, the food is authentic, spicy and cheap at restaurants such as **Chez Le Bebe** (114 NE 54th Street) and **Gourmet Creole** (8427 NE Second Avenue). To taste Haitian hard dough bread (served piping hot) and pastries filled with meat and salt cod, the **New Florida Bakery** (46 NE 62nd Street) tops the list.

Once you have satisfied your stomach, head over to the **Caribbean Marketplace** (5927 NE Second Avenue) to buy Haitian primitive art, wood carvings and ice-cream. The marketplace, which opened in 1990, is itself a work of art, and in 1991 won an American Institute of Architects' award for its bold Caribbean design and splashy bright colours. However, because Little Haiti is perceived as a crime-heavy neighbourhood, this shopping complex has failed to draw many tourists. It remains open, but in January 1997 the city foreclosed on the centre and its fate is unknown. Next door, you can find books on Haiti and its culture at **Libreri Mapou** (5919 NE Second Avenue). Owner Jan Mapou also sells his home-made kremas – a cream liquor made with eggs and rum.

Bolder tourists might want to investigate **Ray's Farm** (7630 NE First Avenue; 754 0000), a proper farm (goats, chickens etc) in the middle of a pretty dodgy urban area. It's the last known address of a lost hippy tribe, and on Saturday nights becomes Imagine restaurant, a showcase for progressive sounds (call to get directions). And if British visitors get homesick for Blighty, there's even a little bit of England in Little Haiti. Pub-cum-music venue **Churchill's Hideaway** (5501 NE Second Avenue) serves English beer as well as the country's chow.

Design District

South of Little Haiti is the Miami Art and Design District, also referred to as the Arts and Design Village, located from NE 36th to 41st Streets and from NE Second Avenue to N Miami Avenue.

Lying in the shadow of Downtown Miami, the area has slowly rebounded in recent years from being considered unsafe to luring South Beach artists and photographers in search of cheaper studio space to rent. Some shop owners would like to think the district will be the next South 1Beach, but its proximity to economically depressed neighbourhoods mitigates against it.

Once a vast pineapple grove, the area was known as Decorators Row in the early 1920s, when home design shops set up shop. Until recently, the district was open only to private clients. It is trying to shake off that perception by drawing more public foot traffic by not keeping the doors locked, but many shops still opt for the door buzzer.

Top choices for antique shopping include **Twery's** (160 NE 40th Street) and **Evelyne S Poole** (3925 N Miami Avenue). There are tons of furniture stores to peruse, including the **Portfolio Collections** (3841 NE Second Avenue) and **LaVerne Galleries** (90 NE 39th Street). Most showrooms offer fine European or Asian-style furniture and many are located in four malls called Plazas 1, 2, 3 and 4, found along NE Second Avenue starting from 38th Street. Note that some of these stores are open by appointment only.

The most eclectic stores can be found on 40th Street between NE Second Avenue and N Miami Avenue: try **Alexandria Diez** (51 NE 40th Street), which specialises in intricate wrought-iron furniture work and **World Resources** (No.56), which sells rare Asian and African wares and furniture and mass-produced versions of its originals.

In addition to furniture showrooms, tiny cafés are popping up everywhere. The **Piccadilly Garden Restaurant & Lounge** (35 NE 40th Street), a charming garden café with waterfalls and tropical bromeliads, serves up US food with a continental twist. For basic French cuisine, there's **Chacuterie** (3612 NE Second Avenue), while **Stephans Gourmet Deli** (2 NE 40th Street), with outdoor tables, is the mainland branch of the popular South Beach deli. The **Uptown Grill** (Mid II building, 444 NE Second Street) offers good sandwiches, salads and daily grilled fish specials in the bright atrium of this decorators' showroom.

You should visit this charming district with its streets dotted with potted bougainvilleas during the day because most shops close at about 5pm. As few people actually live here, there's really nothing in the way of nightlife. The Piccadilly, however, remains open for dinner.

There are also a few art galleries in the district. **Adamar Fine Arts** (177 NE 39th Street) focuses on contemporary Latin American art (for more information, *see chapter* Museums & Galleries). The **Florida Museum of Hispanic & Latin American Art** (1 NE 40th Street) has a permanent collection of contemporary Latin art and holds monthly exhibitions.

Miami in Context

History

In its 100-year existence, Miami has welcomed everyone from real estate entrepreneurs to refugees as it evolved into the multicultural metropolis it is today.

SPANISH ARRIVAL

Although the finger-shaped peninsula of Florida has been inhabited for at least 10,000 years, little is known about the lives of the earliest settlers, descendants of Central and South American Indians. Detailed written records began only with the arrival of one of Spain's greatest explorers.

Juan Ponce de León had sailed with Christopher Columbus on his second voyage to the Americas in 1493 and later conquered Puerto Rico for Spain. His reward was to be made governor of the island in 1510, but the spirit of adventure never left him. During his term as governor, he constantly heard tales from Puerto Rico's Native American inhabitants about a mythical island called Bimini, believed to be somewhere north of Cuba (which De León had surveyed with Columbus). Bimini was said to be teeming with gold reserves and to possess a magical spring whose waters had the power to restore youth and heal the sick.

Seduced by the tales, De León repeated them to King Ferdinand V of Spain in 1512. Within days, he was provided with a boat, a crew and orders to find, conquer and colonise Bimini. When his expedition sighted land on 27 March 1513, De León believed he had succeeded. Landing just north of the site of present-day St Augustine, on Florida's north-eastern coast, he made a claim in the name of the king and, because he had first seen land on Easter Sunday, known in Spanish as Pascua Florida ('Festival of Flowers'), decided to name the region Florida. Believing that he had discovered an island, De León tried to circumnavigate it, looking for the fountain and the gold; finding neither, he eventually gave up and returned to Puerto Rico in 1514.

Juan Ponce de León, Florida's 'discoverer'.

St Augustine, the US's oldest colonial town.

Many different Indian tribes inhabited Florida and the surrounding area. Some, like those in Cuba, had been friendly and welcomed the Spanish colonists with open arms. Others fiercely resented the invaders. When De León returned to Florida in 1521 with two shiploads of horses, cattle, tools, seeds and people to start a new Spanish settlement, he came under attack and, badly wounded, was forced to flee. He died in Cuba a few weeks later.

The legend of Florida, however, lived on. During the next few years, a host of young Spaniards tried and failed to establish a permanent settlement, chiefly in the hope of finding the rumoured reserves of gold, but only to be beaten back by the Indians. By the 1560s, interest was starting to wane, but when a massive French force, led by Jean Ribaut, arrived in 1562 to claim the new territory for France, the Spanish realised they had to take action or risk losing Florida altogether.

STRUGGLES FOR CONTROL

Pedro Menéndez de Avilés, captain-general of the Spanish fleet, was ordered to destroy the French colony, Fort Caroline. In 1565, Ribaut and his followers were captured and executed, leaving Menéndez free to establish St Augustine, the oldest continuous European settlement in the US. The French attempted, but failed, to retake the town and St Augustine became a key trading centre.

But the bloodshed did not stop there. In 1586, Britain attempted to get in on the act, sending Sir Francis Drake to lead a naval bombardment that razed St Augustine. For the next 150 years, the English, Spanish and French all vied with the Indians for control of the 'new world', establishing colonies, forts and missions and engaging in bloody confrontation after bloody confrontation. Spain had the upper hand until the Seven Years War (1757-1763, aka the French and Indian War) between Britain and France, in which Spain sided with France. In the First Treaty of Paris, which ended the war, the Spanish ceded Florida in return for the strategically important port of Havana, which the British had captured in 1762.

Under British rule, Florida was divided into two separate colonies, East and West, leaving the surviving Indian tribes, who had joined forces with the Creek Indian tribes that had been pushed down into Florida after repeatedly losing out to the might of the American army, undisturbed in the inland area. Collectively, the new Indians called themselves the Seminole (meaning 'wild one' or 'runaway') and would soon prove to be a force to be reckoned with. The British held on to the area during the American War of Independence (1775-1783) but the Second Treaty of Paris which brought peace also handed Florida back to Spain.

THE US TAKES OVER

From around 1814, US troops made a series of raids into Florida, claiming they were attempting to capture escaped slaves from the neighbouring state of Georgia. They left the Spanish well alone but killed hundreds of Indians (who regularly gave refuge to escaped slaves and had begun intermarrying with them). The scale of the slaughter matched that elsewhere in America, with the Indians slowly being wiped out. The true intention was to remove the Indians completely and take control of the region in order to wrest it from the Spanish. The conflict became known as the First Seminole War (1817-1819). The strategy worked. Led by General (later President) Andrew Jackson, the US troops captured the city of Pensacola in May 1818 and deposed the Spanish government. Spain formally ceded Florida to the US in 1819.

Thousands of colonists soon began to arrive, pushing the Indians further and further south. In 1832, a new treaty was drawn up and the Indians were told they would have to move to a new territory west of the Mississippi. Their chief, Osceola, refused, thrusting his knife into the unsigned treaty as a show of defiance. A few weeks later, 110 US soldiers led by Major Francis Langhorne Dade on a routine patrol were slaughtered by the Indians (and runaway slaves who had joined them), sparking off the Second Seminole War.

The cost to both sides, financially and in lives, was enormous. In 1837, the US agreed to negotiate and Osceola entered one of their camps under a flag of truce. It was a ruse. He was captured and imprisoned, but still the war raged on. In the end, the US spent more than $40 million and lost 2,500 soldiers before the majority of the Seminoles – around 4,000 of them – finally relented and moved to Arkansas. A few refused to leave, fleeing instead to the Everglades where they remain today.

THE MAKINGS OF MIAMI

In 1845, Florida became the 27th state to join the Union and, for a short time at least, there was peace. It was also around this time that what would eventually become the City of Miami began to take shape. During the war, the US had established a limestone fortress, Fort Dallas, on the north bank of a river that flowed through southern Florida. When the soldiers left, the fort became the base for a tiny village established by William H English, which he called Miami.

In the meantime, railroads and steamboats had appeared in the north of the state, bringing prosperity and better links with the rest of the Union. William D Moseley was elected state governor and took control of a population that numbered 87,445, of which 39,000 were black slaves. The vast majority of the white population considered slaves an essential and acceptable part of everyday life and the newly accepted state began to feel increasingly isolated as dissent about the use of slaves led to the formation of the Republican party (trading in slaves had already been abolished in 1808).

Henry Flagler, the father of Miami.

Although it had the beginnings of a small community, Miami would never have become the major city it is now had it not been for one of the US's greatest pioneers, Henry Flagler. Flagler, who had made his $50 million-plus fortune as an associate of a certain John Rockefeller in the Standard Oil company, first came to Florida in the 1880s because of his wife's frail health and its all-year-round good climate. He decided to move into the railroad and hotel business. Starting in St Augustine, his railroad slowly worked its way down the east coast, stopping at each major town to build a plush hotel. With newspapers extolling Florida's weather (so warm that citrus fruits could be grown), it soon became a major tourist destination for the wintering rich – the only people who could afford to stay at Flagler's luxurious hotels.

Another railway magnate, Henry Plant, began building the Atlantic Coastline Railroad on the opposite coast, from Jacksonville down to Tampa, and more investors and settlers began to flood in.

ONE WOMAN'S VISION

At the start of the 1890s, the area around Miami comprised nothing more than a few plantations and trading posts. The first proper community, some way south of the Miami River, was Coconut Grove, but it was only when Julia Tuttle's husband died and she decided to relocate from Cleveland to a plot of land north of the river that things really started to move.

Tuttle had a vision – a city to rival anything else in the US – and she knew how to make it reality. She approached Henry Plant and asked him to extend his railroad to Miami. He turned her down. Undeterred, Tuttle went to Henry Flagler, whose own railway line stopped at Palm Beach, just 66 miles to the north. He kindly explained that he could see no benefit in extending his line down to Miami because there was simply nothing there.

Tuttle knew all too well that without the railroad, the tiny settlement would be too isolated to ever become prosperous. For example, sending a letter from Palm Beach to Miami, 66 miles away, took at least two months. The letter went to a lighthouse community at Jupiter and then by Indian river steamer to the railhead at Titusville. From there it travelled by train to New York, then by steamer to Havana. The final leg of the journey was made by a trading schooner which docked at the mouth of the Miami River – a journey of 3,000 miles in all. The postal service was eventually speeded up with the introduction of the 'barefoot mailman' who, for $600 a year, would literally walk the journey along the beach once a week. But even this wasn't enough to turn Miami's fortunes. In the end, it took an act of nature.

In the winter of 1894-5, a killer frost devastated most of the orange crop in the north of the state, but Miami, further south and well within the

When Abraham Lincoln became the first Republican president in 1860, Florida responded by withdrawing from the Union and joining other southern slave states in the Confederacy. Though the Civil War hardly touched South Florida, most of the major towns in the north (with the exception of Tallahassee) were captured by Union forces early in the war. There was only one large-scale engagement, the Battle of Olustee in February 1864, which proved to be one of the last Confederate victories. On 10 May 1865, federal troops entered Tallahassee and the US flag flew once more. Slavery was abolished and a new state constitution was adopted, allowing Florida to be re-admitted to the Union in 1868.

THE RAILWAY APPROACHES

The 1862 Homestead Act promised 160 acres of land free to any citizen who would stay on them for at least five years and, during that period, effect some improvement. Among the early takers was Edmund Beasley, who in 1868 moved into the bayside area now called Coconut Grove. In 1870, William Brickell bought extra land on the south bank of the Miami River and Ephraim Sturtevant acquired the area known as Biscayne. In 1875, his daughter, Julia Tuttle, went to see him there and fell in love with the area, though it would be another 16 years before she returned.

'tropical zone', escaped the freeze. According to legend, Tuttle sent Flagler a handful of orange blossoms to show that her crop was unaffected. When she agreed to give Flagler half her land (300 acres) and some of William Brickell's, the hard-nosed businessman finally agreed to begin work.

When the first locomotive arrived in Miami on 15 April 1896, all 300 residents turned out to greet it – some of the old-timers had never seen a train and fled to the woods at its approach. Thousands of new settlers and investors flocked down in anticipation of the boom that would surely follow. Tuttle's dream was about to come true.

BIRTH OF A CITY

The shallowness of Biscayne Bay had hindered the growth of the area, but the railroad meant that machines, supplies and people could easily get to Miami, which rapidly began to take shape. A month after the arrival of the railroad, the first newspaper, the *Miami Metropolis*, rolled off the press. In July, Miami was granted city status. In September, the first school opened. Flagler used some of his newly acquired land to build the enormous, plush Royal Palm Hotel, with the intention of encouraging visitors to spend money. More and more tourists began to visit, responding to advertisements in newspapers and magazines that described Miami as 'the sun porch of America', 'where winter is turned to summer'.

Considering Florida's earlier attitude to slavery, it is ironic that blacks were to become so tied to Miami's history. The first shovel of earth that began construction of the Royal Palm Hotel was dug up by the Reverend AW Brown, who was black, as was WH Arston, who signed the original city charter. When the city was incorporated, a third of the original voters were former slaves despite the fact that elsewhere in Florida blacks had few rights. However, immediately after incorporation, the blacks were disenfranchised.

To ensure growth took place in an organised fashion, the city's founders laid out a basic grid plan to the north and south of the river, only to see most of the wooden buildings destroyed in a fire in December 1896. Perhaps it was the shock of seeing her dream go up in flames, but Julia Tuttle died unexpectedly soon afterwards, at the relatively young age of 48. Miami's founding mother may have gone but the city was quickly rebuilt and attracted ever-growing numbers of tourists – and some less welcome visitors.

During the 10-week Spanish-American War in 1898, 7,000 US troops were stationed in Miami, waiting to be shipped down to Cuba. They amused themselves by using coconuts for target practice and swimming naked in the bay, much to the chagrin of the local residents, who did their best to make them feel unwelcome. The church-going black community was a particular target and, on several occasions, the tension escalated into violence with several blacks being killed. It seems that between the residents and the mosquitoes, the soldiers were indeed made miserable. One wrote home: 'If I owned both Miami and Hell, I'd rent out Miami and live in Hell.'

Temperance evangelist Carry Nation patrolled Miami's 'dens of the sinful'.

THE TWENTIETH CENTURY

With the new century came new settlers. Both population and town began to grow rapidly; a business district, banks, movie theatres and a rival newspaper, the *Miami Evening Record*, were set up. There were also so many drinking dens and gin houses that the main thoroughfare became known as 'whiskey street', prompting the arrival of Carry Amelia Nation, 'the Kansas Cyclone'.

A six-foot tall, powerfully built woman, she was known for striding into 'the dens of the sinful' armed with bricks, a hatchet and a Bible and declaring: 'Men. I have come to save you from a drunkard's fate!' She would throw her bricks at the bar, breaking the glasses and bottles, then shout 'God be with you!', and leave. The wife of a chronic alcoholic, she saw it as her task to rid the world of the evil of alcohol, seeing her name as divine providence: Carry A Nation. She stormed into Miami in 1908 and sold copies of her newsletter, 'Smasher's Mail', but was prevented from doing much 'good work' by the concerned citizens who kept a close eye on her every move.

Carry probably had a point. Such easy access to alcohol and so many single men (who had settled there to seek their fortunes) was never destined be a good combination. But even then law enforcement was hardly Miami's strong point. Its first marshal, Young F Gray, was a bandy-legged Texan who loved to drink, and was frequently so drunk that he needed help to mount his bicycle. As well as being the city's first cop, he was also the first to be suspended after being found drunk on duty once too often.

THE FIRST BOOM

Governor Napoleon Bonaparte Broward, in office from 1905-1909, began major drainage of the Everglades to reclaim more land. By 1913, 142 miles of canals had been constructed and Henry Flagler had extended his railroad all the way down to Key West. Government Cut (later to become the Port of Miami) was dug across the lower end of the future Miami Beach to improve access to the harbour, creating Fisher Island in the process.

John Collins, a visionary rather than a businessman, saw potential in the area and borrowed money to build a bridge from Miami to the beach. His money ran out halfway through but he was bailed out by Carl Fisher, who had made a fortune by inventing a new kind of car headlight; in return, Fisher was given much of the land on the beach. By the start of World War I, Miami was in the middle of one of its most rapid periods of growth.

Fisher could see the true potential of the beach and began removing its trees and dredging the sea around it, creating his vision of paradise. Within a year, the area had its first hotels, swimming pools, restaurants and casinos. It was the ultimate playground of the rich. Elsewhere in Miami, many

of the wealthy visitors who had spent winters in the city decided to move there permanently, building fabulous waterfront estates, including Vizcaya.

THE ROARING TWENTIES

Miami's population doubled between 1920 and 1923. Some of the newcomers were drawn by slick advertising campaigns which promoted equally slick community developments, such as the 3,000-acre Coral Gables. Described by its developer George Merrick as the City Beautiful, the Gables was designed as a vision of paradise on earth – and carefully regulated to stay that way. Rigorous local laws are still in force now: residents are forbidden to park their boats in the front driveways of their houses; they are not allowed to remove trees without permission or keep more than four pets; houses can only be painted one of a selected number of pastel colours and lawns must be kept neat, otherwise they are cut by city workers who then send a vast bill for the service. In return, the citizens get to live in a development that reflects the best of Spanish and Italian design, where plazas, fountains and stunning arches seem to grace every tree-lined street.

But not all of the new residents were quite so well to do. Somehow, prohibition and its 'anti-saloon laws' never really hit Miami. With rum runners able to smuggle freely along the impossible-to-patrol coast, it wasn't long before everyone in the US knew of the supposed haven. The widespread notion that prohibition actually made people drink more, promoted disrespect for the law, generated organised criminal activity and popularised the image of the 'gangster', certainly held true in Miami. Before long, the city was virtually overrun

1920s brochures extolled Miami's charms.

Boats tossed out of the Miami River by the 1926 hurricane.

with mobsters and illegal liquor, giving rise to the nickname 'the leakiest spot in America'.

It was for this reason that the old courthouse, once the venue for public hangings, was replaced in 1926 by a much larger building. So large, in fact, that for the next 50 years the Dade Country Courthouse was to be Miami's tallest building. It remains in use, and as busy as ever, today.

There was a building boom all over Miami, some of the growth being 'controlled' by a plan to divide the city into four geographic sections and rename some of the districts and streets – a move deemed necessary because the US Post Office threatened to discontinue mail delivery because of the city's outdated street system. Prices rocketed as people rushed to be part of the latest land boom. Hotels, airports and other amenities sprang up. Miami Beach alone suddenly had 15,000 residents.

Everyone was so busy making money and plans that when the *Miami Tribune* warned, in early September 1926, of an impending tropical storm, few people paid much attention. The hurricane hit in the middle of the night of 26 September, when winds of up to 128mph smashed their way through the city. More than 100 people died, thousands were left homeless, boats were thrown onto the road and most bayside developments were flooded.

The hurricane damage was just being mended and the economy had barely recovered when the Great Depression and a statewide recession brought on by the 1929 Wall Street Crash descended. As if that weren't enough, the north of Florida was invaded by Mediterranean fruit flies, which destroyed more than 60 per cent of the citrus groves. For many, it seemed that the city was finished, a sentiment echoed by dozens of newspaper headlines that screamed: 'Miami is wiped out!'

UP FROM THE ASHES

Many of the millionaires who had profited during the boom years, including George Merrick and one-time mayor John 'Ev' Sewell, were wiped out by the fall in real estate prices. But, even though the founding financiers had gone, the mix of beautiful beaches, a fantastic climate and seemingly endless potential remained, so new money soon flowed in and was warmly received.

A group of mostly Jewish developers began building a lot of small, moderne-style hotels on Miami Beach along Collins Avenue and Ocean Drive, adding to Miami's fast-growing Jewish community and establishing what would later become the art deco district. With the hotels came tourists and with the tourists came renewed prosperity. Pan American Airways launched a service connecting Miami with dozens of other major cities, including many in South America. Miami was soon established as 'the gateway to Latin America' and the population grew steadily.

On 15 February 1933, just before President Franklin Roosevelt's inauguration, 18,000 Miami residents witnessed an attempt to change the course of history. Roosevelt, who was on vacation, agreed to make a public appearance at Bayfront Park. In the crowd, unemployed bricklayer Guiseppe Zangara fired five shots, wounding five people

A brief history of Cuba

Even if hundreds of thousands of Cubans had not moved to Miami, the history of the two places would still be inexorably linked. Cuba was the main supply base for Spanish expeditions to Florida at the time when the peninsula was being discovered and, because of its strategic importance, the subject of fierce rivalry between its Spanish owners and the US.

The Cubans themselves wanted independence from Spain. The biggest revolt came in 1868 and, after 10 years of fighting, the Spanish finally granted many concessions, though continued to rule with a iron rod. In February 1895, the revolution resumed under the leadership of Cuban writer and patriot José Marti. The suspicious sinking of the US battleship *Maine* in Havana harbour in 1898 gave the US an excuse to join the revolutionaries, setting off the 10-week Spanish-American War. When Spain relinquished control, the US finally took over.

For the next 20 years, there were several major insurrections against the US, each one met unyieldingly by squadrons of troops. The US invested heavily in the island and controlled its finance, industry and agriculture, with the US receiving most of its sugar from Cuba. Wealthy Cubans travelled regularly to the US to gamble, drink or simply buy clothes.

After World War I, numerous Cuban presidents tried and failed to improve the lot of their people. Things started to look better in 1940 when Fulgencio Batista, former head of the Cuban senate, became president and started reforms. But Batista lost his office after one term and Cuba became embroiled into World War II. In 1952, Batista took power once more with the support of the army and attempted to crush an uprising by a young lawyer, Fidel Castro, whom he sent into exile. Then he began his dictatorship.

In December 1956, Castro invaded Cuba with around 80 supporters. Seventy were killed on landing but Castro himself and a handful of others fled to the mountains and started a guerrilla army which harassed the Batista government, winning considerable popular support – and also the tacit backing of the US government. In March 1958, Castro called for a general revolt; as his support grew so Batista's dwindled. Late that year, President Eisenhower announced an arms embargo against the Cuban government. On 1 January 1959, Batista fled, leaving Castro in control.

Almost immediately, anti-Castro Cubans began to flood into Miami. For many, it seemed they had left just in time. Castro had promised to hold free elections but never did. Instead he nationalised every major business – even the US-owned ones – and took over billions of dollars worth of property. Had the Cubans stayed, they would have lost everything.

A small brigade of exiles in Miami, with the backing of President Kennedy, were trained by the CIA to invade the island and restore US interests. But the 1,300-strong force – known as 'Brigade 2056' – was expected and met by the Cuban army soon after landing at the Bahia de Cochinos (Bay of Pigs) on the south coast on 17 April 1961. Nearly 100 were killed and the rest (including the father of pop singer Gloria

including Chicago mayor Anton Cermak. Roosevelt, however, escaped unharmed. Zangara was sentenced to 80 years for attempted murder, but when Cermak died he was executed for murder.

Once in power, Roosevelt launched a package of reconstruction programmes to better the lives of many Americans. Young men and not-so-young war veterans were drafted to build parks and new public buildings, which, in Miami, included fire stations, highways, public housing and social clubs. A hurricane struck on Labor Day 1935, killing 400 people and wiping out much of the new construction work, but, once again, Miami found the will to rebuild the damage and continue. There was, however, resentment about Jewish involvement in southern Miami Beach. Slowly, the Beach became segregated, with 'Gentiles Only' signs appearing in the northern part, just as the tide of anti-semitism was also rising across the Atlantic.

WORLD WAR II

The battles in Europe and the Far East seemed a long way off until the US naval base at Pearl Harbour was bombed without warning by the Japanese on 7 December 1941. The US entered the war, and no-one was sure what would happen next. Florida's extensive coastline was seen as a particularly weak link in the US's defence, and tourism, by then the mainstay of Miami's economy, dropped off dramatically. Everyone's worst fears were confirmed in February 1942 when, in full view of thousands of horrified Miami residents, a fleet of German submarines attacked and sank four tankers in a torpedo attack just off the main harbour. More attacks quickly followed: with most of the US Navy's major ships out in the Pacific Ocean, German U-boats found they could attack Florida virtually at will. While the US never had to face the equivalent of the Blitz, were launched from Cuba. Castro responded by mobilising thousands of Cuban troops and calling the blockade an act of war.

At first it seemed the crisis would be resolved by negotiation but, by the Friday, US spy planes revealed work on the missile sites had actually speeded up. Subsequent spy planes were fired on and the US air force was put on standby. Within two days, the Russian premier, Khrushchev, agreed to meet all the US demands.

In December 1965, twice-daily 'Freedom Flights' began bringing thousands of Cubans to Miami; by the time they ended in 1973, the city's Cuban population had reached 300,000. In 1980, Castro decided to rid himself of Cuba's more troublesome citizens. He temporarily lifted exit restrictions and announced that anyone who wanted to leave Cuba could do so. Around 125,000 took up the offer using a flotilla of boats and rafts from the docks at Mariel harbour. Among the 'Marielitos' were some 25,000 criminals and mental patients, who would soon add to Miami's social and economic woes.

During the 1990s, as the USSR collapsed, Castro found his subsidies drying up. In 1995, 21,000 Cuban rafters arrived in Miami, which prompted the US government to announce that future rafters would be returned to Cuba. An increasingly rigorous interpretation of immigration legislation means that effectively Cubans have lost their special status and are now treated like any other would-be emigrants. In 1996, Clinton passed the Helms-Burton Act, imposing trade sanctions on foreign businesses with interests in Cuba, thereby causing a rift between the US and its European and Canadian allies. Cuba is now attempting to boost its own tourist trade in order to support itself.

Refugees arriving in Key West, 1980.

Estefan) were taken prisoner. After this, Castro was unable to enter diplomatic or trade relations with the US, so turned to the USSR, which provided both economic and military aid, much to the chagrin of the US.

When, in 1962, the US government learned that the USSR had nuclear weapon bases in Cuba, the world spent a full week on the brink of nuclear war. On Monday 22 October, President Kennedy announced an air and sea blockade of Cuba to prevent any more equipment being moved there. He demanded the removal of all weapons from the island and threatened to attack the Soviet Union if missiles

the submarines ensured that those who lived in Miami would never feel the war was more than a few hundred feet away, and what little tourism remained quickly died away.

Ironically, the war would later save Miami. The warm climate was deemed perfect for training new soldiers and by the end of 1942, nearly 150 hotels had been converted into barracks and others into temporary hospitals for the wounded. By the time World War II was over, one-quarter of all officers and a fifth of enlisted men in the US Army Air Corps had passed through Miami.

The shortage of manpower brought about by the war improved the lot of Miami's growing black community. In the late 1940s, the first black police officer was appointed to patrol the 'coloured district' and an all-black municipal court was set up. The city's first black judge was appointed and, for the first time, blacks were allowed into the Orange

Bowl Stadium, albeit restricted to sitting in the end zone. Beaches remained segregated, however, adding to the underlying racial tensions which occasionally exploded into violence. In 1951, Carver Village, a black housing project in a formerly white neighbourhood, was repeatedly bombed. Several synagogues and a Miami Shores church were attacked because of their pro-black sympathies and activities.

It was around this time that the gangsters returned to Miami, in force. No-one was quite sure how they managed to evade the law until the publishers of the *Miami Herald* and *Miami Daily News* got together to launch a campaign to drive the gangsters out. In July 1950, the Crime Commission of Greater Miami held live television hearings of court cases. Corruption was discovered at every level of government and eventually the county sheriff was removed from office. But the most

Miami memorials

Miami is a city that likes to hold onto its past and honour those who have contributed to making the city what it is today. From the Ponce de León Plaza in Coral Gables to a planned tribute to those who were killed in the ValuJet plane that crashed in the Florida swamps just west of Miami in 1996, celebrations of history are everywhere. To those visiting from places that have a longer history, their relative newness gives them a particular resonance.

Perhaps the most famous is the **Holocaust Memorial** (corner of Dade Boulevard and Meridian Avenue, Miami Beach, pictured), which is dedicated to the six million Jews who died at the hands of the Nazis and is a poignant reminder that Miami is home to one of the largest concentrations of Holocaust survivors in the world.

The **Bay of Pigs** monument (SW Eighth Street, at 13th Avenue, Little Havana), also known as the Brigade 2506 Memorial, with its eternal flame, commemorates the ill-fated Bay of Pigs invasion. The Cuban theme continues at the **Plaza de la Cubanidad** (W Flagler Street and SW 17th Avenue), a memorial fountain dedicated to José Marti who led Cuba's fight for independence from Spain. The nearby trees are an essential part of the monument, representing mourners who grieve for the loss of their

homeland. Of equal importance to many Cubans is the **Ermita de la Caridad** (3609 S Miami Avenue), a shrine on the bayfront purchased by the Catholic Church and arranged so that worshippers will be facing Cuba as they pray.

The **Woodlawn Cemetery** in Little Havana contains the grave of Carlos Prio Socarras, onetime president of Cuba, deposed in 1952 by Fulgencio Batista. His tombstone carries the red, white and blue of the Cuban flag. Further down the road at the Graceland Cemetery (SW Eighth Street), the **Cuban Mausoleum** remembers the rafters who lost their lives at sea attempting to make the 90-mile journey to Miami.

The man who many believe was more responsible for the development of South Florida than any other, Henry Flagler, has not been forgotten. In addition to having his name on the main Downtown street, there is also a **Flagler Memorial Monument** on a little island just to the west of Miami Beach, accessible only by private boat.

In typical Miami style, the city also honours the famous by naming streets after them. Look out for the **Julia Tuttle Causeway, Andy Gibb Drive** in South Pointe Park, **Ronald Reagan Avenue** in Little Havana and **Arthur Godfrey Road** (named after a 1950s TV light entertainer) in Miami Beach.

---

welcome postwar change was that thousands of soldiers who had trained there returned with their families. Once again, Miami was on the up.

RISING TENSIONS
Immediately after the 1959 Cuban revolution, Miami became home to thousands of anti-Castro immigrants. What started as a trickle became a flood as daily flights brought nearly 100,000 Cubans to the city within a few months. Although the first wave was mostly from Cuba's affluent middle class, later arrivals were far poorer and found themselves competing with Miami's poorest blacks for jobs and housing. When a recession hit in the 1970s, the worst since the 1930s, unemployment soared and violent, race-related confrontations became the norm – although this did little to stop the flow of Cubans to the city. By 1973, there were more than 300,000 in Miami.

The Jewish community also grew rapidly, in the mid-1970s matching the number of Cubans and becoming one of the largest concentrations of Jews in the US outside New York. Miami became particularly attractive to the older Jewish generation: 75 per cent of those living there were aged over 60.

In the summer of 1980, an all-white jury in Tampa, on the west coast of Florida, acquitted a white policeman of beating to death black insurance agent Arthur McDuffie. The anger of Miami's incensed African-American community boiled over into a riot that claimed 18 lives and levelled parts of Liberty City. The disruption lasted for three days and caused damage worth $80 million. The following week – as thousands of 'boat people' begin to arrive from Haiti, fleeing their own dictatorship and attracted by the success of the Cuban immigrants – *Time* magazine ran a cover story about Miami headlined 'Paradise Lost?'.

The Mariel boatlift in 1980 bought 125,000 Cuban refugees to Miami. With the new arrivals came thousands of criminals and mental patients, part of a plan by Castro to rid himself of the dregs of Cuban society. Cubans soon established themselves as the premier drugs dealers in the area, not hesitating to shoot rivals out of business. Miami briefly but notably became Murder Capital USA, with 621 violent deaths in the the city in 1981 alone.

In 1985, a cocaine ring was discovered at Miami airport. More than a ton of coke went through the airport each week, a quarter of all the cocaine being smuggled into the US. As *Miami Vice* began to top the TV ratings, customs officials announced that, in real-life Miami, drugs were now worth more than the city's real estate business.

BOUNCING BACK

With international attention focused on the area, the city councillors realised something had to be done to prevent Downtown Miami and South Beach from being overrun by drugs dealers and down-and-outs. The art deco district received federal protection, a new transport network was developed and fashion photographers began staging shoots in South Beach, sparking its transformation into a hip, happening area buzzing with clubs, restaurants and bars. 1985 saw the election of Xavier Suarez, Miami's first Cuban-born mayor, and at last it seemed that someone was working to reduce racial tension. Two years later, the city had become safe enough for the Pope to visit and a host of sporting events, from the Miami Grand Prix to basketball exhibitions and football matches, brought in even more tourists. The latest boom was in full flow. Even 1992's Hurricane Andrew, which left more than 150,000 homeless, failed to halt the rise. Predicted to strike the city dead

Xavier Suarez, Miami's first Cuban mayor.

centre, it spared the City of Miami but hit South Dade, causing total damage worth $30 billion.

In 1994, the Summit of the Americas brought Clinton and every Latin American and Caribbean president (except Castro, of course) to Miami. In 1996, the city celebrated its centennial and the government announced that Southcom, US military command for all of Central and South America and the Caribbean, will move from Panama to Miami. Today, with tourism in Greater Miami worth $13½ billion a year and Miami recognised as an international banking centre, the gateway to both Europe and Latin America with the largest cruise port and second busiest airport in the US, Julia Tuttle's dream could not have come more true.

Key events

3,000BC Tequesta Indians, early Miami inhabitants, appear as a culture.
1513 Juan Ponce de León lands in Florida, claiming it for Spain.
1763 Spain cedes Florida to Britain.
1783 Spanish gain control again.
1817-1819 First Seminole War.
1819 Spain hands Florida to the US. It becomes a US territory in 1821.
1835-1842 Second Seminole War.
1845 Florida joins the Union, then withdraws during the American Civil War and is re-admitted in 1868.
1896 Henry Flagler's railroad arrives in April. Miami is granted city status in July.
1905-1913 Government Cut dug; Everglades drained to provide more land for building; Miami Beach blossoms.
1926 Hurricane hits, destroying much of the city, and Miami slides into recession, exacerbated by the Wall Street Crash of 1929.
1930s Hundreds of art deco hotels built on Miami Beach.
1935 Labor Day hurricane.
1941 US joins World War II; thousands of US troops train in Miami.
1959 Fidel Castro takes power in Cuba; 100,000 Cubans flee to Miami.
1961 Kennedy launches attack on Bay of Pigs.
1962 Cuban Missile Crisis.
1980 Liberty City riots and Mariel boatlift.
1992 Hurricane Andrew hits South Florida.
1994 Summit of the Americas held in Miami.
1996 Miami celebrates its centennial – and goes bust.
1997 Referendum held on the continued existence of the City of Miami.

Miami Today

It's a city of extremes, the melting pot reached meltdown point. Nothing stays the same in the blast furnace that is Miami, says Tim Schmand.

'May you live in interesting times'
Ancient Chinese curse

'I live in Miami so you don't have to'
The author

Miami is the American empire's primary outpost in the Caribbean and, perhaps, its last Cold War installation. It's a place where the potatoes and gravy of the country's heartland are replaced by the islands' rice and beans. Where English can seem like a second language and the most arcane news out of Cuba is discussed on Spanish-language talk-radio shows as if divining the future through the entrails of a dove.

It's a dangerous place for kids, 53 dead of gunshots in 1996, and for pedestrians – on average 100 are killed by automobiles each year. Only New York City has a higher rate of AIDS. But it can also be a refuge, from both oppressive governments and cold winters, and a place to celebrate life. It hosts the United States' biggest street party, and on South Beach people both straight and gay stagger from club to club searching for the antidote to the ennui of the 1990s.

Dade County, Miami's regional government, is the sixth poorest county in the US – yet in 1997 it gave the local professional basketball team a 30-year sweetheart lease on some of the region's most valuable property, promising them an additional $8.5 million each year if only they'd please, please stay in Dade. It is arguably the capital of art deco and streamline moderne, the architectural styles of the 1930s that provide South Beach's elegantly kitschy stage where tourists can be parted from their money. It's a place of salsa-hot merengue roll of hips down Calle Ocho, gangsta strut and pop down NW Seventh Avenue and the flight of white anglos up Interstate 95, all gone to look for America north of the Broward County line.

MIAMI, CUBA

Miami may today be an international city, but for the first 65 years of its existence it was primarily an inward-looking resort town, focusing ruthlessly on its own survival. If the tourists wanted it, the tourists would get it, laws be damned. During Prohibition, when the manufacture and sale of alcohol was prohibited in the US, booze flowed through Miami like water. Though gambling was

illegal, posh casinos operated with impunity through to the late 1940s, and a 1936 magazine article reported: 'Miami whores are cheap… Usually the charge is $3 – but they will take $1'.

In 1958, as the civil rights movement was taking hold and tourism leaders prayed for a cold winter in the north-eastern US, Miamians paid scant attention to the turmoil in Cuba. Miami had hosted Cuba's toppled leaders before. They led quiet lives. They didn't interfere with the Season. What could change? On New Year's Day 1959, Cuban leader Fulgencio Batista fled the island. Fidel Castro ascended to power and his alignment with the Soviet Union unleashed a wave of immigration that changed Miami, South Florida and the entire United States. Miami was quickly transformed from a tourist mecca into a Cold War outpost. During the 1960s, the University of Miami grew to be the largest CIA installation outside of Virginia. South Florida's coastline is said to have hosted the world's third largest navy, and there are reports of up to 12,000 CIA operatives plotting the overthrow of the Castro regime. And despite the funds, the plans, the threats, Fidel Castro has held power for more than 38 years.

He has proven himself a wily character, from whom Machiavelli might have learned a few things. Fidel can, as he has in the past, unleash waves of immigration, which strain South Florida's social services and wreak havoc with tourism. Purge the highest ranks of his military at the merest hint of dissatisfaction. Confound Miami's exile community with seemingly erratic behaviour – beginning a dialogue with one faction while the Cuban Air Force shoots down two unarmed civilian planes representing another.

Most daringly, in 1997 Fidel Castro invited Pope John Paul to visit Cuba. A wily man embraces his enemy if it suits his needs. The title of Fidel's book, *History Will Absolve Me*, may contain the clue to his greatest desire. Castro wants history to treat him well, and he would shake hands with the devil, or in this case the Pope, to achieve that end. If the meeting comes off, Fidel Castro and Pope John Paul – arguably the late-twentieth century's foremost communist and anti-communist – will join together to ensure something that hasn't happened in Cuba since the early 1950s, a peaceful transition of power.

One may ask why a guidebook about Miami, Florida, USA, would devote so much space to Fidel

Miami's volatility extends to its weather, as spring 1997's twister proved.

Castro. Maybe because Miami, since 1959, has been evolving from the seasonal American resort it was during its first 65 years into suburban Havana. The story is in the numbers, but we won't bore you with a long-winded discussion of demographics. All you need to understand is that the migration of native-born English speakers has been offset by immigrants from Spanish-speaking countries, primarily Cuba but from other Latin American nations as well. No other twentieth-century US city has undergone such a rapid change in population. While New York and Los Angeles have had more immigrants, neither surpasses Miami in the percentage of the population those immigrants represent. And Miami's Cubans are the American success story. In the 30-plus years since their arrival, they have risen to the top of South Florida's business and governmental agencies. They are the power base.

THE MELTDOWN POT

Miami is not a southern US city, like Atlanta or Memphis or Nashville. It is a newly imagined place. While some have dubbed it the Capital of Latin America, one imagines Santiago, Lima, Buenos Aires or Bogota disputing that claim. But Miami, with its modern infrastructure and stable currency, has become the region's capital of capital, where the Venezuelan bolivar can be converted to US dollars or dollars to Colombian pesos. Miami is a looking glass, where a Latin American sees the US and a New Yorker sees Latin America. It's retro-nothing and prepared to be post-everything – post-colonial, post-military dictatorship, post-Cold War, post-Fidel, post-Anglo hegemony, post-millennium, post-post-post. It is the future.

Miami is a lesson in the fluidity of national boundaries, the ephemeral sense of a country's language and the continuing shift of population and power that someday someone will call history. Miami is a creation of technology and foreign policy – marketing and the marketplace. It's a breach in the fire-wall between the north and the south, between English and Spanish. The ground shifts everyday beneath Miami. It is a dream, a night vision, and we may wake up one morning and discover it gone.

A 1996 Northeastern University study ranked Miami as the most volatile city in the US. The study focused on civil disturbances and riots, but there are greater forces at work in Miami than merely angry locals. In most large US cities every time a cop stops a car in an inner-city neighbourhood, it is a potential riot. Any time a concert sells out or a professional sports team wins a championship, civil disturbances are possible.

But in no other US city would a few people taking refuge in Havana's Peruvian Embassy unleash an influx of 125,000 refugees like the 1980 Mariel boatlift. Nowhere else would see anything like the 70,000 Nicaraguans who came to Miami in the 1980s as a result of the United States's proxy war against the Sandinistas. Or the Haitians who took to barely seaworthy boats after Jean Bertrand Aristide, the nation's first democratically elected president, was overthrown in a coup d'état. Or where a summer dust storm in the Sahara desert can develop into a hurricane whose winds and rain are powerful enough to scour the land of everything natural and man-made in the slot between Cuba and the Bahamas. Miami is a place that can – and has – changed overnight.

Miami crime

The statistics will tell you crime in Miami is down for the third year in a row, but watch the news any night and you have the sense you are living in a post-apocalyptic city. In both its length and its often bizarre quality, Miami's rap sheet is as violent and highly coloured as anything you'll find in the books of schlock-comic crime writers such as Carl Hiaasen and Elmore Leonard. Murder is almost a daily occurrence and robbery so rife that it barely gets a mention. Car-jackings are on the up, as are the 'Good-Samaritan-turned-sour' stories. Sadly, Floridians are being forced to turn their back on strangers who ask for help and, likewise, refuse help when it is offered.

In 1996, 128 people were killed in the 40sq mile police district of the City of Miami, with guns being the preferred murder weapon. That is roughly one murder per 2,800 people. In many countries this would be deemed epidemic (in Manhattan the figure for 1996 was one murder per 7,437) – and even that's a 58 per cent drop on the 1980 figure. On the streets, in the deprived inner-city areas, it is the 'drugs, poverty, more drugs' cycle that leads to violent assault, robbery and even murder... the more bizarre, the more Miami.

South Florida has long been associated with organised crime (Al Capone had a permanent suite at the exclusive Biltmore hotel), but the traditional mafia-type brotherhoods tend to stick to Fort Lauderdale. In Miami, organised crime is almost exclusively drug-related. In 1996, the small special investigative department at Miami City Police seized 180½ kilos of cocaine and $40,889,000 in cash – this does not include seizures by other agencies. Coastguard boats tally their busts with symbols on the side – a snowflake is cocaine, a marijuana leaf cannabis. Most of the narcotics come from Colombia and Miami is a veritable washing machine for drug-related cash. With the city's strong Latin American and Hispanic communities, it is easy for South American drug barons to blend in.

Domestic violence accounts for many of the fatal assaults, but it appears that child/wife battery in the city has a particularly sadistic edge. And although many citizens have become anaesthetised to the drug-related murders, the community was outraged in February 1997 when four-year-old Kendia Lockhart was murdered, her body burnt and her arms amputated. Her father was charged with her death. Then there was the woman who, worried that her grand-daughter was not being well cared for, killed the toddler and stashed the body in her freezer – alongside packs of chips and frozen peas.

On a less sinister note, the wackiest crime in recent times has to be the theft of $3.9 million from a Brinks armoured vehicle. But this was no ordinary heist – the truck overturned in one of the poorest neighbourhoods, spilling out millions in notes, coins and food stamps. Word spread quickly – pennies from heaven – and within seconds locals descended on the area. Like myriad vultures, they collected nearly all the contents of the van before police arrived. The money has never been recovered. And it seems that robbery – there

STRANGER THAN FICTION

Though we locals know it as a strange town, even we wonder about day-to-day life in Miami. Elections in Nicaragua, Guatemala, Haiti and Jamaica are followed as closely as those held locally, and, of course, the politicians visit, campaign for votes, raise funds. Religious sensibilities clash over questions of animal sacrifice, and when the United States Supreme Court affirms the right to sacrifice, a local santeria priest celebrates by killing 14 animals.

We have Willie and Sal, a couple of local boys who made good operating a $2.1 billion cocaine import trade. The federal government takes an interest and begins prosecution. A number of witnesses succumb to sudden and violent deaths. The Feds lose the case. The despondent top local prosecutor goes to a topless bar for a bit of company and to drown his sorrows. One magnum of champagne and a lap dance later, there's a scuffle, and for some unexplained reason, the prosecutor bites the dancer. He resigns from office shortly thereafter.

A 400lb (plus or minus) politician flees the country rather than testify under oath about the alleged theft of his car – did it occur at his upper-class Coral Gables town home, or, as witnesses reported, outside an inner-city crack house where he purportedly cavorted about in his voluminous boxer shorts? Local politicos are quick to point out

were 5,187 in the Miami City police district in 1996 – gets stranger by the day. In January 1997, a home invader burst into a Bay Harbor Islands apartment, said 'I'll break your arm and kill you, if you don't pay the $21,500 you owe to the people in Venezuela', and then proceeded to take jewellery as the bewildered resident looked on.

Why crime is so prolific and quite so wacky is a subjective issue, but a combination of geography, weather and wealth certainly seems to flush the criminals this way. The almost constant fine climate makes it an ideal location for all types of wheeling and dealing. Miami and the surrounding areas are just a short hop away to freedom – by sea or air – and many of Florida's criminal residents are either lying low before stepping off the mainland US or have just arrived. It's also handy for the Everglades, where it's easy to make things disappear. For those who have already done the deal/ deed, there are few places as fashionable to spend your loot, and with celebrities as neighbours and pools at every condo, no-one's going to blink an eyelid if you splash out the odd million.

However, although crime is present in every district (like any big city), do not expect to see gun-toting bandits on every corner. The basic rule of 'look for the poverty and you will see the crime' is an unfortunate reality. Stick to well-lit, commercial districts or the more affluent residential areas, because there ain't no Don Johnson keeping watch on these streets.

● For more advice on tourist safety, *see chapter* **Essential Information**.

they're not indicted, merely being investigated.

In preparation for a visit by a congressional fact-finding probe into overcrowding at the Krome Detention Center, Immigration and Naturalization Service employees release some detainees and hide others from the visiting delegation. Cuban teens practice elaborately choreographed *quince* dances in a dry-cleaner's parking lot on Bird Road, while, further west in the Everglades, Cuban commando groups prepare for an invasion of Cuba. Russian mobsters plot to purchase a decommissioned submarine from the former Soviet Union and use it to smuggle drugs to the US. And, yeah, all Latin performers' credentials must be checked at the Broward County line: did they disavow the Castro regime? Are they good freedom-loving/Castro-hating/right-thinking individuals? If not – watch out. In support of Cuban liberty, we are willing to deny liberties in Miami.

It is a town where cross-cultural communications seem to require United Nations intervention. In 1997, African Americans outraged over their failure to make progress in Miami's booming economy staged a day of protest, Black Out '97. Black workers were asked to boycott their jobs and attend a rally in Downtown. That same day, the Cuban community honoured three civilian fliers shot down a year earlier by the Cuban Air Force. The Cuban community saw the Blacks as indifferent to their concerns and, strangely enough, that's just what the Black community thought. In spite of this lack of communication, diversity is celebrated as one of Miami's most valuable resources. But quite frankly, it has yet to demonstrate itself as an asset for the smooth governing of a region, at least in Miami's instance.

MIAMI ICED?

In 1996 a corruption scandal and the revelation of the City of Miami's near bankruptcy threatened the end of the city. A group of land owners and attorneys began a petition and secured enough signatures to put the question to a vote (yet to take place as we go to press). They propose dissolving the city government and transferring its functions to the larger Metropolitan Dade County government. Miami had just celebrated its 100th anniversary and its demise seemed somehow fitting: it took a round hundred years for the city government to fulfil all its useful functions; now it should pass on.

And there appeared, at first, significant support for dissolution, but polling data suggests the citizens of the City of Miami, the only people allowed to vote on the issue, are overwhelmingly opposed to the idea. That's not surprising considering the freight the name and the very idea of Miami carries. 'Balseros' – Cuban refugees who fled the island by raft – were not headed to Dade County or *Estados Unidos*, but Miami. The same could be said for Haitian boat people, Nicaraguan contras and refugees from the northern states, fleeing that region's oppressive winters. Each wave of immigrants brought their own imagined Miami. You can't vote to dissolve your dream, even if it occasionally borders on a nightmare. In the unlikely event that the citizens vote for abolition, don't worry: the idea of Miami will still be here.

So why live in Miami? Why bother to visit? The weather is excellent. Miami Beach may possess the best urban beach in the US. The Everglades offer the solitude of a wilderness less than two hours away. And 100 years ago, this place wasn't even here. London, Paris, and New York all have established social orders that change slowly, if at all. Miami has no order. It's a community of competing agendas, where a loss one day can become a win the next. It's a place where time is compressed – where something is happening or about to happen all the time. It's a community on edge.

There may be more fun places to visit, easier places to know, but there are few more interesting places than Miami.

● Tim Schmand is a writer living in South Miami.

Miami by numbers

Population of Dade County	**2.06 million**	Native species of palm	**15**
Population of Miami Beach	**92,000**	Capacity (in passengers) of world's	
Population of City of Miami	**400,000**	largest cruise ship, registered at	
Latin proportion of Greater		Port of Miami (the *Destiny*)	**3,400**
Miami population	**50%**	Fall in Dade County's	
Miles of coastline in Greater Miami	**84**	murder rate 1990-1996	**25%**
Elevation	**12ft**	Fall in Dade County's	
Average surf temperature		robbery rate 1990-1996	**33%**
on Miami Beach	**74°F**	Percentage of US limes supplied by	
Average air temperature	**75°F**	Dade County before Hurricane Andrew	**75%**
Visitors who stayed at least		Percentage of US limes supplied by	
one night in Miami in 1996	**13.6 million**	Dade County after Hurricane Andrew	**50%**
Total impact of visitor expenditure		Top speed of 1997 tornado	**112mph**
per man, woman and child	**$7,227**	Annual value of fashion shoots	
Median household income		to Dade County in 1995	**$115 million**
(Dade County)	**$31,618**	Number of fashion shoots, movies and	
Most frequently spoken languages		commercials in Dade County in 1995	**5,000**
(other than English and Spanish),		Incidents of rock throwing	
in descending order	**Creole, Yiddish,**	reported to the Florida Highway	
	German, Italian, Portuguese, Chinese,	Patrol July 1996-January 1997	**43**
	Sanskrit/Hindi, Tagalog	Tons of trash picked up in	
Number of taxi cabs	**1,827**	Miami Beach after New Year 1997	**30,000**

Latin Miami

Over half of Dade County's population is of Latin origin – and it's a half with clout. We track Miami's metamorphosis from Capital of Exile into Capital of the Americas.

Greater Miami is hailed as Cuba's second city, dubbed 'Capital del Exilio,' the Capital of Exile. Cubans are the largest Latin group in Dade County, totalling close to 700,000 out of a population of two million and representing about 60% of the total Latin enclave. Also in the Latin mix are Nicaraguans who fled the Sandinistas, monied professionals from the Spanish-speaking South American countries and labourers from Guatemala. For people who want out of South America, Miami is often the first stop.

CUBAN CLOUT

In contrast to other cities in the US, such as Los Angeles, where the Latin population has little political power, Cubans hold important banking positions and wield strong political muscle in Dade County. After the 1996-97 elections, Miami, Hialeah and Coral Gables all had Cuban mayors. In 1996, the new position of executive Dade County mayor went to Alex Penelas, the youngest son of a Cuban exile family, praised by supporters as presidential material, given that he was born in the US, a constitutional requirement for the man at the White House. In the US House of Representatives, Miami's Cuban-born Ileana Ros-Lehtinen (daughter of a Bay of Pigs veteran) and Lincoln Díaz-Balart (ironically, a nephew of Fidel Castro) are among the loudest Republican voices ranting against the bearded old man in charge in Havana. They are evidence of the Republican majority among Cubans in Florida, although since 1995 the number of Democrats has increased among Cubans and Latins in general, mostly to the anti-immigration legislation sponsored by the Republicans.

Curiously, Cubans did not always aim for this political power. Though there was a Cuban community in Miami during the 1950s, the great exodus began after Fidel Castro's rise to power in 1959. Those who left their country after 1959 have generally considered themselves political exiles, not immigrants. Forced by the Cuban government to relinquish all their property and money, those coming to the US after 1960 arrived as political refugees without a penny in their pockets. While driven to succeed economically, for years Cubans in Miami were slow to become US citizens or play any role in local politics. The general idea was to go back to Cuba as soon as Castro fell, an event that

has been predicted quite persistently, and quite fallaciously, every single year for almost 40 years.

BREAKING THE EMBARGO, BOTH WAYS

The Strait of Florida, spanning a mere 90 miles from Key West to the northern coast of Cuba, is often described as a tropical version of the Berlin Wall, making Miami a kind of West Berlin for Cuba. Travel is strictly restricted and regulated in both directions. A US embargo forbids 'trading with the enemy' or travelling to Cuba, with the exception of one family visit per year for those with close relatives there. Journalists and academics going to Cuba to do research must get a special permit from the US Treasury Department. For its part, the Cuban government scrutinises the request of any Cuban in the US who wants to visit the island, and reserves the right to deny entry.

The placards displayed at any of several Cuban demonstrations that occur throughout the year would lead one to think that Cubans in Miami are strong supporters of the US embargo, unsuccessfully cheered for decades as the tool that will choke Fidel Castro and bring him to his knees. Yet, as vexed customs officials at the airport often point out, Miami Cubans are the ones who most often violate the embargo by going to Cuba through a third country, usually Mexico or the Bahamas.

This situation has created a lucrative business for some people in Miami. Those who go most frequently often sell their weight allowance at $10 a pound or more, serving as couriers to other Cubans who are unable or unwilling to visit their family while Castro remains in power. Travellers return with their coveted allowance of cigars and rum, which they resell at a huge profit in Miami's black market. Meanwhile, in Cuba, transactions in US dollars have been decriminalised, spurring the development of family-owned businesses in spite of strong government restrictions in this otherwise officially Marxist-Leninist country. Visitors also take dollars to their family, something that is also forbidden by the US embargo. For instance, a recent visitor to Havana got around by hiring a driver with car at $30 a day. The driver had a 1956 Chevy, which he had bought for $2,500 with money that his sister had sent him from Hialeah. The '56 Chevy is his livelihood.

In addition to dollars, Cubans who visit the island often take their families large quantities of cheap merchandise that's hard to find in Cuba and which their relatives will resell at a profit. Favourite goods for this purpose include ballpoint pens, cigarette lighters, plastic watches and T-shirts. Numerous stores in Little Havana, centred on SW Eighth Street, cater to these travellers. They sell gusanos, duffel bags specially designed for travel to Cuba, named for their tubular shape that's reminiscent of a worm (gusano) but also a humourous appropriation of the term, since 'gusano' has been the label used by Fidel Castro to insult those that oppose him or leave the country.

These same stores sell all kinds of cheap wares. Calle Ocho, or SW Eighth Street, has one of the biggest concentrations of 'dollar' stores in Miami, in which everything costs a dollar or less. Many of these goods, made of 100 per cent authentic plastic, will not get to the end of their long journey from Hong Kong or Taiwan until they shine under Cuban skies. Some political observers consider the situation in Cuba in the late 1990s similar to that of Poland and other formerly Eastern Block countries in the late 1980s. What Cubans in Miami are doing today is similar to what the Polish community of Chicago (the largest outside Poland) was doing ten years earlier: serving as suppliers for the increasing number of family-owned businesses in a crumbling Soviet-style centralised economy. Meanwhile, Cubans in Miami live in constant expectation of the day when change will come.

The Cuban government too profits from the embargo and the hostility of the US government by charging $160 for an entry permit to any Cuban who wants to return for a visit. This is why many Cuban exiles refuse to ask for one, feeling that it is demeaning to pay for a permit from a government they despise. This attitude, in turn, increases the demand for the courier business. Discussions on this topic seem to fill the airwaves of the mostly Cuban-run Spanish-language radio stations in Miami. To go or not to go to Cuba, that seems to be the most passionate question.

Meanwhile, in spite of the embargo, there's no lack of US products in Cuba at government-owned dollar stores. Cubans and visitors can buy all sorts of US products which make their way into the country by circumventing the US embargo through Panama, such as Coca-Cola, Kodak film and even condoms with the US flag printed on the box. These goods are sold by the government in dollars at high prices, and bought by people in Cuba with the dollars brought by their relatives in Miami, all part of an unavowed system of state-run capitalism that flourishes in spite of the continued socialist rhetoric. While newspaper headlines in Miami often blow the whistle on people involved in this trade, the situation is evidence to many Cubans and Americans that the embargo is not only ineffective, but downright counterproductive.

In the US, the embargo now allows for increased cultural exchanges and improved communications, making it legal to import recorded music and books from Cuba. In practical terms, it means that the most complete selection in the world of excellent Cuban music, from the 1940s to the present, is to be found in the numerous record stores blasting popular tunes through their speakers along Calle Ocho, particularly Casino Records, at SW Eighth Street and 12th Avenue. Don't expect to hear any recent music from Cuba on the airwaves of Miami, though: a station that tried to air it in 1996 was forced to change its programming after being accused of 'treason to the Cuban cause' and receiving an anonymous bomb threat, a tactic dear to old-guard anti-Castro groups in Miami. Do expect to hear and see a lot of Gloria Estefan, a most popular resident celebrity who arrived in Miami as a baby in the arms of her mother and whose father was a personal bodyguard to dictator Batista's wife. You may even run into Gloria in person at Allioli or Lario's on the Beach, her two restaurants, or, at a SoBe club, catch a glimpse of Madonna, whose child was fathered by a New York Cuban with family ties in Miami.

The incident with the radio station is evidence of generational differences among Cubans. Gino Latino, the assumed name of the DJ concered, is a young announcer born in Miami to Cuban parents. He typifies first generation Cuban-Americans who have never been to Cuba, but who nevertheless feel a great bond with its culture. Ironically, this cultural bond, instilled by their immigrant parents, often implies a rejection of the older generation's political intolerance.

A NOSTALGIA CULTURE

Miami drips with nostalgia for Cuba, only a 40-minute plane ride away, but physically absent for almost 40 years. Yet visitors to Miami won't find large murals painted on the outside of buildings, attempting to bring back memories of the lost, native landscape, nor folkloric scenes adorning the entrance to Cuban restaurants. Unlike cities in the US with a large Mexican population where the visual muralist tradition predominates, literate Cuban culture has made Miami a palimpsest of bilingualism. Words, words, words abound everywhere! They are in large block type, unadorned, loudly marking restaurants, stores, barbershops and car dealerships in patriotic red, white, and blue, conveniently the national colours of both Cuba and the US.

For those in the know, nostalgia is conveyed by the names of the businesses. Small shops are named after famed large department stores in pre-1959 Havana. La Moderna Poesía, one of the best and largest Spanish-language bookstores in the whole country, at SW Eighth Street and 52nd Avenue, lives up to its renowned predecessor in Havana. Small doctor's offices are named after reputable private medical clinics in pre-1959 Havana. Caballero Funeral Home boasts 'Since 1857' at its front entrance, referring to its founding in Havana, not Miami, for the latter was not established until almost 30 years later.

Nostalgic decorations are reserved for indoors. The murals, the paintings and the photographs of Cuba are to be found on the interior walls of restaurants and barbershops. La Carreta Restaurant, located at SW Eighth Street and 37th Avenue (and whose sign imitates that of its famed namesake in Havana), is lined with large-format, back-lit photographs of Cuba. Habana Vieja Restaurant, at 3622 SW 22nd Street, displays paper-maché tableaux of typical Havana scenes by the acclaimed Scull sisters, artists and personality twins now in their 60s, who often add a splash of kitsch to cultural events around the city with their outrageously coordinated outfits and hats.

Nostalgia can take peculiar forms: 'I don't understand why they left if they now pay in Miami to see me.' These words, attributed to Fidel Castro, are a reference to Armando Roblán, a seasoned actor who has made a career since 1959 imitating the leader in green uniform, first in Cuba, then in Miami. People don't of course pay to see Castro in Miami, but rather Roblin's hilarious caricature of him. Roblin keeps updating his impersonations of Castro at Teatro Trail, 3713 SW Eighth Street.

LATIN DIVERSITY

Back in the 1970s, the mayor of Miami was not Cuban, but Puerto Rican, a group that has US citizenship from birth, but which accounted for less than seven per cent of the Latin population in Miami. Back then, Cubans were not very interested in local politics. The big change in attitude came after the Mariel Boat Lift of 1980, which brought almost 125,000 Cubans to US shores in a matter of months. Negative media coverage of the Cuban Marielitos, due in part to Castro's strategy of mixing common criminals and mental patients with those seeking to leave, prompted Cubans to play a more determining role in Florida politics.

The success of Cubans in Miami has often been cause for friction with other Latin groups. By virtue of their status as political refugees, Cubans have qualified for a variety of Federal programmes not available to other Latin American immigrants. While Federal law has been strict on undocumented aliens from Mexico and other Latin American countries, it actually encouraged migration from Cuba through the Cuban Adjustment Act, which since the 1960s has automatically granted political asylum to any Cuban who touches US shores.

As Cubans have become affluent, they have moved to the more upscale suburbs. Waitresses at Cuban-owned restaurants are often not Cuban but recent arrivals from other countries. A section of what's still considered Little Havana is now known as Little Managua, due to its large population of Nicaraguans, numbering over 75,000 citywide, the second largest Latin group in Miami. Cubans and Nicaraguans were often allies in political rallies during the years of Nicaragua's Sandinista government. But tensions have often sprung up between the two groups owing to the fact that Nicaraguans did not receive the favourable treatment generally granted to Cubans. Wealthy bankers, engineers, businessmen, investors and developers from Colombia, Venezuela, Peru, and Argentina complete the urban Latin scene, while farm labourers from Guatemala and Mexico harvest crops in rural areas of Homestead.

THE CAPITAL OF THE AMERICAS

Because of its increasingly diverse Latin American community and its growing importance as a major banking and trading post between the US and Latin America, Miami likes to see itself as the Capital of the Americas, the place where north and south converge for mutual benefit. The 1994 Summit of the Americas reinforced the city's own perception of itself as 'Capital of the Americas' as it welcomed the 34 prime ministers and presidents of all the nations of the Americas, with the one notable exception of Cuba. The opportunity was used by Cuban exiles to stage a peaceful march of 40,000 protesters calling for democratic freedoms and human rights in an island painfully lacking in both.

Bolstering Miami's claim to capital status is the fact that it has also become a major player in the music, TV and movie industries. Together with Sony, the Estefans have helped build a recording industry, with a large studio in Miami Beach. Popular Spanish-language TV programming is taped and beamed out of Miami to the rest of the United States and Latin America. Cuban-born Cristina Saralegui hosts her own daily talk show, *El Show de Cristina*, claimed to be the most widely watched TV programme in the world.

The contradiction in all of this is that if Miami is to live up to its own vision as Capital of the Americas, it means it must relinquish its provincial title of Capital del Exilio, a term cherished by those very people who have most contributed to internationalising it. Having hostile relations with the neighbouring country to which its population is closest won't help Miami grow to its envisioned status. Many expect US-Cuba relations to slowly but surely head toward normalisation, as with Vietnam and China. And what if Castro finally does fall or dies? Will Cristina and the Estefans, and all the Cuban politicians, bankers and investors who are now US citizens immediately repatriate themselves in a frantic effort to finally claim that capital status for Havana? After all, there's certainly some truth to the rumour that in spite of their professed pro-US stance, they all secretly feel that Havana is the city that rightfully deserves to be Capital of the Americas. Next year in Havana? Yes! And they'll say it again next year, and the year after, and the one after that.

Rafting to freedom

The experience of Cuban rafters, or balseros, coming to US shores has been a determining cultural factor in Cuba and Miami. The topic has served as inspiration for writers, filmmakers, painters (such as Luis Cruz Azaceta in the US), and installation artists, such as Kcho (who lives in Cuba but has exhibited in New York and Miami). The home-made rafts themselves have frequently been exhibited in art galleries from Miami to New York.

Political or cultural events organised by Cubans in Miami often prompt the display of a Cuban raft at the entrance or in the lobby. The Cuban Museum of the Americas (1300 SW 12th Avenue; 858 8006), whose mission is to preserve Cuban art in the US, has a collection of drawings by children who arrived in rafts. Different selections from that collection have been exhibited at various events.

Throughout all this, 'Hermanos al Rescate' (Brothers to the Rescue), a private organisation of Cuban pilots, has played a prominent role in searching the perilous, shark-infested waters of the Strait of Florida for rafters. During the great exodus of 1994 over 37,000 balseros were rescued by Brothers to the Rescue and the US Coast Guard during the summer months. As new immigration accords between the US and Cuba have mandated the repatriation of balseros intersected at sea by the US Coast Guard, the number arriving on US shores has considerably diminished. Those who do make it to land are generally allowed to stay. Efforts are being made to turn into a museum the building in Key West formerly used by Hermanos al Rescate to receive balseros.

Architecture

From high-tech high-rises to desirable deco, Miami's architecture fuses the shock of the new with the schlock of the old.

Beach Patrol HQ, *Miami Beach: a nautical theme complements its beachfront location.*

In its one-century existence, Miami has had more boom-to-bust and boom-again streaks than most Las Vegas high rollers. Between hurricanes, unbridled real-estate speculation and waves of mass immigration, the city has grown in fits and starts; brought to the brink of destruction and then rebuilt even bigger and more expansive. Critically dependent on tourist dollars, it sells itself to the world with images of fanciful art deco buildings and gleaming Downtown high-rises reflected in the calm waters of Biscayne Bay. Left on the cutting room floor are the thousands upon thousands of uninspired structures so common to suburban US sprawl. Unlike many cities that grew up around natural harbours or in sheltering mountain valleys, the banks of the Miami River on the edge of the mosquito-infested Everglades were an unlikely setting for a metropolis. The young city was carved out from tropical marshland, while Miami Beach across the bay was little more than a spit of sand and thick mangroves. Even today the view from highway overpasses or upper-storey windows is of a remarkably green and tropical city.

The best of Miami architecture recognises in some way the city's tropical setting or its multicultural pulse, though some of the most endearing buildings, such as the Moorish designs in Opa-Locka, are in fact costly follies built by developers determined to imprint their own grand visions on the young city. Apart from George Merrick and his masterplan for the bucolic streets of Coral Gables, few succeeded. Yet, for better or worse, as a reflection of a city determined to lure millions of tourists and new residents, Miami's hotels, shopping areas, office buildings and homes stand as architectural monuments to the capricious whims of popular taste.

Walking tours focusing on Miami Beach's art deco architecture are offered by the **Miami Design Preservation League** (MDPL) on Thursdays at 6.30pm and Saturdays at 10.30am. They leave from the Art Deco Welcome Center at 1001 Ocean Drive (at 10th Street) and cost $10. Equipment for self-guided audio tours can be rented daily from 11am until 4pm for $5. Call 672 2014 for more information. MDPL also offers bicycle tours of the district on the first and third Sundays of the month at 10.30am; book on 674 0150.

Weekday tours of the district are also offered by **Donna Zemo's Deco Tours**; call 531 4465 for more information. A wider range of tours touching upon Greater Miami's history and development are offered by the **Historical Museum of Southern Florida**. Led by the very knowledgeable Doctor Paul George, these range from walking tours of various neighbourhoods to boat rides up the Miami River. Times, departure points and costs vary; call 375 1625 for more information. Other tours focusing on Miami history are organised by the **Dade Heritage Trust** (358 9572) during the Dade Heritage Days festival, usually held in April and early May. For more information on tours, *see also chapter* **Sightseeing**.

SOUTHERN COMFORTS

Miami was never really a true Southern city and possesses none of the antebellum architecture associated with the American South. When Commodore Ralph Munroe set out to build a residence for his family in Miami in 1891, he applied his knowledge of boat building to the design of the **Barnacle**, a large wooden home with wide verandahs, typical of the Caribbean. Built (before the age of air conditioners) to let breezes and light carry through the house, it has survived the worst winds and rains that nature could throw at it. More diminutive but equally representative of Miami's pioneer days is the **Flagler Palm Cottage**. Erected in 1897 in Dade County pine, this bright yellow cottage is the last surviving example of the homes built by railroad magnate Henry Flagler to attract residents to the new city.

Surviving examples of the turn-of-the-century wooden homes of **Coconut Grove's Bahamian community** can be seen along Charles Avenue between SW 37th Avenue and Main Highway. Long and narrow, with rooms built in a linear fashion, these were commonly referred to as 'shotgun cottages' because a bullet could travel straight through the front door and out the back.

Barnacle State Historic Park

3485 Main Highway, at Charles Avenue, Coconut Grove (448 9445). Bus 42, 48. **Open** 9am-4pm Fri-Sun. **Guided tours** 10am, 11.30am, 1pm, 2.30pm, Fri-Sun. **Admission** including house tour $1; free under-5s. Arrive half an hour early to sign up for afternoon tours.

Flagler Palm Cottage

66 SE Fourth Street, between NE First Avenue & Miami Avenue, Downtown. Bus 6, 8, 48, 95/Metromover Fort Dallas Park. The interior of the house is not open to view.

Deco double-take

In Miami Beach today 'deco', as in art deco, means dollars; so much so that the strip of art deco hotels with restaurants along Ocean Drive is now Florida's second most popular tourist attraction after Walt Disney World. But as much as Miami Beach may seem gaga over deco, strict design guidelines limit the ability of architects to build modern interpretations of the deco style. Rather, architects are encouraged to design new buildings to be harmonious with the prevailing deco style, without copycatting its principal elements.

Today it is the architects of fast-food restaurants on Miami Beach who are the most obvious heirs to the art deco legacy. Trying to reflect deco without being deco in itself has lead to some interesting highs in fast-food architecture. Check out the neo-Mediterranean deco of the Burger King at the corner of 17th Street and Alton Road, and the bold and chunky ornamental bands on the front of the McDonald's at 1601 Alton Road, at 16th Street. It's up for grabs whether the Burger King at 1100 Fifth Street, at Lenox Avenue, is deco-influenced or not, but its huge round window is the ultimate in the ship porthole motif.

SPANISH ROOTS

The two most popular architectural styles in Miami during the boom years of the 1910s and 1920s were Mission and Mediterranean. Mission, based on the eighteenth-century Spanish missions built in California, is noted for its relatively simple design with ornamentation saved for the roof line and entrance. A particularly romantic and fine example is the 1917 **Plymouth Congregational Church** in Coconut Grove.

More flamboyant, with surface carvings, geometric patterns and terracotta-tiled roofs, the Mediterranean style has endured as the favourite of property developers to this day. Good examples of period Mediterranean buildings can be found on South Bayshore Drive in Coconut Grove and throughout Coral Gables. George Merrick, the developer of Coral Gables, crowned his graceful suburban city with an elegant, Spanish Renaissance-style **City Hall** (1928) and an imposing Baroque palace, the **Colonnade Building** (1925), the headquarters of his real estate company. Today the Colonnade houses upscale shops and is woefully overshadowed by the adjacent Colonnade Hotel, built in the 1980s.

Plymouth Congregational Church

3400 Devon Road, at Main Highway, Coconut Grove (444 6521). Bus 42, 48. **Open** 9am-5pm Mon-Fri.
Ask in the church office to visit the main sanctuary; otherwise open during Sunday morning services at 10am.

Coral Gables City Hall

405 Biltmore Way, at SW 42nd Avenue/Le Jeune Road, Coral Gables (446 6800). Bus 42, 52, 56, J. **Open** 9am-5pm Mon-Fri.

Colonnade Building

169 Miracle Mile, at Ponce de Leon Boulevard, Coral Gables. Bus 40, 72. **Open** individual shops open at varying hours.
The Colonnade Hotel, into which the building is incorporated, is at 180 Aragon Avenue (441 2600).

FLIGHTS OF FANCY

Ever the resourceful salesman, Merrick offered those not taken by the Mediterranean style the opportunity to live in a number of '**International Villages**', which reflect French Norman, South African Dutch and even Chinese design. Perhaps the only more audacious appropriator of styles was developer Glenn H Curtiss, who envisioned a city lifted straight from the pages of *The Arabian Nights*. Minarets, domes and Moorish-style arches can be found scattered throughout the City of Opa-Locka, though today greatly altered and in varying degrees of upkeep because of the area's relative poverty. The 1926 **City Hall** is the best example of this quixotic urban dream.

Coral Gables International Villages

South African Dutch-style houses on SW 42nd Avenue, between Riviera Drive & Maya Avenue; French Norman along the 400 block of Vizcaya Avenue, at SW 42nd Avenue/Le Jeune Road; Chinese homes along the 5100 block of Riviera Drive, between Sansovino & Castania Avenues & Maggiore Street. *See also chapter* **Coral Gables**.

Opa-Locka City Hall

777 Sharazad Boulevard, at Ali Baba Avenue, Opa-Locka (688 4611). Bus 21, 27, 28. **Open** 9am-5pm Mon-Fri.
Ask at the library inside the city hall if someone is available to give you a tour of the building.

PASTEL PARADISE

Unlike the grandiose power-tripping of its distant New York or Chicago relatives, Miami Beach art deco is as giddy an assemblage of motifs and influence as any 1920s flapper decked out in strands of beads, bracelets and dangling earrings. More than 800 buildings from the 1920s and 1930s survive in the city's historic district, between South Pointe Park at the island's tip and Dade Boulevard. Their survival is due to the vision of a handful of activists who in 1976 founded the Miami Design Preservation League. In 1979 much of South Beach was listed in the National Register of Historic Places.

Miami Beach's unparalleled collection of art deco buildings owes its existence to two important events: the Paris Exposition Internationale des Arts Decoratifs et Industriels Moderne of 1925 and the great hurricane of 1926. With most of Miami Beach's buildings destroyed, architects had a free hand to marry a renewed interest in decorative arts with the current fascination for industrial design. Ship portholes, wheel crankshafts and streamlined wings were incorporated into building designs. Bas reliefs on buildings reflected Miami's tropical setting, with flamingos and palm trees popular motifs. Angular shapes and geometric patterns predominate, while whimsical decorative touches incorporate such far-flung elements as Mayan and Egyptian themes.

The building at **685 Washington Avenue**, which has housed a number of restaurants and is currently vacant, is a particularly good example of early 1930s art deco. Squared columns with carved floral decoration flank the doorway and rise up towards a low, stepped, temple-like 'ziggurat' roof with small spire. A nice bit of tropical deco is architect Russell Pancoast's 1936 **Peter Miller Hotel** (1900 Collins Avenue). An angular central tower which serves as the entrance to the building is crowned with a low and broad Mediterranean-style sloping tile roof. And no better example of the nautical influence on art deco design exists than the **Beach Patrol headquarters** (1001 Ocean Drive, at 10th Street), which not only features porthole windows but a facade shaped like the bow of an ocean liner.

In the late 1930s, the taste turned to streamlining facades, with more rounded edges and banding above windows reducing some of the early emphasis on playful surface decoration. The **Cardozo Hotel** (1300 Ocean Drive) is a good example of both relatively simple surface styling

*A palm tree joins the shape-play at the **Atlantis** condominium (see page 101).*

and prominent rounding of the facade and windows. A striking example of streamline line applied to what is known as Depression moderne is the **Miami Beach post office** at 1300 Washington Avenue. A classical, central rotunda is topped with a shallow dome and an ornamental lantern. The external facade is virtually unadorned, while the interior features a WPA-era mural and attractive brass detailing.

Many Miami Beach buildings of the 1920s and 1930s are a hybrid of the art deco and streamline styles that is seen nowhere else. One such hybrid is the **Governor Hotel**, designed by noted deco-era architect Henry Hohauser and built in 1939, a hidden jewel on quiet 21st Street (at number 435, just east of Washington Avenue). Gentle setbacks in the facade are highlighted by vertical fluting and banded, eyebrow-like trim over the windows. Glass panels are etched with flamingos and tropical themes, and the lobby still has the original chequerboard tile floor.

Some of the historic district's present bright colour schemes may be a bit more fanciful than when the buildings were actually built, but they nonetheless shine brilliantly in the abundant sunlight. The buildings take on an even more raffish personality at night when washed in neon light. The cool blue of the **Colony Hotel sign** (Ocean Drive, between Seventh & Eighth Streets) is a particular postcard favourite. More subtle but noteworthy is the illuminated band of glass blocks along the undulating facade of the **Sterling Building** (927 Lincoln Road, between Jefferson & Michigan Avenues).

TROPICAL TOWERS

Miami's infatuation with Spanish architecture was so great that during a two-year period between 1925 and 1926 developers commissioned no less than three replicas of Seville's 800-year-old Giralda Tower from the architectural firm of Schultz and Weaver: the Miami News Tower (known today as **Freedom Tower** after its more recent use as a processing center for Cuban refugees), currently unoccupied, the **Biltmore Hotel** in Coral Gables and the no-longer-extant Roney Plaza Hotel on Miami Beach. Vultures seem particularly fond of circling the pyramid-crowned tower of the somewhat less graceful but appropriately sturdy and solid **Dade County Courthouse**, built in 1926.

The 1938 **Alfred I Dupont Building** in Downtown Miami is the city's finest example of Depression-era modern. The second-floor bank lobby features handsome brass grill work, inlaid marble floors and a very unexpected wood beam ceiling hand-painted with scenes from Florida's history. A monument to the boom-to-bust banking scandals of the 1980s, the **NationsBank** building (constructed in 1987, and still popularly called the Centrust building after the failed bank for which it was built), is contemporary Miami's most distinctive skyscraper, with a three-tiered curved exterior atop a square cube. It is particularly striking when lit up at night.

Freedom Tower
600 Biscayne Boulevard, at Sixth Street, Downtown. Bus 3, 9, 10, K, T/Metromover Freedom Tower. Currently unoccupied and closed to the public.

Biltmore Hotel
1200 Anastasia Avenue, at Granada Boulevard, Coral Gables (445 1926). Bus 52, 56, 72. Public areas and restaurants are open to visitors.

Dade County Courthouse
73 W Flagler Street, at NW First Avenue, Downtown (275 1155). Bus 3, 16, 95, C, S/Metrorail & Metromover Government Center. **Open** 9am-5pm Mon-Fri.

Alfred I Dupont Building
169 E Flagler Street, between NE First & Second Avenues, Downtown (374 3677). Bus 3, 16, 95, C, S/ Metromover Miami Avenue. **Open** 8am-6pm daily. The second-floor bank lobby is open during banking hours, generally 9am-3pm, but can be viewed through the locked gates at other hours when the building is open.

NationsBank
100 SE Second Street, at NE First Avenue, Downtown (539 7100). Bus 2, 6, 9, 10, K/Metromover Miami Avenue. **Open** public lobby 8am-6pm daily.

FUTURE PERFECT
As captured in the opening sequence of Miami Vice, the **Atlantis** condominium (1982) at 2025 Brickell Avenue (between 20th & 21st Roads) is recognisable as 'the building with the hole in it' – a reference to the 37ft cube cut from the building's centre on the 12th floor. Within the open cube are a spa bath, a red circular staircase and a palm tree. A signature product of world-renowned local firm Arquitectonica, the Atlantis is joined on the same street by two of the company's equally colourful and witty plays on angles and shapes: the **Imperial Building** at 1627 Brickell Avenue (between 16th & 17th Roads) and the **Palace Building** at 1541 Brickell Avenue (between 15th & 16th Roads), also begun in 1982. All are private condominium residences, not open for tours, but readily visible from Brickell Avenue.

Woggles and cheeseholes

Morris Lapidus never saw a curve he didn't love. It was hard angles that he banished from his architectural repertoire. For many years, the architect and designer of numerous Miami Beach hotels, including the lavish Eden Roc and Fontainebleau (opened in 1954), was also banished from the realm of what was considered good taste. Upon seeing the Fontainebleau Hotel, the mayor of the French town of the same name is supposed to have remarked, 'this is not Fontainebleau, but bouillabaisse'. Having started out designing department store interiors, Lapidus approached the design of resort hotels with the idea that people wanted to be sold on the idea of a dream vacation, hotels offering theme environments being as much the focus of a vacation as the destination itself. His lobbies often featured a grand staircase that led nowhere in particular, but served well as a runway for guests to strut up and down. Strange, biomorphic shapes he called 'woggles' floated above the lobby, supported by improbable 'beanpoles' which disappeared up into 'cheeseholes' cut out of the ceiling.

While many of his interiors have since been altered, the strange shapes of the sun shelters and planters that Lapidus designed for the conversion of Lincoln Road into a pedestrian mall have been refurbished and are today a cherished symbol of the area's eccentric personality. Morris, now a feisty 95-year-old, has lived long enough to see himself rehabilitated by the profession which once scorned him, and has been dubbed the Architect of the American Dream.

Where do you find out what's happening in London?

http://www.timeout.co.uk

Time Out

Your weekly guide to the most exciting city in the world

Miami Eating
& Drinking

Restaurants & Cafés

Dining out is one of Miami's great pleasures, whether you want to be seen on the scene or carbo-load at a Cuban cafeteria.

With over 6,000 licensed restaurants to choose from, dining out in Miami has become a bona fide eat, see and be seen sport in the same league as rollerblading on Ocean Drive. Reflecting the influences of the Caribbean and Latin America, Miami's restaurants offer an exotic and sultry sophistication. There's a major buzz surrounding this city's dining scene – and not just because everyone's cellphones are ringing with reservation confirmations.

It hasn't always been this way. Miami was once the laughing stock among highbrow epicureans, who turned their noses up at the city's only dining tradition: the ghastly, unhip, unsophisticated Early Bird Specials: cheap, 4-6pm meal deals for early-to-bed oldies. While the Early Bird still has many Miamians lining up pre-sunset at various eateries, others, young and old, are queuing at some of the nation's most avant-garde, award-winning establishments in the hours closer to the break of dawn.

Groundbreaking chefs such as Mark Militello, Allen Susser, Jonathan Eismann and Norman Van Aken have used Miami's tropical offerings to establish the phenomenon known as 'Floribbean' or New World cuisine, fusing local ingredients into culinary masterpieces. These days, Miami is right up there with New York and San Francisco on the esteemed map of trend-setting, new-wave cuisine.

WHERE TO EAT

South Beach offers an entirely new world of edible, palpable glitz and glamour, embracing everything from the avant-garde couture cuisine of the *Lifestyles of the Rich and Famous* set to uber-trendy sushi and Italian restaurants. Hors d'oeuvres in Beach area restaurants take the form of the droves of Hollywood celebrities. People tend to wear their Saturday night best in the hope of being spotted by Calvin Klein for his next ad campaign. Dress code? Basically a free for all, with a heavy emphasis on loud Versace print shirts, jeans, black, black and more black.

South Beach's sleek and chic cuisine does have its price, however. Beach restaurants are notorious for slow and arrogant service; by the time you get your cutting-edge dish of pan-roasted, pan-seared whatever, that trend will likely have been long over. Many restaurants include a 15 per cent gratuity 'for

your convenience' (hence the lazy service), but often neglect to tell you, so don't be afraid to ask and don't be afraid to adjust it for better or worse if need be. Many also provide valet parking, at reasonable to astronomical rates, for those too cool or impatient to search in vain for a precious parking space.

For a quieter, more conservative dining experience, Coral Gables is a foodie's heaven. The Gables is home to some of the city's most acclaimed, diverse and expensive establishments, which play host to many of Miami's power lunches and dinners and other clandestine tête-à-têtes. Yuppies love the Gables because every restaurant reflects an upwardly mobile sensibility. They can be a bit stuffy, but that's an acceptable trade-off for the first-rate food. Dress code is a bit more austere, but elegant.

Little Havana is Miami's gift to all who desire the sights, tastes and sounds of old world Cuba. For some of the best Cuban food, hit Calle Ocho (SW Eighth Street) and sample the culture's most authentic comestibles at traditional streetside cafeterias or restaurants. The feel ranges from laidback to a pace as frenetic as the language spoken – Spanish is more common here than English.

Miami Beach, Downtown, Coconut Grove and Key Biscayne all boast water views. Yet, while water may be ideal for scenic purposes, it isn't always ideal for seafood. Miami's seafood is good, but not, unlike the Keys, remarkable. Stone crabs are the most celebrated crustaceans in this city but are only available between October and May.

The average prices given are for a typical meal. Thus, in a restaurant, they include three mid-priced courses (no wine), in a deli a sandwich and dessert.

South Beach

Fifth Street & below

Big Pink

157 Collins Avenue, between First & Second Streets, South Beach (532 4700). Bus H, W. **Open** noon-4am daily. **Average** $23. **Credit** AmEx, MC, V.

As the newer but less nouveau relation of Nemo (*see below*), Big Pink captures the feel of a hip, New York-style diner right down to the hustle, bustle and noise level. An open kitchen serving run-of-the-mill pizzas, sandwiches, salads and hamburgers also offers an authentic TV dinner on a tray complete with compartments and dessert. The family-style table arrangement promotes camaraderie among diners. Popular with the after-club crowd.

Century

140 Ocean Drive, between First & Second Streets, South Beach (674 8855). Bus H, W. **Breakfast** 6am-11am, **lunch** 11am-5pm, **dinner** 6.30-11pm, daily. **Average** $33. **Credit** AmEx, DC, MC, V.

On the desolate southern tip of Ocean Drive, the Century is an expensive place where hipsters go to be away from the mainstream. Attached to a hotel favoured by fashionistas (such as Thierry Mugler) and celebrities, the Century offers California cuisine in an ultra-modern setting, with video footage on some nights from the latest catwalk shows.

China Grill

404 Washington Avenue, at Fifth Street, South Beach (534 2211). Bus C, H, K, W. **Lunch** 11.45am-5pm Mon-Fri. **Dinner** 6pm-midnight Mon-Thur, Sun; 6pm-1am Fri, Sat. **Average** $40. **Credit** AmEx, DC, MC, V.

With portions large enough to feed the entire Asian continent, the cavernous China Grill is a culinary experience that should be shared by many. That is, if you are lucky enough to land a reservation at a decent hour. Unless your surname is Stallone or Nicholson, you may find yourself indulging in China Grill's Pan Asian cuisine at the unfashionable hour of 6pm or indigestion-inducing midnight. But with incomparable broccoli rabe dumplings, outrageous crispy spinach (not low-fat, but so good it's even Oprah's favourite), lobster pancakes and a killer dessert sampler, this hub of South Beach flashiness is well worth the wait, so find a spot at the packed bar, read the excerpts from Marco Polo's diary engraved in the mosaic floor and keep your eyes open for everybody who's anybody.

Joe's Stone Crab

227 Biscayne Street, between Washington & Collins Avenues, South Beach (673 0365). Bus H, W. **Lunch** 11.30am-2pm Tue-Sat. **Dinner** 5-10pm Mon-Thur, Sun; 5-11pm Fri, Sat. **Average** $35. **Credit** AmEx, DC, Disc, MC, V.

Unless you grease one of the secret service-like maitre d's with some hard cash, you'll be waiting for those famous cold claws for up to two hours, sometimes more. Joe's is an institution that attracts locals, tourists and celebrities (Ivana claims it as her favourite). It ranks up there as one of the country's most profitable restaurants, serving seasonal stone crabs (Oct-May only) with a 'secret' mustard sauce, garlic creamed spinach, French-fried sweet potatoes, coleslaw and hash browns. For non-seafood lovers, fried chicken and liver and onions are the way to go. Save room for the key lime pie – considered the best in town. Joe's has a takeout shop for those who can't face the queues – take your claws outside for a picnic in South Pointe park.

L'Entrecote de Paris

413 Washington Avenue, between Fourth & Fifth Streets, South Beach (673 1002). Bus C, H, K, W. **Dinner** 6pm-1am daily. **Average** $22. **Credit** MC, V.

In a prime spot in the up-and-coming SoFi (South of Fifth Street) area straight across from the hustle and bustle of China Grill (*see above*), this unassuming bistro is a favourite with Europeans and those who'd rather enjoy the hype from afar. Despite its limited but almost bargain-priced menu of steak, chicken or salmon (all accompanied by a salad and fantastic frites), L'Entrecote's few yet strategically placed tables inside and out are always full.

Nemo

100 Collins Avenue, at First Street, South Beach (532 4550). Bus H, W. **Lunch** noon-3pm Mon-Sat. **Brunch** noon-3pm Sun. **Dinner** 7pm-midnight Mon-Sat; 6pm-11pm Sun. **Average** $40. **Credit** AmEx, MC, V.

Chef Michael Schwartz, formerly of Wolfgang Puck's Chinois in LA, has given people a reason to cross over to the more desolate yet quickly developing side of Collins Avenue. Hollywood types head this way to sample Nemo's finest organic fare (*Good Morning America*'s 'sweetheart' Joan Lunden was rumoured to have a little tryst in the bathroom here with actor Steve Guttenberg), which includes wok charred salmon with roasted pumpkin seeds, crispy prawns with salsa, and an addictive white bean and olive oil purée in which to dip the hot, crusty, home-made bread.

Eating as an event

Admit it. You love to eat. Anyone who says they don't is lying. That, or, they've never been to Miami. Miami recognises this gastronomic passion and makes eating more than a necessity with a slew of food-oriented activities and festivals guaranteed to keep you off your diets.

Gourmet magazine and the Miami Beach Film Society have merged two of life's greatest pleasures – food and film – into a series of fabulous theme dinners at Miami Beach's popular eateries with menus derived from some of the cinema's most delectable flicks, such as *Like Water for Chocolate*, *Eat Drink, Man Woman* and *The Last Supper*. Prix fixe dinners are all inclusive. For more information, call 673 4567.

At the Hotel Astor, get dressed up for the monthly Chef's Table dinner party, which plays to various over-the-top themes such as Gilligan's Rasta Island and Viva Las Vegas, complete with costumed diners and waiting staff, period music, party favours and activities. Fantastic fun. For more information, call 534 2433.

Then there are the annual food festivals, which bring out the masses who are enticed into buying food tickets in order to sample the goods, often on street stalls and stands. The following are the most popular:

Taste of the Grove (444 7270): A January food fest at which Coconut Grove's most popular restaurants offer their best dishes amid live music and entertainment.

Carnaval Miami/Calle Ocho (644 8888): A 23-block celebration of Latino food and heritage. Held in March.

South Florida International Food & Wine Festival (445 1926 ext 2090): Gourmet food frenzy reigns in Coral Gables in April.

Taste of the Beach (672 1270 ext 17): Yearly pig-out on South Beach, featuring the area's yummiest restaurants as well as live entertainment. Usually held in May. The success of the event depends on good weather.

Savannah

*431 Washington Avenue, between Fourth & Fifth Streets,
South Beach (604 8080). Bus C, H, K, W.* **Dinner** 7pm-
12.30am daily. **Average** $35. **Credit** AmEx, DC, MC, V.
You may find Garbage's Shirley Manson, Butch Vig, Duke
Erickson and Steve Marker, Liza Minnelli or Larry
Fishburne holed up in the sleek and soulful back lounge of
Miami Beach's latest restaurant/haute spot. Not only is it the
first true Southern cooking establishment to arrive in a town
saturated with sushi and Pan Asian cuisine, but its simple
chic décor is as soothing and comforting as its cornbread.
Wooden floors, soft lighting and a baby grand turn the con-
summation of fried chicken into an art form rather than a
greasy mess. Savannah creates a retro-cool culinary experience out of traditional soulfood with such delights as a mod
version of macaroni and cheese with leeks, and sassed up
sweet potato creme brulée.

Smith and Wollensky

1 Washington Avenue, South Beach.
Carnivores unite! National steakhouse Smith and Wollensky
has landed at the tip of South Beach, at South Pointe to be
specific, in the form of a cavernous, 550-seat space with one
of the best views in the city. S&W hails from meat-loving
New York and Chicago, so you can be assured that your slab
o' beef here is a choice one. Due to open in November 1997.

Tap Tap

*819 Fifth Street, between Jefferson & Meridian Avenues,
South Beach (672 2898). Bus C, K.* **Dinner** 5.30pm-
midnight Mon-Thur, Sun; 5.30pm-1am Fri, Sat. **Average**
$25. **Credit** AmEx, MC, V.
Enjoy a taste of the Caribbean at this funky, artsy restaurant, which pays homage to Haitian culture with colourful
wall murals, Haitian music and art and a bohemian crowd
that gathers for art shows, poetry readings and pseudo intellectual conversation. For the ethno-phobic, there's vegetable
stew, but you should try the goat – it tastes like chicken.

10th Street & below

Astor Place

*Hotel Astor, 956 Washington Avenue, at 10th Street,
South Beach (672 7217). Bus C, H, K, W.* **Lunch**
11.30am-2.30pm Mon-Sat. **Brunch**12.30-2.30pm Sun.
Dinner 7-11pm Mon-Thur; 7pm-midnight Fri; 6pm-
midnight Sat; 6-11pm Sun. **Average** $40. **Credit** AmEx,
MC, V.
Cowboy chic is one way to describe this Southwestern-
influenced haute spot located at the base of the recently
renovated Hotel Astor. Chef Johnny Vinczenz creates a
culinary frenzy with 'Caribbean Cowboy' dishes such as corn-
crusted snapper in a boniato mash, garlic pineapple chicken
and a shrimp 'martini' that's out of this world. Desserts aren't
shabby either: the Study of Chocolate is a must-have for all
chocoholics. Comfy booths, soothing lighting in a relaxed,
airy atmosphere makes this Place one of the beach's most
desirable. Soothe your hangover at Sunday brunch by paying penance with some Deviled Eggs from Hell.

Boulevard Bistro

*740 Ocean Drive, between Seventh & Eighth Streets,
South Beach (532 9069). Bus C, H, K, W.* **Breakfast**
9am-11am, **lunch** 11am-5pm, **dinner** 5pm-midnight,
daily. **Average** $35. **Credit** AmEx, DC, MC, V.
Don't be put off by the over-friendly hostess brandishing the
menu in the faces of passing pedestrians. She's just confident that what the Boulevard's got to offer is worth stopping
for. On a street where every seat is a good one, this café
boasts prime seating and an excellent Mediterranean-
influenced seafood menu. The warm goat's cheese salad – a
bed of arugula and endive mounted by a frisbee-sized, phyl-
lo dough-encrusted hunk of goat's cheese – is orgasmic.

Dab Haus

*852 Alton Road, between Eighth & Ninth Streets, South
Beach (534 9557). Bus F/M, S, W.* **Dinner** 4-11pm Mon-
Thur, Sun; 4pm-midnight Fri, Sat. **Average** $20. **Credit**
DC, MC, V.
Ale-house-cum-restaurant offering German beers and gar-
lic-heavy food such as wienerschnitzel, garlic soup and
honey-garlic baked brie.

Farfalla

*701 Washington Avenue, at Seventh Street, South Beach
(673 2335). Bus C, H, K, W.* **Dinner** 6pm-midnight,
Mon-Thur, Sun; 6pm-1am Fri, Sat. **Average** $25. **Credit**
AmEx, DC, MC, V.
A popular Aspen- and LA-based trattoria, Farfalla does well
in Miami with its wood-burning stove serving up excellent
pizzas and huge portions of pasta to a young, well-travelled
crowd. On Wednesday nights, unescorted women get free
meals; prepare to brave a mob.

Follia

*929 Washington Avenue, between Ninth & 10th Streets,
South Beach (674 9299). Bus C, H, K, W.* **Dinner** 6.30-
11pm Mon-Thur, Sun; 6.30pm-1am Fri, Sat. **Average**
$30. **Credit** AmEx, DC, Disc, MC, V.
After changing hands numerous times, this trendy Italian
restaurant finally solved its identity crisis by paying more
attention to its reputation as part of the club scene than to
its cuisine. Bouncers, not maitre d's, stand at the door await-
ing your arrival.

I Paparazzi

*Breakwater Hotel, 940 Ocean Drive, between Ninth &
10th Streets, South Beach (531 3500). Bus C, H, K, W.*
Breakfast 8am-noon, **lunch** noon-5pm, daily. **Dinner**
5-11.45pm Mon-Thur, Sun; 5pm-12.45am Fri, Sat.
Average $38. **Credit** AmEx, DC, MC, V.
Expensive and overrated Italian food is accepted at this popular Ocean Drive attraction because of its live music, which
has prompted the management to place velvet ropes on the
street to contain the pedestrian onlookers.

Larios on the Beach

*820 Ocean Drive, between Eighth & Ninth Streets, South
Beach (532 9577). Bus C, H, K, W.* **Open** 11.30am-
midnight Mon-Thur, Sun; 11.30am-2am Fri, Sat.
Average $27. **Credit** AmEx, DC, MC, V.
Miami's sweetheart Gloria Estefan may be a partner in this
Cuban eatery, but she's not the only reason that it is consis-
tently packed, with a wait of up to two hours at weekends.
The classic Cuban dishes get a so-so rating from the Cubans,
but a better one from those who aren't as fluent in the cui-
sine. Good music.

Mango's Tropical Café

*900 Ocean Drive, at Ninth Street, South Beach (673
4422). Bus C, H, K, W.* **Open** 11am-4am daily. **Average**
$15. **Credit** AmEx, Disc, MC, V.
After a few rum runners in this festive Caribbean-style café,
you won't care that the fare is just mediocre. Mango's is all
about atmosphere, with its loud, live, salsa music guaranteed to get even non-dancers out of their seats.

Mezzaluna

*834 Ocean Drive, between Eighth & Ninth Streets, South
Beach (674 1330). Bus C, H, K, W.* **Lunch** noon-4.30pm
Mon-Sun. **Dinner** 5pm-midnight Mon-Thur, Sun; 5pm-
1am Fri, Sat. **Average** $20. **Credit** AmEx, DC, MC, V.
The sidewalk tables at Mezzaluna, in whose LA branch Nicole
Brown Simpson ate her last meal, are rather cramped, so head
straight inside. Here you'll find a more relaxed setting beneath
the sky-painted fresco ceiling. The brick-oven pizzas, tagli-
olini with shrimp in a white wine sauce, and black linguine
with spicy sauce are all highly recommended.

*Order from an album cover menu at muso hangout the **Sushi Rock Café** (page 114).*

*Go funky and folksy at Haitian favourite **Tap Tap** (page 106).*

"Three things you should know, Love. The name's Mel. The drink's Tanqueray Sterling Vodka. And how unreasonable I can be if you forget the first two."

IMPORTED
Tanqueray
Sterling
VODKA

CHARLES TANQUERAY & C.O
LONDON, ENGLAND

Drink responsibly, Love.

Imported Vodka, 40% and 50% Alc./Vol. (80° and 100°), 100% Grain Neutral Spirits. ©1997 Schieffelin & Somerset Co., New York, N.Y.

Sumptuous pan-Asian food and celeb sightings pull 'em in at hip hotspot **China Grill** *(p105).*

Moe's Cantina

616 Collins Avenue, between Sixth & Seventh Streets, South Beach (532 6637). Bus C, H, K, W. **Dinner** 5pm-2am daily. **Average** $18. **Credit** AmEx, MC, V.
Though Pancho Villa may not have sipped his tequila here, supermodel Niki Taylor and a bevy of beautiful people have. Moe's is heavy on atmosphere – the only thing to remind you that you're still in South Beach and not Mexico are the model types who gather here in droves and even eat the (decent) food. Beware of roaming banditos in the form of shot girls who will harass everyone at your table until someone lets them pour tequila down their throat. Just make sure to chase it with some of Moe's spectacular salsa.

The Naked Earth

901 Pennsylvania Avenue, at Ninth Street, South Beach (531 2171). Bus C, H, K, W. **Open** noon-11pm Mon-Thur; noon-midnight Fri, Sat; noon-5pm Sun. **Average** $8. **Credit** MC, V.
Is it a lounge, a furniture store or a gallery? Well, The Naked Earth is many things but, most significantly, it is the only pure vegan restaurant on South Beach. Inexpensive.

News Café

800 Ocean Drive, at Eighth Street, South Beach (538 6397). Bus C, H, K, W. **Open** 24 hours daily. **Average** $25. **Credit** AmEx, DC, MC, V.
The place that practically invented the sport of South Beach people-watching, News Café is the reigning king of Ocean Drive. Whether you come by foot, blade, Harley or Ferrari, you should wait for an outside table, which is where you need to be to fully appreciate the News experience. Service is notoriously slow and often arrogant, but the menu, while not necessarily newsworthy, has some good bites, such as the Middle Eastern salad, fruit salad, hamburgers and omelettes. An extensive collection of national and international newspapers and mags from the in-house shop will keep you occupied while you wait. There's a branch in the Streets of Mayfair mall (2901 Florida Avenue) in Coconut Grove (774 6397).

The Official All Star Café

Edison Hotel, 960 Ocean Drive, between Ninth & 10th Streets, South Beach (531 2744). Bus C, H, K, W.
Based on the New York sports-themed restaurant of the same name, co-owned by athletic heavy hitters such as Monica Seles, Andre Agassi and Shaquille O' Neal, this new eatery is due to open in the autumn. The menu pays homage to sports food: wings, burgers and salads. The Pat Riley outdoor patio offers poolside dining and a sidewalk café.

Puerto Sagua

700 Collins Avenue, at Seventh Street, South Beach (673 1115). Bus C, H, K, W. **Open** 7.30am-2am daily.
Average $23. **Credit** AmEx, DC, MC, V.
Surrounded by trendy restaurants, this trad Cuban diner has been around forever, holding its own with paella-style chicken and rice, ham croquettes and pork chops. It's frequented by nocturnal creatures after a quick shot of energy-boosting Cuban coffee and a media noche before heading into the dawn.

Sport Café

538 Washington Avenue, between Fifth & Sixth Streets, South Beach (674 9700). Bus C, H, K, W. **Open** noon-1am daily. **Average** $25. **Credit** AmEx, Disc, MC, V.

Welcome to Florida.
Now hit a local attraction.
(smash crabs and feel great at The Crab House Seafood Restaurant)

Seriously Fresh Seafood.
79th Street Causeway, Miami (305) 868-7085.
8291 International Drive, Gooding's International Plaza (407) 352-6140.
8496 Palm Parkway, Vista Centre Shoppes (407) 239-1888.
Locations also in North Miami, Ft. Lauderdale, and Palm Beach

International
Agenda

The best weekly entertainment
listings from around the world

Amsterdam Berlin London Madrid New York Paris Prague
Every Wednesday in *Time Out*
Every Friday in *El País*
http://www.timeout.co.uk

The bean scene

As trendy a city as Miami is, there was one fad that took a while to catch on: coffeehouse chic, maybe because for decades, Cuban cafeterias have been pouring café cubano, café con leche and cortaditos to caffeine addicts used to stronger stuff and therefore uninterested in the burgeoning coffee craze. Unlike most other major cosmopolitan cities, Miami does not have a Starbucks on every corner, but that doesn't necessarily mean the city doesn't know its coffee.

Big Star Coffee

1259 Washington Avenue, between 12th & 13th Streets, South Beach (532 0012). Bus C, H, K, W. **Open** 7am-11pm Mon-Thur, Sun; 7am-1am Fri, Sat. **No credit cards**.
This small storefront coffee shop may lack the bohemian beat of Java Junkies (*see below*), but is a good stop for a quick latte, iced coffee or cigar before moving on. There are only one or two tables outside and inside is kind of tight, but if you've got time to spare, hang out and watch the body beautifuls grab their shots of espresso before they head upstairs to the popular Club Body Tech gym.

The Coffee Beanery

638 Collins Avenue, between Sixth & Seventh Streets, South Beach (674 8829). Bus C, H, K, W. **Open** 7.30am-midnight Mon-Fri; 8am-midnight Sat, Sun. **Credit** AmEx, DC, MC, V.
A touch of Seattle grunge hits South Beach and Sunny Isles in the form of this coffeehouse, specialising in hazelnut coffees and frozen coffee concoctions. Board games, newspapers and magazines aplenty.

Coffee Buzz

731 Lincoln Road, between Euclid & Meridian Avenues, South Beach (672 6908). Bus C, G, K, L, S. **Open** 9am-11pm Mon-Thur, Sun; 9am-midnight Fri, Sat. **No credit cards**.
The latest caffeine buzz house on the Road.

Java Centrale

2334 Ponce de Leon Boulevard, at Aragon Avenue, Coral Gables (569 3083). Bus 24, 37, 40. **Open** 6.30am-11pm Mon-Fri; 7am-11.30pm Sat; 8am-11.30pm Sun. **Credit** MC, V.
With bright lights and a chilly atmosphere, this is the coffee version of fast food, serving light meals and okay coffee. Not somewhere you'd really want to hang around while writing your novel.

Java Junkies

1446 Washington Avenue, at Espanola Way, South Beach (674 7854). Bus C, H, K, W. **Open** 7am-5am daily. **Credit** AmEx, DC, Disc, MC, V.
Java Junkies is possibly the closest thing to an authentic coffeehouse in a city that, oddly, has yet to succumb to a trend that has overtaken the nation. People tend to linger here for hours, making it difficult to secure a table.

Joffrey's

3434 Main Highway, at Fuller Street, Coconut Grove (448 0848). Bus 42, 48. **Open** 7am-midnight Mon-Thur, Sun; 8am-2am Fri, Sat. **Credit** (over $5) AmEx, DC, MC, V.
This chain-operated coffeehouse brews a flavourful array of gourmet coffees and features a luscious assortment of cakes and pastries guaranteed to keep you coming back for more. With an airy interior and plenty of tables outside, Joffrey's is a big winner among walkers, bikers, rollerbladers and slackers alike.
Branch: 660 Lincoln Road, South Beach (673 5474).

Luna

775 NE 125th Street, between NE Seventh & Eighth Avenues, North Miami (892 8522). Bus 10, 75, G. **Open** 10am-midnight Mon-Thur; 10am-1am Fri, Sat; noon-midnight Sun. **No credit cards**.
This arty coffeehouse (we love the barbershop chair) right across from the Museum of Contemporary Art provides the perfect environment for discussing the exhibition you've just seen. Ask for espresso or cappuccino made with caffeinated water for extra zing.

The décor's not fancy and the outdoor seating overlooks a parking lot, but you don't go to Sport Café for the scenery, but for the authentic, cheap, home-made Italian food. If you're fortunate enough to visit when the owner's mother is in town, make sure to sample the home-made lasagna or gnocchi.

Thai Toni

890 Washington Avenue, at Ninth Street, South Beach (538 8424). Bus C, H, K, W. **Dinner** 5.30-11pm Mon-Thur, Sun; 5.30pm-midnight Fri, Sat. **Average** $25. **Credit** AmEx, MC, V.
Toni of Toni's Sushi (*see below*) had the vision to open the first Thai restaurant in the district. Good service and fresh ingredients are a plus, as are the comfy, high-backed chairs – but if you like spicy, say so, as most dishes tend to be mild.

16th Street & below

Allioli

Cardozo Hotel, 1300 Ocean Drive, at 13th Street, South Beach (538 0553). Bus C, H, K, W. **Breakfast** 6am-11am daily. **Open** 11am-11.30pm Mon-Fri, Sun; 11am-1am Sat. **Average** $35. **Credit** AmEx, DC, Disc, MC, V.

Euro-Mediterranean meets South Beach deco at Gloria Estefan's second Ocean Drive eatery, named after the Spanish word for garlic mayonnaise. Located at the legendary Cardozo Hotel, used in the film *Birdcage*, Allioli's cool, ambient Spanish music, assortment of tapas and paellas and gorgeous modern interior make for excellent dining.

Charlotte's Chinese Kitchen

1403 Washington Avenue, between 14th Street & Espanola Way, South Beach (672 8338). Bus C, H, K, W. **Lunch** noon-3pm Mon-Sun. **Dinner** 3-11pm Mon-Thur, Sun; 3pm-12.30am Fri, Sat. **Average** $25. **Credit** MC, V.
Finding good Chinese food in Miami is about as easy as finding snow. Charlotte's comes close, but not close enough, with a basic Szechuan menu and divey, hole-in-the-wall space that puts diners off. Take out instead, or try the newer branch.
Branch: 744 41st Street, Miami Beach (535 1555).

Chrysanthemum

1248 Washington Avenue, between 12th & 13th Streets, South Beach (531 5656). Bus C, H, K, W. **Dinner** 6-11pm Tue-Thur, Sun; 6pm-midnight Fri, Sat. **Average** $30. **Credit** AmEx, DC, MC, V.

Gourmet sarnies aren't just for cissies at **Le Sandwicherie.**

Not exactly an eat-out-of-the-container Chinese restaurant, Chrysanthemum puts a gourmet spin on Szechuan and Pekinese cuisines with innovative and delicious items such as the wonton ravioli appetiser in spicy ginger and garlic sauce, steamed whole fish in ginger and scallion sauce, and basil shrimp with snow peas.

11th Street Diner

1065 Washington Avenue, between 10th & 11th Streets, South Beach (534 6373). Bus C, H, K, W. **Open** 24 hours Mon, Wed-Sun; 1am Tue-8am Wed. **Average** $15. **Credit** AmEx, DC, MC, V.
The original 1948 structure of this diner was dismantled and shipped down from Wilkes Barre, Pennsylvania, of all places, and set up on the corner of busy 11th Street. This popular round-the-clock spot attracts a motley crew of celebrities, club kids and curious tourists and is famous for its slow service but above-average diner fare.

Escopazzo

1311 Washington Avenue, between 13th & 14th Streets, South Beach (674 9450). Bus C, H, K, W. **Dinner** 6pm-midnight Mon-Thur; 6pm-1am Fri, Sat; 6-11pm Sun. **Average** $30. **Credit** AmEx, DC, MC, V.
The name may mean 'crazy' but the only sign of insanity here is the fact that there are only 15 tables to accommodate the steady following of die-hard fans who consider Escopazzo's Italian fare to be primo. Dim lighting, home-made risotto de journo, excellent pasta and doting service justify the slightly expensive prices.

The Frieze Ice Cream Factory

1626 Michigan Avenue, at 16th Street, South Beach (538 0207). Bus C, G, K, L, S. **Open** noon-midnight Mon-Thur, Sun; noon-1am Fri, Sat. **Average** $3. **No credit cards.**
If you're gonna blow your diet and skip the sugar-free, fat-free, frozen yogurt for the real thing, you'll want to do it here, where the ice-cream is home-made and imported by some of the area's top restaurants. The usual flavours are a safe bet, but the adventurous can try unusual ones such as tomato.

Front Porch Café

1420 Ocean Drive, between 14th & 15th Streets, South Beach (531 8300). Bus C, H, K, W. **Open** 8am-10.30pm daily. **Average** $13. **Credit** AmEx, DC, Disc, MC, V.
One of the quainter and less posey spots on Ocean Drive, Front Porch is the preferred breakfast and lunch venue among locals looking for good food and service sans attitude. Enjoy homestyle French toast with bananas and walnuts, omelettes, fresh fruit salads and pizzas and classic breakfast pancakes (with bacon and syrup if you're feeling really decadent). Breakfast is served whenever you want it.

Grillfish

1444 Collins Avenue, at Espanola Way, South Beach (538 9908). Bus C, H, K, W. **Dinner** 6-11pm Mon-Thur, Sun; 6pm-midnight Fri, Sat. **Average** $25. **Credit** AmEx, DC, MC, V.
With not much pomp and circumstance, this place has proved its staying power by serving simple but super-fresh seafood (grilled, sautéd or over pasta) at very reasonable prices in an unpretentious yet stylish setting.

Le Sandwicherie

229 14th Street, between Collins & Washington Avenues, South Beach (532 8934). Bus C, H, K, W. **Open** 10am-4am Mon-Thur, Sun; 10am-5am Fri, Sat. **Average** $6. **No credit cards.**
Open until the crack of dawn, Le Sandwicherie is South Beach's only gourmet sandwich bar, catering to the tattoo artists who work next door – that's Emerson on the picture above – hungry clubbers, limo drivers and anybody else who likes a good ham, turkey, tuna or veggie sandwich with or without eight or so toppings served on freshly baked French bread or a croissant.

Lulu's

1053 Washington Avenue, between 10th & 11th Streets, South Beach (532 6147). Bus C, H, K, W. **Open** 11am-midnight Mon-Thur; 11am-1am Fri, Sat. **Average** $25. **Credit** MC, V.

Any Miami Elvis sightings are likely to occur here, in the kitschest soulfood joint this side of Memphis. After chowing down on fried chicken or a fried peanut butter and banana sandwich (Elvis' fave), head upstairs to the shrine built to the King.

Maiko Japanese Restaurant & Sushi Bar
1255 Washington Avenue, between 12th & 13th Streets, South Beach (531 6369). Bus C, H, K, W. **Lunch** noon-3pm daily. **Dinner** 6pm-midnight Mon-Thur; 5pm-2.30am Fri, Sat. **Average** $28. **Credit** AmEx, DC, MC, V.
One of the first Japanese restaurants to hit the Beach, Maiko recognises that trendoids can tire of sushi by offering wonderfully prepared teriyakis, tempuras and yakisobas, as well as fresh sushi rolls.

Mezzanotte
1200 Washington Avenue, at 12th Street, South Beach (673 4343). Bus C, H, K, W. **Dinner** 6pm-midnight Mon-Thur, Sun; 6pm-2am Fri, Sat. **Average** $40. **Credit** AmEx, DC, Disc, MC, V.
You don't go to Mezzanotte for a quiet, romantic Italian meal but for a bacchanalian feast. The loud music often provokes patrons to get up and dance on the tables; before you scoff, you may find yourself doing the table hustle, too, since your food won't be arriving anytime soon. After building up a raging appetite from all that dancing, reward yourself with a fabulous risotto al porcini, gnocchi bolognesa or osso bucco.
Branch: 3390 Mary Street, Coconut Grove (448 7677).

Miami Subs
1101 Washington Avenue, at 11th Street, South Beach (534 2838). Bus C, H, K, W. **Open** 10am-3am daily. **Average** $6. **Credit** AmEx, Disc, MC, V.
The only fast-food sub shop to offer Dom Perignon, Miami Subs' good spicy fries and an attached Baskin Robbins make this Florida chain a popular one with the on-the-go crowd. Open until the wee hours, Miami Subs is also a hangout for bored teenagers who lack the fake IDs required to get them into the local clubs.

Osteria del Teatro
1443 Washington Avenue, at Espanola Way, South Beach (538 7850). Bus C, H, K, W. **Dinner** 6pm-midnight Mon, Wed, Thur, Sun; 6pm-1am Fri, Sat. **Average** $45. **Credit** AmEx, DC, MC, V.
So what if the beach's best, albeit priciest, Italian restaurant is located directly under the mangy Cameo Theatre? With panoramic windows facing a busy intersection and divine cuisine, it's worth every penny.

Pucci's Pizza
1447 Washington Avenue, between 15th Street & Espanola Way, South Beach (673 8133). Bus C, H, K, W. **Open** noon-5am daily. **Average** $5. **No credit cards.**
You may think the people lining up on Washington Avenue are waiting to get into a club, but think again. They're all waiting to satiate their cravings for the beach's closest thing to New York pizza. Slices are slinging till the small hours, and for the weight-conscious there's even a low-fat version.
Branch: 651 Washington Avenue, South Beach (673 8177).

Royal Canadian Pancake House
1216 Washington Avenue, between 12th & 13th Streets, South Beach (604 9983). Bus C, H, K, W. **Open** 4.30am-10pm Mon, Fri-Sun; 7am-10pm Tue-Thur. **Average** $10. **Credit** MC, V.
Whoever said size doesn't matter obviously never dined in this pancake house, whose motto is 'pancakes make people happy'. Not graduates from the Aunt Jemima school of pancakes, these come in gourmet flavours such as chocolate chip and banana. It's one size fits all, and that size is massive: one order is enough for two. Don't fill up on the complimentary chocolate chip cornbread before trying the trademarked 'womlette', a hybrid of a waffle and an omelette.

Cuisine to go

Whether you're sick of room service or don't feel like dressing to the nines just to eat a good meal, there are plenty of local services that will bring the food to you for a small charge. There's even one that will bring a waiter to serve you in bed. Ask your concierge if they have a copy of the service's menu guide or *We Deliver* magazine or call the service directly. A word to the impatient and the starving: these services often take longer than it would for you to get dressed and get the food yourself.

A la Car (892 2226): This service exists in South Beach and the nobby Aspen, Colorado, so you know it's gotta be good. Local delivery from some of the best restaurants in South Beach, Miami, North Miami and North Miami Beach. $15 minimum order, $3.99 for delivery within the same area; outside your area, the charge is 20% of the food total.

Entree Express (447 3783): The premier delivery service. Food from high-end restaurants and special services such as dinner in bed or outdoors, waiter service and special requests. For dessert: hard-to-find tickets to sold-out area events. Prices vary.

Teledine (672 3463): Delivery from popular Miami Beach restaurants to South Beach, Mid-Beach, North Beach, Downtown, Brickell, Surfside and Bal Harbour until midnight. Delivery $3.50-$10 depending on where you are; five per cent discount for cash.

Telephone Take-Out (466 9300): Food from 28 table service restaurants in the Aventura area delivered to anywhere from Hollywood Beach Boulevard to Bal Harbour. $3 delivery charge.

San Loco Tacos
235 14th Street, between Collins & Washington Avenues, South Beach (538 3009). Bus C, H, K, W. **Open** 11am-5am Mon-Thur, Sun; 11am-6am Fri, Sat. **Average** $7. **No credit cards.**
Home-made burritos, tacos, quesadillas and enchiladas: real good, real cheap, real fast.

Spiga
Hotel Impala, 1228 Collins Avenue, between 12th & 13th Streets, Miami Beach (534 0079). Bus C, H, K, W. **Dinner** 6pm-midnight daily. **Average** $20. **Credit** AmEx, DC, Disc, MC, V.
A quiet favourite with locals and luminaries who want to enjoy a fantastic meal free of South Beach hype, this intimate Italian restaurant is elegant and unpretentious, concentrating on food rather than fanfare. Once the bruschetta with grilled eggplant is brought to the table, it is evident that Spigais in a different class. The garlicky gnocchi with tomato and basil is an incredible illustration of how simple doesn't mean bland. The pungent gorgonzola polenta appetiser is a meal in itself, and risotto with bay scallops is excellent.

Sushi Hana
1131 Washington Avenue, between 11th & 12th Streets, South Beach (532 1100). Bus C, H, K, W. **Dinner** 5pm-1am Mon-Thur; 5pm-2am Fri, Sat. **Average** $25. **Credit** AmEx, DC, Disc, MC, V.

What's the squeeze?

More popular than coffeehouses are juice bars. Here's the juice on some of Miami's most popular thirst-quenchers:

Athens Juice Bar

6976 Collins Avenue, between 69th & 70th Streets, Miami Beach (861 2143). Bus G, H, J, L, S. **Open** 8am-7pm Mon-Sat; 11am-5pm Sun. **Credit** MC, V.
Freshly squeezed juices, fruit salads.
Branch: 1214 Washington Avenue, South Beach (672 4648).

Hollywood Juice Bar

704 Lincoln Road, between Euclid & Meridian Avenues, South Beach (538 8988). Bus C, G, K, L, S. **Open** noon-9pm Mon-Thur, Sun; noon-10pm Fri, Sat. **Credit** MC, V.
Shakes heavy on berries, bananas and vitamins.

Smoothie King

1525 Alton Road, at 15th Street, South Beach (672 6595). Bus F/M, S. **Open** 9am-9pm Mon-Sat; 10am-9pm Sun. **Credit** AmEx, MC, V.
Popular with the power-lifting set.
Branch: 1232 S Dixie Highway, Coral Gables (669 0013).

South Beach Smoothie

1229 Washington Avenue, between 12th & 13th Streets, South Beach (531 5633). Bus C, H, K, W. **Open** 10am-11pm Mon-Sat; 11am-9pm Sun. **No credit cards.**
Highest-quality, all-fruit, no-preservative shakes, with or without pure vitamin supplements
Branch: 1549 Sunset Drive, South Miami (666 2153).

Joining the abundance of sushi houses in the Beach area, Sushi Hana is considered by many to be one of the best. That's debatable, but the place is always packed, open late and reasonably priced.

Sushi Rock Café

1351 Collins Avenue, between 13th & 14th Streets, South Beach (532 2133). Bus C, H, K, W. **Lunch** noon-3pm, **dinner** 5pm-midnight, daily. **Average** $28. **Credit** AmEx, DC, MC, V.
Almost every rock star who comes to town stops at Sushi Rock for a quick fix (Aerosmith's Steven Tyler and Joe Perry ate here almost nightly during their Miami recording sessions and David Lee Roth drowned his post-Van Halen sorrows in saké many a night).This sushi house rocks with its fresh assortment of sushi, hand rolls and traditional Japanese cuisine, funky atmosphere and hip, late-night crowd. The only sushi house where you can trade your Peter Frampton album-cover menu for a Donna Summer one over a Madonna Roll.

Thai House

1137 Washington Avenue, between 11th & 12th Streets, South Beach (531 4841). Bus C, H, K, W. **Lunch** noon-3.30pm Mon-Fri. **Dinner** 5-11.30pm Mon-Fri; 4-11.30pm Sat, Sun. **Average** $23. **Credit** AmEx, MC, V.

Average to good Thai food served on an excellent strip of Washington Avenue. Enjoy tasty favourites such as pad thai, sautéed chicken in chilli paste, sweet and sour vegetables and shrimp curry while observing the inebriated parade of bar hoppers stumbling on their way.

Tita's

1445 Pennsylvania Avenue, at Espanola Way, South Beach (535 2497). Bus C, H, K, W. **Dinner** 6.30-11pm Mon-Thur, Sun; 6.30pm-midnight Fri, Sat. **Average** $20. **Credit** AmEx, DC, MC, V.
Hidden on the remote corner of Pennsylvania Avenue and Espanola Way, this industrial-chic Southwestern haunt has acquired a reputation for excellent food at great prices. A tortilla stuffed with cactus, roasted garlic and spinach, and fish in blue cornmeal are a couple of the innovative offerings.

Toni's New Tokyo Cuisine & Sushi Bar

1208 Washington Avenue, at 12th Street, South Beach (673 9368). Bus C, H, K, W. **Dinner** 6pm-1am Mon-Thur, Sun; 6pm-1am Fri, Sat. **Average** $30. **Credit** AmEx, MC, V.
The granddaddy of all South Beach sushi establishments, Toni's has been serving some of the freshest fish around for 10 years. Despite its late 1980s neon lighting and pricey menu, many swear by this place.

Lincoln Road & above

The Beehive

630A Lincoln Road, between Pennsylvania & Euclid Avenues, South Beach (538 7484). Bus C, G, K, L, S. **Open** noon-midnight daily. **Average** $20. **Credit** AmEx, DC, MC, V.
Lincoln Road's diner offers an eclectic menu in a friendly atmosphere. Choose from specialities such as baby back honey-barbecued ribs or blue cheese pizza with ham. Outdoor tables are usually full, but that doesn't mean you have to sit in the less-than-atmospheric inside. Ask to sit in the secluded but serene courtyard, and visit the loungey back bar.

Blue Door

Delano Hotel, 1685 Collins Avenue, at 17th Street, South Beach (672 2000). Bus C, G, H, L, S. **Breakfast** 7am-11am Mon-Sun. **Lunch** 11.30-3pm Mon-Sun. **Dinner** 7pm-midnight Mon-Thur, Sun; 7pm-1am Fri, Sat. **Average** $50. **Credit** AmEx, DC, MC, V.
Smack dab in the middle of the linen-draped lobby of Ian Schrager's so-chic-it-hurts Delano Hotel, the Blue Door is one to visit if you enjoy seeing and being seen. But the main viewing, er, dining area isn't the only option. There's also a kitchen area in the lobby with a long buffet table bearing an impressive gourmet lunch and, during cocktail hour, a sleek champagne and caviar bar; the Blue Door also extends its service out on the verandah. The contemporary US cuisine is unusual (swordfish with green-apple reduction), but not the main reason people don their best Armanis and scramble for a table. Hint: Madonna was once part-owner and you may witness a virtual who's who in fashion and entertainment.

Café Papillon

530 Lincoln Road, between Drexel & Pennsylvania Avenues, South Beach (673 1139). Bus C, G, K, L, S. **Open** 8am-midnight daily. **Average** $15. **Credit** AmEx, DC, MC, V.
Yet another Euro-style café, Café Papillon is known mostly for its gourmet coffees and decadent cakes imported from Italy, but it also offers some great sandwiches, including goat's cheese, grilled eggplant and roasted peppers on focaccia and a biscotti cookie with each coffee ordered.

Da Leo Trattoria

819 Lincoln Road, between Jefferson & Meridian Avenues, South Beach (674 0350). Bus C, G, K, L, S. **Dinner** 6-11pm daily. **Average** $22. **Credit** AmEx, DC, MC, V.

Another restaurant popular more for its prices and locale (bang in the middle of Lincoln Road Mall) than for its food, Da Leo prides itself on its Italian authenticity with basic home-style pasta and meat dishes. It has a more informal pizzeria across the road called Pizza e Via Da Leo

Lincoln Road Café

941 Lincoln Road, at Michigan Avenue, South Beach (538 8066). Bus C, G, K, L, S. **Open** 8am-midnight daily. **Average** $10. **Credit** AmEx, Disc, MC, V.
A locals' favourite, this down-to-earth Cuban-accented café is very popular for its cheap breakfasts. For $4.85, you can indulge in a hearty portion of eggs any style with bacon, ham or sausage. Lunch and dinner specials are delicious and also cheap; try the ubiquitous rice and beans or a chicken fricassee with plantains. Live music is an occasional perk.

Lucky Cheng's

600 Lincoln Road, at Pennsylvania Avenue, South Beach (672 1505). Bus C, G, K, L, S. **Breakfast** 10am-3pm, **lunch** 11.30am-5pm, daily. **Dinner** 7-11pm Mon-Thur, Sun; 7pm-midnight Fri, Sat. **Average** $30. **Credit** AmEx, DC, MC, V.
Planet Hollywood's got nothing on Lucky Cheng's as far as glitz, glamour and beautiful women are concerned. But there's a catch. The beautiful waitresses are actually men in drag. With two successful establishments in New York and New Orleans, there was no way this place could avoid South Beach, a mecca for men who like to dress up. The Thai-Chinese cuisine, however, is rather unremarkable. Stick to the bar, have a mai-tai and check out the drag show.

Norma's on the Beach

646 Lincoln Road, between Pennsylvania & Euclid Avenues, South Beach (532 2809). Bus C, G, K, L, S. **Lunch** noon-3pm Tue-Sun. **Dinner** 6-11pm Tue-Thur; 6pm-midnight Fri, Sat; 5.30-10.30pm Sun. **Average** $35. **Credit** AmEx, DC, Disc, MC, V.
Why jet off to Jamaica for the finest Caribbean ingredients when they are flown straight to Norma's? The offspring of two acclaimed restaurants in Jamaica, Norma's cooks up island specialities such as Beggar's Purse, sautéed ground sirloin, mushrooms, peas and onions topped with gorgonzola mashed potatoes, Rasta Chicken, chicken with callaloo and, of course, jerk pork, tuna and chicken wings. With entrées $16-$32, it's not cheap, but at least it saves you the airfare.

Pacific Time

915 Lincoln Road, between Jefferson & Michigan Avenues, South Beach (534 5979). Bus C, G, K, L, S. **Dinner** 6-11pm Mon-Thur, Sun; 6pm-midnight Fri, Sat. **Average** $40. **Credit** AmEx, DC, MC, V.
A Lincoln Road standout, Pacific Time is nationally acclaimed as a leader in Pacific Rim cuisine – a fusion of Chinese, Japanese and Thai that is a blissful assault on the senses. Chef/proprietor (and former model) Jonathan Eismann cooks up Vietnamese warm batter-dipped bananas, saké roasted sea bass, wok sautéd yellowfin tuna and a chocolate bomb (baked to order), all of which are guaranteed to take you into a time zone that's out of this world.

South Beach Brasserie

910 Lincoln Road, at Jefferson Avenue, South Beach (534 5511). Bus C, G, K, L, S. **Lunch** 11.30am-4pm, **tea** 4-6pm, daily. **Dinner** 6-11pm Mon-Thur, Sun; 6pm-1am Fri, Sat. **Average** $40. **Credit** AmEx, DC, Disc, MC, V.
Before you vow not to check out another celebrity-owned restaurant, head to actor Michael Caine's latest triumph. Housed in a former Jehovah's Witness Temple, this is the only place on South Beach where you can order something called bangers (sausages to you anglophobes) and still feel elegant. With its British and 'Mediterr-asian' accents, everything here – escargot, chopped salad, linguine with prawns, grilled ahi tuna – is just smashing.

Where to find the best

Best chic eats
Astor Place (South Beach)
China Grill (South Beach)
Savannah (South Beach)
The Forge (Mid-Beach)
The Blue Door (South Beach)
Nemo (South Beach)

Best for brunch
Astor Place (South Beach)
The Forge (Mid-Beach)
Grand Café (Coconut Grove)
Nemo (South Beach)
Sunday's on the Bay (Key Biscayne)

Best for people-watching
Blue Door (South Beach)
11th Street Diner (South Beach)
The Forge (Mid-Beach)
News Café (South Beach)
Van Dyke Café (Lincoln Road)

Best for waterside-dining
Big Fish (Downtown)
Monty's (Coconut Grove)
Rusty Pelican (Virginia Key)
Shooter's (North Miami Beach)
Sunday's on the Bay (Key Biscayne)

Best for celeb-spotting
Blue Door (South Beach): Calvin Klein, David Geffen, Kate Moss, Johnny Depp.
China Grill (South Beach): You name it, they've been here. Christy's: Rod Stewart, George Bush.
The Forge (Mid-Beach): kd lang, Quentin Tarantino, Billy Baldwin, Oliver Stone.
Nemo (South Beach): Antonio Sabato Jr, Steve Guttenberg, Joan Lunden.
Savannah (South Beach): Oprah Winfrey

Van Dyke Café

846 Lincoln Road, at Jefferson Avenue, South Beach (534 3600). Bus C, G, K, L. **Open** 8am-1am Mon-Thur, Sun; 8am-2am Fri, Sat. **Average** $20. **Credit** AmEx, DC, MC, V.
News Café's two-floor Lincoln Road offshoot may be jazzier, but otherwise it's not much different from the original. A major people-watching outpost, Van Dyke has a nearly identical menu to that of its Ocean Drive sibling, but its warm, wood-floored interior, jazz bar, accessible parking and an intense chocolate soufflé make it a less frenzied alternative.

Wolfie's

2038 Collins Avenue, at 20th Street, South Beach (538 6626). Bus C, G, H, L, S. **Open** 24 hours daily. **Average** $20. **Credit** DC, MC, V.
Mobster Meyer Lansky had a booth here and when Frank Sinatra and his Rat Pack played the Marco Polo Hotel, they'd always stop at this beach landmark/deli. Despite less than stellar food (the pickles on the table probably date from the same era), Wolfie's is still a popular 24-hour dining option. If you're lucky, you'll get a waiter or waitress who'll reminisce about the old days over a cup of coffee.

World Resources

*719 Lincoln Road, between Euclid & Meridian Avenues,
South Beach (535 8987). Bus C, G, K, L, S.* **Open** noon-
11pm daily. **Average** $25. **Credit** AmEx, DC, Disc, MC, V.
It's too bad the people behind this Thai restaurant-cum-fur-
niture gallery weren't as resourceful with the sometimes
disappointing food as with the concept. The inside tables are
surrounded by antiques, art and furniture from all corners
of the globe (all for sale), outdoor seating is plentiful and
there's usually live music of various ethnicities. For a sweet
tooth, the Thai iced coffee is a perfect alternative for dessert.

Yuca

*501 Lincoln Road, at Drexel Avenue, South Beach (532
9822). Bus C, G, K, L, S.* **Lunch** noon-4pm Mon-Sat;
1-5pm Sun. **Dinner** 6-11pm Mon-Thur; 6pm-midnight
Fri, Sat; 5-11pm Sun. **Average** $45. **Credit** AmEx, DC,
Disc, MC, V.
With a name that stands for Young Upscale Cuban
Americans, it's no wonder that this restaurant's high-priced
Nuevo Cubano cuisine has earned Yuca both rave reviews
from gourmands and scoffs from old-world purists who consider it a travesty to pay top dollar for sweet plantains
stuffed with dried cured beef, even if it does come in a fancy
presentation. Less heavy on the grease and the pocketbook
is the upstairs club, where Albita, 'the Cuban kd lang', and
other performers give you a hearty show that's well worth
the outrageous $25 plus two-drink minimum cover charge.

Mid-Beach

Arnie & Richie's

*525 41st Street, between Prairie & Royal Palm Avenues,
Miami Beach (531 7691). Bus C, F/M, J, K, T.* **Open**
6am-9pm Mon-Thur, Sun; 6am-6pm Sat. **Average** $15.
Credit AmEx, MC, V.
Corned beef on rye, chicken soup, salami and other cold cuts
and Jewish favourites at this popular New York-style deli.

The Forge

*432 41st Street, between Royal Palm & Sheridan
Avenues, Miami Beach (538 8533). Bus C, F/M, J, K, T.*
Brunch noon-3pm Sun. **Dinner** 6pm-midnight daily.
Average $40. **Credit** AmEx, DC, MC, V.
Local legend has it that Al Capone is alive and well in this
restaurant's acclaimed wine cellar. A rococo-lover's fantasy,
The Forge is a multi-chambered, ornately decorated (and
priced) monument known for its decadent wines, steak and
fish. There is a spa menu for the calorie-conscious, who may
choose to work out by touring the wine cellar (ask your waiter). Wednesday nights are raucous: the who's who of Miami
gather for a dinner/dancing/schmoozing scene that's a weekly ritual for the rhinestoned, gold-laméd, gregarious set.

The Oasis Café

*976 41st Street, at Alton Road, Miami Beach (674
7676). Bus C, F/M, J, K, T.* **Open** 11am-10pm Mon-
Thur; 11am-11pm Fri, Sat; 5-10pm Sun. **Average** $15.
Credit AmEx, MC, V.
Mid Beach's secret hideaway, offering huge Middle Eastern
platters at reasonable prices.

Pan Coast

*Indian Creek Hotel, 2727 Indian Creek Drive, between
27th & 28th Streets, Miami Beach (531 2727 ext 353).
Bus C, F/M, G, H, L.* **Breakfast** 7-11.30am Mon-Fri;
8am-noon Sat, Sun. **Dinner** 6-11pm Mon, Wed-Sun.
Average $35. **Credit** AmEx, DC, Disc, MC, V.
Nestled in a cosy-chic room and Napa-Valley-ish patio off
the lobby of this quaint hotel, the Pan Coast restaurant is
unassuming, but its Pacific Rim gusto is wonderfully lavish.
Hailing from the prestigious Cordon Bleu school in London,
Chef Mary Rohan is a whizz, especially when it comes to

shellfish and overall presentation. Scallop wontons in a pungent ginger sauce,tempura shrimp with mustard miso sauce,
guava soy barbecue pork tenderloin are all as pretty as they
are delicious; Space Age loungey music and a celestial chocolate espresso cake will have you reaching Nirvana.

North Beach

Café Prima Pasta

*414 71st Street, between Byron & Collins Avenues,
Miami Beach (867 0106). Bus L, K, R.* **Lunch** noon-
2.30pm Mon-Sat. **Dinner** 6-11pm Mon-Thur, Sun; 6pm-
midnight Fri, Sat. **Average** $25. **No credit cards**.
A bright spot on a dingy street, this tiny café's home-made
pastas pack 'em in, with crowds of carbo-hungry people
spilling out onto the sidewalk. The scent of the garlic and oil
dip wafting outside makes the wait bearable.

Lemon Twist

*908 71st Street, between Rue Bordeaux & Bay Drive,
Miami Beach (868 2075). Bus L.* **Dinner** 6pm-midnight
daily. **Average** $18. **Credit** AmEx, MC, V.
Marinated olives in garlic and oil begin your journey into
North Beach's newest, hippest Mediterranean eatery and a
complimentary shot of the eponymous house spirit will complete it. In between, expect congenial service and excellent
pasta and meat dishes at terrific prices.

Surfside to Golden Beach

Coco's Sidewalk Café

*9700 Collins Avenue, at 97th Street, Bal Harbour (864
2626). Bus G, H, J, S, T.* **Open** 11.30am-8.30pm daily.
Average $25. **Credit** AmEx, MC, V.
Like its fellow Bal Harbour shops, this café is scenic but its
prices obscene. Save your money for couture and stick to cuisine – pizza, salads, meatloaf, grilled chicken – elsewhere.

The Rascal House

*17190 Collins Avenue, at 171st Street, Sunny Isles (947
4581). Bus E, K, S, V.* **Open** 24 hours daily. **Average**
$15. **Credit** AmEx, MC, V.
Queuing at this landmark deli can be quite time-consuming,
but never dull as the cacophony of New York, Boston and
Chicago accents will keep you entertained until you're seated
in an ancient 1950s vinyl booth, where a waitress pushing
70 will bring you classic corned beef, brisket or potato pancakes and, if you're lucky, a doggy bag to wrap up the rolls
and danish left in your complimentary bread basket.

Key Biscayne

Linda B's Steakhouse

*320 Crandon Boulevard, Key Biscayne (361 1111). Bus
B.* **Dinner** 5.30pm-midnight daily. **Average** $25. **Credit**
AmEx, DC, MC, V.
The steaks here are right out of the *Flintstones*: giant. But
there's nothing prehistoric about this paean to prime rib and
porterhouse. The service is excellent, the décor light and airy.

Rusty Pelican

*3201 Rickenbacker Causeway, Virginia Key (361 3818).
Bus B.* **Lunch** 11.30am-4pm daily. **Dinner** 5-11pm Mon-
Thur, Sun; 5pm-midnight Fri, Sat. **Average** $25. **Credit**
AmEx, DC, Disc, MC, V.
With breathtaking views of the city skyline, the Rusty
Pelican is a wonderful and romantic place if you're in the
mood for five-star atmosphere rather than food, which in this
case is unimpressive. Instead, have a few drinks, enjoy the
views and head somewhere else to eat.

The stilettos are out at quirky Downtown favourite **Big Fish**.

Sunday's on the Bay

5420 Crandon Boulevard, Key Biscayne (361 6777). Bus B. **Lunch** 11.30am-5pm Mon-Sat. **Brunch** 10.30am-3.30pm Sun. **Dinner** 5pm-2am Mon-Wed, Sun; 5pm-2.30am Thur-Sat. **Average** $25. **Credit** AmEx, DC, MC, V.
A semi-smart place to kick back, relax and enjoy the view amid the sounds of local reggae and islands-influenced bands. The seafood-oriented menu is decent, but can't compare with the magnificent waterfront sunsets. Best for Sunday brunch.

Downtown Miami

Big Fish

55 SW Miami Avenue Road, off N Miami Avenue & SW Sixth Street, Downtown (373 1770). Bus 6, 8. **Open** 11am-11pm daily. **Average** $25. **Credit** AmEx, MC, V.
This unassuming seafood shack on the Miami River is definitely a big fish in the little pond of Downtown restaurants. Featuring a spectacular waterside setting, Big Fish has a corking view of the Miami skyline and some of the freshest catches around, including lobster, shrimp and grouper and shrimp. Its paella (for two) takes half an hour to cook up but is well worth the wait. This place can be hard to find. Cross Brickell Avenue Bridge, heading south, and take the first right (SW Fifth Street). The road narrows under a bridge; the restaurant is just on the other side.

Capital Grille

444 Brickell Avenue, at SE Fourth Street, Downtown (374 4500). Bus 95/Metromover Knight Center. **Lunch** 11am-3pm Mon-Fri. **Dinner** 5-10pm Mon-Thur, Sun; 5-11pm Fri, Sat. **Average** $40. **Credit** AmEx, DC, Disc, MC, V.
Located on the Capital Hill of Miami's business movers and shakers, Capital Grille is the quintessential location for a power lunch, dinner or cocktail. Like the conversations that occur here, the food is quite heavy, with beef sirloin, filet mignon and prime rib among the offerings.

East Coast Fisheries

360 W Flagler Street, at N River Drive, Downtown (372 1300). Bus 11, 77. **Open** 11am-10pm Mon-Thur, Sun; 11am-11pm Fri, Sat. **Average** $25. **Credit** AmEx, MC, V.
Housed in an industrial two-storey structure by the Miami River, this recently renovated seafood warehouse featured in the Miami-filmed, Jack Nicholson-Michael Caine vehicle *Blood and Wine*. The rustic atmosphere is complemented by a monstrous menu of delicacies such as Florida lobster, king crab legs and jumbo shrimp with an artichoke-crab stuffing.

Fishbone Grill

650 S Miami Avenue, at SW Seventh Street, Downtown (530 1915). Bus 6, 8. **Open** 11.30am-10pm Mon-Thur; 11.30am-11pm Fri; 5.30-11pm Sat. **Average** $18. **Credit** AmEx, DC, Disc, MC, V.
Attracting the nearby Brickell Avenue business crowd, Fishbone Grill is a small restaurant with a reputation as one of Miami's best seafood establishments. In addition to the menu of practically anything that swims cooked in the open kitchen, it's famous for jalapeno cornbread, pizzas and salads.

The Fish Market

1501 Biscayne Boulevard, at 15th Street, Downtown (374 4399). Bus 3, 16, 48, 95, S/Metromover School Board. **Lunch** 11.30am-2.30pm Mon-Fri. **Dinner** 6-10pm Mon-Wed, Sun; 6-11pm Mon-Sat. **Average** $35. **Credit** AmEx, DC, Disc, MC, V.
Hidden inside the Crowne Plaza Miami Hotel (formerly The Omni), this upscale, elegant restaurant is considered one of the best places for seafood in the entire city, boasting only the freshest fish, including Florida lobster.

Greenwich Village

1001 S Miami Avenue, at SE 10th Street, Downtown (372 1716). Bus 6, 8, B/Metrorail Brickell/Metromover Tenth Street/Promenade. **Lunch** 11.30-3pm Mon-Fri. **Dinner** 5.30-11pm Mon-Sun. **Average** $25. **Credit** AmEx, DC, Disc, MC, V.

Off the beaten path, this country-style Italian restaurant is a great place to grab a dinner before heading to an event at the nearby Miami Arena. Pasta dishes are praiseworthy, as is the Caesar salad, which some consider one of Miami's best.

Joe's Seafood
400 NW North River Drive, at NW Fourth Street, Downtown (374 5637). Bus 77. **Open** 11am-10pm Mon-Thur, Sun; 11am-11pm Fri, Sat. **Average** $20. **Credit** AmEx, DC, MC, V.

Not to be confused with Joe's Stone Crab on South Beach, Joe's Seafood is a charmingly rugged, Latin-accented, fish market/restaurant overlooking the Miami River. Seafood dishes are numerous and fresh, but the main reason diners come here is for the relaxed air of the simple and good life on the commercially travelled Miami River.

Porcao
801 S Bayshore Drive, at SE Eighth Street, Downtown (373 2777). Bus 24, 48, 95, B/Metromover Eighth Street. **Open** noon-midnight daily. **Set meal** $25. **Credit** AmEx, DC, MC, V.

The bright cheery pig on the logo of this churrascaria – whose name sounds and looks like 'pork out' – says it all. And pigging out is taken to new heights and weights here as you enter the world of rodizio, an endless feast of meats and 37 salads that keep coming at you until you burst.

Smitty's
3195 NE Second Avenue, between NE 31st & 32nd Streets, Downtown (573 3162). Bus 9, 10, 36, J. **Open** 6am-3pm Mon-Fri; 7am-2pm Sat. **Average** $10. **Credit** AmEx, MC, V.

Serving only breakfast and lunch, this downhome eatery's menu is a nice change from the mass-produced fare offered by neighbouring fast-food establishments. A popular lunch spot, it has been cooking its burgers to order and whipping up home-made pancakes, meatloaf and other US favourites in sizeable portions for more than 50 years.

S&S Diner
1757 NE Second Avenue, between NE 17th & 18th Streets, Downtown (373 4291). Bus 9, 10. **Open** 6am-7.30pm Mon-Fri; 6am-2pm Sat. **Average** $10. **No credit cards.**

S&S has had them lining up at its counter diner since the 1940s. As one of Dade County's oldest eating establishments, its staying power is in the family recipes – classic diner food and blue plate specials such as meatloaf, roast turkey, fried chicken and a slew of side dishes.

Tobacco Road
626 S Miami Avenue, at SW Seventh Street, Downtown (374 1198). Bus 6, 8. **Open** 11.30am-2am Mon-Sat; noon-midnight Sun. **Average** $20. **Credit** AmEx, DC, Disc, MC, V.

In keeping with its nitty-gritty image as Miami's oldest bar, 'the Road' is an institution favoured by professionals, barflies and professional barflies who simply want to sling back a beer or two or three in a bluesy atmosphere. Also a live music venue, this Road is well travelled, known for its crowded Friday happy hours. Tuesday night is lobster night, when 100 lobsters go for $9.99 a piece. Get there by 6pm to be sure of your catch. Otherwise, choose from typical, often greasy bar fare such as hamburgers and buffalo wings.

Bayside Marketplace

Hard Rock Café
401 Biscayne Boulevard, at NE Fourth Street, Downtown (377 3110). Bus 3, 16, 48, 95, C/Metromover College/ Bayside. **Open** 11am-11pm Mon-Thur, Sun; 11am-midnight Fri, Sat. **Average** $20. **Credit** AmEx, DC, MC, V.

Located on the water with a giant guitar revolving on the roof, at least Miami's rendition of this worldwide chain has a good view. Other than that and Gloria Estefan's bustier, this Hard Rock is like all the rest, typically known for long queues and lots of noise. Call ahead: on some nights you may catch a special musical act or event.

Los Ranchos
401 Biscayne Boulevard, at NE Fourth Street, Downtown (375 0666). Bus 3, 16, 48, 95, C/Metromover College/ Bayside. **Open** 11.30am-11pm Mon-Thur, Sun; 11.30am-midnight Fri, Sat. **Average** $28. **Credit** AmEx, DC, MC, V.

Carnivores will agree that this Nicaraguan chain restaurant is one of the better places to satisfy a meat jones with steak, steak and more steak. Los Ranchos is rated for its churrasco, a Nicaraguan-style grilled flank steak with chilli salsa, and other South American specialities.

Coral Gables

The Bistro
2611 Ponce de Leon Boulevard, between Valencia & Almeria Avenues, Coral Gables (442 9671). Bus 40, 72. **Lunch** 11.30am-2pm Tue-Fri. **Dinner** 6-10.30pm Tue-Thur; 6-11pm Fri, Sat. **Average** $30. **Credit** AmEx, DC, Disc, MC, V.

Romantic French bistro with classic French food and friendly, informal service.

Café Kolibri
6901 Red Road, at San Ignacio Avenue, Coral Gables (665 2421). Bus 37, 72. **Open** 7.30am-10pm daily. **Average** $22. **Credit** AmEx, DC, Disc, MC, V.

This trendy, healthfood-oriented café offers organic fare, a pleasant ambiance and a bar with a comprehensive wine list.

Caffe Abbracci
318 Aragon Avenue, between Le Jeune Road & Salzedo Street, Coral Gables (441 0700). Bus 42, 56, J. **Lunch** 11.30am-2.30pm Mon-Fri. **Dinner** 6-11pm Mon-Thur, Sun; 6pm-midnight Fri, Sat. **Average** $35. **Credit** AmEx, DC, MC, V.

There's a reason why the name of this exquisite restaurant means 'hugs'. Caffe Abbracci will embrace you and your appetite with congenial staff, a lovely atmosphere and possibly the city's best Italian cuisine. How can you resist the home-made black and red ravioli filled with lobster in pink sauce, risotto with porcini and portobello mushrooms, or the famous grilled veal chop topped with tricolore salad, with mixed berries served in a caramel basket for dessert?

Caffe Baci
2522 Ponce de Leon Boulevard, between Andalusia & Valencia Avenues, Coral Gables (442 0600). Bus 40, 72. **Lunch** noon-3pm Mon-Fri. **Dinner** 6-11pm Mon-Thur; 6-11.30pm Fri, Sat. **Average** $35. **Credit** AmEx, DC, MC, V.

Finally, a cosy, gourmet eatery that serves Italian fare the way it should be served – in colossal portions. The risotto and pasta dishes are fantastic, as are the desserts.

Christy's
3101 Ponce de Leon Boulevard, at Malaga Avenue, Coral Gables (446 1400). Bus 40, 72. **Lunch** 11.30am-4pm Mon-Fri. **Dinner** 4-11pm Mon-Thur; 4-11.45pm Fri; 5-11.45pm Sat; 5-11pm Sun. **Average** $40. **Credit** AmEx, DC, Disc, MC, V.

You can almost taste the power surging through this elegant, English-style restaurant where George Bush may be sitting at one table and Rod Stewart at another – but the best thing about Miami's premier steak house is the superlative lamb chops, steaks and prime rib. Whatever you choose, be sure to preface it with Christy's classic Caesar salad.

Darbar

276 Alhambra Circle, between Ponce de Leon Boulevard
& Le Jeune Road, Coral Gables (448 9691). Bus 42, 56,
73, J. **Lunch** 11.30am-2.30pm Mon-Sat. **Dinner** 6-10.30pm
Mon-Sun. **Average** $32. **Credit** AmEx, MC, V.
Looking for a little spice in your food? This flavourful Indian
restaurant is the place, where a mouth-watering mix of 15
spices go into the chicken, shrimp and vegetables dishes.
The tandoori is top-notch as is the English-made Indian beer.

The Heights

2530 Ponce de Leon Boulevard, at Valencia Avenue,
Coral Gables (461 1774). Bus 40, 72. **Lunch** noon-
2.30pm Mon-Fri. **Dinner** 6-11pm Mon-Thur; 6pm-
midnight Fri, Sat. **Average** $35. **Credit** AmEx, MC, V.
Innovative, North Californian cuisine reaches a new loftiness
at this two-storey restaurant, which was originally – but is
no longer – affiliated with Pacific Time. Salads include Costa
Rican hearts of palm with steamed asparagus and sweet
leeks in citrus vinaigrette; entrées include a vegetarian portobello mushroom steak with toasted vegetable couscous,
sweet snow peas and shitake mushrooms, and pan-roasted
sea bass in citrus juices with truffled celery root and yukon
gold potatoes. You'll love the famous chocolate bomb or dark
chocolate smores dessert.

John Martin's

253 Miracle Mile, between Ponce de Leon Boulevard &
Salzedo Street, Coral Gables (445 3777). Bus 24. **Open**
11.30am-midnight Mon-Thur; 11.30am-1am Fri, Sat.
Average $22. **Credit** AmEx, DC, Disc, MC, V.
Adding a little spring to Irish cuisine is this popular pub and
restaurant, featuring such traditional favourites as shepherd's pie and good ol' American hamburgers, as well as a
steak in whiskey and mushroom sauce and a selection of
beers that will have you doing a jig in no time.

Le Festival

2120 Salzedo Street, at Alcazar Avenue, Coral Gables
(442 8545). Bus 42, J. **Lunch** 11.45am-2.30pm Mon-Fri.
Dinner 6-10.30pm Mon-Thur; 6-11pm Fri, Sat. **Average**
$30. **Credit** AmEx, DC, MC, V.
This City Beautiful landmark will take you back to the pre-
cholesterol-conscious days of heavy French-style sauces.
Pâté, cheese soufflé, duck a l'orange and steak are good
enough to make you forget about your arteries for a night.

Norman's

21 Almeria Avenue, at SW 37th Avenue, Coral Gables
(446 6767). Bus 37. **Lunch** noon-2pm Mon-Fri. **Dinner**
6-10.30pm Mon-Thur; 6-11pm Fri, Sat. **Average** $45.
Credit AmEx, DC, MC, V.
Gourmet magazine says Norman's is the best restaurant in
South Florida. Some even say it's the best in the United
States. Gifted chef and cookbook author Norman Van Aken
(whose own favourite restaurants, incidentally, are Astor
Place, Nemo and Savannah) takes New World cuisine to yet
another plateau with signature dishes such as rhum and pepper painted grouper, seared foie gras on toasted Cuban bread
and rioja-braised lamb shanks. The open kitchen setting and
smart clientele make Norman's a required, albeit expensive,
dining experience.

Red Fish Grill

9610 Old Cutler Road, between SW 93rd & 101st
Streets, Coral Gables (668 8788). Bus 65. **Dinner**
5-10pm Tue-Sun. **Average** $30. **Credit** MC, V.
Hidden away in scenic Matheson Hammock Park, Red Fish
Grill offers spectacular waterside dining. Eat fresh fish
dishes – sautéd snapper, pan-seared tuna and pan-fried crab
cakes – in a panoramic setting.

Restaurant Place St Michel

Hotel Place St Michel, 162 Alcazar Avenue, at
Ponce de Leon Boulevard, Coral Gables (446 6572).
Bus 40, 72. **Breakfast** 7-9.30am, **lunch** 11.30am-
2.30pm, daily. **Dinner** 5-10.30pm Mon-Thur, Sun; 5-
11.30pm Fri, Sat. **Average** $35. **Credit** AmEx, DC,
MC, V.
Experience la bonne vie at this charming little European
restaurant that's hailed for its crêpes and game and fish dishes, all of them as inviting as the intimate and romantic
ambiance in which they're served.

Tutti's

4612 Le Jeune Road, between Alminar Avenue & Blue
Road, Coral Gables (663 0077). Bus 56. **Open** 11am-
10pm Mon-Thur, Sun; 11am-midnight Fri, Sat. **Average**
$22. **Credit** AmEx, DC, Disc, MC, V.
Welcome to Tuscany in the Gables. Tutti's countrified interior and large portions of pastas, pizzas and classic Tuscan
cuisine make this well-priced restaurant a popular one, even
if it reeks of the sweet smell of roasted garlic.

La cocina Cubana

Until Cuba becomes a hot resort destination
once again, Miami will undoubtedly continue to
serve up the nation's best Cuban food, no exceptions. Like nearly all ethnic foods, Cuban cuisine
has its trademark dishes, most of which are
obscenely caloric (the Cubans love to fry), yet
wonderfully savoury. The Cuban menu is carbo-
heavy, revolving around beans and rice. It is
also very sauce-laden, with an emphasis on meat
– mostly pork and steak – and plantains.

The following is a translation of some of the
most popular Cuban delicacies. *Buen provecho!*

Arroz con pollo A savoury combination of chicken and
yellow rice.

Bistec palomilla Thin steak doused in an oily mixture
of minced onions and parsley.

Boniato Similar to a sweet potato.

Chorizo Full of flavour, this Spanish garlic sausage is
heavy on the fat.

Churros An elongated doughnut-like Cuban pastry often
accompanied by café con leche.

Masas de puerco Pork chunks.

Media noche The Big Mac of Cuban food, this sandwich
is filled with ham, pork and cheese.

Mojo A marinade used to spice up vegetables, consisting
of hot olive oil, lemon juice, sliced raw onion, garlic, water
and a touch of pepper and cumin.

Moros y cristianos A ubiquitous Cuban side dish: black
beans and white rice.

Sofrito The basis for many stews, meat dishes and the
ever-present black beans, sofrito is a sauce made of onion,
green pepper, oregano and ground pepper in olive oil.

Verdes Fried green plantains.

Yuca A signature ingredient in many Cuban dishes, this
tuber can be found in many forms: chunks, slices or fries.

Coconut Grove

Café Med
*CocoWalk, 3015 Grand Avenue, at Virginia Street,
Coconut Grove (443 1770). Bus 42, 48.* **Open** 11am-
midnight Mon-Thur, Sun; 11am-1am Fri, Sat. **Average**
$25. **Credit** AmEx, DC, MC, V.
Average Italian cuisine on the lower level of the Grove's fre-
netic CocoWalk complex. Good people watching.

Café Sci Sci
*3043 Grand Avenue, at McFarlane Road, Coconut Grove
(446 5104). Bus 42, 48.* **Lunch** noon-3pm Tue-Sun.
Dinner 3pm-12.30am Mon-Thur, Sun; 3pm-1am Fri, Sat.
Average $30. **Credit** AmEx, MC, V.
Though not as pretentious as its name suggests, Café Sci Sci
(pronounced she-she) is one of the Grove's most expensive
eateries, serving good but not grandiose Northern Italian
cuisine – either on the cramped and busy sidewalk, or inside,
where the ambiance is often better than the food.

Café Tu Tu Tango
*CocoWalk, 3015 Grand Avenue, at Virginia Street,
Coconut Grove (529 2222). Bus 42, 48.* **Open** 11.30am-
midnight Mon-Wed, Sun; 11.30am-1am Thur; 11.30am-
2am Fri, Sat. **Average** $22. **Credit** AmEx, MC, V.
While you tempt your palate with the various tapas, roaming artists may be dipping onto their palettes and creating
masterpieces right before your eyes in the Grove's restau-
rant-cum-artist's-loft. You're encouraged to order and share
many different items, which vary from black bean soup to
spicy chicken egg rolls. The sangria is pretty good here, and
enough of it may help you interpret the many paintings that
cover the interior.

The Chart House
*51 Chart House Drive, at S Bayshore Drive, Coconut
Grove (856 9741). Bus 48.* **Dinner** 5.30-11pm Mon-Thur;
5.30-11.30pm Fri, Sat; 5-10pm Sun. **Average** $25. **Credit**
AmEx, DC, Disc, MC, V.
This steak and seafood house is overpriced and overrated
but it does have a great location on Sailboat Bay and possibly the best salad bar around.

The Cheesecake Factory
*CocoWalk, 3015 Grand Avenue, at Virginia Street,
Coconut Grove (447 9898). Bus 42, 48.* **Open** 11.30am-
midnight Mon-Thur; 11.30am-1am Sat; 11.30am-11.30pm
Sun. **Average** $25. **Credit** AmEx, MC, V.
If the thought of 30 kinds of cheesecake doesn't appeal to
you, study a copy of the glossy, spiral-bound menu while
you wait for a table and you'll be sure to find something that
does. Huge, meal-sized salads can feed two or three, while
the unusual pastas, such as Caesar salad pasta, and great
sandwiches are also on the large size. The rich and chunky
cheesecakes – peanut butter cookie dough, Jack Daniels and
even a 'lite' version – are worth straying from your diet.

Chiyo
*3390 Mary Street, at Grand Avenue, Coconut Grove (445
0865). Bus 42, 48.* **Lunch** noon-2.30pm Mon-Fri.
Dinner 5.30pm-midnight daily. **Average** $25. **Credit**
AmEx, DC, Disc, MC, V.
Nestled in the upstairs corner of the barren Mayfair shopping mall, Chiyo is worth the search, especially if you're on
a quest for good sushi in the Grove, rolled out in a bright
setting that pays homage to late 1980s neon. Note: while the
fish may be fresh here, so are many of the waitstaff.

Dan Marino's
*CocoWalk, 3015 Grand Avenue, at Virginia Street,
Coconut Grove (567 0013). Bus 42, 48.* **Open** 11.30am-
2am Mon-Wed, Sun; 11.30am-3am Thur-Sat. **Average**
$18. **Credit** AmEx, DC, MC, V.
Unless you're a football fanatic, don't bother coming to this
sports bar and don't expect exquisite cuisine. Little more
than a museum to Marino's football career, this so-called bar
and grill attracts a rowdy college crowd.

Grand Café
*2669 S Bayshore Drive, at 27th Avenue, Coconut Grove
(858 9600). Bus 48.* **Breakfast** 7am-11.30am, **lunch**
11.30am-3pm, **dinner** 6-11pm, daily. **Average** $40.
Credit AmEx, DC, MC, V.
The name may as well refer to the prices, but grand, indeed,
is how you'll feel in this opulent dining room in the Grand
Bay Hotel, with an exquisite regional American menu and
unparalleled service. Appetisers and entrées are as rich as
they sound, and include pan-seared Florida crab cakes, foie
gras and baked macadamia and ginger crusted salmon. The
Sunday brunch is renowned and possibly the best around.

Greenstreet Café
*3110 Commodore Plaza, at Main Highway, Coconut
Grove (567 0662). Bus 42, 48.* **Open** 7am-11.30pm Mon-
Thur, Sun; 7am-1am Sat. **Average** $20. **Credit** AmEx,
MC, V.
A bustling sidewalk café with excellent salads and sand-
wiches, seating and Sunday brunch.

Johnny Rockets
*3036 Grand Avenue, at McFarlane Road, Coconut Grove
(444 1000). Bus 42, 48.* **Open** 11am-1.30am Mon-Thur;
11am-4.30am Fri, Sat; 11am-2.30am Sun. **Average** $10.
Credit MC, V.
Happy Days lives on at this shiny 1950s- and 1960s-style
hamburger joint, where at any moment the waiting staff are
likely to break into a chorus of 'Jailhouse Rock'. Inside is
an old-fashioned soda counter where you can order from a
small menu featuring run-of-the-mill hamburgers, cheese-
burgers, shakes and fries.

Kaleidoscope
*3112 Commodore Plaza, at Main Highway, Coconut
Grove (446 5010). Bus 42, 48.* **Lunch** 11.30am-3pm
Mon-Fri. **Dinner** 6-11pm Mon-Sat; 5.30-10.30pm Sun.
Average $28. **Credit** AmEx, DC, Disc, MC, V.
Standing the test of time, Kaleidoscope has been a permanent fixture in the ever-changing Grove for 23 years with its
appealing second-floor balcony and dining room above
Commodore Plaza. The French Continental menu with a
tropical flair features an eclectic array of entrées including
crusted rare seared yellowfin tuna in a warm ginger soy
vinaigrette, duck in an orange chutney glaze and pastas such
as tortellini with spicy gulf shrimp and sun-dried tomatoes.

Modern Art Café
*2801 Florida Avenue, at Mary Street, Coconut Grove,
(461 1999). Bus 42, 48.* **Open** 11.30am-midnight Mon-
Thur, Sun; 11.30am-2am Fri, Sat. **Average** $25. **Credit**
AmEx, DC, Disc, MC, V.
Like a work in progress, it took this mammoth eatery quite
a while before it was unveiled to the public (one reason being
the threat of a lawsuit over the restaurant's original name:
Picasso Café). When it did open, people noticed the funky-
museum-like interior (complete with gift shop) sooner than
the New World Bistro cuisine. Like art, the food here is a matter of personal taste. Quesadillas with pork, crab cakes with
cilantro ketchup and spring rolls in a funky, lively atmosphere may produce a finer appreciation of Modern Art.

Monty's
*2550 S Bayshore Drive, at Aviation Avenue, Coconut
Grove (858 1431). Bus 48.* **Open** 11am-3am daily.
Average $30. **Credit** AmEx, DC, MC, V.
The Walt Disney World of waterfront dining, Monty's has
long been a Grove institution where you can eat shrimp or
stone crabs before renting a boat and heading out. Though

the indoor dining room overlooking the water is quite scenic, it's also a little stuffy and overpriced. The outside tiki hut area is more popular with the younger, happy-hour set for its laid-back Key West aura and seafood bar menu.

Paulo Luigi's

3324 Virginia Street, at Florida Avenue, Coconut Grove (443 7433). Bus 42, 48. **Lunch** 11am-4pm Mon-Fri. **Dinner** 4pm-1am Mon-Sat; 4-11pm Sun. **Average** $20. **Credit** AmEx, DC, Disc, MC, V.
Before CocoWalk landed in the middle of the Grove, this romantic Italian eatery was one of the area's most popular. Located behind the complex, it is now even more of a local favourite thanks to its almost hidden site. With good pizza and pasta dishes at reasonable prices, it is one of the better, less commercial neighbourhood haunts.

Senor Frog's

3008 Grand Avenue, at Virginia Street, Coconut Grove (448 0999). Bus 42, 48. **Open** 11.30am-2am Mon-Sat; 11.30am-1am Sun. **Average** $20. **Credit** AmEx, DC, MC, V.
For those who have been to the various Senor Frog's scattered around Mexico, this Grove outpost is a bit bland and more on the mellow side. For those who haven't, this Frog is a hopping good time with standard Mexican cuisine and good margaritas. Follow the mariachi band and request seating in the outdoor courtyard.

Taurus

3540 Main Highway, between Charles & Franklin Avenues, Coconut Grove (448 0633). Bus 42, 48. **Open** 11.30am-2.30am daily. **Average** $22. **Credit** AmEx, DC, MC, V.
A locals' roadside hangout located on the more pastoral end of Main Highway, Taurus takes you on a beer and burger-heavy timewarp to the days of pre-Gap, pre-Banana Republic Coconut Grove. A little bit country, a little bit rock 'n' roll, this happy-hour haven is a jeans and T-shirt establishment.

Little Havana

Casa Juancho

2436 SW Eighth Street, between SW 24th & 25th Avenues, Little Havana (642 2452). Bus 8, 22. **Open** noon-midnight Mon-Thur, Sun; noon-1am Fri, Sat. **Average** $27. **Credit** AmEx, DC, MC, V.
Respectable Spanish cuisine with an amusement-park flair: strolling musicians, hanging hams and a lively crowd.

Hy Vong

3458 SW Eighth Street, between SW 34 & 35th Avenues, Little Havana (446 3674). Bus 8, 37. **Open** 6-11pm Tue-Sun. **Average** $18. **No credit cards**.
A gem of a hole in the wall serving delicious Vietnamese cuisine at bargain basement prices.

Islas Canarias

285 NW 27th Avenue, at NW Third Street, Little Havana (649 0440) Bus 27. **Open** 7am-11pm daily. **Average** $15. **Credit** MC, V.
Tiny family-style Cuban restaurant that's always brimming with hungry diners who swear this is the best Cuban eatery in town. Reasonable prices and specialities such as the garlic-smothered steak keep 'em coming.

La Carreta

3632 SW Eighth Street, at SW 36th Avenue, Little Havana (447 0184). Bus 8, 37. **Open** 24 hours daily. **Average** $12. **Credit** DC, MC, V.
Cuban chain restaurant with plenty of nostalgia for pre-Castro Cuba, sugarcane plants growing on the front lawn, large portions and a backroom cafeteria for the imbibing of coffee, pastries and sugarcane juice.

Vietnamese crowd-pleasers at **Hy Vong**.

La Esquina de Tejas

101 SW 12th Avenue, at SW First Street, Little Havana (545 0337). Bus 12. **Open** 7am-10pm daily. **Average** $17. **Credit** AmEx, DC, Disc, MC, V.
Cheap, classic Cuban food is offered here, where Ronald Reagan once stopped to schmooze with Hispanic voters. A choice spot for pork, ham, and cheese sandwiches.

Versailles

3555 SW Eighth Street, at SW 36th Avenue, Little Havana (445 7614). Bus 8, 37. **Open** 8am-2.30am Mon-Thur; 8am-3.30am Fri; 8am-4.30am Sat; 9am-2am Sun. **Average** $14. **Credit** DC, MC, V.
Almost as famous as its palatial namesake in France, Versailles is a kitschy, iconoclastic Cuban diner with wall-to-wall mirrors, a constant buzz of activity and a mammoth, unabridged menu featuring every dish known to the culture.

North Dade

Biz Bistro

Aventura Mall, 19575 Biscayne Boulevard, at NE 195th Street, Aventura (931 8448). Bus 3, 9, E, S. **Lunch** 11.30am-4pm, **light meal** 4-5.30pm, daily. **Dinner** 5.30-11pm Mon-Fri; 5.30-11.30pm Sat; 5.30-10.30pm Sun. **Average** $30. **Credit** AmEx, DC, Disc, MC, V.
Despite its cheesy name and location within the Aventura Mall, Biz Bistro, owned by Jack Nicholson's former personal chef, is a respectable, upscale restaurant serving mostly Italian food in a jazz-influenced atmosphere.

Chef Allen's

19088 NE 29th Avenue, at NE 190th Street, North Miami Beach (935 2900). Bus S, V, Biscayne Max. **Dinner** 6-10pm Mon-Thur, Sun; 6-11pm Fri, Sat. **Average** $40. **Credit** AmEx, DC, MC, V.

*Cuban goes glitzy at **Versailles** (page 121).*

If anyone deserves to have a restaurant named after them, it's chef Allen Susser, winner of the James Beard award (and just about every other award going) and reigning king of New World cuisine. Everything here is out of this world, speaking the luscious language that is distinctly 'Floribbean', infusing fantastic fish and meat with exotic ingredients such as key lime and mangos, making every meal seem like a culinary trip to paradise. Desserts and soufflés are divine and should be delved into no matter how full you are.

Gourmet Diner
13951 Biscayne Boulevard, at NE 139th Street, North Miami (947 2255). Bus 3, 28. **Open** 11am-11pm Mon-Fri; 8am-11.30pm Sat; 8am-10.30pm Sun. **Average** $17. **No credit cards**.
The only diner around where you can order escargot, this is not your average greasy spoon. Arugula and endive salads with goat's cheese, pasta salads and meat dishes give it gourmet standing. Prices aren't astronomical.

Mark's Place
2286 NE 123rd Street, at N Bayshore Drive, North Miami (893 6888). Bus G. **Dinner** 6.30-11pm Mon-Thur; 6-11pm Fri-Sun. **Average** $40. **Credit** AmEx, MC, V.
Excellence marks the spot where chef Mark Militello presides, fashioning a new breed of cuisine from basic Florida ingredients. Caribbean lobster with sweet plantain mash, conch creole sauce and stewed hearts of palm; saffron linguine with Gulf shrimp, seared tomatoes, roasted chillies, black olives, capers and rapini; rare sesame seared tuna with oriental vegetables, jasmine rice, pickled ginger, wasabi and ponzu, salad 'Tarpon Spring' with Peruvian potatoes and roast garlic aiolli are a mere sampling of Mark's mealtime magic.

Oggi
1740 79th Street Causeway, at E Treasure Drive, North Bay Village (866 1238). Bus L. **Lunch** 11.30am-2.30pm Mon-Fri. **Dinner** 6-10.30pm Mon-Thur; 6-11.30pm Fri, Sat; 5.30-10.30pm Sun. **Average** $22. **Credit** AmEx, DC, MC, V.

Despite being tucked away in a neighbourhood strip mall – and despite the relatively unimaginative food – this Italian establishment remains popular. It offers freshly made pasta and other stodgy items in a pseudo neo-classical ambiance. Expect boring faves such as cannolis and mozzarella caprese.

Prezzo
18831 Biscayne Boulevard, at NE 188th Street, North Aventura (933 9004). Bus 3, V, Biscayne Max. **Lunch** noon-3pm, **pizza & salad only**, 3-5pm, daily. **Dinner** 5.30-10.30pm Mon-Thur; 5-11.30pm Fri, Sat; 5-10pm Sun. **Average** $25. **Credit** AmEx, Disc, MC, V.
The wood-burning pizzas and large portions of pasta are good and reasonably priced in this garlic-heavy hub of the Aventura scene – but not necessarily worth getting a beeper from the frazzled hostess and waiting up to an hour for it to vibrate you to a table.

Shooter's
3501 NE 163rd Street, at NE 35th Avenue, North Miami Beach (949 2855). Bus E, H, V. **Open** 11.30am-midnight Mon-Thur; 9am-midnight Fri-Sun. **Average** $25. **Credit** AmEx, DC, Disc, MC, V.
Long before Aaron Spelling decided to make Shooter's the one and only hangout for his angst-ridden characters on *Melrose Place*, this Shooter's (no relation) was – and is – the one and only hangout for the angst-ridden kids of North Miami Beach with its dockside drinking and fair pasta, salads and burgers.

Shula's Steak House
7601 NW 154 Street, at Miami Lakes Drive, Miami Lakes (820 8102). Bus 83, E. **Breakfast** 6.30am-11am daily. **Lunch** 11.30am-2.30pm Mon-Fri. **Dinner** 6-11pm Mon-Sat; 6-10pm Sun. **Average** $40. **Credit** AmEx, Disc, MC, V.
A famous steak house not only because its owner Don is the former Miami Dolphins coach but because the steaks are excellent and humungous. The guts and the glory: finish one of their porterhouses and get your name on a plaque.

Toojay's

3585 NE 207th Street, east of 34th Court, Aventura
(936 9555). Bus 3. **Open** 8am-9pm Mon-Fri; 8am-10pm
Sat, Sun. **Average** $15. **Credit** AmEx, Disc, MC, V.
A busy deli in the Shoppes at the Waterways Mall, offering
large, pricey salads, sandwiches and wicked chocolate cake.

South Dade

Kon Chau

8376 Bird Road, between SW 83rd & 84th Avenues,
Southwest Dade (553 7799). Bus 40, 87. **Open** 11am-
10pm Mon-Sat; 10am-10pm Sun. **Average** $12. **Credit**
MC, V.
Damn good dim sum, damn cheap.

Romano's Macaroni Grill

12100 SW 88th Street, at SW 121st Avenue, Kendall
(270 0621). Bus 56, 88. **Open** 11.30am-10.30pm Mon-
Thur, Sun; 11.30am-midnight Fri, Sat. **Average** $22.
Credit AmEx, DC, Disc, MC, V.
Opera-singing waiters, an 'honor system' featuring pour
your own wine and a delicious assortment of pastas and pizzas contribute to the fun of this loud chain restaurant. You
can't book, but call ahead to let them know you're coming.

Shorty's BBQ

9200 S Dixie Highway, at Dadeland Boulevard, South
Miami (670 7732). Bus 1, 52/Metrorail Dadeland South.
Open 11am-11pm daily. **Average** $12. **Credit** MC, V.
This friendly Country& Western-style barbecue pit is one of
the last vestiges of pre-developed, pre-trendy Miami. Enjoy
great barbecue chicken, ribs and sauce at long picnic tables.

Siam Lotus

6388 S Dixie Highway, at SW 63rd Avenue, South
Miami (666 8134). Bus 52, 65, 73/Metrorail Dadeland
North. **Open** 11.30am-10.30pm Mon-Sat; 4-10.30pm Sun.
Average $20. **Credit** AmEx, MC, V.
This shack-like eyesore shouldn't be judged on looks: it serves
some of the best Thai food around. The pad thai alone should
convince you that beauty is in the mouth of the beholder.

Tropical Chinese

7991 SW 40th Street, at SW 79th Avenue, Southwest
Dade (262 1552). Bus 40. **Open** 11am-11pm daily.
Average $28. **Credit** AmEx, DC, MC, V.
It is hard to find decent Chinese food in this city, but follow
the countless Chinese families for enough south and you'll
discover it in the middle of a nondescript strip mall. This is
the place for Hong Kong-style Chinese food, with the best
dim sum in the area and the most enticing entrées.

Restaurants by cuisine

Brazilian: Porcao (p118).
Burgers & traditional American: Dan Marino's
(p120); Hard Rock Café (p118); Johnny Rockets (p120);
The Official All Star Cafe (p109); Rusty Pelican (p116);
Shooter's (p122); Smitty's (p118); Taurus (p121);
Tobacco Road (p118).
Cafés & sandwich bars: Café Kolibri (p118); Café
Papillon (p114); The Cheesecake Factory (p120); Coco's
Sidewalk Café (p116); Front Porch Café (p112);
Greenstreet Café (p120); Le Sandwicherie (p112); Miami
Subs (p113); News Café (p109); The Oasis Café (p116);
Van Dyke Café (p115). *See also box* **The Bean Scene**.
Californian: Century (p105); The Heights (p119).
Chinese: Charlotte's Chinese Kitchen (p111);
Chrysanthemum (p111); Kon Chau (p123); Lucky
Cheng's (p115); Tropical Chinese (p123).
Cuban: Islas Canarias (p121); La Carreta (p121); La
Esquina de Tejas (p121); Larios on the Beach (p106);
Lincoln Road Café (p115); Mango's Tropical Café
(p106); Puerto Sagua (p109); Versailles (p121); Yuca
(p116).
Contemporary American: Blue Door (p114).
Delis: Arnie & Richie's (p116); Toojay's (p117);
Wolfie's (p115).
Diners & grills: The Beehive (p114); Big Pink (p104);
11th Street Diner (p112); Gourmet Diner (p122); The
Rascal House (p116); Shorty's BBQ (p123); S&S Diner
(p118).
Fish & seafood: Big Fish (p117); East Coast
Fisheries (p117); Fishbone Grill (p117); The Fish
Market (p117); Grillfish (p112); Joe's Seafood (p118);
Joe's Stone Crab (p105); Monty's (p120); Red Fish Grill
(p119); Sunday's on the Bay (p117).
French: The Bistro (p118); Kaleidoscope (p120); Le
Festival (p119); Restaurant Place St Michel (p119).
German: Dab Haus (p106).
Haitian: Tap Tap (p106).
Ice-cream: The Frieze Ice Cream Factory (p112).
Indian: Darbar (p119).

International: Café Tu Tu Tango (p120); South
Beach Brasserie (p115).
Irish: John Martin's (p119).
Italian: Biz Bistro (p121); Café Med (p120); Café Prima
Pasta (p116); Café Sci Sci (p120); Caffe Abbracci (p118);
Caffe Baci (p118); Da Leo Trattoria (p114); Escopazzo
(p112); Farfalla (p106); Follia (p106); Greenwich Village
(p117); I Paparazzi (p106); Mezzaluna (p106);
Mezzanotte (p113); Oggi (p122); Osteria del Teatro
(p113); Paulo Luigi's (p121); Prezzo (p122); Pucci's
Pizza (p113); Romano's Macaroni Grill (p123); Spiga
(p113); Sport Café (p109); Tutti's (p119).
Jamaican: Norma's on the Beach (p115).
Japanese: Chiyo (p120); Maiko Japanese Restaurant
& Sushi Bar (p113); Sushi Hana (p113); Sushi Rock
Café (p114); Toni's New Tokyo Cuisine & Sushi Bar
(p114).
Mediterranean: Allioli (p111); Boulevard Bistro
(p106); Lemon Twist (p116).
Mexican: Moe's Cantina (p109); San Loco Tacos
(p113); Senor Frog's (p121).
New World: Chef Allen's (p121); Mark's Place (p122);
Modern Art Café (p120); Norman's (p119).
Nicaraguan: Los Ranchos (p118).
Pan Asian & Pacific Rim: China Grill (p105); Nemo
(p105); Pacific Time (p115); Pan Coast (p116).
Pancakes: Royal Canadian Pancake House (p113).
Posh American: Grand Café (p120).
Southern: Lulu's (p112); Savannah (p106).
Southwestern: Astor Place (p106); Tita's (p114).
Spanish: Casa Juancho (p121).
Steakhouses: Capital Grille (p117); The Chart House
(p120); Christy's (p118); The Forge (p116); L'Entrecote
de Paris (p105); Linda B's Steakhouse (p116); Shula's
Steak House (p122); Smith and Wollensky (p106).
Thai: Siam Lotus (p123); Thai House (p114); Thai
Toni (p111); World Resources (p116).
Vegan: The Naked Earth (p109).
Vietnamese: Hy Vong (p121).

Bars

Cocktails on the beach, cheap beer and pool tables or a cool martini and an even cooler crowd – you can drink until dawn at Miami's watering holes.

Fifteen years ago only a handful of nightclubs, most of them seedy, served the metropolitan Miami area after 2am (the closing time demanded by most liquor licences issued by the state of Florida). Then came Miami Beach's makeover into a shiny new club capital; suddenly, nocturnal Miamians had a wealth of options for drinking and dancing into the small hours.

Nowadays, savvy locals advise visiting friends to take along sunglasses when stepping out for a night on the town; so many saloons keep cranking all through the night that novice revellers have been known to lose track of time and emerge from a bar or club only to be brutally reminded by Miami's retina-searing sun that morning has broken. Some bars still close at 2am; many others don't start hopping until that time. Alcohol can legally be sold until 5am.

Most of the action takes place in two areas: South Beach (Miami Beach south of 23rd Street), aka 'the Beach'; and Coconut Grove, aka 'the Grove'. The Beach in particular has achieved worldwide renown for its preponderance of

exclusive, star-studded, glittery nightspots. But you don't have to be a model or a Latin pop star to join in the fun. There is no shortage of exotic alternative destinations full of colourful characters.

BOOZE & THE LAW

Like most of the US, Florida has harsh under-age drinking and drunk-driving countermeasures. You must be 21 to purchase or consume alcohol in Florida; be prepared to show photographic ID. Get busted behind the wheel of an automobile with more than the equivalent of about two drinks in your system, and you can expect jail time and punitive fines in the order of thousands of dollars. For serious bar-hoppers and club-crawlers, it pays to stay on the Beach; the higher hotel rates are offset by the freedom to stagger back and forth between as many cocktail lounges and gin joints as you want. Should you get too snookered to walk, cheap and omnipresent taxis can quickly and painlessly shuttle you home. Don't be afraid to ask the bartender to call one for you.

*Old Jack keeps the kids in line at local favourite the **Irish House**.*

Washington Avenue

So many bars have cropped up on the 600 block of Washington Avenue (between Sixth and Seventh Streets) on South Beach that massive crowds form and spill out into the street in front of the most popular clubs, necessitating police crowd-control procedures. Dance clubs such as Bash and Union Bar pull in hormone-driven hordes, as do a handful of more or less interchangeable bars (including the ones we've listed below), all of which offer some combination of dancefloor and billiards tables. For all, catch bus C, H, K or W.

Bar 609
609 Washington Avenue (673 5609). **Open** 10pm-5am Thur-Sat. **Credit** AmEx, MC, V.

Charlie Brown
623 Washington Avenue (534 3834). **Open** 9pm-5am Fri-Sat. **Credit** AmEx, DC, Disc, MC, V.

Chili Pepper/Brandt's Break
621 Washington Avenue (531 9661). **Open** 9pm-5am Wed-Sat. **Credit** AmEx, MC, V.

Society Hill
627 Washington Avenue (534 9993). **Open** 10pm-5am Wed-Sun. **Credit** AmEx, DC, Disc, MC, V.

The Beaches

South Beach

The Abbey
1115 16th Street, between Alton Road & Lenox Avenue, South Beach (538 8110). Bus F/M, S, W. **Open** 1pm-5am daily. **No credit cards.**
A former hole-in-the-wall known as the Knotty Pine, the Abbey recently jumped on the microbrewery bandwagon, but didn't sell its classic dive-bar soul in the process. It's the microbrewery for people who hate microbreweries.

Berlin Bar
661 Washington Avenue, between Sixth & Seventh Streets, South Beach (674 9300). Bus C, H, K, W. **Open** 9pm-2am Mon-Thur, Sun; 9pm-4am Fri, Sat. **Credit** AmEx, DC, MC, V.
Laid-back elegance at a premium price makes this a fave hangout of well-heeled conversationalists seeking refuge from the youthquake masses streaming in and out of Berlin's noisy dance-oriented neighbours. It attracts a slightly older, better-dressed and less frenetic clientele who believe an expensive drink is a small price to pay for a little sanity. The chocolate martinis have a small but rabid following.

Chamber Lounge
2940 Collins Avenue, at 30th Street, South Beach (673 0338). Bus C, F/M, G, H, S. **Open** 10am-5am Mon-Wed, Sat, Sun; 1pm-5am Thur, Fri. **No credit cards.**
A hotel basement bar that wouldn't feel out of place in New York or Boston, the Chamber is a cosy little hangout where you can drink until 5am every night of the week.

The Clevelander
1020 Ocean Drive, between 10th & 11th Streets, South Beach (531 3485). Bus C, H, K. **Open** 11am-5am daily. **Credit** AmEx, DC, MC, V.
Casually dressed locals and tourists gather around the pool bar at this loud pick-up spot. Patrons too drunk to make conversation have a choice of leering at other patrons or checking out the flesh parade on Ocean Drive's busiest corner.

821
821 Lincoln Road, between Jefferson & Meridian Avenues, South Beach (531 1188). Bus A, F/M, G, L, S. **Open** 5pm-3am daily. **No credit cards.**
Hip, artsy, gay-friendly locals make up the lion's share of this blessedly non-attitudinous Lincoln Road hangout's clientele. Writers, performance artists, ultra-low-budget film

makers, bisexual models and drag queens rub shoulders at the bar or grind hips on the tiny dancefloor; the easygoing, anything-goes ambience makes this stop a favourite of straight couples looking for a third hand. Performances by campy rock band Frosty are not to be missed. *See also chapter* **Gay & Lesbian**.

Irish House
1431 Alton Road, between 14th Court & 15th Street, South Beach (534 5667). Bus F/M, S, W. **Open** 11am-2am Mon-Sat; 1pm-2am Sun. **No credit cards.**
The best neighbourhood bar on South Beach sits on the west side of the island, safely removed from the maddening crush of the Deco District. Locals overdosing on glitz and fabulousness love the laid-back atmosphere; sunburnt tourists, heroin-thin models and expensively dressed poseurs seem to have difficulty finding the place. This beer-and-burger joint doesn't serve hard liquor (beer and wine only), which translates into a convivial crowd of mildly buzzed funseekers rather than a morose bunch of future cirrhosis cases. The two pool tables, four TV sets, bumper pool and foosball tables, and three dart boards all see plenty of action. And wizened old Jack – a rail-thin, seventyish employee whose job it is to monitor the action and keep the kids in line – makes the club a safe haven for women who don't want to be pestered by lotharios in testosterone overdrive.

Jams Tavern & Grill
1331 Washington Avenue, between 13th & 14th Streets, South Beach (532 6700). Bus C, H, K, W. **Open** 1pm-5am daily. **Credit** AmEx, DC, MC, V.
Cheap beer, a no-bullshit attitude and edible, affordable bar food attract a steady stream of locals to this sports bar in the heart of Washington Avenue's frenzied club district.

Lost Weekend
218 Espanola Way, between Collins & Washington Avenues, South Beach (672 1707). Bus C, H, K, W. **Open** 4.30pm-5am daily. **Credit** AmEx, Disc, MC, V.
Billiards tables abound at this appropriately named watering hole that's situated just across the street from the long-running gay nightclub Warsaw.

Mac's Club Deuce
222 14th Street, between Collins & Washington Avenues, South Beach (531 6200). Bus C, H, K, W. **Open** 8am-5am daily. **No credit cards.**
Eclectic is far too tame a word to describe the bizarre mix of South Beach denizens who hunker down and liquor up at Club Deuce every night of the week. From transsexual

hookers to nightclub glitterati to down-and-out locals to visiting celebrities like Quentin Tarantino, Club Deuce attracts the funkiest, motliest, coolest, scariest crowd of any bar on the South Florida nightlife landscape. And it's easy to see why: ideal mid-South Beach location; strong, reasonably priced drinks; comfortably shabby décor (spruced up with a little neon left over from a *Miami Vice* shoot); and possibly the hippest jukebox south of Manhattan.

Moe's Cantina

616 Collins Avenue, between Sixth & Seventh Streets, South Beach (532 6637). Bus C, H, K, W. **Open** 5pm-midnight daily. **Credit** AmEx, MC, V.
Skip the so-so food at this trendy Mexican restaurant-cum-models'-hangout and stick to the bountiful margaritas and beautiful-people watching.

Penrod's

1 Ocean Drive, at Biscayne Street, South Beach (538 1111). Bus H, W. **Open** 11am-1pm Mon-Thur, Sun; 11am-1am Fri, Sat. **Credit** AmEx, MC, V.
Two decades ago owner Jack Penrod made a mint with a Fort Lauderdale nightspot that became the number-one destination of college spring breakers vacationing along the infamous Fort Lauderdale strip. But when Fort Lauderdale poobahs made the economically disastrous decision to chase away the college kids and try to lure more sedate – and higher-spending – conventioneers, Penrod took his concept south and became one of the first big nightlife prospectors to stake a claim in South Beach. While Miami Beach does only a tiny fraction of the spring-break business that once flocked to Fort Lauderdale, Penrod's perpetuates that drunken frat-boy vibe with bikini contests, beach volleyball, poolside and ocean-view drinking, an impressive array of TVs tuned into major sporting events and no shortage of *Baywatch* wannabes.

Wet Willie's: *naff cocktail central.*

The Raleigh

1775 Collins Avenue, at 18th Street, South Beach (534 1775). Bus C, G, H, L. **Open** 5pm-midnight Mon-Thur, Sun; 5pm-1am Fri, Sat. **Credit** AmEx, DC, MC, V.
Miami's best martinis are shaken not stirred in this elegant hotel bar. The Raleigh's bartenders take the art of mixing very seriously and would sooner engage 007 in mano-a-mano combat than indulge his habit of substituting vodka for gin.

Ted's Hideaway

124 Second Street, between Ocean Drive & Collins Avenue, South Beach (no phone). Bus H, W. **Open** 8am-5am daily. **No credit cards.**
Ted's reeks of stale beer (at least you hope that's what it reeks of). No telephone. Horrible food. And a two-for-one happy hour from 2-4am. It takes guts to remain a quintessential dive bar when all around you court the trendy, the upscale, the youthful: Ted's doesn't give a goddamn and that's what makes it special.

Wet Willie's

760 Ocean Drive, at Eighth Street, South Beach (532 5650). Bus C, H, K, W. **Open** 11am-2am Mon-Thur; 11am-3am Fri, Sat. **No credit cards.**
This is Naff Central of Ocean Drive. Lurid is the word: for the crowd, the vibe and most particularly the slushy cocktails, which are dispensed from barrel-sized vats in sherbert colours and go under such names as Attitude Improvement and Call-a-Cab – and those are some of the more tasteful examples. Food and décor are nothing to write home about – but after an evening here you won't be able to hold a pen. On two storeys with a roof terrace overlooking Ocean.

North Beach

Happy's Stork Lounge

1872 North Bay Causeway, at East Treasure Drive, North Bay Village (868 9191). Bus L. **Open** 11am-5am daily. **Credit** MC, V.
If Martin Scorsese had made *Mean Streets* in Miami, he'd have shot much of it here. Off-duty cops, hard-drinking journalists, an eerie, flickering neon sign and a host of shady-looking characters speaking in hushed tones give this place a wonderfully seedy feel.

Surfside to Golden Beach

Molly Malone's

166 Sunny Isles Boulevard, near Collins Avenue, Sunny Isles (948 3512). Bus E, H, K, S, V. **Open** 11am-3am daily. **Credit** MC, V.
Sea cows and mad cows alike frequent Molly Malone's, the only Irish pub in the world where you can study manatees from the back porch. This tavern on the Intracoastal Highway offers the expected Irish beers on tap – Guinness, Harp, Bass and Murphy's Amber – and a fully stocked bar to help wash down tunes from the eclectic jukebox.

Virginia Key

Bayside Hut

3501 Rickenbacker Causeway, Virginia Key (361 0808). Bus B. **Open** 11.30am-10pm Mon-Thur; 11.30am-midnight Fri, Sat; 11.30am-9.30pm Sun. **Credit** AmEx, MC, V.
Small, and tucked away between a boat storage yard and the decomposing concrete hulk of Miami Marine Stadium, the Bayside Hut (not to be confused with the tourist-oriented Bayside Marketplace in Downtown) remains popular with insiders who appreciate the waterfront setting, the fresh seafood and the spectacular views (especially at night) of the Miami skyline from across Biscayne Bay.

*Make like Flipper and get down to **Jimbo's**.*

Jimbo's

Off the Rickenbacker Causeway at Sewerline Road, Virginia Key (361 7026). Bus B. **Open** 6am-6.30pm daily. **No credit cards.**

Hands down the most-difficult-to-find and even more-difficult-to-describe watering hole in Miami. What do you call a place that started as a gathering spot for shrimping trawlers and mutated into a combination of disparate enterprises – a bocce court, a fish-smoking oven, a dollar-a-can beer-drinking hangout, a tropical lagoon where they shot *Flipper*, a collection of vacant faux-Bahamian shacks rented out for hundreds of TV, photo and movie shoots from *Miami Vice* to *True Lies* – linked only by owner-manager Jimbo Luznar's proprietorship? The term 'bar' doesn't begin to do Jimbo's justice. Shrimpers, crusty old sea dogs and even City of Miami politicos gravitate to this sanctuary just minutes from Downtown. Precious few South Florida attractions can compete with the simple pleasure of sipping beer on Jimbo's dock while watching manatees loll in his lagoon. One caveat: under no circumstances let the owner hustle you into a game of bocce – he never loses unless he's setting you up.

Key Biscayne

Sundays on the Bay

5420 Crandon Boulevard, Key Biscayne (361 6777). Bus B. **Open** 11.30am-11.45pm Mon-Wed; 11.30am-1am Thur-Sun. **Credit** AmEx, Disc, MC, V.

A one-time hotspot for coke smugglers, who would pull right up to the bar in their cigarette boats, Sundays was recently seized by the federal government as part of a massive drug money laundering bust. It's lost some of its lustre since its mid 1980s heyday, but still makes a refreshing stop for beachgoers returning from the public beach at Crandon Park.

The Mainland
Downtown

1800 Club

1800 N Bayshore Drive, at NE 18th Street, Downtown (373 1093). Bus 16, 36, 62, A, T. **Open** 11.30am-3am daily. **Credit** AmEx, MC, V.

The city's powerbrokers quaff three-martini lunches during the day; at night the 1800 Club serves as an unofficial rallying point for fans of Miami's professional hockey and basketball teams (which play at the nearby Miami Arena).

Tobacco Road

626 S Miami Avenue, at SW Seventh Street, Downtown (374 1198). Bus 6, 8. **Open** 11.30am-5am Mon-Fri; noon-5am Sat. **Credit** AmEx, DC, Disc, MC, V.

Even when the stages are silent, Miami's premier blues club, former speakeasy and supposed holder of the city's first liquor license still qualifies as one of the city's finest drinking establishments.

Coral Gables

Duffy's Tavern

2108 SW 57th Avenue, between SW 21st & 22nd Streets, Coral Gables (264 6580). Bus 24. **Open** 10am-12.45am Mon-Sat; 10am-11.45pm Sun. **No credit cards.**

A favourite hangout of UM football players (past and present), Duffy's prides itself on its jock-friendliness.

Coconut Grove

Flanigan's Laughing Loggerhead

2721 Bird Avenue, between SW 40th Street & 27th Avenue, Coconut Grove (446 1114). Bus 22, 27, 42. **Open** 11.30am-5am daily. **Credit** AmEx, Disc, MC, V.

A Grove institution, the Loggerhead stocks some 200 bottled beers and serves up a delectable blackened dolphin sandwich (among other basic but succulent selections such as ribs and juicy, two-fisted hamburgers). A fishing motif prevails, with aged wooden walls plastered with Hemingway-esque photos of anglers and their prodigious catches.

Monty's

2550 S Bayshore Drive, at Aviation Avenue, Coconut Grove (858 1431). Bus 48. **Open** 11.30am-4pm, 5-11pm, Mon-Thur, Sun; 11.30-4pm, 5pm-midnight, Fri, Sat. **Credit** AmEx, DC, Disc, MC, V.

An outdoor raw (seafood) bar located next to a marina, Monty's has been popular with Groveites for decades.

Mine's a...

Long days in the sun demand their own particular alcoholic accompaniments. What should you put in your cooler for a day on the beach – and, more importantly, what do you reply when that attractive stranger offers to buy the newly sun-kissed you a drink?

For its sheer thirst-quenching abilities, beer is top of the list, and with nearly 3,000 varieties on the US market (as opposed to a mere 300 20 years ago), you don't have to stick to Bud. However, don't expect to find your favourite import or obscure microbrew: arcane Florida state law permits the sale of beer only in certain sizes of bottle, which rules out metric and non-standard quantities.

Miami has lived up to its reputation for lagging behind the rest of the US with its reluctance to join in the national enthusiasm for 'craft-beers', beers made in locally owned microbreweries and brew pubs. The first two labels to call Miami home hardly bode well for fans of fresh, hearty suds. Neither Hurricane Reef nor Firehouse offer much to distinguish themselves from the popular, nationally distributed microbrews such as Samuel Adams, Anchor Steam and Pete's Wicked.

Equally, brewpubs are finding it hard to get a foothold in Miami. Since the closure of the South Pointe Seafood House and its in-house brewery, the only place you can get real beer on tap in South Beach is **The Abbey** (*see above* **South Beach**), which serves a hoppy, crisp lager – and even that is contracted out to a microbrewery in Key West. On the mainland, **Don Gambrinu's Brewery House and Restaurant** in suburban Miami Lakes (6685 Eagle Nest Lane; 556 0502) ties the microbrew concept in with a 300-seat eaterie. Be warned: the stuff you get in both these places is substantially stronger than commercial beer.

If you're not partial to beer, there are other options. The old reliable martini has enjoyed renewed popularity in Miami (as it has throughout the US) with the resurgent hipness of lounge culture. The short shots of choice are Cuervo tequila and the viscous, vile-tasting Jagermeister. Students of Latin culture may want to start with Cuba Libres (glorified rum and Cokes) and work up to the legendary libation known as the mojito – a drink that originated in Cuba's countryside, became all the rage among Havana's high society and virtually disappeared after Castro seized power. Today you can only find this classic cocktail – a mixture of rum, sugar, lime juice, ice, soda water and the mysterious mint-like yerbabuena leaf – in and around Miami's Little Havana district and at the more clued-in South Beach restaurants, such as **Yuca** (501 Lincoln Road).

Thatch-roofed, open-walled, mini tiki huts surround a stage where tasteful reggae and calypso bands do their best to persuade the floral-print-shirted minions to dance.

The Taurus
3540 Main Highway, between Franklin & Charles Avenues, Coconut Grove (448 0633). Bus 42, 48. **Open** 11.30am-2.30am daily. **Credit** AmEx, DC, MC, V.
A few doors down from the Coconut Grove Playhouse, the Taurus restaurant serves some of the Grove's best steaks, and the adjoining bar boasts more colourful Grove old-timers per barstool than any other bistro.

Tavern in the Grove
3416 Main Highway, between Grand Avenue & Fuller Street, Coconut Grove (447 3884). Bus 42, 48. **Open** 3pm-3am daily. **Credit** AmEx, MC, V.
Fresh-faced UM coeds frequent this no-nonsense hole-in-the-wall in the heart of the Grove.

Virtua Cafe
3390 Mary Street, at Grand Avenue, Coconut Grove (567 3070). Bus 42, 48. **Open** 11.30am-1am Mon-Thur, Sun; 11.30am-2am Fri, Sat. **Credit** MC, V.
This interactive virtual reality entertainment emporium comes complete with a bar, restaurant, retail store, Internet hookups and all the latest cyberific gizmos to enable you to blast away virtual invaders from outer space.
e-mail: corporat@virtuacafe
website: http://www.virtuacafe.com

North & South Dade

Ukelele Bar
10950 Biscayne Boulevard, between NE 109th & 110th Streets, North Miami (891 9203). Bus 3. **Open** 11am-1am daily. **No credit cards.**
Basic neighbourhood bar in a fast-deteriorating neighbourhood.

Fox's Sherron Inn
6030 S Dixie Highway, between SW 60th & 61st Avenues, South Miami (661 9201). Bus 37, 52, 57, 65. **Open** 11am-1.30am Mon-Sat; 5pm-midnight Sun. **Credit** AmEx, MC, V.
Dark and cold as a crypt, with commodious red vinyl booths and a full food menu to complement the well-stocked bar, Fox's has been pouring tall, stiff drinks since 1956.

Hooligan's Pub & Oyster Bar
9555 S Dixie Highway, at Dadeland Boulevard, South Miami (667 9673). Bus 1, 52, 65. **Open** 11am-4am Mon-Thur, Sun; 11am-5am Fri, Sat. **Credit** AmEx, DC, MC, V.
The archetypal yuppie sports bar: TVs everywhere, cheap chicken wings, draught beer specials, plenty of parking.

Your Father's Moustache
7232 SW 59th Avenue, at SW 73rd Street, South Miami (665 9996). Bus 37, 57, 72. **Open** 11am-2am Mon-Wed; 11am-5am Thur-Sat; 2pm-2am Sun. **Credit** AmEx, MC, V.
Well-lit, clean restrooms, friendly owner: this quiet little place in one of Miami's premier neighbourhoods is a local favourite.

Miami Shopping
& Services

Shopping & Services

Getting conspicuous about consumption.

Miami isn't a city big on sidewalks and there are few spots where walking is encouraged: really just South Beach, Coconut Grove, Coral Gables' Miracle Mile and Downtown Miami. Fortunately, the shopping here is good fun: more diverse and individual than most of the air-conditioned mega-malls offering generic department-store fare. All these areas have more to offer than just shops, and are relatively well-connected transport-wise. However, outside them, you'll be better off with a car.

The current trend is towards upmarket open-air shopping malls, a promenade of top-quality names – Ralph Lauren, Williams-Sonoma, Bloomingdale's – in a cushy theme-park setting. **The Falls** in Pinecrest, Southwest Dade, for example, is set around an elaborate but shallow running brook, with the occasional bench and bridge for you to catch your breath between purchases. At Fort Lauderdale's mega discount mall, **Sawgrass Mills**, you can dine in an air-conditioned jungle squawking with animatronic toucans. It's a jungle in there. More often than not, a movie mall of six or more screens is part of the package, plus one or more big chain eateries.

Miami is nicknamed the gateway to Latin America and many rich South Americans shop here, sometimes in bulk, but mostly in upscale Bal Harbour, where Chanel, Gucci, Prada and Bulgari cater to their wallets. For the more adventurous who want to feel the heartbeat of the city, go downmarket and stroll through Downtown Miami, where you'll think you just made a left turn to Puerto Rico. There are umpteen luggage, electronics and sporting goods stores here, windows popping with outlandish Brazilian high heels, street carts selling fruit and Cuban coffee everywhere. Most of the proprietors here are Cuban or Central American transplants and conduct business as they would in the old country – so expect to haggle and hustle. Imported knock-off merchandise floweth over. You get what you pay for, so spend wisely and get receipts.

Thanks to relatively low rents and sales tax (6.5 per cent on top of the marked price), prices are generally a bit cheaper here than in New York or LA, though the selection is slimmer. Unlike in New York, there's usually a forgiving return policy (read the fine print on your receipt) and a 30-day exchange clause for credit. Remember that the shelf life of most shops is short, so call before making a long journey, and make sure you get written guarantees (and a helpline number for electronics).

If you're taking goods out of the country, remember that you will be liable for duty and tax above a certain value ceiling (£145 in the UK).

One-stop
Malls

Bal Harbour Shops

9700 Collins Avenue, at 96th Street, Bal Harbour (866 0311). Bus G, H, K, R, S. **Open** 10am-9pm Mon-Fri; 10am-7pm Sat; noon-7pm Sun.
The oh-so-exclusive Bal Harbour Shops, built in the next city north from Miami Beach in the late 1960s, is nicknamed Miami's Rodeo Drive. In this three-storey, modernist Bali Hai, you'll find big-bucks labels like Prada, Tiffany's, Chanel, Gianni Versace and Bulgari rubbing padded shoulders with the more affordable Gap and Banana Republic and department stores Neiman Marcus and Saks Fifth Avenue. There's also an American Express Travel office.

Bayside Marketplace

401 Biscayne Boulevard, at NE Fourth Street, Downtown (577 3344). Bus 3, 16, 48, 95, C/Metromover College/Bayside. **Open** 10am-10pm Mon-Thur; 10am-11pm Fri, Sat; 11am-8pm Sun.
Pricey mall fun as it's on the water (sightseeing boat tours run from here). Arrive by motorboat and dock, or just park your car in the lot. The stores? Foot Locker for athletic shoes, Roland the Hatter, Brookstone for great gadgets, plus outdoor kiosks selling arts and crafts from Latin America. There's a food court plus Miami's Hard Rock Café and street entertainment every night.

CocoWalk

3015 Grand Avenue, at Virginia Street, Coconut Grove (444 0777). Bus 42, 48. **Open** 11am-10pm Mon-Thur, Sun; 11am-midnight Fri-Sat. **Credit** varies.
Locals of this boho burg rued the arrival of corporate America in the form of this multi-storey semi-outdoor mall. At least it has a slightly funky feel, as malls go, with a handful of gift/jewellery market stalls and terrace seating at the cafés. Otherwise it's all the usual names: Gap, Victoria's Secret, Banana Republic, plus eating joints and a 16-screen cinema.

Dadeland Mall

7535 SW 88th Street, at SW 72nd Avenue, Kendall (665 6225). Bus 87, 88/Metrorail Dadeland North/Dadeland South. **Open** 10am-9pm Mon-Sat; noon-5.30pm Sun.

The first air-conditioned supermall fronts Burdine's, a local department store (with a separate complex for home furnishings) as its flagship. There's also Arango design, Sharper Image, Saks Fifth Avenue, Lord & Taylor and a spectacular two-storey Limited-Express store.

The Falls

8888 SW 136th Street, off S Dixie Highway (US 1), South Dade (255 4570). Bus 1, 52, 65. **Open** 10am-9pm Mon-Sat; noon-6pm Sun.
The only Bloomingdale's in town is this themed megamall's big draw. You'll also find Crate & Barrel, Pottery Barn, Macy's, J Crew, Williams-Sonoma and Mark Cross.

Loehmann's Fashion Island Mall

2855 NE 187th Street, at Biscayne Boulevard, North Miami Beach (932 0520). Bus 3, V. **Open** 10am-9pm Mon-Sat; noon-6pm Sun.
Loehmann's women's markdown paradise is the hub of this new open-air mall just south of Aventura Mall, its antithesis. Also, a sprawling Barnes & Noble, Gap and a cineplex.

Omni International Mall of Miami

1601 Biscayne Boulevard, at NE 16th Street, Downtown (374 6664). Bus 3, 16, 48, 95, C/Metromover School Board. **Open** 10am-9pm Mon-Sat; noon-5.30pm Sun.
Generic merchandise for middle-of-the-road customers. Homeboy territory at weekends. Its proximity is a plus (it's across the bridge from South Beach). There's also cheap parking, cheap movies, Cruise Penney's department store, Gap, Express, Wolf Camera and Bentley's Luggage.

The Streets of Mayfair

2911 Grand Avenue, between Mary & Virginia Streets, Coconut Grove (448 1700). Bus 42, 48. **Open** hours vary, according to each store.
These two malls (a cineplex in each) are back to back in downtown Coconut Grove. They're popular with high school

Reflecting on the **Collectibles Market***.*

kids who cruise en masse at weekends. Concessions include Banana Republic, Gap, Express, Victoria's Secret, Borders Books, Music & Café, Oak Feed Natural Food Store, Blockbuster Music and Planet Hollywood.

Department stores

Bloomingdale's

The Falls, 8778 SW 136th Street, at S Dixie Highway, South Dade (252 6300). Bus 1, 52, 65. **Open** 10am-9.30pm Mon-Sat; noon-6pm Sun. **Credit** AmEx, MC, V.
High-end yet affordable goods for sophisticated consumers: Polo, Donna Karan, Moschino, Chanel, plus housewares for the gourmet, great purses and shoes.

Burdine's

Dadeland Mall, 7303 SW 88th Street, at SW 72nd Avenue (662 3400). Bus 87, 88/Metrorail Dadeland North/Dadeland South. **Open** 10am-9.30pm Mon-Sat; noon-6pm Sun. **Credit** AmEx, MC, V.
Though its South Beach branch is still catching up with the neighbourhood, Burdine's has been a Florida staple for decades. This branch is the best for fashion and lingerie.
Branch: 1675 Meridian Avenue, Miami Beach (674 6300).

Macy's

Aventura Mall, 19535 Biscayne Boulevard, at NE 195th Street (937 5485). Bus 3, 9, E, S. **Open** 10am-9.30pm Mon-Sat; 10am-6pm Sun. **Credit** AmEx, MC, V.
The All-American department store. The housewares department at Aventura is extensive. Fine ready-to-wear.
Branch: The Falls, 9100 SW 136th Street, South Dade (278 3385).

Neiman-Marcus

Bal Harbour Shops, 9700 Collins Avenue, at 96th Street, Bal Harbour (865 6161). Bus G, H, K, R, S. **Open** 10am-9pm Mon-Fri; 10am-7pm Sat; noon-7pm Sun. **Credit** AmEx.
Poshest of the posh. Almost like shopping on Madison Avenue. There's a designer salon (Richard Tyler, Mizrahi, Donna Karan), plus Robert Clergerie shoes, Bobbi Brown make-up and special gift and costume jewellery departments.

Markets & fairs

The Art Deco Street Festival

Ocean Drive, between Fifth & 15th Streets, Miami Beach (672 2014).
On January 16-19, 1998, from noon to midnight, Ocean Drive will be packed with rows of international vintage booths selling everything from moderne and art deco furniture and clothing to rare French movie posters. Food booths sell wienerschnitzel, fresh-squeezed lemonade and plenty besides. An annual jam-packed event.

Espanola Way Flea Market

Espanola Way, between Washington & Drexel Avenues, Miami Beach. Bus C, H, K, W. **Open** noon-sundown Sun.
This hippie's bazaar of ethnic handicrafts and vintage stuff is a junker's dream. Small but lively.

Miami Beach Convention Center

1901 Convention Center Drive, at 17th Street, Miami Beach (673 7311). Bus C, H, K, W.
A major venue for shows: Antique Jewellery & Watch Show, Sept 24-25 and Oct 14-15, 1997; The Original Miami Beach Antique Show, Jan 26-29, 1998; Barnes Antique Show, Nov 18-19, 1998.

Outdoor Antique & Collectibles Market

Between 16th & 17th Streets and Lenox & Washington Avenues (information 673 4991), South Beach. Bus C, G, K, L, S. **Open** Oct-June 10am-5pm every 2nd & 4th Sun.

Sink your teeth into some tasty bargains at **Sawgrass Mills**.

Down artsy Lincoln Road mall, sellers come from all over to hawk retro: Wakefield dressers, 1960s chandeliers, Fiestaware, doodads and frocks. Fun flea.

Thunderbird Swap Shop
3291 W Sunrise Boulevard, Fort Lauderdale (1-954-791 7927). **Open** 8.30am-6pm Mon-Fri; 7.30am-6.30pm Sat, Sun. **Credit** varies.
This is one of the last great drive-ins (70-plus acres). During the day, it doubles as a country music concert hall and a live circus show and it has the hustle bustle of a real Southern country fair. You'll see plenty of bonafide rednecks and enterprising Latinos here selling rusty auto parts, knock-off merch, and some used and vintage items. Best buys are at the huge farmer's market, nursery and gold jewellery depot. Thursday is peak day.

Discount department stores

Best Buy
8450 S Dixie Highway, at SW 83rd Street, in Dadeland Station, South Dade (662 7073). Bus 1, 52, 87, 88/Metrorail Dadeland North. **Open** 10am-9pm Mon-Sat; 11am-6pm Sun. **Credit** AmEx, Disc, MC, V.
Everything from CDs to cellphones, computers, cameras, electronics, fridges – you name it, this warehouse has it.

Marshall's
16800 Collins Avenue, at 170th Street, Miami Beach (446 8575). Bus E, K, S, V. **Open** 9.30am-9.30pm Mon-Sat; 11am-6pm Sun. **Credit** AmEx, Disc, MC, V.
'Never, never, never pay full price' is the motto of Miami's No.1 discount store. Markdowns on designer clothing, housewares, furnishings, gourmet foods, accessories, luggage, athletic shoes. Women's undies cost from $1.99; there's also affordable children's wear.
Branches: 20515 Biscayne Boulevard, Aventura (937 2525); 13619 S Dixie Highway, South Dade (253 3962).

TJ Maxx
8765 SW 136th Street, at S Dixie Highway, South Dade (255 5498). Bus 1, 52, 65. **Open** 9.30am-9.30pm Mon-Sat; noon-6pm Sun. **Credit** AmEx, Disc, MC, V.
Not as large or sophisticated as Marshall's, Maxx's has no DKNY. Seek and you shall find.

Ross Dress for Less
18495 Biscayne Boulevard, at NE 184th Street, North Miami Beach (933 0098). Bus 3, 9. **Open** 9.30am-9.30pm Mon-Sat; 11am-7pm Sun. **Credit** AmEx, Disc, MC, V.
Much like Maxx's, Ross's is an also-ran in the discount department store stakes, but there's plenty to choose from.

Target
8350 S Dixie Highway, at SW 83rd Street, in Dadeland Station, South Dade (668 0262). Bus 1, 52, 87, 88/Metrorail Dadeland North. **Open** 8am-10pm daily. **Credit** AmEx, Disc, MC, V.
Overwhelmingly inexpensive. There's clothing, small appliances, house and garden, foodstuffs, drugstore items, sports and gym equipment, and much else. Tie a balloon to your companions: Target is so big, you may never see them again.

Factory outlets

Sawgrass Mills
12801 W Sunrise Boulevard, Sunrise, in Broward County (1-954 846 2350). Shuttle buses run from Miami Beach hotels Mon-Sat. **Open** 10am-9pm Mon-Sat; 11am-8pm Sun.
The Star Wars of discount malls dwarfs most airports: it's over a mile long, covering 170 acres, and is one of Florida's top tourist draws. Designed by postmodernists Arquitectonica, Sawgrass now houses Barneys, DKNY, Joan & David, J Crew, Neiman Marcus, Target, and Sport Authority. There's a foreign currency exchange centre, five ATMs, an 18-cineplex, plus a food court.

Speciality

Fedco

1605 Washington Avenue, between 16th Street & Lincoln Road, Miami Beach (531 5583). Bus C, H, K, W. **Open** 8.30am-9pm Mon-Sat; 10am-5pm Sun. **Credit** Disc, MC, V.
No visit to South Beach is complete without a rummage around this discount drugstore, the octogenarian's paradise. The grandad of pharmacies, 29 years old, it's jam-packed with bottom-priced goods and wacky blue-haired grannies.

Loehmann's

7135 SW 117th Avenue, off SW 72nd Street, Kendall (596 5500). Bus 56, 72. **Open** 10am-9pm Mon-Sat; noon-6pm Sun. **Credit** Disc, MC, V.
Designer markdowns for women only: Gottex swimsuits, Calvin undies, Moschino, Karan couture leftovers. If you don't mind trying on clothes in front of blue-haired ladies in bulging support hose (the dressing room's like a locker room), you'll find bargains. Merchandise credit exchange only, so no cash refunds.
Branch: 18703 Biscayne Boulevard, North Miami Beach (932 4207).

Office Depot

100 NE First Avenue, at NE First Street, Downtown (372 3311). Bus 9, 10, 11, 77, K/Metromover First Street. **Open** 8am-6pm Mon-Fri; 9am-3pm Sat. **Credit** AmEx, Disc, MC, V.
Bulk supplies for business or home. Alternatively, you can shop for a nice-priced computer or fax here.
Branch: 15033 S Dixie Highway, South Dade (235 9884).

Sally Beauty Supply

1529 Alton Road, between 15th & 16th Streets, Miami Beach (532 9691). Bus F/M, S, W. **Open** 9am-7pm Mon-Sat; 11am-5pm Sun. **Credit** AmEx, Disc, MC, V.
A chain of cosmetic and fashion supplies for the professional beautician and do-it-at-homers. Hair colours, nail appliqués, generic Aveda hair product line (Aura).

Arts & entertainment

Books

The 9th Chakra

817 Lincoln Road, between Jefferson & Meridian Avenues, Miami Beach (538 0671). Bus C, G, K, L, S. **Open** 2-8pm Mon; noon-11pm Tue-Thur; noon-11pm Fri, Sat; 2-9pm Sun. **Credit** AmEx, MC, V.
In case you were wondering, your ninth chakra is in your neck, the silver cord to your soul. This metaphysical bookstore has been here for six years. Psychic consultations cost $40 for half an hour; astrological natal charts $30. There are also ritual packages for love and health; feng shui tools; Kama Sutra books, edible oils, tantric videos and honey dust for your partner.

Barnes & Noble Booksellers

18711 Biscayne Boulevard, at Loehmann's Fashion Island, North Miami Beach (935 9770). Bus 3, V. **Open** 9am-11pm daily. **Credit** AmEx, DC, Disc, MC, V.
The trouble with these megachains is they're stacked with Book-of-the-Month club mainstream American pulp. Not the place to find eclectic reading matter, but worth a stroll.
Branch: 7710 N Kendall Drive, Kendall (598 7292).

Books & Books in Miami Beach

933 Lincoln Road, between Jefferson & Michigan Avenues, Miami Beach (532 3222). Bus C, G, K, L, S. **Open** 10am-11pm Mon-Thur, Sun; 10am-midnight Fri, Sat. **Credit** AmEx, DC, Disc, MC, V.

This literary marketplace is the mating ground for South Beachers who read (and is also the only bookstore on the island). Now that the Russian Bear Café serves mochaccino and gourmet nibbles in-house, you can daydream al fresco on Lincoln Road or gaze upon the madding crowd from the air-conditioned picture window.
Branch: 296 Aragon Avenue, Coral Gables (442 4408).

Borders Book Shop

3390 Mary Street, at the Mayfair, Coconut Grove (447 1655). Bus 42, 48. **Open** 10am-11pm Mon-Thur, Sun; 10am-midnight Fri, Sat. **Credit** AmEx, Disc, MC, V.
The largest branch of this slightly alternative bookstore chain, Borders is the antidote to its glitzy next-door neighbour, Planet Hollywood. There's cappuccino in the cosy café, of course, a good selection of photography books, a large children's and magazine section, even music upstairs.
Branches: 19925 Biscayne Boulevard, Aventura (935 0027); 9205 S Dixie Highway, South Dade (665 8800).

Grove Antiquarian Books

3318 Virginia Street, at Florida Avenue, Coconut Grove (444 5362). Bus 42, 48. **Open** 11am-7pm Mon-Sat. **Credit** AmEx, Disc, MC, V.
A cache of eclectic, bookish, arty fare. Safely tucked away from surrounding mall-rat mania, this cubbyhole is a book lover's delight. Excellent fine art, twentieth-century literature and Floridiana.

Kafka's Used Book Store

1460 Washington Avenue, between 14th Street & Espanola Way, Miami Beach (673 9669). Bus C, H, K, W. **Open** 10am-10pm Mon-Thur, Sun; 10am-midnight Fri, Sat. **No credit cards.**
Not Manhattan's Strand, but give it time. Mostly used paperbacks, some hardbacks. Great beach reading at hostel prices.

Lambda Passages Bookstore

7545 Biscayne Boulevard, at NE 75th Street, Miami (754 6900). Bus 3, 16. **Open** 11am-9pm Mon-Sat; noon-6pm Sun. **Credit** AmEx, DC, Disc, MC, V.
Tucked away in the edgy red light district of Biscayne Boulevard, this store has an ample selection of new and used gay and lesbian books. Good for videos. Coffee and cookies are sold at the gay-owned florist's entered from the bookstore. For more gay books, see **GW – the Gay Emporium** *listed under* **Specialist & Gifts.**

Murder on Miami Beach

16850 Collins Avenue, at 168th Street, Sunny Isles (956 7770). Bus E, S, V. **Open** hours vary; call for details. **Credit** A,Ex, MC, V.
A cosy bookstore for mystery lovers.

The Seeker of the Light

536 Lincoln Road, between Drexel & Pennsylvania Avenues, Miami Beach (531 1455). Bus C, G, K, L, S. **Open** 11am-10pm Mon-Thur; 11am-midnight Fri, Sat; noon-8pm Sun. **Credit** AmEx, DC, Disc, MC, V.
'Come in. You will feel the Light' reads the ad. It must be true as there's always a crowd perusing the well-lit aisles of this 'bookstore for the enlightened age'. Boasting the biggest selection of books on astrology, esoterica and all things spiritual, it's also a folksy new age centre, offering bilingual Tarot readings, aura photography, yoga classes, reiki, past-life regression, and our personal favourite, brain dormancy.

Cameras & electronic

The countless electronics stores in downtown Miami, downtown Miami Beach and Lincoln Road are notorious. Unless you're particularly savvy (an ex-employee of Nikon), don't mess with these jocks. They're known for selling goods that've fallen off the truck, so to speak. Watch for missing guarantees and never leave without a receipt (including the names of sales staff) and an explanation of the return/exchange policy. Generally, it's better to shop in established retail houses.

Office Depot (*see above* **Discount**) has an electronics department that sells Apples, Canons, Hewlett-Packards, Brother faxes, cellphones, and the like. Sadly, its prices are better than its service.

Aperture Professional Supply

1330 18th Street, between Bay Road & West Avenue, Miami Beach (673 4327). Bus F/M, S, W. **Open** 10am-4pm Mon-Fri. **Credit** AmEx, MC, V.

Pros can hire camera gear here – Canon, Nikon, Hasselblad – buy film and rerent studio space (535 6375) at this all-purpose facility. Some amateur autofocus equipment.

CompUSA

8851 Southwest 136th Street, at S Dixie Highway, across the street from The Falls, South Dade (234 5600). Bus 1, 52, 65. **Open** 10am-9pm Mon-Sat; 11am-6pm Sun. **Credit** AmEx, DC, Disc, MC, V.

The computer supermarket. Everything in IBM, PC and Macintosh soft- and hardware, from outlandish computer games to state-of-the-art laptops, modems, CD-Roms. Aisles of books, accessories and technobrats hogging terminals. **Branch**: 900 Park Center Boulevard, North Dade (620 1800).

Computer Village

1140 S Dixie Highway, between Turin & Augusto Streets, Coral Gables (667 7400). Bus 48, 52, 65/Metrorail University. **Open** 9.30am-6pm Mon-Fri; 9.30am-5pm Sat. **Credit** AmEx, DC, Disc, MC, V.

The Apple Mac garage: where to have your PowerBook, Hewlett-Packard laser printer and the like repaired. The computer nerds who work here give personal service and advice.

One Hour Photo

Bayside Marketplace, Downtown (377 3686). Bus 3, 16, 48, 95, C/Metromover College/Bayside. **Open** 10am-10pm Mon-Thur; 10am-11pm Fri, Sat; 11am-9pm Sun. **Credit** AmEx, DC, Disc, M, V.

One Hour is expensive but one of the few places in the city where you can have your film developed quickly. Also provides a full range of photographic and video products. Price for developing a 24-exposure roll of 35mm film: about $9.

Tropicolor Photo

1442 Alton Road, between 14th & 15th Streets, Miami Beach (672 3720). Bus F/M, S, W. **Open** 9am-8pm Mon-Sat; 11am-6pm Sun. **Credit** AmEx, Disc, MC, V.

An all-purpose neighbourhood photo print processing lab with colour Xerox and passport ID services. Best prices.

Music & video

Blockbuster Video

1501 Alton Road, at 15th Street, Miami Beach (538 0614). Bus F/M, S, W. **Open** 10am-midnight daily. **Credit** AmEx, Disc, MC, V.

The biggest video rental chain also hires out VCRs. A massive choice of new releases plus children's videos, subtitled foreigns, classics, gore.

Casino Records

1208 SW Eighth Street, between SW 12th & 13th Avenues, Little Havana (856 6888). Bus 8, 12. **Open** 9am-9pm Mon-Sat; 10am-5pm Sun. **Credit** AmEx, DC, Disc, MC, V.

Another great place to find Cuban discos (records), which, reportedly, are easier to buy here than in Havana.

Do Re Mi Music Center

1829 SW Eighth Street, between SW 18th & 19th Avenues, Little Havana (541 3374). Bus 8, 17. **Open** 10.30am-8pm Mon-Sat. **Credit** AmEx, Disc, MC, V.

The house of Latin music, be it romanticos (ballads) or salsa.

Island Trading

1330 Ocean Drive, between 13th & 14th Streets, Miami Beach (673 6300). Bus C, H, K, W. **Open** 11am-8pm Mon, Tue, Sun; 11am-10pm Wed, Thur; 11am-11pm Fri, Sat.* **Credit** AmEx, Disc, MC, V.

A hand-picked selection of authentic happenin' Afrique and Caribe CDs on maverick Island Record labels – Mango, Quango, Cup of Tea.

New Concept Video

749 Lincoln Road, between Meridian & Pennsylvania Avenues, Miami Beach (674 1111). Bus C, G, K, L, S. **Open** 10am-midnight Mon-Fri; 10am-11pm Sat, Sun. **Credit** AmEx, DC, Disc, MC, V.

Independent video rentals specialising in edgy cinema, hard-to-find foreign films, indies and triple XXX fare.

Revolution Records & CDs

1620A Alton Road, between 16th Street & Lincoln Road, Miami Beach (673 6464). Bus F/M, S, W. **Open** 11am-9pm Mon-Sat; noon-7pm Sun. **Credit** AmEx, Disc, MC, V.

A cosy nook of used CDs and cassettes peppered with 1960s memorabilia, Madonna posters, James Dean-alia.

Spec's Music

501 Collins Avenue, at Fifth Street, Miami Beach (534 3667). Bus C, H, K, W. **Open** 10am-1am Mon-Sat; 10am-midnight Sun. **Credit** AmEx, Disc, MC, V.

The largest music megastore in Miami boasts two floors of listening stations, music equipment, mags, paraphernalia and an in-store café.

Yesterday & Today

1614 Alton Road, between 16th Street & Lincoln Road, Miami Beach (534 8704). Bus F/M, S, W. **Open** noon-8pm Mon-noon-9pm Thur, Fri; noon-8pm Sat; 1-7pm Sun. **Credit** AmEx, Disc, MC, V.

The house of house – house music, that is. A hip-hop deejay's hang-out with all the latest sides and headphones. Cool selection, used CDs too.

Toys & games

FAO Schwarz

9700 Collins Avenue, at 96th Street, Bal Harbour (865 2361). Bus G, H, K, R, S. **Open** 10am-9pm Mon-Fri; 10am-7pm Sat; noon-7pm Sun. **Credit** AmEx, DC, Disc, MC, V.

Where to go for that mini Mercedes Benz your five-year-old demanded. Goods are pricey but choice. Top-drawer teddy-bears and dolls: upmarket diversions for youngsters.

Toys RUs

6325 S Dixie Highway, at SW 63rd Avenue, South Dade (662 1911). Bus 65, 72/Metrorail South Miami. **Open** 9.30am-9.30pm Mon-Sat; 11am-7pm Sun. **Credit** AmEx, Disc, MC, V.

Santa shops here. It's a playhouse of toys at low prices, with several branches in town, all with the latest kids' stuff.

FW Woolworth

410 Lincoln Road, between Drexel & Washington Avenues, Miami Beach (531 8173). Bus C, G, K, L, S. **Open** 9am-8.45pm Mon-Sat; 10am-5.45pm Sun. **Credit** AmEx, Disc, MC, V.

Test-ride a go-ped at **Fritz's Skate Shop**.

This Miami Beach institution is the largest sundries store in town, with a fun beach and toy department. It's stacked with inexpensive knick-knacks, souvenirs, cosmetics, domestics and midnight snacks. The original 1950s diner counter still serves grilled cheese sandwiches.

Sport & outdoor

2theXtreme
700 Lincoln Road, between Euclid & Meridian Avenues, Miami Beach (538 1390). Bus C, G, K, L, S. **Open** 11am-8pm Mon-Fri; 11am-10pm Sat; noon-8pm Sun. **Credit** AmEx, MC, V.
Supertech extreme sports boy (and girl) toys brought to you by homeboy rapper-extreme, Vanilla Ice. They include top-of-the-line jet skis, Harleys, motorcross bikes, rollerblades, plus state-of-the-art accoutrements (not cheap) for the extreme athlete who likes livin' on the edge.

Fritz's Skate Shop
601 Collins Avenue, at Sixth Street (532 0054). Bus C, H, K, W. **Open** 10am-8pm Mon-Thur, Sun; 10am-10pm Fri, Sat. **Credit** AmEx, DC, Disc, MC, V.
Rollerblades for rent ($8 per hour; $24 per day; $15 overnight – including insurance) or sale. Free group lessons are held on Sunday mornings. Or buy a California go-ped, a motorised scooter, for about $600.
Branch: 726 Lincoln Road, Miami Beach (532 1954).

Grey Taxidermy
712 NW 12th Avenue, Pompano Beach, Broward County (1-954 785 6456). No public transport. **Open** 9am-5pm Mon-Fri. **Credit** AmEx, Disc, MC, V.
Want to turn your fishing triumphs into trophies? You bag it, they'll stuff it. The lobby is lined with many fine examples of life-like stiffs, furry, feathered and finned.

Miami Beach Bicycle Center
601 Fifth Street, at Washington Avenue, Miami Beach (674 0150). Bus C, K. **Open** 10am-7pm Mon-Sat; 10am-5pm Sun. **Credit** AmEx, DC, Disc, MC, V.
Cruisers and mountain bikes can be rented for $14 a day, $50 a week, or by the hour. State-of-the-art cycles and paraphernalia from Cat Eye, Oakley and RockShox, plus clothing and shoes. Excellent bike repairs.

Sports Authority
8390 S Dixie Highway, at SW 83rd Street, in Dadeland Station, South Dade (667 2280). Bus 1, 52, 87, 88/Metrorail Dadeland North. **Open** 10am-9pm Mon-Sat; 10am-6pm Sun. **Credit** AmEx, Disc, MC, V.
A sporting goods superstore: 39,000sq ft of scuba gear, Coleman camping equipment, Remington tents, tennis rackets, golf bags, Timberland and Wolverine boots, and over 50 'blades. Prices promised to match the lowest on market.
Branch: 18499 Biscayne Boulevard, North Miami Beach (682 0717).

Xisle Surf Shop
437 Washington Avenue, between Fourth & Fifth Streets, Miami Beach (673 5900; surf report: 534 7873). Bus C, H, K, W. **Open** 10am-7pm Mon-Fri; 10am-6pm Sat; noon-6pm Sun. **Credit** AmEx, MC, V.
This is where to buy the *Baywatch* props and body gear – surf jams, thongs, shades (Arnettes, Dragons, Black Fly Oakleys), surfboards, boogie boards, wakeboards, skateboards. Staff don't rent surfboards, only the styro version (not as impressive, but they work).

Fashion

General

Banana Republic
800 Collins Avenue, at Eighth Street, Miami Beach (674 7079). Bus C, H, K, W. **Open** 10am-9pm Mon-Thur; 10am-10pm Fri, Sat; 10am-8pm Sun. **Credit** AmEx, Disc, MC, V.
Two-floor store with a winding staircase. Chic and sensible clothes, shoes, gymwear and jewellery are stocked. You'll also find Banana Republic at the Bal Harbour Shops, Falls and CocoWalk malls.

Gap
673 Collins Avenue, between Sixth & Seventh Streets, Miami Beach (531 5358). Bus C, H, K, W. **Open** 10am-9pm Mon-Thur; 10am-10pm Fri, Sat; 11am-8pm Sun. **Credit** AmEx, DC, Disc, MC, V.
A loft of classic American casuals. Great sales from $3.99 up. The lingerie department (Beach store only) premières stylish but comfortable undies. Good value.
Branch: 401 Biscayne Boulevard, Downtown (539 9603) and in malls including Bal Harbour and CocoWalk.

Laundry Industry
666 Collins Avenue, between Sixth & Seventh Streets, Miami Beach (531 2277). Bus C, H, K, W. **Open** 11am-8pm Mon-Sat; noon-6pm Sun. **Credit** AmEx, MC, V.
The black and white of it all. Cousin of the New York SoHo store, with basic separates that will cure any fashion victim.

Designer

Given South Beach's rep as Model City, fashion-shoot capital of the world and club central, you might expect Miami to have a native fashion industry. Well, it does, but it exists more to satisty the shopping appetites of visiting Latin Americans than to give DKNY a run for its money. Miami's Fashion District is a desolate area of factories and warehouses crammed with over-ornamented goods. There's one success story in the local world of high fashion: Cuban-American couturier Fernando Garcia, whose Alta y Baja Costura (High & Low Couture) counts Bergdorf's among its international clientele. His range retails at **Magazine**.

Betsey Johnson
805 Washington Avenue, at Eighth Street, Miami Beach (673 0023). Bus C, H, K, W. **Open** 11am-7pm Mon-Wed; 11am-8pm Thur-Sat; noon-6pm Sun. **Credit** AmEx, MC, V.
Kicky designer boutique for girls who refuse to grow up.

Magazine
229 Eighth Street, between Collins Avenue & Ocean Drive, Miami Beach (538 2702). Bus C, H, K, W. **Open** 11am-8pm Mon-Sat; noon-7pm Sun. **Credit** AmEx, DC, Disc, MC, V.
Next to the Moschinos, Gaultiers and Comme des Garçons in this groovy boutique, fabu Cubano Fernando Garcia showcases his slinky line of decolletage-friendly haute couture. Check out the Matinée store down the street for sale items and more footwear. The proprietors are Brit ex-pats.

Nicole Miller
656 Collins Avenue, between Sixth & Seventh Streets, Miami Beach (535 2200). Bus C, H, K, W. **Open** 11am-8pm Mon-Thur; 11am-10pm Fri, Sat; noon-6pm Sun. **Credit** AmEx, MC, V.
Tropical cocktailwear and smart clothing for the modern woman with the perfect figure. Evening gowns are fitted in this couture salon with its Parisian feel.

Romanoff
Bal Harbour Shops, 9700 Collins Avenue, at 96th Street (Romanoff Women's Apparel: 866 2222; Romanoff II: 865 7775). Bus G, H, K, R, S. **Open** 10am-9pm Mon-Fri; 10am-7pm Sat; noon-7pm Sun. **Credit** AmEx, MC, V.

Barbra Streisand shopped at Romanoff (and at full price, too). Designer bargains can be found at the sequel, Romanoff II, a chic closet of Euro haute-couture markdowns from seasons past: Comme des Garçons, Gaultier, selected Prada footwear.

Todd Oldham
763 Collins Avenue, between Seventh & Eighth Streets, Miami Beach (674 8090). Bus C, H, K, W. **Open** 11am-9pm Mon-Sat; noon-7pm Sun. **Credit** AmEx, MC, V.
A fun house filled with Todd's pop op fashions. Home toys for girls and boys.

Versace Jeans Couture
755 Washington Avenue, between Seventh & Eighth Streets, Miami Beach (532 5993). Bus C, H, K, W. **Open** 11am-7pm Mon-Sat; 10am-6pm Sun. **Credit** AmEx, DC, Disc, MC, V.
Gianni lives! This is practically an extension of his winter palazzo on Ocean Drive. Over-the-top *Dynasty* couture, swimsuits and nouveau regalia for the home.

Accessories & jewellery

For those whose shopping capacity exceeds their luggage capacity, throughout downtown Miami and South Beach (Lincoln Road Mall) are countless mom 'n' pop shops selling quality and functional throwaway luggage – Samsonite, American Traveler, Halburton, expandable nylon bags from $20, briefcases and backpacks, too. Genial haggling is okay.

Bentley's Luggage & Gifts
Omni International Mall, 1601 Biscayne Boulevard, at NE 16th Street, Downtown (358 6466). Bus 3, 16, 48, 95, C/Metromover School Board. **Open** 10am-9pm Mon-Sat; noon-5.30pm Sun. **Credit** AmEx, DC, Disc, MC, V.
A long-standing tony luggage shop, also selling wallets etc.
Branch: 8888 SW 136 Street, South Dade (278 8403).

*For funky threads, head to **Todd Oldham**.*

Seeing a Santeria

It's almost unconstitutional *not* to practise Santeria in Miami, after a celebrated court case established the right. A relative of voodoo, the Cuban branch of the African Yoruba religion is widely followed here, be it under the guise of Catholicism or superstition. Yes, animal sacrifices do go on in the hinterlands of Hialeah. If this doesn't deter you, visit a *botanica*.

On the outside, most *botanicas* look like curio shops, but make no mistake, those aren't knick-knacks in the window but spiritual supplies and so should be treated with respect. (Don't come to a botanica for a laugh or you'll cause offence. Respectful tourists – only – are tolerated). The room is rife with *santos* (representations of saints, some with magnets for your dashboard), religious candles, *milagros* (Mexican silver charms for whatever ails you), bead necklaces, furry animal pelts, big iron nails and horseshoes.

If your interest is piqued, ask for the resident *consulta*, a spiritual advisor who'll take you into the back room and tell your future: she'll throw cowrie shells and consult playing cards; you'll throw money, preferably cash, about $21. After the *consulta* spills your fortune (only the good

news, not the bad), a cure and/or ritual is prescribed. This can be the beginning of a long relationship, much like an initial visit to the shrink, and just as expensive, maybe a couple of hundred dollars, depending on your karma. If perchance someone's put an evil spell on you, you may be asked to return the next day for a cleaning. You may be instructed to wear light clothing and BYOB, a litre of white rum for the *orishas*. The gods like rum, even cheap rum. Not to worry. No goat's or chicken's blood is shed on public premises. A baptism of olive branches dipped in holy water is more like it. And an amulet to go, perhaps. Sometimes a fetish is prepared for you packed with herbs. Say thank you. And remember when someone greets you with 'Can I help you?' it's not a rhetorical question.

Botanica Esperanza
901 SW 27th Avenue, at SW Ninth Street, Little Havana (642 2488). Bus 8, 27. **Open** 9.30am-5.30pm Mon-Fri; 9.30am-2pm Sat. **Credit** AmEx, Disc, MC, V.

Botanica Nena
902 NW 27th Avenue, between NW Ninth & 10th Streets, Little Havana (649 8078). Bus 7, 27. **Open** 8am-6pm Mon-Fri; 8am-4pm Sat. **No credit cards**.

Fendi
Bal Harbour Shops, 9700 Collins Avenue, at 96th Street (861 6666). Bus G, H, K, R, S. **Open** 10am-9pm Mon-Fri; 10am-7pm Sat; noon-7pm Sun. **Credit** AmEx, DC, MC, V.
Beautiful handcrafted jewellery cases with secret compartments, overnight bags and to-die-for purses.

Joya
527 Lincoln Road, between Drexel & Pennsylvania Avenues, Miami Beach (534 5191). Bus C, G, K, L, S. **Open** 11am-8pm Mon-Thur; 11am-10pm Fri, Sat; noon-7pm Sun. **Credit** AmEx, Disc, MC, V.
That's Spanish for jewellery, which Tim, the owner, crafts when he's not stocking the store with goodies for your home.

Louis Vuitton
9700 Collins Avenue, at 96th Street, in Bal Harbour Shops, Bal Harbour (866 4470). Bus G, H, K, R, S. **Open** 10am-9pm Mon-Fri; 10am-7pm Sat; noon-7pm Sun. **Credit** AmEx, DC, Disc, MC, V.

Maya Hatcha
3058 Grand Avenue, between Fuller Street & Main Highway, Coconut Grove (446 0921). Bus 42, 48. **Open** 11am-6pm Mon-Wed; 11am-9pm Thur-Sat; 1-6pm Sun. **Credit** AmEx, DC, Disc, MC, V.
Great selection of hand-crafted ethnic jewellery and clothing: Mexican silver, African beads. Been here since the 1960s.

Morays
224 SE First Street, between NE Second & Third Avenues, Downtown (374 0739). Bus 11, 16, 77/Metromover First Street. **Open** 10.30am-5pm Mon-Fri. **Credit** AmEx, DC, Disc, MC, V.

The oldest jeweller's downtown (50 years), Morays stocks every watch brand you could possibly think of, from Cartier through to Bertolucci. Located in the Little Switzerland of Miami near the Seybold Building arcade, which houses ten floors of jewellers, engravers and watchmakers. Speaking Spanish helps here.

Roland Your Hatter
17 N Miami Avenue, between E Flagler & NE First Streets, Downtown (374 6263). Bus 6, 8, 9, 11, 77/Metromover Miami Avenue. **Open** 9am-5pm Mon-Sat. **Credit** AmEx, DC, Disc, MC, V.
Your Panama stockist. Roland's brims with tropical pith helmets, cowboy hats, porkpies, Gilligan hats and straws. No-one leaves here bareheaded.

Whittall & Shon
1319 Washington Avenue, between 13th & 14th Streets, Miami Beach (538 2606). Bus C, H, K, W. **Open** 11am-10pm Mon-Thur; 11am-9.30pm Fri, Sat; 11am-9.30pm Sun. **Credit** AmEx, MC, V.
Flowered Easter bonnets here amid the skivvies and tees perused by local gay traffic.

Beachwear

Connie Banko Swimwear
5607 SW 74th Street Avenue, South Miami (667 1535). Bus 37, 57, 72/Metrorail South Miami. **Open** 9.30am-4.30pm Mon-Sat. **Credit** AmEx, MC, V.
The Esther Williams of swimsuits. For 30 years, Connie has tailored swimsuits guaranteed to accentuate the positive and

camouflage the negative. Come in for a fitting or choose from her line of ready-to-wear. Custom-made takes about a week and costs from $90. Your pattern is kept on file.

Dolce Vita
422 Espanola Way, between Drexel & Washington Avenues, Miami Beach (672 8801). Bus C, H, K, W. **Open** 10am-8pm daily. **Credit** AmEx, MC, V.
Designer swimwear – not just bikinis but, yes, one-pieces: La Perla, Guess, Sauvage. Plus pareos (colourful scarf wraps) and imported sandals.

Ritchie Swimwear
800 Ocean Drive, at Eighth Street, Miami Beach (538 0201). Bus C, H, K, W. **Open** 10am-9pm Mon-Sat; 10am-8pm Sun. **Credit** AmEx, MC, V.
Wild bikinidom: bright tangas, strings, one-pieces fit for a *Baywatch* babe. All made in Miami. Mix-and-match bikini tops and bottoms cost from $60.
Branch: 3401 Main Highway, Coconut Grove (443 7919).

Children's
See also above **Department stores.**

Camille's Lollipops & Rainbows
809 NE 125th Street, between NE Eighth & Ninth Avenues, North Miami (891 5437). Bus 10, 75, G. **Open** 10am-6pm Mon-Fri; 10am-5pm Sat. **Credit** MC, V.
Slightly worn goods, mostly quality toys and clothing.

The Children's Exchange
1415 Sunset Drive, at SW 54th Avenue, Coral Gables (666 6235). Bus 37, 72. **Open** 9.30am-5pm Mon-Fri; 10am-4.30pm Sat; noon-5pm Sun. **Credit** Disc, MC, V.
The Saks Fifth Avenue of children's used clothing: Tommy Hilfiger, Polo, Yes. It also has toys.

Consigning Women's Kids
King's Bay Shopping Center, 14429 S Dixie Highway, at SW 144th Street,South Dade (233 5992). Bus 1, 52, 57. **Open** 10am-6pm Mon, Tue, Thur-Sat; 10am-8pm Wed. **Credit** MC, V.
Everything for the nursery is sold at this clearing-house for budget-wise mums and mums-to-be. Cribs for travellers, and portable playpens are rented out to air-travellers whose luggage allowance doesn't let them bring them. Stock also includes used strollers, toys, walkers and bedding.

Consignment Corner
8265 SW 82nd Avenue, Kendall (235 0958). Bus 1, 52, 57. **Open** 10am-5pm Mon, Tue, Thur, Fri; 10am-7pm Wed; 11am-5pm Sat. **Credit** AmEx, Disc, MC, V.
Nearly-new wear for kiddies and pregnant mums. Some toy collectibles.

Gap Kids
Bayside Marketplace, 401 Biscayne Boulevard, Downtown (539 9334). Bus 3, 16, 48, 95, C/Metromover College/Bayside. **Open** 10am-10pm Mon-Thur; 10am-11pm Fri, Sat; 11am-8pm Sun. **Credit** AmEx, MC, V.
Cute cheery gear for infants and tots, brought to you by the same Californian company that dresses mum and dad. The starter kit: Barbie Gap (blonde or black), $45.
Branches: 2982B Grand Avenue, Coconut Grove (445 4070); 8888 SW 136th Street, South Dade (235 2814).

Kidding Around
The Falls, 8888 SW 136th Street, at S Dixie Highway, South Dade (253 0708). Bus 1, 52, 65. **Open** 10am-9pm Mon-Sat; noon-6pm Sun. **Credit** AmEx, Disc, MC, V.
This pricey kids' boutique sells hand-picked quality fashion and furniture for tots and infants. Fun swimwear.

Marshall's
20515 Biscayne Boulevard, at NE 205th Street, Aventura (937 2525). Bus 3, 9, E, S. **Open** 9.30am-9.30pm Mon-Sat; 11am-6pm Sun. **Credit** AmEx, Disc, MC, V.
Discount designer baby and children's clothing (Oshkosh, Ralph Lauren) and accessories.
Branch: 13619 S Dixie Highway, South Dade (253 3962).

Clubwear/street fashion

Deco Denim
1301 Washington Avenue, between 13th & 14th Streets, Miami Beach (534 9397). Bus C, H, K, W. **Open** 10am-10pm Mon-Sat; 10am-9pm Sun. **Credit** AmEx, DC, Disc, MC, V.
Top to bottom jeanswear: a barn of Levis, Calvins and Ralphs, with a kids' starter section. Branch at 645 Collins.

Ete
714 Lincoln Road, between Euclid & Meridian Avenues, Miami Beach (672 3265). Bus C, G, K, L, S. **Open** 11am-10pm Mon-Thur, Sun; 11am-11pm Fri, Sat. **Credit** AmEx, DC, Disc, MC, V.
The original South Beach lifestyle boutique with a New York state of mind. What to buy: casuals, swimwear, cool hats, bags, shoes, shades, bath toys, fun costume jewellery.

Ona Saez
915 Washington Avenue, between Ninth & 10th Streets, Miami Beach (534 2445). Bus C, H, K, W. **Open** noon-11pm Mon-Fri; noon-midnight Sat, Sun. **Credit** AmEx, DC, MC, V.
An Argentine designer who shows off his line of kicky clubwear and accessories in this salon.

Pervert
1220 Washington Avenue, between 12th & 13th Streets, Miami Beach (535 1191). Bus C, H, K, W. **Open** 11am-10pm Mon-Thur; 11am-midnight Fri; noon-midnight Sat; noon-8pm Sun. **Credit** AmEx, DC, MC, V.
House music plays while you shop for cool hip hop gear, Phat Farm tees, B-boy hats, backpacks, surf decals.
Branch: 1655 Meridian Avenue, Miami Beach (535 2292).

Rampage
The Falls, 8888 SW 136th Street, at S Dixie Highway, South Dade (278 1212). Bus 1, 52, 65. **Open** 10am-9pm Mon-Sat; noon-6pm Sun. **Credit** AmEx, DC, Disc, MC, V.
Skinny fly girls shop here: American People, Girls Rule hip hop sportswear, Converse sandals, Steve Madden heels, sexy undies, trinkets, disco make-up. Very NYC, but nice prices.

Eyewear

Au Courant
Bal Harbour Shops, 9700 Collins Avenue, at 96th Street, Bal Harbour (866 2020). Bus G, H, K, R, S. **Open** 10am-9pm Mon-Fri; 10am-7pm Sat; noon-7pm Sun. **Credit** AmEx, DC, Disc, MC, V.
One of the first see-and-be-seen posh optical shops.

Eyeglass Emporium
552 Arthur Godfrey Road, at Prairie Avenue, Miami Beach (534 2288). Bus C, F/M, J, T. **Open** 10am-6pm Mon-Fri; noon-3pm Sat, Sun. **Credit** AmEx, Disc, MC, V.
A bazaar of classic and contemporary styles for the entire family at fair prices. Optometrist on the premises.

Meir Ben-Nissan MD
1674 Meridian Avenue, between Lincoln Road & 17th Street, Miami Beach (538 1201). Bus C, G, K, L, S. **Open** 9.30am-5.30pm Mon-Fri. **Credit** AmEx, MC, V.
He's the optometrist local eyeglass merchants recommend.

South Beach Eyes
*760 Ocean Drive, between Seventh & Eighth Streets,
Miami Beach (538 9966). Bus C, H, K, W.* **Open** noon-
8pm Mon-Thur; noon-9pm Fri; noon-10pm Sat; noon-7pm
Sun. **Credit** AmEx, DC, Disc, MC, V.
This rad museum of contemporary eyewear boasts a con-
noisseur's plate of name designers: Kata, Yohji Yamamoto,
Lafont, Kirk Original, Morgenthal Frederics, Blinde Optics.

Shoes

Exotik Shoes
*1423 Washington Avenue, between 14th Street &
Espanola Way, Miami Beach (532 1252). Bus C, H, K, W.*
Open 10am-11pm daily. **Credit** AmEx, DC, Disc, MC, V.
Great selection of functional funky shoes: Timberland,
Birkenstocks, Vans, platforms, clogs.
Branch: 3448 Main Highway, Coconut Grove (448 0085).

Foot Locker & Lady Foot Locker
*Omni Mall International, 1601 Biscayne Boulevard, at
NE 16th Street, Downtown (577 8309). Bus 3, 16, 48,
95, C/Metromover School Board.* **Open** 10am-9pm Mon-
Sat; noon-5.30pm Sun. **Credit** AmEx, Disc, MC, V
Hip-hoppers stop here for Reeboks, Nikes, Adidas and New
Balance – at competitive prices.

Just for Feet
*3000 Grand Avenue, at Virginia Street, Coconut Grove,
(443 7463). Bus 42, 48.* **Open** 10am-midnight Mon-Thur;
10am-1am Fri, Sat; 11am-10pm Sun. **Credit** AmEx, MC, V.
A superstore chain of athletic footwear for wannabe Michael
Jordans.

Kenneth Cole
*190 Eighth Street, at Collins Avenue, Miami Beach (673
5151). Bus C, H, K, W.* **Open** 11am-9pm Mon-Sat; noon-
7pm Sun. **Credit** AmEx, MC, V.
The only free-standing KC boutique in town showcases his
line of courant footwear and bags.

Mars
*1035 Washington Avenue, between 10th & 11th Streets,
Miami Beach (673 8040). Bus C, H, K, W.* **Open** 10am-
10.30pm Mon-Thur; 10.30am-11pm Fri, Sat; noon-8pm
Sun. **Credit** AmEx, Disc, MC, V.
Bright beach footwear and clothing. Multicoloured Hush
Puppies, Converse sneakers – fashion brand-names that
make rich pickings for Euro tourists, who have to pay half
as much again at home.

Neiman-Marcus
*9700 Collins Avenue, at 96th Street, in Bal Harbour
Shops, Bal Harbour (865 6161). Bus G, H, K, R, S.*
Open 10am-9pm Mon-Fri; 10am-7pm Sat; noon-7pm Sun.
Credit AmEx.
The shoe department makes you want to fly to Manhattan
for more Clergeries and Karans. The best curated selection
of designer shoes in town. Watch for the end-of-season sales.

Star Shoes & Boots
*440 Espanola Way, between Drexel & Washington
Avenues, Miami Beach (532 8599). Bus C, H, K, W.*
Open 9.30am-7pm Mon-Sat; 11am-8pm Sun. **Credit** MC,
V.
As the name says – plus leather in luggage and jacket form.
Branch: 835 Washington Avenue, Miami Beach (532
8229).

Wild Pair
*76 E Flagler Street, between N Miami & NE First
Avenues, Downtown (358 0635). Bus 3, 16, 95, C,
S/Metromover First Street.* **Open** 9.30am-6pm Mon-
Thur; 9.30am-7pm Fri, Sat; 10am-5pm Sun. **Credit**
AmEx, Disc, MC, V.
The $10 sale rack of discontinued styles is the big attraction
in this designer knock-off footwear store. The Downtown
branch caters for the disco-Latin and art student crowd.
Branches: 401 Biscayne Boulevard, Downtown (374
2262); **Athletic Addict** 1574 Washington Avenue,
Miami Beach (673 9838).

Pounding the beat takes its toll on your feet: getting a shoeshine on Calle Ocho.

Underwear

See also above **Department stores** *and* **Discount department stores**.

Flash Lingerie

Bal Harbour Shops, 9700 Collins Avenue, at 96th Street, Bal Harbour (868 4465). Bus G, H, K, R, S. **Open** 10am-9pm Mon-Fri; 10am-7pm Sat; noon-7pm Sun. **Credit** AmEx, DC, Disc, MC, V.

Imported top-range sexy Madonna goods: Hanro, La Perla.

Victoria's Secret

The Falls, 8888 SW 136th Street, at S Dixie Highway, South Dade (232 8560). Bus 1, 52, 65. **Open** 10am-9pm Mon-Sat; noon-6pm Sun. **Credit** AmEx, Disc, MC, V.

Playmates shop here for moderately priced lingerie, corsets, pyjamas, bras. Also a potpourri and fragrance counter. All very safe and tasteful.

Branch: CocoWalk, 3015 Grand Avenue, Coconut Grove (443 2365).

Vintage

Beatnix

1149 Washington Avenue, between 11th & 12th Streets, Miami Beach (532 8733). Bus C, H, K, W. **Open** 1-10pm Mon-Thur, Sun; 2-11pm Fri, Sat. **No credit cards**.

Extensive stock of used and vintage clobber, especially basketball jerseys and cool 1960s retro accessories.

Love Me 2 Times

831 Washington Avenue, between Eighth & Ninth Streets, Miami Beach (672 0225). Bus C, H, K, W. **Open** 11am-9pm Mon-Thur; 11am-10pm Fri, Sat; noon-8pm Sun. **Credit** AmEx, MC, V.

A quaint but hip selection of nicely priced girl-boy Flower Power wear for the 1990s. Always a basket of under $10 items. Mostly small sizes.

Miami Twice

6562 SW 40th Street (Bird Road), between SW 65th & 67th Avenues, South Miami (666 0127). Bus 40, 73. **Open** 10am-7pm Mon-Sat; noon-6pm Sun. **Credit** AmEx, DC, MC, V.

The retro department store frequented by prop-buyers. An extensive Bakelite jewellery and accessories collection as well as furnishings – 1950s dinettes, Fiestaware, lunch-boxes and the like. Clothing, clothing, clothing.

Too Much

1667 Michigan Avenue, between Lincoln Road & 17th Street, Miami Beach (673 0265). Bus C, G, K, L, S. **Open** 1-7pm daily. **Credit** AmEx, Disc, MC, V.

Sonny & Cherwear. A cubbyhole of vintage dresses dating from the 1950s to the 1970s. From the floor to the ceiling there's an eclectic choice of velvets, lace, crochet, bonnets and bellbottoms in wild colours, plus purses and platform shoes. Named after the shop that featured in the cult 1960s British film *Smashing Time*.

Services

Clean Machine

226 12th Street, between Collins & Washington Avenues, Miami Beach (534 9429). Bus C, H, K, W. **Open** 24 hours daily. **Credit** AmEx, Disc, MC, V.

This 24-hour full-service laundrette/dry cleaner's/art gallery is where wafer-thin models do their laundry inbetween shoots. Or use the 'Wash & Fold' service, charged by the pound. Giant outdoor dryers on the back patio make this a neighbourhood hang-out.

Branch: 1629 Jefferson Avenue, Miami Beach (674 1939).

Maria's Alteration Shop

1622A Alton Road, between 16th Street & Lincoln Road, Miami Beach (674 1552). Bus F/M, S, W. **Open** 8am-4pm Mon-Wed; 8am-5pm Thur, Fri; 8am-noon Sat. **No credit cards**.

Around since 1962, Maria and her seamstresses will fix a hem for $6. Homey atmosphere, like visiting your aunt.

Mark's Quality Cleaners & Laundry

1201 20th Street, off Alton Road, Miami Beach (538 6275). Bus F/M, S, W. **Open** 6.30am-9pm Mon-Thur; 6.30am-7pm Fri; 7am-6pm Sat. **Credit** AmEx, MC, V.

Where high society comes to drop off tuxes and ballgowns. The prices will take you to the cleaners, but it's worth it: staff are pros. Same-day service if in by 10am, or Mark's will pick up and deliver. Excellent for alterations, leatherwork, and major repairs.

Non Stop Prop Shop Inc

1800 Bay Road, at 18th Street, Miami Beach (534 8771). Bus F/M, S, W. **Open** 8am-6pm Mon-Fri; noon-5pm Sun. **Credit** AmEx, MC, V.

The busiest wardrobe and prop rental in town. Where to rent a tux or feather boa on South Beach.

Western

Robert's Western Wear

5854 S Dixie Highway, at SW 58th Avenue, South Miami (666 6647). Bus 72/Metrorail South Miami. **Open** 10am-6pm Mon-Wed, Sat; 10am-9pm Thur, Fri. **Credit** AmEx, Disc, MC, V.

Urban cowboys get their gear at this long-established ranch. Boots, hats, jeans, you name it.

Food & drink

The Bagel Factory

1427 Alton Road, between 14th & 15th Streets, Miami Beach (674 1577). Bus F/M, S, W. **Open** 5.30am-3pm daily. **No credit cards**.

The only place in town you'll find an authentic New York bagel (55¢): onion, chocolate chip, raisin pumpernickel, sesame seed, poppy seed or plain. Lox and cream cheese, too.

Biga

1710 Alton Road, between 17th Street & Dade Boulevard, Miami Beach (538 3335). Bus F/M, S, W. **Open** 7.30am-6pm Mon-Sat; 8am-3pm Sun. **Credit** AmEx, MC, V.

If you're packing for a nouvelle picnic, pick up an olive loaf or sourdough breads here. Baked daily on the premises.

Captain Frank's Fleet

On Watson Island docks, off MacArthur Causeway/Interstate 395, between Miami & Miami Beach (372 1060). Bus C, F/M, K, S. **Open** until sunset daily. **No credit cards**.

If no one answers the phone, it's 'cause it's a payphone next to the dock where Capt Frank sells lobsters under a shanty for under $10, plus shrimps, squid, conch, yellowtail tuna.

Epicure Market

1656 Alton Road, between 16th Street & Lincoln Road, Miami Beach (672 1861). Bus F/M, S, W. **Open** 10am-7pm Mon-Sat; 10am-6pm Sun. **Credit** AmEx, MC, V.

Pricey but worth it, especially the kosher deli, where a daily menu of prepared foods (frozen, too) have kept most of Miami Beach in matzoh ball soup for years. Gourmet standards are reached. There are also fresh fruits and vegetables weighed by a greengrocer, an excellent butcher and a bakery.

Natural Food Market at South Beach
*1011 Fifth Street, at Michigan Avenue, Miami Beach
(535 9050). Bus C, K.* **Open** 9am-10pm Mon-Sat; 11am-
9pm Sun. **Credit** AmEx, Disc, MC, V.
It has a branch in South Miami, but this one's bigger, with
its own parking lot and outdoor dining area. The better to
eat the goodies in, lovingly prepared daily by the staff.
There's an ample vitamin and cosmetics section, including
homoeopathic cures and aromatherapy products.

Norman Brothers Produce
*7621 SW 87th Avenue, at SW 76th Street, South Miami
(274 9363). Bus 72, 87.* **Open** 8am-7pm Mon-Sat; 10am-
6pm Sun. **Credit** AmEx, Disc, MC, V.
A busy Southern-style open-air market with a fresh selection of tropical fruits and vegetables and its own bakery. Gift
baskets and parcels available.

Oak Feed Natural Food Market
*Streets of Mayfair Mall, 2911 Grand Avenue, between
Mary & Virginia Streets, Coconut Grove (448 7595). Bus
42, 48.* **Open** 9am-10pm Mon-Sat; 10am-10pm Sun.
Credit AmEx, DC, MC, V.
The original natural foodstore in Miami used to feed hippies
in the 1960s. The 1990s version is air-cooled with a prepared
foods section, and a good restaurant that's Buddha-inspired.

Volpe Liquors
*1631 Washington, between 16th & 17th Streets, Miami
Beach (538 0809). Bus C, H, K, W.* **Open** 8am-11.30pm
daily. **Credit** AmEx, Disc, MC, V.
Domestic and imported liquor, wine, beer, Evian, can be
delivered seven days a week.

Whole Foods Market
*Waterways Shoppes, 3565 NE 207th Street, at NE 34th
Avenue, Aventura (933 1543). Bus 3, 9.* **Open** 9am-
10pm daily. **Credit** AmEx, MC, V.
The biggest health food grocery store in town (part of a
national chain) is a bit out of the way, but serves great
gourmet natural food to go. And they bake their own breads.

Local produce

For the real deal in farmer's markets, head down
the Tamiami Trail (SW Eighth Street) and turn
south down the ole trucking route on Krome
Avenue/SW 177th Avenue towards Homestead,
where 'U-Pic-Em' (self-pick) stalls are the order of
the day. In this vast stretch of farmland, you'll see
scenes from the real South, workers (mostly
migrant Mexicans and local blacks) breaking their
backs picking corn and tomatoes. But you'll also
encounter toasted tourists hauling fruits and veg
to the road stands during the November to May
season. If you join them, be sure that the field
you're harvesting has a sign posted U-Pic-Em. The
agricultural police, not to mention the local farmers, don't take kindly to poachers. Afterwards,
mosey over to one of the larger farmer's markets
for a fresh milkshake and home-baked muffin.

Knaus Berry Farm
*15980 SW 248th Street, at SW 159th Avenue,
Homestead (247 0668). Bus 35, 70.* **Open** Nov-April
only; call for details.
These farmers are devout German Baptist snowbirds who've
been farming here for years. Known for their delicious strawberry milkshakes, they also make wonderful organic baked
goods. Call ahead, as they're only open during the season
(around Thanksgiving until the end of April).

Lincoln Road Farmers Market
*Lincoln Road Mall (between 16th & 17th Streets and
Alton Road & Washington Avenue), Miami Beach.*
Every first and third Sunday (the schedule isn't hard and
fast), there's a small neighbourhood farmer's market in the
centre of Lincoln Road Mall, around Meridian Avenue. Biga,
a local gourmet bakery, sells baguettes and yummy rolls
cheap, and vendors sell beautiful fresh fruits and vegetables,
orchids, coffees, coconuts and honeys.

Rainbow Farms
*18001 SW 177th Avenue, at SW 180th Street, South
Dade (258 0421). No public transport.* **Open** mid-Dec-
end Mar 8am-5pm daily. **No credit cards.**
Rainbow Farms run lots of the U-Pic-Em stands on Krome
Avenue (238 7057) and also has this headquarters. It has a
picnic area and is kid-friendly, with picking fields especially reserved for children.

Robert is Here
*19900 SW 344th Street, between SW 197th & 202nd
Avenues, Homestead (246 1592). No public transport.*
Open 8am-7pm daily. **No credit cards.**
'Gateway to the Everglades' is the logo. Located on the edge
of historic Florida City, this farmer's market is known for its
fresh fruit milkshakes. It also sells its own line of tropical
salad dressings and honey made from indigenous flora. It
survived Hurricane Andrew and is a Florida institution.

Ethnic

All of the big supermarkets, like Publix, have an
ethnic section for Latin condiments, kosher and
deli foods and Asian specialities. Sedano's supermarkets, located throughout Little Havana, cater
largely to the Cuban-American palate.

Asia Market
*9531 SW 160th Street, off US 1, South Dade (232
2728). Bus 1, 52.* **Open** 9.30am-6.30pm Mon-Sat; 11am-
5pm Sun. **No credit cards.**
Fresh, frozen and canned foods from China, Japan, the
Philippines and Korea. This mom-and-pop store is well-
stocked with vegetables and imported rices, plus some
novelty and drugstore items.

La Brioche Dorée
*4017 Prairie Avenue, between W 40th & 41st Streets,
Miami Beach (538 4770). Bus C, F/M, J, T.* **Open**
7.30am-5pm Mon-Fri, Sun. **No credit cards.**
To-die-for almond croissants, éclairs, desserts, baguettes,
and brioche. The best French bakery in town.

Daily Bread
*2486 SW 17th Avenue, between SW 24th Terrace & US
1, Miami (856 0363). Bus 17, 24.* **Open** 8.30am-6pm
Mon-Sat. **Credit** MC, V.
Middle Eastern and Greek groceries, pastries, and cheeses.
Great falafels.

Lorenzo's Italian Supermarket
*16385 West Dixie Highway, between NE 163rd &
164th Streets, North Miami Beach (945 6381). Bus 3,
83, H.* **Open** 8am-7pm Mon-Sat; 8am-6pm Sun. **Credit**
MC, V.
The largest, most extensive Italian supermarket in town,
with a section for fresh vegetables and imported items. If you
can't find it here, you'll have to fly to Little Italy in New York.

Oriental Mart
*9529 S Dixie Highway, at SW 95th Street, South Dade
(661 4509). Bus 104.* **Open** 9.30am-9pm daily. **Credit**
MC, V.
Japanese and Korean food, wine and gifts.

Thai Market
7339 SW 45th Street, between SW 73rd & 74th Avenues, South Dade (267 0880). Bus 40, 73. **Open** 11am-7pm daily. **No credit cards.**
Authentic foodstuffs from Thailand.

Interiors

Miami's **Design District**, which caters primarily to trade professionals but has recently been trying to open up to individual buyers too, lies on the outskirts of Downtown Miami. Furniture showrooms and architectural offices occupy two main bi-level structures: **MID I**, 4100 NE Second Avenue (576 7571); and **MID II**, 4141 NE Second Avenue (576 5515). Decorative items, kitchen, bathroom fixtures and tiles are displayed in the **Miami Decorating & Design Center**, 3930 NE Second Avenue (573 8116). Most showrooms are open Monday to Saturday until 5pm. As is the case with most areas in the process of gentrification, there's always a risk of petty crime, so keep your wits about you. Park only in patrolled security lots or where there's foot traffic. *See also chapter* **Little Haiti & Design District**.

Arango
Dadeland Mall, SW 88th Street, at SW 72nd Avenue, Kendall (661 4229). Bus 87, 88/Metrorail Dadeland North/Dadeland South. **Open** 10am-9pm Mon-Sat; noon-5.30pm Sun. **Credit** AmEx, MC, V.
This top art and design shop has been around for over 20 years. Comparable to the MOMA store, it's excellent for gifts for the home.

Bed, Bath & Beyond
8380 S Dixie Highway, at SW 83rd Street, in Dadeland Station, South Dade (662 7691). Bus 1, 52, 87, 88/Metrorail Dadeland North. **Open** 9.30am-9.30pm Mon-Sat; 10am-7pm Sun. **Credit** AmEx, Disc, MC, V.
A superstore of household goods and gadgets at everyday prices, conveniently located at the Dadeland Metrorail stop. Everything from designer trash cans to anti-allergen bed covers, comforters and drapes.

Boca Bargoons Decorative Fabrics
15801 S Dixie Highway, at SW 158th Street, South Dade (255 1718). Bus 1, 52. **Open** 9.30am-6pm Mon-Sat. **Credit** AmEx, DC, MC, V.
A roomful of designer upholstery at discount prices.

Central Hardware
545 Arthur Godfrey Road, at Prairie Avenue, Miami Beach (531 0836). Bus C, F/M, K, J, T. **Open** 8am-6.30pm Mon-Fri; 9am-5pm Sat; 10.30am-3.30pm Sun. **Credit** AmEx, Disc, MC, V.
A Beach institution, stocked with everything you need for the home and garden. Knowledgeable clerks give you personal service. There's a hand-picked selection of small appliances, throw rugs, housewares (great gifts), beach and barbecue things, even a 24-hour photo lab.

Crate & Barrel
The Falls, 8888 SW 136th Street, at S Dixie Highway, South Dade (971 9977). Bus 1, 52, 65. **Open** 10am-9pm Mon-Sat; noon-6pm Sun. **Credit** AmEx, Disc, MC, V.
Contemporary home and garden stuff, à la Martha Stewart. Good value; great crockery.

Details
1031 Lincoln Road, between Lenox & Michigan Avenues, Miami Beach (531 1325). Bus C, G, K, L, S. **Open** 11am-9pm Mon-Thur; 11am-10pm Fri; 11am-11pm Sat; 11am-8pm Sun. **Credit** AmEx, MC, V.
Furniture, flamboyant furnishings and oodles of decorative knick-knacks. Great bath stuff, mirrors, frames, lamps.

Jamson Whyte
832 Collins Avenue, between Eighth & Ninth Streets, Miami Beach (535 2224). Bus C, H, K, W. **Open** noon-8pm Mon-Wed, Sun; noon-10pm Thur-Sat. **Credit** AmEx, MC, V.
Airy showroom of top-of-the-range tropical furniture from Africa and Asia.

Lunatika
1019 Lincoln Road, between Lenox & Michigan Avenues, Miami Beach (534 8585). Bus C, G, K, L, S. **Open** 11am-8pm Mon-Thur; 11am-9pm Fri, Sat; noon-6pm Sun. **Credit** AmEx, MC, V.
Contemporary lampdom. A roomful of ingenious illumination – Milano sconces, abstract drops, and what have you.

Pottery Barn
The Falls, 8888 SW 136th Street, at S Dixie Highway, South Dade (238 0331). Bus 1, 52, 65. **Open** 10am-9pm Mon-Sat; noon-6pm Sun. **Credit** AmEx, Disc, MC, V.
Shabby-chic furniture, stylish furnishings for home and office, dishware, bath things, frames.

Williams-Sonoma
Bal Harbour Shops, 9700 Collins Avenue, at 96th Street, Bal Harbour (861 1822). Bus G, H, K, R, S. **Open** 10am-9pm Mon-Fri; 10am-7pm Sat; noon-7pm Sun. **Credit** AmEx, Disc, MC, V.
The hearth: a cosy gourmet's paradise of top-of-the-range kitchen utensils, appliances, and dinnerware.
Branch: 8888 SW 136th Street, South Dade (256 9929).

World Resources
719 Lincoln Road, between Meridian & Pennsylvania Avenues, Miami Beach (534 9095). Bus C, G, K, L, S. **Open** 4-11.30pm daily. **Credit** AmEx, DC, Disc, MC, V.
Shop for Balinese beds, drums, gongs, incense, batiks, crystals and candles while listening to live sitar music and eating sushi (or Thai) under the stars.

Retro

Dish
939 Lincoln Road, between Jefferson & Michigan Avenues, Miami Beach (532 7737). Bus C, G, K, L, S. **Open** noon-10pm Mon-Thur, Sun; noon-11pm Fri; noon-midnight Sat. **Credit** MC, V.
Retrieved institutional crockery from the Jockey Club, Mr Donut and the *Queen Mary*. A relative of Fish's Eddy in Manhattan.

Modernism Gallery
1622 Ponce de Leon, between Mendoza & Zamora Avenues, Coral Gables (442 8743). Bus 42, 73, J. **Open** 9am-5pm Mon-Fri; noon-5pm Sat. **Credit** AmEx, MC, V.
An intelligent collection of twentieth-century furniture, including Gilbert Rohde, Noguchi, and Heywood Wakefield. Excellent stockists – if you don't see it, they'll find it.

Pop
1151 Washington Avenue, between 11th & 12th Streets, Miami Beach (604 9604). Bus C, H, K, W. **Open** noon-11pm Mon-Sat; 2-11pm Sun. **Credit** AmEx, DC, MC, V.
Collectable toys from the 1950s onwards. It's top pop time-capsule stuff: pure Americana, Ken and Barbie, sci-fi robots. The Jetsons live here.

Just what I've always wanted

Five crucial souvenirs of Miami

◀ **Alligator heads**: $15-$40 approx, depending on size, from souvenir shops on Tamiami Trail

Flamingo saltwater taffy: ▶ $5-$12 (depending on size), from souvenir shops at Miami International Airport

Santeria oils: $2-$7, from botanicas throughout Miami

▲ **Snowstorm calendar**: $4.99, from Woolworths

◀ **Crab claw keyring**: $3, from Joe's Stone Crab

tiffanydonnakaransasak
ellentracylancômehugo
bosscalvinkleinbernardaud
guessungarocanalikeds
tommyhilfigervalentino
coachfendikiplingswatch
villeroy&bochmontblanc
tagheuermikimotodkny
prescriptivesralphlauren
charismaferragamopolo
annekleingundchristofle
braun
spode bloomingdale's
shiseidolenoxbobbibrown
duéperduédiornicolemille

There's a gift waiting for you. Simply stop by our Visitors Center
with this ad and a same-day Bloomingdale's receipt.* We'll also tell you
about our special events, hold all of your packages, and offer shopping
assistance in over 10 languages.

Town Center at Boca Raton, 561-394-2000   The Falls-Miami, 305-252-6300
Palm Beach Gardens, 561-625-2000   Aventura opening in November

Not all collections available in all stores.   *Limit one per customer.

Senzatempo

*815 Washington Avenue, between Eighth & Ninth Streets,
Miami Beach (534 5588). Bus C, H, K, W.* **Open** 10.30am-
6pm Mon-Fri; 12.30-7pm Sat. **Credit** AmEx, MC, V.
Posh vintage Euroretro antiques: Eames, Bertoia, choice
Patek Philippe watches.

Stone Age Antiques

*3236 NW South River Drive, at NW 32nd Street,
Northwest Dade (633 5114). Bus 32, 36, J.* **Open** 9am-
5pm Mon-Fri. **No credit cards**.
Some would call this a junkyard, not a splendid selection of
maritime antiques, Western gear and movie props. It's
anchored on the Miami River; its logo: 'The Real Man's Store'.

Health & beauty

Agua

*Delano Hotel, 1685 Collins Avenue, at 17th Street,
Miami Beach (672 2000). Bus C, G, H, L, S.* **Open** 9am-
7pm daily. **Credit** AmEx, MC, V.
When Madonna spas here she closes the place down, so call
first, then tan naked on the roof solarium, get a massage,
facial or hot herbal bath in minimalist Starck-ian splendour.
An 18 per cent gratuity is added.

Aveda Environmental Lifestyle Store

*932 Lincoln Road, between Jefferson & Michigan
Avenues, Miami Beach (531 9580). Bus C, G, K, L, S.*
Open 11am-9pm Mon-Fri, Sun; 11am-11pm Sat. **Credit**
AmEx, MC, V.
Twenty-first century chic, with lots of attitude over
aromatherapy. It's pricey, of course, but has a great stock,
especially in hair products. Tip: pick up the generic brand,
Aura, for half the price at Sally's Beauty Supply (*see above*
Discount).

Brownes & Co Apothecary

*841 Lincoln Road, between Jefferson & Meridian
Avenues, Miami Beach (532 8703). Bus C, G, K, L, S.*
Open 10am-10pm Mon-Thur, Sun; 10am-11pm Fri; 10am-
11.30pm Sat. **Credit** AmEx, Disc, MC, V.
Beauty's only skin deep; globetrotting supermodels know
this. That's why they shop at this bazaar for hard-to-get
cosmetics : Shu Uemura, Trish McEvoy, Kiehl's, Aveda,
LeClerc poudres, Phytotherathrie natural hair care, Dr
Hauschka skin care products and Geo Trumper for men.

The Center for Enlightenment

*538 Lincoln Road, between Drexel & Pennsylvania
Avenues, Miami Beach (534 1998). Bus C, G, K, L, S.*
Open noon-10pm Mon-Thur, Sun; noon-midnight Fri,
Sat. **Credit** AmEx, Disc, MC, V.
Free lectures daily: how to meditate, nutritional healing etc.
Sign up for workshops with master life instructors or sim-
ply drop in and have your runes read in the tea room.

Imagen Medical Day Spa

*300 Arthur Godfrey Road, at Pine Tree Drive, Miami
Beach (673 0666). Bus C, F/M, K, J, T.* **Open** hours
vary, phone for details. **Credit** AmEx, MC, V.
This place looks like a doctor's office that's also a beauty
spa, that is, your friend can have a facial and a pedicure while
you get a little rhinoplasty adjustment or warts singed off.
Maybe a little breast enhancement. Perfect for Miami Beach
where everybody's perfect.

MAC

*650 Collins Avenue, between Sixth & Seventh Streets,
Miami Beach (604 9040). Bus C, H, K, W.* **Open** 11am-
9pm Mon-Sat; noon-6pm Sun. **Credit** AmEx, Disc, MC, V.
The supermodel's make-up choice. Marvellous makeovers
from pros on the premises. With RuPaul and kd lang as mas-
cots, you'd never guess it's owned by Estee Lauder.

Vidal Sassoon

*660 Collins Avenue, between Sixth & Seventh Streets,
Miami Beach (672 3600). Bus C, H, K, W.* **Open**
10.45am-7pm Tue, Fri; 10am-6pm Wed, Thur; 9am-4pm
Sat. **Credit** AmEx, MC, V.
A new addition to this salon empire. Cuts from $45-$70,
including a head massage.

*A spa for your car – **The Detailers Car Wash**, page 147.*

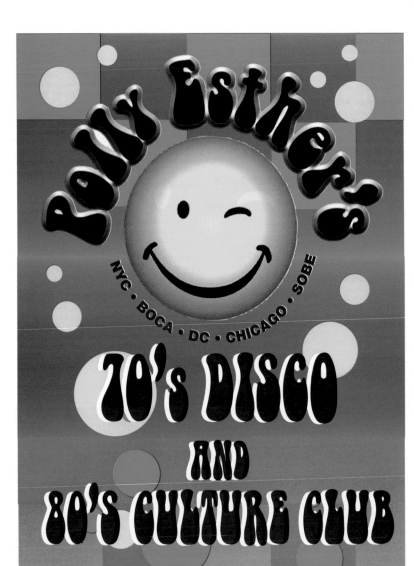

Polly Esther's

NYC • BOCA • DC • CHICAGO • SOBE

70's DISCO AND 80's CULTURE CLUB

841 Washington Ave.
South Beach, Miami
305-535-5633
Fax 305-535-8332

99 S.E. 1st Ave.
Boca Raton, Florida
561-447-8955
Fax 561-362-8960

Walgreen Drug Stores

1845 Alton Road, at Dade Boulevard, Miami Beach (531 8868). Bus A, F/M, R, S, W. **Open** 24 hours daily, including prescriptions. **Credit** AmEx, Disc, MC, V.
Late-night pit stop for snacks and to fix what ails you. You'll also find inexpensive household items, small appliances, cosmetics and beach paraphernalia.
Branches (not 24 hour): Miami Beach NE 167th Street, North Miami Beach (652 7332); 122 Biscayne Boulevard, Downtown (893 6860).

Specialist & gifts

Dapy

Aventura Mall, 19575 Biscayne Boulevard, at NE 195th Street, Aventura (933 8847). Bus 3, 9, E, S. **Open** 10am-9.30pm Mon-Sat; 10am-6pm Sun. **Credit** AmEx, Disc, MC, V.
A toy bazaar for the kid in you. Inflatables, trinkets, reissued collectibles, stuffed animals, Monroe-abilia, beach paraphernalia and much, much more.

The Detailers Car Wash

3400 S Dixie Highway, at Bird Avenue, Coconut Grove (444 1255). Bus 22, 40, 42, J/Metrorail Douglas Road. **Open** 7am-9pm Mon-Sat; 9am-7pm Sun. **Credit** AmEx, DC, Disc, MC, V.
How to wash your car and marry a millionaire, well, almost. Single yuppies converge here to nosh on free bagels and cream cheese while their leased Beamers take a bath.

Flowers & Flowers

925 Lincoln Road, between Jefferson & Michigan Avenues, Miami Beach (534 1633). Bus C, G, K, L, S. **Open** 9am-10pm Mon-Thur; 9am-midnight Fri, Sat; noon-6pm Sun. **Credit** AmEx, DC, Disc, MC, V.
Extraordinary floral works of art. A delicate Parisian sensibility goes into stocking these gifts of love – rare scents, decoratives, vases, frames.

Gold Kiosk

Delano Hotel, 1685 Collins Avenue, at 17th Street, Miami Beach (672 2000). Bus C, H, G, L, S. **Open** 7am-midnight Mon-Thur, Sun; 7am-1am Fri, Sat. **Credit** AmEx, MC, V.
Everything for the global traveller, from Philippe Starck miniatures and Kiehl's sunblock to erudite erotic reading matter, by way of foreign mags and smokes, supermodel cosmetics, Eurokinis, Kate Spade bags and cool shades. Plus the famous Philippe Starck lemon squeezer.

GW – the Gay Emporium

720 Lincoln Road, between Euclid & Meridian Avenues, Miami Beach (534 9177). Bus C, G, K, L, S. **Open** 11am-10pm Mon-Thur, Sun; 11am-11pm Fri, Sat. **Credit** AmEx, MC, V.
Gay goodies. Feather boas, kinky sexwear, black leather S&M gear, monogrammed CUM towels, dildos, dildos, dildos. The upstairs book loft has a good selection of new gay fiction and non-fiction, as well as gay travel guides.

The Historical Museum Gift Shop

The Historical Museum of South Florida, 101 W Flagler Street, at NW First Avenue, Downtown (375 1492). Bus 3, 16, 95, C, S/Metrorail Government Center. **Open** 10am-5pm Mon-Wed, Fri, Sat; 10am-9pm Thur; noon-5pm Sun. **Credit** AmEx, MC, V.
Pure Floridiana – Southern cracker cookbooks, postcards, alligator souvenirs, Seminole Indian arts and crafts.

Miami Wedding Services

20533 Biscayne Boulevard, Suite N-122, at NE 205th Street, Aventura (933 4489). Bus 3, 9. **Open** 9am-6pm, by appointment only. **No credit cards**.

Street-level shopping on Flager Street.

Florida is an easy place for non-nationals to marry; this lot can help you through the admin and arrange the ceremony itself, anywhere you fancy, from the beach to the Everglades.

The Store of Knowledge

The Falls, 8888 SW 136th Street, at S Dixie Highway, South Dade (238 7774). Bus 1, 52, 65. **Open** 10am-9pm Mon-Sat; noon-6pm Sun. **Credit** AmEx, Disc, MC, V.
A toy emporium for big and little kids: ingenious board and computer games, crosswords, train sets, sci-fi knick-knacks.

Straighten Up, the Organizer Store

1229 Lincoln Road, between Alton Road & West Avenue, Miami Beach (538 0775). Bus F/M, S, W. **Open** 9am-7pm Mon-Sat; 10am-6pm Sun. **Credit** MC, V.
Gadgets for home and travel: shelving, containers, and office accessories to simplify your life.

Tattoos by Lou

231 14th Street, between Collins & Washington Avenues, Miami Beach (532 7300). Bus C, H, K, W. **Open** 11am-2am Mon-Thur, Sun; 11am-3am Fri, Sat. **Credit** AmEx, MC, V.
Lou's not around anymore but his legend lives on. Tattoos cost from $50, depending on the design. Body piercing starts at $55, including jewellery, for a belly button or nipple. Quick and simple. Tongues $75; genitalia pricey, dicey.

Travel by Design

1210 Washington Avenue, between 12th & 13th Streets, Miami Beach (673 6336). Bus C, H, K, W. **Open** 9am-5pm Mon-Fri. **Credit** AmEx, Disc, MC, V.
Your hip travel agent. Laid back but gets the job done.

The Wolfsonian Museum Gift Shop

1001 Washington Avenue, at 10th Street, Miami Beach (531 1001). Bus C, H, K, W. **Open** 11am-6pm Tue, Wed, Fri, Sat; 11am-9pm Thur; noon-5pm Sun. **Credit** AmEx, MC, V.
A range of goods relevant to this museum of twentieth-century propaganda art: architectural books, postcards, unique *objets* of design, decorative art, and jewellery.

Stogie wonderland

Over the last decade, the cigar, long associated with crusty old fogies, has reclaimed its reputation as a status symbol. It nows boasts its own magazine, *Cigar Aficionado*, and even (choke, choke) cologne. Miami's Cuban connections and outdoor existence have proved fertile ground for the weed to flourish. Many a smoky conversation is overheard regarding possession of prized Cohibas (Che's and Fidel's fave), contraband smuggled in from Havana through Nassau or Moscow. Castro reputedly chomps on specially made Esplendidos: length seven inches; ring gauge 47.

These days, lipstick lesbians (and Madonna) give new meaning to the male-dominated tradition, tongueing Amaretto-dipped Davidoffs in the most exclusive cigar salons, such as the Forge's **Cuba Club** (432 41st Street; *see chapter Restaurants & Cafés*), which every Wednesday is the appointed watering hole for South Beach's wannabe rich and famous.

Miami's transplanted Cuban population never lost its burning desire to stoke a few. They roll their own, like back in the old country, in factories based in Little Havana. For a crash course in stogie-ology, visit the **Caribbean Cigar Company**. Watch rows of veteran cigar rollers turn brown leaves to gold, or ask the *torcedor* in the window of the company's South Beach store to roll you a fresh maduro Havana Classico.

A good cigar is easy to find. There's a cigar lounge on every other corner and a box stashed behind any reputable bar. Even the neighbourhood liquor store keeps a well-lit humidor stocked with a fresh supply. Accessories: fancy cigar scissors or a portable guillotine cutter does the trick. Make a clean cut, leaving $\frac{1}{8}$ inch of the cap intact, and don't fire up with matches of high sulphur or wax. Butane is recommended. Be it a 35¢ cigarillo, a Macanudo (Jamaican-Mexican-Dominican tobacco mix wrapped in Connecticut Shade) or Tom Jones's choice, the oily but tangy Havana Montecristo, remember this: suck hard but don't inhale.

Bill's Pipe & Tobacco Shop
2309 Ponce de Leon Boulevard, between Aragon & Giralda Avenues, Coral Gables (444 1764). Bus 24, 42, 52, 56, J. **Open** 10am-6.30pm Mon-Fri; 10am-4pm Sat. **Credit** AmEx, MC, V.

Caribbean Cigar Factory
Factory: *6265 SW Eighth Street, between SW 62nd & 63rd Avenues, Miami (267 3911). Bus 8, 73.* **Open** 9am-5.30pm Mon-Fri. **Credit** AmEx, Disc, MC, V. **Shops**: 760 Ocean Drive, between Seventh & Eighth Streets, Miami Beach (538 6062); 2992 McFarlane Road, at Main Highway, Coconut Grove (445 3922).

The Cigar Connection
534 Lincoln Road, between Drexel & Pennsylvania Avenues, Miami Beach (531 7373). Bus C, G, K, L, S. **Open** 11am-7pm Mon-Wed, Sun; 11am-10pm Thur; 11am-11pm Fri; 11am-midnight Sat. **Credit** AmEx, MC, V.

El Crédito Cigars
1106 SW 8th Street, at 11th Avenue, Little Havana (858 4162). Bus 8, 12. **Open** 8am-5.30pm Mon-Fri; 8am-4pm Sat. **Credit** AmEx, DC, Disc, MC, V.
Cigars may be the trendy vice of the moment, but at El Crédito's musty factory they are a way of life. Cigar rollers who look so much the part you'd think Central Casting rounded them up, practise their art in the Little Havana factory. The staff are friendly and will walk you around their stock, which includes the highly rated La Gloria Cubana line of cigars.

Holy Smoke
1052 Ocean Drive, between 10th & 11th Streets, Miami Beach (674 9390). Bus C, H, K, W. **Open** 1pm-2am Mon-Thur, Sun; 1pm-3am Fri, Sat. **Credit** AmEx, Disc, MC, V.

Smokers Road
630 South Miami Avenue, between SW Sixth & Seventh Streets, Downtown (375 8178). Bus 6, 8, 24, 48, 95/Metromover Fifth Street. **Open** 9.30am-11.30pm Mon-Thur; 9.30am-2am Fri; 1pm-2am Sat. **Credit** AmEx, MC, V.
Men flock here in the middle of the night to have a puff. Smokers Road rolls its own brand and sells it out of the box, a large wooden chest on the floor. It's like a men's club, with poker and dominoes in one corner.

Tequesta Cigars
220 71st Street, Suite 207, between Abbott & Collins Avenues, Miami Beach (868 7422). Bus G, H, J, L, S. **Open** 9am-5pm Mon-Fri. **Credit** MC, V.

Arts & Entertainment

Clubs

Here's the hit list of the hottest, hautest, hippest nightspots.

Miami is a nocturnal creature's dream come true. Some people in this city don't even come out until the sun goes down, when out of the sun-drenched stupor of daytime everything seems to come alive, thanks in part to the customary pre-going-out ritual known as a nap. Much like New York, to which this city's nightlife has been compared in countless 'what's hot, what's not' articles, Miami is sleep-deprived. Things here don't get going until late: it's a no-no to be seen at a club before 11pm, at the earliest. This is especially true of South Beach (or, as some say, the 'SoHo of the South'), the hub of nocturnal activity where the cheerleaders of the

*High-end cabaret at the **Tropigala** (p155).*

chic elite gather in droves. The stomping ground of the bold and the beautiful, South Beach (not 'SoBe', unless you want to be pinned as a tourist) plays host to some of Miami's trendiest, most star-studded (albeit ephemeral) clubs and a rainbow spectrum of club kids, stiletto-heeled drag queens, fashion victims and trendoids all carousing within a mere few blocks. Where else but in sexy, sweaty South Beach could you dance the dreadful macarena before a crowd that includes Ivana Trump, Adnan Kashoggi and the latest Hollywood starlet? Striking a pose is possibly the area's most celebrated nocturnal pastime. For a more intimate taste of South Beach nightlife as locals know it, it is best to go out during the week, as weekends tend to draw the undesirables and 'causeway crowds' hailing from all points away from the Beach.

Although South Beach may be the epitome of Miami cool to some, it is not necessarily the only place to party. Downtown Miami is experiencing a slow renaissance with a sparse scattering of alternative and Latin clubs frequented by those on the cutting edge who consider the Beach passé. Coconut Grove, while not exactly a club town, offers a great nighttime pedestrian scene of inebriated college kids and tourists clad in shorts and sandals. Then there's Little Havana, for a spicy take on Cuban nightlife; and even the suburbs (yes, even Miami has 'em) have filled their nightlife void with one or two clubs worthy of a visit.

BARS WITH ATTITUDE

While South Beach clubs are sizzling in their own right, certain bars in the area are swank alternatives and draw a chic following. The **Rose Bar** at the Philippe Starck-designed Delano Hotel (1685 Collins Avenue, at 17th Street) is the hautest, while the bars at the **Hotel Astor** (956 Washington Avenue, at 10th Street) and restaurants **Nemo** (100 Collins Avenue, at First Street) and **China Grill** (404 Washington Avenue, at Fifth Street) are also quite hip. Then there's the **Berlin Bar** (661 Washington Avenue, between Sixth & Seventh Streets), an upscale watering hole with the air of a private nightclub. Dress to impress.

LICENSING LAWS & COVER CHARGES

You have to be 21 to drink alcohol in the US so few clubs will admit under-21s (Cameo sometimes has over-18 nights, but phone first to check). Take photo ID, even if you're much older. By law, clubs

How to crash a party

When it comes to parties, Miami will throw one at the feeblest of excuses. The opening of the new Texaco station. New carpeting at a club. Whatever. At any given time, you can always find an event of some sort. And more often than not, celebrities of varying degrees will be in attendance; local celebs may even throw their own. For some, party-crashing is a hobby. Others live for it. You, too, can find yourself hobnobbing with the rich and famous if you know how to play the game right.

Step 1: Gather your sources. The *Miami Herald* has more than a few columnists ready to dish the dirt on the hot-ticket fêtes. Local freebie newspapers such as *New Times* and beach papers such as *The SunPost*, *Wire* and *Fashion Spectrum* magazine (widely available all over South Beach in shops, cafés, hotels and street-corner boxes) are also worth checking. Local tabloid TV show *Deco Drive* (Channel 7, 7.30pm-8pm, Mon-Fri) is up on celebrity activities, and promo invitations are strewn around in stores, restaurants and other public places.

Step 2: Get on the phone. Information numbers and contact people are usually listed on event-related publicity. If not, certain entertainment PR firms usually handle such events; Susan Brustman and Associates (573 0658) and Gordon Sloan Diaz-Balart (381 6500) are the bigger ones. Call them. If they can't help, call the local nightlife columnists and they may help you.

Step 3: Pitch yourself as somebody important and essential to the situation. You hear Julio Iglesias is having a shindig at his house on Indian CreZek Island in conjunction with the National Academy of Recording Arts and Sciences – say you're a music writer for (fill in the blank) publication. Be creative, assertive and convincing (but remember, posing as an actual individual is a crime). If that fails, give yourself a royal-sounding surname and throw it out to whoever is in charge. This also applies to getting on guest lists at clubs. If worse comes to worst, get dressed, go to the venue and lose yourself in the crowd of invited guests. When they walk in, so do you. You hope.

Step 4: Never let them see you sweat. Once inside, just blend in and try to look like you were born there. Don't act conspicuous. Probably half the people there just did what you did.

must stop serving alcohol at 5am; at some places this means that if you're already in the club you won't have to leave but can carry on partying until 8am, when they can start selling booze again. Most places remain open until 3am, 4am and sometimes 5am, at which time they are still so packed you may experience the inevitable transitional shock of coming out and seeing daylight.

Cover charge policies vary. Women often get in gratis while men have to cough up the cash. Many places don't charge cover, a convenient courtesy that allows you to club hop and club owners to jack up the prices of drinks. You'll need cash to pay the admission charge.

DRESS CODES

Individuality is welcomed as far as dress is concerned, but discretion is encouraged when hitting the more exclusive nightspots. Certain clubs are more than willing to turn away anybody who isn't decked out in the latest couture. In general, casual dress is discouraged – but going out in a Dior ballgown is also scoffed at (unless you're coming from a black-tie gala). Not to fret. If all else fails, black is the universal (non) colour of choice and a safe bet. Shabby chic is also acceptable. Certain places allow jeans and others don't, so you may want to phone in advance.

DRUGS

Drugs are forbidden. Having experienced a series of drug busts in the late 1980s and early 1990s, many Miami clubs are super-strict when it comes to narcotics and have strategically placed narcs and police officers waiting to grab the next offender. Typical drugs of choice among club kids are ecstasy, cocaine and rohypnol, the so-called date rape drug. Fortunately, Miamians never bought into the supposed heroin-chic crap, although heroin has experienced something of a clandestine club resurgence. Either way, drugs and clubs are a lethal cocktail and you will get busted. That's a guarantee.

● **Miami clubs open and shut down with alarming frequency and are often closed for private parties, so always call ahead.**

Dance clubs

For gay clubs, *see chapter* **Gay & Lesbian**. For Latin music clubs with dancing, *see chapter* **Music**.

South Beach

Amnesia
136 Collins Avenue, at First Street, South Beach (531 5535). Bus H, W. **Open** 11pm-5am Thur-Sat; 5pm-2am Sun. **Admission** $10 Thur-Sat; $5 Sun.

You can dance if you want to

Just when you thought it was safe to put away the polyester, the bell-bottoms and that glowing disco-ball keyring, you come to Miami and discover that disco culture is alive and well in the city known mainly for its own Latin-influenced hip-hop and rap. What Seattle is (or was) to grunge, Miami is, for better or worse, to disco. And this is not a new development either. Some of the disco era's cheesiest and most recognisable figures actually live in the Magic City – the Bee Gees, Miami residents, recorded parts of the now-legendary *Saturday Night Fever* soundtrack in North Miami's Criteria Studios. And we mustn't forget that Miami native KC wouldn't have been shakin' his booty without the help of the band named after the very state of Florida.

Visit any club in Miami and you're bound to hear at least one song that pays homage to the era of tackiness. Disco nights, such as the Cameo's Flashback Disco on Sundays, have been packing in hordes of retro nightcrawlers who still consider *Le Freak* to be chic. New York-based Polly Esther's also recognised the demand for all disco, all the time, and packed up their eight-tracks and moved right into South Beach, providing a continual musical timewarp for those who dare to go back.

But dastardly disco isn't the only dance craze heating up Miami's and, in some cases, the nation's airwaves. After Luther Campbell of raunchy local rap group 2 Live Crew (remember *Me So Horny?*) took a lot of flak for his controversial lyrics and provocative character, the intensity of Miami's hip-hop scene lessened, with many clubs (including Campbell's own) closing down. Other than Cameo, there is now no particular venue that offers hip-hop acts. But a new brand of Miami-inspired dance music has emerged from the hip-hop and rap cultures in the form of local groups such as the Quad City DJs, whose infectious 'Come on Ride the Train, Ride it', sparked a whole new, albeit ridiculous dance known appropriately as The Train. More than one local group – The Bayside Boyz and Los del Rio – is responsible for the unfortunately unforgettable macarena, the 1990s' very own song and dance version of the hustle. And who could forget the (too) many versions of the song 'Whoop, There it is', made popular by 95 South, a group named after Florida's very own interstate? And to make matters worse, remember Vanilla Ice? 'Ice, Ice, Baby' is also, we must confess, a Miami song.

Fortunately, in the interest of preserving Miami's hipness quotient, there is a clearly audible saving grace in the form of local DJ-doctored mega dance mixes of popular songs, which have helped push other dance music out of the spotlight and into the bargain bins. Madonna's 1996 version of the Andrew Lloyd Webber *Evita* classic 'Don't Cry for me Argentina' was toyed with by a local Miami DJ and transformed into a very danceable anthem that skyrocketed up the nation's dance charts. Many of Gloria Estefan's more soporific ballads have also been spun into dance favourites, all by local club DJs. And while the Miami club scene may not be as DJ-oriented as in, say, London or New York, there are certain star DJs, such as Power 96's DJ Laz, DJ Abel of Salvation and 'Sista' Marc Leventhal who spins the best of soul and funk at Liquid's Fat Black Pussycat on Mondays.

Miami's brand of dance music is even available on CD, allowing you to enjoy the sounds of the city even when you're long gone. Bash nightclub has a series of CDs known appropriately as Bash, The CD, featuring compilations of some of the club's most requested tunes. There is even a CD compilation, called Tea Dance, of the popular Sunday afternoon tea dances, and the White Party, a local gay fundraising party that has achieved national status, also has its own locally produced, eponymously titled CD. As host city of the annual Winter Music Conference, the largest music industry convention in dance history, and with local indie dance labels cranking out CDs as fast as some songs' rpms, it is evident that Miami is no longer a one-hit wonder in the constantly rotating turntable of dance music.

This open-air, multi-levelled, multi-chambered disco theme park offers insane one-nighters, including its famed foam parties at which buckets of bubbles are dumped onto sweaty dancers, thus conveniently masking their various lewd and lascivious activities; bacchanalian, Sunday-afternoon, gay-oriented tea dances on Sunday afternoons featuring big-name DJs; and a host of other events and parties guaranteed to provide you with a night to remember (assuming your memory's in any state to function).

Bash
655 Washington Avenue, between Sixth & Seventh Streets, South Beach (538 2274). Bus C, H, K, W. **Open** 10pm-5am Mon-Sat; 11pm-5am Sun. **Admission** $15 Fri, Sat.
A mainstay of the ever-changing South Beach club scene, Bash offers dance music indoors and world music on the outdoor patio. Weekends tend to attract the younger 'causeway crowd' but during the week Bash remains true to its name

The 1970s are stayin' firmly alive at **Polly Esther's** (see page 154).

and usually hosts at least one or two private parties for the fashion and entertainment communities. And did we mention that Simply Red's Mick Hucknall and bad boy actor Sean Penn are co-owners?

Cameo

1445 Washington Avenue, at Espanola Way, South Beach (532 0922). Bus C, H, K, W. **Open** 11pm-5am Thur-Sun. **Admission** $7-$10; women free before midnight.

Housed in a renovated art deco theatre, the Cameo is a rowdy, slightly seedy dance duplex that could benefit from a bit more renovation. Nevertheless, it is a choice venue for national hip-hop-oriented music acts and remains a big draw for the 18-plus crowd with (in)famous one-nighters such as Sunday's Flashback Disco and Friday's Hot Bodies Contest.

Groove Jet

323 23rd Street, between Collins Avenue & Dade Boulevard, between Collins Avenue & Dade. **Open** 11pm-5am Tue, Thur-Sun. **Admission** $10 after midnight.

Last time we visited, the Smashing Pumpkins' leader Billy Corgan was sitting amid the broken glass and mirrors of the outdoor patio. Woody Harrelson was also here, as were the latest members of the Calvin Klein supermodel set. And the list goes on. Despite its relatively remote location, the Groove attracts the jet set with its techno-influenced front room, soulful back room and some intricate hiding spots for the antisocial. The premier spot for nocturnal creatures who refuse to go home before 6am, Groove Jet shares owners with New York's younger, wildly successful star-magnet, Jet Lounge.

Jazid

1342 Washington Avenue, between 13th & 14th Streets, South Beach (673 9372). Bus C, H, K, W. **Open** 9pm-4am Mon-Sat. **Admission** free.

Smoky and sultry, illuminated by flickering candelabras, Jazid is the kind of place where you'd expect to hear Sade's *Smooth Operator* on constant rotation. While the downstairs features live jazz, sometimes on acid, upstairs there's a DJ spinning the very best of soul and funk. A cool, mellow crowd of models, Euros and locals looking for a little reprieve from the mainstream mayhem.

KGB

637 Washington Avenue, between Sixth & Seventh Streets, South Beach (534 5420). Bus C, H, K, W. **Open** 11pm-5am Tue, Thur-Sun. **Admission** $10.

The Cold War is long over and the only thing cold about this Soviet-chic nightclub is the large assortment of vodkas available at the loungey upstairs VIP vodka bar. There's a communal feeling of peace and Latin-influenced music in the rooftop garden and a red-hot techno dance area on the ground floor. Somewhat militant doormen eventually part the red ropes for all who dare enter.

Liquid

1439 Washington Avenue, at Espanola Way, South Beach (532 9154). Bus C, H, K, W. **Open** 11pm-5am Mon, Fri-Sun. **Admission** $10.

This club kid haven is owned by Ingrid Cassares, Madonna's pal and Miami's very own nightlife diva (nepotism factor: Madonna's brother Christopher Ciccone recently designed the super-swanky downstairs lounge). It frequently attracts major celebs as well as a serious dance crowd that couldn't care less if David Geffen or Johnny Depp were in the secret VIP room. In a futile attempt to recreate a Studio 54 ambience, the velvet ropes may seem impenetrable but in fact part for just about anybody who's willing to be scrutinised for a while. On Mondays, when the enormously popular, *Shaft*-inspired Fat Black Pussycat clubnight is held, the entrance moves to the alley. Sunday night is gay night.

The Living Room at the Strand

671 Washington Avenue, between Sixth & Seventh Streets, South Beach (532 2340). Bus C, H, K, W. **Open** 8.30pm-5am daily **Admission** $10 Mon-Thur; $15 Fri, Sat.

An air of arrogance and a slightly sinister blood-red interior have placed this hipper-than-thou lounge high on the itinerary of the bar-hopping, scene-sucking in-crowd. But this Living Room isn't comfy enough for every lounge potato: beware of the so-called 'door Nazis' who get their thrills from rejecting the sea of people that gathers here, admitting only six-foot model-types.

MG Club
524 Ocean Drive, between Fifth & Sixth Streets, South Beach (532 8420 ext 325). Bus H, W. **Open** 10pm-5am Thur-Sat. **Admission** free.
An intimate space located in the basement of the Mare Grande Hotel (hence MG) featuring Cozy Monday's, an evening of jazz. Possibly the only spot on Ocean Drive not overcrowded with tourists.

Polly Esther's
841 Washington Avenue, between Eighth & Ninth Streets, South Beach (535 5633). Bus C, H, K, W. **Open** 11pm-5am Wed, Thur, Sun; 10pm-5am Fri, Sat. **Admission** $10.
For better or for worse, the decade of dreadful fashion and disco music is alive and well in this campy 1970s club where every night is a scene out of *Saturday Night Fever*, complete with cheesy music from Abba to the Village People, authentic memorabilia, wall-to-wall magazine covers strewn with teen idols such as John Travolta and David Cassidy, and a fun Brady Bunch wall with a hole cut in the middle so you, too, can experience the thrill of being a Brady kid.

Salvation
1775 West Avenue, between Alton Road & Dade Boulevard, South Beach (673 6508). **Open** 10pm-5am Fri-Sun. **Admission** $12-$15.
For those seeking liberation from the cookie-cutter mould of lame Saturday-night dance clubs, Salvation is the place. Housed in an old warehouse, it's not only spacious (though every space is always filled) but features some of the world's best DJs spinning the latest dance mixes and a bevy of beautiful men for whom Salvation has become a weekly ritual. Most popular on Saturdays.

Semper's
645 Washington Avenue, between Sixth & Seventh Streets, South Beach (673 0302). Bus C, H, K, W.
This elegant, upscale, members-only nightclub was one of the most popular spots for the international jet set during the height of the South Beach renaissance. After a five-year hiatus, Semper's recently reopened and aims once again to be the epicentre of café society, but it has had its problems so may have closed again by the time you read this.

Twist
1057 Washington Avenue, between 10th & 11th Streets, South Beach (538 9478). Bus C, H, K, W. **Open** 1pm-5am daily. **Admission** free.
If you're claustrophobic (or homophobic, for that matter) then Twist is not for you, because it will have you twisting and contorting just to find a space on the way-crowded dance floor. A very popular, two-storey, late-night gay dance club with a good vibe and energetic crowd.

Warsaw
1450 Collins Avenue, at Espanola Way, South Beach (531 4555). Bus C, G, H, K, W. **Open** 9pm-5am Wed-Sat. **Admission** $5 after 11.30pm Wed-Fri.
A South Beach institution, this gay dance club attracts scantily clad, body-conscious men from all over the world. Sights and sounds are spectacular, not to mention on the verge of being X-rated, so don't expect any signs of demure dancing.

Downtown

Les Violins
1751 Biscayne Boulevard, between NE 17th & 18th Streets, Downtown (371 8668). Bus 3, 16, 32, 36, 95.
Rumba and tango. Legs and muscles, too. Yowza, yowza, yowza. Boogie nights are alive and well in this Cuban mainstay with a Brazilian floorshow. Les Violins was damaged by fire in spring 1997 but should have reopened by the time this guide is published.

Pecs appeal at the endorphin-generating **Salvation**.

Coconut Grove

Club St Croix

3015 Grand Avenue, at Virginia Street, Coconut Grove (446 4999). Bus 42, 48. **Open** 8pm-3am Mon-Thur, Sun; 7pm-5am Fri, Sat. **Admission** $4-$5 Thur-Sat; free Mon, Tue, Sun.

Experience the enticing rhythms of the islands at this island-themed tropical dance paradise. Wednesday is Ladies' Night, which means that women escape the $4 charge.

Sticky Fingers

3399 Virginia Street, at Grand Avenue, Coconut Grove (461 3313). Bus 42, 48. **Open** 6pm-2am Tue, Wed, Sun; 6pm-4am Thur-Sat. **Admission** $5-$10 after 10.30pm Thur-Sat.

Neither the most enticing name nor the most enticing place, this is a club-cum-restaurant with something of an identity crisis. It's a cross between a big band-style supper club and your classic discotheque. No relation to Bill Wyman's operation of the same name in the UK.

North Dade

Bermuda Bar

3509 NE 163rd Street, at NE 35th Avenue, North Miami Beach (945 0196). Bus E, H, V. **Open** 5pm-4am Wed, Thur; 5pm-6am Fri; 8pm-6am Sat; 8pm-4am Sun. **Admission** $5-$10.

Large dance club frequented by young, suburban professionals. Wednesday night is Ladies' Night.

Kitchen Club

11220 Biscayne Boulevard, at NE 112th Street, Miami Shores (754 0777). Bus 3. **Open** 11pm-5am Fri; midnight-5am Sat. **Admission** varies.

Even after moving locations three times, this Friday and Saturday night haven has a faithful following of Goth-influenced clubbers and ravers. Whip out the black lipstick or you just won't fit in.

South Dade

Café Iguana

Town & Country Center, 8505 Mills Drive, at SW 88th Street & SW 117th Avenue, West Kendall (274 4948). Bus 56, 88. **Open** 5pm-5am Mon-Fri; 7pm-5am Sat, Sun. **Admission** $5 Fri, Sat.

Weekends here draw flocks of suburbians-turned-club lizards who come for the local scene and music that varies from Latin to country. Special events such as the *Playgirl* magazine Men of Miami contest are often hosted here.

Marsbar

Town & Country Center, 8505 Mills Drive, at SW 88th Street & SW 117th Avenue, W Kendall (271 6909). Bus 56, 88. **Open** 8pm-5am Wed, Thur, Sat; 6pm-5am Fri. **Admission** $2 Thur; $5 after 9pm Fri, Sat.

Ignore the fact that this club is located in a strip mall. Marsbar is the hip alternative to South Beach, featuring a chic (albeit suburban) elite consisting of black-clad club kids dancing to cool New Order-ish music.

West Dade

La Covacha

10730 NW 25th Street, at NW 107th Avenue, West Dade (594 3717). No public transport. **Open** 11.30am-8pm Mon-Wed; 11.30am-midnight Thur; 11.30am-4am Fri-Sun. **Admission** $5 after 9pm Fri-Sun.

Latin dance hall with an energetic disco atmosphere. A fave among young Cuban and Latino dance enthusiasts.

Club Tropigala

Fontainebleau Hilton, 4441 Collins Avenue, at 44th Street, Miami Beach (672 7469). Bus G, H, J, L, S. **Open** 7pm-11pm Wed, Thur, Sun; 7pm-2am Fri, Sat. *Shows* 8.30pm Wed, Thur; 8pm Fri-Sun. **Admission** $15.

Ricky Ricardo's big-band Tropicana nightclub meets *Showgirls* – Latin-style, of course. These are major floorshow productions that will take you back to the days when every outing to a nightclub was a gala. If you can't go to Las Vegas, then get your high kicks here.

Cigar club

Cuba Club

432 41st Street, between Royal Palm & Sheridan Avenues, Miami Beach (604 9798). Bus C, F/M, J, K, T. **Open** 7pm-2am Mon, Tue, Thur-Sat; 7pm-3am Wed; 7pm-midnight Sun. **Admission** free; annual membership $250; cigar humidor $4,000.

With the stogie craze still smokin', the owners of the pristine Forge restaurant (*see chapter* **Restaurants**) decided that they'd build a temple to the art of cigar-smoking. The result was the Cuba Club, with its elaborate decor, chandeliered VIP smoking room and a vault that contains the privately owned humidors of some of Miami's most famous smokers, among them Madonna, Michael Caine and Sylvester Stallone. Memberships to this club cost in excess of $3,000, but you need not be a member to light up inside.

For one night only

Some clubs are only good on certain themed nights. Here's a list, but remember: these are very erratic and change quite often.

Monday

Fat Black Pussycat at **Liquid** – soul and funk speakeasy à la *Superfly* and *Shaft*. To discover the password necessary for admittance, call 531 6576

Wednesday

Fashion Night at **Bash**
Amateur Strip Contest at **Warsaw**
Chi-chi dinner party extravaganza at **The Forge** (*see chapter* **Restaurants & Cafés**)

Thursday

Phunky Town at **Polly Esther's**
Back Door Bambi at **Liquid** – a kinky night of deep house; call the hotline on 672 8351

Saturday

Boys' night out at **Salvation**
Un-Social Club at the smoky and sultry **Jazid** – a calm, cool and collected crowd

Sunday

Jet Set – Esquivel-esque vibes at **821** (*see chapter* **Bars**)
Ratpack Night – kings of swing hit the **Berlin Bar**

Comedy clubs

Comedy clubs in this city are few and far between. It's not that Miami doesn't have a sense of humour, it's just that there's so much amusement to be found elsewhere, we guess.

The Improv

Streets of Mayfair, 3390 Mary Street, at Grand Avenue, Coconut Grove (441 8200). Bus 42, 48. **Shows** 8.30pm Mon-Thur, Sun; 8.30pm, 10.45pm, Fri; 7.45pm, 10pm, midnight, Sat; 8.30pm Sun. **Admission** $10 Mon-Thur, Sun; $12 Fri, Sat. **Credit** AmEx, MC,V.
New comedy club chain featuring national and local talent.

Punch 59

Edge Theater, 405 Espanola Way, between Drexel & Washington Avenues, South Beach (1-954 583 4577). Bus C, H, K, W. **Shows** 9pm Thur. **Admission** $5. **No credit cards**.
On Thursday nights this small South Beach theatre hosts a showcase of surprisingly witty local acts.

Drag clubs

Nathan Lane's dolled-up character in *Birdcage* did no justice to the reigning drag queens of South Beach, where the movie was filmed. There's an entire subculture of drag queens in this neck of the woods, led by drag royalty such as Adora and Kitty Meow. There are as many drag queens as there are MAC lipstick shades, and most have better figures, hair, clothing and make-up than some of the area's working models. In addition to the street parade of drag queens that begins when the sun goes down, the queens actually perform in full regalia, lip-synching anything from Shirley Bassey to Madonna at various South Beach venues. A long-running tradition is **Mulberry Mondays**, when Adora and her crew of dazzling divas do their thing; the venue changes frequently so keep your ears open. **Lucky Cheng's** Chinese restaurant on South Beach (600 Lincoln Road, at Pennsylvania Avenue; 672 1505), where the waitresses are waiters in drag, presents a cabaret twice a night featuring Adora's many girls. For $10 the performers will 'sing' your requested song. Do not miss this just because you don't look as fabulous as the girls. It's truly a spectacular sight. Plus, you'll pick up some fabby beauty and fashion tips.

Sex clubs

The popularity of nightclubs featuring 'sophisticated adult entertainment' (ie strippers) has soared in recent years. Ubiquitous, upscale, brass-and-mirrors joints with the words 'Gold' or 'Platinum' in their names offer valet parking, charge up to $15 at the door, sell absurdly overpriced drinks and cater to affluent male patrons who think nothing of investing $20 per three-minute song for a close-up view of undulating breast implants.

More than 60 Miami area bars (up from about half a dozen such venues two decades ago) lure customers with totally nude female dancers who writhe suggestively on raised stages. The old-fash-

*She is a he: a lip-synching 'waitress' at **Lucky Cheng's**.*

ioned striptease has given way to 'lap dancing' and 'friction dancing', barely legal variations on the old bump-and-grind wherein the dancer coyly brushes various body parts against the client's crotch. Therein lies the rub: customers are strictly prohibited from touching dancers, but dancers can touch customers. The bigger the tip, the longer and more intimate the contact.

Glitzier clubs discreetly funnel such activity into expensive champagne rooms. The clubs strictly maintain this fine line between titillation and prostitution; there is no quicker and surer path to get tossed out of a club than to proposition a dancer. (Police raids are extremely rare, although one often reads about strip club owners getting busted for high-level drug dealing, tax evasion, money laundering or the like.)

It wasn't always thus. Some 25 years ago, motorcycle gangs ran Miami's dens of iniquity. Prostitution and drug sales (mostly speed) flourished. The dancers weren't much to look at and the patrons tended to be down-and-outers. The cops eventually drove the bikers out of the business by the mid-1980s, just in time for a new breed of proprietor to take over. These were the halcyon years of the cocaine trade, when swarms of enterprising Miamians became overnight millionaires. Droves of beeper-packing young Latin men crowded the late-night meccas, killing time between arriving shipments. Inevitably, the realisation dawned that high-volume cash businesses were marvellous places not just to spend money, but to launder it. And what better way to impress a heavy-hitting customer or South American supplier than to surround him with nubile young women from your very own flesh pit?

Nouveau-riche small businessmen flooded the market with capital, transforming seedy dives into plush nightspots. No longer sleazy-looking holes-in-the-wall, strip clubs gained respectability. Nowadays they cater less to drug dealers than to professional athletes and business-lunching corporate types. Most advertise that they welcome couples, although in reality few women muster the courage to enter these male-dominated sanctuaries. (There are no gay strip clubs per se, although many gay dance clubs, both male and female, feature nude go-go dancers.) Only one club – North Miami Beach's La Bare – stages male dancers who strip for women. And how's this for a double standard: according to Florida law, the boys are not allowed to bare all, but must hide the goods with G-strings. Maybe La Bare should change its name to La Cover Up.

Bare Necessity

9100 South Dixie Highway/US 1, between SW 90th & 92nd Streets, South Miami (670 2373). Bus 1, 52, 65/ Metrorail Dadeland South. **Open** noon-6am Mon-Fri; 2.30pm-6am Sat; 2.30pm-5am Sun. **Admission** free over-21s; $10 18-21s.

Converted from a notorious rock 'n' roll bar, Bare Necessity used to host live bands playing Zeppelin. Now the entertainment consists of naked women who dance to Zeppelin.

Breaching the velvet ropes

In a retro attempt to recreate the exclusivity of clubs in the mould of New York's infamous Studio 54, many of South Beach's night spots have invested heavily in the concept of impenetrable velvet ropes, the gateway to all things fabulous. Illusion plays an important role: amassing a huge crowd in front of an empty club will create demand, so while it may seem impossible to part the ropes unless you're a skinny-rib model or accompanied by an A-list celebrity, it can usually be done with a bit of patience. Even the Berlin Wall had to crumble eventually.

The door guards tend to let women and men accompanied by women through first (unless, of course it's a gay establishment). Beyond this, the key to playing Moses of the Night and parting the red ropes lies in the following tactics:

Once you're through, you can set yourself another challenge. Nearly every club has a VIP room or section, set away from the crowds; it is a status symbol but not (as you might expect) reserved exclusively for celebs and luminaries.

The key to entry into the VIP room is simple: call ahead. Most clubs will be happy to accommodate you as long as you fulfill the required one- or two-bottle minimum necessary to keep your derrière in place (champagne is most popular, but vodka or other liquor is OK, too). We didn't say being a VIP was cheap, did we?

Do

● Emit that 'Don't hate me because I'm beautiful' air of confidence.
● Dress to impress.
● Be cordial.
● Look important.
● Call ahead (and try to weasel your name on the guest list to avoid the above).

Don't

● Name-drop or call out bouncers' names.
● Under- or overdress.
● Act too excited to be there.
● Bribe the doormen (although many will take your cash offerings, this is a major faux pas).

Nothing but the best

*Clubkids get a draught of **Liquid** refreshment.*

Best all-round dance club: **Salvation**
Best heterosexual dance club: **Liquid**
Best mellow club: **Jazid**
Best retro club: **Polly Esther's**
Best club for a secret rendezvous: **Cuba Club**
Best loungey club: **The Lounge at Liquid**
Best one-nighter: **Fat Black Pussycat at Liquid**
Most clubby non-club: **The Rose Bar at the Delano**

Hotel
Best club for spotting models: **KGB**
Best star-gazing club: **Liquid**
Most difficult to get into: **The Living Room at the Strand**
Best music: **Groove Jet**
Best escape from Miami: **Amnesia**
Best late-night: **Groove Jet**

Deja Vu

2004 Collins Avenue, at 20th Street, South Beach (538 0355). Bus C, G, H, L, S. **Open** noon-5am Mon-Sat; 6pm-5am Sun. **Admission** free during day; midnight-5am $10 plus $10 drink minimum.

The City of Miami Beach prohibits the sale of alcoholic beverages in strip clubs. You can't buy liquor at Deja Vu, but you will find some of the hottest dancers in South Florida. And it's located in South Beach.

La Bare

2355 Sunny Isles Boulevard, at Biscayne Boulevard & NE 163rd Street, North Miami Beach (945 6799). Bus 3, E, H, V. **Open** 8pm-2am Mon-Thur, Sun; 8pm-3am Fri, Sat. **Admission** $10 women over 21; $15 women 18-21; no men allowed.

Miami's only strip club for women, and it's currently in danger of being closed down.

Miami Gold

17450 Biscayne Boulevard, at NE 174th Street, North Miami Beach (945 6030). Bus 3, V. **Open** 3pm-6am Mon-Fri; 5pm-6am Sat; 9pm-5am Sun. **Admission** $10.

Porno-film superstars often perform special shows at this pricey club which is located just a few blocks north of

Solid Gold, *below* (to which it's no relation). The bars' proximity to each other encourages club-hopping.

Solid Gold

2355 Sunny Isles Boulevard, at Biscayne Boulevard & NE 163rd Street, North Miami Beach (956 5726). Bus 3, E, H, V. **Open** noon-4am Mon-Fri; 4pm-4am Sat, Sun **Admission** $10; women allowed in only when accompanied by a man.

This long-standing high-rollers' favourite, located in the same building as La Bare, employs over 100 showgirls. Also in danger of being shut down. Women can go, but only in the company of men – and it's hardly one the husband's going to want to take you to.

The Trap

13690 NW Seventh Avenue, at NW 136th Street, North Miami (681 1756). Bus 28, 77, E. **Open** noon-1am Mon-Sat; 6pm-1am Sun **Admission** free; one-drink minimum.

Coming on more like a neighbourhood pub than a strip club, The Trap has won *New Times'* Best Strip Joint award for four years running. Attractive dancers who actually converse with customers, drink prices that aren't that much higher than they are in a regular bar and free admission have won it a loyal local following.

Film

Miami isn't Hollywood but the movies are big business here: you can go actor-spotting in South Beach, see a film being made on the city's streets or even watch one in a cinema.

Just as Miami Beach has gone through several boom-and-bust cycles, so has the motion picture industry engaged in an on-again, off-again affair with the area that dates back nearly 80 years.

In 1917, legendary Miami politico John 'Ev' Sewell persuaded silent film star Cissy Fitzgerald to let himself and other investors incorporate a production company bearing her name – but the enterprise soon folded. Undaunted, Sewell convinced aviation pioneer Glenn Curtiss to take a flyer on Miami Studios, a Hialeah production facility also backed by *Miami Herald* owner Frank Shutts and other prominent local businessmen. In 1922, director Rex Ingram accepted an invitation to shoot his next film at Miami Studios with silent film great Ramon Navarro; local bigwigs gleefully predicted a mass exodus from Hollywood to South Florida. But weather delays and inexperienced local workers made Ingram's shoot a near-disaster; he high-tailed it out of town as soon as he finished principal photography and excoriated Miami Studios in interviews. Word of the unpredictable climate and the studio's ineptitude spread. The deadly hurricane of 1928 killed off any last hopes of revitalisation.

Miami may have blown its chances of becoming an East Coast Hollywood, but, more recently, it has become one of the world's hippest and hottest locations for film shoots (*see box* Who said crime doesn't pay?). However, the same seductive tropical charms, natural and otherwise, that long ago earned Miami the nickname 'The Magic City' also seduce and mesmerise film-makers into making mystifying choices. How else to explain the bizarre decisions by internationally acclaimed directors who have come here to shoot in recent years?

What voodoo logic persuaded Indian director Mira Nair (*Salaam Bombay!*) that she could credibly convey the Cuban-American experience in *The Perez Family* using non-Latin actors such as Marisa Tomei and Anjelica Huston? What mysterious force charmed Spanish writer-director Fernando Trueba (maker of *Belle Epoque*) into believing he could successfully make a screwball comedy (*Two Much*) out of a Donald Westlake crime novel – and do so in English with Antonio Banderas, a Spaniard whose command of the English language is only slightly more polished than the director's own? Based on positive

box-office results, one could argue that Mike '*The Graduate*' Nichols succeeded in transposing *La Cage aux Folles* from gay Paree to even gayer SoBe in *The Birdcage*, but no-one who saw the original would go so far as to suggest that Nichols' version surpasses it. And where exactly did producer Joel Silver get the notion that Cindy Crawford could act? It's hard to recall a more ridiculous excuse for a movie than *Fair Game*.

Some stars work here; others play here. A few do both. Madonna, Sylvester Stallone and Cher have bought homes and invested in businesses in the area; civic booster Sly is actively pursuing the construction of a full-blown movie studio and state-of-the-art production facility in town and has lent his name and funds to the perennially cash-strapped Miami Film Festival. Michael Caine has opened a restaurant. Mick Hucknall and Sean Penn have invested in popular nightspot Bash. And on any given weekend you can find the likes of Robert De Niro, Johnny Depp, George Clooney, Salma Hayek, Stephen Dorff, Jack Nicholson, Pedro Almodóvar and a smattering of Baldwin brothers navigating the shark-infested waters of South Beach nightlife.

MAINSTREAM & INDEPENDENTS

Cinema and Miami both celebrated their centenaries in 1996. But, despite sharing the same number of birthday candles and despite Miami's popularity with visiting film-makers and celebs, the celluloid art form does not exactly thrive here (the city does not support a single repertory cinema). Simply put, tourists do not come to Miami to see movies. They're more likely to visit a nightclub in the hope of catching a real-life glimpse of an actor than to venture into a cinema to see the same thesp in action. During the day, active Miamians pursue a plethora of outdoor pleasures; at night, the world's trendiest bars, restaurants and night-clubs beckon. Who has time – or money – left over for going to the cinema? And let's face it, watching the world go by from a sidewalk café on South Beach can be as surreal, unpredictable and entertaining as vintage Fellini.

Of course, the big hits put (mostly adolescent) backsides on seats, just as they do anywhere, but smaller, independent and European films suffer acute difficulty attracting an audience. Such films

Cobb's Mayfair 10, *from decadence to opulence.*

tend to open in South Florida months after they premiere in New York or LA, and then they may play for as little as a week. Similarly, video rental stores focus on big Hollywood releases to the exclusion of smaller, riskier fare.

However, there is a pocket of hope for connoisseurs and bootstrap film-makers. The Alliance Film/Video Co-op conducts a variety of film-making workshops and classes, sporadically screens classic and avant-garde films, and makes available to its members editing and production facilities at discount prices. Housed in an old office building just across South Beach's upscale Lincoln Road Mall from the related Alliance Cinema, the co-op is the hub of underground film-making in South Florida. Whether you want to rent equipment on the cheap or just chat with kindred spirits who know as much about Buñuel, Brakhage and Kenneth Anger as they do about George Lucas, check out the Alliance Co-op at 924 Lincoln Road, Suite 208, Miami Beach, FL 33139 (538 8242).

TICKETS & INFORMATION

It is customary to buy tickets in cash at the box office just prior to the start of a film, but you should book for opening-night spectaculars. The going rate for admission is around $6.50, but most cinemas offer discounts for students (with college ID) and senior citizens. Prices are often reduced for early afternoon and twilight showings.

Both the daily *Miami Herald* and the weekly *New Times* newspapers publish fairly accurate and comprehensive film listings. The *Herald*

covers every film that opens in Miami but its reviews (most of which run in the Friday Weekend section) are substantially shorter than those in *New Times*. The latter may go into greater depth but publishes only two or three reviews per week (written by self-important LA-based critics who occasionally miss films of particular local interest). You can call the free service 888 FILM (3456) for a schedule of what's playing where and when, one-line film summaries and credit card bookings.

South Beach has possibly the city's best-programmed cinema in the **Alliance** (*see below*), but currently lacks big commercial multi-screeners. Your best bet by car would be to cross the MacArthur Causeway and go to the Omni 10 at 1601 Biscayne Boulevard (448 2088); by bus head north on the L or H to the Cobb's Byron-Carlyle at 500 71st Street (866 9623).

The cinemas

The advent of multiplexes has resulted in an explosion in the number of movie screens – and a corresponding implosion in average screen size. Several multi-screens, generally those situated in relatively affluent neighbourhoods like Coconut Grove, have experimented with dedicating a screen or two to films that would have traditionally wound up making the rounds of art houses. In general, however, European, Asian, South American and smaller independent US films are limited to a handful of tiny cinemas.

Interesting multiplexes

AMC CocoWalk 16

3015 Grand Avenue, at Virginia Street, Coconut Grove (448 7075). Bus 42, 48. **Open** 12.30-10pm Mon-Thur, Sun; 12.30pm-1am Fri, Sat. **Tickets** $6.50 adults; $4.50 students, senior citizens; $3.75 under-13s. **Credit** AmEx, Disc, MC, V.

The AMC chain has formalised its dedicated-to-small-films policy under the category 'Gourmet Cinema'. This 16-screener, located in the bustling, upscale CocoWalk shopping and dining complex, often features as many as three non-Hollywood films playing at any one time.

AMC Fashion Island

18741 Biscayne Boulevard, between NE 187th & 191st Streets, North Miami Beach (931 2873). Bus 3, V. **Open** 12.30-10pm Mon-Thur, Sun; 12.30pm-1am Fri, Sat. **Tickets** $6.50 adults; $4.50 students, senior citizens; $3.75 under-13s. **Credit** AmEx, Disc, MC, V.

A North Miami Beach version of the AMC CocoWalk 16, but situated in a discount mall.

Cobb's Mayfair 10

3390 Mary Street, at Grand Avenue, Coconut Grove (447 9969). Bus 42, 48. **Open** 1-11pm Mon-Thur, Sun; 1pm-1am Fri, Sat. **Tickets** $6.50 adults; $4.50 students, senior citizens; $3.75 2-11s. **Credit** MC, V.

During the go-go early 1980s, the obscenely opulent Mayfair arcade (imported Italian tile mosaics, fountains galore, brass-and-glass elevators) catered to the shopping whims of cash rich cocaine cowboys. Rumours abound as to the role that money-laundering played in the Mayfair's construction and early tenant base. Lately, however, spurred by competition from nearby CocoWalk, the once-snooty mall has openly courted more upper-middle-class trade with the addition of a Border's bookstore, a Planet Hollywood restaurant and a 10-screen cinema. First-time visitors are invariably flummoxed by the layout: the difficult-to-find box office is on the first floor while the cinema itself occupies the third. As with CocoWalk, finding parking on a Friday or Saturday night can be a frustrating experience.

Regal Cinemas California Club VI

850 Ives Dairy Road, at NE 199th Street & 10th Avenue, North Dade (652 8558). Bus 91. **Open** 1-10.30pm daily. **Tickets** $6.50 adults; $4.50 students; $4 children, senior citizens. **No credit cards.**

It's not as likely to host non-Hollywood fare as the multiscreens listed above, but the California Club nonetheless deserves mention for its giant, state-of-the-art main auditorium. If you want to see a blockbuster, this is the place.

Classic, foreign & experimental

Alliance Cinema

927 Lincoln Road, between Jefferson & Michigan Avenues, South Beach (531 8504). Bus A, F/M, K, L, S. **Open** 8-10pm Mon-Thur; 6pm-midnight Fri; 4pm-midnight Sat; noon-10pm Sun. **Tickets** $6 non-members; $4 members, shows before 6pm. **No credit cards.**

Week in and week out, South Beach's smallish Alliance books the most stimulating and challenging fare in the city. Films may take a while to arrive but if it's worth seeing it will arrive at the Alliance at some point – and no other Miami cinema books a fraction as many films of interest to the gay community.

Alcazar Cinematheque

235 Alcazar Avenue, between Le Jeune Road & Ponce de Leon Boulevard, Coral Gables (446 7144). Bus 40, 42, J. **Open** 7.30-9.30pm Mon-Fri; 3.30-9.30pm Sat, Sun. **Tickets** $6. **No credit cards.**

One of a pair of small art-house cinemas in Coral Gables, the Alcazar and the Astor (*below*) specialise in European and independent US movies.

Astor Art Cinema

4120 Laguna Street, between Bird Road & Shipping Avenue, Coral Gables (443 6777). Bus 37, 40, 42/Metrorail Douglas Road. **Open** 7.30-9.30pm Mon-Fri; 3.30-9.30pm Sat, Sun. **Tickets** $6. **No credit cards.**

Like the Alcazar (*above*), the Astor specialises in European and indie US product, with the odd revival thrown in for good measure. Owner Cesar Soto is always on the lookout for quality Spanish-language films.

Bill Cosford Cinema

Second floor, Memorial Building, University of Miami, off Campo Sano Avenue & University Drive, Coral Gables (284 4861). Bus 48, 52, 56. **Open** screenings vary; call for schedule. **Tickets** $5 adults; $3 students, senior citizens. **No credit cards.**

Located on the University of Miami campus, the Cosford offers an eclectic mix of Asian, European and art-house fare. Named after the late *Miami Herald* film critic Bill Cosford and completely renovated with a gift from his family, it is roomier and plusher than most first-run cinemas.

Florida International University

University Park Campus, Graham Center, SW Eighth Street & 107th Avenue (348 2461). Bus 8, 11, 24, 71. **Open** 8pm Wed. **Tickets** free.

Cinema Wednesdays offers classic movies for free. Open to non-students as well as the FIU community.

Louis Wolfson II Media History Center

Metro-Dade Public Library, 101 W Flagler Street, at NW First Avenue, Downtown (375 4527). Bus 3, 16, 95, C, S/ Metrorail & Metromover Government Center. **Screenings** 1pm Tue, Thur. **Tickets** free.

The Wolfson Media History Center hosts a weekly programme called Video Rewind in the main auditorium of the Downtown branch of the Metro-Dade Public Library. Director Steve Davidson unearths selected historical videos from the centre's massive archives. Even if you don't care for the scheduled screenings, nostalgia buffs and anyone with even a passing interest in Miami's past should drop by the archive and check out some of the amazing footage of Miami through the years.

Miami Art Museum

101 W Flagler Street, at NW First Avenue, Downtown (375 3000). Bus 3, 16, 95, C, S/Metrorail & Metromover Government Center. **Open** screenings vary; call for schedule. **Tickets** free with museum admission.

Films about art and artists.

Discount

While there are no repertory houses per se, several Miami cinemas cater to budget-conscious moviegoers who don't mind seeing films that opened months earlier. Unfortunately these are a schlepp away from the main tourist areas.

Apollo Theater

3800 W 12th Avenue, at W 38th Street, Hialeah (826 6606). Bus 29, 54, 73. **Open** screenings vary; call for a schedule. **Tickets** $1.50.

Favorite Cinemas

4650 W 17th Court, between W 46th & 49th Streets, Hialeah (557 9888). Bus 29, 33, 54. **Open** noon-10pm daily. **Tickets** $1.50.

Super Saver Cinema
11501 Bird Road, at SW 115th Avenue, South Dade (227 0277). Bus 40, 71. **Open** 12.30-10pm daily. **Tickets** $1.50.

University VII
1645 SW 107th Avenue, at SW 16th Street, South Dade (223 2700). Bus 8, 24, 71. **Open** 7.30-9pm Mon-Fri; 2.30-9pm Sat, Sun. **Tickets** $1.50.

Film festivals

Ironically, for a town that can't muster year-round support for foreign, independent and art-house cinema, Miami has a glut of film festivals.

Anti-Film Festival
Information 538 8242. **Date** Feb.
A heartfelt response to the glitz, glamour and hype surrounding the infinitely more commercial Miami Film Festival, the Anti-Film Festival is mounted by the Alliance Film/Video Co-op to screen its members' edgy, avant-garde work. Inspiration and creativity sometimes compensate for what the films lack in budget.

Fort Lauderdale International Film Festival
Information 1-954 563 0500. **Date** Nov.
Taking more of a grab-bag attitude than the Miami Film Festival's notoriously selective (and subjective) approach, the rapidly growing, corporate-sponsored FLIFF screens several dozen films every November. The emphasis is on US independents, especially the work of Florida filmmakers,

Who said crime doesn't pay?

Although films from many different genres have capitalised on Miami's unique charms, crime stories dominate made-in-Miami movies. Many blame (or praise) that insanely popular mid-1980s TV series *Miami Vice* for cultivating Miami's image as a tropical Casablanca, replete with fast cars, faster women and Colombian drug dealers battling chic Armani-clad lawmen. However, sex, crime and South Florida share a long and illustrious cinema history.

The Miami Story (1954) and *Miami Expose* (1956) set the tone before Sonny Crockett and Rico Tubbs were born. In 1964, a debonair super spy known as 007 first encountered arch-nemesis Goldfinger by the pool at Miami Beach's

Fontainebleau Hotel. (Bond, in his Roger Moore incarnation, came back to the Everglades to film *Live and Let Die*, pictured above.) Soon after, Frank Sinatra (whose off-screen fraternisation with mafiosi is well documented) got into the hardboiled gumshoe act as tough-talking private dick Tony Rome in the film of the same name with '60s sex kittens Jill St John and Raquel Welch.

Legend has it that Gerard Damiano borrowed mob money to shoot the most popular and notorious porn film of all time, *Deep Throat*, in Miami in the early '70s. In 1977's *Black Sunday*, lethally beautiful terrorist Marthe Keller used sex to lure wacko Bruce Dern into a plot to blow up the Goodyear blimp during the Super Bowl at Miami's although Euro fare has become a larger part of the mix. Several of its top offerings screen at Miami's Bill Cosford Cinema.

Italian Film Festival

Information 532 4986. **Date** One week in Nov.
The newest kid on an increasingly crowded block, this festival celebrates the cream of Italy's current cinematic crop.

Miami Film Festival

Information 377 3456. **Date** Feb.
The grand-daddy of all South Florida film festivals, the Miami fest launched in 1984. Unlike Utah's better-known Sundance festival, which was founded a year later and draws film-lovers and industry types, the Miami festival sells most of its 32,000 tickets to locals starved of quality films. US audiences first encountered the work of Pedro Almodóvar, Régis Wargnier, Fernando Trueba and Lasse Hallström here;

no film festival in North America rivals MFF for showcasing new Spanish-language works. The festival usually spans the first fortnight in February and supplements the always intriguing roster of films with gala parties, meet-the-filmmaker forums and a smattering of free seminars and lectures.

Queer Flickering Light

Information 531 0903. **Date** one week in early June.
Dedicated to the works of gay and lesbian film-makers from around the US, QFL is gaining a national reputation.

South Beach Film Festival

Information 532 1233. **Date** April.
Maintaining an office a floor below the Alliance Film/Video Co-op, the game but struggling SBFF is open to shorts, animation, experimental works and full-length documentaries and narratives. It unspools in Lincoln Road's Colony Theater.

Orange Bowl stadium. Nebbish ne'er-do-well honeymooner Charles Grodin dumped his Jewish bride on Miami Beach and took off after WASP princess Cybill Shepherd in *The Heartbreak Kid*. William Hurt melted under Kathleen Turner's *Body Heat* in 1981. And two decades after Bond met Goldfinger, Al Pacino's Tony Montana watched in disgust from the deck of the same Fontainebleau Hotel pool in *Scarface* as his Marielito pal Manolo suggestively wagged a tongue at American babes in teenie-weenie bikinis.

The mid-1980s double whammy of *Miami Vice* and *Scarface* begat a string of cheesy, straight-to-video drugs-and-crime productions such as *Miami Cops* (starring the original Shaft, Richard Roundtree), *Miami Supercops*, *Miami Horror* and *Miami Vendetta*. Even the lowbrow *Police Academy* series got into the act. The rash of trash led to a post-*Vice* backlash, epitomised by 1990's *Miami Blues*, which starred Fred Ward, Alec Baldwin and Jennifer Jason Leigh in a dark and cynical adaptation of cult crime-fiction master Charles Willeford's Hoke Moseley novel.

Miami Blues cleared the decks for a new breed of crime story in the 1990s. Laughs edged out larceny in Jim Carrey's shamelessly silly 1993 hit, *Ace Ventura: Pet Detective*. Sylvester Stallone and Sharon Stone tangoed for cash in 1994's equally (but unintentionally) laughable *The Specialist*. Comeback kid John Travolta cemented his post-*Pulp Fiction* star status by playing a Miami loanshark gone Hollywood in 1995's *Get Shorty*. And Antonio Banderas's career took a giant step in the other direction following his turn as a love-struck gallery owner/con man in 1996's *Two Much* – a film destined to be remembered less for its own merits than for Banderas's real-life Heartbreak Kid act, ditching his wife for his co-star Melanie Griffith.

In 1995, Martin Lawrence and Will Smith gave *Miami Vice* a wisecracking, black-on-black makeover in *Bad Boys*. Cindy Crawford proved her ability to stretch as an actress less compelling than her ability to stretch a wet T-shirt in the incoherent spy drama *Fair Game*, while Demi Moore bared all for her art (again) in *Striptease*, based on the novel of the same name by *Miami Herald* columnist Carl Hiassen. 1996's *Curdled* served Grand Guignol with salsa.

Lately, the pace has only speeded up – as in *Speed II*. *Blood and Wine* reunited Jack Nicholson with his *Five Easy Pieces* director Bob Rafelson. A dozen years after portraying the archetypal Cuban heel in *Scarface*, Al Pacino returned to South Florida as an Italian wise guy (opposite Johnny Depp, pictured below) in *Donnie Brasco*. And, in the ultimate confirmation of Miami's evolution into a hip film-making mecca, Quentin Tarantino has declared his intention to get behind the cameras for the first time since *Pulp Fiction* to direct the motion picture adaptation of Elmore Leonard's South Florida-based novel *Rum Punch*.

So you can forgive anyone who works in the film industry in Miami for getting the adage wrong. For them, crime pays handsomely, indeed.

Museums & Galleries

Beach town it may be, bimboid it ain't. Miami's arts scene is thriving, diverse and accessible.

The visual arts in Miami tend to get upstaged by the area's natural attributes, as most locals and tourists typically prefer a day at the beach to viewing an exhibition indoors. But the lack of crowds is one advantage for the culturally minded in Miami, and those who abandon the obvious lures of South Florida's 'sun-n-fun' for its more obscure museums and galleries will discover an active local art scene that is as diverse as the city's population.

Miami has experienced a significant cultural awakening in the past decade, with a marked increase in artistic activity during the past few years. The number of museums and galleries has grown significantly, and the Metro-Dade County Art in Public Places programme has dotted the urban landscape with site-specific projects, among them South Beach's decorative new electric buses. Miami's public art tends to be aesthetically pleasing rather than conceptually challenging – this is apparent on arrival at Miami International Airport, where Christopher Janney's 'Harmonic Runway' greets international passengers in the Concourse A arrivals corridor with a rainbow spectrum reflected through coloured glass and the sound of native birds and frogs, and Michele Oka Donner has inlaid the terrazzo floor with bronze sea creatures and shells.

While Miami is not a centre for cutting-edge art, internationally recognised artists do show here, and important travelling exhibitions from major institutions in New York and elsewhere in the US often come to the **Museum of Contemporary Art** in North Miami, the **Bass Museum** in Miami Beach, the **Miami Art Museum** in Downtown, Coral Gables' **Lowe Art Museum** and Florida International University's **Art Museum**. Further afield, the **Museum of Art** in Fort Lauderdale (1-954 525 5500) and the **Norton Museum** on West Palm Beach (1-561 832 5196) are worth a day trip. All these venues feature a disparate exhibition schedule that mixes contemporary and historical shows and work by locals and non-locals, often with an emphasis on Latin American art.

The immigration of artists from Cuba and other Latin American countries has made Miami a showplace for Caribbean and South American culture. At any given time, exhibits of artefacts as varied as pre-Columbian ceramics, Mexican modernist paintings, Cuban refugee rafts and Haitian voodoo flags are on display in institutions around town. There is no definitive cultural centre here, and museums and galleries are spread over the various cities that make up Greater Miami – if you want to see what's out there, it's easier with a car.

ART FAIRS

Miami's compartmentalised art world comes together in early January (usually around the first weekend), when the highly commercialised Art Miami fair is held at the Miami Beach Convention Center and a more interesting, alternative contemporary art fair takes over two floors of the nearby Raleigh Hotel. A lot of out-of-town collectors and curators make the trip, lured by the warm winter weather, and local galleries and museums put on their most spectacular shows. In general, more noteworthy exhibitions are mounted during high season in winter, but museums and galleries are open through the summer, when they're a good place to take refuge from the afternoon heat.

Museums

All Miami's museums offer extensive educational programmes that include lectures, films, music and Saturday afternoon activities for children. See the weekly *New Times* calendar section or the *Miami Herald*'s Weekend section for information about exhibitions and programming. The free *Southeast Gallery Guide* can be picked up in most galleries.

Art & culture

The American Police Hall of Fame & Museum

3801 Biscayne Boulevard, at 38th Street, Buena Vista, Miami (573 0070). Bus 3, 16, 62, J, T. **Open** 10am-5.30pm daily. **Admission** $6 adults; $4 seniors; $3 under-12s. **Credit** MC, V.

The nation's only memorial honouring US police officers who have died in the line of duty, this museum is easy to

*Driven up the wall at the **Police Hall of Fame**.*

spot – it's got a real police car embedded in the facade of the building. The names, ranks, cities and states of more than 6,000 murdered officers are engraved in white marble on the first floor. Certainly unique, the Police Hall of Fame has displays of guns, handcuffs, billy clubs and the like, as well as 'pursuit vehicles' and execution devices, including a guillotine and an electric chair (which you can sit in). There's even a crime scene set – visitors are invited to solve the murder.

The Art Museum at Florida International University

PC Building Room 110, University Park Campus, SW Eighth Street & 107th Avenue, Westchester (348 2890). Bus 8, 11, 24, 71. **Open** 10am-9pm Mon; 10am-5pm Tue-Fri; noon-4pm Sat. **Admission** free.

This small, first-floor museum on the south campus of Miami's public university habitually offers ambitious collective exhibitions. Shows have explored such subjects as Dada, Cuban modernism, fashion and art, and Latin American folk art. Work by FIU professors and students is also shown periodically. A substantial collection of notable outdoor sculpture by Alexander Calder, Jonathan Borofsky, Isamu Noguchi and others, on loan from a local collector, is on display on the FIU campus (pick up a list of the works and a map at the museum).

Bass Museum of Art

2121 Park Avenue, between 21st & 22nd Streets, South Beach (673 7530). Bus C, G, H, L, S. **Open** 10am-5pm Tue-Sat; 1-5pm Sun. **Admission** $5 adults; $3 students, senior citizens; free under-6s; free or by donation every second and fourth Wed of the month. **Credit** MC, V.

Miami Beach's only fine art museum, the Bass is located in a cosy 1930s art deco building that was once a public library. Made of keystone coral rock, it was designed by acclaimed

local architect Russell Pancoast, son-in-law of Miami Beach pioneer John Collins. The Bass is named after a family of benefactors who donated their collection of European art to the City of Miami Beach in the 1960s. Pieces from the collection are on display in one of the museum's galleries: most are minor works created by followers of Peter Paul Rubens and other masters, and highlights include 'The Tournament', an enormous sixteenth-century Flemish tapestry. European visitors are unlikely to be wowed by the Bass's holdings, but the museum also hosts consistently fine temporary shows smartly installed in the limited two-storey space. These have included art about AIDS, costumes from Fellini's films and the works of surrealist Meret Oppenheim. Films relating to exhibition themes are shown in the museum's auditorium every weekend and occasional classical and jazz concerts are offered. The Bass also runs an art camp for children during summer and Christmas holidays.

Historical Museum of Southern Florida

Metro-Dade Cultural Center, 101 W Flagler Street, at NW First Avenue, Downtown (375 1492). Bus 3, 16, 95, C, S/Metrorail & Metromover Government Center. **Open** 10am-5pm Mon-Wed, Fri, Sat; 10am-9pm Thur; noon-5pm Sun. **Admission** $4 adults; $2 6-12s; free under-6s. **Credit** AmEx, MC, V.

This quaint museum offers a family-friendly exhibit on the history of Miami and its disparate residents, from the Miccosukee Indians and the Anglo-American pioneers who founded the city to the Cuban immigrants who started arriving as political refugees in the 1960s. The slightly kitsch display features dioramas recreating the natural environment, Indian artefacts and a short slide show on local history. Temporary shows have featured Cuban cigar labels and Florida landscape art. The gift shop has a large selection of Florida vintage postcards and books on local history, architecture and wildlife, as well as plastic alligators and other souvenirs for children.

Lowe Art Museum

University of Miami, 1301 Stanford Drive, at Ponce de Leon Boulevard, Coral Gables (284 3603). Bus 48, 52, 56. **Open** 10am-5pm Tue, Wed, Fri, Sat; noon-7pm Thur; noon-5pm Sun. **Admission** $4 adults; $3 senior citizens; $2 students; free UM students, under-12s. **Credit** (shop only) AmEx, MC, V.

The recently expanded Lowe Museum on the University of Miami's pastoral campus has an important collection of pre-Columbian gold and silver objects. Its holdings of over 8,000 works also include Navajo and Pueblo Indian textiles and baskets, Renaissance and Baroque paintings and Latin American art. Historical shows here have focused on Southeast Asian ceramics, early American paintings and Haitian art. Work by contemporary local artists is also shown.

Miami Art Museum (MAM)

Metro-Dade Cultural Center, 101 W Flagler Street, at NW First Avenue, Downtown (375 3000). Bus 3, 16, 95, C, S/Metrorail & Metromover Government Center. **Open** 10am-5pm Tue, Wed, Fri; 10am-9pm Thur; noon-5pm Sat, Sun. **Admission** $5 adults; $2.50 students, senior citizens; free under-12s. **Credit** AmEx, MC, V.

Long suffering from an identity crisis, the decade-old Center for the Fine Arts was renamed the Miami Art Museum in 1996. Formerly showing only temporary exhibitions, it is now a collecting museum of modern and contemporary art. Nascent collection or no, the museum has enduring problems. Its fortress-like building (designed by Philip Johnson) opens onto a plaza that's unbearably hot in summer, when homeless Miami residents take refuge by the entranceway fountains. The exhibition schedule is consistently hit-or-miss – the chief curator's post has been vacant for several years. Some wonderful travelling shows have been seen here, such as 1996's Sacred Art of Haitian Vodou, and a projects gallery features site-specific installations, often by local artists. But plenty of mediocre group shows find their way here, too.

Miami Dade Community College Centre Gallery

300 NE Second Avenue, at NE Third Street, Downtown (237 3278). Bus 9, 10, K, T/Metrorail & Metromover Government Center. **Open** *9am-5pm Mon-Fri.* **Admission** *free.*

Of several public galleries maintained by the community college, the Centre Gallery on the Downtown campus is the most visited. Shows are invariably interesting, focusing exclusively on contemporary art by international artists and covering a broad range of timely themes, from performance art to new technology. Exhibition openings attract large crowds of students, local artists and collectors.

Metro-Dade Public Library

Metro-Dade Cultural Center, 101 W Flagler Street, at NW First Avenue, Downtown (375 2665). Bus 3, 16, 95, C, S/Metrorail & Metromover Government Center. **Open** *9am-6pm Mon-Wed, Fri, Sat; 9am-9pm Thur; 1-5pm Sun.* **Admission** *free.*

The main branch of the public library features evocative public art by California conceptual artist Edward Ruscha. The commanding first-floor cupola, for example, is painted with evocative clouds and a quote from *Hamlet*: 'Words Without Thoughts Never to Heaven Go'. Changing photography and painting exhibitions installed in the first-floor auditorium provocatively explore Miami architecture, history, immigration and other community-related themes. The Louis C Wolfson Media Center is a film and TV archive that holds regular (usually free) screenings and seminars.

Museum of Contemporary Art (MOCA)

770 NE 125th Street, between NE Seventh Court & Eighth Avenue, North Miami (893 6211). Bus 10, 16, G. **Open** *10am-5pm Tue-Sat; noon-5pm Sun.* **Admission** *$4 adults; $2 students; free under-12s.* **Credit** *MC, V.*

The mission of Miami's newest museum is to stay on the art world's cutting edge. Inaugurated in 1996, MOCA showcases the latest contemporary trends, taking a broader view of art than other local institutions with intallations and multimedia shows that have emphasised video and manipulated photography. Group shows take place in the museum's warehouse-like main gallery and adventurous installations, often by up-and-coming Miami artists, in a smaller, separate space. The museum's curator/director, Bonnie Clearwater, has a taste for the conceptual, but work in traditional media, such as Mexican modernist paintings, have also featured. Artists' films are screened in the courtyard.

Rubell Family Collections

95 NW 29th Street, between N Miami Avenue & NW First Avenue, near Design District (573 6090). Bus 6. **Open** *1-4pm Fri-Sun or by appointment.* **Admission** *free.*

The biggest and boldest contemporary art collection on public display in Miami belongs to Mera and Don Rubell, private collectors from New York, who have housed their holdings in a split-level warehouse space near Downtown. Important works by just about every artist who's graced the cover of a US art magazine in the past 15 years are included, from 1980s names like Jeff Koons, Cindy Sherman, Keith Haring and Jean-Michel Basquiat to current art-world darlings such as Janine Antoni and Paul McCarthy. Exhibitions change periodically, and the public also has access to the collection's extensive library of art books and journals.

Sanford L Ziff Jewish Museum

301 Washington Avenue, at Third Street, South Beach (672 5044). Bus C, H, W. **Open** *10am-5pm Tue-Sun.* **Admission** *$5 adults; $4 children, students, senior*

citizens (over-55s); $10 family ticket; free under-6s; free Sat. **Credit** *(shop only, $30 minimum) AmEx, MC, V.*

With financial support from Florida's large Jewish community, this converted synagogue opened as a museum in 1995. A fascinating permanent display documenting the history of Jewish life in Florida includes photos of the gentile-only hotels that were common in Miami Beach in the 1920s and 1930s. Silver goblets, elaborate menorahs and other religious artefacts donated by local families are also on view. Temporary exhibitions focus on religious art and Judaica.

Vizcaya Museum & Gardens

3251 S Miami Ave, at 32nd Road, Coconut Grove (250 9133). Bus 48/Metrorail Vizcaya. **Open** *house 9.30am-5pm; gardens 9.30am-5.30pm daily.* **Admission** *$10 adults; $5 6-12s; free under-6s.* **Credit** *AmEx, MC, V.*

There's something surreal about this expansive Italian Renaissance-style villa standing incongruously within a US city that's only 100 years old. Formerly the winter home of Chicago industrialist James Deering, the Vizcaya is a first-rate copy of European design. The high ceilings and open courtyard were designed to allow the sea breezes to function as natural air-conditioning, though now climate damage has made it necessary for the courtyard to be glassed over. Tours are given of the 34 rooms packed with period furniture and art, but most notable are the grounds: 10 acres of gorgeous gardens and fountains on the shore of Biscayne Bay.

Science & nature

Fairchild Tropical Garden

10901 Old Cutler Road, at SW 101st Street, Coral Gables (667 1651). Bus 65. **Open** *9.30am-4.30pm daily.* **Admission** *$8 adults; free under-13s.* **Credit** *AmEx, Disc, MC, V.*

Resembling a rainforest in the middle of the city, Fairchild is the largest (83 acres) tropical botanical garden in the continental US. You'll find every conceivable variety of palm tree, tropical flowers and fruit trees, lily pools, orchids, waterfalls and 11 ponds. The garden was founded by plant explorer David Fairchild, and is still used for botanical research. Wander the landscape at will or take a free guided walk or tram tour led by staff members. Special events include flower shows, kids' days and cooking demonstrations; the spring mango festivals draw big crowds. Check out the gift shop for offbeat gardening accessories, plant books and botanical art.

The Gallery of Transportation

165 Aragon Avenue, at Ponce de Leon Boulevard, Coral Gables (529 8599). Bus 40, 72, J. **Open** *noon-5pm Mon-Fri.* **Admission** *free.*

Museum-grade scale models of planes, trains and automobiles (and boats), plus transport-related art by local artists.

Miami Museum of Science & Space Transit Planetarium

3280 S Miami Avenue, at SW 32nd Road, Coconut Grove (854 4247). Bus 48/Metrorail Vizcaya. **Open** *Museum 10am-6pm daily. Laser shows 8.30pm, 9.30pm, 10.45pm, midnight, Fri, Sat.* **Admission** *Museum $9 adults; $7 students, senior citizens; $5.50 3-12s; free under-3s; half-price after 4.30pm Mon-Fri. Laser shows $6 adults; $3 senior citizens, 3-12s. Observatory free.* **Credit** *(shop only) AmEx, MC, V.*

Miami's science museum is decidedly low-tech, but it offers the kind of exhibits on natural wonders that thrill kids. Adults will have fun, too, viewing campy scientific displays that include a skeleton riding a bicycle while a recorded voice sings 'The leg bone connected to the foot bone'. Temporary exhibits have featured mechanical dinosaurs, pirate ship booty and the Internet. Native birds and animals found injured in the wild are nursed back to health in a small zoo in the back of the museum. Nostalgic baby-boomers and freaky high schoolers flock to the trippy laser light shows – Laser Beatles, Laser Pink Floyd, Laser Led Zeppelin – that are a Planetarium staple.

Galleries

Galleries can be found clustered together in several parts of the city, generally reflecting the character of the neighbourhood where they're found. **Coral Gables**, which has a large number of Cuban-American residents, is sometimes referred to as the 'Latin American art capital' for the galleries that line its main thoroughfare, Ponce de Leon Boulevard, and the intersecting streets. An evening gallery walk is held on the first Friday of each month. Free vans shuttle people from gallery to gallery, and the event has a upmarket cocktail party air that's far from bohemian: business suits and ties outnumber black jeans.

Things are more casual over on **Lincoln Road Mall** in South Beach, where a bathing suit and rollerblades is seen as an acceptable outfit. Gallery nights happen here on the second Saturday of the month. Unfortunately, rents have increased as the area has become trendy, and there aren't many galleries left. In depressing contrast to just two years ago, when there were some really innovative spaces, this gentrified pedestrian mall has been taken over by pricey restaurants and designer houseware stores. The main artistic attraction on the mall now is artcenter south florida, a worthy non-profit organisation that owns several formerly commercial buildings converted into low-rent artists' studios and two alternative galleries.

High rents on South Beach and in other parts of the city have led to the creation of a new gallery district in several warehouses on the fringes of Coral Gables off **Bird Road**, where the most experimental art in Miami can now be found. The **Design District** holds occasional gallery walks; check newspaper listings for details. Admission is free to all these galleries.

South Beach

Alliance Gallery
927 Lincoln Road, between Jefferson & Michigan Avenues (531 8504). Bus A, F/M, K, L, S. **Open** 7.30pm-midnight Mon-Fri; 3.30pm-2am Sat; 11.30am-10pm Sun. **No credit cards**.
Works by young area artists are exhibited in the lobby of the Alliance Cinema, an art movie house and centre for underground culture. Shows have included William Keddell's 3-D landscapes and Damian Rojo's quasi-religious wall constructions recalling Mexican ex-votos (popular religious artworks).

Barbara Gillman Gallery
939 Lincoln Road, between Jefferson & Michigan Avenues (534 7872). Bus A, F/M, K, L, S. **Open** noon-6pm Tue-Fri; noon-7pm Sat; by appointment Sun. **Credit** AmEx, DC, Disc, MC, V.

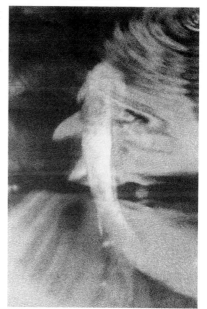

Work by Michelle Sas at **Pallas** *(p170).*

Longstanding Miami art dealer Gillman has a changing display of work in various media. Look for Herman Leonard's black-and-white photo portraits of American jazz greats and Dina Knapp's kitschy vinyl collages of tropical scenes incorporating old postcards and other Florida memorabilia.

Books & Books
933 Lincoln Road, between Jefferson & Michigan Avenues (532 3222). Bus A, F/M, K, L, S. **Open** 10am-11pm Mon-Thur, Sun; 10am-midnight Fri, Sat. **No credit cards**.
This artsy bookshop and coffee hangout regularly exhibits formidable works by photojournalists and local artists. **Branch**: 296 Aragon Avenue, at Salzedo Street, Coral Gables (442 4408).

Continuum Gallery
927 Lincoln Road, between Jefferson & Michigan Avenues (538 3455). Bus A, F/M, K, L, S. **Open** noon-4pm Tue-Fri. **No credit cards**.
Tucked into a corner of the Sterling Building, next to Books & Books, Continuum offers diverse group and solo shows by contemporary artists.

Espanola Way Art Center
405 Espanola Way, between Washington & Drexel Avenues (673 6248). Bus C, H, K, W. **Open** 6-10pm Tue-Fri; noon-8pm Sat; or by appointment. **No credit cards**.
Visitors are welcome to check out the studios in this funky artists' building off Washington Avenue. Group shows and individual artist's installations are hung in the lobby.

artcenter south florida
Art 1035 & Art 1037, 1035 & 1037 Lincoln Road, between Michigan & Lenox Avenues (534 3339). Bus A, F/M, K, L, S. **Open** 5pm-10pm Wed-Fri; 2-10pm Sat. **Credit** Disc, MC, V.

Two alternative exhibition spaces run by the non-profit artcenter south florida (previously known as South Florida Art Center) show a wildly disparate range of offerings with an edge. Painting, photography, video work, sculpture, ceramics and installations have been shown in this loft space, and it has also been used for performances, poetry slams and panel discussions on contemporary art. Shows reflect the cultures of Miami's diverse communities: photos of Haitian street murals; the work of Cuban artists who arrived with the Mariel boatlift; an installation that cunningly examines myths of Black American culture; drawings by schoolchildren; portraits of drag queens. Down the street at 800 Lincoln Road, the smaller Art 800 gallery (674 8278; open 5-10pm Thur-Sat) shows the output of artists who are members of artcenter south florida. Work can also be viewed and bought in the artists' studios in this building, nearby at 850 Lincoln Road and a block up at number 924, where the art centre's offices are located. The office maintains a databank of local artists and staff can provide information on artists' residencies, grants and other cultural programmes in Florida. Artsite at 1655 Lenox Avenue (674 8278; open by appointment only) is also an artcenter south florida facility, showing smaller exhibitions.

Tap Tap

819 Fifth Street, between Jefferson & Meridian Avenues (672 2898). Bus C, K. **Open** 5.30pm-midnight Mon-Thur, Sun; 5.30pm-1am Fri, Sat. **Credit** AmEx, Disc, MC, V.
Some of the best examples of Haitian art in the city can be found in this South Beach restaurant, a hangout for local artists and musicians, where murals depicting voodoo spirits and Caribbean landscapes cover the walls and are painted on the tables. Paintings on canvas, cut-out metal sculptures and colourful beaded and sequinned silk flags are also on show. Some are for sale; ask for Gina Cunningham or Peter Eves, the restaurant's owners and resident Haitian culture experts. *See also chapter* **Restaurants & Cafés**.

Vanity Novelty Garden

(534 6115). **Open** by appointment only. **No credit cards.**
Tamara Hendershot's amalgamation of works by Southern self-taught artists is the best collection of its kind in Miami: this is the place for authentic, eccentric Americana. Hendershot's brightly painted bungalow on South Beach is packed with paintings and objects by 'outsider' artists: the insane, the elderly, the handicapped, uneducated artists who make art 'in spite of themselves'. A former New York photo editor, Hendershot is a picturesque character who wears vintage dresses and lives with 20 cats and a dog. She specialises in Florida artists, including the celebrated black painter Purvis Young, known for his expressionist works depicting horses, musicians and Haitian boat people; Milton Schwartz, an institutionalised genius whose meticulous collages combine religious and pop culture images; and Willie Eaglin, a blind man who hooks abstract rag rugs that exhibit a brilliant sense of colour. Hendershot also has work by artists from throughout the Southern US, such as well-known Alabama painter Thornton Dial. Prices are very reasonable, starting at $50. This is a private home so please ring to make an appointment and get the address.

Coral Gables

All the following galleries are on (or very near) Ponce de Leon Boulevard, between Camilo and Madeira Avenues.

Americas Collection

2440 Ponce de Leon Boulevard, at Andalusia Avenue (446 5578). Bus 40, 42, 72, J. **Open** 10.30am-5pm Mon-Fri; noon-5pm Sat. **Credit** AmEx, MC, V.
This gallery, specialising in Latin American painting, caters to a conservative clientele. Work is of high quality but not particularly adventurous.

Artspace/Virginia Miller Gallery

169 Madeira Avenue, between Douglas Road & Ponce de Leon Boulevard (444 4493). Bus 37, 42, J. **Open** 11am-6pm Mon-Sat. **No credit cards.**
One of Miami's oldest galleries, Virginia Miller offers an eclectic selection of contemporary painters from Latin America and elsewhere.

Elite Fine Art

3140 Ponce de Leon Boulevard, between Santander & San Sebastian Avenues (448 3800). Bus 40, 72, J. **Open** 11am-6pm Mon-Fri. **Credit** AmEx, MC, V.
As the name suggests, Elite is a rather stuffy high-end gallery where preferred guests are served espresso on a silver tray. But get past the posing and this space is worth a look, especially for those interested in Latin American painting. The gallery features work by artists ranging from masters such as Cuban surrealist Wifredo Lam and Colombian Fernando Botero to young artists from different Latin American countries. Paintings are generally on a large scale, and styles tend toward lyrical, 'magic realism' and figurative paintings. Owner Jose Martinez Canas is well-versed in the history of Latin American painting.

Gary Nader Fine Art

3306 Ponce de Leon Boulevard, between Sarto & Camilo Avenues (442 0256). Bus 40, 72, J. **Open** 11am-6pm Mon-Fri. **Credit** AmEx, MC, V.
Every January, Nader hosts a Latin American art auction in his gallery. The rest of the year he shows mainly work by Latin American masters.

Margulies Taplin Gallery

3310 Ponce de Leon Boulevard, between Sarto & Camilo Avenues (447 1199). Bus 40, 72, J. **Open** 10am-5pm Tue-Fri; 11am-3pm Sat; or by appointment. **No credit cards.**
Near the Nader showroom, this handsome gallery usually features works by contemporary artists from Florida and elsewhere, with an emphasis on abstract and conceptual multimedia works.

Quintana Gallery

3200 Ponce de Leon Boulevard, between San Sebastian & Romano Avenues (444 6331). Bus 40, 72, J. **Open** 10am-6pm Mon-Fri; by appointment Sat. **No credit cards.**
The work of the hottest artists in Latin America – those typically featured in German art show Documenta and at the international biennies – can be found here. Colombian art dealer Fernando Quintana opened this elegant space on Ponce de Leon in 1996 and his shows have been of consistent interest: a museum-quality retrospective of Jean-Michel Basquiat's work was outstanding. Among those represented by the gallery are Mexican sculptor and painter Miguel Angel Rios and Haitian artist Edouard Duval-Carrie.

Design District

This area is on the northern edge of Downtown Miami, east of the North-South Expressway (1-95). It is mainly taken up with design showrooms interspersed with a few galleries.

Bakehouse Art Complex

561 NW 32nd Street, between NW Fifth & Sixth Avenues (576 2828). Bus 6, 77, J. **Open** 10am-4pm Tue-Fri. **Credit** MC, V.
Artists' studios housed in an old bakery are open to the public. Group shows are mounted in the communal gallery of this non-profit centre, whose eclectic residents include painters, sculptors, a jeweller and a lighting designer.

The Wolfsonian: an object lesson

The heir to a family fortune made from movie theatres, Mitchell Wolfson Jr (now in his fifties) has spent his life travelling the world and collecting twentieth-century artefacts. While many would have dismissed articles such as World's Fair souvenirs, obsolete radios and old postcards as junk, Wolfson (known to all as Micky), realised their immense historical and aesthetic value. The hundreds of thousands of items now housed in the Wolfsonian museum illustrate how political and societal change is promoted and perceived through everyday objects, patriotic posters and memorabilia, typography and book design, architecture and fine art.

The Wolfsonian opened in 1996 in a magnificent art deco building in South Beach that was formerly a storage warehouse. The museum displays changing exhibitions from the collection, devoted to what Wolfson refers to as 'the arts of reform and persuasion', dating from the dawn of the modern machine age at the turn of the century to the end of World War II. The collection includes streamlined clothes irons, water pitchers and other household items that embody the birth of transatlantic travel and furniture with the stepped angles of skyscrapers as well as work by major twentieth-century designers. The nascent excitement of space-age technology is present in a vacuum cleaner with flashing 'headlights' and a glowing, electric blue glass radio. Wolfson amassed a good deal of material from the world wars, particularly Nazi propaganda and fascist art. These include a Braille copy of *Mein Kampf*, a Hitler pin-cushion, a metal grating with a swastika motif, a bust of Mussolini's head with an exquisite streamlined design and Italian Futurist paintings.

Exhibitions at the Wolfsonian are expertly curated to maximise the effect of the stories that objects such as these can tell, individually and collectively, and it hosts regular evening lectures. A visit to this unique museum is a must for anyone interested in design or history, but it is by no means a special-interest institution. There are so many nuances to the displays, so many takes to these objects, that even children who cannot grasp the historical context will be delighted by the visual aspects (there are also special exhibits for children with small furniture and low-hung paintings).

No expense was spared in the renovation of the museum's immensely elegant building; so much was spent, in fact, that the Wolfsonian began having financial problems shortly after it opened. Management of the museum is expected to be taken over by Florida International University, under an agreement to make it a public institution.

The Wolfsonian
1001 Washington Avenue, at 10th Street, South Beach (531 1001). Bus C, H, K, W. **Open** 11am-6pm Tue, Wed, Fri, Sat; 11am-9pm Thur; noon-5pm Sun. **Admission** $5 adults; $3.50 students, senior citizens; free under-6s; free or by donation 6-9pm Thur. **Credit** AmEx, MC, V.

Lucio Rodrigues Gallery

4100 NE Second Avenue, at NE 41st Street (576 3666).
Bus 9, 10. **Open** 11am-5.30pm Tue-Fri; 11am-4pm Sat.
Credit AmEx, MC, V.

Brazilian art is the focus of this gallery, and group shows are the norm. Symposia on subjects relating to Brazilian culture are sometimes held here.

Pallas Photographic Gallery

50 NE 40th Street, between N Miami Avenue & NE First Avenue (573 7020). Bus 9, 10. **Open** 10am-6pm Mon-Fri; 1-4pm Sat. **Credit** AmEx, Disc, MC, V.

A high-quality photographic lab and gallery (pro photographers note: considering the amount of photo-shoots that are done here, good labs are few and far between), Pallas has monthly shows and stocks black-and-white prints of work by Miami-based photographers. These include homoerotic male nudes by Andrew Melick, documentary shots of rural Tennessee by Paul Morris and Robert Torske's portraits of Quichua Indians in Ecuador. Pallas will also take special orders, and can obtain work as requested on themes such as Florida landscapes, urban scenes or Americana, or by a specific photographer.

Bird Road Warehouse District

The emergent Bird Road Warehouse District is located between Bird Road and Shipping Avenue, on the eastern edge of Coral Gables where it meets Coconut Grove. The nearest Metrorail station is Douglas Road, an easy walk away, or you can catch bus 37, 40 or 42. All three of the galleries listed below opened in 1997.

Ambrosino Gallery

3095 SW 39th Avenue (445 2211). **Open** 11am-5pm Mon-Fri; by appointment Sat. **Credit** AmEx, MC, V.

Young Venezuelan art dealer Genaro Ambrosino's 4,000sq ft raw concrete warehouse is the most spectacular gallery space in Miami. Ambrosino shows decidedly non-commercial work by nationally known artists such as Donald Lipski and young local artists, including Glexis Novoa, Ana Albertina Delgado, filmmaker Tag Purvis and environmental installation artist Conrad Hamather. Mainly large-scale works are shown. Frequent evening events are held in the space, such as collaborative performances by video artist Charles Recher and experimental musicians Alfredo Triff and Gustavo Matamoros, all based in Miami. Openings also feature screenings and music.

Fredric Snitzer Gallery

3078 SW 38th Court (448 8976). **Open** 10am-5pm Tue-Sat. **Credit** AmEx, MC, V.

Snitzer became internationally known in the early 1990s for showing the politically charged work of young artists coming to Miami from Cuba. Although the gallery still represents some Cuban artists, notably Jose Bedia, Ruben Torres Llorca and Consuelo Castaneda, Snitzer has lately moved towards a more pluralistic exhibition programme. Many prominent Miami-based artists show here, including sculptor Carol Brown and the up-and-coming British artist Mark Handforth, who in 1996 installed a huge satellite dish that took up the whole gallery. Originally from Philadelphia, the charismatic Snitzer has been dealing art in Miami for two decades, and is a great source of information on local artists and art trends.

Galerie Douyon

3080 SW 38th Court (445 6624). **Open** 11am-5pm Tue-Sat. **Credit** AmEx, MC, V.

Next door to Snitzer, Douyon tends to feature innovative work by contemporary artists from Haiti and South America.

Gimme five:

An increasing number of artists are choosing Miami as a place to live and work. Some are drawn by the low studio rents and relaxed atmosphere virtually devoid of the pressures of competition prevalent in the major international art centres. Others are attracted to South Florida's natural assets or its Caribbean flair. Miami is removed, but not isolated: cosmopolitan New York is only a short plane ride away. And for Latin American artists, Miami is a place where they can enjoy the opportunities of the US while remaining connected to their own culture. Artists here are as diverse as the rest of the population and thus there is no defined local 'school' or style. As proven by these five outstanding artists, everyone heeds their own muse in Miami.

Jose Bedia

A practitioner of the Afro-Cuban religion Palo Monte, Bedia combines spiritual symbology with a contemporary sense of space and materials in work that is at once primitive and sophisticated. Immigration and

self-discovery are themes in paintings that employ images of animals and Bedia's own mythological beings. He is best known for his large, gritty installations incorporating painting and found objects. Since leaving Cuba in 1991, Bedia has exhibited at New York's Museum of Modern Art and has had a one-man travelling show organised by the Philadelphia Museum of Art. He is represented in Miami by the Fredric Snitzer Gallery.

Robert Chambers

A Miami native, Chambers' work (opposite, top) recalls Pop happenings and the performances of 1970s action artists. His installations convey a sense of movement: billowing lengths of coloured silk hang from the gallery ceiling; a fleet of small boats crowd the floor. Chambers has a fascination for machines, and he's rather like a mischievous mad scientist, filling rooms with soap bubbles or firing a cannon from the roof of a museum. He has taught at New York University and is now a faculty member of the University of Miami's art department. Chambers has shown in Miami at the Museum of Contemporary Art and Ambrosino Gallery.

Miami artists to look out for

Edouard Duval-Carrie

Duval-Carrié's colourful works carry on the Haitian tradition of art inspired by the voodoo religion and the island's social and political travails. His post-modern interpretations of typical images from Haitian popular culture can be celebratory or cynical. Duval-Carrié, who has been living in Miami since the early 1990s, maintains close ties to Haiti and has represented the country in international exhibitions such as the Sao Paulo and Havana bienniales and at the Atlanta Olympic Games. His best-known paintings are expressive caricatures of the Duvalier family that illustrate the corrupt practices of their former political regime. More recently, his work has taken the form of Veves, or depictions of voodoo deities, whose images Duval-Carrié has

cast in bronze, recalling statues of classical Greek gods. The Quintana Gallery in Coral Gables shows his work.

Teresita Fernández

A Cuban-American who grew up in Miami, Fernández is known for her minimal, provocative installations. A meticulous artist, her work often deals with proportion and space, creating subtle optical illusions: she has turned a gallery into a sort of communal shower room, displayed two similar tables of different sizes, and painted a large museum room to look like an empty swimming pool. Her spray-painted walls are pictured bottom left. Fernández is not represented by a Miami gallery, but has shown at the Museum of Contemporary Art and other venues.

Tag Purvis

Filmmaker Tag Purvis projects his 16mm short films onto gallery walls and the outside of buildings, where they appear like moving paintings. One infamous work, an image of two men kissing, has caused controversy on two occasions when it was projected locally. Other works have included a poetic meditation on the loss of friends to AIDS, and several films dealing with aspects of rural life in the his native Mississippi. Purvis has participated in various international film festivals and is now working on a feature film about growing up as a homosexual in the American South. He is represented by the Ambrosino Gallery and works in a studio at the artcenter south florida.

Media

How to turn on, tune in and pick up the dope.

Newspapers

The best-read and most reliable newspaper (not just in Miami but in the whole of southern Florida) is the *Miami Herald*. Covering both international and national news, both paper and its reporters became internationally renowned during the days when Miami was the murder capital of the USA and the *Herald* set itself the task of tracking down and naming those responsible. One former reporter, Edna Buchanan, won a Pulitzer prize for documenting more than 5,000 violent deaths and has since become a best-selling crime novelist. Other columnists to look for include Pulitzer prize winner Liz Balmaseda and funny-man Dave Barry. Carl Hiaasen is the locals' favourite for his sensible, no-nonsense take on Miami's madness. However, the *Herald* is the only major paper in town, and media watchers note that it often sings a tune of civic boosterism that's uncomfortably rosy. Of late the paper has not been as zealous in going after fishy business; notably at City Hall, where a major budget scandal found the city desk napping.

Other national coverage comes from the *New York Times*, which produces a Florida edition, as does the *Wall Street Journal*. All titles are available from shops and vending machines all over the city. On a more provincial level, the *Orlando Sentinel*, the *Fort Lauderdale Sun Sentinel* and the *Palm Beach Post* cover the major local news stories in the Tri-County area and beyond. They, too, are widely available.

On Sunday, the *Miami Herald* has almost too many sections to count, let alone read. They include a nifty classified section and a comprehensive TV guide for the week ahead. The Friday edition has a Weekend section with movie and theatre reviews, restaurant listings and details of pretty much everything going on in Miami.

The same service, in more alternative fashion, is provided by *New Times*, free from clubs, bars and drop bins all over town. *New Times* often picks up the ball the *Herald* drops when it comes to investigative journalism. At times, however, it picks up the ball and runs on and on with it for more pages of minutiae than necessary. *New Times* reviewers are more feisty than their *Herald* peers and more apt to zero in on what's new and happening.

Business readers are catered for by *Miami Today*, another weekly tabloid ($1 at newsstands; free at local banks, offices, etc) and the *Daily Business Review*, while legal eagles can turn to the *Miami Review*.

Minorities are also well catered for. The *Miami Times* and *Caribbean Today* cover the black community, while the *Christian Community Newspaper* and *The Gospel Truth* give readable and unbiased coverage of world and local events. The *Jewish Journal* gives the lowdown on one of the city's largest ethnic communities. There are also smaller community newspapers, such as *Community News* and the *Pinecrest Tribune*, available all over. Full of pictures of the kind of people (and pets) that question the whole notion that Miami is a place where anyone has any fun at all, they give you a sometimes uncomfortably close-up view of what life here is really like.

Magazines

Though not strictly magazines, the publications that cover the Miami Beach area devote so much space to pictures of beautiful people doing this and that that they hardly count as newspapers. Among the titles you will come across are *South Florida*, *South Beach*, *Travel Host* and the self-regarding glossy *Ocean Drive*, all full of ideas on where to go, what to do and who to be seen with, and all available from hotel lobbies and bins. There is also *Wire*, devoted to the party scene, with a weekly clubbing diary and a calendar section to help you decide which parties are worth crashing. Check out publisher and editor Andrew Delaplaine's 'Barbs' column for an opinionated and amusing tongue-lashing of local Miami Beach officials.

The best place to buy international titles is **News Café** (*see chapter* **Restaurants**), conveniently also one of South Beach's most crucial haunts.

*Print junkies get their fix at **News Café**.*

TV news crews are a frequent sight in never-uneventful Miami.

Latin American

The largest Spanish-language daily in the United States is Miami's *El Nuevo Herald*, published by the *Miami Herald* and free with it but compiled by a separate staff. There is some carry-over of stories from the English edition, but *El Nuevo* has its own columnists, reporters, reviewers and editorial board. Often the paper will have more complete international news than its English-language cousin. Neither paper seems to be able to to say 'boo' about Cuba without upsetting somebody in town and causing a protest outside the *Herald* building. However, that more political niche is more than adequately filled by other Spanish-language papers such as *Libre* and *El Diario Americas*. The free weekly *Exito*, a lifestyle title in the loose mould of *New Times*, can be picked up all over town. Be warned that if you buy your *Herald* way outside a Spanish-speaking neighbourhood, *El Nuevo* may not be included.

Radio

Music can generally be found anywhere on the FM band, while, as is the case with the rest of the world, the poorer sound quality of AM channels tends to restrict them to a mainly talk-based product. In addition to a great deal of Spanish and Creole language programming, you can also find shock jocks by the dozen. Spanish-language talk radio here is a world of its own, where political rivals are still fighting long-ago Latin American revolutions and

will go as far as to challenge each other to on-air duels. The initials for each station may seem intriguing, but rarely mean anything worth knowing.

FM

In Miami they like round numbers, so frequencies are often rounded up when people talk about a particular station.

88.9 WDNA Community public radio.
89.7 WMCU Christian programming and music.
90.5 WVUM The University of Miami's station; lots of grungey, student-style rock and alternative music.
91.3 WLRN An affiliate of the highly regarded National Public Radio system. Good classical and jazz at times. The best station to tune to to find out if a hurricane is on its way.
92.3 WCMQ (aka FM 92) Spanish music.
93.1 WTMI Classical and easy listening.
93.9 WLVE Also known as Love 94, this channel plays non-stop jazz.
94.9 WZTA Advertises itself as the home of 'real rock' and as such is everything you would expect from an AOR music station. Tunes to cruise down the freeway by.
95.7 WXDJ (aka EL Zol 95) Salsa.
96.5 WPOW (aka Power 96) The latest dance sounds.
97.3 WFLC (aka Coast 97.3) Adult contemporary rock.
99.1 WEDR (aka 99 Jamz) Urban contemporary and R&B to play air guitar along to.
99.9 WKIS (aka Kiss FM) Don't be fooled by the name, this is the home of good ol' country music.
100.7 WHYI (aka Y-100) Contemporary pop stuff.
101.5 WLYF (aka 101.5 Lite FM) Easy listening.
102.7 WMXJ (aka Magic 102.7) Plays the oldies, but not too oldies, from the Supremes to the Beatles.
103.5 WPLL (aka Planet Radio) A semi-nostalgic trip down to the 1980s and early 1990s.
105.1 WHQT (aka Hot 105) A mix of R&B with a sprinkling of adult contemporary and soul. Sunday morning gospel show.

105.9 WBGG (aka Big 106) Classic rock.
106.7 WRMA (aka Romance) Contemporary Spanish and Latin American sounds.
107.5 WAMR (aka Amor) Spanish contemporary music with 'larger than life' DJs.

AM

560 WQAM Talk with a strong emphasis on sport.
610 WIOD News, entertainment, talk and sports.
710 WAQI Radio Mambi: Spanish talk – loud, passionate and controversial. If you ever wanted to know just how much Fidel Castro is hated in Miami, listen in.
790 WAXY Talk.
830 WACC The latest news in Spanish, including sports results and coverage. Also known as Radio Acción.
940 WINZ News and sport.
980 WWNN Describes itself as a 'self-help' radio station.
1080 WVCG A virtually non-stop diet of religious talk.
1140 WQBA Spanish talk shows with the latest news.
1170 WAVS Caribbean news and talk.
1210 WCMQ Spanish news/talk.
1260 WSUA Spanish/Creole news and talk.
1360 WKAT 'International variety'.
1400 WFTL All talk with a heavy emphasis on entertainment. Good for reviews and tips on where to go.
1450 WOCN Spanish, Brazilian and Creole news and talk.
1490 WMBM Miami's only gospel radio station.
1560 WRHC Spanish news/talk.
1580 WSRF A wide mix of ethnic news, reviews and talk.

Television

What with Miami being the gateway to Latin America, it comes as no surprise to find that it's the base for MTV's Spanish-language programming – which, strangely, is not carried on local cable. Other Latin product is made here, too, including the variety-fest *Sàbado Gigante*, shown in 18 Latin American countries. Attending a taping will be one of the wildest things you could do in Miami, even if – or perhaps because – you don't speak the language. For details, call 471 8262 (and be prepared for a Spanish answerphone message).

Finding channels may not be as simple as you may think. With almost a dozen cable companies in the area, each structuring their output differently, you will find different stations on different channel numbers in adjacent houses. Some hotels issue station guides; otherwise, flick through the channels until you come across the **Preview Channel**, which has a split-screen format and gives you listings for the next two hours on each channel. Using this as your guide, you should be able to work out what is what.

CNN is excellent for overall news, as is its sister network, **Headline News**. Upstart 24-hour news network **MSNBC** is notable for replacing the same old talking heads with younger, more racially mixed commentators. Some local news reports, particularly on **Channel 7** (Fox), tend to be sensational, as if dedicated to proving that reality is more bizarre and disturbing than even the writers of *Miami Vice* could conceive of. **ESPN** has the best sports coverage and you should also be able

to find **Comedy Central, Nickelodeon, The Weather Channel** and **HBO**. There are also the Spanish language stations **Telemundo** and **Univision**, which seem to show little apart from hugely popular soaps, though the new Spanish-language news network **CBS-Telenoticias** has some meat to it. The local public access cable station, **Channel 3**, while not as extreme as New York's, is still worth a look to see what the more eccentric members of the community get up to.

Websites

There is a huge variety (particularly in terms of quality) in Miami's Internet offerings. At one end, there are functional community networks, at the other slick websites put out by conference organisers. Start at **http://www.miami.thelinks.com** for a multiplicity of Miami links including museums, sports, hotels, businesses and something like 50 sites that claim to be city guides.

http://www.miamiandbeaches.com
The Greater Miami & The Beaches Convention & Visitors Bureau site includes comprehensive details of Miami's attractions and facilities. You can also reserve accommodation.

http://www.southbeach.org
Good for information on what's happening in the most happening part of Miami. Useful stuff plus the purely vibey: hair tips from Don King, anyone?

http://metronetwork.com/metroguide/mia/
One of the better city guides, with all-round info, including good kids' stuff and a today's events section. Links in to the equivalent night guide site.

http://www.downtownmiami.com
A nostalgic look at the Miami area with a chat area, an events finder (including movie guide) and a local businesses search.

www.tourist.com/miami/events
Lists virtually every forthcoming event taking place in the Miami area from harvest festivals to Billfish tournaments (whatever *they* are).

http://www.herald.com
A virtual rendition of the *Miami Herald* that's clear and easy to use. The Herald's travel site is **www.goflorida.com**.

http://ci.miami.fl.us
The official City of Miami guide and as such the only one to provide you with a welcome message from the mayor. As well as information on history, businesses and attractions, the site also features live links with surveillance cameras in the area – so you can check the weather before you leave.

http://ci.miami-beach.fl.us
Miami Beach's official site, with lots of good info including a virtual tour of the area.

http://www.greatermiami.com
Stats, facts and contacts from the Greater Miami Chamber of Commerce.

http://www.state.fl.us
The state of Florida's info site, with vast amounts of user-friendly data on everything from climate to contacts.

Music

Miami compensates for its lack of classical clout with a buzzing Latin American beat and a downhome local rock scene.

Classical

For years, area movers and shakers have been plotting and scheming to build a humungous performing arts centre in Downtown Miami, as a spectacularly upscale home for orchestras, ballet companies and so on. Meanwhile, in our lifetimes, the **Florida Philharmonic** under conductor James Judd, the **New World Symphony** under Michael Tilson Thomas, the **Miami Chamber Symphony**, the **Florida Grand Opera** and a plethora of touring companies can be found at numerous venues in Dade County and in the next two counties north, Broward and Palm Beach.

Judy Drucker and her Concert Association of Florida bring in major acts – such as the National Symphony Orchestra, the National Orchestra of France, the Saint Paul Chamber Orchestra with Bobby McFerrin and the American Ballet Theatre – during the year. Most of these shows take place at the Dade County Auditorium and the events are highly regarded. The ubiquitous New World Symphony (which might be found playing for free at South Pointe Park one week and teeming with guests such as Korean violin babe Chee-Yun or hunky stringfellow Pinchas Zukerman the next) is always worth a listen.

Orchestras

The New World Symphony Orchestra

Lincoln Theater, 555 Lincoln Road, at Pennsylvania Avenue, South Beach (673 3331). Bus C, G, K, L, S. **Open** box office 9am-5pm Mon-Fri; one hour before show. **Tickets** $19-$50. **Credit** AmEx, DC, Disc, MC, V.

Hailed for its trademark balance of technical brilliance and youthful zeal, this orchestral academy offers gifted graduates of the US's most prestigious music schools an intensive learning and performing experience at a career-entry level under the artistic direction of conductor Michael Tilson Thomas. Since its 1988 debut, the New World Symphony has performed in venues worldwide, from Carnegie Hall to Wolf Trap to Paris's L'Opéra Bastille and has been broadcast on the BBC, LWT and PBS's 'Great Performances' series. From its headquarters in South Beach's grand old Lincoln Theater, the NWS presents a complete season of concerts from October to May. Performances include full orchestra, chamber music pops and family concerts. Free concerts and musicians' forums take place on Mondays.

Cosy and comfortable for more intimate shows, the Lincoln is a 785-seater converted cinema. It epitomises art deco streamline moderne, complete with rounded corners and elaborate stylised floral bas-relief panels.

Major venues

Dade County Auditorium

2901 W Flagler Street, at SW 29th Avenue, near Little Havana (545 3395). Bus 11, 27. **Open** box office 10am-5pm Mon-Fri; until showtime on performance days. **Tickets** vary. **Credit** (until 5pm) MC, V.

Built in 1951, the DCA made history early on by breaking the colour barrier (singer Marianne Anderson performed here) and as the first US venue to stage an upstart named Luciano Pavarotti (in 1954). Excellent acoustics, easy accessibility from anywhere in Dade, and free on-site parking (for most events) are reasons that the Florida Grand Opera calls this home. The Florida Philharmonic regularly appears here, too. Shame about the aesthetics: in terms of design and décor it has little more to offer than a high school auditorium.

Gusman Center for the Performing Arts

174 E Flagler Street, between NE First & Second Avenues, Downtown (372 0925). Bus 3, 16, 95, C, S/ Metromover Miami Avenue. **Open** box office noon-3pm, 5-6pm, daily; two hours before performance. **Tickets** prices vary. **Credit** MC, V.

The most beautiful – and underused – of all South Florida venues, the Gusman opened in 1926 as a movie theatre in the heart of Downtown Miami. Today, it hosts a smattering of concerts throughout the year and for 10 days in February returns to its celluloid roots as the venue for the Miami Film Festival. With excellent sightlines and acoustics and a ceiling that looks like a summer night sky, the Gusman is a true jewel that dances with financial death on a regular basis (one recent benefactor was local boy Sylvester Stallone).

Jackie Gleason Theater

1700 Washington Avenue, at 17th Street, South Beach (673 7300). Bus A, F/M, G, K. **Open** box office 10am-5.30pm Mon-Fri; noon-showtime Sat, Sun; until showtime on performance days. **Tickets** prices vary. **Credit** AmEx, MC, V.

Next to the Miami Beach Convention Center, this 2,700 seater is home to Broadway shows, the Miami City Ballet (considered one of the top five in the nation) and a variety of entertainment including modern and classical dance, pop concerts, the Florida Philharmonic Pops Series and international acts from the Russian Ballet to Jewish and Colombian folkloric companies. It opened in 1951 as the Miami Beach Auditorium. During the 1960s, Jackie Gleason taped his variety television series here, and in 1987, upon the Great One's death, it took his name.

Other venues

AT&T Amphitheatres

Bayfront Park, 301 Biscayne Boulevard, at NE Third Street, Downtown (358 7550). Bus 3, 16, 48, 95, C/ Metromover College/Bayside.
South Pointe Park, 1 Washington Avenue, at Harley Street, South Beach (673 7224). Bus H, W.
Both **Open** tickets available at door on day of show. **Tickets** prices vary. **No credit cards.**
Both are pleasant sites for outdoor concerts of varying types.

Coral Gables Congregational Church

3010 DeSoto Boulevard, between Catalonia & Malaga Avenues, Coral Gables (448 7421) Bus 52, 56, 72. **Open** church office 8.30am-4.30pm Mon-Fri; 4.30pm-showtime on performance days. **Admission** $20. **Credit** AmEx, MC, V.

An old building in a nice neighbourhood, and setting for an ungodly amount of important music. The open-minded minders of CGCC bring in a bounty of non-mainstream, often highbrow musical events.

Gusman Hall

University of Miami, 1414 Miller Drive, at San Amaro Drive, Coral Gables (284 6477). Bus 52, 56/Metrorail University. **Open** doors open one hour before performance. **Tickets** prices vary. **No credit cards.**

Not to be confused with the Gusman Center in Downtown, this campus hall hosts the Festival Miami every October, a series of concerts featuring University of Miami faculty and invited guest performers playing jazz, classical and contemporary, plus year-round recitals, student performances and guest concerts.

Temple Beth Am

5959 N Kendall Drive, at SW 59th Avenue, South Miami (667 6667). Bus 57. **Open** temple office 9am-5pm Mon-Thur; 9am-4pm Fri; tickets available on day of show. **Tickets** prices vary. **No credit cards.**

Temple Beth Am offers a concert series of classical music performed primarily by soloists, both local and national. It takes place from October to May on Sunday afternoons.

Latin

From the salsa that blares from car radios and floor shows at Cuban restaurants to Latin rock concerts and tango bars, Miami moves to a Latin beat. Hispanic residents make up more than half of the city's population, and music is the most public expression of their various native cultures. Restaurants and clubs all over Miami offer recorded and live music, catering to any one of the many Hispanic communities, with hard-driving Dominican merengue, lilting Mexican rancheras, pulsating Afro-Cuban rumba and the popular Cuban and Puerto Rican mix of rhythms known everywhere as salsa. The crowd at most of these places is made up of Spanish speakers; non-Hispanics are welcome, but it can be hard for the uninitiated to know where to go to dance or just listen.

Big Latin names from salsa singer Celia Cruz to the Mexican rock group Mana appear frequently at larger venues like the James L Knight Center, the Jackie Gleason Theater and the Bayfront Amphitheater; frequent free concerts celebrating Latin American holidays are also celebrated at Bayfront (*see below* **Rock**). The annual Latin Jazz Festival in February brings in venerable names and up-and-coming acts from all over the country.

Class acts shake their stuff at **Café Nostalgia** *(page 128).*

You got me dancing

It's a myth: Latins aren't born shaking their hips. They have to learn like the rest of us. That fact is made evident by all the Argentines learning tango and the Cubans taking rueda classes nightly in Miami. Dance lessons are currently in vogue here for anyone who's not already a sought-after partner on the floor. Some people go to find a partner, others attend with their mates. The whole thing seems a little corny and stepping out can be embarrassing at first, but in Miami, knowing how to dance to Latin rhythms can seem like a necessity. The results are worth it. Classes everywhere range from absolute beginner to advanced.

The most fun place in town to learn rueda (the fundamental Cuban dance that is the basis of salsa) and other Cuban-rooted moves and arm-twisting salsa variations is at **Club Mystique** (Hilton Hotel, 5101 Blue Lagoon Drive, off NW 57th Avenue; 262 1000). Thursday night (9pm) classes attract a big crowd: this is something of a singles scene. A DJ plays music all night so students can stay after the class is over and practise what they've learned. Classes are free. Some of the best teachers in town are the **Salsa Lovers**. Their well-attended salsa classes ($6 only) for all levels are on Mondays and Wednesdays at the Blue Banquet Hall (9843 SW 40th Street, between SW 98th & 99th Avenues; 220 7115).

Gaucho's Café (2901 SW Eighth Street, at SW 29th Avenue, Little Havana; 649 9494) holds tango lessons ($10) on Tuesdays and Thursdays, 8-11pm. Classes are small and everyone moves at their own place. Teacher Jimena Quiroga can have you doing the basic steps in three lessons.

The Tango Argentino dance party is held on Saturdays at **Arthur Murray** dance school (2916 Ponce de Leon Boulevard, between Palermo & Catalonia Avenues, Coral Gables; 444 6136) and Wednesdays at the **Elks Club** (22 Giralda Avenue, between SW 37th Avenue & Ponce de Leon Boulevard, Coral Gables). Classes, at $10, are from 7.30-10.30pm; after that, the party begins. For more information, call 1-305 446 9444 or 267 6923.

And the Calle Ocho Festival in March (*see chapter* **By Season**) is a humungous, sweaty, street carnival where bands perform on stages placed every few blocks on people-packed SW Eighth Street.

INFORMATION

At any time of year, you'll find the most complete Latin music listings in the Spanish weekly newspaper *Exito* and in the Viernes (Friday) guide published by *El Nuevo Herald*. Check *New Times* for extensive listings in English. Or start by tuning into some Latin music on one of the many Spanish-language radio stations: 98.3 FM features commercially minded salsa and merengue that can be rather manic, but it's not bad for driving down the highway; WAMR (107.5 FM) plays exclusively Latin love songs. The best Latin music on the radio is broadcast from 8-10pm nightly on community radio station WDNA (88.9 FM). Its Latin Fusion programme offers a smorgasbord of music from all over Latin America, past and present, with an emphasis on Cuban music by musicians living in Cuba and in exile. For more information on Latin radio stations, *see chapter* **Media**.

Cabaret

Victor's Café
2340 SW 32nd Avenue, between SW 23rd & 24th Streets, Little Havana (445 1313). Bus 24. **Open** *restaurant* noon-midnight daily; *upstairs cabaret* 9pm-3am Sat. **Admission** $20. **Credit** AmEx, DC, MC, V.
This restaurant offers a taste of 1950s Havana with a revue called Asi es mi Cuba ('This is my Cuba') on Saturdays, modelled after the shows at Cuba's Club Tropicana. Dancers, musicians and showgirls make for an extravaganza: Las Vegas entertainment, Latin-style.

Cuban

Café Nostalgia
2212 SW Eighth Street, at SW 22nd Avenue, Little Havana (541 2631). Bus 8, 22. **Open** 9pm-3am Thur-Sun. **Admission** $10 Fri, Sat. **Credit** AmEx, MC, V.
The kind of smoky hole-in-the-wall that breeds good music, Café Nostalgia is a hangout for recent emigrés from Cuba and attracts an artsy crowd. The house band, Grupo Nostalgia, includes some of the best musicians in the city. The first set starts around 10pm, and the small dancefloor soon gets crowded; things get really hot after midnight when local musicians and visitors from New York or Havana habitually drop in. The jam session continues to the wee hours. Get a lesson in Cuban music history between sets, when rare footage of performances by pre-revolutionary Cuban musicians are projected on a screen over the stage.

Crossway
1850 NW Le Jeune Road, at NW 18th Street, Northwest Dade (871 4350). Bus 7, 42, J. **Open** 4pm-4am Fri; 6pm-4am Sat; 4pm-midnight Sun. **Admission** $8 Fri, Sat; $5 Sun. **Credit** AmEx, DC, Disc, MC, V.
Located in a Howard Johnson hotel near the airport, this club's featured performer is Israel Kantor, a noted Cuban soul singer known for his playful improvisational style and music that's great for dancing. Kantor, a star in Cuba with the dance band Los Van Van before he came to Miami in the 1980s, performs on Saturday nights.

Follia
929 Washington Avenue, between Ninth & 10th Streets, South Beach (674 9299). Bus C, H, K, W. **Open** *restaurant* 6.30-11pm Mon-Thur, Sun; 6.30pm-1am Fri, Sat; *club* 7pm-4am Fri, Sat. **Admission** free. **Credit** AmEx, DC, Disc, MC, V.
On Wednesday nights, singer Luis Bofill from Grupo Nostalgia brings a group of Cuban musicians to South Beach to perform for the cocktail crowd at this Italian restaurant, which has a stage and some sofas in the back of the dining room. This smooth Latin lounge act combines romantic vocals and deft conga playing.

Yuca
501 Lincoln Road, at Drexel Avenue, South Beach (532 9822). Bus C, G, K, L, S. **Open** noon-4pm, 6-11pm Mon-Thur; noon-4pm, 6pm-midnight Fri, Sat; 1-11pm Sun. **Admission** $25 plus two-drink minimum Fri & Sat for Albita show. **Credit** AmEx, DC, Disc, MC, V.
The reigning queen of the Cuban music scene is Albita Rodriguez, who appears at this upscale nouvelle Cuban restaurant on Fridays and Saturdays (11pm), packing the place with trendy Cuban-American locals and informed out-of-towners. A show woman of deserved renown, Albita

arrived in Miami from Havana four years ago. Since then, she has sung at such soirées as Madonna's birthday party and Clinton's inaugural celebration, and has recorded two albums on Emilio Estefan's Sony imprint, Crescent Moon Records. Albita's androgynous look has earned her the nickname 'the Cuban kd lang' (Lang herself drops by when she's in town), but it's the singer and her band's talent that really deserve attention. Covering the basic Cuban musical styles from rhythmic sones to romantic bolero ballads, her voice never falters, and in between numbers she works the crowd with a vengeance. After four years of performing constantly at Yuca and other venues, Albita's show has gotten a bit pat for jaded locals, but first-timers are sure to be impressed. What makes it all come together is the singer's incredible backing band. It's hard to take your eyes off any of the three women musicians – keyboardist Viviana Pintado, slinky-hipped flute player Mercedes Abal, and Julia Serrano, who plays the Cuban tres guitar with jaw-dropping virtuosity. The place is full every night Albita performs; be prepared to part with at least $50 each. You won't get in without a reservation; make it as far in advance as possible.

Flamenco

Casa Panza
1620 SW Eighth Street, between SW 16th & 17th Avenues, Little Havana (643 5343). Bus 8, 17. **Open** 11am-11pm Mon, Wed; 11am-1.30am Tue, Thur-Sun. **Admission** free. **No credit cards.**
The Tuesday and Thursday night fiestas at this small Spanish tavern are legendary. A young professional crowd eats, drinks and dances around the tables until the early hours of the morning while a guitarist plays and sings flamenco on a tiny stage, accompanied by two stomping female dancers in traditional costume. Owner Jesus Lopez runs about urging the customers to let loose – he's liable to have the whole place doing the macarena. Fridays and Saturdays are more sedate, with a great classical guitarist playing romantic, Latin-tinged dinner music.

Miro Café
448 Espanola Way, at Drexel Avenue, South Beach (538 6476). Bus C, H, K, W. **Open** noon-midnight Wed, Thur, Sun; noon-2am Fri, Sat. **Show** 10pm Wed, Fri, Sat. **Admission** free. **Credit** AmEx, DC, MC, V.
Guitarist Paco Fonta and his group get going on Friday and Saturday at this cosy corner restaurant in South Beach with flamenco music and dancing. Attracts a young, largely European crowd.

Latin jazz

Mojazz Café
928 71st Street, at Bay Drive, Miami Beach (865 2636). Bus L. **Open** Wed, Thur, Sun 8.30pm-1am; 8.30pm-2am Fri, Sat. **Show** 9.30pm. **Admission** $6-$10. **Credit** MC, V.
Latin jazz concerts are held periodically in venues around town, but percussionist Luis Miranda's gig on the first Thursday of each month at Mojazz is the one steady date on every aficionado's calendar. An esteemed sideman, Miranda has played with Dizzy Gillespie, Machito, Chico O'Farrill and Charlie Parker. An informal, Miami Beach neighbourhood jazz club, Mojazz is nice place to have a few drinks or a light dinner while you listen to the music.

Tango

Gaucho's Café
2901 SW Eighth Street, at SW 29th Avenue, Little Havana (649 9494). Bus 8, 27. **Open** noon-5pm Mon; noon-11.30pm Tue-Thur; noon-12.30am Fri, Sat. **Show** 10pm. **Admission** free. **Credit** MC, V.

This restaurant in a strip mall across from a McDonald's doesn't look like much, but once inside, it's just like being in Buenos Aires. Live tango music is performed on Fridays and Saturdays by a stellar trio. Ruben Stefano (who used to play with Xavier Cugat's Orchestra) is on keyboards, Oswaldo Barrios plays the accordion-like bandoneon that gives the tango its winsome, nostalgic sound, while the restaurant's owner Lito Quiroga sings in a rocks-and-gravel voice. The group sticks mostly to the classics made famous by tango legend Carlos Gardel. The regulars here are Argentine immigrants, who often start singing along. Some seductive twist and turns are executed on the dancefloor by everyone from young girls to elegant old men with pomaded hair. Dance lessons are given on Tuesdays and Thursdays.

Dance clubs

Centro Espanol

3615 NW S River Drive, at NW 36th Street, Northwest Dade (634 5845). Bus 32, 36, J. **Open** 10am-10pm Mon-Wed, Fri, Sun. **Admission** free. **No credit cards**.
There's nothing high-toned about this place, a gay disco some nights of the week (when it's known as On the Waterfront; *see chapter* **Gay & Lesbian**). Sunday afternoon is the time to dance to recorded salsa and merengue or the occasional live band. Located in a dodgy neighbourhood next to the Miami River, Centro Espanol has a restaurant, a pool hall and an outdoor dance area and bar that looks like something you'd find in the Central American countryside. The clientele is working class, the beers are two bucks and the dancefloor is crowded. There's a lot of local colour and people are friendly, but this is the underbelly of Latin Miami: a working knowledge of Spanish is recommended. Unescorted women proceed with caution.

Club Mystique

Hilton Hotel, 5101 Blue Lagoon Drive, off NW 57th Avenue, Northwest Dade (262 1000). Bus 7. **Open** 5pm-3am Wed; 5pm-4am Thur; 5pm-5am Fri; 8.30pm-5am Sat; 8.30pm-3.30am Sun. **Admission** $10-$20 Fri, Sat. **Credit** AmEx, DC, Disc, MC, V.
Miami's long-standing salsa palace is packed on weekends with serious dancing couples and singles after partners. It's an informal place where regulars create a family atmosphere and the emphasis is on dancing rather than drinking.

Excalibur

117 NW Le Jeune Road, between NW First & Second Streets, Northwest Dade (644 6007). Bus 11, 42, J. Call for more information.
Housed in a former medieval-theme restaurant built like a castle, this recently opened club has become the place to see the best in New York salsa. Larry Harlow, Cheo Feliciano and Oscar D'Leon have been among the featured musicians. Even when it's crowded, the cavernous interior provides plenty of room for dancing. The crowd is a mix of recent Latin American immigrants, young Cuban-Americans and Americans. Don't expect much English to be spoken.

La Covacha

10730 NW 25th Street, at NW 107th Avenue, West Dade (594 3717). No public transport. **Open** 11.30am-8pm Mon-Wed; 11.30am-midnight Thur; 11.30am-4am Fri-Sun. **Admission** $5 after 9pm Fri-Sun. **No credit cards**.
An open-air Cuban-style roadhouse, La Covacha offers great barbecue and dancing. A young crowd of bilingual Miamians frequents the place, owned by a Cuban-American former model. DJ-programmed music varies from salsa and merengue to techno and Spanish house. Latin rock nights on Sunday are very popular, featuring the latest music and videos from Latin America and Spain. Live bands from Argentina or Mexico sometimes perform.

Studio 23

247 23rd Street, between Collins & Park Avenues, South Beach (538 1196). Bus C, G, H, L, S. **Open** 8pm-4am Fri, Sat. **Admission** free. **Credit** AmEx, MC, V.
A high cheese factor is the main draw of this tacky Latin joint on South Beach, where you're likely to see characters who look like they belong in an episode of *Miami Vice*. A DJ plays salsa and merengue hits through the night.

Rock, roots & jazz

Over the years Miami has become known as a sonic garden from which sprouts little else but disco/dance/Latin music, a rep the area still can't shake. One reason for this is that Latin and disco acts tend to live here (Gloria Estefan, Madonna, Jon Secada, the Bee Gees) while almost everything else is, in typical Miami fashion, transient. Big acts such as Aerosmith and REM come to record albums, then travel on. Some bands grow up in Miami, build their chops here, then move away to embrace fame and fortune, among them country superstars the **Mavericks**, who quit town for Nashville.

But media images and outside perceptions have never done this city justice. There's a thriving and idiosyncratic local scene that has spawned acts of national stature – even if they have had to move out to achieve it. You might catch one of these 'gonnabees' gigging around town. Many South Florida acts are moving into the realm of the universally known, and the disparity among them illustrates the expansive aural zeitgeist. In the past year or two: Fort Lauderdale's **Marilyn Manson**, a horrific and fairly shocking knock-off of Alice Cooper/Iggy Pop, escaped from the South Beach clubs to record best-selling major label albums and receive constant MTV play. Soulful eccentric **Nil Lara** has successfully fused Latin rhythms with classic rock in a seamless hybrid that won him a recording contract on Capitol Records and glowing notices from rock critics across the land. **Mary Karlzen**, a fixture on the scene for years with all-blonde girl rockers Vesper Sparrow, struck out on her own with a Mary Chapin-Carpenter-esque country-rock sound that garnered her a deal with Atlantic Records and yielded the critically lauded but commercially unsuccessful album *Yelling at Mary*. The lovely and girlish **Amanda Green**, sort of a Cyndi Lauper meets Liz Phair, has glommed rave reviews on her first tour after playing and recording locally.

The Mavericks, by the way, are an aberration; Miami has never been much of a country-music place and the Mavs played at rock clubs while establishing themselves.

THE LOCAL SCENE

Stalwart local heroes both new and old keep the ragtag local rock scene running. A straight-up rocker with a golden voice, **Diane Ward** is a must-see songstress who long ago deserved

Fight them on the beaches to get to the one and only **Churchill's**.

national recognition and a big-time label deal. **Manchild**, inescapably linked to Hendrix because they're a white-guys rhythm section fronted by a left-handed black guy who can make the guitar talk in tongues, can draw a thousand people to a club show and, excepting a recent hiatus, play just about every night of the week at some venue or another. Super-psychedelic **Al's Not Well** is both a sonic and visual treat. Songstress **Magda Hiller**, always on the verge of being discovered, can play three-hour shows you can't pull yourself away from, mixing sweetness with rawer material and throwing in covers of anyone from Neil Young to Dusty Springfield. And **Iko-Iko**, Miami's senior blues band, has of late adopted a rockin' style rife with bayou voodoo influences to become one of the most stomping bands in the Southeast. Look for them at Tobacco Road, where they were house band for years and still pop in for performances guaranteed to get your mojo working.

Miami is also home to some of the rudest music you'll find. **Harry Pussy, To Live and Shave in LA**, the **Laundry Room Squelchers** and other so-called noise bands drive away customers and damage ear drums around the nation (and even in Europe) from the South Florida homebase. Locally, these dissonant displays usually take place at Churchill's Hideaway. Anything involving Rat Bastard – one of whose bands, **Scraping Teeth**, achieved national fame (infamy?) a couple of years ago when *Spin* magazine declared it the Worst Band in America – is sure to be different.

Miami-style punk has spun off into far-flung musical substyles, from the straight-ahead post-Velvet Underground snarl of the **Eat** and the Pixies-ish intensity of the **Holy Terrors** to the arsenic cocktail camp of **Frosty** and the skewed, hallucinogenic anarchy and barely controlled mayhem of **Kreamy Lectric Santa** and **Los Canadians**.

You'd think that a tropical metropolis like Miami would be teeming with great reggae and world-beat bands and venues; sadly, nothing could be further from the truth. Listless mercenaries butcher half-hearted Bob Marley and Third World covers in the tourist-trap bars along South Beach's Ocean Drive; try Coconut Grove's **Hungry Sailor** (3426 Main Highway, at Grand Avenue; 444 9359) for a change of pace.

That doesn't mean there's no black music: rap and hip-hop have thrived here. While Luther Campbell's **2 Live Crew** didn't invent the concept of mixing raw, blatantly lascivious lyrics with urgent bass-and-drum driven dance music, the *Me So Horny* guys certainly did their share to popularise raunchy rap. No Miami artist has made quite as much noise – literally or figuratively – on the national rap or dance scenes since, but Miami's ascendancy as a club mecca has made it a natural locale for a dance industry shindig known as the **Winter Music Conference**. For one wild week in March, dozens of nationally renowned dance artists descend on South Beach, and visiting national DJs like Todd Terry, Frankie Knuckles and Little Louie Vega guest spin in local clubs.

VENUES

The best clubs are those willing to stage acts of sundry ilks on any given night. Clubs with capacities of around 200 are the best places to catch exciting and varied bands and solo acts that may someday be known worldwide but for now remain our little secrets. **Tobacco Road**, Miami's oldest bar, mixes rock, blues, Cajun and Brazilian. Little Haiti's **Churchill's Hideaway**, a British pub and rock hub, might feature hardcore thrashing one night and lilting reggae the next. **Rose's** on South Beach delves deep into the rock scene but also relies on funk and Latin rock. This eclecticism means that with careful picking and choosing, you can catch an outstanding concert in an intimate atmosphere and end up having drinks with the performers after the show. Or it can mean you waste an hour enduring some real schlock.

Major venues

AT&T Amphitheatre at Bayfront Park

For listings, see above Classical: Other venues.
Outdoors site in Downtown and location of an excellent annual reggae festival in August saluting Bob Marley (who died in Miami and whose family performs at the big event each year). This is also the place where a pseudo-riot broke out during a Pearl Jam concert.

Cameo

1445 Washington Avenue, at Espanola Way, South Beach (532 0922). Bus C, H, K, W. **Open** 11pm-5am Thur-Sun. **Tickets** prices vary. **No credit cards.**
Major rap shows, edgy rock acts and various hip-hop haps throw down in a supersize old movie theatre in the heart of art deco land. Master reggae/hip-hop selector Waggy Tee packs the youngbloods in till the wee hours on Saturday evenings; on Sunday nights the Cameo stages Flashback Disco, Miami's longest-running 1970s hangover.

Miami Arena

721 NW First Avenue, at NW Seventh Street, Downtown (530 4400). Bus 2, 6, 7/Metrorail Overtown/Arena/ Metromover Arena/State Plaza. **Open** box office 8.30am-5pm Mon-Fri; until 8.30pm on performance days. **Tickets** prices vary. **Credit** AmEx, Disc, MC, V.
Home of the Miami Heat and Florida Panthers sports teams (both of which will be moving to new arenas soon), this functional (and not much else) building holds about 15,000 and is the site of most major touring concerts in Miami.

Rock

Cheers

2490 SW 17th Avenue, between SW 24th Terrace and US 1, near Downtown (857 0041). Bus 17, 24. **Open** 8pm-2am Wed-Sun. **Admission** $5. **No credit cards.**
The spot for hardcore punk, grunge, ska, slop, thrash and trash. And genres that fall near that. Monstrous moshing and pierced bodies galore.

Churchill's Hideaway

5501 NE Second Avenue, at NE 55th Street, Little Haiti (757 1807). Bus 2, 54. **Open** 11am-3am Mon-Sat; noon-3am Sun. **Admission** varies. **No credit cards.**
A firmly established rock dive owned and operated by Brit ex-pat Dave Daniels, the Church is the hub of Miami's underground rock scene, with live music from neophyte garagesters making their world debuts to highly regarded

touring acts whose onstage behaviour is a bit much for more civilised venues. Top local bands usually fill weekend bills; week nights are hit and miss. No pretensions, minimal door charges and cheap prices on several dozen varieties of beer (no hard liquor). You never know what you'll get, but if it's ballsy bands and beer-swilling good times you're looking for, Churchill's is the place to begin your search.

Rose's Bar & Music Lounge

754 Washington Avenue, between Seventh & Eighth Streets, South Beach (532 0228). Bus C, H, K, W. **Open** 5pm-5am daily. **Admission** varies. **No credit cards.**
Ambitious and not too pretentious as South Beach goes, offering some great music in a room that's only okay for sightlines and acoustics.

South Beach Pub

717 Washington Avenue, between Seventh & Eighth Streets, South Beach (532 7821). Bus C, H, K, W. **Open** 9.30pm-4am daily. **Admission** varies. **No credit cards.**
A reliable line-up of local rock talent.

Stella Blue

1661 Meridian Avenue, between Lincoln Road & 17th Street, South Beach (532 4788). Bus C, G, K, L, S. **Open** 5pm-2am Mon-Thur, Sun; 5pm-5am Fri, Sat. **Admission** $3-$22. **Credit** AmEx, DC, MC, V.
New and more upscale than other rock joints, this one's tasteful and big enough for not overly popular touring acts. Bring extra money if you intend to eat or consume alcohol with your music; drinks and food don't come cheap here.

Tobacco Road

626 S Miami Avenue, at SW Seventh Street, Downtown (374 1198). Bus 6, 8. **Open** 11.30am-5am Mon-Fri; noon-5am Sat. **Admission** varies. **Credit** AmEx, DC, Disc, MC, V.
Holder of Miami liquor license number 001, the Road for the past two of its nine decades has been a favourite of discerning but fun-loving music fans. Creaky and comfortable, with excellent food and a bountiful range of libations (including many hard-to-find limited editions), the Road features live music downstairs every night and fills its upstairs cabaret on Thursdays with radio madmen the Beast and Baker's original music series and on Fridays and Saturdays with touring acts, mostly blues.

Jazz & blues

The blues are poorly represented in Dade County, though you can catch them further north in Broward County. **Tobacco Road** (*see above*) brings in bigger acts – the walls there are covered with signed photos of just about every top blues act of the past few decades – and there are occasional festivals. The fledgling **Blues Power Club** (3701 NE Second Avenue, at NE 37th Street, Design District; 576 1336) is also worth checking out. Old-school R&B and soul still find an audience at Carol City's **Studio 183** (2860 NW 183rd Street, off NW 27th Avenue, North Dade; 621 7295), where the likes of Bobby Womack and Clarence Carter hold court. Jazz doesn't fare much better, though the **MoJazz Café** (*see above* **Latin**) is highly recommended for both its ambience and the talent it books on a nightly basis. The **Van Dyke Café** (846 Lincoln Road, at Jefferson Avenue; 534 3600) jazzes up South Beach with excellent acts seven nights a week.

Sport & Fitness

Miami's climate and water-bound location make it perfect for outdoor activities of all kinds.

The Great Outdoors

So many people have moved to the Miami area for its outdoor splendours that those outdoor splendours have been greatly reduced (the houses for these interlopers to live in have to go somewhere). This Catch-22 hasn't completely obliterated the Everglades and Atlantic shoreline – yet. Those are the big draws – the ocean on the east and the magnificent swamp to the west (*see chapter* **The Everglades**) – but there are many parks of varying types throughout the urban area.

Aviation

Miami boasts a number of ways to get high without side-effects. Try **Action Helicopter** (858 1788) for rentals, charters and instruction; **Aerotaxi** (1-800 472 5070) for charters; **Biscayne Helicopters** (252 3883) for sightseeing tours; and **Blackhawk** (983 3606) for tours of the Bahamas, Keys, Orlando and South Florida. **Pan Am Air Bridge** (1-800 424 2557) now owns Chalks, a 77-year-old outfit that flies by small seaplane (with pontoons) to Bimini and Paradise Island; it's an excellent way to see the sea from the air, and romantically charming to boot. **Miami City Flights** (861 0077) takes groups of three to nine people to the Bahamas, the Caribbean and Mexico. Call for more information and prices. *See also chapter* **Sightseeing**.

Canoeing & kayaking

The trick is not finding a place to row your own, but finding a place to rent the craft and equipment. Most locals exploit these hobbies year round, meaning they own the necessary stuff. For rentals, accessories and guided tours, try **Urban Trails Kayak Rentals**, 10800 Collins Avenue, Miami Beach (947 1302).

Cycling

Biking offers the best way to enjoy South Florida's most scenic areas because, frankly, auto traffic here sucks. Which is also why most locals choose the paved bike routes around town over simply wandering the roadways. Virginia Key and Key Biscayne are joined by the **Rickenbacker Causeway**, which is elevated (to allow for the boat traffic below) between the mainland and each island, making this the closest thing to mountain biking you'll find. It's a bit strenuous, but the route affords spectacular ocean views and plenty of spots to break for a refreshing dip. Easier on the legs and equally spiritually uplifting are the paths cut into the Everglades (for details, *see chapter* **The Everglades**).

Within the urban jungle, Coconut Grove's paths run along some of the priciest, leafiest and most attractive residences as well as the most neon-laden nightspots outside South Beach. Pedal north along **Bayshore Drive** to see even nicer abodes, including those of Sly Stallone and Madonna Ciccone. Call a bicycle shop for specifics (about bike paths, not celebrities) and organised outings.

Aventura Riders

Whole Foods Market, The Waterways Shoppes, 3575 NE 207th Street, Aventura (937 4463).
This group of bike owners meets every Sunday at 10am for a moderately paced 20-mile ride around the neighbourhood.

Mangrove Cycles

260 Crandon Boulevard, Key Biscayne (361 5555).
Open 9.30am-6pm Tue-Sat; 11am-5pm Sun.
Single-speed cruisers cost $7 for 2 hours, $10 per day. Multi-speed bikes are $12 for 2 hours, $18 per day.

Miami Beach Bicycle Center

601 Fifth Street, at Washington Avenue, South Beach (674 0150). **Open** 10am-7pm Mon-Sat daily.
Mountain bikes and cruisers cost $14 per day, $50 per week.

Fishing

Florida Bay, Biscayne Bay, the Intracoastal Waterway, the Gulfstream, the Everglades, countless lakes and canals – you don't have to travel to the Keys or the Caribbean to catch fish. All kinds of fish – from tiny freshwater bream to giant sailfish and half-ton sharks. The somewhat pricey charter boats will guide you to spots for giant tarpon and elusive bonefish and other big-game finny prey. The party boats generally dock or anchor off a reef for snapper, grouper and similar good eating. Any bridge will do – the causeways connecting Miami Beach to the mainland are especially popular among locals. You don't need a saltwater fishing licence if you fish from a charter boat or pier that charges admission, but you do if you fish from shore or rent your own boat. Licenses are available from the Dade County Tax Collector's Office (140 W Flagler Street, Miami; 270 4916) or bait and tackle shops, and cost $7 for three days, $17 for seven days.

Fishing gear

Visit any big retailer (such as K-Mart) or sporting goods outlet (such as Sports Authority; *see chapter* **Shopping**) or a bait and tackle shop. Try **A Fisherman's Paradise** at 3800 NW 27th Avenue, Northwest Miami (634 1578) and 17730 S Dixie Highway, South Dade (232 6000) for a vast selection of all things angling. **Crook and Crook** (2795 SW 27th Avenue, Coconut Grove; 854 0005) sells live and rigged bait plus the gear to go with it, while **Gordon's** (2627 SW 27th Avenue, Coconut Grove; 856 4665) has bait and tackle. Also try **Haulover Marine Center**, 15000 Collins Avenue, Miami Beach (945 3934).

Charter boats

Charter boats take up to six people. Half-day excursions (4½hrs) cost $450; full-day trips (8½hrs) are $650. Try one of the following outfits:

L&H Crandon Marina *Key Biscayne (361 9318).*
A charter boat service specialising in sailfishing and, in the summer, dolphin (not the sea mammal but a schooling fish that makes for excellent eating).
Mark the Shark *Biscayne Bay Marriott Marina, Downtown (759 5297).*
You want to catch a shark, you call Mark. Also guides for other large species.

Reel Time Sport Fishing *2560 S Bayshore Drive,*
Coconut Grove (856 5605).
Sailfish, wahoo, dolphin.
Blue Waters *Castaways Docks, 16375 Collins Avenue,*
Miami Beach (944 4531).
All Shark *(949 2948)* and **Therapy** *(945 1578):*
Haulover Marina, Collins Avenue & 108th Street, Miami
Beach.

Party boats

The best way for novices to get a feel for deep-sea fishing is
to board a party boat (usually 65-85 footers). These take out
8 to 50 people and provide guests with tackle, bait and
instruction. Costs vary from $24-$40 for half- or full-day
trips. All you have to do is reel in your catch and have a good
time. Drinks and food are offered on some at a nominal
charge. Contact one of the following:

Blue Sea II *1020 MacArthur Causeway, Watson Island*
(554 7373).
Reward II *Dock A, Miami Beach Marina, 300 Alton*
Road, South Beach (372 9470).
Kelley Fleet *(945 3801): Haulover Marina, Collins*
Avenue & 108th Street, Miami Beach.

Golf

Florida's sunny climate means that golfing is a very popular activity, and there are plenty of courses to choose from.

Biltmore Golf Course

1210 Anastasia Avenue, at Granada Boulevard, Coral
Gables (460 5364). Bus 52, 72. **Open** 6.30am-7pm Mon-
Fri; 6am-7pm Sat, Sun.
This upscale, 18-hole, par 71 course is made hazardous by
the lovely Coral Gables Waterway and costs about $20 per
round including cart.

Crandon Golf Course at Key Biscayne

6700 Crandon Boulevard, Key Biscayne (361 9129). Bus
B. **Open** 7am-sunset daily.
Non-residents pay $43 per round. Fee includes tax, cart and
some inspiring ocean views. An 18-hole, par 72 course.

Doral Golf Resort

4400 NW 87th Avenue, at NW 41st Street, Northwest
Miami (592 2000). Bus 36, 87. **Open** 7am-6pm daily.
Features the Blue Monster (home of the Doral-Ryder Open
tournament) as one of four 18-hole courses and a nine-hole
beginner's course. Prices are $90-$160.

Fontainebleau Golf Club

9603 Fontainebleau Boulevard, at NW 97th Avenue & W
Flagler Street, Northwest Miami (221 5181). Bus 7, 11,
87. **Open** 7am-7.30pm daily.
Two 18-hole courses plus a floodlit driving range, tournaments and instructors. Rates vary by season and decrease
later in the day. Price is about $34 per round for two people,
including taxes and cart.

Hang-gliding

No mountains, hills or cliffs around here. But…

Miami Hang Gliding

2550 S Bayshore Drive, at Aviation Avenue, Coconut
Grove (285 8978). Bus 48. **Open** 10.30am-6pm Tue-Sun.
The other day James Tindle was up for nearly four hours
reaching an altitude of nearly 6,500ft. You're welcome to join
him, although you'll probably only get to 1,000ft. Tindle and
crew will teach you what to do and send an instructor up
with you. High ground lacking in these parts, a boat pulls
you until you reach the right height: the line is then released
and you're a bird. Down below you'll see Stiltsville (a small
community of houses built in the ocean), Vizcaya and other

Head for the big blue astride a jet-ski.

cool land- and watermarks. You land in the water, which
Tindle describes as 'smooth and fun'. Couples welcome; there's
no charge to stay on the boat and watch your partner fly.

Horseriding

Southwinds Equestrian Center

6201 SW 122nd Avenue, off SW 64th Street, South
Dade (279 0189). Bus 56, 72. **Open** 9am-9pm Mon-Fri;
9am-6pm Sat, Sun. **Lessons** $35 for a 30-minute private
class or a one-hour group class.
English riding lessons, show circuit, lighted arenas.

Jet-skis & waterbikes

Extremely popular among practitioners, intensely disliked
by those opposed to the noise and potential danger (a boat
carrying famous musical couple Emilio and Gloria Estefan
not long ago crashed into a waterbiker with fatal results).
Water bikes cost about $10 per hour, wave runners about
$50 per hour. If you must cause a wake, try these:

Haulover Marine Center *15000 Collins Avenue,*
Miami Beach (945 3934). **Open** 8am-4pm daily.
Key Biscayne Boat Rentals *3301 Rickenbacker*
Causeway, Virginia Key (361 7368). **Open** 9am-5pm
Mon-Fri; 8.30am-6.30pm Sat, Sun.
Sun HydroBike Rentals *1200 Crandon Boulevard,*
Key Biscayne (365 0309). **Open** 10am-sunset daily.

Sailing

Try **Miami Beach Sailing**, 121 Ocean Drive, Miami Beach
(532 7245), or **Sailboats of Key Biscayne**, 4000 Crandon
Boulevard, Key Biscayne (361 0328). For those who know
how to sail, the latter is the place to rent a boat. If you need
someone to take you, you must make a reservation and pay
an extra $10 per hour.

Scuba & skin diving

Although most locals head down to the Keys for their underwater exploring, there are spots in Biscayne Bay worth a
look. Most dive shops offer lessons (in heated pools), equipment rental, air for tanks and chartered trips. The best of
them are listed below. *See also box* **Reefer madness**.

Adventure Bound Sports *17633 S Dixie Highway,*
South Dade (232 4442).
Austin's Diving Center *10525 S Dixie Highway,*
South Dade (665 0636).
Divers Den *12614 N Kendall Drive, Kendall (595 2010).*
Scuba Sports *16604 NE Second Avenue, N Miami*
Beach (940 0926).
Divers Paradise *4000 Crandon Boulevard, Key*
Biscayne (361 3483).
Offers daily dive trips and specialises in the wrecks in the bay.

And you thought beaches were for relaxing.

Swimming

Plenty of beaches, natch, but freshwater stroking is also widely available. Most hotels have pools and there are many public pools (call the Dade County Parks and Recreation Department on 533 2000 for a list). The most interesting public pool is the Venetian Pool (*see above* **Aqua aerobics**).

Participation sports

Beach volleyball

Penrod's

1 Ocean Drive, at Biscayne Street, South Beach (538 1111). Bus H, W. **Open** 11am-11pm Mon-Thur, Sun; 11am-1am Fri, Sat. **Credit** AmEx, MC, V.
The mecca of many things Miamian, South Beach serves as the hotspot for this burgeoning sport – whether you're there to play or spectate. The fratty beach club Penrod's has six courts and provides volleyballs (you'll need a $25 refundable deposit and photo ID). There are other courts marked off further north around the 10th Street hub.

Bowling

If you insist on wasting time indoors, or just have to get that kegling fix, there are plenty of alleys listed in the phone directory, including these two. Many of the larger lanes also have pool tables, video games, restaurants and bars.

Bird Bowl

9275 Bird Road, between SW 92nd & 93rd Avenues, Southwest Miami (221 1221). Bus 40. **Open** 8.30am-midnight Mon-Thur, Sun; 8.30am-3am Fri; 9am-3am Sat. **Admission** $3 per person per game; $1.50 shoe rental.

Don Carter's Kendall Lanes

13600 N Kendall Drive, at SW 137th Avenue, Kendall (385 6160). Bus 88. **Open** 24 hours daily. **Admission** $3.25 per person per game; $2 shoe rental.

Ice-skating

Miami Ice Arena

14770 Biscayne Boulevard, at NE 147th Street, North Miami Beach (940 8222). Bus 3, 28. **Open** 11am-2pm, 5-7pm, Tue; 7.30-10pm Wed; 11am-2pm Thur; 8pm-midnight Fri; 10am-noon, 1-5pm Sat; 1-5pm, 7-10pm, Sun. **Admission** $3-$8; $2 skate rental.
Enjoy recreational ice-skating or ice hockey games here.

Gold Coast Ice Arena

4601 N Federal Highway, at 46th Street, Pompano Beach (1-954 943 1437). No bus. **Open** 10am-12.30pm, 1.30-4pm, Mon-Wed; 10am-12.30pm, 1.30-4pm, 8.15-10pm, Thur; 10am-12.30pm, 1.30-4pm, 8.15-11.15pm Fri; 1.30-4pm, 8.15-11pm, Sat. **Admission** $5-$6; $2 skate rental.
A 30-minute drive north of Miami, this rink is where the Florida Panthers professional ice hockey team practises. Anyone can skate every day all year round.

In-line skating

Get in line to in-line skate around the trendier sections of town. South Beach, with its insurmountable lack of parking and consistently congested traffic, is infested with low rollers who wheel everywhere – into nightclubs, restaurants, hotel lobbies. Some retailers even post 'No Blading' signs at their storefronts. Ocean Drive along the beachfront ranks as the most popular spot; for the less confident there are beach paths. The no-cars-allowed Lincoln Road Mall provides a nice variation on the deco theme. Coconut Grove's old streets and active nightlife also offer a good wheel, as does Key Biscayne.

Fritz's Skate Shop

601 Collins Avenue, at Sixth Street, South Beach (532 0054). Bus C, H, K, W. **Open** 10am-8pm Mon-Thur, Sun; 10am-10pm Fri, Sat. **Credit** AmEx, DC, Disc, MC, V.
Sales and rentals ($8 an hour).
Branch: 726 Lincoln Road, South Beach (532 1954).

Sergio's Skate Zone

180 Crandon Boulevard, Suite 116, Key Biscayne (361 6610). Bus B. **Open** 9am-7pm Mon-Fri; 9am-5pm Sat, Sun. **Credit** AmEx, MC, V.
Sales and rentals. Group lessons cost about $10 (inc skates).

Skate 2000

1200 Ocean Drive, at 12th Street, South Beach (538 8282). Bus C, H, K, W. **Open** 9am-9pm Mon-Thur, Sun; 9am-10pm Fri, Sat. **Credit** AmEx, Disc, MC, V.
Free lessons at 10am on Sundays: if you need rental skates ($8 an hour) come to the shop, otherwise meet at the 10th Street boardwalk.

Pool & billiards

Bars and bowling alleys generally have pool tables, but to get cued in at a dedicated pool parlour, try **Jillian's Billiard Club**, 12070 SW 88th Street, Kendall (595 0070); **New Wave Billiards**, 1403 SW 107th Avenue, Kendall (220 4790) and **Wesley's** (15346 W Dixie Highway, North Miami). On South Beach's Washinton Avenue, there are **The Diamond Club** (No.1242; 531 2114) and **Brandt's Break** (No.621; 531 9661). Even these joints aren't exclusively for racking and whacking – other diversions such as booze and video games go with the territory. Pool games cost about $10 per hour.

Rollerhockey

Roller hockey games are held on Fridays at 5pm and Saturdays at 9am at **Skate 2000** in South Beach (*see above* **Rollerblading**): all you need is your skates. For more information, call 538 8282.

Hockey World

14382 Biscayne Boulevard, at NE 143rd Street, North Miami Beach (949 6990). Bus 3, 28. **Open** 10am-8pm Mon-Sat.

All the hockey equipment you could need.

Tennis & racquetball

Wealthier South Floridians have tennis courts in their backyards and there are public and private courts around town in numbers that attest to the popularity of net games here. Call the Dade County Parks & Recreation Department (532 2000) for information about public courts.

Salvadore Park Tennis Center

1120 Andalusia Avenue, between Columbus Boulevard & Cordova Street, Coral Gables (460 5333). Bus 24. **Open** 8am-10pm Mon-Fri; 8am-7pm Sat, Sun. **Admission** $4.30-$5 per person per hour.

Tropical Tennis

Tropical Park, 7900 SW 40th Street, at SW 79th Avenue, Southwest Miami (223 8710). Bus 40. **Open** 11am-8pm Mon-Fri; 9am-8pm Sat, Sun. **Admission** $1.85-$2 per person per hour.

YMCAs

For general YMCA information, call 358 5077.

Carver YMCA

401 NW 71st Street, at NW Fourth Avenue, Northwest Miami (759 3317). Bus 2, L. **Open** 6.30am-8pm Mon-Fri, Sun; 9am-2pm Sat. **Admission** $5 per day.

Basketball courts, gym, aerobics, karate classes.

Southwest YMCA

4300 SW 58th Avenue, between SW 42nd & 44th Terraces, Southwest Miami (665 3513). Bus 40, 72. **Open** hours vary depending on facility. **Admission** $5 per day.

Swimming pool, basketball court, racquetball courts.

Fitness

Thanks to the bare necessity of clothing in these climes, many South Floridians muscle up enough to be worth a gawk as they strut their buff stuff. Flat bellies, fat-free thighs, firm chests and the rest are regularly paraded along South Beach and in downtown Coconut Grove.

Aqua aerobics

Venetian Pool

2701 DeSoto Boulevard, at Toledo Street, Coral Gables (460 5356). Bus 24, 72. **Open** 11am-5.30pm Tue-Fri; 10am-4.30pm Sat, Sun.

An all-wet workout beats the heat every Tuesday and Thursday at 5pm. Classes cost $6, pool admission included.

Dance

Most visitors simply hit the nightclubs of South Beach and let the music move them. But for more serious light-trippers, there are lots of schools and classes. *See also chapter* **Music**.

Kendall Dance Studio *8838 SW 129th Street, off SW 87th Avenue, Kendall (233 8700)*:
Ballroom for beginners through advanced.
Lorraine Florido Dance Academy *7401 Miami Lakes Drive, off SW 67th Avenue, Miami Lakes (824 9465)*.
Jazz, ballet, tap, modern.

Mid-Eastern Dance Exchange *350 Lincoln Road, at Washington Avenue, South Beach (538 1608)*.
A collective of serious belly dancers, available to perform or teach you in their rehearsal space. Beginners welcome. Veils and finger cymbals are sold.
Momentum School of Dance *3601 S Miami Avenue, at Alatka Street, Coconut Grove (858 7002)*.
Ballet, jazz, modern, tap.

Gyms

Narcissism, thy middle name is Miami. Buff boys and lithe ladies proudly parade their pecs up and down Ocean Drive and in area nightclubs. Tone up to join them at **Club Body Tech** (1253 Washington Avenue, South Beach, 674 8222); note that homophobes are extremely unwelcome here – the workout facilities are great but many locals regard Body Tech as a heavy guy-guy pick-up spot. Alternatively, try **Gridiron** (1676 Alton Road, South Beach, 531 4743), owned by former Miami Dolphins football player John Bosa. Off the Beach, try **Bally's**, which has various locations (call 1-800 777 1117 for your nearest) or **Olympia** at 20311 Biscayne Boulevard, Aventura (932 3500). For gay gyms, *see chapter* **Gay & Lesbian**.

Yoga

Siddha Yoga Meditation Center

1700 SW Third Avenue, at SW 17th Road, near Downtown (856 4407). Bus 24/Metromover Brickell.
Call for times and cost of classes.

Yoga by the Sea

501 96th Street, at Byron Avenue, Bal Harbour (861 8245). Bus G, K, R, S, T. **Classes** 6.30pm Mon; 9.30am Sat. **Cost** $9.

Yoga Institute of Miami

9350 S Dadeland Boulevard, Suite 207, at SW 93rd Street, Kendall (670 0558). Bus 1, 52, 65/Metrorail Dadeland South. **Classes** 5.30pm Mon; 9.30am, 7pm, Tue; 5.30pm Wed; 9.30am, 6.30pm Thur; 10am Sat. **Cost** $15.

Spectator sports

Apart from the Miami Dolphins' famous undefeated NFL season in 1972, South Florida boasts little in the way of tradition and only a blurry image as a home of top-notch pro sports teams. So what explains the championship fever infecting fans of all major sports these days? Well, Miami does boast lots of fast cash and people who know how to sling it around. Thus, the forever mediocre Dolphins acquire premier coach Jimmy Johnson, and the NBA's Miami Heat sign a pair of all-stars as well as premier coach Pat Riley. The ice-hockey team, the Florida Panthers, zips to the 1996 Stanley Cup Finals (under coach Doug MacLean) while pro baseball's Florida Marlins begin signing free agent superstars left and right and land top coach Jim Leyland.

The result is that this sun- and drug-drenched forever-on-vacation annex of Latin America has quickly become Jock City, USA. Already fielding highly successful (though highly felonious) football teams and a winning baseball programme, the University of Miami has also seen its basketball team emerge as a Big East contender. The other good news in the local sports world is that the city remains sun- and drug-drenched – meaning tickets are never as hard to come by as they should be with all this winning going on.

TICKETS & INFORMATION

The *Miami Herald* provides adequate listings. Tickets can be purchased at each venue's box office or through **Ticketmaster** (with credit card by phone at 350 5050 or with cash only at outlets all over town); service charges are high. So-called ticket brokers (scalpers) offer better seats at higher prices to most events; they advertise in the classified sections of local papers.

American football

Both on and off the field, the collegiate Hurricanes tend to provide a better show than the professional Dolphins. With players regularly caught in violations of laws and league rules, the Canes still manage to put together winning seasons, capturing four national championships since the early 1980s. Pro Player Stadium, home of the Dolphins, is slated to host the Super Bowl in 2000. The season runs from the last week of August to the penultimate week of December.

Reefer madness

Less than 100 years ago, Miami's beaches were snow-white, the water crystalline and untainted, and the indigenous flora and fauna abundant. It's a beautiful image that troubles now; after decades of unrelenting exploitation and sprawling residential and commercial development – much of it built before the word 'ecology' entered the lexicon and savagely wasteful – it's a wonder there's anything left at all. But there is, and most of it can be found around irregularities in the ocean floor, rising breaks in the otherwise desert-like flatness.

Three natural reefs run along the Florida coast, formed by coral that grew over thousands of years when sea level rose during the meltdowns after the Ice Age. They extend from about 300m offshore to about two miles out. The nearest to shore, First Reef, runs north from Homestead and is not considered worth diving. It lies too far offshore to swim to, but is only 20-30ft below the surface, so you could snorkel if desperate.

These underwater ecosystems developed gradually, intermittently and over a vast period of time. The barriers formed by the reefs and nooks and crannies therein make excellent habitat for all types of aquarian plants and animals – parrotfish and snappers, crabs and eels, anenomes and fans, coral and barracudas, to name just a few. And reefs build on themselves. Yet they are incredibly fragile bits of natural construction; one wrong turn by a ship's captain can take out large chunks and obliterate thousands of years' worth of nature's handiwork (unfortunately, such accidents occur with alarming frequency).

Human encroachment has, of course, exacerbated the problem. In the 1970s, expansion of the Port of Miami – where all those giant cruise ships dock – required dredging and filling operations that ravaged vast quantities of sealife.

Finally, in 1981, Dade County recognised the importance of reefs, and decided not to wait for the next ice age to correct the problem. The county implemented the Artificial Reef Program, which has successfully synthesised 23 new 'reefs' by strategically sinking ships (more than 60, so far), concrete, limestone boulders, army tanks, prefabricated modules, and even a 727 jet liner in an effort to jumpstart Mother Nature. As the years go by, lifeforms set up shop at these man-made bulkheads and reef-like ecosystems develop. It might not be completely natural, but at least it marks an attempt – and by all accounts a successful one – for humankind to fix what it broke. The City of Miami Beach oversees the programme, which is funded by the Port of Miami and state grants. The old Miami Beach watertower is the next man-made structure destined for the troubled waters offshore.

There are numerous individual artificial reefs within the 23 official sites. Some of these have been engineered specifically for diving. Most offer fine fishing. In fact, though the programme was initiated for habitat restoration and enhancement, it has provided a big lift to the charter dive industry, boosted commercial fishing and brought smiles to countless recreational anglers.

The best artificial reefs, and the most accessible from South Beach, lie directly east of the Fountainebleau Hilton hotel. You need a boat. Some are as shallow as 40 feet, so you can snorkel, but diving is better (visibility permitting). This area is known as the Wreck Trek and includes Billy's Barge, a Haitian shrimp boat, the Boulders, the Matthew Lawrence and the Army Tanks – all within about a half-mile radius.

Three highly recommended artificial reef charter operators are **H2O Scuba** (956 3483), **Bubbles** (856 0565) and **Tarpoon** (887 8726). For more details on what the sea has to offer, contact **Miami Beach's Water Sports Marketing Council** by calling 1-888 728 2262 or 672 1270.

Miami Dolphins
Pro Player Stadium, 2269 NW 199th Street, at NW 27th Avenue, North Dade (623 6100). Bus 27, 83. **Tickets** $17-$42.

University of Miami Hurricanes
The Orange Bowl, 1501 NW Third Street, between NW 14th & 16th Avenues, near Downtown (643 7100). Bus 7, 12, 17. **Tickets** $18-$30; call 284 2263 or 1-800 462 2637.

Auto racing
The Metro-Dade Homestead Motorsports Park (1 Speedway Boulevard, Homestead) hosts the Grand Prix of Miami, which begins the Indy Car World Series each February (tickets cost $40-$200) and the Jiffy Lube Miami 300 in November for stock cars. Other events are scheduled throughout the year. Call 230 7223 for more information. At Hialeah Speedway (3300 W Okeechobee Road, Hialeah; 821 6644), stock cars lap it up every Saturday night under the lights. Tickets cost $8; free for under-12s.

Baseball
The Florida Marlins play at Pro Player Stadium (*see above* **American football**); tickets cost $2-$25. The University of Miami Hurricanes play on campus at Mark Light Field, 6201 San Amaro Drive, Coral Gables (284 4171). The Florida International University Golden Panthers play at FIU Field, on the University Park Campus at SW 17th Street and 117th Avenue, South Dade (348 3161). Tickets for college games cost $3-$5. The pro season runs from April through September; the college season from February through May.

Basketball
Both the NBA's Miami Heat and the University of Miami Hurricanes play at Miami Arena, 721 NW First Avenue, Downtown (530 4400). Tickets for Heat games cost $15-$29; for Canes games $9-$13. Florida International University's Golden Panthers hoop it up at the Golden Panther Arena on the University Park campus (*see above* **Basketball**); tickets cost $3-$7. The pro baseball season is from November to April; the college season begins and ends a month earlier.

Greyhound racing

Flagler Dog Track
401 NW 38th Court, at NW Seventh Street, Northwest Dade (649 3000). Bus 7, 37. **Racing** *1 Jun-30 Nov* 7.30pm Mon, Wed, Fri, Sun; 12.30pm, 7.30pm, Tue, Thur, Sat. **Admission** $1-$3.

Hollywood Greyhound Track
Pembroke Road & US 1, Hallandale (1-954 454 9400). Bus Broward County Transit 1, board at Aventura Mall. **Racing** *1 Dec-31 May* 7.30pm Mon, Wed, Fri, Sun; 12.30pm, 7.30pm, Tue, Thur, Sat. **Admission** $1-$3. Poker and simulcasts of parimutuels are available at both tracks year-round.

Horse racing
Three flat courses divide seasons so one is always open. In addition to the thoroughbreds running live, the tracks also simulcast racing from other venues around the country.

Calder Race Course
21001 NW 27th Avenue, at NW 215th Street, North Dade (625 1311). Bus 27, 91. **Open** late May-early Jan. **Admission** $2-$4.

The Florida Panthers in action.

Gulfstream Park
US 1, between Hallandale Beach Boulevard & Ives Dairy Road, Hallandale (931 7223). Bus 3. **Open** early Jan-mid Mar. **Admission** $2-$4.

Hialeah Park
2200 E Fourth Avenue, between E 22nd & 33nd Streets, Hialeah (885 8000). Bus 28, 37, L/Metrorail Hialeah. **Open** mid Mar-late May. **Admission** $2-$4. This landmark track, struggling to stay open due to a lack of patronage, is worth visiting even when no racing is scheduled, thanks to its floral splendour, vintage charm and, of course, those famous flamingoes.

Ice-hockey
Round here, ice is the stuff you put in the cooler to keep the beer and soda cold; ice is what you add to tea; Ice is the local has-been with the first name Vanilla. Encase ourselves in padding and skate around on the frozen stuff swinging big wooden sticks? No way. Yet Miami has embraced pro hockey in a big way – for two reasons. A number of transplanted New Yorkers set the pace (and explain to natives what a blue line is), and our team wins. Last year the Cats made it to the NHL finals, losing to Colorado but still proudly wearing the slippers of a Cinderella. Also, fans here became (in)famous for tossing fake rats onto the ice, a practice since prohibited by the NHL; even the New Yorkers here have failed to adequately explain the rubber rat thing. The season is from October through May.

Florida Panthers
Miami Arena, 721 NW First Avenue, at NW Seventh Street, Downtown (530 4400). Bus 2, 6, 7/Metrorail Overtown/Arena/Metromover Arena/State Plaza. **Tickets** $12-$34.

Jai-alai
A fast, fascinating import from the Basque region of the Pyrenees, jai-alai is fun to watch even if you don't bet.

Dania Jai Alai
301 E Dania Beach Boulevard (A1A), at US 1, Dania (945 4345). Bus Broward County Transit 1, board at Aventura Mall. **Games** noon, 7.15pm, Tue, Sat; 7.15pm Wed-Fri; 1pm Sun.

Miami Jai Alai
3500 NW 37th Avenue, between NW 34th & 36th Streets, Northwest Miami (633 6400). Bus 36, J. **Games** noon, 7.10pm, Mon, Wed, Sat; 7.10pm Thur, Fri.

Theatre & Dance

Miami's performance scene may not be as established or diverse as London's or New York's, but you can find surprisingly innovative and engaging work – if you look hard enough.

When people think of Miami, they imagine palm trees, sand, ocean and nightclubs. They do not tend to think cultural mecca. However, perhaps because of an influx of people from the north (New York, New England and Chicago) and the south (Latin America), the area has enjoyed a burgeoning interest in theatre and dance in the past decade. Both national acts coming here on tour and indigenous drama and dance companies have been finding wider audiences for an eclectic mix of work.

INFORMATION & TICKETS
For performance information, call the venues or dance companies direct or check the listings in *New Times* and the Weekend section of the *Miami Herald*'s Friday edition. For comprehensive, up-to-the-minute information about the local dance scene, call **Florida Dance Association**

(237 3413), which publishes the bi-monthly *Florida Dance Calendar* with details of who's doing what, when and where.

You can usually buy tickets direct from the venue's box office or the dance company's office both in advance and on the day of the show; tickets for major companies and venues can also be purchased through **Ticketmaster** on **358 5885** (note that service charges range from $4.75 to $5.50 per ticket).

Theatre

Although numerous experimental theatre companies bubble to the surface each year and wow the public with out-there work, such small, under-funded ventures have to scrounge for performance space and tend not to survive very long. If you have a taste for truly experimental work, you have to catch it on the run in Miami. Mainstream and contemporary text-based offerings, however, abound from companies that are lucky enough to maintain permanent homes. You won't find theatres clustered in one district along the lines of New York's Broadway or London's West End (venues tend to be split between Coral Gables Coconut Grove, Downtown and South Beach), but with a decent map and good directions, devotees can satisfy their live theatre cravings.

Major venues

Actors' Playhouse
280 Miracle Mile, between Salzedo Street & Ponce de Leon Boulevard, Coral Gables (444 9293). Bus 24, 40, 42, J. **Tickets** $26.50 Wed, Thur, Sun; $29.50 Fri, Sat. **Credit** AmEx, MC, V.
After establishing its reputation and building a loyal audience in a strip mall-based theatre for 10 years, this company recently moved to refurbished quarters in a renovated 600-seat (plus 300 in the works) art deco movie house on this street of fancy shops and restaurants in one of Miami's classier neighbourhoods. The company relies on a somewhat formulaic mix of war-horse musicals (*Man of La Mancha*, *Brigadoon*), what they like to call 'contemporary musicals', and comedies (Neil Simon's *Laughter on the 23rd Floor*, Ray Cooney's *Funny Money*). Once in a while, the company pulls out the stops with an awe-inspiring rendition of something unexpected, such as 1996's marvellous production of the musical *Big River*. It also runs a first-class children's theatre with shows throughout the year on Saturday afternoons.

*Popular fare at **Actors' Playhouse**.*

Coconut Grove Playhouse
*3500 Main Highway, at Charles Avenue, Coconut Grove
(442 4000). Bus 42, 48.* **Tickets** Main stage $30 Tue-
Thur, Sun; $35 Fri, Sat; Encore Room $22 Tue-Thur, Sun;
$27 Fri, Sat; $10 under-24s; $10 discount on day of show
6-7pm, cash only. **Credit** AmEx, Disc, MC, V.

Undoubtedly the grand-daddy of Miami's theatre scene, the
Playhouse opened its doors as a regional theatre in 1956 and
immediately made history with the US premiere of Beckett's
Waiting for Godot. A venue for national tours throughout
the 1960s, the Playhouse enjoyed the artistic directorship of
Jose Ferrer for several years before New Yorker Arnold
Mittelman took over the reins in the mid-1980s. Initially,
Mittelman took some heat from critics for his fluff programming but he has redeemed himself in recent seasons,
blowing the town away with a production of *Death of a
Salesman* with Hal Holbrook and a revival of *Who's Afraid
of Virginia Woolf?* starring Elizabeth Ashley and Frank
Converse. The Playhouse is home to two theatres: the 1,100-
seat main auditorium and the cosier Encore Room, which
has nightclub-style seating around a postage stamp stage
and often features plays by local writers.

Smaller venues

Florida Shakespeare Theatre
*Biltmore Hotel, 1200 Anastasia Avenue, at Granada
Boulevard, Coral Gables (446 1116). Bus 52, 56, 72.*
Tickets $22-$26; $19-$23 students, senior citizens.
Credit AmEx, MC, V.

Hurricane Andrew literally blew the roof off FST's permanent home in August 1992 and the company limped along
for the next four years, raising funds, mounting a show here
and there and performing Shakespeare for elementary
schools. It finally opened the doors of its plush new digs during the 1996-97 season: a state-of-the art, 154-seat theatre in

the grounds of the elegant Biltmore Hotel. Under the artistic
direction of Juan Cejas, one of the most innovative directors
in town, FST concentrates on contemporary US playwrights
plus a couple of Shakespeare plays a year. Open-air
Shakespeare productions are planned, once the adjacent 500-
seat amphitheatre is completed.

New Theater
*65 Almeria Avenue, between Douglas Road & Galiano
Street, Coral Gables (443 5909). Bus 24, 42, 52, 56, J.*
Tickets $20 Wed, Thur, Sun; $25 Fri; Sat; $7 students.
Credit AmEx, MC, V.

Located in a small but welcoming storefront just blocks
away from the Actors' Playhouse and FST, this 11-year-old,
70-seat theatre serves as an inspiration to the area's newer
smaller venues. It presents a careful blend of modern
classics, new pieces by up and coming playwrights and the
controversial. Recent productions have included Tennessee
Williams' *The Glass Menagerie*, Richard Kalinowski's *Beast
on the Moon*, the Miami premiere of Terrence McNally's
Love! Valour! Compassion and the South Florida debut of
Tony Kushner's *Angels in America*. Shows are marked by
intelligent direction, well-crafted staging, fastidious attention to detail and solid production values.

50-seats & under

Area Stage
*645 Lincoln Road, between Meridian & Pennsylvania
Avenues, South Beach (673 8002). Bus C, G, K, L, S.*
Tickets $18 Thur, Sun; $20 Fri, Sat; $8 under-25s.
Credit MC, V.

Husband-and-wife team John and Maria Rodaz opened Area
on Lincoln Road in 1989 when the pedestrian mall was still
a low-rent artist district and not the chi-chi hotspot it is
today. As galleries and studios folded to make way for

Miami City Ballet

No-one who wanders the streets of South Beach
can fail to notice the Miami City Ballet: it
rehearses and teaches in a storefront on Lincoln
Road, through whose bay windows the dancers
are clearly visible to passers-by. Well, if you've
got something to be proud of, why not show it
off? Miami's premier classical dance company is
a world-class group. Founded by former New
York City Ballet principal Edward Villella in
1985, the 45-member ensemble, drawn from
major-league companies such as the New York
City Ballet, Paris Opera Ballet, Dance Theater
of Harlem and Deutsche Opera Berlin, has garnered a national and international reputation
over the past decade.

Villella, an Italian kid from Bayside, New
York, where a future as a male ballet dancer
would not normally be in the cards, studied at
New York's Maritime Academy and won
acclaim as a baseball player and a boxer before
landing on his toes as one of the US's most celebrated male principals in the New York City
Ballet. In 1960, he made ballet history with his

stunning performance in the revival of NYCB
impresario George Balanchine's 1929 masterpiece *Prodigal Son*. Thirty-two years later,
Villella entitled his biography *Prodigal Son*.

He also keeps Balanchine's legacy alive
through the repertoire of the Miami City Ballet.
Villella founded the company in 1985, a decade
after he was forced to curtail his career in New
York owing to debilitating dance-related injuries.
The company also performs the work of modern
choreographers Paul Taylor and Jose Limon. New
pieces by Peruvian-born resident choreographer
Jimmy Gamonet de los Heros are composed in the
neo-classical style yet lend both a contemporary
and a Latin flavour to the repertoire.

The Miami City Ballet performs in Florida
from September to April and is usually on tour
the rest of the year.

Miami City Ballet
*905 Lincoln Road, between Jefferson & Michigan
Avenues, South Beach (532 4880). Bus C, G, K, L, S.*
Open box office 10am-5pm Mon-Fri. **Tickets** $16-$46.
Credit AmEx, MC, V.

upscale shops and restaurants, Area hung on to its intimate 49-seat space for dear life and, happily for audiences, still remains on the Road. Despite the area's gentrification, the company sticks close to its rough and ready roots. Each year it consistently produces the most honest and passionate work in town, mounting contemporary pieces that other theatres do not seem to want to touch, from Beckett and Pinter over the years to more recent offerings like Loretta Greco's *Passage*, an inventive political saga of Cuban rafters crossing the Florida Straits, Mario Vargas Llosa's *La Chunga* and Nicholas Wright's *Mrs Klein*, a problematic yet compelling play about psychoanalyst Melanie Klein.

Edge Theater

405 Espanola Way, between Drexel & Washington Avenues, South Beach (531 6083). Bus C, H, K, W. **Tickets** $12; $10 students, senior citizens. **No credit cards.**

This small space on the top floor of a building housing galleries and lofts, on one of South Beach's most charming streets, packs in a local crowd enthusiastic about its contemporary offerings. Artistic director Jim Tommaney disdains what he calls 'suburban dramas', programming instead playwrights like David Mamet, David Henry Hwang and Harold Pinter, with a heavy emphasis at times on Tennessee Williams, and another emphasis on sexual parodies including nudity, bondage and simulated onstage sex. The space also showcases the work of new and unknown playwrights. Productions tend to be more ambitious than polished but they get an A for effort.

3rd Street Black Box

230 NE Third Street, between NE Second & Third Avenues, Downtown (371 9619). Bus 3, 9, 10, 16, K/ Metromover College North/College/Bayside. **Tickets** $12; $8 students, senior citizens. **No credit cards.**

Founded by a firebrand group of graduates of Miami's New World School of the Arts, 3rd Street set up shop in 1995 in the back of an Asian restaurant in Downtown Miami – a bold move given that the area rolls up its pavements at night. Marked more by enthusiasm and a catch-as-you-can programming philosophy than by a distinct artistic vision, the theatre has presented an eclectic mix of musicals (Jones and Schmidt's offbeat *Celebration*), comedies (Israel Horowitz's *Line*) and dramas (Rafael Lima's *Hard Hats*), as well as original works by local artists including one-person shows about Judy Garland and Anais Nin.

Theatre series

The Broadway Series

(Information on whole series & tickets 1-800 939 8587). Jackie Gleason Theater for the Performing Arts, 1700 Washington Avenue, at 17th Street, South Beach (673 7300). Bus A, F/M, G, K. **Tickets** prices vary. **Credit** AmEx, MC, V.

A staple in Miami, Fort Lauderdale and Palm Beach, the Series brings national touring productions of Broadway and off-Broadway shows to audiences who never make it to New York to catch the hits. In Miami, the shows are mounted at the 2,700-seat Jackie Gleason Theater, a conventional auditorium with less-than-fabulous acoustics which also hosts comedians, cabaret acts and just about every acclaimed national and international touring dance company that comes this way. Depending on your taste, you can catch recycled crowd-pleasers such as *Grease* and *Cats* or more sophisticated fare such as Edward Albee's *Three Tall Women*, Terrence McNally's *Master Class* and Christopher Plummer in *Barrymore*. The 1997-1998 season (Oct-May) is scheduled to include *Chicago*, *Rent*, *Show Boat* and *Full Gallop*, the acclaimed one-woman show about Diana Vreeland.

City Theater

PO Box 248268, Coral Gables, FL 33124 (information 284 3355). **Tickets** $12-$36. **Credit** AmEx, MC, V.

One of Miami's most dynamic new theatres, showcasing the city's finest local acting, directing and design talent, this company launched Summer Shorts, a spirited marathon festival of one-act plays taking place over three weekends in June and July 1996. The festival is now scheduled to take place each year at the University of Miami's Jerry Herman Ring Theater in Coral Gables; ring the above number for more details.

Miami Light Project

841 Lincoln Road, Miami Beach, FL 33139 (531 3747). **Tickets** $15-$20. **Credit** AmEx, MC, V.

Miami Light presents a glittering annual season (Oct-May) of innovative theatre, music and dance luminaries (*see below* **Dance series**). Recent visitors have included Spalding Gray, Eric Bogosian, Danny Hoch, Margo Gomez, Roger Guenveur Smith and the Los Angeles-based Latino comedy troupe Culture Clash. Miami Light also stages the annual, weekend-long Here and Now Festival in June, showing in-progress, cutting-edge performance works by local theatre, dance, visual and spoken-word artists.

Hispanic theatre

Bridge Theater

Miami Beach Woman's Club, 2401 Pinetree Drive, at 24th Street, Miami Beach (886 3908). Bus K. **Tickets** prices vary. **No credit cards.**

Although Hispanic culture has impacted on life in Miami in innumerable ways – Anglos and Hispanics live side by side, go to school together, eat in each other's restaurants, enjoy each other's music – crossover in the theatre world has been minimal because each culture persists in presenting drama in its own language. With a commitment to bringing the work of Hispanic and Hispanic-American playwrights to English-speaking audiences through English-language productions, the Bridge has gone far in connecting the two worlds dramatically.

International Hispanic Theater Festival

Information 445 8877). **Tickets** $15; some free events. **Credit** AmEx.

Taking place during the first two weeks in June for the past 12 years, this festival is considered one of the most important gatherings of Hispanic theatre practitioners in the world. It draws companies performing classical, contemporary and experimental work in Spanish, Portuguese and English from Spain, the Caribbean, South and Central America, Mexico and the US. Shows take place in venues all over town and there are also symposiums, lectures and workshops. The 1998 festival runs from 30 May to 15 June.

Teatro Avante

235 Alcazar Avenue, between Le Jeune Road & Ponce de Leon Boulevard, Coral Gables (445 8877). Bus 42, 52, 56, J. **Tickets** $15. **Credit** AmEx.

Run by Cuban-born Mario Ernesto Sanchez, this Hispanic-language theatre has consistently presented literary Hispanic drama, where other theatres in the Spanish-speaking scene tend toward nightclub acts, vaudeville-style comedies and melodramas. Like many small arts enterprises, Avante has suffered financial setbacks, and in 1996 Sanchez leased his theatre to Alcazar Cinematheque which programmes art films, but the company still manages to produce two or three live works a year, mostly in Spanish with an occasional English offering. Sanchez is also the director of the prestigious Hispanic Theater Festival (*see above*).

*Members of the **Mary Street Dance Theatre** (page 192) are put through their paces.*

Further afield

The **Pope Theater Company** (262 South Ocean Boulevard, Manalapan; 1-800 514 3837) offers inventive interpretations and dazzlingly designed productions of the most daring new theatre in the country. Although the beautiful mid-sized theatre, with not a single bad seat surrounding its three-quarter thrust stage, is an hour-plus drive north of Miami, for theatre addicts it is worth the ride. Slightly closer to Miami is the **Caldwell Theater Company** (7873 North Federal Highway, Boca Raton; 1-561 930 6400), a regional theatre featuring sometimes excellent renditions of a standard mix of classical and contemporary fare.

Closer still is the **Hollywood Boulevard Theater** (at 1938 Hollywood Boulevard, Hollywood; 1-954 929 5400), with its pastiche of occasionally fabulous, other times inane productions from works by Noel Coward and Wendy Wasserstein to musicals by Maltby and Shire. Next door, the **Florida Playwrights Theater** (1936 Hollywood Boulevard; 1-954 925 8123) serves up slightly less mainstream but more consistently satisfying productions of work from the likes of Craig Lucas and Christopher Durang. Each summer, FPT performs two Shakespeare plays in repertory; it's the Bard on a shoestring budget, done remarkably well.

Dance

Miami's diverse dance landscape supports the classical to the modern to the cutting edge but, although companies like Miami City Ballet and Ballet Flamenco La Rosa have permanent rehearsal spaces, not one company listed here has a permanent performance space. Productions are mounted in large and small venues around Miami and on stages in the neighbouring northern counties of Broward and Palm Beach.

Major dance companies on tour tend to roost at the multi-purpose **Jackie Gleason Theater of the Performing Arts** in South Beach (673 7300; *see above* **Theatre**). In recent seasons, TOPA has played host to Dance Theater of Harlem, Lar Lubavitch, Bill T Jones, St Petersburg Ballet of Russia and American Ballet Theater. Local troupes, including the Miami City Ballet, also perform there. Dance performances are also held at the smaller **Colony Theater** in South Beach (1040 Lincoln Road, at Lenox Avenue; 674 1026), with seating for 465 and good sightlines from any seat in the house. The **Gusman Center for the Performing Arts** in Downtown (174 E Flagler Street, at NE Second Avenue; 372 0925), a wonderfully ornate 1926 landmark, seats 1,700 and offers excellent acoustics for theatre, music, film and dance; Mark

Morris performed there recently. Local companies also mount shows at the **Louise O Gerrits Theater** at the New World School of the Arts in Downtown (25 NE Second Street, between N Miami & NE First Avenues; 237 3541).

Modern

Freddick Bratcher & Company
Information 448 2021. **Tickets** $18.50; $10 students, senior citizens. **Credit** Ticketmaster only.
Choreographer/dancer Bratcher toured with the Alvin Ailey and Martha Graham companies before bringing his dynamic Ailey-esque interpretations of jazz and modern dance to Miami in 1976. In 1980 he founded his own dance ensemble, whose 10 members reflect the multi-ethnic makeup of the region. The troupe's energetic, theatrical, often whimsical and diverse repertoire includes dances set to songs by Nina Simone, blues by Mose Allison and compositions by Bach. Always popular is *DeGhettoized Boho Hip Hop*, set to a blend of rappings by Kool G Raps and the pop musings of Harry Nilsson. Committed to bringing dance to inner-city kids, the company also performs and leads workshops in schools and youth centres.

Houlihan & Dancers
Information 531 3260. **Tickets** $12; $7 students, senior citizens. **Credit** AmEx, MC, V.
Gerri Houlihan, a graduate of the Julliard School and the Lar Lubavitch troupe, founded this company in 1991. Marked by a blend of athleticism and lyricism and set to scores ranging from Bach and Mendelssohn to all percussion, her original choreography walks the line between traditional and contemporary. The company's six dancers perform in Miami in autumn and spring, touring for much of the rest of the year.

Karen Peterson & Dancers Inc
Information 378 6626. **Tickets** $8-$15; $2 discount disabled, students, senior citizens. **No credit cards.**
Self-proclaimed as Florida's 'mixed-ability' dance company, this unique troupe features three able-bodied dancers and four disabled dancers in manual and electric wheelchairs. Under the guidance of Karen Peterson, who founded the company in 1990, dancers share in the composition of works which explore the dimensions of being disabled through modern dance structures. The 1997-98 season includes collaboratively created pieces to music by Bach, Meredith Monk and percussionist Gabrielle Roth, as well as a number called *Beyond Words* in which personal stories and text combine with movements to honestly examine the experience of being physically challenged. The company also offers classes.

Mary Street Dance Theatre
Information 573 7376. **Tickets** $10; $8 students, senior citizens. **No credit cards.**
Founded in 1985 by Miami-based choreographer and dancer Dale Andree, this company has become a mainstay of the city's modern dance scene. Along with extensive community outreach – performing and teaching at hospitals, community centres, correctional institutes and schools – the troupe performs on local stages. Recently, Andree has moved from conventional choreography, in which every movement in a piece is plotted before a dancer interprets it on stage, to creating improvisational work before a live audience – a risky but ultimately rewarding change that infuses performances with an exciting and unpredictable energy.

Momentum Dance Company
Information 858 7002. **Tickets** $15-$25; $7 students, senior citizens. **Credit** MC, V.
A 15-year-old company directed by Delma Iles featuring an extensive programme of performances for adults and children throughout the year in Miami. The troupe has premiered over 60 new works, primarily by Florida choreographers, as well as offering selections by modern dance pioneers such as Doris Humphreys, Isadora Duncan, Eleanor King and Anna Sokolow. The company often collaborates on projects with artists in other disciplines, including poets, fashion designers, architects, photographers and visual artists and has commissioned scores by contemporary composers.

World dance

Ballet Flamenco La Rosa Company
555 17th Street, at Pennsylvania Avenue, South Beach (672 0552). Bus C, G, K, L, S. **Tickets** $15-$25. **No credit cards.**
A professional flamenco dance company performing traditional and contemporary flamenco works to live music in a theatre setting. Founded by Ilisa Rosal, Ballet Flamenco has earned a reputation for melding flamenco with other styles of music and dance such as Middle Eastern, Afro-Cuban, Indian, jazz, blues and tap. The troupe's repertoire ranges from a complete dramatic flamenco work called *The Trojan Women* to a dialogue between tap and flamenco entitled *Ritmo Azul* to a collaboration between flamenco, Celtic, African, North African and Middle Eastern styles of dance set to a composition by world music artist Loreena McKennit. Rosal and company also offer daily classes in all styles of dance, music and theatre.

Dance series & festivals

Write to or telephone the organisations below for more details.

Community Concert Series
1688 Meridian Avenue, Suite 1001, Miami Beach, FL 33139 (538 2121). **Tickets** free-$40. **Credit** AmEx, MC, V.
A popular local concert series (Sept-May) presenting national and local music, Community Concerts also sponsors local dance troupes, as well as bringing in outside artists such as Menaka Thakker, a classical Indian dance and music troupe.

Cultura del Lobo
Miami-Dade Community College, Wolfson Campus, Suite 1410, 300 NE Second Avenue, Miami, FL 33132 (237 3010). **Tickets** $10-$50. **Credit** AmEx, MC, V.
This varied year-round series with a multicultural slant presents music, dance, and visual art shows. Last year it hosted the exuberant Dance Africa Miami Festival featuring Urban Bush Women, Philadelphia choreographer Rennie Harris, Brazil's Ballé Folclórico and the Soweto Street Beat Dance Company.

Florida Dance Festival
Florida Dance Association, 300 NE Second Avenue, Miami, FL 33132 (237 3413). **Tickets** $10-$75. **Credit** AmEx, MC, V.
This 20-year old festival (originally based in Tallahassee and then in Tampa) makes a permanent move to Miami in June 1998. Nearly 300 classes, workshops, performances and special events celebrate dance as art and as a means of personal, political, religious and social expression. The 1998 festival runs 14-27 June. Venues vary, so call for details.

Miami Light Project
841 Lincoln Road, Miami Beach, FL 33139 (531 3747). **Tickets** $15-$20. **Credit** AmEx, MC, V.
Along with music and theatre (*see above* **Theatre series**), Miami Light brings choreographers and dance companies to town, such as the Brussels-based dance-theatre company Wim Vandekeybus; Dance Alloy, from Pittsburgh, along with performance artist Ann Carlson; and the New York choreographer Molissa Fenley.

Miami in Focus

Gay & Lesbian

Miami's queer community may be less politicised than elsewhere but there is no lack of gay goings-on, notably in the pink-tinged world of South Beach.

Gay Miami makes no apologies for living up to its reputation as a place of hedonistic excess. The well-earned stereotype has the scene divided between pumped muscle boys and Latin men with well-oiled hips. While gays in Miami come in all shapes and sizes and have interests beyond the gym and salsa dancing, the city does lack the kind of queer diversity found in New York or San Francisco. In a place of warm breezes and salutary nights, activism usually translates into dancing in the streets at one of the many AIDS fundraisers throughout the year. Likewise, the women's community is less visible than in other big cities. A primary reason is that many Latina lesbians still live at home or keep close relations with their families. While the boys start the night with a bar crawl, the girls may be enjoying a barbecue organised by a local gay church. Miami being such an outdoor city, gay sporting and camping groups are popular with both men and women.

South Beach is the scene-stealer when it comes to bars and clubs. Lincoln Road is probably the gay-friendliest area in town, where you can walk hand-in-hand without encountering nasty stares. Miami's Latin community may be outwardly conservative, but many families have an uncle or aunt who is gay and elaborate Latin drag shows draw a good-sized straight crowd.

Resources

Tourist information on gay and lesbian Miami, particularly South Beach, is available from the **South Beach Business Guild** (534 3336/1-888 893 5595). The Guild, which serves as the local gay chamber of commerce, holds general meetings that are open to the public and a good place to meet local gay and lesbian business professionals. Meetings are held at 10am on the last Thursday of the month at Tita's Restaurant, 1445 Pennsylvania Avenue, at Espanola Way, South Beach.

For general information on organisations serving the gay community, call **Switchboard of Miami** (358 4357). **Project YES** (663 7195) co-ordinates services and social groups serving gay youth. **Gay Alcohol Anonymous** (573 9608) meetings are held at the Lambda clubhouse, 410 NE 22nd Street (between NE Fourth & Fifth Avenues) in Miami. The **Dade Human Rights Foundation** publishes a monthly gay community calendar and resource guide; call Dennis Leyva on 673 7000 ext 6127 for a copy. *Out Pages*, the Florida gay community's telephone book, has a website with listings at http://www.outpages.com. A list of upcoming gay and lesbian events in Florida can be found at Destination Florida (the *Miami Herald*'s Florida travel website) on http://www.goflorida.com.

In 1992, the city of Miami Beach adopted a human rights ordinance that prohibits discrimination based on sexuality. Specific legal questions can be addressed by the **Gay and Lesbian Lawyers Association** (665 3886).

Newspapers & magazines

For what's happening in the bars and clubs, check out *Hot Spots*, *Scoop* and *Wire*, plus *The Contemporary Women* for events in the women's community. *TWN* is South Florida's (free) gay newspaper and *Fountain* is a lifestyle monthly. *Perra* covers the gay Latin scene. All are available from drop boxes and gay venues and bookstores. The Out & Around column in the Neighbors section of the Sunday *Miami Herald* focuses on gay life in South Florida.

HIV & AIDS

New studies indicate that HIV transmission in Miami is still at epidemic proportions. The combination of a sexy, tropical atmosphere with easy access to drugs and millions of holidaymakers looking for a good time has constantly stymied AIDS-prevention efforts. For specific information on HIV and AIDS, call **Health Crisis Network** at 751 7751. The **Body Positive Resource Center** (175 NE 36th Street, between North Miami Avenue and Biscayne Boulevard, near the Design District; 576 1111) offers workshops, a gym and art centre for people with AIDS. The **People With AIDS Coalition** (573 6010) can help with issues of discrimination.

Accommodation

No need to be nervous about approaching the reception desk of virtually any hotel in Miami Beach with your boyfriend or girlfriend and asking for a queen-sized bed. The local tourism commission actively courts gay tourists, and hoteliers have developed a taste for the queer dollar. Rooms are often booked months in advance for busy winter weekends and during holidays the normal rates are often jacked up. Gay-specific lodgings include:

Colours – The Mantell Guest Inn

255 W 24th Street, at Collins Avenue, Miami Beach, FL 33140 (reservations & front desk 531 3601/fax 532 0362). Bus C, F/M, G, H, L. **Rates** single; $89 double; $149 suite. **Credit** AmEx, MC, V.
This hotel on the northern edge of South Beach offers small, plain rooms, but a nice pool area and knowledgeable staff.

European Guest House

721 Michigan Avenue, between Seventh & Eighth Streets, South Beach, FL 33139 (reservations & front desk 673 6665/fax 672 7442). **Rates** single or double $59-$69 with shared bathroom; $70-$89 with private bathroom. **Credit** AmEx, Disc, MC, V.

*Have an unforgettable night at **Amnesia**.*

Well-promoted abroad in gay publications, the Guest House is unfortunately not one of the better examples of that 'gay touch' when it comes to appealing décor and basic tidiness, but it is inexpensive.

The Island House

715 82nd Street, between Harding & Collins Avenues, North Beach, FL 33154 (reservations 1-800 382 2422/front desk 864 2422/fax 865 2220). Bus G, H, S, T. **Rates** *$69 single; $79-$99 double with fridge; $129*
suite with kitchenette and bar. **Credit** AmEx, Disc, MC, V.
This men-only guest house is a little way from the South Beach action, but then it's closer to the nude beach at Haulover Park. Rooms are unremarkable, but clean. There is a Jacuzzi and clothing-optional patio.
Branch: 1428 Collins Avenue, South Beach (864 2422).

The Jefferson House

1018 Jefferson Avenue, between 10th & 11th Streets, South Beach, FL 33139 (reservations & front desk 534 5247/fax 534 5953). Bus C, H, K, W. **Rates** *$95 single, double; $150 suite.* **Credit** AmEx, MC, V.
Comfortable, friendly and on a quiet residential block, the Jefferson is often booked in advance by return visitors. Sun deck and dipping-pool.

South Florida Hotel Network

1688 Meridian Avenue, at 17th Street, South Beach, FL 33139 (538 3616/fax 538 5858). Bus C, G, K, L, S. **Open** *9am-6pm Mon-Fri; 9am-3pm Sat.*
This gay-owned reservation service is a good one-stop call to find lodgings and the lowdown on local events.

Bars & clubs

Miami gay clubs are long on hi-energy music and high-gear cruising, but short on the kind of creative environments and outrageous fashions typical of London or New York. Things are simpler here and a lot more primeval. Jeans, tank-tops and cocky smile are all the attire you'll need for the bars, while in the big South Beach dance clubs the look of choice is no shirt and the loopy smile of club-drug bliss. Latin nights at clubs are a bit dressier (not only will men actually keep their shirts on, there may even be collars on them). There are no women-specific venues in Miami, but there are women's nights and a handful of bars are women-friendly. There are also a number of once-a-week gay nights which move venues every few months. Check local publications such as *Wire* for listings. *See also chapter* **Clubs**.

South Beach

Amnesia

136 Collins Avenue, at First Street, South Beach (531 5535). Bus H, W. **Open** *11pm-5am Thur-Sat; 5pm-2am Sun.* **Admission** *$10 Thur-Sat; $5 Sun.*
Sunday tea dances, with the action unfolding right under the stars in this open-air club, are a South Beach must. The amphitheatre setting, with seating cascading up around the dancefloor, affords a great way to take in the scene and de rigueur drag show.

821

821 Lincoln Road, between Jefferson & Meridian Avenues, South Beach (534 5535). Bus C, H, K, W. **Open** *5pm-3am daily.*
A mixed bar, but heavily gay and lesbian, with stylish décor and changing art shows. It's right in the thick of the action on Lincoln Road so not surprisingly it gets pretty busy. The background dance music tends to jar the smooth martinis. Thursday is Ladies Night.

Circuit central

Miami didn't invent the circuit party – a travelling dance event of muscle, music and club drugs – but it did take these once largely underground gay raves and put them squarely on the map of queer recreational geography. The **White Party** and **Winter Party** are Miami's big annual circuit events, but virtually any weekend at South Beach clubs serves as a circuit training ground. And the SoBe party-boy has become the universal symbol of the 'no pecs, no sex' crowd of hyper-masculinity; looking like Tarzan, walking like Jane – and reputed to talk like Cheetah.

Circuit parties are almost always organised as AIDS fundraisers, and the events themselves are very much a psychological reaction to the horrors of AIDS. As men wasted away and died left and right, survivors pumped their bodies and took to the dancefloors, hell-bent on celebrating life and reclaiming sex as something to be enjoyed, rather than feared. Many regulars speak of an incredible bonding with their fellow man, a sentiment which may not always come from the bottom of the heart, but is certainly made all the easier to accept when you are lost in a sea of 3000 gyrating men.

Like any subculture, circuit parties have developed their own language and rituals. You may want to go up and 'dock' (dance together) with a guy in a very 'cunti' (hot-looking) pair of shorts, who may well offer you a 'bump' (hit) of 'K' (ketamine, a popular drug), which could land you in a 'K-hole' (a state of near-suspended animation owing to ketamine being an animal tranquiliser). Glucose helps prevent slipping into K-holes, hence all those boys dancing with lollipops in their mouths. Circuit Noize, 'a rag custom-designed for crazed party boys', has a website at http://www. circuitnoize.com.

For more information on the White Party (always held on the last Sunday in November) and White Party week events, call **Health Crisis Network** at 751 7775. For Winter Party information (held in March), call **Advance Damron Vacations** (1-800 695 0880).

Hombre

925 Washington Avenue, between Ninth & 10th Streets, South Beach (538 7883). Bus C, H, K, W. **Open** 8am-5am daily.

When it's late at night and the head you're thinking with doesn't rest on your shoulders, this long-time South Beach bar is the place to find others who think like you do.

Loading Zone

1426A Alton Road, between 14th Street & 14th Court, behind Domino's and Subway, South Beach (531 5623). Bus K, S, W. **Open** 7pm-5am daily.

This is about as raw and industrial-looking a club as SoBe offers, plus the added touch of leather. Very cruisey and refreshing after one too many sneers by stuck-up pretty boys in other clubs.

Liquid

1439 Washington Avenue, at Espanola Way, South Beach (532 9154). Bus C, H, K, W. **Open** 11pm-5am Mon, Fri-Sun. **Admission** $10.

Have a sugar daddy and don't have to get up to go to work tomorrow morning? Then join the other hardcore and hard-muscled party-boys who crowd the dancefloor till way past bedtime. Dance-music gods Junior Vasquez and Todd Terry make this their Miami home.

Pump at Zen

1203 Washington Avenue, at 12th Street, South Beach (673 2817). Bus C, H, K, W. **Open** 10am-5pm Fri. **Admission** $10.

Friday night, hi-energy dance party with the big boys.

Rex

409 Espanola Way, between Washington & Drexel Avenues, South Beach (534 0061). Bus C, H, K, W. **Open** 10pm-5am daily.

A new dance-bar for mingling and meeting.

Salvation

1775 West Avenue, between Alton Road & Dade Boulevard, South Beach (673 6508). Bus K, S, W. **Open** 10pm-5am Fri-Sun. **Admission** $12-$15.

It's 3am on a Saturday night and you can taste the steroids, the testosterone and endorphins in the air as a thousand-plus muscle boys groove shirtless to very deep dance tracks. PECtacular.

Twist

1057 Washington Avenue, between 10th & 11th Streets, South Beach (538 9478). Bus C, H, K, W. **Open** 1pm-5am daily.

Two-level bar with an outdoor patio on the second floor, a small dancefloor and a pool table. Everyone starts their evening here and many stay late, finding it a good alternative to the packed and pricey clubs.

Venus Envy

1427 West Avenue, between 14th Street & 14th Court, South Beach (673 1717). Bus K, S, W. **Open** 10pm-4am Sat. **Admission** $7.

Mermaids, glamour gals and their pals frolic every Saturday night at the Venus Envy parties at Starfish. Mary D, who promotes the popular Thursday night for women at the 821 bar (*see above*), has resurrected the Starfish restaurant as an elegant place for the ladies to play. Intimate cocktails (9-11pm), followed by dance music until late.

Warsaw

1450 Collins Avenue, at Espanola Way, South Beach (531 4555). Bus C, G, H, K, W. **Open** 9pm-5am Wed-Sat. **Admission** $5 after 11.30pm Wed-Fri.

*A diverse crowd tests the water at **Splash**.*

Nearly a decade ago, Warsaw put gay South Beach on the map, and it certainly isn't coasting on its reputation . From foam parties to go-go boys and duelling drag queens, Warsaw has never let the crowd down and the good-sized dancefloor remains packed.

West End

942 Lincoln Road, at Michigan Avenue, South Beach (538 9378). Bus C, H, K, W. **Open** noon-5am daily.
South Beach's one true unpretentious gay bar, with pool table and cheap drinks. Locals tend to stop in after work, and some never seem to leave. Girls often rule the pool table.

Sunny Isles

Boardwalk

17008 Collins Avenue, at 170th Street, Sunny Isles (949 4119). Bus E, K, S, V. **Open** 6am-5am daily; strip shows 10pm-4.30am.
Miami's premier strip bar, where the boys hail from Brazil, the Dominican Republic and many far-off ports. The atmosphere is a tad sleazy, and the crowd a good deal less pretty than the performers. **Park Place** next door (17032 Collins Avenue; 949 4112; open 3pm-6am daily) is a bit more peppy, with cute bartenders and dance music.

The Mainland

Eagle

1252 Coral Way (SW 22nd Street), between SW 12th & 13th Avenues, near Coral Gables, Miami (860 0056). Bus 12, 17, 24. **Open** 8pm-3am Mon-Thur, Sun; 8pm-4am Fri, Sat.
For those who insist on leather in Miami's tropical heat, this is the town's only serious leather-Levi venue.

Whittall & Shon: the best gear, hands down.

On the Waterfront

3615 NW S River Drive, at NW 36th Street, Northwest Dade (635 5500). Bus 32, 36, J. **Open** Thur, Sat; times vary. **Admission** free.
Take a deep breath and be brave: this bar on the seedy Miami River is worth the adventure of getting there. Gay and lesbian Latin couples crowd the dancefloor as the music switches back and forth from Latin to Top 40 pop tunes. If you don't know the steps, the grand ladies of Latin drag are there to show you how it's done.

Ozone

6620 Red Road (SW 57th Avenue), one block off US 1, South Miami (667 2888). Bus 48, 52, 72/Metrorail South Miami. **Open** 9pm-5am daily. **Admission** women $5-$10 daily; men $5 Fri-Sun.
Large South Miami club notable for its bustling Sunday Latin night with drag divas and machismo in ample supply.

Splash

5922 S Dixie Highway, at Sunset Drive, South Miami (662 8779). Bus 37, 57, 72/Metrorail South Miami. **Open** 4pm-3am Mon-Thur; 4pm-5am Fri, Sat. **Admission** $3-$5.
Friendly dance club not far from the University of Miami, often featuring dancers, performers and theme nights popular with a diverse crowd. On Fridays, the club hosts Miami's most popular evening for women, 'Girls in the Night'.

Restaurants & cafés

With so many gay patrons and waiting staff, virtually every restaurant in South Beach qualifies as a 'gay' restaurant. Here are some of the particularly 'family'-friendly ones, to be joined by the time this guide is out by a branch of Balans, a London hotspot, at 1024 Lincoln Avenue.

Hollywood Juice Bar

704 Lincoln Road, between Euclid & Meridian Avenues, South Beach (538 8988). Bus C, G, K, L, S. **Open** noon-9pm Mon-Thur, Sun; noon-10pm Fri, Sat.
Need a strawberry, banana and apple juice smoothie or a protein powder and wheat-grass juice concoction? Bladers with gym bags zip in for the juices and healthy snacks.

Jeffrey's

1629 Michigan Avenue, at Lincoln Road, South Beach (673 0690). Bus C, H, K, W. **Open** 6-11pm Tue-Sat; 5-10pm Sun.
This romantic bistro was made for hand-holding and kissing over candles. Prices are moderate to expensive.

Lucky Cheng's

600 Lincoln Road, at Pennsylvania Avenue, South Beach (672 1505). Bus C, H, K, W. **Open** 10am-5pm, 7-11pm Mon-Thur, Sun; 10am-5pm, 7pm-midnight, Fri, Sat.
Is that a false eyelash in my lo mein? Could be, at this Asian cuisine restaurant (recently relocated to larger premises) with drag waitresses who perform during dinner. Often the crowd is made up of straight tourists come to gawk – but call to find out about special drag shows. Inexpensive to moderate.

The Palace

1200 Ocean Drive, at 12th Street, South Beach (531 9077). Bus C, H, K, W. **Open** 9am-midnight Mon-Thur, Sun; 9am-1am Fri, Sat.
Right on Ocean Drive across from the entrance to the gay beach, they could serve sawdust here and the place would still be packed with those taking in the view of naked torsos. The salads and sandwich fare is good, the bar a popular hangout and the music a redux of last night at the clubs.

The orange juice lady

If the Miami lesbian and gay community may seem a bit superficial and disorganised, consider that it is amazing gays can even show their face in Dade County. In 1977, Anita Bryant, a one-time beauty queen, singer of saccharine inspirational ballads and spokesperson for the Florida Citrus Commission, led a heated battle against gay rights in Miami. The riots at Stonewall in New York may have birthed the gay and lesbian civil rights movement, but it was the battle in Miami that brought the issue of homosexuality before more people around the globe than ever before.

The faithful took it as a sign from God that, within hours of the Dade County Commission passing an ordinance protecting against discrimination based on sexuality, it snowed for the first time in Miami. Bryant set out to reclaim Dade County for god-fearing Christians. Very cleverly, she and her handlers focused their campaign not against homosexuality per se, but on saving children from recruitment by homosexuals. In their view, if teachers could not be fired for being gay, then Miami's children would not be safe from indoctrination into becoming homosexual. Bryant and her efforts were widely criticised by prominent figures and media across the US, Europe and Australia. And across the globe, gays and lesbians used their opposition to Bryant's campaign as a rallying point to organise their own communities. If only that had been true in Miami itself, where the gay community ended up fighting internally about how best to confront Bryant.

On 7 June 1977, Dade County voters overwhelmingly chose to overturn the county

ordinance and roll back protection for gays and lesbians. Bryant did not even bother to hold a victory party, saying that she was instead at home with her family, like any good wife. Twenty years later, Bryant is long gone from Miami, now performing in regional theatres throughout the South. Dade County still does not have a law protecting gays and lesbians from discrimination, but local gay leaders admit they have their eye on the prize and are getting ready to test the waters again.

Shopping

GW 'The Gay Emporium'
720 Lincoln Road, between Euclid & Meridian Avenues, South Beach (534 4763). Bus C, H, K, W. **Open** 11am-10pm Mon-Thur; 11am-11pm Fri, Sat.
The Beach's main gay bookstore, with a good selection of gay and lesbian fiction, magazines, condoms, lube and leather accessories. The eye-catching, safer-sex artworks, by Lazaro Armaral, change monthly.

Il Libra
637 Lincoln Road, at Pennsylvania Avenue, South Beach (531 1884). Bus C, H, K, W. **Open** 11am-9pm daily.
If it's skimpy, tight or just too cute, it's here: from clubwear to sleepwear and underwear. Shares premises with Liberty House, which offers fashion for men and women.

Whittall & Shon of Miami
1319 Washington Avenue, between 13th & 14th Streets, South Beach (538 2606). Bus C, H, K, W. **Open** 11am-10pm Mon-Thur; 9am-11.30pm Fri, Sat; 11am-9.30pm Sun.

Even big boys need to don feathers and beads sometimes. Tight muscle T-shirts share the limelight here with a wall of hats that just scream fabulous.

Gyms & baths

What churches are to Rome, gyms are to South Beach. Working out is religion in a city where no-one seems to own a shirt. Many offer daily and weekly memberships. Here are the gay faves.

Club Body Tech
1253 Washington Avenue, between 12th & 13th Streets, South Beach (674 8222). Bus C, H, K, W. **Open** 6am-10.30pm Mon-Fri; 8am-9pm Sat; 9am-8pm Sun. **Day membership** $14.
Even Adonis would find himself feeling a bit self-conscious toning up here, with supermodels and the most genetically gifted people on earth blasting their abs. Still, this is one of Miami's best-equipped gyms and the staff are helpful.

Club Body Center

2991 Coral Way, between SW 27th & 32th Avenues,
near Coral Gables (448 2214).
The Sunday poolside barbecues here are quite a bit different than those held up the road at nearby churches. Themed body contests include the ever-popular 'Mr Third World Miami'. There's a gym, but that's not why you came. Call for opening times.

The David Barton Gym

Delano Hotel, 1685 Collins Avenue, between 16th & 17th
Streets, South Beach (674 5757). Bus C, G, H, L. **Open**
6am-midnight Mon-Fri; 8am-9pm Sat, Sun. **Day**
membership $20; $15 if staying in the Delano or nearby hotels.
Related to the trendy gyms of the same name in New York. Celebs staying in the Delano often put in an appearance.

Gridiron

1676 Alton Road, between Lincoln Road & 17th Street,
South Beach (531 4743). Bus K, S, W. **Open** 5.30am-
11pm Mon-Fri; 8am-8pm Sat; 8am-6pm Sun. **Day**
membership $9.
Probably the most popular gym with locals, there's a decent camaraderie here; even if it's just to disguise the pre-bar cruising happening at the weight stacks.

Idols Gym

1000 Lincoln Road, at Michigan Avenue, South Beach
(532 0089). Bus K, S, W. **Open** 24 hours Mon-Sat; 10am-
7pm Sun. **Day membership** $10.
This is where the big boys – and we mean BIG – come to grunt and groan as they bench press weights equal to small Japanese cars. On Saturday nights, there's a DJ and anyone can work out for $5.

Outdoor activities

Beaches

South Beach's **12th Street Beach** is where the beef comes to grill. Strutting and gossiping goes on all day every day between the towels and the beach chairs (which are available for rent). Even some of the lifeguards, both male and female, get in on the act. Nude sunning and swimming are permitted at the northern end of Miami Beach at **Haulover Park**; the gay section of the nude beach is to the north of the lifeguard tower. The best place to park is in the second parking lot heading north on Collins Avenue.

Cruising areas

Those who like their sexual encounters al fresco will find Miami a mixed blessing. On one hand, the city's sultry flavour will have your gay-dar going off in supermarket aisles and shopping malls. On the other, cruising in parks has become a risky endeavour. Many once-popular cruising grounds have been fenced off. **Flamingo Park**, in the middle of South Beach, is still ground-zero for nocturnal naughtiness, with the handball courts doubling as a backroom, but police patrols have been stepped up and arrests are common. Likewise, the nearby alleys are also under police surveillance. Less risky is seeing who is taking in the night air

along the beach between **19th** and **23rd Streets**. The gay beach at Haulover Park should be avoided at night due to gang activity.

Sports

Besides a car, the other four wheels everyone in South Florida seems to have are inline skates. Even more than pumping iron, blading along Ocean Drive and Lincoln Road is a must of gay life. Many of the South Beach skate shops (*see chapter* **Sport**) offer classes and there will more than likely be a few fellow queer novices to crash into, so don't worry if your technique is lacking. The **Southeastern Great Outdoors Association** (667 2222) puts together gay and lesbian camping trips, clothing-optional sails and bike rides in the Everglades and local parks. The **Sunshine Athletic Association** (1-954 776 2322) organises gay and lesbian tennis matches, bowling, sailing and other sporting opportunities.

Esther Williams and Mark Spitz wannbes can join the gay swimming club for a workout on weekday evenings; call 534 9428 for details of times and locations. Gay volleyball games get underway at 5pm at the 12th Street beach. Look out for the nets strung between pink poles with rainbow colours. Women's softball games are played most Sundays in Flamingo Park; call Yvonne on 538 3861 for further information.

Religion

Three gay Metropolitan Community Churches serve Miami:
South Beach MCC *2100 Washington Avenue, at 21st*
Street, South Beach (532 2287).
Christ Church MCC *7701 SW 76th Avenue, off*
Sunset Drive, South Miami (284 1040).
Grace Church MCC *10390 NE Second Avenue, at NE*
103rd Street, Miami Shores (758 6822).

South Florida's gay synagogue, **Congregation Etz Chaim** (1-954 714 9232), is located in Fort Lauderdale, but at times offers services in South Beach. **Holy Wisdom Interfaith Community** at 4639 SW 75th Avenue, south of Bird Road/SW 40th Street, South Miami (264 5777) offers a variety of religious services and programmes. Call each congregation for service times.

Intellectual pursuits

Books & Books, in Miami Beach and Coral Gables, host a monthly gay and lesbian reading group; call 442 4408 for details. Community issues are discussed on the second Monday of the month (7-9pm) at **The Roundtable**; call Steve Baird at 372 2442 for location. The monthly **Lavender Salon** is a forum for exploring queer theory and issues, as well as hosting guest speakers; call 864 8888 for details on place, date and time.

Business

Whether you want just the fax or a full-blown video conference, here's all you need to know to do the business.

It's hard to believe that just over a century ago Miami's main industry was the milling of starch products from local roots. Today, it's often referred to as the Business Capital of the Americas, with international trade the city's bread and butter. Miami International Airport is the busiest international air cargo centre in the United States and the Port of Miami the most important shipping hub for the Caribbean and South America. Fresh flowers (nearly 100,000 boxes of them daily) make their way from South America to Europe and the rest of the world via Miami, while machine products and computer equipment from Asia are transferred from giant freighters onto smaller ships heading out to ports throughout the Americas.

Miami's growth into an economic powerhouse rests on the wide availability of trade services in the city: more international banks than any other US city other than New York and hundreds of freight brokers, shipping agents and lawyers specialising in international commerce. Among the fastest-growing local industries benefiting from the import-export boom are producers of medical equipment, pharmaceuticals, textiles and electronics. Seeking to capitalise on the fast-growing economies in Latin America, media giants ranging from MTV to Sony and Reuters have all set up Spanish-language broadcast ventures and marketing offices in Miami, making the city the new 'Hollywood of the Americas'.

When it comes to doing business, a few minor factors need to be remembered. As with the rest of the US, meetings are far more informal but in Miami and particularly on South Beach, extremely so. Also, remember that most dates are written out month, day, year so 2/8/98 refers to February, not August. If in doubt, check.

Information

Beacon Council
80 SW Eighth Street, Suite 2400, Miami, FL 33130 (579 1300/375 0271 fax).
The main organisation dedicated to attracting new business to Dade County.

Miami Beach Chamber of Commerce
1920 Meridian Avenue, Miami Beach, 33139 (672 1270).

Coconut Grove Chamber of Commerce
2820 McFarlane, Coconut Grove, FL 33133 (444 7270).

Coral Gables Chamber of Commerce
50 Aragon Avenue, Coral Gables, FL 33134 (446 1657).

Florida Gold Coast Chamber of Commerce
1100 Kane Concourse, Bay Harbor Islands, FL 33154 (866 6020).

Conventions

Not all of Miami's 12 million annual visitors head straight to the beach. Around three million have to attend conventions, meetings or seminars first. Conventions are big business in Miami and getting bigger. In 1985 there were 291 separate events which attracted more than 300,000 delegates. By 1995, there were 675 conventions pulling in almost a million visitors. Among the major events held in the area are Art Miami each January, attracting 10,000 international visitors; the South Florida Auto Show, which pulls in an incredible 300,000; and the Miami Boat Show in February, which, not surprisingly, attracts a mighty 350,000.

There are two main convention centres: the enormous **Miami Beach Convention Center**, which has a massive, million square feet of exhibition space, and the smaller **Coconut Grove Convention Centre**. When it comes to attending either, the closer you can stay, the more stress-free your life will be. The sad truth is that the convention centres are a little too large and a little too successful for their own infrastructure. For the major conventions, finding somewhere to stay can be a nightmare. The best advice is to book as early as possible. For Miami Beach Convention Centre, the best places to stay are any of the hotels between about 15th and 24th Streets, all of which are within walking distance. South or north of these, it makes more sense to take a cab – not necessarily either quick or easy in rush hour – though the new electric shuttle bus may facilitate more convenient commuting from points south. Some hotels will offer cheaper rates for particular conventions – ask. If you get caught out at short notice and find everything booked up, try the **Florida Hotel Network** (1-800 538 3616).

Miami Beach Convention Centre
1901 Convention Centre Drive, between 17th Street and Dade Boulevard, Miami Beach (673 7311/673 7435 fax). E-mail: http://ci.miami-beach.fl.us
This is one of the best designed convention centres in the US and can handle four major events or one mega meet at any one time. It takes up four blocks in Miami Beach's art deco district and is only minutes from the beach. The main halls are all on one level and are surrounded by 70 meeting rooms. Parking is difficult, with only 800 spaces, though a further 2000 can be found at the 17th Street Garage.

Coconut Grove Convention Centre
2700 Bayshore Drive, Coconut Grove (579 3310/579 3393 fax). E-mail: http://mailbox@miami.ci.@miami.fl.us
Renovated in 1989, this centre on the edge of Biscayne Bay is home to a variety of events: shows for antiques and jewellery, guns and knives, and boats; concerts and trade shows.

Import/export

Miami Free Trade Zone
2305 NW 107th Avenue, Northwest Miami (591 4300/591 1808 fax). **Open** 8.30am-5pm Mon-Fri. **Credit** varies depending upon vendor.
One of the largest duty-free trade centres in the US for international import-export, the center is open to anyone with a business card interested in buying wholesale products ranging from textiles to electronics.

Libraries

Metro-Dade County Public Library
101 W Flagler Street, at NW First Avenue, Downtown (375 2665). Bus 3, 16, 95, C, S/Metrorail Government Center. **Open** 9am-6pm Mon-Wed, Fri, Sat; 9am-9pm Thur.
As well as 1.5 million books and a team of helpful, knowledgeable staff, the main library has local and national newspapers on CD-ROM. You can print off selections for free. There are also computer links to the Internet and community and business services. The Miami Beach regional branch, at 2100 Collins Avenue (535 4219), has fewer books but the same business facilities.

Publications

Besides the main newspaper, the *Miami Herald*, there is also the *Daily Business Review*, which, though sometimes seeming a little biased towards financial markets, gives thorough coverage of everything you need to know to be successful in Miami. The free weekly *Miami Today* is rated as one of the best business newspapers in the US. It profiles local business players, details their latest plans and has a handy calendar listing up-and-coming events.

Shops & services

Aircraft charter

Avior Aircraft Charters
12011 SW 144th Street, Homestead (255 0568).
On-demand charter service and tours of Florida, the Bahamas and the Caribbean. Avior has access to a range of aircraft from small propjets to longer-range models. Flights can go out 24 hours daily from any airport.

Miami Air International
5000 NW 36th Street, Suite 307 (871 3300).
Specialises in cruises, incentives and corporate travel. Its fleet includes Boeing 727s with a capacity of 173 passengers.

Cellular phones

Florida Cellular
20401 NW 2nd Avenue, Northwest Dade (655 1202). **Open** 10am-6pm Mon-Fri; 9am-5pm Sat. **Credit** M, V.
Sells a whole range of products.

Express Cellular Rentals
815 NW 37th Avenue, Northwest Miami (871 9430). **Open** 9.30am-6.30pm Mon-Fri. **Credit** AmEx, DC, Disc, M, V.
Daily, weekly or monthly rentals plus sales and servicing on most popular models of mobile phones.

Couriers

Courier services listed all go worldwide. Addresses given are for the main office; staff will be able to inform you of your nearest drop-off point.

DHL
2176 NW 82nd Avenue, at NW 21st Street, Northwest Miami (471 0490). **Open** 8am-8pm Mon-Fri; 9am-4pm Sat. **Credit** AmEx, DC, Disc, M, V.
Ring for details and drop-off deadlines from this delivery company, which has a reputation for offering good rates.

Federal Express
2100 NW 82nd Avenue, at NW 21st Street, Northwest Miami (1-800 463 3339). **Open** 8am-7.15pm Mon-Fri; 8am-5pm Sat. **Credit** AmEx, DC, Disc, M, V.
Well represented in Miami with numerous offices and distribution centres across the city.

UPS
6001 E Eighth Avenue, Hialeah (1-800 742 5877). **Open** 8.30am-7pm Mon-Fri. **Credit** AmEx, M, V.
Account holders can phone any time during the business day for a pick-up; non-account holders must call a day in advance.

Computers

Compunet Inc
6600 NW 27 Avenue, Suite 207, Northwest Miami (693 5553). **Open** 8.30am-5pm Mon-Fri. **Credit** AmEx.
Sells, leases and services most major brands of computer, including laptops. Also offers a consulting service to help you get your machine to work in the US.

Micro Informatica Corp
99 SE Fifth Street, Downtown (418 3200). **Open** 9am-6pm Mon-Fri. **Credit** DC, M, V.
One of several branches of this chain in the Miami area. Sells most types of computer but only services its own models.

Executive car rental

Corporate Car USA
1995 NE 142nd Street, North Miami (949 8888). **Open** 24 hours daily. **Credit** AmEx, DC, M, V.
Offers executive sedans, limousines, vans, mini-buses, wheelchair-equipped vehicles and motorcoaches.

Interpreters & translators

Language Service Bureau
1000 Quayside Terrace, Tower 1, Suite 307, Miami (891 0019).
Can deal with most European languages or will be able to find someone who can help. The company works in a range of media and can provide support services.

Professional Translating Services
44 W Flagler Street, Suite 540, Downtown (371 7887).
Provides US court-certified translation of legal documents, books and manuals as well as court interpreting.

Legal & Technical Translations, Inc
7335 SW 130th Street, South Dade (252 0606).
Legal & Technical specialises in translations from Portuguese and Spanish. Services include US court-certified translations of contracts, books and technical manuals; consecutive and simultaneous translating; conference interpreting and tape transcription.

Message services

Ding a Ling Answering Service
1421 NE 163rd Street, North Miami Beach (940 1932). **Open** 8.30am-5pm. **Credit** AmEx, Disc, M, V.
Will take messages on your behalf 24 hours a day and can also assist you in setting up your own voicemail service.

Mail Boxes Etc

7930 NW 36th Street, Northwest Miami (591 1554).
Open 8am-7pm Mon-Fri; 9am-5pm Sat. **Credit** AmEx,
Disc, M, V.
There are several branches of this popular chain in Miami.
As well as the obvious service, the 'etc' refers to extras such
as packaging and shipping and mail forwarding.

Office equipment

Nemesio Office Equipment

2400 B NW 94th Avenue, Northwest Miami (471 4448).
Whatever item of equipment you forgot to bring with you,
you should be able to find it here.

Office services

Kinko's

*600 Brickell Avenue, at SE Sixth Street, Downtown (373
4910). Bus 6, 8, 24, 48, 95/Metromover Fifth Street.*
Open 24 hours daily. **Credit** AmEx, Disc, M, V.
Somewhat surprisingly, considering the huge number of
business visitors, office services are hard to find in Miami,
particularly on South Beach, where the hotels tend to monop-
olise (and overcharge) for all such services. However, all the
Miami branches of America's premier chain of copy shops
feature the usual helpful, friendly staff as well as on-site use
of computers, typesetting, printing, photocopying, fax and
phone facilities and courier services via Federal Express.

Words on the Beach

*1657 Drexel Avenue, between Lincoln Road and 17th
Street, Miami Beach (534 9673). Bus C, G, K, L, S.*
Open 9am-7pm Mon-Fri; noon-5pm Sat. **Credit** MC, V.
No Kinko's on the Beach, unfortunately: this is your best
alternative for printing, photocopying and word processing.

Office rental

International Corporate Park

1890 NW 107th Avenue, Northwest Miami (594 5900).
A 300-acre park, providing industrial warehouse space.
Rentals are available through an arrangement with Easton
Babcock real estate companies.

Secretarial services

Brickell Executive Colony

1110 Brickell Avenue, Suite 340, Downtown (358 3554).
This small but efficient and reliable chain will produce
perfect resumes, send faxes and carry out other secretarial
services for you.

Videoconferencing

Worldwide Videoconferencing

46 SW First Street, Suite 100, Downtown (373 9997).
Open 24 hours daily. **Credit** MC, V. **Rates** $400-$2,000
per hour.
Can link you up to other videoconferencing suites around the
world, allowing you to see as well as speak to those at the
other end of the line.

Women in business

The *Women's Business Journal*, held at most libraries and
free from the Barnes & Nobles at 18711 NE Biscayne
Boulevard, Aventura, and 152 Miracle Mile, Coral Gables,
features contacts and information about networking, business activities and courses. The Journal also publishes the
Let's Network guide to Women's Business Organisations in
South Florida. Credit card orders on 1-800 966 3336.

Women's Chamber of Commerce of Dade County

446 6660.
Promotes women-owned and women-run business throughout the area.

Getting online

If you have laptop and modem with you (or
plan to rent), you will want to be able to pick
up your e-mail while you're away. However,
prepare for headaches. Few of the UK
Internet service providers have local dial-ups
in the US (and those that do may make an
extra charge). Check with your provider
before you go. Online service providers, such
as **America Online** and **CompuServe**, are
more likely to have local access, but may
make a 'roaming' charge for use outside your
home country (see below for details). If you
do want to access the net in this way, you will
need to change the settings on your modem
to dial the new number.

The other way to pick up and send mail is
via POP3, offered by most (but not all) service providers. POP3 allows you to access
your home e-mail account from any net-connected terminal with e-mail software, such as
those at the Miami-Dade County Library (*see*
Libraries) or Virtua Café (*see chapter* **Bars**).
Ask your provider for more details.

If you're away for long enough, it may be
worth setting up your own US Internet
account. (You can then access your home
account via POP3.) Many companies offer
free month-long trial periods – check the computer press for current offers.

If you are dialling in from a hotel room,
bear in mind that extension lines out of digi-
tal switchboards won't carry the signal. You
will either need to ask nicely at the office if
they have a spare direct line you can borrow,
or to stay at a hotel that offers data ports.
Listings in our **Accommodation** chapter
pick out those that do. As top-end hotels, such
as the Marlin, become more aware of the
demand for net access, they are starting to
install net-connected terminals in rooms.

AOL dial-up 358 9147; support 1-703 448 8700;
roaming charge £4 per hour.
CompuServe dial-up 262 9325; support 1-614 718
2800; no roaming charge.
MSN dial-up 358 6951; customer service 1-813 557
0613; technical support 1-813 557 0613; roaming
charge $2.50 per hour.

Children

How to keep your children entertained when beach life palls.

For families travelling with children, the seemingly endless stretch of shoreline in South Florida serves as an inherently kid-friendly backyard where toddlers and teens can while away hours playing in the waves in the aquamarine ocean or dozing in the sun. Except that the sun is very strong and parents, despite abundant sunscreen and hats (which kids hate to wear anyway), may find they want alternative options, especially during the peak sun hours of 10am to 2pm. Besides, it occasionally does rain in Miami. But don't fret: the city and its environs offer family activities to spare. Many of the best are a drive away, so you should think about renting a car, if only for a day.

One of the best family-friendly beaches here is Crandon Park Beach on Key Biscayne; for details of this and other beaches and attractions, *see chapter* **Sightseeing**. For toyshops and kids' clothing stores, *see chapter* **Shopping & Services**.

INFORMATION

The larger (and usually more expensive) hotels provide babysitting services, day camps and activities in-house. If you're staying in a smaller place or want to get away from your lodgings for an afternoon, check the *Miami Herald*'s Weekend section in the Friday edition and *New Times* for weekly listings of children's events. If you plan an outdoor excursion, don't forget sunblock, hats, sunglasses and bottled water for the entire clan.

Babysitting

Nurse Finders
6175 NW 153rd Street, Miami Lakes (823 8448).
Open 8.30am-5.30pm Mon-Fri (answering service after hours).
In business for 20 years, this licensed and bonded agency has offices in major cities around the country. The Miami branch serves all the major hotels in Miami Beach, Coral Gables, Coconut Grove and Downtown and babysitters will also come to small hotels or private homes (they provide their own transportation). All babysitters have had criminal background checks and are trained in first-aid. On call 24 hours a day, the service's hourly charges are $14 for up to two children, $17 for three or four children and $19 for five or more children (4 hours minimum).

Accommodation

South Beach sports back-to-back hotels but partying in the streets can render early bedtime for kids obsolete. Further north in Miami Beach you can find more family-oriented though pricey lodgings, such as the glamorous Fontainebleau Hilton and Eden Roc. Hotels on streets in the 70s are quieter still and much less expensive, as are a string of hotels and motels in Surfside in the 80s and 90s; also in the 90s is the upscale Sheraton Bal Harbour, which is popular with well-to-do families. Further north lies Sunny Isles, lined with a range of accommodations from inexpensive motels to four-star resort hotels. You won't be in the heart of the South Beach action but you will be on the ocean and you can drive to SoBe in five to 40 minutes (depending on how far north you are). For detailed information on hotels, *see chapter* **Accommodation**.

Restaurants & cafés

Miami's warm weather and laid-back Latin American flavour exert an influence on family schedules. Parents, grandparents, aunts and uncles stay out until all hours with large broods of kids along Miami Beach's **Lincoln Road** and at Downtown's **Bayside Marketplace**, two outdoor enclaves of shops, galleries and restaurants that are off-limits to cars.

Stroll and people-watch along Lincoln Road after dusk, then sit down with the kids at **Da Leo's Pizza Via** (826 Lincoln Road, between Jefferson & Meridian Avenues; 530 0803), a casual spin-off of the restaurant's more elegant bistro across the road. The waiters are incredibly patient with infants and toddlers and an ample selection of small pizzas on the menu will satisfy the most distractable young appetite. Pasta dishes, daily specials, wine and beer are available for mom and dad.

Bayside's indoor food court, outdoor stalls selling fruit drinks and snacks, live bands and street performers will keep the kids fed and entertained. In South Beach, numerous outdoor cafés make eating out with kids fairly easy during the day but night-time dining on crowded, trendy Ocean Drive or in upscale restaurants on Washington Avenue can be trying, with nary a kid's menu in sight. A better bet is the Fontainebleau Hilton's **Trop-Art Café** (4441 Collins Avenue, between 44th & 45th Streets; 538 2000), which has a children's menu and crayons on every table, or the outdoor deck of **Jimmy Johnson's Bar & Grill** (4525 Collins Avenue, between 45th & 46th Streets; 672 6224), overlooking the Miami Beach boardwalk and the ocean, and serving kid-proof burgers and nachos.

*Learning indispensable adult skills at **Miami Youth Museum** (page 206).*

Recreation

The **Actors' Playhouse** in Coral Gables (280 Miracle Mile; 444 9293) runs a great children's theatre with shows on Saturday afternoons. **Shores Performing Arts Theatre** in Miami Shores (9806 NE Second Avenue; 751 0562) also offers shows for kids, as does **Momentum Dance Company** (3601 S Miami Avenue; 858 7002); for more details, *see chapter* **Theatre & Dance**.

For a truly star-studded show, join the **Southern Cross Astronomical Society** on Saturdays (usually 8-10pm) for star-gazing in Bill Sadowski Park, 17555 SW 79th Avenue, at SW 176th Street, in South Dade (255 4767).

Dade County Fair & Exposition

Tamiami Park, SW 24th Street & 112th Avenue, South Dade (223 7060). Bus 24, 71. **Open** 19 Mar-5 Apr 1998 3-11pm Mon-Fri; 10am-11pm Sat, Sun. **Tickets** $7 adults; $5 6-12s; free under-6s.

A Miami institution since 1950, the annual Dade County Fair lasts for 18 days in March and April. A 30-minute drive from Miami Beach, it used to be a traditional agricultural event with prizes for livestock and student craft and science projects, but now, in addition to the cows, goats, lambs, rabbits, chickens and guinea pigs, has expanded into a large amusement park with a vast array of rides. Very family-oriented, it also has seven venues for live entertainment including 9ft puppets, Disney character shows, magic acts and bands.

Lummus Park

10 Ocean Drive, between Fifth & 15th Streets, South Beach (673 7730). Bus C, G, H, K, W. **Open** 24 hours daily.

An open stretch of grass and a cement walkway, perfect for cycling, rollerblading, skateboarding and pushing strollers, located between the beach and the street, parallel to South Beach's café-ridden Ocean Drive. Playgrounds bookend either end of the park, a cement wall skirts the sand and benches pepper the area. Older kids can join volleyball games played on the beach. Check newspapers for music and dance performances or firework displays.

Miami Beach Public Library

2100 Collins Avenue, at 21st Street, South Beach (535 4219). Bus C, G, H, K, W. **Open** 10am-8pm Mon, Wed; 10am-5.30pm Tue, Thur-Sat.

The Miami Beach branch of Miami's extensive library system. Although the building is located on a rather rundown stretch of Collins Avenue, the children's room is spacious and features puzzles, boardgames, a menagerie of stuffed animals and videos and books for under-13s. Twenty-minute storytime sessions are held on Tuesdays at 10.30am and Wednesdays at 7pm (kids come in their pyjamas), and there is a maths and science workshop every Saturday at 10am. The Miami-Dade Public Library in the Metro-Dade Cultural Center (101 W Flagler Street, at NW First Avenue; 375 2665) in Downtown also has a good kids' section.

Scott Rakow Youth Center

2700 Sheridan Avenue, at Pine Tree Drive, Miami Beach (673 7767). Bus G, K. **Open** 11am-8pm Sun. **Admission** $3.

During the week this multipurpose facility acts as an after-school centre for local kids but Sunday is family day for tourists as well as natives. The centre has an ice-skating rink for kids aged nine and above (open 3-4.45pm, $1 for skate rental), a bowling alley (1-5pm, $1.25 shoe rental) and an outdoor swimming pool (1-5pm), plus pool and ping-pong.

South Pointe Park
1 Washington Avenue, between Ocean Drive & Second Street, South Beach (673 7224). Bus H, W. **Open** 5am-midnight daily.
The southernmost tip of South Beach offers a relaxing getaway from the frantic see-and-be-seen pace of the rest of SoBe. Located next to the beach, the park has an amphitheatre (check newspaper listings for free music and dance events), a large playground, picnic shelters, a fishing pier and fields for baseball, football and other activities.

Museums

Of the museums listed in our **Museums & Galleries** chapter, the **Miami Museum of Science & Space Transit Planetarium** is particularly good for kids. The Planetarium has daily star displays and laser music shows at weekends, and the observatory is open on Saturday evenings (8-10pm), weather permitting. The **Historical Museum of Southern Florida** is also fun.

Miami Youth Museum
Miracle Center, Level U, 3301 Coral Way, between SW 32nd & 34th Avenues, Miami (446 4386). Bus 24, 37. **Open** 10am-5pm Mon-Thur; 10am-9pm Fri; 11am-6pm Sat, Sun. **Admission** $4; free first Fri of the month 5-9pm. **Credit** MC, V.
Located in the corner of a multi-floored shopping mall, this hands-on fun centre with educational exhibits features a mini-supermarket complete with faux food that can be loaded into pint-sized shopping carts and checked through working, kid-sized cash registers. Other displays include a television studio where children can operate a technician's board or anchor the evening news, a police car, a fire engine and interactive art-making exhibits. The museum also holds arts and crafts workshops.

Museum of Discovery & Science
401 SW Second Street, at SW Fifth Avenue, Fort Lauderdale (1-954 467 6637). **Open** 10am-5pm Mon-Sat; noon-6pm Sun. **Admission** $6 adults; $5 senior citizens, 3-12s. *Combi ticket to museum & IMAX show* $12.50; $11.50 senior citizens; $10.50 3-12s. **Credit** AmEx, MC, V.
Make a day trip out of a visit to this stupendous science museum in Fort Lauderdale, a 45-to 60-minute drive north of Miami. Before or after getting your science fix, visit the neighbouring **Museum of Art** (1 E Las Olas Boulevard; 1-954 763 6464), stroll the nearby **Riverwalk** alongside the boat-lined New River and check out **Cheeseburger Cheeseburger** (708 E Las Olas Boulevard;1-954 524 8824).
At the science museum itself, a 52ft tall kinetic energy sculpture called the Great Gravity Clock dominates the courtyard entrance; kids will be so mesmerised it will be hard to get them inside. Once you do, they will be treated to permanent exhibits such as Choose Health, featuring hands-on displays about fitness, nutrition and personal health; Gizmo City, a 'metropolis' including virtual reality games, computer activities and manipulative displays from 'The Factory' to 'The Sports Complex'; and Florida Ecospaces, displaying live native animals and plants. There's also Space Base, which looks at space flight and exploration and has space travel simulations, and KidScience, an interactive educational play area for toddlers. Visiting exhibits have covered such subjects as the brain, music and extinct species. The state-of-the-art IMAX cinema screens 3-D films daily.

Flora & fauna

Some of Miami's main animal draws, all reliable diversions, are listed and reviewed in the **Sightseeing** chapter. They are the world-class **Metrozoo**, the can't-fail-with-kids **Seaquarium**, whose shark presentation goes down particularly well, and the **Parrot Jungle & Gardens**, where children can hand-feed the birds in the petting zoo.

Equestrian Center
Tropical Park, 7900 SW 40th Street, Bird Road & Palmetto Expressway, South Dade (554 7334/226 8315). Bus 40, 56, 87. **Open** 8am-4pm Sat, Sun.
Watch thoroughbreds, rodeo horses and quarter horses perform for free in weekend shows at Tropical Park, about five miles from Downtown Miami.

Simpson Park
55 SW 17th Road, off S Miami Avenue, Downtown (856 6801). Bus 24, 48, B. **Open** 8am-3.30pm Tue-Fri;10am-5.30pm Sat.
This historical park, one of South Florida's oldest and smallest (8.5 acres), is a haven full of wildlife: butterflies, raccoons, opossums, squirrels, lizards and frogs. Free nature and boat tours are given to local school children, but others may tag along, too.

Further afield

Biscayne National Underwater Park
9700 SW 328nd Street, at SW 97th Avenue, Homestead (230 7275/230 1100). No public transport. **Open** 8am-5.30pm daily. **Credit** AmEx, MC, V.
A trip to South Florida is not complete without a glimpse of the area's spectacular but sadly endangered coral reefs and marine wildlife. About 1½ hours south of Downtown Miami, this sprawling expanse of waterways and islands remains less frequented by visitors than many other parks, ensuring more private and unspoiled underwater adventures. Reservations are required for three-hour glass-bottom boat trips (10am daily; $19.95 adults; $17.95 senior citizens; $9.95 under-12s) and snorkelling (1.30pm daily; $27.95 for three hours). Certified divers can book on scuba diving trips (9am Wed; 8.30am Sat, Sun; $35 for four hours).

Butterfly World
Tradewinds Park South, 3600 W Sample Road, Coconut Creek (1-954 977 4400). **Open** 9am-5pm Mon-Sat; 1-5pm Sun; last admission 4pm. **Admission** $10.95 adults; $8.95 senior citizens; $6 4-12s. **Credit** AmEx, MC, V.
North and inland of Fort Lauderdale, off I-95, Butterfly World, as you might expect, has plenty of exotic butterflies, in a tropical rainforest setting, as well as a breeding laboratory, museum, insectarium and English rose garden.

Everglades National Park: Shark Valley
Tamiami Trail (US 41), 18 miles west of Krome Avenue, Ochopee (221 8455). No public transport. **Open** 8.30am-6pm daily. **Admission** $8 per vehicle. *Tram rides* $8 adults; $7.20 senior citizens; $4 under-12s. *Bicycle rentals* $3.25 per hour. **Credit** AmEx, Disc, MC, V.
Drive about an hour from Downtown Miami and you find yourself smack in the middle of Florida wilderness. The Shark Valley area offers tram tours through a 15-mile loop of sawgrass prairie, otherwise known as the Everglades. You can also walk or cycle the loop. Bring your own bikes or rent them; cycles with training wheels are available although you can request a kid's seat for a child weighing up to 40lb. There are plenty of short walking trails within half a mile of the visitor centre, and from a deck behind it you can observe wildlife, including alligators, wading birds and fish.

Miami Survival

Survival

All you need to know to avoid trouble in paradise.

Emergencies

Ambulance, fire brigade or police
911 (free from payphones)

Non-emergency police inquiry
595 6263

Coast Guard
Marine emergencies 535 4368/air emergency 536 5611

Crisis Counselling Service
358 4357
Trained volunteers are on hand 24 hours a day to help you through any kind of emotional crisis.

Locksmith
A Key To U *(628 3733/beeper 882 9402)*
This company has a 24-hour emergency call-out service for apartments, cars and commercial buildings. It can also repair most types of locks and cut new car keys.

Poison Hotline
1-800 282 3171
Staff can provide information on a wide range of poisons including medical overdoses and exposure to hazardous chemicals. Will refer patients to 911 if necessary.

Rape Hotline
585 7273
A confidential counselling and support service. Staff won't file a report to the police unless you ask them.

Suicide Hotline
358 4357
If you're depressed or suicidal call this number for confidential support and comfort.

Airlines

Air Jamaica 1-800 523 5585; **Aeromexico** 526 5880; **Air Canada** 1-800 776 3000; **Air France** 1-800 237 2747; **Alitalia** 1-800 223 5730; **American** 358 6800; **British Airways** 1-800 247 9297; **Delta** 448 7000; **Iberia** 1-800 772 4642; **KLM** 1-800 374 7747; **Laker Air** 1-800 269 1318 Laker Air (Miami departures); 1-954 202 0444 (Fort Lauderdale departures); 1-888 525 3724 (Orlando departures); **Northwest** 1-800 225 2525; **Swissair** 1-800 221 4750; **TWA** 1-800 892 4141; **United** 1-800 241 6522; **Virgin** 1-800 862 8621

Consumer

Better Business Bureau
625 0307/1-900 225 5222 premium rate recorded information line.
Information on all sorts of reliable businesses in your area; can also be used to file information on those which fail to come up to scratch.

Taxi Complaints Line
375 2460

Driving

All passengers must wear seatbelts, even when travelling in the back seat, or face fines of up to $150. Speed limits vary according to the type of road but are around 30mph in built-up areas. Occasionally, if you approach a school, for example, the limit will drop to as low as 15mph: keep a look out – fines are quite stiff. Driving while drunk (or under the influence of drugs) can result in a fine of up to $5,000 and a possible prison sentence. Not having your driving licence on you while driving is also an arrestable offence. Technically, you don't need an international driving licence, but some rental companies demand one and it can be useful as photo ID. For general driving info, *see* chapter **Essential Information**.

AAA Emergency Road Service
1-800 222 4357
Members receive free towing and roadside service, as do members of international affiliates such as the UK's AA, depending on the terms of their membership. Non-members can join over the phone but existing members have priority. There are offices throughout Florida (Miami's most central branch is at 4770 Biscayne Boulevard #850; 571 0360), which dispense maps and advice to members.

Road conditions hotline
470 5349

Parking

Trying to find somewhere to park in South Beach, particularly at weekends, is an absolute nightmare. The local joke is that the reason so many cars cruise the area is not to attract members of the opposite sex but because it's impossible to find anywhere to stop. It's probably a good excuse, since cruising along Ocean Drive is now illegal and the majority of the central parking bays are open to residents only or have been leased out by restaurants. There are **designated parking areas** off Collins Avenue at 15th and 16th Streets and at Lincoln Lane and Washington, close to the Convention Center, but both are a way from the main action. The further north you go, from 26th Street and above, the more free spaces you are likely to find. The main **parking lots** are on 13th Street between Collins and Ocean, on Seventh Street between Collins and Washington and on 12th Street between Drexel and Washington (in the police building).

If you decide to take a chance on street parking, remember that South Beach is notorious for having hordes of wardens. Depending on your budget, you may not be too worried if you receive a ticket. They cost $18 dollars if paid within 30 days but then rise to $45. If your rental car is ticketed, the company will chase you.

Clamping hasn't yet reached Florida but if you cause an obstruction, you'll be towed away. If your car goes missing on Miami Beach, call **Beach Towing** on 534 2128. If they don't have it, then try the police. In Downtown Miami, there are plenty of meters and plenty more high-rise parking garages, almost on every street corner, but they are expensive. You'll need bucket loads of quarters for both so it's worth remembering that a few of the major tourist attractions, such as the Metro-Dade Cultural Center, offer visitors heavily discounted parking.

When parking on the streets, particularly in central areas, you may be approached by vagrants asking for 'spare change' to 'watch over your car'. With break-ins and thefts from cars endemic, it may be a worthwhile investment. And if you do have spare change, don't leave it on the dashboard – it can take as little as that to encourage a thief to break in.

Foreign consulates

The countries listed below all have consulates in Miami and can help you if you lose your passport or suffer some other emergency. If your country isn't on this list, call directory information for Washington (1-202 555 1212) for the number of your consulate there.

Antigua & Barbuda 381 6762; **Argentina** 373 1889; **Austria** 325 1561; **Bahamas** 373 6295; **Barbados** 442 1994; **Belgium** 932 4263; **Belize** 751 5655; **Bolivia** 358 3450; **Brazil** 285 6200; **Canada** 579 1600; **Chile** 373 8623; **Colombia** 448 5558; **Costa Rica** 871 7485; **Denmark** 446 0020; **Dominican Republic** 358 3220; **Ecuado**r 539 8214; **El Salvador** 371 8850; **Finland** 871 8212; **France** 372 9798; **Germany** 358 0290; **Guatemala** 443 4828; **Haiti** 859 2003; **Honduras** 447 8927; **Hungary** 448 4989; **Israel** 358 8111; **Italy** 374 6322; **Jamaica** 374 8431; **Japan** 530 9090; **Korea** 372 1555; **Luxembourg** 373 1300; **Mexico** 716 4977; **Netherlands** 789 6646; **Nicaragua** 220 6900; **Norway** 358 4386; **Panama** 371 7031; **Paraguay** 374 9090; **Peru** 374 1305; **Portugal** 444 6311; **Senegal** 371 4286; **Spain** 446 5511; **Suriname** 593 2163; **Switzerland** 274 4210; **Taiwan** 443 8917; **Thailand** 445 7577; **Togo** 371 4286; **Tunisia** 576 5049; **Turkey** 371 4286; **United Kingdom** 374 1522; **Uruguay** 443 9764; **Venezuela** 577 3834.

Health & medical

Doctors

Dade County Medical Association
324 8717
Call for doctor referrals (9am-5pm Mon-Fri).

Hospitals

Be forewarned that in Miami, as in other parts of the US, you'll be charged a fortune for even the most basic medical care. Just a basic consultation with a doctor will cost you about $100. Having full insurance cover, preferably with a low excess, is the only way to feel at ease; keep the details with you and leave a copy with someone at home. If it's not an emergency, try one of the many walk-in clinics, which are cheaper, friendlier and more numerous than hospitals. They include the **Stanley C Myers Community Health Center** at 710 Alton Road (538 8835), a public clinic which charges you according to how much you earn. Others can be found in the local white pages. For full-blown emergencies, dial 911 or head for the nearest emergency room. The one at Mount Sinai Medical Centre in Miami Beach is considered the best but also charges the most.

Coral Gables Hospital
3100 Douglas Road, Coral Gables (445 8461).
Has a 24-hour emergency department and also a high-capacity outpatient unit with same day-surgery on offer. In some cases, free transport can be arranged.

Cedars Medical Center
1400 NW 12th Avenue, Downtown (325 5511).

Blown away

A dust storm swirls out of the Sahara Desert and begins a slow rotation west, gaining speed over the vast distance of the Altantic Ocean. East of the Lesser Antilles, it develops an eye, and is named by meteorologists. It grows more powerful. By the time it has passed through the slot between Cuba and the Bahamas it has developed into a storm whose winds and rain can be strong enough to scour the land of everything natural and man-made when it hits land. And the land it hits is Florida. The hurricane season runs from June to October and during the course of a year there may be as few as two or as many as 20 blowing in. However, dramatic though that might seem, there is little cause for concern for visitors. The majority blow themselves out or remain at sea rather than striking the mainland. Having been devastated several times in the past, Miami also has a sophisticated early warning system which ensures that when the 'big one' does arrive, it is unlikely to be a surprise. The National Hurricane Centre in Miami can give 24 hours warning of a possible hit, and public radio and most TV stations then give out the latest storm information and evacuation plans. Be prepared to evacuate your hotel, even if the weather does not appear threatening when the warning is issued.

Tornados, such as the one which hit Miami in spring 1997, are part of the same weather system, but despite their dramatic appearance, are considerably less destructive. They are also less predictable, so there will be no warning. Most of Miami's buildings are robust enough to suffer only minor damage, even if they are directly in a tornado's path, so staying inside is probably the safest thing to do. Alternatively, stay out (preferably within bolting distance) and enjoy one of nature's greatest free shows.

Hurricane warnings/weather updates
229 4522

Metro-Dade Stormwater Utility Flood Zone Hotline
372 6685

Flooding complaints
372 6688

Transport information
638 6700

Gator life

More than Mickey Mouse, the one critter truly associated with Florida is the alligator. About a million live in the fresh waters of the state, from canals to golf course ponds, dining on small to medium-sized mammals (deer included) and fish. There are approximately 11,000-13,000 complaints a year about too-close-for-comfort encounters filed by humans against their sharp-toothed neighbours. Only 18 or so involve attacks, though the number has been rising steadily since the 1980s. In March of 1997, an 11-foot, 450-pound gator attacked and killed a three-year-old boy wading in a pond in Volusia County, north of Orlando. The last previous attack was in 1993 when a gator broke the neck of a 70-year-old woman in Sumter County, between Orlando and Occala. In total, alligators, which are found abundantly in rural and urban waterways alike, have killed only eight people in Florida over the last 50 years. Florida's 21 licensed alligator trappers captured and killed 4,799 gators last year. Though they're not paid for their service, trappers are allowed to sell the animal's meat, teeth and hide – an adult gator can yield $400. Recreational and indiscriminate killing is prohibited, but alligators are commercially raised for their meat.

Though there's a healthy population of alligators in the Everglades, they are rather puny by gator standards. Researchers are worried that pollution and changes in water-flow patterns are taking their toll on the reptiles, whose weight is averaging less than 200 pounds. By contrast, in Central Florida gators can weigh almost three times as much. The largest specimen ever captured in the state came from the Panhandle and was a massive 14 feet long and 600 pounds heavy.

Alligators, while generally wary of humans, have grown less so as development has encroached on their habitat. Some think nothing of sunning themselves on the shoulder of the roads that cut across Florida's swampy interior,

such as the aptly named Alligator Alley (US 75). The best place to view alligators is from the walkways of the Everglades National Park, where again, having grown accustomed to humans, they often will bask in the sun at the edge of the paths. Depending on how brave you're feeling, it is possible to stand just a few feet away and snap a picture, but remember, an alligator can lunge about 30 feet in a matter of seconds. Be particularly careful in approaching cute alligator babies – momma gator may be lurking just behind some tall grass and will be very protective of her kin.

Has private rooms and an international centre specialising in dealing with foreign patients.

Health South Doctor's Hospital
5000 University Drive, Coral Gables (666 2111).
Three hundred or so beds, a 24-hour emergency department and a sports medicine and health and fitness institute.

Jackson Memorial Hospital
1611 NW 12th Avenue, Miami (585 1111/emergency room 585 6901).
The main county hospital.

Mount Sinai Medical Center
4300 Alton Road, Miami Beach (674 2121).
Well equipped and therefore expensive.

Children's Hospital
3100 SW 62nd Avenue, Southwest Miami (666 6511).
A specialist emergency room and good outpatient services.

The Women's Center
Boca Raton Community Hospital (1-561 362 5000).
Features a centre for breast examination and treatment of cancer as well as a range of other services.

Abortion/contraception/STDs

Planned Parenthood of Greater Miami
2900 Bridgeport Avenue, Coconut Grove (441 2022).
Care for men and women, including birth control supplies, counselling, testing and treatment for sexually transmitted diseases and pregnancy testing.

Women's Care
68A NE 167th Street, North Dade (947 0885).
Private clinic specialising in abortions and gynaecology.

Aids/HIV
See also chapter **Gay & Lesbian**.
Community Alliance Against AIDS *243 3852*
HIV/AIDS Hotline *751 7751*

Alcoholism
Alcoholics Anonymous *371 7784*
Alcohol Helpline *1-800 252 6465*

Dental
For referrals, call **AAA Referral Service** 1-800 733 6337, or 1-800 336 8478) or, for the **Dental Society**, 667 3647.

Optical

Pearle Vision
7901 Biscayne Boulevard, at NE 79th Street, Miami (754 5144). Bus 3, 16, 33, L. **Open** 9am-6pm Mon-Fri; 9am-4pm Sat. **Credit** AmEx, Disc, M, V.
If your glasses get broken or you lose a contact lens, Pearle Vision can issue you with a new set in around an hour.

Pharmacies/drug stores
See chapter **Shopping & Services**.

Disabled

As with most of the US, disabled travellers are likely to find Miami relatively easy to get around. Miami's Deco District, with its 1930s proportions, provides some tight angles and tiny lifts for wheelchair users to negociate, but even the smallest of hotels often have ramps and lifts fitted, and all public buildings, which include museums and libraries, must by law have wheelchair access and suitable toilet facilities.

In Miami, beach-lovers have wheelchair access at Crandon Park on Key Biscayne and the North Shore State Recreation Area on Miami Beach. Most buses have specially low entrances, set spaces and grips, and both the Tri-Rail and Metromover are fully wheelchair accessible.

Orlando's theme parks all offer leaflets on the suitability or otherwise of their various attractions. Walt Disney World's Epcot and MGM Studios are both OK for wheelchair users, with the Magic Kingdom less impressive, and following a recent trend Universal Studios Florida is excellent, with all but one ride accessible to people and their wheelchairs.

The **Society for the Advancement of Travel for the Handicapped** (1-212 447 7284/fax 1-212 725 8253), though New York based, can offer information and services for disabled travellers planning trips to all parts of the States.

Deaf Services Bureau
1320 S Dixie Highway, Suite 760, Coral Gables (1-305 668 4407/TDD 668 3323).
Provides a wide range of services including information, interpreting, counselling and legal representation, and also runs a 24-hour crisis line.

Florida Relay Service
200 South Biscayne Boulevard, Suite 600 (1-305 579 8644/1-800 955 8770/TDD 1-800 955 8771)
Operates a round-the-clock service connecting TDD (Telecommunications Devices for the Deaf) users with those who do not have TDD phones. State-wide.

Metro-Dade Transit Agency Special Transportation Service
1-305 263 5406
Will provide door-to-door transport for disabled people who are unable to use public services. At least three weeks notice are needed – contact them well in advance of your trip.

Miami Lighthouse for the Blind
601 SW Eighth Avenue (1-305 856 2288).
Provides a wide range of information on how the blind can make the most of Miami's attractions and facilities.

Metro-Dade Department of Human Services and Independent Living
1335 NW 14th Street (1-305 547 5444/547 7355 fax).
D-SAIL is a referral and information service for the physically disabled. Staff can offer advice on suitable hotels and van rental. Its opposite number in Orlando is the Centre for Independent Living on 1-407 623 1070.

Foreign newspapers

The best, though not the most convenient, place for international titles is **Worldwide News**, 1629 NE 163rd Street (940 4730). A range is also stocked at **News Café** (*see chapter* **Restaurants & Cafés**), **Bus Terminal News**, 327 Alhambra Circle, Coral Gables (443 7979) and **Plaza News**, 7900 Biscayne Boulevard, Little Haiti (751 6397).

Late

Socially, Miami is a very late city – things don't get started until at least 10pm or 11pm. Thus late-opening clubs, bars and restaurants are the norm, especially in South Beach. However, for more practical needs, there are few 24-hour facilities, with the exception of a handful of drugstores and launderettes and a sex shop or two (*see chapter* **Shopping & Services**). If you need to change money after office hours, you will need to cash a travellers cheque or use an ATM.

Our pick of late-opening restaurants on South Beach are **11th Street Diner**, **La Sandwicherie**, **Pucci's Pizza** and **San Loco Tacos**. Good 24-hour operations are **News Café** and **Wolfie's**. In Little Havana, **Versailles** stays from 2.30am-4.30am. For all, *see chapter* **Restaurants & Cafés**.

Left luggage

Fear of terrorism combined with a spate of thefts mean that the shiny blue lockers at Miami International Airport are no longer available to the public. There are a few lockers at the Greyhound terminals both Downtown and near the airport (*see chapter* **Getting Started**). If it's your last day and you are heading for the airport, try checking your bags in in early (eight hours shouldn't be a problem, even for a domestic flight), or ask to leave them at your hotel after check-out time.

Legal problems

If you're challenged by a police officer, do exactly as you're told and don't make any sudden movements. Though most Florida cops are tourist friendly, some hard cases have itchy trigger fingers. If you find yourself arrested and accused of a serious crime, you will be allowed one phone call. You are best calling your consulate, whose staff should be able to help smooth over the logistical difficulties. If you do not have a lawyer in mind, the court will appoint one for you. Otherwise, you can call the **Florida Bar Association** (1-800 342 8060) for a referral. Miami is not yet as sue-happy as some other US cities, but with so many rollerbladers about, you can't be too careful.

If you are arrested, particularly for driving offences, never attempt to pay a fine straightaway. The move may be misconstrued and you may find yourself charged for attempting to bribe a police officer.

Legal Line
573 6339
Free information and advice on personal injury, entertainment law, real estate, consumer and immigration law.

Lost property

Call 375 3366 for items lost on Metro-Dade Transit (Mon-Fri 8am-4.15pm), 876 7377 for Miami International Airport. Otherwise, call the non-emergency police line on 595 6263.

Post offices/poste restante

Main post office
2200 Milam Dairy Road, west of Miami International Airport (639 4280). Bus 73. **Open** 7am-7pm Mon-Fri; 8.30am-2pm Sat.

Miami Beach Post Office
1300 Washington Avenue, Miami Beach, FL 33139 (599 1787). Bus C, H, K, W. **Open** 8am-5pm Mon-Fri; 8.30am-2pm Sat.

Downtown/General Delivery
500 NW Second Avenue, Miami, FL 33101 (639 4284). Bus 2, 7, 21/Metrorail Government Center. **Open** 8-5pm Mon-Fri; 9am-1.30pm Sat.

Also the address for general delivery – if you need to receive mail but don't know where you'll be staying, you can have it sent here. Have it marked General Delivery followed by your name. You must pick up such mail in person; you'll need photographic identification.

Coral Gables Post Office
251 Valencia Avenue (599 1795).

Coconut Grove Post Office
3191 Grand Avenue (599 1750).

Public toilets

Restrooms can be found in large stores, shopping malls, bars, restaurants, museums, gas stations, public beaches, large car parks and railway and bus stations. Sometimes they are clean. Sometimes they need cleaning. Some cafés and restaurants may ask you to buy something but if you're feeling mean, ask to use the telephone, invariably located next to the restrooms, and sneak in.

Reference libraries

Metro-Dade County Public Library
101 W Flagler Street, at NW First Avenue, Downtown (375 2665). Bus 3, 16, 95, C, S/Metrorail Government Center. **Open** 9am-6pm Mon-Wed, Fri, Sat; 9am-9pm Thur.
This excellent library has literally millions of books, as you'd expect. It also, less predictably, doubles as a venue for free lectures and concerts for the public, as well as children's events. There are computers which you can book to use, local and national newspaper archives, a superb collection of material on the history of Florida and Miami and, to top it all, helpful staff and a great ambiance. And on hot days, the air conditioning is a boon. The Miami Beach branch is at 2100 Collins Avenue (535 4219).

Working the cruise liners

It might be nigh on impossible to get a visa to work in the US, but it's not so hard to get one for working off its shores. With three million passengers leaving for cruises out of the Port of Miami, the industry is booming – and someone has to keep all those people fed and entertained. Seeing the world while working on a cruise ship ranks right up there for many people with such quixotic dreams as joining the circus or becoming a Vegas showgirl. No nine-to-five commute, getting to escape foul weather and being surrounded by people having a good time. What could be better than that?

'Sometimes people have misconceptions about working on a ship,' says the hotel employment manager for Royal Caribbean Cruise Lines, one of the major players. 'For the guests, it's very nice. For the employees it is hard work. It's very similar to working in a hotel.'

Royal Caribbean has at any time 10,855 people on five-week to eight-month contracts to staff its 10 ships. They come from 27 countries, but all

are at least 21 years old. Obviously, few suffer from seasickness or at least do their damnedest not to show it. And while employment brings with it a Seaman's Visa from the US, it often does not allow for more than 12 hours of shore leave each time the ship comes into a US port.

There are 72 different positions which Royal Caribbean hires for, ranging from waiters to stewards and entertainers. Salaries vary widely depending on experience and seniority. Better known entertainers may be hired on short-term contracts, but the line has its own corps of onboard talent who rehearse in Miami dance studios when a ship is in port. Unlike the characters on TV's *The Love Boat,* who often seemed to live and eat better than the passengers, crew members may be assigned to share cabins, and all eat in the crew dining room.

If you'd like to be among them, contact the cruise line of your choice. Addresses and numbers are listed in the phone book.

Religious services

St Patrick Catholic Church
3716 Garden Avenue, Miami Beach (531 1124).

Coconut Grove United Methodist
3713 Main Highway, Coconut Grove (443 0880).

Christ Episcopal Church
3481 Hibiscus Street, Coconut Grove (442 8542).

First Baptist Church of Miami Beach
2816 Sheridan Avenue, Miami Beach (538 3507).

First Church of Christ Scientist
410 Andalusia Avenue, Coral Gables (443 1427).

Ismailia Cultural Centre
2045 NE 151st Avenue, North Dade (944 1710).

Jehovah Witness Kingdom Hall
300 W 40th Street, Miami Beach (532 8588).

Plymouth Congregational Church
3400 Devon Road, Coconut Grove (444 6521).

All People's Synagogues
7455 Collins Avenue, Miami Beach (861 5554).

Spanish vocabulary

good morning/afternoon	**buenos días**
good evening/good night	**buenas noches**
hello	**hola**
good-bye	**adiós**
please	**por favor**
thank-you	**gracias**
excuse me	**perdóneme**
I'm sorry, I don't speak Spanish	**Lo siento, no hablo Espanol**
Do you speak English?	**¿Habla usted Ingles?**
How much is...?	**¿Cuanto cuesta?**
Please can I have the bill?	**La cuenta, por favor**

one	**un, uno** (m), **una** (f)		
two	**dos**	three	**tres**
four	**cuatro**	five	**cinco**
six	**seis**	seven	**siete**
eight	**ocho**	nine	**nueve**
ten	**diez**	eleven	**once**
twelve	**doce**	thirteen	**trece**
fourteen	**catorce**	fifteen	**quince**
sixteen	**dieciseis**	seventeen	**diecisiete**
eighteen	**dieciocho**	nineteen	**diecinueve**
twenty	**veinte**	twenty-one	**veintiuno**
thirty	**treinta**	forty	**cuarenta**
fifty	**cincuenta**	sixty	**sesenta**
seventy	**setenta**	eighty	**ochenta**
ninety	**noventa**	one hundred	**cien**
one hundred and one	**ciento uno**		
one hundred and ten	**ciento diez**		
five hundred	**quinientos**		
one thousand	**mil**		

Students

There are two main universities in Miami, the state-run Florida International University and the private University of Miami. The FIU has a strong arts bias while the UM is geared more geared towards science and is renowned for its medicine courses. The Miami-Dade Community College is the main county-sponsored public college, with its main centre in Downtown Miami. It's rated highly nationally, and has good language labs with short courses available.

Anybody wishing to enroll should approach the American institutions direct. Non-nationals will need to prove that they can support themselves during their stay and apply for an F-1 or M-1 visa. The M-1 is for vocational courses where practical training includes work experience, while the F-1 is for purely academic courses. Details and information on both can be obtained from the Immigration and Naturalisation Service on 536 5741. You may also hear of the J-1 visa, which gives you a social security number and therefore allows you to take a job, but it is only really applicable to students on exchange schemes and people who want to work in summer camps. For details of this scheme in the UK, contact **BUNAC**, 16 Bowling Green Lane, London, EC1R 0BD (0171 251 3472); or Camp America, 37A Queen's Gate, London, SW7 5HR (0171 581 7373/581 7333 brochure line).

Florida International University
University Park, South Dade (348 2363).

Miami-Dade Community College
300 NE 2nd Avenue, Downtown (237 3000).

University of Miami
PO Box 248025, Coral Gables FL 33124-2230 (284 2271).

Telegrams

Western Union has branches all over the City. Call 1-800 325 6000 to find the nearest one to you. As well as transferring money, they will also send telegrams.

Visas

Under the Visa Waiver Program, citizens of the UK, Japan, Australia, New Zealand and all West European countries (except for Portugal, Greece and the Vatican City) do not need a visa for stays of less than 90 days (business or pleasure), as long as they have a passport that is valid for the full 90-day period and a return ticket. An open standby ticket is acceptable. Canadians and Mexicans do not need visas but must have legal proof of their residency. All other travellers must have visas. Full information and visa application forms can be obtained from your nearest US embassy or consulate. The **US Embassy Visa Information Line** in the UK is on 0891 200 290. In general, send in your application at least three weeks before you plan to travel. Visas required more urgently should be applied for via your travel agent.

Do not overstay your visa. Yes, you might be given a few days' grace, but you might not. If you want to apply for an extension – though the odds are not good – contact the **US Immigration & Naturalisation** service at 7880 Biscayne Boulevard (536 5741). Staff consider that everyone applying for an extension is planning to work illegally. Unless you can prove otherwise, you will have a very hard time.

Working in Miami

Though it might seem as if every other waiter/ress is European, working visas are nigh on impossible to get, and trying to find casual work is difficult. US labour laws are strict and companies which hire illegal aliens face substantial fines. Not only will you face deportation but you will seriously jeopardise your chances of returning to the US. Your best bet is to look for work on the cruise liners that operate out of the Port of Miami, which can employ non-US nationals since they sail international waters, and enjoy your downtime here (*see box* **Working the cruise liners**).

Central Park SUMMERSTAGE '97

Brought to you by

MILLER BREWING COMPANY

Supported by

New York City's favorite FREE music, dance, and spoken word festival. Every summer.

The Radisson Empire Hotel in NYC is pleased to offer special weekend packages for SummerStage visitors. Package includes discount hotel, VIP passes to concerts, souvenirs, dinner or lunch for two at the Hard Rock Cafe, passes to local clubs and more.

Call 800-333-3333 (US and Canada only)
or 212-265-7400 for details.

Visit us in NYC

Radisson
E·M·P·I·R·E

Pick up a copy of TIME OUT NEW YORK when you arrive this summer for a complete schedule of Central Park SummerStage events.
Call the CPSS hotline at 212-360-2777 or check out our website at www.SummerStage.org for calendar details.

Central Park SummerStage is a project of the City Parks Foundation in cooperation with the City of New York/Parks and Recreation

Beyond Miami

Getting Started

All you need to know to use Miami as a base for exploring south and central Florida.

The state of Florida contains three distinct areas, each with its own geo-physical attributes and culture. In winter, temperatures in North Florida routinely dip into the 30°Fs and 40°Fs at night and often get even colder. While Central Florida is more moderate, the area around Orlando also experiences cold spells during winter, which many visitors are unprepared for. In South Florida, however, winter temperatures rarely dip lower than the 50°Fs, and then infrequently. Culturally, North Florida is an adjunct of the American Deep South, which it borders; Central Florida resembles the heartland of the US, a south-eastern slice of the Midwest; and South Florida is a stew bubbling with chunks of Latin America, the Caribbean, New York City and a remnant of the Old South. Travel between areas can cause culture shock; be forewarned.

The Florida peninsula is long, narrow and flat, but nowhere in the state will you be more than 60 miles away from saltwater – either the Atlantic Ocean on the east coast or the Gulf of Mexico on the west. And if you look skyward instead of straight ahead, remarkable dense and textured cloud formations may well visually suggest the mountains that Florida lacks.

TIMING YOUR TRIP

One thing to keep in mind when you plan your trip: as temperatures in Florida soar, vacation prices plunge. From late April and early May, when the weather is usually gorgeous, hotel, car rental and other prices dip. As summer progresses, vacation deals turn into vacation steals throughout the state. It is, however, family travel time, so queues at the many kid-oriented theme parks in Central Florida are enormous, augmented by Latin American families escaping their winter. In other places, including Miami and most of South Florida, you'll be able to walk right into many of the hottest restaurants and nightspots without waiting at all. Of course, you do have to consider your tolerance for steamy humid weather, as well as your enthusiasm for hurricanes, the annual season for which runs from June to the end of November.

Information

Tourist information

The Sunday *Miami Herald* contains a travel section (Section J), which always has information

about Florida travel and events. Destination Florida, an interactive online travel guide to Florida, is accessible at www.goflorida.com.

Florida Tourism

PO Box 1100, Tallahassee, FL 32302 (1-904 487 1462/ fax 1-904 414 9732).
2701 Le Jeune Road, Suite 406, Coral Gables, FL 33134 (1-305 442 6926).
ABC Florida, PO Box 35, Abingdon, Oxfordshire, United Kingdom, OX14 4SF.
This private outfit, which has taken over the functions of the Florida Division of Tourism, offers a very useful holiday pack containing a vacation guide, maps and other information. It's free to US addresses from the US offices and £2 (cheques to ABC Florida) within Britain from the UK branch.

Camping & outdoors

More information can be found on the following website: www.floridacamping.com.

Association of RV Parks & Campgrounds

1340 Vickers Drive, Tallahassee, FL 32303 (1-904 562 7151/fax 1-904 562 7179). **Open** 8.30am-5pm Mon-Fri.
Contact the Association for a copy of *Florida Camping Guide.*

Florida Department of Environmental Protection

Division of Recreation & Parks, MS 535, 3900 Commonwealth Boulevard, Tallahassee, FL 32399-3000 (1-904 488 9872/fax 1-904 922 4925). **Open** 8am-5pm Mon-Fri.
Contact the Department to request a free copy of the comprehensive *Guide to Florida State Parks.*

Transport

Driving

For driving tips and car rental companies, *see chapter* **Getting Around**. The best maps for drivers are from the Triple A or Rand McNally, from bookstores, and the official Florida Transportation Map (part of the Florida Tourism pack; *see above*).

American Automobile Association (AAA)

(1-800 596 2228). **Open** 24 hours daily.
Florida Division, 1000 AAA Drive, Member Services Department 68, Heathrow, FL 32746.
4770 Biscayne Boulevard, Suite 850, Miami, FL33137 (1-305 571 0360). **Open** 8.30am-5.15pm Mon-Fri.
The fabulous Triple A provides excellent – and free – maps, guidebooks, specific travel routes (TripTiks) and towing services to member of the AAA or an affiliated organisation (such as the British AA). You can fax specific requests to 1-800 350 7437: include your membership number, a daytime telephone number and date of departure.

Cruise America Motorhome Rentals

7740 NW 34th Street, Miami, FL 33122 (1-305 591 7511). **Open** 9am-5pm Mon-Sat.
RV and motorbike rental agency.

Worldwide Motorhome Rentals

(recorded information 1-800 350 8031/office 1-702 452 7712/fax 1-702 452 5919. **Open** *office* 8am-5pm Mon-Fri.
If you want to hire a recreational vehicle (RV), contact this independent information and reservation service. Services include free delivery and pick-up, free airport pick-up and drop-off and free unlimited generator use. You must book early. You can check their website at www.wwmhr.com.

Air

It is generally advised that you book any internal US flights through an agent in your home country, or as part of your international ticket. However, this is not necessarily the cheapest way, except, perhaps, at the height of tourist season (Christmas to Easter) or on public holidays. Do your research. In Florida, consult the Sunday *Miami Herald* travel section and its Guide to Lowest North American Air Fares, or contact a local travel agent. Reduced-rate return fares are usually cheapest on weekdays, and often require seven-day advance booking and a Saturday stopover. Flights from Fort Lauderdale are often cheaper than from Miami.

The following airlines have regular flights from Miami to various points in Florida: **American Eagle** (1-800 433 7300), **United** (1-800 241 6522), **Continental** (1-800 525 0280) and **Comair (Delta)** (448 7000). Some ValuJet, which was the hottest and fastest growing US discount airline until one of its jets plunged into the Everglades in May 1996, is now probably the safest airline in the US because of close government scrutiny, but no longer flies out of Miami – though it does fly from Fort Lauderdale.

Bus

Greyhound

1-800 231 2222.
Stations: 700 Biscayne Boulevard, at Bayside Marketplace, Downtown Miami (1-305 379 7403). Bus 3, 16, 48, CS/Metromover Freedom Tower, 4111 NW 27th Street, at 41st Avenue, near Miami International Airport (1-305 871 1810). Bus 7, 37, 42, J.
Credit AmEx, Disc, MC, V.
Long-distance bus service from Miami to points north and south. Travel is cheaper Mon-Thur, and buying a return ticket at the time of departure will save 5-15%. Private bus companies can be booked through most travel agents.

Rail

Amtrak

1-800 872 7245.
Station: 8303 NW 37th Avenue, at NW 79th Street, near Hialeah (1-305 835 1221). Bus 32, 42, L/Metrorail Tri-Rail.
Long-distance train service. You can travel from New York to points on the east coast of Florida, including Miami. The connecting bus service (available only to rail passengers), provides a service to Orlando, Tampa, Key West, West Palm Beach and other points. Its bus service between Orlando and Fort Myers can be accessed by any traveller. Return tickets are substantially cheaper than two one-ways.

Tri-Rail

1-800 874 7245.
Commuter rail line that runs the 70-plus miles between Miami and Fort Lauderdale and the Palm Beaches. It links with Miami's rapid transit system Metrorail and various Miami bus routes. Fares vary by zones.

Fantasy islands

Ah, the Caribbean: calm waters, soft breezes, cool drinks and friendly island natives. Paradise revisited; or, more aptly, paradise designed, courtesy of your cruise ship operator. After hearing mounting complaints from passengers of aggressive souvenir hawkers, unscrupulous local taxi drivers and overcrowded island beaches, the major cruise ship lines have given up trying to find as-yet-unspoilt tropical paradises. What God cannot provide, Royal Caribbean Cruise Line can: CocoCay island.

A spit of Bahamian sand has been turned into the ultimate fantasy island, with smiling locals (ferried in from neighbouring islands) serving up bountiful island buffets, playing calypso music and leading snorkelling adventures to the nearby reef where there is a sunken replica of Blackbeard's pirate ship and a submerged plane (seized from drug smugglers). Other cruise lines are buying their own islands, six at present, including Disney, which plans to launch its own ships in 1998.

Some travel writers have taken the cruise lines to task for sanitising the travel experience, but financial analysts note that selling unencumbered pleasure is a sure way to make tidy profits. Not surprisingly, after downing one or two glasses of the local libation, the CocoLoco cocktail, and writing a postcard to the folks back at home in the snow, even the most hardened sceptics are given to letting their criticism disappear with the tide.

Cruises

The **Port of Miami** (1-305 371 7678) is one of the busiest passenger and freight ports in the world. More than three million cruise passengers embarked in 1996. There are (controversial) plans afoot to expand the existing 12 passenger terminals with up to four more, on the Downtown waterfront.

You can book cruises (three-11 nights) to points as geographically and culturally diverse as the east and west coasts of Mexico, Puerto Rico, France, Haiti, St Thomas, Jamaica, Key West, Colombia, the Panama Canal and most of the Caribbean island paradises. Try **Carnival Cruise Lines** (1-800 327 9501); **Discovery Cruise Line** (1-800 937 4477); **Norwegian Cruise Line** (1-305 436 0866); **Royal Caribbean Cruise Lines** (1-305 379 4731); **Dolphin Cruise Line** (1-305 358 2111); **Majesty Cruise Line** (1-800 222 1003). Cruises vary hugely in duration, facilities and price.

Check local travel agents and the *Yellow Pages* under 'Cruises'. Websites include cruise magazines Porthole (www.porthole.com) and Smith's CruiseLetter (www.chevychase.com.cruise). You can get terrific, up-to-date information about individual ships through the Cruise Ship Center (www.safari.net./market/CruiseShipPage.html) and cruise reviews from Cruises Inc (www.cruisesinc.com).

The Everglades

Discover an antidote to the urban in this unique environment of mangrove swamps, coastal islands and some really wild wildlife.

The most defining feature of Florida is neither its miles of beaches, nor the ubiquitous mouse a man named Disney set loose on the state more than a quarter of a century ago. It is the Everglades. Commonly thought of as swamp, the Everglades is actually more a shallow, bankless river, or a 'River of Grass', as the 106-year-old environmentalist Marjory Stoneman Douglas called it in her famous book of the same name. The Everglades occupy the southernmost 80 miles or so of the state, of which the Everglades National Park at the tip, on which this chapter focuses, is just a part.

The natural course of the river flows the hundred miles from Lake Okeechobee to Florida Bay at a rate of 100 feet per day, with the water's depth varying from as much as three feet to as little as three inches. An extensive system of canals and levees built this century has disrupted the natural flow of water into the Everglades, leading to continual problems with the quantity – and quality – of the water that does finally reach the park. More than six million South Florida residents, tens of millions of annual tourists, hundreds of industries and thousands of species of plants, birds, fish and animals rely on the River of Grass for clean water.

Although the US's second largest national park, the Everglades (founded in 1947) is not as obviously stunning as some of its more mountainous Western cousins. As such, its true beauty cannot be appreciated from the windows of a camper speeding along the roads between rest-stops. Even exploring the Everglades on a noisy airboat ride climaxes when the driver turns off the engine and leaves you floating silently in endless sawgrass.

The Everglades is the only National Park in the US to be recognised by the United Nations as both an International Biosphere Reserve and World Heritage Site. It is home to plant and animal life found both in the West Indian tropics and in more temperate northern zones. The idea of South Florida as a meeting point of north and south is nowhere more true than here.

As full of wildlife as the Everglades may seem, it is in fact a troubled sanctuary of last report for many species. The number of wading birds in the southern area has declined from 265,000 in the 1930s to 18,500 today. Only 10 Florida panthers are thought to still live in the park, and although the Everglades has never had a large population of black bears, they are more reluctant than ever to show themselves to visitors.

Still, the park does teem with life. Deer exist in good numbers and this is the only place in the world where alligators and crocodiles co-habit. The alligators are far more abundant, with the crocodiles keeping to the saltier waters nearer the coast. During a walk along one of the park's trails, you are likely to be greeted by turtles, butterflies, frogs, rabbits, possibly a snake, and many of the 350 species of birds who either reside in the park or make it a migratory rest stop.

A River of Grass is actually far too limiting a definition for the variety of plant life within the Everglades: saw palmetto (commonly called sawgrass) may be dominant overall, but there are more than 1,000 kinds of seed-bearing plants and 120 types of trees. Mangrove and various hardwood tree hammocks (islands of land) dot the expanses of sawgrass, and in the summer, flowering plants add splashes of colour to the green canvas.

Marshmallow-scoffing racoons; the **Coopertown Restaurant**.

PLANNING YOUR TRIP

The dry season – November to May – is the best time to visit the Everglades. South Florida's ravenous mosquito population is more than happy to welcome you in the summer, as are the staff of air-conditioned gift shops on the park's edges which charge double for bottles of suntan lotion. Heavy summer and fall rains can also sometimes flood parts of the Everglades, including the popular Shark Valley trail.

Numerous tourist shops along the Tamiami Trail sell water and soft drinks, and many have cafés. In Florida City and Homestead, there are shops and small restaurants, as well as an abundance of fruits and freshly baked sweets at the Robert Is Here fruit market. There are also shops and restaurants in Everglades City. Water fountains, soda vending machines and restrooms can be found at all visitor centres within the park.

It is advisable year-round (but especially in summer) to bring suntan lotion, a hat and sunglasses. Mosquito repellent is essential in the summer.

In terms of access, the park can be divided into two main areas: the northern section, accessed by Shark Valley and Everglades City; and the southern section, accessed by the Main Visitor Center near Homestead and Florida City. There is no public transport into either area.

Everglades National Park

40001 State Road 9336, Homestead, FL 33034-6733 (1-305 242 7700). **Open** 8am-5pm daily.

Northern access

Shark Valley & Gulf Coast Visitor Centers

Twenty-five miles west of the Florida Turnpike, Shark Valley is the most accessible part of the Everglades from Miami and makes for a perfect half- or full-day outing. The Tamiami Trail (US 41), which leads here, is the old, mostly two-lane road across the southern part of the state, running along the park's northern boundary. Plans call for stretching the park's boundaries a few miles east

and south to protect against encroaching development. To accomplish this would involve the government buying out some of the businesses on the park's edge, which exist for the tourist trade and are relics of a simpler, albeit tackier, era. The airboat tour operators, Miccosukee Indian village tours and alligator wrestling shows along the Tamiami Trail are pleasantly worn at the edges, though for the most part lacklustre. As impressive as it is to watch man muzzle a gator, it is far less an example of traditional Indian culture than of Florida's myriad ways of luring dollars out of tourists.

At **Coopertown** (the sign says 'population 8', but it's a big overstatement), they have been running airboat tours for more than 50 years. The guides are knowledgeable and this may be the best of several places to take an airboat ride – if only for having a beer before or after in the Coopertown Restaurant, whose walls are covered with decades of Everglades memorabilia including alligator heads and claws. Given that the number of daily customers appears to equal the town's boasted population, stick to a bag of chips. The Miccosukee Restaurant is a safer bet, and there's a small museum devoted to Indian life in the Everglades.

Shark Valley (admission $8 per car) features a 13-mile paved road leading to an observation tower overlooking the heart of the Everglades. The Visitor Center (242 8455) is open 8.30am-5pm daily. Two-hour guided tram tours run hourly from 9am-4pm during the peak season (Dec-Apr), less frequently off-season, and cost $8 adults, $7.20 senior citizens, $4 under-13s; you might need to book three weeks in advance during winter. But it's more fun to either bring a bicycle or rent one there ($3.25 per hour) – then you can stop at your leisure to explore and take short diversions on paths into the hammocks. Even a walk of a mile or two will bring many surprise encounters with the park's inhabitants, including alligators who delight in napping on the road with near – but not absolute – indifference to visitors. This is not Walt Disney World, so proceed with caution.

On an airboat ride; pool at **The Rod & Gun Club Lodge** *(p221).*

Less than 10 miles further west along Tamiami Trail from Shark Valley, the road passes through **Big Cypress National Preserve**, with its tracts of cypress and pine trees growing among the swampy terrain. The tiny town of **Ochope** boasts the US's smallest post office, which measures a little more than seven by eight feet. The 'panther crossing next 5 miles' sign is worth a snapshot.

South of SR 29 from the Tamiami Trail is **Everglades City**, the gateway to the **Ten Thousand Islands**. This is where the Everglades meets the Gulf of Mexico, and the coastline fractures into thousands of islands, many thick with mangroves. The town itself is not much to write home about, though a new, high-tech IMAX theatre with video shows on the Everglades will soon be built to lure more visitors. Mother Nature's existing reality may not come with air-conditioning, but the environment is incredibly lush and rich in wildlife. For information, as well as permits for backcountry camping within the park, visit the **Gulf Coast Visitor Center** (1-941 695 3311, open 7.30am-5pm daily) in town on SR 29.

Porpoises and some of Florida's remaining 1,200 manatees, or sea cows, can be found in the waters of the Ten Thousand Islands and even the noble American bald eagle can be sighted. The easiest way to get on the water is with Everglades National Park Boat Tours. Ninety-minute tours ($13 adults, $6.50 6-12s) of the nearby islands, Indian shell mounds and an overview of the area's ecology start at 9am and leave every 30 minutes until 4.30pm.

A number of local concerns rent canoes and kayaks by the hour or day, as well as rentals for overnight camping trips in the Ten Thousand Islands and along the 99-mile Wilderness Waterway trail leading south to the Flamingo Visitor Center.

North American Canoe Tours

107 Camilla Street, Everglades City (1-941 695 3299).
Open *1 Nov-15 April* 9am-5pm daily. **Rates** *Canoes* $16 4hrs from noon; $20 first day; $18 each additional day. *Kayaks* $30-$45 per day.
This is the rental side of The Ivey House B&B (*see below*).

Everglades National Park Boat Tours

Gulf Coast Visitor Center (1-800 445 7724 Florida only/1-941 695 2591). Open 8.30am-5pm daily. **Rates** *Canoes* $18 per day 8.30am-5pm; $36 overnight.
If you plan to canoe down to Flamingo, they charge $150 to bring your car to meet you, or they'll pick you up in Flamingo and bring you back to Everglades City for $100.

Getting there

From Miami, head west on I-395 to SR 821 south (aka the Florida Turnpike). Take the US 41/SW Eighth Street (Tamiami Trail) exit; the Shark Valley entrance is about 25 miles west. If you want to go to Everglades City and the park's Gulf Coast Visitor Center, continue west on the Tamiami Trail and then head south on SR 29 (about a 2½-hr drive from Miami).

Where to stay

Shark Valley can be reached in an hour from hotels on Miami Beach, and there is no accommodation (apart from primitive campsites) in this section of the park. About 40 miles further west, in Everglades City, near the Gulf Coast Visitor Center, there are a limited number of hotels. Local RV (recreational vehicle) sites will permit camping, though they're not really designed to make you feel at one with nature. Along the Wilderness Waterway are a number of chickees (covered wooden platforms elevated above the open water) for camping. During the winter, campsites ($10) on the islands and chickees must be reserved in person at the Gulf Coast Visitor Center.

Holy cows

Manatees are the gentle giants of Florida's waters. Also known as sea cows, these plant-eating, aquatic mammals have large, seal-like bodies and beaver-like tails. They grow from nine to 13ft and weigh up to 3,000lb. Once found throughout the Caribbean and South America, the species may have been totally eradicated from waters south of the equator by massive hunting. The majority of manatees today live in bays, shallow rivers, canals and estuaries (either fresh- or saltwater) around the Florida coast. Manatees are particularly vulnerable to injury from boats and fishing lines and more than 900 of Florida's estimated population of 1,700 are marked with distinctive scars. In 1996, toxic red tide (an infestation of waters by micro organisms) was responsible for 150 manatee deaths, the most ever recorded. Divers, swimmers and boaters are required to stay out of designated sanctuaries, and boaters must adhere to all speed signs.

Unfortunately for the manatee, their good disposition and natural curiosity means they are not afraid of people. If you are fortunate enough to be approached by a manatee while swimming, do not touch it unless it touches you first and return the friendly gesture with a gentle, open-hand hello. While manatee sighting is never easy, during the winter months they are fond of gathering in warmer, shallow waters, particularly the warm discharge flows from electric power plants on the west coast of Florida.

To report manatee injuries, harassment or sightings of tagged animals, call the Save the Manatee Club on 1-407 539 0990.

The Captain's Table

102 E Broadway (mailing address PO Box 530), Everglades City, FL 34139 (1-800 741 6430/1-941 695 4211). **Rates** *27 Dec-30 Apr* double $75; suite with kitchen $95; *1 May-26 Dec* double $55; suite $70.
All rooms have private bathrooms and there is an Olympic-sized pool, heated in the winter.

The Ivey House

PO Box 5038, Everglades City, FL 34139 (1-941 695 3299). **Open** 1 Nov-15 Apr. **Rates** $50.
This is based at the same address on Camilla Street as North American Canoe Tours (*see above*).

On the Banks of the Everglades

201 West Broadway (mailing address PO Box 570), Everglades City, FL 34139 (1-941 695 3151/1-888 431 1977). **Rates** $40-$110.
B&B in an old bank with four rooms with shared bathrooms and five apartments with kitchen and private bathrooms. Breakfast is served in the bank's walk-in vault.

The Rod & Gun Club Lodge

200 Riverside Drive (mailing address PO Box 190), Everglades City, FL 34139 (1-941 695 2101). **Rates** Nov-May $85; June-Oct $50.

Southern access

Main, Royal Palm & Flamingo Visitor Centers

Rebuilt and expanded after the original buildings were damaged by Hurricane Andrew in 1992, the **Main Visitor Center** houses educational exhibits, a small cinema and a bookshop. The centre is open 7.30am-5.30pm daily; admission $10 per car.

Just inside the park is the **Royal Palm Visitor Center** (also 242 7700). This sub-centre serves as the head of the Gumbo Limbo and the Anhinga walking trails, which take in the abundant wildlife within Taylor Slough, the smaller of the two main sloughs, or marshy bogs, within the park (the other is Shark River Slough in the centre of the park). The animals and birds here are known for their ease around humans and this is considered one of the best wildlife photography areas in the park.

Except for the swampy terrain of the Slough, the Everglades here is more wooded than the northern part of the park. At **Long Pine Key**, there are picnic areas within the slash pine forests and on the banks of numerous small lakes. Just under 13 miles west of the Main Visitor Center is **Pa-hay-okee** (the Indian name for the Everglades, meaning 'Big Water') **Overlook Trail**. A board-walk leads to an observation tower from where you can watch some of the park's larger birds, such as vultures and hawks, fly over their domain.

The road dips south from here, first passing some small hammocks of stately mahogany trees, and on to the mangrove forests which signal the approaching shoreline of Florida Bay. Just before the **Flamingo Visitor Center**, 38 miles from the park entrance, is Mrazek Pond, noted as a viewing spot for some of the park's more exotic waterfowl.

The area around the Flamingo Visitor Center is very much the jewel of the Everglades. The scenery is right out of Robinson Crusoe, with a variety of walking and canoe trails through dense mangrove forests and along the calm, island-filled waters of Florida Bay. Sunset by Eco Pond is a must, when hundreds of ibis and other birds seek out their favourite tree-top perches for the night.

Flamingo is also the gateway for water trips to campsites up and down the coast and unspoilt beaches like Cape Sable. Local concessions rent canoes, kayaks, motorboats and even houseboats. Fishing is permitted, but check with the ranger's office for licensing requirements and restrictions.

AmFac

Flamingo Lodge Marina & Outpost Resort (1-941 695 3101). **Open** sunrise-5pm daily. **Rates** *Bicycles* $3 per hour; $17 24 hours. *Canoes* $8 per hour; $40 24 hours. *Kayaks* single $11 per hour; $50 24 hours; double $16 per hour; $60 24 hours.
Also ask about organised canoe tours and camping trips.

Getting there

From Miami, head west on I-395 to SR 821 south (aka the Florida Turnpike). When the Turnpike ends in Florida City, take the first right turn through the centre of town and follow the signs to the park entrance on SR 9336 – make sure you take a left turn when you come to local landmark Robert Is Here fruit market. The Main Visitor Center is about 1½hrs from Miami.

Where to stay

Outside the park, there are numerous motels and hotels in Homestead and Florida City. Inside the park, the only motel-style accommodation is the Flamingo Lodge at the Flamingo Visitor Center, at the park's southernmost tip. There are managed campsites at Long Pine Key, Flamingo and Chekika; during the winter you must book primitive campsites ($10) in person at the Flamingo Visitor Center. Alternatively, you could stay at Key Largo, which is about a 45-minute drive from the Main Visitor Center and has unparalleled snorkelling and many hotels.

Best Western – Gateway to the Keys

1 Strano Boulevard, Florida City, FL 33034 (246 5100). **Rates** $89-$107 15 Dec-15 Apr; $69-$85 14 Apr-14 Dec.

Days Inn of Homestead

51 S Homestead Boulevard (US 1), Homestead, FL 33033 (245 1260). **Rates** $86-$149 Nov-Apr; $45-$57 Apr-Oct.

The Flamingo Lodge

1 Flamingo Lodge Highway, Flamingo, FL 33034 (1-800 600 3813/1-941 695 3101). **Rates** two people 15 Dec-31 Mar $95; 1 May-31 Oct $65; 1 Nov-14 Dec $79.

Katy's Place

31850 SW 195th Avenue, Homestead, FL 33033 (246 0783). **Rates** $85 shared bathroom; $125 private bathroom.

Fort Lauderdale & Palm Beach

North from Miami, the coast life continues in cities that rival it for interest, influence and beach-based hedonism.

The urban sprawl north of Greater Miami has long been viewed as a retirement hotbed for the northeastern and mid-western states. But there's a lot more to it than the sum of its suburban parts.

The towns that sprouted like weeds along oil tycoon Henry Flagler's railroad from Palm Beach to Miami once had their own character and microhistorical purpose. The car, blind planning and real estate frenzy eventually blurred town borders, creating what is known as the Tri-County area (Dade, Broward and Palm Beach Counties). Fortunately, recent civic efforts to renovate city centres have brought back some distinction.

The area grew largely out of Miami's ills. What began years ago as 'white flight' – families fleeing north in search of safer neighbourhoods, better schools and cleaner streets – now includes any ethnic group with the bucks to get out of crime-conscious Miami. But as with most of suburbia, the blight they've escaped is now encroaching on their cookie-cutter neighbourhoods and cloned malls. The trend now is to move west, hacking away at the Everglades and farmlands. The good news is you can avoid this suburban wasteland; there's rarely a need to venture west of I-95 unless you're Everglades-bound or shopping at Sawgrass Mills. The most colourful portion remains the strip of land hugging the Atlantic. Here 'olde Florida' – anything before air-conditioned 1960 – exists in all its fascinating gaudiness as pseudo-Mediterranean palaces stand beside Jetsonian motels.

In general, the further north you journey, the more pristine it gets. Venture off the main drag in Boca Raton and you'll find gardens more manicured than in Fort Lauderdale. There are laws in Boca forbidding open garage doors, offensively coloured garbage cans and the parking of pick-up trucks in certain areas. Matters get even more regimental in Palm Beach; grass is clipped at its edges so that nature and concrete never touch. Outlawed pink plastic flamingos give way to ceramic lawn jockeys, their once-black skin now painted a politically correct white. Despite growing pains and over-clipped bougainvillaea, even the most jaded visitor will find the shore and surrounding lushness

intoxicating. Both Broward and Palm Beach Counties offer an oasis from the pace of Miami.

There are two ways to travel: via I-95, the main freeway, or US 1 (also known as Federal Highway) which slowly winds through every town. I-95 is fast, riddled with accidents and quite dull; US 1 is an eternal stretch of fast-food joints, no-tell motels and auto lots. The towns below are listed from south to north.

TELEPHONE CODES

New telephone area codes are **1-954** for **Broward County** and **1-561** for **Palm Beach County**. You need to use the code only if you're calling from outside the area; for example, calling Fort Lauderdale (in Broward County) from Miami (in Dade County).

Getting there & around

Note that train and bus services are infrequent, not visitor-friendly and sometimes a hassle; bus terminals are usually located in unsavoury neighbourhoods and train stations are often desolate and usually automated. It's easier and better to rent a car (*see chapter* **Getting Around**).

By car

From Miami take **I-95** or **US 1** north. For **Hollywood**, exit at Hollywood Boulevard east. For **Fort Lauderdale** (about 30 minutes from Miami), from I-95 take I-595 east and follow signs for 'Ft Lauderdale US 1 north'; once on US 1, turn right on 17th Street. This leads to the beach and major hotels. From Fort Lauderdale to **Delray Beach**, the fastest route is via I-95; the most scenic is via A1A (Ocean Drive). Exit at Atlantic Avenue east (not to be mistaken with the Atlantic Avenue exit in Pompano Beach). For both **West Palm Beach** and **Palm Beach** (a one-hour drive from Miami), exit I-95 at Okeechobee Boulevard east.

By train

Tri-Rail (1-800 874 7245) commuter trains operate on an infrequent schedule. From the Miami airport station, 14 trains depart daily to points north, including **Hollywood**, **Fort Lauderdale** (35 minutes from Miami) and **Palm Beach** (one hour). Miami-Fort Lauderdale return fare is about $4-$6; Fort Lauderdale-Palm Beach return costs about $4-$7.

By bus

Greyhound (1-800 231 2222) has 20 buses daily from the Miami terminal (4111 NW 27 Street; four blocks from Miami

Take a water taxi to explore Fort Lauderdale's 300 miles of waterways.

International Airport) to downtown **Fort Lauderdale** (515 NE Third Street); return fare is $7 and the journey takes about one hour. From Fort Lauderdale, 16 buses run daily to **West Palm Beach** (100 Banyan Boulevard at Flagler Street); return fare to both destinations is around $9. For information on local buses in Broward County, call 1-954 357 8400, in Palm Beach 1-561 233 4287.

Hallandale, Hollywood & Dania

There's little reason to stop among the cavernous condominiums of **Hallandale**, just north of the county line. It's a town for the elderly, and driving can be maddening. If you fancy betting, however, there's **Gulfstream Park**, South Florida's premier thoroughbred horse track, open mid-January through March (Hallandale Beach Boulevard and US 1; 1-954 454 7000). For the dogs, go to the **Hollywood Greyhound Track**, open from December to April (831 N Federal Highway; 1-954 454 9400).

A favourite among the working class and petty mafioso (or at least those who look the part), **Hollywood** enjoys a low profile that's welcome after self-conscious South Beach. French Canadians trek here during winter and take over the beachfront **Broadwalk**: an asphalt promenade lined with souvenir shops, inexpensive restaurants and biker bars. At night it's abuzz with the sound of French voices and the smell of heavy cigarette smoke, which frequently overpowers the ocean's breeze. Free outdoor concerts are held year-round on Mondays, Tuesdays and

Wednesdays at 7.30pm at the **Hollywood Beach Bandshell** (Johnson Street and the Broadwalk; concert line 1-954 921 3400). The music featured runs the gamut from big band, Latin and jazz to rock 'n' roll and country – with line dancing lessons thrown in free. Here you'll find the largest global concentration of elderly ladies with peroxide-drenched hair. It's quite a sight.

Travel three miles west on Hollywood Boulevard and you'll hit downtown. It's been spruced up with pedestrian-friendly features and new cafés and galleries have been trickling in, causing some developers to predict (yet) another South Beach. Two small black box theatres and a few galleries on adjacent Harrison Street are reason enough to visit. **My Thai Café** (2003 Harrison Street; 1-954 926 5585) is a bright culinary spot, as is **Sushi Blues Café**, a sushi bar with live jazz (1836 S Young Circle; 1-954 929 9560).

Dania's claim to fame is its antique shops, lining several blocks on US 1 and Dania Beach Boulevard. The other main attraction is jai alai, reputedly the fastest game in the world; this Basque import includes parimutuel betting. Games are held year-round at the **Dania Jai Alai Palace** (301 E Dania Beach Boulevard; 1-954 927 2841). While in the area, try the **Rustic Inn Crabhouse** (4331 Anglers Avenue; 584 1637). This local favourite is worth the drive for its famous garlic crabs, presented with newspapers to catch the fish squirt, bibs, mallets and service as rustic as the name.

Fort Lauderdale

Fort Lauderdale is the glossy American Dream: well-tended beaches filled with bodies beautiful, glittering waterways dotted with private yachts, and cosy neighbourhoods. More relaxed than Miami and less stodgy than its neighbours in Palm Beach, Fort Lauderdale has been on a redevelopment spree with impressive results.

The best introduction to the city is by water. Dubbed 'the Venice of America', Fort Lauderdale boasts over 300 miles of waterways. During the 1920s, finger islands were built atop mangrove swamps, causing eco-havoc; waterfront mansions replaced the muck and millionaires parked yachts outside their bedrooms. The **Water Taxi** (1-954 467 6677) covers most of the area and stops virtually anywhere, with many waterside restaurants and hotels having their own stop. An all-day pass costs $15 and allows unlimited boardings.

More traditional sightseeing cruises, with an informative commentary, are offered on Mississippi-style paddle wheelers: the **Jungle Queen** (801

Gay Fort Lauderdale

The 1960 Connie Francis cult film, *Where The Boys Are*, set in Fort Lauderdale, has ironically lived up to its name. Gay men have been fleeing their intolerant Ohio burgs for years in search of sun, boys and, perhaps, Connie. The town has a large, politically established gay and lesbian community that's diverse in race and age and not as ravesome as South Beach's.

For the men, there's a deluge of bars, though you can skip many unless you fancy addled rent boys. The beach to be seen at is at Ocean Drive and St Sebastian Street, while **The Floridian Restaurant** (1410 E Las Olas Boulevard; 1-954 463 4041) is open 24 hours and very gay-friendly. The bar and club scene is constantly changing but hotspots at the moment include weekends at the **Copa** (2800 S Federal Highway; 1-954 463 1507); Fridays at **Electra** (1600 SE 15th Avenue; 1-954 764 8447); Saturdays at **The Saint** (1000 State Road 84; 1-954 525 7883); and Sundays and Mondays at **Cathode Ray** (1105 E Las Olas Boulevard; 1-954 462 8611). Check out free *Hotspots* or *Scoop* magazines for listings of gay restaurants, bars, hotels and services.

Seabreeze Boulevard; 1-954 462 5596) and the **Carrie B** (SE Fifth Avenue and the New River; 1-954 768 9920). Full-day ocean cruises – gambling, dining and entertainment on ships that either cruise nowhere or to the Bahamas – embark from Port Everglades (17th Street and Eisenhower Boulevard). The most popular are **Discovery** (1-954 525 7800) and **Sea Escape** (1-954 925 9700).

Tourist central is **Fort Lauderdale Beach**, a sliver of land hemmed in by the Intracoastal Waterway and the Atlantic Ocean. Long famous as the Spring Break stomping ground for northern collegians, the city wised up several years ago after one too many intoxicated undergrads fell off a hotel balcony. Hotels refused college bookings. Ocean Drive (A1A) – aka 'the strip' – was made one-way, discouraging the all-American pastime of cruising. Along with extensive renovation, a brick promenade for joggers, inline skaters and bikes replaced parking spaces. A deco-style, neon-streaked 'wave wall' was built, the sand was replenished and the arrival of upmarket cafés transformed the area.

For a glimpse of the former beach scene, visit the infamous **Elbo Room** (Las Olas Boulevard and A1A), a Custer's Last Stand for the young, shirtless and inebriated. Located appropriately near all this water is the **The International Swimming Hall of Fame** (1 Hall of Fame Drive; 1-954 462 6536). The Olympic-sized pools are open all year to the public (except when competitions are scheduled) for a nominal charge.

Several palm trees north on A1A looms the new **Beach Place**, a multi-level Mediterranean villa for shopping/dining/drinking that faces the beach. The shops are nothing not found in an airport; the draw is food and drink and meeting after-work yuppies. Among the more popular eateries is the sexist Hooters (Hooter, breasts, geddit?), part of a Florida chain. Its hot chicken wings are acclaimed, although the top-heavy all-female wait staff are its raison d'être. It also boasts a stunning view of the surf – should anyone look in that direction.

The beach along this stretch is the most popular. A day spent here and you'll think that most of twentysomething USA – both sexes – has had some form of breast augmentation. Call it Baywatch East. The water is clean and manned with lifeguards; parasailing, chair and umbrella concessions dot the shoreline as well as bicycle and skate rentals. For a bit more quiet and a lot more greenery, stroll north to the **Hugh Taylor Birch State Park** (Sunrise Boulevard and A1A): a lovely nature reserve with a tunnel leading to the beach, barbecue pits on the Intracoastal Waterway and smooth roads for cycling or skating.

For a taste of the Deep South with Mediterranean spice, head for **Las Olas Boulevard** (between 15th Avenue and Federal Highway), the epicentre of trendy Fort Lauderdale.

One of the few places where people walk, this oak-lined stretch of shops, galleries and al fresco restaurants teems on weekends. Some highlights are **Zan(Z)Bar**, a South African bistro at 602 E Las Olas Boulevard, **O Hara's Pub** for live jazz (No.722), and **Mark's Las Olas** restaurant (No.1032) for imaginative dining.

Head west on Las Olas Boulevard and you'll hit the redeveloped downtown. Along the New River lies an attractive esplanade, Riverwalk, which winds from Las Olas Boulevard to the **Broward Center for the Performing Arts** (201 SW Fifth Avenue; 1-954 462 0222), a multi-use complex that brings in touring theatre productions. Downtown boasts the **Museum of Discovery and Science** (401 SW Second Street; museum 1-954 467 6637; IMAX Theater 1-954 463 4629); for more information, *see chapter* **Children**. Nearby is the **Fort Lauderdale Museum of Art** (1 E Las Olas Boulevard; 1-954 763 6464). Further west is Himmarshee Village, the historic section of the city. It has a Key West feel and offers some distinctive cafés and bars and a busy microbrewery.

Twelve miles west of Fort Lauderdale is the monolithic **Sawgrass Mills Outlet Mall** (12801 W Sunrise Boulevard; 1-954 846 2350). Laid out in the shape of an alligator (as if shoppers notice), it claims to be the largest outlet mall in the world and is home to the wildly popular **Rainforest Café**, where you can dine in the eye of a simulated hurricane. On returning from shopping nirvana/hell, stop into the **Mai Kai** (3599 N Federal Highway; 1-954 563 3272) for the campiest happy hour this side of Honolulu; it's a massive pre-Disney tiki hut serving fabulous tropical drinks.

Where to stay

For the genuine Fort Lauderdale experience, try staying on or near the beach at one of the many moderately priced hotels that stretch along A1A.

Lago Mar Resort

1700 S Ocean Lane, Fort Lauderdale, FL 33316 (1-954 523 6511). **Rates** $180-$275.
A family-owned resort landmark.

Riverside Hotel

620 E Las Olas Boulevard, Fort Lauderdale, FL 33301 (1-954 467 0671). **Rates** $159-$229.
Olde Florida style, fabulous location.

Tourist information

Friday's Showtime section of the local *Sun-Sentinel* newspaper offers extensive entertainment and dining listings, as does *XS*, a free weekly found throughout Broward County.

Fort Lauderdale Chamber of Commerce

512 NE Third Avenue, Fort Lauderdale, FL 33301 (1-954 462 6000/fax 1-954 527 8766). **Open** 8.30am-5pm Mon-Fri.

More cash, less flash in Palm Beach.

Greater Fort Lauderdale Convention & Visitors Bureau

1850 Eller Drive, Fort Lauderdale, FL 33316 (1-954 765 4466/fax 1-954 765 4467). **Open** 8.30am-5pm Mon-Fri.
Check the website at http://www.co.broward.fl.us/sunny.

Boca Raton & Delray Beach

Once in Palm Beach County, you'll hit Boca Raton – gated communities, reproduction antiques shops and the nouveau riche. It's no surprise that a place named in Spanish after a rodent's mouth should be the home of the infamous tabloid *The Globe* (the even more infamous and outrageous *National Enquirer* is in nearby Lantana). Boca is also known for its omnipresent pink stucco buildings and rawhide-tanned Linda Evans clones. Nowhere are both more apparent than in **Mizner Park** (Federal Highway between Palmetto Park Road and Glades Road), a recent shopping development that emulates some sort of Euro-glitz. Also of interest is the lovely beachside Boca Raton Hotel & Club, a lavish 1920s hotel, and the International Museum of Cartoon Art.

If you want to stop between Fort Lauderdale and the Palm Beaches, make it Delray Beach, an intimate town with an artistic bent, wide beaches, younger people and navigable traffic. In fact, it's cheaper to stay here than in Palm Beach, which is only a short drive away. **Atlantic Avenue** is the main drag and, like most neighbouring towns, has revamped its sidewalks, lights and landscaping. It is lined with mom-and-pop shops, galleries and downhome cafés serving bargain breakfasts. The **Twilite Café** (205 E Atlantic Avenue; 1-561 272 4330) is the funkiest and feels like small-town America. At night, the **Musician's Exchange** (213 E Atlantic Avenue; 1-561 274 8300) is popular for jazz and blues. For homesick Brits, there's the **Blue Anchor Pub** (804 E Atlantic Avenue; 1-561 272 7272), which serves pub grub and 14 draught beers, eight of them British. The owners, former *Daily Mirror* editors, were regulars at the old Blue Anchor in London's Chancery Lane. On hearing the facade had been saved from razing, they shipped it to Florida and opened for business.

Where to stay

The Seagate Hotel & Beach Club
400 S Ocean Boulevard, Delray Beach, FL 33483 (1-561 276 2421/fax 1-561 243 4714). **Rates** $154-$238.
Lovely, spacious, kitchen-equipped suites with beachfront dining and pool.

Tourist information

Greater Delray Beach Chamber of Commerce
64 SE Fifth Avenue, Delray Beach, FL 33483 (1-561 278 0424/fax 1-561 278 0555). **Open** 9am-5pm Mon-Fri.

Unlike most of Florida, the city of Palm Beach does little to encourage tourists. The only visitors this small island town really wants are those they already know – those who would prefer to pick up a bauble from Tiffany's than a sea shell from the beach. It's still the winter playground of corporate heirs, obscure royalty and American blue blood, and a place where the world at large must be content with admiring exteriors and window shopping. Unless you pull a Kennedy, there's little reason to stay on the island overnight. It's best to lodge elsewhere and make a day trip to the island. Public beaches are all but

Beach Babylon

Forget about the rhapsodised strength and morality of the US middle classes – if you want proof that the US was built, and is still run, by that ruthless, amoral, white, Anglo upper echelon of Yankee blue blood, you need only cross the Royal Poinciana Bridge to Palm Beach. Here lies the single greatest concentration of wealth and scandal in the US. Palm Beach confounds the typical US city: it is both a holy shrine to the American Dream of capitalism and a racist, anti-semitic, class-driven anomaly in a country that spouts egalitarian rhetoric. One thing it's never been is boring.

Once Henry Flagler laid railroad tracks and set up camp on the island with his first hotel, the Vanderbilts followed in their private railcar, with the rest of society fast on their heels. Palm Beach soon replaced milder St Augustine as the place to be for 'the season' (mid-December through mid-April). The Rockefellers, Carnegies, Mellons, Phippses, Drexels, Stotesburys and Morgans fled their frozen northern mansions for winter suites at Flagler's grand resorts. Soon hotel stays were out and building one's own palatial summer cottage was de rigueur. Self-made men like Woolworth, Wanamaker, Post, Hutton, Dodge, Firestone, Kennedy and Pulitzer arrived with wives and mistresses in tow. Displaced and homeless royalty from Europe and the Near East followed, adding international intrigue and long-winded names to guest lists. Hence began a succession of affairs, divorces, scandals and fab parties that would make *Hello!* magazine blush. Among the folly:

● Joseph Kennedy invited film star Gloria Swanson to his new winter home, whereupon he seduced her on arrival; decades later, his grandson, William Kennedy Smith, acted in similar fashion with a local woman and was

brought up on rape charges in a highly publicised trial that rocked the island. Yet Kennedy men and their voracious appetites were already the stuff of local legend. A few years earlier, David Kennedy, son of senator Robert Kennedy, died of an apparent drug overdose in a Palm Beach hotel suite. Old time WASP Palm Beachers still sniff and claim that the Irish Catholic Kennedys were never Palm Beach material anyway.

● From cereal to sublime: CW Post invented Grape Nuts and amassed such a fortune that his daughter, Marjorie Merriwether Post, and then her husband EF Hutton built a mansion in 1926 for $8 million. Mar-a-Lago was the pre-eminent place for lavish costume parties and entertaining. That same property was sold to Donald Trump in 1985 for a mere $5 million. With the devaluation, so went the entertaining; Ivana reportedly used plastic hotel champagne buckets. Mercifully, after the divorce, Donald turned it into a private club.

● From the sublime to the ridiculous: future Queen of Mean Leona Helmsley was stabbed in her sleep and pointed a finger at a former maid; it's widely believed her husband Harry did the unsuccessful botch job leading the pair to concoct a wild tale of attempted burglary.

● In 1975, porn publisher Larry Flynt rented a villa from an unsuspecting heiress only to use the grounds as a backdrop for a *Hustler* layout. The town – which regards its fortressed interiors as sacred – was shocked. *Hustler* was banned from all newsstands on the island and the heiress was severely ostracised for not checking references. John Lennon purchased the same estate in 1980 after Yoko had her New York psychic touch pictures of the property (presumably not the ones from *Hustler*) to get the requisite good vibrations. It was the setting for John's reunion with his estranged son Julian. Despite Palm Beach's staidness, John professed to love his new winter home.

● In a town with a bumper crop of divorces, perhaps the most infamous was Peter and Roxanne Pulitzer's in 1982. Making tabloid headlines, the intimate details of their sex life were spelled out: accusations of drug addiction, incest, bad parenting and lesbian trysts with best friend Jacquie Kimberly (wife of heir to the Kimberly-Clarke toilet paper fortune). The sordid private lives of Palm Beachers had never before been made so public and town residents reeled, banishing Roxanne for years – until Prince Charles and Princess Diana made sordid private lives fashionable again.

Conspicuous – but conservative – consumption in Palm Beach's Worth Avenue.

rendered private by restrictive parking. With nothing to do but gawk, abandon the swimsuit and camera, dress stylish and be ready with, 'No, thank you, just looking'.

The **Henry Morrison Flagler Museum** (1 Whitehall Way; 1-561 655 2833) is housed in Whitehall, the former luxury home of the railway magnate who built the east-coast line. As well as admiring the collections of period furniture and paintings, you can take a guided tour, which will give you an overview of Palm Beach history and explain how this oil tycoon was the catalyst for Florida's development. **The Breakers** (1 South County Road; 1-561 655 6611), Flagler's sublime hotel, rises above the royal palms and still serves as the town's charity ball central; it's been said that more money has been raised in the ballrooms of The Breakers than anywhere else in the world. Even if you're not staying here, take a walk inside the Florentine lobby, splurge on afternoon tea or try the famous Sunday brunch.

Worth Avenue is the town's main shopping street. And what a street. Rivalling any pricey shopping hub worldwide, it's worth a look just for the Mediterranean architecture and tranquil courtyards – and of course the wealth on show. Nothing nouveau or cutting-edge here, however; this is where Palm Beach style was born: conservative and slightly aquatic. You'll find Saks, Chanel, Jaeger and Brooks Brothers, as well as many one-of-a-kind shops and galleries.

Mansion-spotting is a bit daunting since most places are surrounded by tall stucco walls covered with vegetation and guarded by retired CIA agents. Most impressive is **Mar-a-Lago** (Southern Boulevard and S Ocean Boulevard), former home of breakfast cereal heiress Marjorie Merriwether Post as well as Donald and the former Mrs Ivana Trump. Since the divorce, Donald has turned it into a private club. For moderate and unpretentious al fresco dining, try **Testa's** (221 Royal Poinciana Way; 1-561 832 0992), which has been serving the Jackie Os of Palm Beach for three-quarters of a century.

West Palm Beach

Railroad magnate Henry Flagler persuaded the black labourers who had helped build his hotel on Palm Beach to move across the Intracoastal Waterway by offering them free land – after he had torched their houses on the island. Thus West Palm Beach was born. It has since eclipsed its affluent neighbour in population and diversity and serves as the county seat.

Downtown's **Clematis Street** is currently undergoing rejuvenation. It's a lively street beginning at the waterfront with a public library, a live theatre, bistros and bars. Walking west you'll find a wine bar with bookshop, a martini bar, a cigar bar (notice a trend?). Hopping in the evening with an array of dining choices, the place looks practically cosmopolitan after lilywhite Palm Beach. Nearby is the **Kravis Center** (701 Okeechobee Boulevard; 1-561 832 7469), a performing arts complex that offers touring Broadway shows, concerts and symphonies. The newly expanded **Norton Museum of Art** (1451 S Olive Avenue; 1-561 832 5196) is one of Florida's most highly regarded museums.

Where to stay

The Breakers

1 South County Road, Palm Beach, FL 33480 (1-561 655 6611/fax 1-561 659 8403). **Rates** *$215-$545.*
If you've got the bucks, this is the place. Ask about special deals, especially off-season. Check the hotel's website at http://www.thebreakers.com. Alternatively, stay at nearby and much cheaper Delray Beach (*see above*).

Tourist information

Palm Beach County Convention & Visitors Bureau

1555 Palm Beach Lakes Boulevard, Suite 204, West Palm Beach, FL 33401 (1-561 471 3995). **Open** *8.30am-5.30pm Mon-Fri.*

Chamber of Commerce of the Palm Beaches

401 N Flagler Drive, West Palm Beach, FL 33401(1-561 833 3711). **Open** *8.30am-5pm Mon-Fri.*

added protection extra fun...

Three way protection for twice the fun.

Hawaiian Tropic's unique Triple Defence System means you can have fun in the sun while wearing the best protection.

1. UVA, UVB & Infrared protection.
2. Exclusive time-released Vitamin Plus complex A,C&E.
3. Waterproof for up to 8 hours.

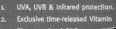

In factors up to 35, our sun protection formulations are made from the purest ingredients for better protection against sunburn and skin damage.

Hawaiian Tropic. We'll add the protection. You have the fun.

The Florida Keys

A string of coral-fringed islands, linked by one of the US's most scenic drives, leads to the tropical bohemia of Key West.

Clapboard houses contribute to Key West's Caribbean feel.

Floridians will tell you that their state is unlike the rest of the US and, in a similar vein, the Keys are unlike the rest of Florida. This group of 45 islands, south of Miami, trails the rounded mainland coast like a procession of tadpoles. A 113-mile roadway links the Keys (from the Spanish 'cayo', meaning small island) to the bottom of the mainland, but that is where any ties with the frenetic Miami pace end. The isles, flanked by the Atlantic Ocean to the south and the Gulf of Mexico to the north and shadowed on both sides by the Florida Reef, a great strip of living coral a few miles off the coast, are rich in marine, bird and plant life. Some of the islands are monstrously overpopulated and lure tourists in vulgar neon. But the further south-west you travel, the more peaceful the backdrop. Finally, in Key West, you'll find the largest collection of nineteenth-century architecture in the US and an island with a predominantly Caribbean feel.

It is not clear when the islands were first inhabited, but it is believed Native American Indians made their home here long before white settlers staked their claim in the nineteenth century. At the beginning, farming communities made a living with fruit orchards and on Big Pine Key a thriving shark factory was established. Cubans, who only had to sail 90 miles from Havana, soon joined the white Americans and today their influence is strongly apparent. Tourism struck in the early 1900s, when engineering tycoon Henry Flagler built his ambitious railway to Key West. Called 'Flagler's Folly', the mammoth project was originally designed to open up trade routes. But the 1935 Labor Day Hurricane put an end to Flagler's 20-year-old vision, when 40 miles of line were washed out to sea. Just three years later, the first Overseas Highway (US 1) was completed and this link tethered the islands to the mainland forever.

Many visitors choose to skip the islands and head straight to Key West. For nature lovers, or those in need of complete tranquillity, this seems a shame. The other islands boast some dramatic national parks, worthwhile tourist attractions and secluded accommodation.

The Keys are generally split into five groups: Key Largo; Islamorada; Marathon and the Middle

Keys; the Lower Keys; and Key West. For detailed lists of accommodation, attractions and dining, contact the individual tourist offices (*see below* **Useful information**).

PHONE CODES
Note that, although the telephone area code for the Keys is the same as for Miami – **1-305** – if you are phoning from Miami or anywhere else outside the Keys, the call does not count as local and you must prefix all phone numbers with the area code. If you are phoning from within the Keys, you don't need to use the code.

Getting there

By car
Head south on I-95, which leads into US 1 (aka Overseas Highway) and keep going straight, over 42 bridges and across 34 islands. The journey to Key West takes about 4½ hours. In places it's gloriously scenic but don't expect to bomb down: most of US 1 is a narrow, two-lane highway and the speed limit is 55mph, often less. **Mile Markers** (MM) – small green signs beside the road – start in South Miami at MM126 and end at Key West with MM0. Addresses en route are followed by their mile marker location: look closely because the signs are not always easy to spot. The Seven Mile Bridge west of Marathon (MM40-47) opened in 1982 beside the original Florida East Coast Railroad and is a remarkable engineering feat, giving excellent views of the Atlantic and Gulf of Mexico. Until you are past Marathon (2½ hours from Miami), the scenery on land is unremarkable. If you're lucky, you may catch a glimpse of the midget Key deer on the Lower Keys, and pelicans accompany you most of the way. Ideally, hire a car in Miami, dump it in Key West and fly back.

By bus
Greyhound (296 9072) operates three buses a day to Key West from Miami International Airport and Biscayne Boulevard in Downtown Miami. There are a number of scheduled stops along the Keys, but you can flag down the bus at any point. The journey from Miami to Key West takes four to five hours and costs $30 one-way, $54 return.

By limo
Island Coaches of Key West (296 4800) charges $150 for a six-person chauffeured limo, $130 for a 10-person van for pick-up from Marathon airport to Key West, one-way. From Miami, the limo costs $325, the van $299.

By air
There are a number of daily scheduled services to Marathon and Key West airports, from Miami and Fort Lauderdale. Prices start at $80 one-way. Contact **Cape Air** (1-800 352 0714), **US Air** (1-800 428 4322) and **American Airlines** (1-800 433 7300). There are no scheduled seaplane flights to the Keys anymore, but **Pan Am** (373 1120) operates on a charter basis. The plane carries 17 people and costs $1,500 one-way from Key West to Miami. The trip includes a scenic tour of the islands and is well worth it if you are feeling rich or have a large group.

Useful information
Key West is the driest city in Florida and sunny nearly all year round. Temperatures during the summer can reach the mid 90°Cs, but cool winds sweep across the Atlantic to the Gulf and keep the heat down. In December, temperatures can drop to the 50°Cs. Throughout the year, afternoon showers are possible and will soak you to the skin within minutes, but they rarely last for more than a couple of hours. Mosquitoes are no more of a problem here than in

any other hot climate (except in the swampy Everglades, where you will get eaten alive). A 24-hour hotline (1-305 229 4522) gives a pre-recorded Florida weather report, as well as tide times.

If you are used to the state of constant alertness that being in Miami brings, you will find the Keys a welcome change. Crime is virtually non-existent in Key West (apart from bicycle theft), but all the same keep a careful watch on your personal belongings. Walking anywhere around Key West at night is far safer than in many areas of the US, but it is advisable to stay clear of the Bahama Village area after dark. The further north-east you travel, the more alert you should be, and in Key Largo revert to savvy-traveller mode.

Florida Keys & Key West Tourist Development Council
3406 North Roosevelt Boulevard, Suite 201, Key West, FL 33041 (1-800 852 3597).
A multilingual operator (1-800 771 5397) is available 24 hours a day for problem-solving (where to find the nearest hospital, etc). Check the website at http://www.fla-keys.com.

Key Largo Chamber of Commerce
10600 Overseas Highway, Key Largo, FL 33037 (1-305 451 1414/1-800 822 1088). Located at MM106. **Open** 9am-6pm daily.

Islamorada Chamber of Commerce
PO Box 915, Islamorada, FL 33036 (1-305 664 4503/ 1-800 322 5397). Located at MM82.5. **Open** 9am-5pm Mon-Fri.

Marathon Chamber of Commerce
12222 Overseas Highway, Marathon, FL 33050 (1-305 743 5417/1-800 842 9580). Located at MM122. **Open** 9am-5.30pm Mon-Fri; 9am-1pm Sat.

Lower Keys Chamber of Commerce
PO Box 430511, Eight Pine Key, FL 33043 (1-305 872 2411/1-800 872 3722). Located at MM31. **Open** 9am-5pm Mon-Fri; 9am-3pm Sat.

Greater Key West Chamber of Commerce
402 Wall Street, Key West, FL 33040 (1-305 294 2587/ 1-800 648 6269). **Open** 8.30am-5pm daily.

Key Largo to the Lower Keys

Key Largo is the largest of the islands and the nearest to Miami, so popular with city weekenders. The neon-clad central strip, with its ubiquitous burger bars and budget motels, can be offputting and the island is not known for its on-shore beauty, but it is compact enough to enjoy for a couple of days, if fast food is your forté. If you do want somewhere nice to eat, try Frank Keys Café (100211 Overseas Highway; 1-305 453 0310), set in a Victorian-style house surrounded by trees. The Everglades are just over the bay and there are numerous thrill and eco-tours available. Key Largo is also home to the *African Queen*, the boat used in the Bogart film (tours of the bay cost $15), and you can dine at Bogie's café at the dockside. The island's main attraction is **John Pennekamp Coral Reef**

Waterworld

The Keys are famed worldwide for their life beneath the water. The natural coral reefs can be appreciated by anyone who can swim, whether a first-time snorkeller or committed diver. Snorkelling and scuba equipment can be hired or bought throughout the Keys. Depending on the location, charter boats will take you to the best sites or you can explore the waters from the beach. First-time divers can train in four days or obtain a resort certificate, which will allow you to scuba with a guide, in a day. The **Florida Keys Marine Sanctuary** (1-305 743 2437) covers the entire island chain, which means that spear fishing is restricted in many areas.

The best known of the undersea parks is the **John Pennekamp Coral Reef**, off Key Largo (1-305 451 1202), where experienced divers can explore sunken wrecks and a 9ft bronze statue, Christ of the Deep. It is also popular for underwater weddings. At the dive shop next to the excellent visitor centre, you can rent snorkelling and diving equipment, join a glass-bottom boat trip and hire motorboats, sailboats, windsurfers and canoes. The park is open 8am-sunset daily; admission is $4 per vehicle plus 50¢ per passenger, $1.50 per pedestrian or cyclist.

Off Islamorada is the **San Pedro Underwater Archaeological Preserve**, which houses the remains of a 1733 Spanish galleon. At Marathon Key, one of the best areas to dive is beneath the **Seven Mile Bridge**. The most unusual event in the diving calendar is the annual **Lower Keys Underwater Music Festival**. Located at the Looe Key National Marine Sanctuary, home to over 150 species of fish, the event usually takes place on the first Saturday in July, when reggae, jazz and classical music is blasted under the reef (call 1-305 872 2411 for dates and details). To take part you must book a place on a local charter.

Sea kayaking is one of the few practical ways to visit the islands and inlets (known as the 'backwaters') north of US 1. The swampy waterways are largely unspoilt and a good place to see the wildlife that noisier craft scare away. The water is calm, meaning that even nervous watergoers can enjoy the mangrove islands and tidal channels without fear (or seasickness). Both guided tours or kayak hire are available; try **Mosquito Coast** on Key West (1-305 294 7178).

Tales of 'the one that got away' in the Keys are hardly necessary, so abundant are the fish. Sports fishing is popular all year round, with marlin, barracuda and sailfish among the big catch. Charter boats, which take four to six people, cost around $550 a day. Individuals can get a half-day-trip on a party boat for $30, which includes tackle, bait and instruction. Islamorada is often considered to be the fishing capital of the world and former US president George Bush hosts the annual bonefish tournament here. Go to any marina on any Key and you will find crews ready to take you to the high seas. Reef fishing is also good entertainment and can be combined with a snorkelling trip. Many outfits offer dive/accommodation packages.

Key Largo's Amoray Dive Resort (1-800 426 6729) also organises underwater weddings. **It's a Dive** (1-305 451 2377) on Key Largo is ranked number three in the US by *Scuba Diving* magazine. At Islamorada, try **Holiday Isle Dive Center** (1-305 664 4145); for Marathon and the Middle Keys, try **Never Enough Charters** (1-305 743 7265); and at Key West, try **Southpoint Divers** (1-800 824 6811). For information about fishing boat charters, contact the individual tourist offices (*see above* **Useful information**).

State Park (*see below* **Waterworld**) and much of the tourist industry (which keeps the isle afloat) is centred on the reef.

Travelling south-west you reach **Islamorada** – a group of six islands also known as the Matecumbes and the Purple Isles. Fishing dominates, but Islamorada is also the first sign of a quieter life – and a good one-night stop en route to Key West. There is a cycle path along the length of the four islands linked by US 1 (the two others are offshore) and there are some pretty, if pebbly beaches. Visit the Chamber of Commerce, which is housed in a bright red railway carriage at MM82.5 (*see above* **Tourist Information**). This compact office has a wealth of local information and some of the most helpful tourism staff you'll ever meet.

Marathon, which has its own airport, screams of tourism, and many say is not worth a visit unless you want to explore the engineering history of the Middle Keys. This island is a sailing community and has the largest year-round population of boat dwellers on the East Coast. You can rent a houseboat here, but don't expect some dinky barge bedecked with flower boxes – for the price you're probably better off staying in a hotel.

If you have time to spare, don't listen to the mainland folk who tell you to steam straight through to Key West. The **Lower Keys** are less

Nature parks

If you're taking a leisurely route through the Keys, it is worth stopping at one of the many national and state parks. These areas are not only rich in wildlife and ecology but are peaceful havens set in breathtaking scenery, and perfect spots to have a picnic or simply cool down. Many are renowned for their snorkelling and fishing, and some have camping areas. Pitching your tent in the parks is a cheap way of staying in the Keys and the sites are well-maintained; off-season you can often find a place away from other campers, beside the sea.

The furthest north is the **John Pennekamp Coral Reef State Park** (1-305 451 1202) at MM102.5, Key Largo, covering 70 nautical square miles of coral reefs, mangrove swamps and seagrass beds (*see also below* **Waterworld**). There are private concessions within the park, offering the usual water-based activities and camping on site. Offshore are two small islands, about one mile from US 1: **Lignumvitae Key State Botanical Site**, which has guided walking tours (winter Mon, Thur-Sun; summer Fri-Sun) through the island's native tropical forest, and **Indian Key State Historic Site**. The latter was inhabited by native American Indians for several thousand years and was once a prosperous wrecking town. Both are accessible by charter boat ($15 adults, $10 under-12s for one island, $25 and $15 for both islands) from MM77.5, Islamorada. Tours run daily except Tuesdays and Wednesdays. For more information, call 1-305 664 9814.

Long Key State Recreation Area (1-305 664 4815), located at MM67.5, is renowned for its marine and bird life. The 635-acre **Bahia Honda State Park** (1-305 872 2353), 12 miles south of Marathon, has one of the best beaches in Florida and is an excellent place to camp and use as a base to visit Key West by day. Bayside cabins are also available.

For detailed information on the parks, contact the Department of Environmental Protection Park Information, Mail Station 535, 3900 Common-wealth Boulevard, Tallahassee, FL 32399 (1-904 488 9872).

---

populated and so may not appeal to action-seeking townies, but they have some unique B&Bs, are teeming with wildlife and are a peaceful respite from their far busier neighbours. It is here that the famous miniature Key deer reside. Adult deer grow to only 2½ft tall. Despite the warning signs along US 1, you are more likely to spot them if you head off down a side road. Many people camp at **Bahia Honda State Park** (*see box* **Nature parks**), as it is close enough to Key West for you to enjoy the nightlife but cheap enough to allow you a few cocktails at sunset.

Dolphins are a big deal in the Keys – for protection, entertainment and even therapy. If you're lucky you might see them on a boat tour, but you can also swim with them and watch them play at a number of sites in the islands north-east of Key West. Contact the **Dolphins Plus Research Centre** on Key Largo (1-305 451 1993), **Theater of the Sea** on Islamorada (1-305 664 2431) and the **Dolphin Research Centre** on Grassy Key (1-305 289 0002).

Key West

Plan to go for a weekend and end up staying a week. Geographically nearer to Cuba than Miami, this happy-go-lucky island is the southernmost point of the US. Known as the Conch Republic (pronounced 'conk'), the pace is slow and visitors are soon lulled into the native regime of just 'being'. The architecture is amongst the prettiest you will see in Florida – a collection of Caribbean and New England-style homes along narrow streets. This is perhaps what makes Key West a favourite haunt of writers and artists, most notably Ernest Hemingway (whose former residence is ruthlessly hawked). It's also a favourite haunt of tourists, who consistently outnumber the local population but manage somehow not to overwhelm them.

Settlers first came to Key West in the early 1800s; a combination of farmers, wreckers and opportunists. Others just happened to chance upon the island and today many residents will admit they never intended to live here, but somehow could not bear to return across the bridge to the mainland. As one local said: 'In the 1970s came the hippies, followed by the gays, and in the 1990s the cruise ship brigade.' Key West was once Florida's wealthiest city, but underwent a slump in the 1940s. Many of the 1970s bohemian set remain, but in recent years the gay community has been responsible for regenerating much of the island.

With few beaches (except at Fort Taylor and the artificial Smathers Beach), Key West is not the place for a bucket-and-spade holiday but keen snorkellers and fisherman will find the coastline worthwhile. You will find that almost everything worth seeing/eating/drinking is at the west of the island in the Old Town, which is split in two by the main drag of **Duval Street**. Walking along Duval and reaching outwards to the leafy streets either side, you will find **Mallory Square**, a hive of shops and eateries, and **Bahama Village**, which is noticeably poorer than most of the Old Town but home to many long-established families. Take your time, take your sunblock and abandon any fast-paced city pretensions.

Sights

Cultural attractions

Most museums and historic buildings are in the Old Town and within walking distance of one another, some offering guided tours. The smaller, privately owned homes are often worth looking at.

Donkey Milk House

613 Eaton Street (1-305 296 1866). **Open** 10am-5pm daily. **Admission** $5 adults; free children. **Credit** (purchases over $20 in shop) AmEx, MC, V.
Owner/curator Denison Tempel lives in this historic house filled with US and European antiques.

Hemingway's House

907 Whitehead Street (1-305 294 1575). **Open** 9am-5pm daily. **Admission** $6.50 adults; $4 6-12s. **Credit** (shop only) MC, V.
See where the literary giant wrote some of his greatest novels. More interesting are the 70 resident cats.

Lighthouse Museum

938 Whitehead Street (294 0012). **Open** 9.30am-4pm daily. **Admission** $6 adults; $2 7-12s. **Credit** MC, V.
If you can be bothered to walk up the 88 steps to the balcony, you get a spectacular view of the island.

Mel Fisher Maritime Museum

200 Greene Street (1-305 294 2633). **Open** 9.30am-5pm daily. **Admission** $6.50 adults; $2 children. **Credit** AmEx, MC, V.
Good for wannabe pirates. Impressive exhibits document maritime history, smuggling, slavery and salvage.

Ripley's Odditorium

527 Duval Street (1-305 293 9694). **Open** 9am-11pm daily. **Admission** $9.95 adults; $8.95 senior citizens; $7.95 students; $6.95 4-12s. **Credit** AmEx, Disc, MC, V.
A peculiar and diverse collection of art, science, nature and just about anything else you can think of to entertain and educate.

Wreckers' Museum

322 Duval Street (1-305 294 9502). **Ope**n 10am-4pm daily. **Admission** $4 adults; 50¢ children. **No credit cards**.
The oldest house in Key West and the former home of merchant seaman Captain Frances Watlington. Offers a chaotic look back in time.

Gardens & places of interest

City Cemetery

Between Margaret and Angela Streets.
Opened in the mid-1800s, this 15-acre cemetery has a collection of strange and witty gravestones. Noteworthy are 'I told you I was sick' and 'Call me for dinner'. Guided tours can be arranged by calling the Historic Florida Keys Preservation Board (1-305 292 6718).

Nancy Forrester's Secret Garden

1 Free School Lane (1-305 294 0015). **Open** 10am-5pm daily. **Admission** $6 adults; $2 children. **Credit** AmEx, Disc, MC, V.
A 25-year labour of love for Nancy and her partner Elliot Wright, containing a unique collection of botanical plants. Nancy is a licensed pastor and also conducts weddings in the enchanted jungle. *See also below* **Where to stay**.

Southernmost point

End of Whitehead & South Streets.
Famous 'I-was-here photo' opportunity. Beware of the 'charming' men who offer to take your picture and then demand a tip.

Sitting on the dock of the bay, Key West.

Wellspring Medicine Garden

800 Amelia Street, at Windsor Lane (1-305 292 2022).
Open 8am-8pm daily. **Admission** by donation.
Garden sanctuary where people are encouraged to 'commune' with nature. Meditation practiced in the evenings. Healing massage available.

Festivals & events

Every evening is the sunset celebration: it's completely free, just walk towards Mallory Square and look out to sea. Tourists and locals gather and high-class buskers, jugglers and acrobatic acts perform as the sun goes down into the Gulf of Mexico in a molten ball.

Every month there is a festival of some sort, but the most famous is the **Fantasy Fest** in October (1-305 296 1817) – the Keys' version of Mardi Gras, a wild 10-day party. The famous week-long **Hemingway Days Festival** in late July, which celebrated the writer's birthday with a literary event, lookalike contest and major fishing tournament, has been cancelled (due to opposition from Hemingway's descendents), but may be revived under another name. Contact the tourist offices for a monthly calendar.

Tours & excursions

Tour on foot and see the historic homes. Pick up a Pelican Path map and guide from any of the tourist booths or write to the Old Island Restoration Foundation, PO Box 689, Key West, FL 33041. The 90-minute **Conch tour train** (1-305 294 5161) and **Old Town Trolley** (1-305 296 6688) give a guided commentary on the town's main attractions. Not recommended for children is the nightly **Ghost Tour** (1-305 293 8009), which leaves from Noah's Ark, 416 Fleming Street.

There are numerous sunset cruises, tours to the coral reefs and glass-bottom boat trips. Try **Fury Catamarans** (1-305 294 8899), the **Schooner Appledore** (1-305 296 9992), and **Discovery Glass Bottom Boat** (1-305 293 0099). Air tours include seaplanes and biplanes; call **Key West Air Service** (1-305 292 5201).

Contrary to popular tourist belief, the Dry Tortugas are not a Tex-Mex snack, but a group of islands 70 miles off the coast of Key West ('tortuga' means turtle in Spanish). The Tortugas National Park (PO Box 6208, Key West, FL 33041) is home to the Civil War monument Fort Jefferson and a wildlife sanctuary. The park is great for a day trip away from the bustle of Key West and excellent for snorkelling and fishing. Visitors must bring all food, water and supplies: there are toilets at the dock but no sinks, showers or rubbish bins, so visitors must remove all items brought into the park. Free

camping is allowed at 10 sites. You can get to the park via the **Yankee Freedom** ferry service (1-305 294 7009), **Sunny Days Catamaran** (1-305 296 5556), **Tortugas Ferry** (1-305 294 7009), **Fort Jefferson Catamaran** (1-305 292 6100) and Key West Air Service.

Eating & drinking

It may have something to do with being at the southern-most point in the US – the sense that you are only a few steps away from falling off the end of the world – that builds the appetite. Whatever the reason, bars and restaurants abound along and around the main strip. The infamous Key lime, a small yellow fruit resembling a lemon, is sold on every corner, in a variety of guises; Key lime pie, juice, marmalade and toffee are worth a try, but beware of poor imitations. Fish, blackened, grilled, fried or baked, is found on most menus and no visitor to the Keys can leave without trying conch, though it may prove a disappointment. This often rubbery-tasting shellfish is best deep-fried and sampled as a fritter. Don't be alarmed by the numerous dolphin dishes offered here – we're talking mahi-mahi fish, not our friend Flipper.

Eating out is not cheap on the main drag but budget travellers can take advantage of free nibbles given out at some bars during happy hour. Bars are open as late as people will drink (officially 4am), but sampling the local cocktails can be expensive. Go for the '2-for-1' deals and check the local *Yellow Pages* and tourist guides for money-off coupons.

Restaurants & cafés

Banana Cafe

1211 Duval Street (1-305 294 7227). **Breakfast & lunch** 8am-3pm, **dinner** 7-11pm, Tue-Sun. **Credit** AmEx, DC, Disc, MC, V.
Watch the world go by at the quieter end of Duval Street. French food, excelling at breakfast and brunch. Live jazz every evening.

Blue Heaven

729 Thomas Street, Bahama Village (1-305 296 8666). **Breakfast & lunch** 6am-3pm, **dinner** 6-10.30pm, daily. **Credit** Disc, MC, V.
Off the beaten track in Bahama Village; you will probably hear the chickens before you smell the food. Dining is outdoors, among domestic bantams and cats. Popular among locals, and you can have your fill without breaking the bank. Art galleries and craft shops on site.

Café des Artistes

1007 Simonton Street (1-305 294 7100). **Dinner** 6-9.30pm Mon-Thur; 6-10pm Fri, Sat. **Credit** AmEx, MC, V.

Exclusive, expensive, award-winning French cuisine (with a tropical twist). Try the Lobster Tango Mango, flambéd in cognac, with a saffron and mango sauce. Booking recommended. Open only in the evenings.

Camille's

703 Duval Street (1-305 296 4811). **Breakfast & lunch** 8am-3pm daily. **Dinner** 6-11pm Tue-Sat. **Credit** AmEx, DC, Disc, MC, V.

Winner of the best locals' local for years. A bustling family-type atmosphere. Crowded, particularly at brunch time, with a menu of Caribbean and European home cooking. Breakfast served until 3pm daily – be prepared to queue.

Gato Gordo Café

404 Southard Street (1-305 294 0888). **Open** 11am-11pm daily. **Credit** AmEx, DC, Disc, MC, V.

Cheap Tex-Mex, big portions and lively atmosphere. Locals come here to snack and drink, especially the margaritas and 30 different types of tequila.

Riviera Pizza

101 Duval Street (1-305 292 5206). **Open** 9am-midnight daily. **No credit cards**.

Cheap and tasty pizza by the slice. Located near the main tourist bars and open until late. Pick up a card inside to get one slice free with every two bought.

Rooftop Café

310 Front Street (1-305 294 2042). **Breakfast** 9-11am, **lunch** 11am-4pm, **dinner** 6-10pm, daily. **Credit** AmEx, Disc, MC, V.

Informal fine dining, overlooking Mallory Square. Try the award-winning lump crab and fresh shrimp cakes or grilled dolphin with macadamia nut sauce.

Bars

Captain Tony's Saloon

428 Greene Street (1-305 294 1838). **Open** 10am-2am Mon-Sat; noon-2am Sun. **No credit cards**.

Just to confuse you, this was Hemingway's original Sloppy Joe's and is opposite the existing venue of that name (*see below*). A tourist hangout, but a lot of fun when it's busy.

Finnigan's Wake

320 Grinnell Street (1-305 293 0222). **Open** 11am-4am Mon-Sat; noon-4am Sun. **Credit** AmEx, Disc, MC, V.

Unpretentious Irish pub, serving a better Guinness than most. A hangout for locals.

Pepe's Café

806 Caroline Street (1-305 294 7192). **Open** 6.30am-10.30pm daily. **Credit** Disc, MC, V.

Cheap beer and free snacks on the bar during happy hour (but don't tell everyone). Good barbecue on Sundays. Popular with locals.

PT's Late Night Bar & Grill

920 Caroline Street (1-305 296 4245). **Open** 11am-4am daily. **Credit** DC, MC, V.

A popular sports bar. Pool tables, TV screens and cheap fast food. Frequented by locals and sports nuts.

Rumrunners

218 Duval Street (1-305 294 1017). **Open** 11am-4am Mon-Sat; noon-4am Sun. **Credit** AmEx, Disc, MC, V.

Another get-extremely-drunk joint, which may have something to do with the Dutch courage measures needed to visit the strip bar upstairs. Lively, hip and full of the holiday crowd. Rumrunners was the scene of a fatal shooting in early 1997, but this was a freak occurrence.

Sloppy Joe's

201 Duval Street (1-305 294 5717). **Open** 9am-4am Mon-Sat; noon-4am Sun. **Credit** Disc, MC, V.

Live bands in a buzzing hangout for the young. Despite the Hemingway memorabilia, the famous former resident had nothing to do with this popular bar.

Shopping

Everything in Key West is expensive, so don't be tempted to buy clothes unless it really is the outfit of your dreams. T-shirt shops breed far more successfully than the beleaguered manatee. There are some unusual shops worth checking out, not because they are exclusive to the Keys but simply because they have interesting buys.

At the **Cuban Leaf Cigar Factory** (310 Duval Street; 1-305 295 9283), you can watch cigars being made before buying. **Capricorn Jewelry** (706B Duval Street; 1-305 292 9338) has a good selection of Native American jewellery. The **Key West Kite Company** (409 Greene Street; 1-305 296 2535) is worth a visit to see all the colourful designs, while **Glass Reunions** (825 Duval Street; 1-305 294 1720)

sells locally made, hand-blown art and household items, but its greatest pull is the ongoing Alpha Romeo sculpture parked outside. Next door is **Pandemonium** (825 Duval Street; 1-305 294 0351), which sells beautiful (and appropriately expensive) handmade tiles.

If you are staying in self-catering accommodation, don't shop at the small supermarkets along the main strips. Tourists are charged higher prices than natives but – if you are feeling confident and/or dishonest – you can try asking for a local's discount (but be warned, they may ask for local ID). **Key Plaza** and **Searstown**, both on N Roosevelt Boulevard, have a good selection of stores, where locals get their supplies. If you get the munchies late at night, head for the 24-hour **Sunbeam Groceries & Deli** (500 White Street; 1-305 294 8993).

Gay hangouts

Bourbon Street Pub
730 Duval Street (1-305 296 1992). **Open** noon-4am daily. **Credit** MC, V.
New Orleans-style bar with the longest 2-for-1 happy hour on Duval (noon-8pm). Weekly shows, including drag acts.

Eight-O-One Bar
801 Duval Street (1-305 294 4737). **Open** 11am-4am Mon-Sat; noon-4am Sun. **No credit cards**.
Live entertainment nightly in the cabaret bar. Quiet room at the back. Popular with locals.

Epoch
623 Duval Street (1-305 296 8521). **Open** *terrace bar* 2-10pm daily; *dance bar* 10pm-4am Tue-Sun. **Credit** AmEx, DC, Disc, MC, V.
Gay-owned and run nightclub, but popular among the straight crowd. 1980s and 1990s dance music, five bars and an outdoor terrace.

Numbers
1029 Truman Avenue (1-305 296 0333). **Open** 11pm-3am daily. **No credit cards**.
Gay strip club. No cover charge. Shows nightly, 11pm-2am.

Where to stay

During the high season in Key West (November to April), accommodation prices soar. At New Year and the October Fantasy Fest, booking is strongly advised. Off-season, you can find good deals at the numerous guest houses and B&Bs, which can be particularly cost-effective if four people share a room with two double beds. Budget accommodation can be found at the youth hostel, near the centre of town or the chain motels. Alternatively, stay in one of the old gingerbread-style family homes. Prices start at $40 per night off-season and run up to $200-plus. If you are staying for a week or more, it might be worth renting a house. Note that the rates given below are for high season, so they will be substantially lower during the off-season.

Key West Condo Vacations (218 Whitehead Street, Key West FL 33040; 1-305 294 7878) rents private homes and condos. **Key West Reservation Service** (715 Front Street, Key West, FL 33040; 1-305 296 7753) is a booking service for hotels, motels and guest houses. For a list of over 55 guest houses and B&Bs, write to the **Key West Innkeepers' Association**, PO Box 6172, Key West, FL 33041.

Denoit's Cottage
512 Angela Street, Key West, FL 33040 (1-305 294 6324). **Rates** $109-$298. **Credit** Disc, MC, V.
A single two-room cottage. Centrally located and a home away from home.

Duval Gardens
1012 Duval Street, Key West, FL 33040 (1-305 292 3379). **Rates** double $120; one-bedroom suite $175. **Credit** AmEx, Disc, MC, V.
Mid-priced, family-run B&B. Access to a private beach resort and free afternoon cocktails.

Island City House
411 William Street, Key West, FL 33040 (1-305 294 5702). **Rates** suites, studio $165-$210; two-bedroom $255-$275. **Credit** AmEx, Disc, MC, V.
Three separate houses overlook a leafy courtyard. Luxurious, understated Colonial-style rooms, some with kitchen.

Nancy Forrester's Secret Garden
1 Free School Lane, Key West, FL 33040 (1-305 294 0015). **Rates** one night $200; more than one night $175. **Credit** AmEx, Disc, MC, V.
One-room studio, which sleeps four, tucked away in the middle of magical botanical garden. *See also above* **Gardens & places of interest**.

Key West Hostel
718 South Street, Key West, FL 33040 (1-305 296 5719). **Rates** members $17; non-members $20. **Credit** MC, V.
Cheap dormitory rooms.

Southernmost Point Guest House
1327 Duval Street, Key West, FL 33040 (1-305 294 0715). **Rates** standard $80-$110; with kitchen $115-$135; suite $150-$175. **Credit** AmEx, MC, V.
A family-run establishment, serving an excellent home-cooked breakfast complete with fresh eggs from resident chickens. Don't remove your sunglasses: the rooms of this historic 1885 house are garish, but they're comfortable.

Getting around

Parking is a pain, the streets narrow and the island small, so you don't need a car. The best way to look around is on foot. Alternatively, bicycles, mopeds and scooters can be hired from between $6-$20 a day and many hotels have rental booths on site. Most firms insist on a credit card for vehicle rentals. Those with ideas of grandeur should try the **Pedicabs** (1-305 292 0077). These two-seater, bicycle-powered rickshaws can be hailed along Duval Street and charge by the minute or journey; check before you board.

You can rent a bicycle by the hour, day or week. Shop around for the best deal; some outfits will offer free pick-up from your hotel. Large rental firms include **The Bicycle Centre**, 523 Truman Avenue (1-305 294 4556); **The Bike Shop**, 1110 Truman Avenue (1-305 294 1073); and **Adventure Bicycle Rentals**, with eight different locations including 1 Duval Street (1-305 293 0441) and 601 Front Street at the Hyatt Hotel (1-305 293 9944). Many firms that rent scooters and mopeds offer group rates and one- or two-seater vehicles. Try **Pirate Scooter**, 401 Southard Street (1-305 295 0000) or **Paradise Rentals** at 105 Whitehead Street (1-305 292 6441) and 430 Duval Street (1-305 293 1112). Taxi companies include **Five Sixes Cab Company** (1-305 296 6666) and **Friendly Cab Company** (1-305 292 0000).

Tourist information

Numerous information booths line Duval Street. They will try to sell you a charter cruise or snorkelling trip, but also provide valuable local advice and money-off coupons. Alternatively, visit the **Greater Key West Chamber of Commerce**, 402 Wall Street (1-305 294 2587) or **Welcome Centre**, 3840 N Roosevelt Boulevard (1-305 296 4444). Gay visitors will find the **Key West Business Guild**, 424 Fleming Street (1-305 294 4603) a useful contact.

Orlando & Walt Disney World

How much fun can a person have? Well, in the Orlando area, quite a lot, actually....

Buy into the American dream and rent a Harley at **Eaglerider** *(see page 248).*

Many people consider Orlando the town that Mickey built. In some ways, that's true. Before Walt Disney World opened in 1971, Orlando was primarily known for its citrus crop. It was a sleepy, landlocked city stranded in the centre of a state that valued beachfront property. But after Mickey and his gang set up shop, Orlando exploded. Everyone wanted to be next to the mouse. Orange groves were levelled and hotels sprang up in their place. Attractions like Sea World, Wet 'n Wild and Universal Studios Florida drew millions. Disney implemented a never-ending expansion policy and tourists flocked here by the planeload.

According to the Orlando/Orange County Convention & Visitors Bureau, more than 36 million visitors came to the Greater Orlando area in 1995. There are an astounding 86,000 hotel rooms with an average occupancy of 79 per cent. The population

has swelled to 1.4 million and most locals are happy because the weather is nice and employment is expected to grow 28 per cent by 2005.

Like any tourist area, Orlando is a party town. The average age is 31 (though it feels younger) and the average activity usually involves drinking. The transient population of tourist-industry workers fuels the party atmosphere and helps make Orlando very apolitical. The vibe can be summarised by the mantra: 'I've got a job, the sun is shining, pass me a beer'. Orlando also has a sizeable gay and lesbian population – unusual for a small, southern city – many of whom work in the tourist industry. Not nearly as flamboyant or activist as similar communities in New York or San Francisco, Orlando's pink community seems to pride itself on being well-integrated within the general population. Many of the city's gay residents live in suburban homes next door to unaware straights.

Culturally, Orlando has a few brights spots, which are slowly getting brighter. Downtown has a vibrant club scene and Orlando has earned a reputation as the rave capital of the US (raves attracting 10,000-plus fans occur regularly just outside town). Orlando plays host to numerous annual festivals of film, Shakespeare, performance art and more. Unfortunately, there's not enough of a regular audience to support venues for many of these art forms. Perhaps it's the legacy of being a tourist town that makes residents think of culture in the same way that they think of attractions – worth a visit once a year.

In the most interesting trend, high-tech has come to town, spurred in part by the steady stream of computer graduates from the University of Central Florida. Major companies such as Time Warner, AT&T, Raytheon and Siemens have divisions in the area. Regional defence contractors, which floundered when peace broke out, recently found salvation by switching to high-tech. One local magazine went so far as to claim that as many Orlando-area residents work in the high-tech sector as in the tourism sector. If this high-tech trend is true, it could influence Orlando's future much more than Disney's next theme park.

ORIENTATION

The Greater Orlando area stretches 30 miles from Sanford in the north to Kissimmee in the south. The topography is flat, with numerous lakes dotting the region. If you avoid the strip malls, it is a beautiful place, with giant oak trees making it feel more like Georgia than Central Florida. I-4 runs on a south-east/north-west route through its centre (though in Orlando itself, it turns north-south). **Downtown Orlando** (*see page 240*) is centrally located just north of the intersection of I-4 and the East-West Expressway. Further north are residential communities such as **Winter Park** (*see page 245*) and corporate office parks. **Walt Disney World** (*see page 252*) and most tourist sites are 10 to 25 miles south of Downtown in a area known to locals as '**The Attractions**' (*see page 246*), focused around I-4 and International Drive (I-Drive). Many tourists spend their whole vacation at the attractions convinced they're seeing Orlando. They're wrong.

Getting there & around

By car

The car is king in Florida. Many tourists love the rental companies' cheap rates, unlimited mileage and freedom to drop off anywhere in the state. Petrol is also much cheaper in the US than in Europe. At large tourist attractions there's usually a daily parking fee of $3-$5, but having a car means that you can come and go as you please. All the major national rental car agencies have operations in Orlando and counters

at Orlando International Airport; for their telephone numbers and web sites, *see chapter* **Getting Around**.

If you're driving to the Greater Orlando area from Miami, you have a choice of three routes:

● **I-95** to **SR 528** (a toll road) runs up the east coast to almost level with Orlando before turning inland. It's direct and fairly cheap. Though I-95 is a big road, it can be crowded with east coast traffic (especially the section from Miami to West Palm Beach). It's a good route if you want to stay near the beaches or visit sights such as the Kennedy Space Center. The drive from Miami takes about five hours.

● The **Florida Turnpike** is the most expensive toll route (South Beach to I-4 near Orlando costs about $15), but the traffic is usually lighter. The turnpike parallels I-95 from Miami north to Fort Pierce, so you can save a few bucks by sticking with I-95 until then. Once the turnpike turns inland, it's a very serene drive through marshes and fields of grass.

● Those searching for authentic rural Florida can follow the twists and turns of **SR 27**, which curves around Lake Okeechobee and heads up the centre of the state. It's a two-lane road much of the way through sugar plantations and small farming towns. There's not much to see or do unless you're interested in bass fishing or the race tracks of Sebring. Our favourite stop is Plantation Paradise (2108 US 27 south in Lake Placid), where everything sold is made with pineapple (try the toothpaste). On the plus side, if you're going to Walt Disney World, SR 27 allows you to bypass Orlando traffic completely. You intersect I-4 west of the park, near Haines City. From Miami, the drive takes about six hours.

By train

If you're arriving by train, you're riding **Amtrak** (1-800 872 7245). There are stations in Winter Park, Sanford, Kissimmee and Orlando. Two trains run daily from Miami to Orlando ($62 one-way, $124 return); the journey takes about 5½ hours. The Orlando station (1400 Sligh Boulevard) is south of Downtown, so you'll need to grab a cab or walk east to Orange Avenue and hop on bus 40 to the Lynx Downtown terminal, from where you can get anywhere.

By bus

Inter-city bus line **Greyhound** (1-800 231 2222) has a main terminal just west of Downtown Orlando at 555 N John Young Parkway (not a great neighbourhood, so don't wander around). Grab local Lynx bus 25 for a short ride to the Downtown Lynx terminal (Pine Street, between Orange and Garland Avenues). There are additional Greyhound stops in Kissimmee and DeBary. Ten buses run daily from Miami to Orlando ($32 one-way, $61 return); the journey takes from 5½ to 11 hours.

Lynx (1-407 841 8240) operates local buses throughout the three counties that make up Greater Orlando. Stops are indicated by a round sign with a paw print. From the Lynx Downtown terminal, you can get anywhere in the area. A one-way ride costs 85¢ and exact change is required. There are discounts if you buy a weekly pass or multi-ticket book. Pick up a bus map at the main terminal or buy a system-wide map/schedule ($3) from local Walgreens drugstores.

By air

Orlando International Airport (1-407 825 2352), located 15 miles south-east of Downtown and 20 miles north-east of Walt Disney World, is serviced by nearly 50 airlines. It has three terminals, each connected to the main building by elevated trains. Besides being modern and efficient, Orlando airport is fastidiously clean; to that end, it forbids the sale of chewing gum on airport property. Two airport information centres, located near entrances to gates 1-59 and gates 60-99, offer multi-lingual personal assistance as well as info on the airport and Central Florida. Currency exchange is available on the baggage claim level and at the international gates. The airport also has 24-hour bank teller machines.

Lynx runs five bus lines from the airport. Bus **42** heads to International Drive and many tourist hotels. The **11** and

51 go to the Downtown terminal via different roads. The 41 follows SR 436 north to Maitland and Apopka while the 52 goes through Pine Castle to the Florida Mall.

Cabs and shuttles are available at the airport without reservations. **Mears Transportation** (1-407 423 5566) and **Transtar Shuttle** (1-407 856 7777) offer continuous shuttles that hit multiple stops: Mears' price to Downtown is $12; both charge $14 to I-Drive. Mears and Transtar also have private town cars. These should be booked 24 hours in advance and the price doesn't include driver's tip (assume 15 per cent). A Mears town car from the airport to the Peabody Hotel is $31; Transtar charges $45 from the airport to I-Drive. Before you hop in a cab, check if your hotel offers a free airport shuttle; many do.

By taxi

Many companies handle taxi and shuttle services within town. Check the *Yellow Pages* phone directory under 'Taxis'. Cabs in or near Downtown Orlando run on a meter system (try Yellow Cab at 1-407 699 9999). Cabs bouncing between hotels and attractions often ignore the meter and charge flat rates; ask before you go. Some hotels offer courtesy shuttles to the attractions for guests. These sound good, until you discover they stop at 10 other hotels on the way.

Ticket brokers

Ticket brokers are standalone businesses offering discounts on attraction tickets and hotel rooms. The discounts vary widely. For instance, it's virtually impossible to get a deal on one-day passes for the Magic Kingdom, Epcot or Universal Studios Florida, but lesser attractions and dinner shows might be discounted 10-15 per cent or more. The benefit of using ticket brokers is that it allows you to skip ticket-buying queues at the theme parks. For that reason, you should buy only real tickets from brokers; don't bother with vouchers, which must then be exchanged for tickets at the gates. Also avoid anything involving a time-share pitch: you really don't need that kind of hassle. One of the best deals that the brokers offer is a four-day Walt Disney World Hopper pass ($199 adults; $160 children). This ticket isn't even sold at Disney. If you use it wisely, it offers entrance to all the Disney attractions for 11 days; restrictions do apply, but it's still worth investigating.

International Visitors Bureau

7670 I-Drive (1-407 351 0002). **Open** 8am-8pm daily; *8445 I-Drive, at Mercado (1-407 351 4110).* **Open** 8am-10pm daily.

Two offices offering hotels, shuttle services, maps, discounted tickets and even currency exchange.

Super Savers Tourist Information Center

2531 E Irlo Bronson Highway (US 192), 1 mile east of Florida Turnpike (1-407 870 7627). **Open** 8.30am-5pm Mon-Sat; 9.30am-5pm Sun.

This family-run business is a good choice if you're staying near Kissimmee. They know everything and are helpful.

Useful information

For information on climate and other travel basics *see chapter* **Essential Information**.

Tourist information

All the major attractions have their own promotional material, and numerous wall displays proffer free brochures, often containing discount coupons for attractions and hotels. Free tourist guides are given away everywhere. Since these are primarily marketing tools, they tend to focus on the lesser attractions and restaurants, but their coupons and maps are nevertheless useful.

A day at the beach

Many visitors are shocked to discover Orlando is landlocked ('Whaddya mean, I can't get a room with an ocean view?'). If you crave sun, fun and sand, jump in a car and head east. The closest waves are in Cocoa Beach, New Smyrna and Daytona Beach, about 50-60 miles from O-Town.

Cocoa Beach, which is a few miles south of the Kennedy Space Center on SR AIA, has a 10-mile strip of shore, Florida's best surfing and the legendary Ron Jon Surf Shop (4151 N Atlantic Avenue; 1-407 799 8888), which treats itself with the high pomp of a Disney attraction. Also check out the Cocoa Beach Pier, which stretches 840ft into the ocean and has three restaurants. It's the place to be seen and be seen being seen.

Daytona Beach is 50 miles north of Cocoa Beach via I-95 or SR 1. Many of Daytona's wide beaches are open to traffic, so you can actually drive a car onto the hard-packed sand. February through March is party central as the town hosts Speed Weeks (three weekends of auto racing), followed by Bike Week (seven days of leather vests and rude comments about Japanese motorcycles), followed by Spring Break (college students get drunk and do stupid things). Local enthusiasm for Spring Break has cooled off somewhat in recent years as residents grew tired of hosing vomit off their lawns. But students still appear each year and Daytona is in no danger of losing its self-proclaimed status as 'The World's Most Famous Beach'.

New Smyrna, 15 miles south of Daytona, has a much calmer vibe and the beaches are free of vehicles. Take I-4 to SR 44 east and you'll find New Smyrna is actually the quickest trip from O-Town, especially since you avoid the Daytona traffic. As for ads touting the proximity of St Petersburg beaches, don't believe the hype. Even if you're staying near the attractions, the closest west coast beaches are 30-40 miles further away than the east coast. Plus, you have to drive through Tampa and a very crowded I-4. Don't consider it unless you're planning on staying overnight in Tampa anyway.

Official Visitors Center of the Orlando Convention & Visitors Bureau

8723 I-Drive, Suite 101, Orlando, FL 32819 (1-407 363 5871). **Open** tickets 8am-7pm daily; information 8am-8pm daily.

Kissimmee-St Cloud Convention & Visitors Bureau

1925 E Irlo Bronson Highway, Kissimmee, FL 34742 (1-407 847 5000). **Open** 8am-5pm daily.

Winter Park Chamber of Commerce

150 N New York Avenue, Winter Park, FL 32790 (1-407 644 8281). **Open** 8am-4.30pm Mon-Fri.

Publications

Orlando has one major daily newspaper, the *Orlando Sentinel* (50¢, Sunday edition $1.50), which is conservative and fairly lame. The *Orlando Weekly* (published on Thursdays) is the town's free 'alternative' paper (mainly an alternative to the *Sentinel*) and offers very complete club and concert listings. Also free are the gay and lesbian weekly *Watermark* and the excellent weekly *Ink Nineteen*, which is dedicated to alternative music and entertainment. *Orlando* is a glossy monthly magazine with local interest features. And if you see *Bitch Rag*, grab it – it's a terrific zine put out by four wacky ladies from Sanford that covers the Orlando scene from their own, highly skewed perspective.

Emergencies

For emergencies, call **911** (or, if you're in a hotel, 9-911). If an ambulance is sent to pick you up, it's supposed to take you to the nearest hospital best suited for your emergency. **Florida Hospital**: Downtown Orlando and Winter Park (1-407 896 6611); Kissimmee (1-407 846 4343). **Orlando Regional Healthcare**: Downtown Orlando (1-407 841 5111); Sand Lake near I-Drive (1-407 351 8500).

Telephones

Note that all Greater Orlando area phone numbers have the area code **1-407**. You need to include the code only if you're calling from outside the area.

Guns 'R Us

Despite the horrifying fact that 16 children die every day from gunshot wounds, the US love-affair with firearms continues. **Shooting Sports of Orlando** (6811 Visitors Circle, across from Wet 'n Wild; 1-407 363 9000) is one of the only places in the state where visitors can rent an honest-to-god, fully automatic weapon for use on the house range. Rifles and handgun can also be rented. Expect to pay about $35, which covers one box or clip of ammunition. No experience? No problem! First-time shooters are welcome and the brochure says 'responsible children of 10 years of age or older are permitted to shoot on the range if accompanied by a parent'. Ahhh, the family that plays together, stays together.

Downtown Orlando

Downtown Orlando has experienced an amazing resurgence. Locals used to complain that there was nothing to do. Now they complain that there's nowhere to park.

Church Street Station was the area's entertainment anchor for 22 years and the only tourist draw. Locals pretty much ignored it and the seedy mess that Downtown had become. In the 1980s, government executives got serious about Orlando's motto (yet another Florida town called 'The City Beautiful') and began cleaning up the place. Lake Eola Park, a former haven for drug dealers, was restored. An aggressive beautification programme planted flowers along roadsides. Cops were put on the streets to reassure people that everything was under control. In the past five years, numerous nightclubs have opened. A thriving house music scene has put Orlando clubs and DJs on the national map, and alternative and college rock bands have made O-Town a regular stop. Young professionals have restored homes in the nearby Lake Eola Historic District. Life has returned to Downtown.

Concentrated in a few square blocks are now upwards of 20 clubs and bars. At weekends, it's not uncommon to see thousands of people strolling around Church Street and Orange Avenue. The area retains a funky, mid-gentrification charm, with old wig shops just a few doors from sky-scrapers and homeless people quietly hanging out in Lake Eola Park. But considering that more skyscrapers are on the drawing board and rents have started to rise, things could change drastically in the future. Right now may well be Downtown Orlando's heyday.

Although Downtown is a large zone that includes residential areas, about 80 per cent of the nightlife occurs in the blocks bordered by I-4 on the east, Rosalind Avenue on the west, Church Street on the south and Amelia Street to the north. This entire area can be covered easily on foot. Street parking is next to impossible, so use one of the many municipal lots: there's one under I-4 near Church Street and another on the corner of Washington Street and Magnolia Avenue. Most are bargain priced at 75¢ an hour. Some lots, such as the convenient one at Boone Avenue and South Street, charge a flat rate of around $3-$5.

General safety rules for travelling in the US also apply in Orlando. Pay attention. Lock your car. Areas to avoid include S Orange Blossom Trail (strip club central) and the west side of I-4 in Downtown (particularly west of N Parramore Avenue and south of the Orlando Arena). The arena's location shouldn't prevent you from going to see an evening event there; just don't get lost driving around at night.

Sights

Church Street Station

129 West Church Street (1-407 422 2434). **Open** 11am-1am Mon-Thur, Sun; 11am-2am Fri, Sat. **Admission** after 6pm (includes all clubs) $17.95 adults; $10.95 4-12s. **Credit** AmEx, Disc, MC, V.

The first stop for tourists, this multi-building complex is its own universe. It boasts turn-of-the-century décor surrounding several restaurants and clubs, as well as retail space and a top-notch video arcade. Due to space, we've listed only the top restaurants and clubs.

Cheyenne Saloon & Opera House: An amazing room built with 250,000sq ft of oak lifted from an Ohio barn. Décor includes Frederic Remington sculptures, original tapestries from Buffalo Bill and Annie Oakley's Wild West Show and chandeliers from the Philadelphia mint. Look around during the day if you don't want to pay admission. Country & Western bands are the entertainment and western BBQ makes up the menu. Country dance lessons are offered every Friday, Saturday and Sunday, 2-5.30pm.

Crackers: Seafood restaurant with some cajun flavour. Victorian décor, many kinds of bottled beers and big-screen TVs for sports.

Lili Marlene's Aviator's Pub: Church Street's best restaurant, serving beef, seafood and poultry in a room full of flight memorabilia. You can even eat on the dining room table and chairs once owned by gangster Al Capone.

Phineas Phogg's: Loud, progressive dance club with ballooning memorabilia. Draught beer costs only 5¢ every Wednesday, 6.30-7.30pm.

Rosie O'Grady's: Located in the former Orlando Hotel. Lots of great furnishings from old banks and railroad terminals and a Dixieland Jazz Revue that's loud and fun. The menu is very limited.

Lake Eola Park

S Rosalind Avenue, between Central Boulevard & Robinson Street.

Witness a rare successful urban renovation. Hunker down and have a picnic in the grass while you watch the world go by or a rent a two-person swan boat ($5 per half-hour) and pedal out to the middle of the lake for a great view.

Terror on Church Street

135 S Orange Avenue (1-407 649 3327). **Open** 7pm-midnight Mon-Thur, Sun; 7pm-1am Fri, Sat. **Admission** $12 adults; $10 under-17s. **Credit** AmEx, JCB, MC, V.

A permanent house of horror featuring high-tech special effects and live actors in extravagant make-up trying to scare the hell out of you. It's kind of goofy, but teenagers and slightly drunk college kids go back again and again for the 20-minute walk-through.

Bars & clubs

Barbarella

70 N Orange Avenue (1-407 839 0457). **Open** 9pm-3am Mon, Fri-Sun.

This dance club has seen better days. Still, it gets huge crowds on weekends. It also has a backyard stage which is a nice place to catch live bands.

The Blue Room

12 W Pine Street (1-407 423 2588). **Open** 8pm-2am Mon-Sat.

One of the coolest new clubs. Elegant without attitude. Spins dance music, but if you're not into moving, there are couches and chairs. Look for DJ Mot.

Cairo

22 S Magnolia Avenue (1-407 422 3595). **Open** 10pm-3am Wed-Sun.

A fashionable, modern dance club. The rooftop lounge is a good place to hang when you need air. Queues down the block on big nights.

The Club at Firestone

578 N Orange Avenue (1-407 426 0005). **Open** 9pm-3am Wed-Sun.

Cited as the best dance club by ravers and Orlando's large gay club contingent, this huge space used to be a Firestone garage. Features killer sound and lighting and the music plays till morning at weekends (no alcohol after 2am). Wander in at 3am and you'll witness an amazing mix of gay, straight, old and young tripping to the beats. Also hosts live shows by big acts. A few blocks north, but it's an easy walk.

Eight Seconds

100 W Livingston Street (1-407 839 4800). **Open** 8pm-3am Thur-Sun.

Downtown's big Country & Western bar. Live bull-riding on Saturdays in the rodeo in the back.

Go Lounge

Wall Street Plaza (1-407 422 1669). **Open** 8pm-2am Mon-Thur, Sat, Sun; 4pm-2am Fri.

A raw, funky space with a billion different bottled beers. The garage in the back sometimes holds a rocking band. Sometimes it holds an old school bus.

Harold & Maude's Espresso Bar

Wall Street Plaza (1-407 422 3322). **Open** 2.30pm-2am Mon-Thur; 2.30pm-3am Fri; 8pm-3am Sat; noon-2am Sun.

Good for a late night cup o' joe, coffee cocktails, ice-cream treats and desserts.

Icon

20 E Central Boulevard (1-407 649 6496). **Open** 9pm-3am Tue-Sat.

Owned by the people who run Cairo (*see above*). Another dance club, this time with a strange, scrap-metal décor. Latin music some nights, club mix on others. Once again, look for DJ Mot spinning.

Jani Lane's Sunset Strip

Second floor, 25 S Orange Avenue (1-407 649 4803). **Open** 10pm-3am Wed-Sat.

Jani used to sing for the pop-metal band Warrant. His club is home to big hair, leather and fishnets. The stage is usually graced by has-been or never-were bands.

Kit Kat Klub

Wall Street Plaza (1-407 422 6990). **Open** 5pm-2am Mon-Fri; 8pm-2am Sat; 6pm-2am Sun.

Very cool, dark space with half a dozen pool tables, good jukebox, velvet curtains, cigars, Botticelli-style prints on the walls, a full bar and a small menu.

SAK Comedy Lab

45 E Church Street (1-407 648 0001). **Shows** 9pm Tue-Wed; 8pm, 9.45pm Thur; 7.30pm, 9.30pm, 11.30pm Fri, Sat.

Voted the best comedy room by *Orlando Weekly* readers. Theatersports shows pit two groups of comics against each other in an improv contest.

Sapphire Supper Club

54 N Orange Avenue (1-407 246 1419). **Open** 10pm-3am daily.

The best club in town to catch live bands. The bar crowd can be loud, which is annoying during quiet acts, but the vibe is good. Check the club's schedule or the *Weekly* to find who's playing. There's an excellent kitchen and a martini menu. Dinner reservations assure you a seat for the show.

added
protection
extra fun...

Three way protection for twice the fun.

Hawaiian Tropic's unique Triple Defence System means you can have fun in the sun while wearing the best protection.

1. UVA, UVB & Infrared protection.
2. Exclusive time-released Vitamin Plus complex A,C&E.
3. Waterproof for up to 8 hours.

In factors up to 35, our sun protection formulations are made from the purest ingredients for better protection against sunburn and skin damage.

HAWAIIAN Tropic.

Hawaiian Tropic. We'll add the protection. You have the fun.

Zuma Beach

46 N Orange Avenue (1-407 648 8363). **Open** 10pm-3am Wed-Sat.

This used to be a great old theatre. Now it's a meat-market dance club where cute girls in bikinis hawk jello shots. It's annoying just to walk past.

Where to eat

Harvey's Bistro

Ground floor, DuPont Center, Livingston Street & Orange Avenue (1-407 246 6560). **Open** 11.30am-10pm Mon-Thur, Sat; 11.30am-11pm Fri. **Credit** AmEx, DC, Disc, MC, V.

An elegant spot for business people that lures locals with the huge portions of its meat-heavy US menu. Especially busy during and after Magic games.

Ichiban

19 S Orange Avenue (1-407 423 2688). **Open** 11am-2pm, 5-10pm, Mon-Thur; Fri; 11am-2pm, 5-11pm, Fri; 5-11pm Sat. **Credit** AmEx, Disc, MC, V.

Moderately priced sushi, teriyaki and tempura, all of it good and served in a relaxed setting.

Kate O'Brien's Irish Pub

24 W Central Avenue (1-407 649 7646). **Open** 11.30am-2am Mon-Sat; 1pm-2am Sun. **Credit** AmEx, DC, Disc, MC, V.

Big comfortable room, Harp on tap (for a particularly bad hangover) and backyard seating. The menu is solid as long as you like Irish food. Check out the all-you-can-eat steam table lunch special ($6.50).

Le Provence Bistros Francais

50 Pine Street (1-407 843 1320). **Open** 5.30-9.30pm Mon-Thur; 5.30-10.30pm Fri, Sat. **Credit** AmEx, DC, MC, V.

A romantic, elegant and upscale French eatery with a good wine list and a superb beef tenderloin with three-peppercorn sauce. Reservations recommended. Open for dinner only.

Manuel's on the 28th

28th floor, DuPont Center, Livingston Street & Orange Avenue (1-407 246 6580). **Open** 6-10pm Tue-Sat. **Credit** AmEx, DC, Disc, MC, V.

You want a romantic view? Come to Manuel's, located 28 floors above Orlando. It features a world cuisine menu that changes quarterly. This is one of O-Town's top restaurants. Reservations are required, as jackets on the gentlemen. Open for dinner only.

NYPD

373 N Orange Avenue (1-407 481 8680). **Open** 11am-9pm Mon-Fri; 1-8pm Sat. **No credit cards**.

Downtown's top pizza, and the more complicated dishes are good, too. Gets crowded with office workers at lunchtime.

Pebbles

17 W Church Street (1-407 839 0892). **Open** 11am-11pm Mon-Wed; 11am-midnight Thur; 11am-1am Fri; 5pm-1am Sat; 5-11pm Sun. **Credit** AmEx, DC, Disc, MC, V.

It's a chain restaurant but you wouldn't know it. Surprisingly good seafood, pasta and poultry with prompt, friendly service and a good wine list.

Sushi Hatsu

24 E Washington Street (1-407 422 1551). **Open** 11am-2.30pm, 5-10pm, Mon-Thur; 11am-2.30pm, 5-11pm, Fri; 5-11pm Sat. **Credit** AmEx, DC, MC, V.

The dining room is bland, but it has the best sushi and sushi chef in town. Prices are inexpensive to moderate.

Shopping

The **Exchange Shopping Emporium** at Church Street Station (1-407 422 2434) is the biggest shopping draw in Downtown. There are 50 speciality shops, most of them geared to tourists, and a fast-food court. A block east is **Church Street Market**, another cluster of retail and food shops on two floors of renovated brick buildings. Retailers include Sharper Image, Brookstone and Haagen-Dazs.

Bad Mood Records

225 N Magnolia Avenue (1-407 246 0072). **Open** noon-10pm daily. **Credit** AmEx, MC, V.

A cool selection of new and used CDs and 12in vinyl for DJs. A great place to pick up flyers for gigs, raves and club events.

Props

50 E Central Boulevard (1-407 278 7222). **Open** 11am-7pm Mon-Fri; 11am-8pm Sat; noon-5pm Sun. **Credit** AmEx, MC, V.

Modern clothes for the clubgoer. Props also has a table full of invites and flyers for the latest club gigs and raves. An essential stop if you plan to dance.

Strong Arm

225 N Magnolia Avenue (1-407 246 8030). **Open** noon-10pm Mon-Thur; noon-midnight Fri, Sat; noon-6pm Sun. **Credit** AmEx, MC, V.

Clothes and paraphernalia for people with body piercings.

Antiques

Since there are a lot of retirees in the area, it follows that there are a lot of antiques. Stores are everywhere, but here are two clusters worth a trip.

Orange Avenue Shoppes

Orange Avenue, between Virginia Drive and Par Avenue, Orlando.

An interesting and varied collection of small shops ranging from standard antique dealers to oddball stores like **Rock & Roll Heaven** (1814 N Orange Avenue; 1-407 896 1952) for vinyl junkies and **Radio Relics** (321 E Evans Street; 1-407 895 0146), one of the best and weirdest shops anywhere for tube radios, televisions and ancient electronic minutiae.

Edgewater Drive Shoppes

Edgewater Drive, between Colonial Drive and Par Avenue, Orlando.

Just west of the Orange Avenue Shoppes, this grouping of stores in College Park offers more country-style antiques, though the variety improves to twentieth-century items around the **College Park Antique Mall** (1317 Edgewater Drive; 1-407 839 1869). Be sure to stop at **Cheap Charlie's Antique Emporium** (643 Lexington Avenue; 1-407 841 2923). Though a bit south of the other stores, this dusty warehouse is crammed with an amazing assortment of junk that, once picked over and cleaned up, you'll find in more upmarket stores at twice the price.

Arts & entertainment

For film fans, there are multiplex movie theatres all over the Orlando area; check the listings in the *Orlando Weekly* to find the nearest. If you want something a cut above the mall crowd, there's only one place to go, though it's a little way out: the **Enzian Theater** (1300 S Orlando Avenue, Maitland; 1-407 644 4662). This single-screen, not-for-profit cinema is the only one bringing in unusual and challenging big-city arthouse films. It also has table service so you can order food and drinks while watching the flick. The Enzian

Spaced out

Just an hour east of Orlando, the Kennedy Space Center (also known as KSC), hub of the US space programme, is hands-down one of the best attractions in Central Florida. Best of all, most of it is free. KSC's Visitor Center boasts a museum and several excellent films and exhibits, including the Rocket Garden, where you can stroll among Mercury and Gemini era rockets (many are surprisingly small). Be sure to take the free Space Shuttle guided tour, which meets in front of the shuttle twice a day. KSC also offers three terrific IMAX films ($5 or $6) shown on five-storey high screens (if ever there was a subject worthy of IMAX, it's space travel).

KSC's primary attraction is a 2½ hour bus tour of the launchpads and vehicle assembly buildings. It costs $8 per adult and $5 per child and is surprisingly bad – the lines are long, the pre-recorded tour is sleep-inducing and you're not allowed off the bus closer than 3½ miles from a launchpad. However, the trip is redeemed by its conclusion, the Apollo/Saturn V Center, which houses a 363ft Saturn V rocket and other well-conceived exhibits.

You can easily spend a full day at KSC, although a half-day (including one or two IMAX films) will probably be enough for most people.

The Center has a friendly, cosy feel and to Orlando-jaded sensibilities there's a refreshing lack of tourist-gouging in the reasonable pricing of foods and merchandise.

If you want to see space hardware in action, note that NASA doesn't allow anyone except astronauts closer than 3½ miles to a launch, although you can see a flying shuttle from virtually anywhere in Central Florida. But if you want to feel the rumble, try the beaches around Titusville (especially the west side of the Indian River) or between New Smyrna and Melbourne.

You can also write three months in advance of a launch to Nasa Visitor Services, PA Pass, KSC, FL 32899, and request a free car pass, which allows you to park a car on a road near the launchpad. If it's too late for that, stop by the KSC Vistor Center and purchase a seat on a NASA tour bus ($10). These air-conditioned double-decker jobs park on the causeway during launches. During landings, the gates are not closed so anyone can show up and watch the shuttle touch down.

Kennedy Space Center

Take SR 405 from Titusville or SR A1A from Cocoa Beach. Follow signs for Kennedy Space Center. Information 1-407 452 2121/launch schedule 1-407 867 4636. **Open** 9am to dusk daily. **Admission** free.

hosts the annual Central Florida Film Festival each June, a growing and increasingly important indie showcase.

For interesting stage plays, check out **Theater Downtown** (2113 N Orange Avenue; 1-407 841 0083) and the **Manhattan South Actors Studio** (1012 N Mills Avenue; 1-407 895 6557). Both do excellent versions of current and original theatrical works. The **Civic Theatres of Central Florida** (1001 E Princeton Street; 1-407 896 7365) produces much larger-scale musicals, dramatic plays and even children's theatre on its three stages.

Art lovers will enjoy the **Orlando Museum of Art** (2416 N Mills Avenue; 1-407 896 4231), which specialises in pre-Colombian artefacts and nineteenth- and twentieth-century US artists associated with Florida. Unfortunately, the same can't be said for science lovers and the **Orlando Science Center** (810 Rollins Street; 1-407 896 7151). This place is a mess. Following a huge and costly expansion, the Science Center's new exhibits are illogical or non-functioning, and an over-reliance on computer terminals makes a visit about as much fun as playing with a CD-ROM, though the IMAX films are cool. Any pretence of exploring nature is dissolved by the plastic trees in the lobby; you'll witness more nature by walking out the door and looking in any direction.

With 2,500 seats, the **Bob Carr Performing Arts Center** (401 W Livingston Street; 1-407 849 2001) is the biggest sit-down theatre space in town. It hosts mid-level events ranging from singer kd lang to touring Broadway productions. It's also home to the Orlando Opera Company (1-407 426 1717) and the Southern Ballet. Complaints have been registered about the acoustics, small stage and lack of a central aisle, but until Orlando comes up with something better, this is it. The **Orlando Arena** (600 W Amelia Street; 1-407 849 2001) – or 'O-Rena' as it's known by locals – is a top-notch, 16,000-seat venue that's home to Orlando Magic (basketball), the Solar Bears (ice-hockey) and the Predators (indoor football). Other events range from big-name rock concerts to ice shows to the circus. The food options are among the best for an arena of this size.

Courtyard at Lake Lucerne
211 N Lucerne Circle East, Orlando, FL 32801 (1-407 648 5188). **Rates** double $105-$110; king $115-$135; suite $135-$165. **Credit** AmEx, MC, V.
A romantic and architecturally interesting 24-room B&B spread through three distinctive buildings. There are no views, since it's located next to a freeway, but the rooms and furnishings compensate.

Harley Hotel of Orlando
151 E Washington Street, Orlando, FL 32801 (1-407 841 3220). **Rates** queen $95; king $105; suite $149. **Credit** AmEx, Disc, MC, V.
About as close to Downtown as you can get without sleeping on Orange Avenue. This is an older hotel, but has several homey touches (free newspapers and Downtown shuttle). Plus, it's just across the street from Lake Eola Park.

Orlando Marriott Downtown
400 W Livingston Street, Orlando, FL 32801 (1-407 843 6664). **Rates** standard $120; double $159; suite $250-$395. **Credit** AmEx, DC, Disc, MC, V.
The best Downtown hotel, located across the street from the O-Rena and the Bob Carr Performing Arts Center.

Orlando Youth Hostel
227 N Eola Drive, Orlando, FL 32801 (1-407 843 888). **Rates** dorm $12 IYHF members, international travellers; double $28.60; double bed, bunk bed $35. **Credit** MC, V.
A 90-bed hostel located across the street from the east end of Lake Eola Park. This is a good location to do some Downtown clubbing from.

Radisson Plaza Hotel Orlando
60 S Ivanhoe Boulevard, Orlando, FL 32801 (1-407 425 4455). **Rates** standard $79-$95; double $95-$114; suite $125-$350. **Credit** AmEx, DC, Disc, MC, V.
A high-rise on the north edge of Downtown. It's nice, but a bit of a hike from the scene. You'll need a taxi.

The Veranda Inn
115 N Summerlin Avenue, Orlando, FL 32801 (1-800 420 6822/1-407 489 0321). **Rates** standard $89; king $169; suite $189. **Credit** AmEx, DC, MC, V.
Located two blocks from Lake Eola Park, this small complex of historic buildings has 11 rooms and suites, most with kitchenettes. The courtyard area has a dipping pool and hot tub. Very gay-friendly.

Winter Park

Just five miles north-east of Downtown Orlando, picturesque Winter Park is the ideal antidote for tourist burn-out. Chartered in 1887 as a winter resort for wealthy Northerners, this mostly upscale burg is a vibrant mix of old money, cellphone-toting yuppies and college students. Although Winter Park looks quite large on a map, its heart is **Park Avenue**, a comfortable eight-block strip more elegant than trendy, bordered on the south by Fairbanks Avenue and on the north by West Swoope Avenue. Smack in the middle of this area is the village green known as **Central Park**, which has a ground-level Amtrak station. Families should plan a lunchtime picnic here as tots will thrill to watch the 1.09pm train roll in.

The Charles Hosmer Morse Museum of American Art
445 Park Avenue (645 5311). **Open** 9.30am-4pm Tue-Sat. **Admission** $3 adults; $1 students. **No credit cards.**
Small but with an excellent collection of Tiffany stained glass. A walking tour takes less than an hour. Be sure to read the strange description cards under each display; instead of scholarly text, these appear to be the words of a cranky senior citizen bursting to express his/her own theories on art.

Cornell Fine Arts Museum
Rollins College Campus (646 2526). **Open** 10am-5pm Tue-Fri; 1-5pm Sat-Sun. **Admission** free.
Set in an attractive lakeside campus setting, this museum has a large and varied painting and print collection as well as the Smith Watch Key Collection: more than 1,200 watch keys, as used prior to stem winding.

The Scenic Boat Tour
312 E Morse Boulevard (1-407 644 4056). **Prices** $6 adults; $3 children. **No credit cards.**
A relaxed, hour-long cruise through old lumber canals, filled with interesting local stories and backyard views of area estates. Boats leave on the hour from 10am to 4pm.

Winter Park Farmers Market
Corner of New England & New York Avenues, a block west of Park Avenue. **Open** dawn-1pm Sat.
Fresh local fruit and veg as well as plenty of picnic food. Be sure to check out Coach Woodruff's BBQ truck.

Where to eat

It's difficult to find a bad meal in Winter Park and just as hard to find anything dirt cheap. Try **Briarpatch** (252 N Park Avenue; 1-407 628 8651) for breakfasts and light, healthy lunches, and **Brandywine's** (505 N Park Avenue; 1-407 647 0055), the best deli on the block, for picnic foods or sidewalk lunches. **La Venezia Cafe** (142 S Park Avenue; 1-407 647 7557) has excellent Italian fare and awesome desserts. **Colony Restaurant** (329 S Park Avenue; 1-407 740 7227) is a newcomer, serving a modern assortment of steaks, seafoods and pastas in a loft setting. **Park Plaza Gardens** (319 S Park Avenue; 1-407 645 2475) is where the after-work crowd hangs. There's a garden restaurant in the back which also handles room service needs for the Park Plaza Hotel. Head a few yards off Park Avenue to **Wm J Sweet's** (122 E Morse Boulevard; 1-407 647 6961), where you can feast on home-made ice-cream and yoghurt with decadent candy and nut mix-ins. North of Winter Park in Maitland is the **Bubble Room** (1351 S Orlando Avenue; 628 3331), chock-full of toys and kitsch theme seating. The food, mainly steaks, is moderately priced and not bad.

Shopping

Power shopping is Park Avenue's main draw. The street is a virtual outdoor mall with lots of greenery and no ugly lighting. National chain stores include **Ann Taylor, Williams & Sonoma, Banana Republic, Orvis, The Gap** and **Caldwell-Massey**. There are dozens of interesting local shops, including several devoted to baby and toddler goodies. Others include **Cigarz** (333 S Park Avenue; 1-407 647 2427), which, as you might guess, rides the premium cigar bandwagon, and **Stamp Cabana** (352 S Park Avenue; 1-407 628 8863), which offers an enormous collection of strange rubber stamps as well as classes on how to create customised greeting cards with stamps. Music fans should head to **Park Avenue CDs** (528 S Park Avenue; 1-407 629 5293), with its smart staff and a hip assortment of new and used CDs ranging from college rock to classical.

Where to stay

The Fortnightly Inn

377 E Fairbanks Avenue, Winter Park, FL 32789 (1-407 645 4440). **Rates** single $75; double $85; suite $95. **Credit** MC, V.

For B&B fans. Built in 1922, each of its five rooms are decorated with assorted antiques and vintage rugs (one room even boasts a Laura Ashley motif, if you like that kind of thing). Rates start at $75 and the hotel is often booked in advance on weekends.

The Langford Resort Hotel

300 New England Avenue, Winter Park, FL 32789 (1-407 644 3400). **Rates** double $75-105; suite $100-200. **Credit** AmEx, DC, MC, V.

A last resort, if that. It peaked somewhere in the 1950s and has been sliding downhill ever since. Avoid, unless slumming is your game.

Park Plaza Hotel

307 S Park Avenue, Winter Park, FL 32789 (1-800 228 7220/647 1071). **Rates** double $80; **suite** $160-185. **Credit** AmEx, DC, MC, V.

Built in 1921, this stately 27-room hotel is hidden on a second floor overlooking Park Avenue and Central Park. It's old, so your bathroom door might not close properly, but the mahogany panelling, antiques and balcony access for most rooms makes up for any shortcomings (Paul Newman and other celebs stay here during the Central Florida Film Festival). Rates increase 20%-25% during special events.

Getting there

By car

Take I-4 to the Fairbanks Avenue exit. Head east on Fairbanks through four miles of dreary strip malls. At Park Avenue, turn left The key area is bordered on the south by Fairbanks Avenue and on the north by W Swoope Avenue. Parking on Park Avenue is possible, but the best bet is to hang a left on Morse Boulevard and park in the free public lots on the other side of the train tracks.

By train

There are two Amtrak trains a day out of Orlando..

By bus

To get to/from Downtown Orlando catch Lynx bus 1 or 9. For Lynx bus information, call 841 8240.

By taxi

A taxi to downtown Winter Park from Downtown Orlando (or vice versa) costs about $11. To go all the way to Walt Disney World from Winter Park, expect to spend $40-$45.

Tourist information

Winter Park Chamber of Commerce, 150 N New York Avenue, Winter Park, FL 32790 (1-407 644 8281).

Attractions Area

'The Attractions' refers to a giant tourist zone clustered around I-4, from Kirkman Road (SR 435) to US 192 (Irlo Bronson Memorial Highway) about 12 miles to the south. Many attractions are on International Drive (known as I-Drive), which runs north-south through this zone and around US 192 near Kissimmee. It is not Orlando but a strange nether world of price-gouging shops and world-famous theme parks. On the plus side, everything is nearby and visitors can get around on foot or by bus. On the downside, its ugly, strip-mall landscape gives Orlando a bad name (repeat after me: this is not Orlando). To confuse matters, the term 'attractions' refers to not only the theme parks but also the rides within those theme parks.

Major attractions

The top three theme parks are **Walt Disney World, Universal Studios Florida** and **Sea World**, followed by **Gatorland, Wet 'n Wild** and **Splendid China**. For Walt Disney World, *see page 252*.

Planning your visit

Conventional wisdom says arrive as early as possible at Walt Disney World and Universal Studios, target favourite rides and hit them first. But there's another strategy – show up in the afternoon. Crowds thin after 3pm as those 7.30am arrivals call it quits. Queues are shorter and the parks are lovely at night, and often have evening entertainment such as fireworks or a concert. You can also split the difference: start early, leave for a midday nap, then return in the evening. Same-day re-admission is free (keep your pass and make sure you get your hand stamped on exit) and you won't have to pay for parking a second time if you save the receipt.

Hours for attractions vary but usually run 9am-6pm; the bigger attractions have extended hours. All prices quoted are for one-day tickets bought at the gate. Multi-day discounts are available as are multi-attraction packages (check out the $94.95 five-day deal for Sea World, Universal Studios and Wet 'n Wild). Other discounts can be found at your travel agent or at ticket brokers (*see above*). Be sure to bring (and use) sunscreen, a hat and sunglasses. A small backpack is a good idea to hold a camera, bottled water and some snacks (outside food is forbidden in the parks, but very few people are hassled about it). Several parks feature water playgrounds where kids get soaked in seconds, so a change of clothes for them and a towel should be included.

UNIVERSAL STUDIOS FLORIDA

1000 Universal Studios Plaza, Orlando (1-407 363 8000). I-4, exit 30B/bus 21, 24, 37, 40, 43. **Open** 9am-7pm daily. **Admission** one-day $39.75 adults; $32 3-9s. **Credit** Disc, MC, V.

When Walt Disney World executives wake up with night sweats, it's Universal Studios Florida they've been dreaming about. It's the only attraction giving the Disney complex a run for its money, and compared to its direct Disney competition (Disney-MGM Studios), many folks declare Universal the winner. Universal's theme park is small but well organised. The motif is studio backlot and it's next door to Universal's real-life Florida production studio – not that anything in the park has very much to do with the real studio (don't believe it when they announce a casting call or an audition as part of a show). If you want to tour the real production studio, ask at Guest Services desks. A proper visit requires a full day or two partial days. Plan to hit the key rides before 11am or after 3pm. Every evening there's a concert as well as the **Dynamite Nights Stuntacular**, a big-thrills stunt show with flames, explosions and speed boats racing around the lagoon.

Fangs for the memory: Jaws at **Universal**.

What to see

Universal's presentations and scripts for its rides are looser than Disney-MGM Studios'; even Universal's worst attractions are worth it if the queues aren't long. On the downside, live actors appear in many Universal attractions and in most cases they're just going through the motions.

If you arrive early, make your first stop **Terminator 2 3D**. With a combination of live actors and panoramic 3-D projection, Arnie and a few co-stars fight to save the world again. Though the plot rehashes the movie, the film footage is new, which is nice. The climactic destruction of the bad guy is spectacular and includes one of the 'coolest' effects you'll experience (that's the only hint we're giving). Next, visit **Back to The Future**, which has the best motion-simulator in any of the parks. It's fast, furious and extremely jarring. If you have a weak stomach, this could be a vomit launch. At the very least, expect to be queasy.

With the big two out of the way, try **Jaws**, a silly boat ride with a silly script (how many times is that damn shark going to come back?). However, you will jump and scream when the latex great white rams your boat. The fake cable network broadcasting to the crowd is quite funny. **Earthquake** opens with a documentary narrated by Charlton Heston explaining how film makers create and shoot an earthquake. Then you're put in a San Francisco subway car to experience a simulated 8.3 quake. Streets crumble, trucks fall through the sidewalk and explode, 65,000 gallons of water rush toward you. It's very impressive. Aim to sit to the front and left of the subway cars for the best view.

As for stage shows, catch **Animal Actors Stage** (featuring trained animals used in films) and **The Wild, Wild, Wild West Show**, which is a stuntman comedy with an energetic cast that delights in mocking other park shows. **The Gory Gruesome & Grotesque Horror Make-Up Show** is funny and informative as it explains the make-up tricks used in real movies. Tots will demand to see **A Day In The Park With Barney**, and worship at the paws of the purple one. If you're tot-free, avoid like the plague. Also skip **ET**, even more of a feelgood Pepsi ad than the movie. It's basically a sled ride through recycled images of the flick.

The biggest miss of all at Universal is **Kongfrontation**; its billboards on I-4 are more exciting than the actual ride. After an endless queue through a mock New York subway station (only the smell of urine is missing), visitors board tram cars which slowly move through the wreckage Kong has caused. You look around, the tram 'driver' shouts 'Oh noooo!' a lot, Kong bumps your tram a bit – and that's all. Ride over. Monitors replay a video of each tram's Kongfrontation. You never saw so many bored faces on one screen.

If all this isn't enough, stay tuned. Universal is in the midst of a multi-billion dollar expansion. A 12-acre entertainment complex will open in 1998 and a second theme park, Islands of Adventure, is scheduled for 1999.

Where to eat

You're in luck: Universal has decent food, though it's not cheap. Make reservations at Guest Services desks for **Studio Stars Restaurant** (a back-lot buffet) and **Lombardi's Landing** (seafood served in a Fisherman's Wharf knock-off) or risk a long line at the **Hard Rock Café**. If you're not interested in table service, try the **International Food Bazaar** for some ethnic treats. For the children, there's a character breakfast at 7.45am where they can munch cereal and toast with the Flintstones, Yogi Bear and others; booking is essential (1-407 224 6339).

SEA WORLD

7007 Sea World Drive, near Orlando (1-407 351 3600). I-4, exit 28/bus 8, 35, 42, 43. **Open** 9am-9pm daily. **Admission** one-day $40.95 adults; $33.90 3-9s. **Credit** Disc, MC, V.

Sea World is the only place to see **Shamu the Killer Whale** and half a dozen excellent shows featuring trained dolphins, whales, sea lions and otters. Every animal show is fabulous: kids and adults alike will be transfixed. At walk-through exhibits, you can pet a sting ray and feed dolphins and sea lions. The whole park is educational, fun and a must-see. Plan on a full-day trip.

Only two shows go wrong at Sea World. The new (and very expensive to build) **Wild Arctic** takes visitors on an motion-simulator helicopter ride to Base Station Wild Arctic where you then tour three, two-storey tanks containing polar bears, walruses, whales and other arctic sealife. The animals are impressive, but the videos and fake base station para-phernalia are distracting and not synchronised with the viewing experience. Try to go when the queue is short. There's a non-motion version too, where the queue is usual-ly shorter and faster. The **Baywatch** water ski show is just plain stupid; it makes one appreciate the intelligence of ani-mals. If you're curious, watch from the lawn behind Mango Joe's Cafe, which makes walking away mid-show easier.

Where to eat

On the food side, service throughout the park is slow. The best bet is the deli at the **Anheuser-Busch Hospitality Center**. Not only are the sandwiches good, but they give away free draught beer (wahoo!). Skip the watery Bud Light stuff and head to the Specialty Brew room to the rear where taps flow with darker, tastier beverages. This alone makes an annual pass worthwhile.

GATORLAND

14501 S Orange Blossom Trail (US 441), near Kissimmee (1-407 855 5496.) I-4, exit 26A/bus 4. **Open** 9am-dusk daily. **Admission** one-day $13.95 adults; $8.95 10-12s; $6.48 3-9s. **Credit** AmEx, MC, V.

Gatorland is one of the few places where visitors can eat the same species they've just watched perform. In operation since 1949, it's the area's oldest (and most reasonably priced) attrac-tion, boasting a comfortable, low-rent ambiance you won't find in the spit and polish mega parks. This 50-acre habitat has hundreds of alligators and crocodiles lurking just below 2,000ft of boardwalk upon which visitors stand. Be sure to buy food and feed the monsters (watch your fingers, those gators jump). You can even pet a baby alligator. A narrated train ride provides an good overview of the property and its mission. Plan on a three-hour visit and catch all three 15-minute shows: **Snakes of Florida, Gator Wrestlin'** and **Gator Jumparoo** (gators leap four feet to grab chicken car-casses hung from a wire). Remember that alligators aren't polite, well-trained animals like the ones at Sea World. They're mean, prehistoric beasts that would just as soon munch the trainer's hand as the chicken he's holding – and that's the fun. Snack on gator ribs and deep-fried gator nuggets at Pearl's Smokehouse (yes, it tastes a bit like chicken).

WET 'N WILD

6200 International Drive, near Orlando (1-407 351 1800). I-4, exit 30A/bus 8, 21, 24, 35, 37, 38, 42. **Open** 10am-6pm daily. **Admission** one-day $24.95 adults; $19.95 3-9s; $12.48 senior citizens. **Credit** AmEx, Disc, MC, V.

The king of water parks and one of the hottest teen pick-up spots in town. Created in 1977 by George Millay (the guy who invented Sea World), it features eight humungous waterslides and a host of more gentle aquatic activities. Brave souls shouldn't miss **Black Hole, Blue Niagara, The Surge, Fuji Flyer** and the scariest of all, **Bomb Bay**. Visitors are loaded into a bomb capsule, the floor suddenly opens and they freefall down a seven-storey, near-vertical slide (78°, to be exact). The non-bomb version is called **Der Stuka** and it's almost as frightening (cross your legs or you'll be wearing your shorts around your neck).

Wet 'n Wild has areas reserved for families with children so they don't get overwhelmed by teens. Women are advised to wear one-piece swimsuits as they stand a better chance of staying on. You should rent a locker for the day but there's no need to rent an inner tube unless you're floating down

Lazy River; bring your own towel and save a few bucks. Plan on a full day (queues can be long). When you tire of water, go next door and putt a free round at Congo River Miniature Golf (it's included in the ticket price).

Parking tip: turn left after the gate and park as near to I-Drive as possible. The street crossing and water park's entrance will be much closer.

SPLENDID CHINA

300 Splendid China Boulevard, Kissimmee (1-407 396 7111). I-4, exit 25B. **Open** 9.30am-7pm daily. **Admission** one-day $26.99 adults; $16.99 5-12s. **Credit** AmEx, MC, V.

One of the strangest attractions in town, Splendid China is filled with more than 60 famous Chinese landmarks, pago-das and buildings all reproduced in miniature (its version of the 4,200 mile Great Wall stretches a half-mile and was con-structed with six million two-inch bricks 'each laid by hand'). It's calming to stroll the grounds and read sanitised history (they fail to mention that little political movement known as Communism) – but it's also hard to avoid a smirk and to think that the place would make an excellent miniature golf course. In its favour, Splendid China offers numerous shows featuring Chinese acrobats, dancers, musicians, comedians and tigers. The shows range from OK to excellent – but don't miss anything featuring the marvellous seven-year-old acro-bat Fang Fang. The upscale Suzhou Pearl Restaurant is authentic and tasty and doesn't require park admission.

Secondary attractions

The fun doesn't stop with $100 million-plus theme parks, and neither does the haemorrhaging of money from your wallet. Orlando has numerous well-established second and third tiers of smaller attractions for when your Disney pass expires. Locations should be clearly marked on free tourist guides and maps.

If you're on I-Drive, **Ripley's Believe It Or Not** (1-407 363 4418) is hard to miss. The building appears to be falling over (believe it or not!). The usual documentation of human freaks and oddities is housed inside. Backyard mechanics will love **Flying Tigers Warbird Restoration Museum** (1-407 933 1942), or Bomberland USA as it's nicknamed. This low-key treat is basically a fix-it shop for WWII airplanes. Visitors can wander free of charge or ante up for a guided tour. While Dad's staring at engines, flower-lovers in your group can check out **A World of Orchids** (1-407 396 1887).

Speed freaks can strap into miniature race cars and spin around the tracks at **Malibu Grand Prix** (1-407 351 9292), **Fun 'n' Wheels** (1-407 363 3500) or **KartWorld** (1-407 396 4800). Should go-karts not impress you, head to **Eaglerider** (1-407 316 8687), where dudes and babes can rent a Harley-Davidson motorbike and fulfil their *Easy Rider* fantasies (you must be 21 and have a motorcycle license). If that's not thrilling enough, there's **Skycoaster** (1-407 248 8449), where up to three people tie themselves to the end of a long cable and swing from a 100ft tower at speeds of 50mph.

Motion-simulator fans can get their fix at **Movie Rider** (1-407 352 0050), which features 70mm film projection and stomach-wrenching chair movements. Of course, nothing matches the visceral thrills of war – and that's why there's **Paintball World** (1-407 396 4199). Teams run through fields shooting at each other with paintball guns, and there's a protected spectator area for pacifists.

If you liked Gatorland, you'll probably like **Jungleland** (1-407 396 1012), which is similar, but less focused on a sin-gle species. Jungleland's road sign could read 'We got lots of animals!'. A less happy scene exists at **Amazing Animals** (1-407 354 1400). Its road sign could read 'We got lots of ani-mals in tiny cages!' Not nice. If you like to hug animals, look for **Green Meadows Petting Farm** (1-407 846 0770), where you can get close to a few hundred farm animals. Big among kids. Horse enthusiasts can saddle up at the stables of **Hyatt Grand Cypress** (1-407 239 1234) or **Horse World** (1-407 847 4343) in Kissimmee. Those who want to get close to nature can explore swamps in person with an organised airboat trip at **Airboat Rides at Boggy Creek** (1-407 344 9550) or **Old Fashion Air Boat Rides** (1-407 568 4307). You can also opt for a do-it-yourself trip at **Airboat Rentals** (1-407 847 3672), where you and three friends can rent a small airboat for $25 an hour. Those who feel lucky and know how to swing a golf club must stop at **Million Dollar Mulligan** (1-407 239 1505), a nine-hole pitch-and-putt course with a hole-in-one challenge worth a million bucks (if you hit it, you could afford to stay at Disney's Grand Floridian next visit).

One last stop to make is **Xanadu, House of the Future**, an eerie, closed-down attraction on US 192 four miles east of I-4. As one Kissimmee official put it, 'It was supposed to be the house of the future, but the future never came'. Truer words were never spoken. This sad, lumpy building looks like a pile of mashed potatoes painted gray. They tried to make it a tourist centre, but that didn't work either. Now it's falling apart and boarded up and if you want a glimpse, you have to peer through dirty windows. If that's not an apt metaphor for the future, what is?

Where to eat

Dinner attractions

Don't stop the entertainment just because it's dinnertime! Orlando offers a host of 'Dinner Attractions' that provide a theme and a show along with plates of convention-grade food. Ticket prices across the board are about $35.95 for adults and $22.95 for kids (3-11s). One price covers all except tipping (15-20 per cent); since you have to pay the ticket price up front, tipping must be handled in cash at the table.

American Gladiators

E Irlo Bronson Highway (US 192), Kissimmee (1-407 390 0000). I-4, exit 25A. **Show** 7.30pm daily. **Credit** AmEx, Disc, MC, V.

Direct from your TV, it's dopey Americana at its best. The Gladiators are muscle-bound guys and gals with one-word names like Laser, Ice and Siren. Having failed to get legitimate sports careers, they compete nightly in a series of contests with titles such as 'Powerball', 'Breakthrough & Conquer' and 'Whiplash' (most are variations on that school-yard classic, 'Kill the Guy with the Ball'). Surprisingly, American Gladiators is big fun, although admittedly that could possibly have something to do with the unlimited beer and wine offered free with dinner.

Arabian Nights

E Irlo Bronson Highway (US 192), Kissimmee (1-407 239 9223). I-4, exit 25A. **Show** 7.30pm daily. **Credit** AmEx, Disc, MC, V.

A 25-act 'magical tour around the world' featuring 50 horses prancing and doing jumping tricks. The razor-thin plot involves a princess searching for her true love. Somehow, they connect Rome, the Wild West, South America, New York, Hollywood and 'the Land of the Mystical Unicorn'. The hit of the show is a Ben Hur-style chariot race.

King Henry's Feast

8984 I-Drive, Orlando (1-407 351 5151). I-4, exit 29. **Show** 7pm daily. **Credit** AmEx, DC, Disc, MC, V.

In a sixteenth-century Tudor castle (or, at least, a stucco building that looks like one), it's King Henry VIII's birthday and he's searching for bride number seven – it could be you! (Just don't ask about the other six.) Festivities include sword- and fire-swallowing, fighting knights, a juggler, music and other suitably medieval-oriented acts.

The green scene

Be wary about betting with strangers when playing golf in Orlando: you might be dealing with a professional. This town is a pro golfer's mecca. At least 50 PGA, LPGA and Senior Tour pros call Orlando home, and there are hundreds of aspiring pros who've moved here looking for a break; just about any of them can kick your butt on the links. The quality of the courses is also extraordinary; there are over 125 of them within a 45-minute drive of Downtown Orlando, many created by renowned designers. Banish the thought of pancake-flat fairways dotted with palm trees; top Central Florida courses feature deep woods and hilly layouts – more like Georgia then the tropics.

Since Orlando is a tourist town, many of the best courses are open to visitors. Walt Disney World's **Palm** and **Magnolia** courses are amazing and host the PGA's Walt Disney World/Oldsmobile Classic and the LPGA's Healthsouth Classic. Arnold Palmer's **Bay Hill** course is a fearsome consumer of hack players. Smart money says that if you can't break 85 at home, don't tee off here.

Jack Nicklaus' crowning design is the near-treeless **Grand Cypress Resort New Course**, inspired by the Old Course at St Andrews, Scotland. Other popular courses include **Mission Inn**, **Grenelefe**, **Timacuan**, **Kissimmee Bay** and **The Oaks**. Duffers should check out **Ventura Country Club** (1-407 282 6590), city-owned **Dubsdred** (1-407 246 3636), **Falcon's Fire** (1-407 239 5445) and **Winter Park Pines** (1-407 894 2121); call public courses direct. You must book for the championship courses; try the booking service **Tee Time USA** (1-800 374 8633/1-904 439 0001).

If you have a hankering to play an exclusive, private course, here's a trick that sometimes works. Tell the golf reservations person you're interested in becoming a club member and want to play a round to see if you like the course. Joining these private clubs costs upwards of $50,000 or more, so be ready to appear wealthy (wearing cut-off shorts and driving a beat-up VW camper van won't cut it). If you've got the cojones for a scam, this method can often secure a round at a course reserved for the power elite.

Keep on (monster) trucking at **Race Rock**.

Medieval Times

E Irlo Bronson Highway (US 192), Kissimmee (1-407 239 0214). I-4, exit 25A. **Shows** 8pm Mon-Fri, Sun; 8.30pm Sat. **Credit** AmEx, Disc, MC, V.

In another castle replica (eleventh-century, this time), knights joust, fight and ride horses in a dirt-covered arena. Obviously more violent than King Henry's love quest. To confirm the illusion, the castle's Hall of Arms houses a collection of authentic period artefacts such as suits of armour and a deed signed and sealed by Pope Pius.

Sleuths

7508 Republic Drive, behind Wet 'n Wild, Orlando (1-407 363 1985). I-4, exit 30A. **Shows** 9pm Mon, Thur, Fri; 6pm Tue, Wed; 6pm, 7.30pm, 9pm Sat; 7.30pm Sun. **Credit** AmEx, DC, Disc, MC, V.

Dinner theatre with an interactive twist. Sleuths rotates a repertoire of nine plays in which the characters mingle with and serve the guests. There's usually a whodunnit cliffhanger which guests are invited to ponder over dinner. Prizes are awarded to successful sleuths.

Wild Bill's Wild West Dinner Extravaganza

E Irlo Bronson Highway (US 192), Kissimmee (1-407 351 5151). I-4, exit 25A. **Show** 7pm daily. **Credit** AmEx, DC, Disc, MC, V.

A Western hoedown hosted by Wild Bill and Miss Kitty with dancehall girls, marksmanship demonstrations, a Texas lariat master, Native American Indian performers and more.

Restaurants

Restaurant choices are endless. Since Orlando is a test-market city, there's always a new concept eatery being built and researched (and usually closed a few months later). All the following are on or near I-Drive.

Of the high-profile, mass-market, fast-food joints, our favourites are **Taco Bell** and **Wendy's**. Both provide satisfying fat content plus the vague feeling that you're eating something healthy. For drive-throughs, try **Checker's**, a regional chain offering tasty variations on the burger theme.

But this is your holiday, so move up the restaurant foodchain to something more special. **Café Tu Tango** (1-407 248 2222) gets high marks from locals and visitors for its creative and trendy 'international tapas' menu. **Bahama Breeze** (1-407 248 2499) is a colourful place to kick back, order a big fruity drink and while away some hours dinning on authentic Caribbean dishes.

For sushi lovers, there are two excellent choices. **Ran-Getsu** (1-407 345 0044) is a long-time fave with a huge following among locals. As well as sushi, it offers Japanese-style steaks and seafood. The new kid on the block is the quieter and more refined **Hanaizuki** (1-407 363 7200), which is winning converts fast. If you seek the thrills of a knife-wielding chef slicing and dicing a few feet from your nose, try **Kobe**, where there's a chef and his grill at every table. Kobe ranks high with extroverts as tables seat 12, so you'll probably meet new friends over sake. They also serve sushi, but folks come for the grill. Kobe has locations on I-Drive (1-407 352 1811) and in Kissimmee (1-407 396 8088).

Traditional seafood can be found at **Fish Bones Restaurant** (1-407 352 0135), where everything is oak-grilled to a tasty finish. For romantic evenings, try **Chattam's Place** (1-407 345 2992), a small but extraordinary oasis tucked into an unassuming professional building. It's low-key and wonderful – and superior to its overhyped neighbour **Christini's** (345 8770), which is the kind of place that salesmen bring their clients when they want to impress them. There's wall after wall of overblown décor, a strolling string trio pressing for tips and an hour-plus wait if you didn't book. The food is OK, but for the prices it should be amazing. The best Indian food on I-Drive can be found at **Passage To India** (1-407 351 3456). Be sure to order several of the different breads and check out the photo and letter from The Cure, who enjoyed a meal here while on tour.

We can't leave this area without mentioning **Race Rock** (1-407 248 9876), home to a ludicrously huge monster truck parked next to I-4 near Sand Lake Road. Think Hard Rock Café. Now, replace the rock 'n' roll memorabilia with auto racing memorabilia. That's Race Rock. Partially owned by racing deity Richard Petty, it's a shrine to the NASCAR set. The building looks a Roman palace with stock cars hanging from the ceiling, motorcycles displayed behind the bar, autographed wheels in cases and car crash replays on the TVs. Happily, the food is well-presented and surprisingly tasty, if a bit overpriced. Try The King, a prime rib reported to be Mr Petty's favourite. And don't be embarrassed to gawk at the décor. That's why it's there.

Shopping

The Florida Mall
Sand Lake Road (SR 482) & S Orange Blossom Trail (US 92) (1-407 851 6255). Bus 4, 7, 42, 43, 52.
A huge upscale mall (particularly for Orlando), this shopping mecca is anchored by Dillard's, Saks Fifth Avenue and Gayfer's and has over 200 other stores. Many new concessions will open by the end of 1997. Very fashionable. Locals make the drive to shop here.

The Mercado
8445 I-Drive (1-407 345 9337). Bus 8, 35, 38, 42.
The Mercado is probably what Disney had in mind when it created Disney Village Marketplace. Over 60 speciality shops on cobblestone streets along with numerous dining options and a regular schedule of nightly entertainment.

I-Drive outlet malls
At the far north end of I-Drive are two factory outlet malls worth visiting. The discounts vary tremendously and some merchandise is reconditioned or discontinued stock. **Belz Factory Outlet World** (I-Drive, one mile north of Kirkman Road) features over 130 merchants, including Converse, Mikasa, Calvin Klein, Reebok and Levi Strauss, spread through four strip malls. On I-Drive between Kirkman Road and Belz is the **International Designer Outlets**, similar to Belz but featuring a better grade of retailer, including Ann Taylor Loft, Off 5th (Saks 5th Ave), Brooks Brothers, Fossil (watches) and Donna Karan. For both, catch bus 8 or 42.

Where to stay

With 86,000 hotel rooms around Orlando, the name of the game is choice. Hotels located near US 192 are less expensive and often fine if Walt Disney World is your primary destination. The downside is that they're in Kissimmee, which can be dull as dishwater unless you're a fan of pick-up trucks. A room inspection is a reasonable request and if you don't like what you see, move on. Haggling is possible at the smaller places, especially if you're a walk-in. Expect to pay at least $45 a night for a private room; the average rate is $67 for single or double. Prices quoted below should be taken only as a rough guide; rates are very volatile. Book early during school holidays. For Disney accommodation, *see page 258*.

American Youth Hostel
4840 W Irlo Bronson Highway, Kissimmee, FL 34746 (1-407 396 8282). **Rates** dorm $13 IYHF members; $16 non-members. **Credit** MC, V.
This 150-bed facility (with some double rooms) is five miles from Walt Disney World's main gate. There are also private rooms and family rooms with kitchens.

Clarion Plaza Hotel
9700 I-Drive, Orlando, FL 32819 (1-407 352 9700). **Rates** standard $149-$169; double $225; suite $338-$507. **Credit** AmEx, DC, Disc, MC, V.
Next to the convention centre, this is an efficient favourite with business travellers. It has a 24-hour market and deli.

Hyatt Regency Grand Cypress
1 Grand Cypress Boulevard, Lake Buena Vista, FL 32836 (1-407 239 1234). **Rates** double with garden view $255-$285; double with pool view $315; private club floor $380; suite $650-$2,500. **Credit** AmEx, DC, Disc, MC, V.

A top-notch resort on the edge of Disney property in the Walt Disney World Village Hotel Plaza. Amenities include golf, tennis, horse-riding, bike rentals, lawn games, boating, a full health club, excellent restaurants and much more. The Magic Kingdom might not seem so interesting once you're here.

Golden Link
4914 W Irlo Bronson Highway, Kissimmee, FL 34746 (1-407 396 0555). **Rates** double $36.95; $3 extra per person. **Credit** AmEx, Disc, MC, V.
Bland, clean rooms, but the rear of the place looks onto Lake Cecile and a small beach where you can rent jet-skis or get waterskiing lessons.

The Peabody Orlando
9801 I-Drive, Orlando, FL 32819 (1-407 352 4000). **Rates** double $240-$300; suite $400-$1,350. **Credit** AmEx, DC, Disc, MC, V.
This 27-floor structure is the most luxurious in town (though it lacks the outdoor perks of the Hyatt Grand Cypress). Amenities galore, terrific restaurants – and twice a day (11am and 5pm) ducks waddle across the lobby from the penthouse to their pool. The Peabody worships ducks, so don't look for them on the menu.

Quality Inn Plaza
9000 I-Drive, Orlando, FL 32819 (1-407 345 8585). **Rates** double $59.95. **Credit** AmEx, DC, Disc, MC, V.
A mammoth hotel that's better than the cheapos but not much more expensive. Solid, but don't expect room service.

Ramada Resort Maingate
2950 Reedy Creek Boulevard, Kissimmee, FL 34747 (1-407 396 4466). **Rates** double $75-$85; suite $200-$275. **Credit** AmEx, DC, Disc, MC, V.
'Maingate' hotels are located in Kissimmee near Walt Disney World's main gates. This Ramada is reliable and popular with tour operators. It has amenities usually found at more expensive places (a big fitness room, VCRs) but is sometimes priced closer to budget level.

Renaissance Orlando Resort
6677 Sea Harbor Drive, Orlando, FL 32821 (351 5555). **Rates** double $249; private club floor $299; suite $600-$900. **Credit** AmEx, DC, Disc, MC, V.
An elegant, upbeat property that serves a great Sunday brunch. Located next door to Sea World. Popular with business travellers and their families.

Vistana Resort
8800 Vistana Center Drive, Lake Buena Vista, FL 32836 (1-407 239 3100). **Rates** one-bedroom suite $149; two-bedroom suite $199. **Credit** AmEx, DC, Disc, MC, V.
Highly regarded one- and two-bedroom villas with kitchens, VCRs, patios and many amenities. A bit like having your own condo.

Rental agencies
If you're travelling with a group or large family, you might want to rent a fully furnished condominium or house – it's like living at home except that you won't have to clean as much. These places often offer the sedentary pace of retirement communities, but if you're at the attractions all day, you might well prefer it like that. **Club Florida Villas** (1-407 396 8831) has condos and houses in a subdivision seven miles east of Walt Disney World. The townhouses of **Orlando Sun Village** (1-407 396 3200) host seasonal visitors and short-termers with its lakefront locations and all the amenities of condo life (pool, tennis, clubhouse). **Feel Like Home** (1-407 438 1613) rents two- and three-bedroom condos five miles east of the Disney complex. Expect to pay about $105-$115 per night for a three-bedroom townhouse or $160-$230 (depending on season) for a three-bedroom house in Kissimme with its own pool.

Walt Disney World Resort

Walt Disney World Resort is huge, and for good reason. In the mid-1950s, Walt opened Disneyland in California and watched in horror as hotels and burger joints boxed in his park. His team bought real estate, built Disneyland to the property line and were then trapped against the neon signs of businesses springing up across the street. Walt wouldn't make that mistake twice.

In 1964, having secretly chosen Central Florida for his next park, Disney began acquiring land south of Orlando using front companies and operatives. Disney's name was never mentioned. Rumours circulated that the buyers were either the government's space programme or billionaire Howard Hughes. By November 1965, when Walt revealed plans for Walt Disney World, he'd acquired 43 square miles of land, making it more than 300 times as large as the California park. He boasted that he had enough space to 'hold all the ideas and plans we can possibly imagine'. Not mentioned was the more obvious benefit of this splendid isolation – Walt would never see a burger joint's sign looming above the walls of the Magic Kingdom. Walt died within a year, but his strategy proved sound. The Magic Kingdom park opened in 1971 and Walt Disney World has expanded its attractions continuously since then. But even now, less than 25 per cent of the property is developed. And at no ground-level point within its parks can visitors see a non-Disney sign.

PLANNING YOUR VISIT

Walt Disney World currently contains three major theme parks – **Magic Kingdom**, **Disney-MGM Studios** and **Epcot** – three water parks – **Blizzard Beach**, **Typhoon Lagoon** and **River Country** – and night-time entertainment complex **Pleasure Island**. There are also more than 21,000 hotel rooms, nearly 800 campsite pitches, five championship golf courses, dozens of restaurants, retail shops, a residential community, nightclubs, a sports complex and more. Expansion is constant. The next attraction to open will be Disney's Animal Kingdom, in spring 1998.

Each major Disney theme park requires a day or two to visit. The smaller parks require as much time as you want to give them (teens might want to live at Blizzard Beach). Don't try to see too much in a short visit; it's more fun if you don't rush. At the front gate of every park you can pick up a guide map/schedule, which is essential for planning your visit. Autumn and January are the slowest periods at Walt Disney World. Really huge queues occur around Christmas, summer and Spring Break (March).

On peak days, Disney sometimes closes parks to everyone except Disney resort guests. Arriving early is the most popular strategy, but the congestion usually clears by 3pm, so afternoon and evening visits should also be considered. Same-day re-admission is free. Gates often open before scheduled opening times for resort guests and closing times vary depending on season and weather.

A dome from dome: **Epcot**, *page 255.*

Parking at the three major Disney parks costs $5 a day per car (if you visit more than one park in a day you don't have to pay again); at the smaller attractions it's free. Inner-park transport (bus, boat and monorail) is free to pass-holders, although some boats are restricted to resort guests.

Lynx buses 33 and 50 take you to Walt Disney World. The 33 is a once-a-day service for Disney employees, leaving Downtown Orlando at 6.30am, so only any good if you really, really want to be at the front of that queue. The 50 runs every hour from 6.45am, again from Downtown (note that it doesn't go along International Drive), with the last service back at 9.45pm. It drops you at the Magic Kingdom ticket centre, from where you can take Disney transport to other park destinations. Journey time is 45 minutes. Reservations for hotels, restaurants and special activities are strongly recommended (call Disney Central on 1-407 934 7639); behind-the-scenes tours can be arranged through the Walt Disney World Resort on 1-407 939 8687.

TICKETS

Each Walt Disney World park charges a separate admission fee. The three major parks all charge a **one-day rate** of $41 for adults and $33 for children (including sales tax). Children are counted as nine years old or less, with under-threes going free. It's almost impossible to get discounts on one-day tickets, although during Spring Break a valid college ID or ISIC card sometimes gets you 25 per cent off the one-day pass (call ahead to check). Travel agents can occasionally get deals, but let's face it, Disney doesn't have much reason to cut prices at the world's most popular tourist destination. There are no multi-day discounts until you hit four days.

Disney's **4 Day Park Hopper Pass** ($153 adults; $122 children) provides four days of unlimited admission to the three major theme parks, internal transport included, but doesn't include entrance to any of the smaller parks. The **4 Day Value Pass** ($137 adults; $110 children) gets you one day in each of the three major parks and a second day in any one major park. A **Five-Day World-Hopper Pass** ($208 adults; $167 children) will get you into all the parks and, if used correctly, is actually valid for 12 days (seven days in the smaller parks followed by five days in the major parks). Multi-day tickets are available at all three major parks. Area ticket brokers (*see page 239*) also sell a **Four-Day Walt Disney World-Hopper Pass** ($199 adults; $160 children).

If you're planning more than one visit in a year, note that at $285 (adults) and $243 (children), an annual pass offers good value.

INFORMATION

The **Walt Disney World Information** number for all enquiries is 1-407 824 4500, and the Walt Disney **website** is at http://www.disney.com. Disabled visitors can request a guidebook on the above number, or its TTD equivalent, 1-827 5141. **The Disney Reservations Center** (1-407 934 7639) is your contact point for booking everything from a cruise to a campsite. AmEx, MasterCard and Visa are accepted in most shops, restaurants (except on-street refreshments) and resorts, as well as for admission.

Admission prices given were correct as we went to press, but are subject to change. They include sales tax and are rounded up or down to the nearest dollar. Note that opening hours can vary depending on the weather and other factors and that occasionally parks limit entrance due to weather, special events or large crowds. Call ahead if you want to be sure.

Major parks

MAGIC KINGDOM PARK

I-4, exit 25B/bus 50. **Open** 9am-10pm daily. **Admission** one-day $41 adults; $33 children.

When the Magic Kingdom Park opened in 1971, it had something for everyone. But Walt Disney World today is far more stratified with each theme park targeted at different demographic groups. By accident or design, the Magic Kingdom has settled into a role as a playland best appreciated by children under 12. Older visitors might relive their childhood or enjoy the carnivalesque atmosphere, but most Magic Kingdom attractions will seem very tame. If you've got tykes, plan on spending a full day or two here, depending on queues and how many times the kids want to ride It's A Small World. If you're childless, a maximum of one day will suffice (late afternoon and evening is an excellent option, especially if the park is open late).

After parking in the Magic Kingdom lot, visitors board a tram to the Transportation & Ticket Center. From there, it's either to the Magic Kingdom gates via monorail (*see box page 254* **How to jump the queue**) or ferry across the Seven Seas Lagoon.

Orientation

At the front gates, grab a guide map, which lays out the attractions, restaurants and guest performers (the Magic Kingdom has an inexplicable penchant for high school marching bands, so don't expect much). The map also lists character appearances for those precious photos ops with Mickey and the gang. The Magic Kingdom is divided into Main Street, USA, which is basically a logistics area and retail strip with the main entrance at one end and Cinderella Castle at the other, and seven themed 'lands' arranged in a circle: Adventureland, Frontierland, Liberty Square, Fantasyland, Mickey's Toontown Fair and Tomorrowland. Smart money says skip all Main Street shops on your way into the park (do you really want to drag around bags of stuff all day? Nooooo). If you must own Disney trinkets, hit the stores as you exit. Most visitors start at one end of the park and work clockwise or counterclockwise. Queues are omnipresent, even for the crappy attractions.

What to see

Tomorrowland

If you get to the park early, run first to the revamped Tomorrowland and hit **Space Mountain**, a terrifying

How to jump the queue

Queues at the Magic Kingdom Transportation & Ticket Center for the express monorail to the Kingdom itself can be frightening in the morning. Not the best way to start a day, huh? Here's a trick: take the 'local' monorail. The express goes directly to the Magic Kingdom while the local goes the opposite direction on the circular track, stopping at two resorts and then the Magic Kingdom. The local is far less crowded and takes only a few minutes longer than the express. Its entrance is just to the left of the entrance for the express.

Also, up to four people can usually ride in the driver's car of each monorail. Big fun for young and old. When you get to the front of the queue, ask an attendant about riding with the driver. You might have to wait for the next monorail, but it's a great view.

Photo call

Everybody wants a shot of the family with Cinderella Castle in the background. But taking the usual photo from Main Street, USA is a drag. There are crowds, parades and too much movement between you and the castle. Instead, head towards Tomorrowland and stop at the walkway's mid-point under the aerial sculptures. Turn left and there's the best, cleanest view of Cinderella Castle in the park, with nothing but lawn and trees in between. Stand against the wall and ask a passer-by to snap a few with your camera.

---

rollercoaster in near-dark. As you hang on for dear life, remember: it used to be faster, but a shower of wigs, glasses, hats and wallets torn from passengers forced Disney to ease back on the throttle. After that, head to the subversive **ExtraTERRORestrial Alien Encounter**, a brilliant lesson on the power of suggestion. Co-designed by *Star Wars* director George Lucas, it borrows tricks used by 1950s horror movie promoters to simulate the sensations of a realistic alien encounter. The effects are very simple and very convincing. Some kids find this too intense and burst out crying. It's the best attraction in the park, bar none. Next, hit **The Timekeeper**, a witty 360° film about time travel, hosted by two cantankerous Audio-Animatronics characters (voices by Robin Williams and Rhea Pearlman). The 'don't bother' list includes **Take Flight**, a dull and dated sled ride through the history of aviation, and **Tomorrowland Speedway**, which features tiny cars crawling along a track at 7mph (yawn).

Mickey's Toontown Fair
You can skip this. This garish cartoon burg is geared to the wee fans. There are more strollers and crying kids here than anywhere in the park. Unless you need a photo with a Disney character, miss it out.

Fantasyland
This feels like a chaotic funfair, complete with carousel rides. It's big, stupid fun to stroll and watch little kids gape. But if those little kids are yours, buck up for long queues on **It's a Small World**, **Mr Toad's Wild Ride** and **Peter Pan's Flight**. The first and third might seem dull to non-tots, but you can't claim to have visited Walt Disney World until you can sing 'It's a small world after all...'

Liberty Square
There are several good attractions but only one essential: **The Haunted Mansion**. This sled ride tours a terrific display of Audio-Animatronics (talking robots designed by Disney in the 1960s). The 999 ghosts, ghouls and goblins on display are friendly, so don't expect a fright. Although it was opened in the 1970s, the details and density of these sets are still impressive.

Frontierland
Head straight for **Big Thunder Mountain Railroad**, an exciting, if smallish rollercoaster that tears through a mountain with excellent scenery on all sides. Next, join the endless line for **Splash Mountain**: Disney's headlining flume offers a few minor plunges and one exceptionally frightening final drop (almost 90ft at 40mph). You will get wet. The trip is filled with Audio-Animatronics characters from the film *Song of the South*, including a fox which appears to be performing an unnatural act with a bear (have your camera

ready). If your kids need to burn off energy, drop by **Tom Sawyer Island**, where they can run through caves, paths and Fort Sam Clemens. Challenge them to find the secret passageway (it's really there.)

Adventureland
This has the classic **Pirates of the Caribbean**, a watery sled ride through an Audio-Animatronics pirate adventure. Sure, the pirates are a bit goofy, but it's fun and kids love it. After that, hit **Jungle Cruise**, a boat tour through tropical waterways filled with wild animals (all Audio-Animatronics). If the cast member playing the captain is any good, the narration will be quite amusing. Day or night, forget **Swiss Family Treehouse**, a fake treehouse you're supposed to climb through (you flew to Florida for this? I don't think so). Even more annoying is **The Tropical Serenade**, 200 Audio-Animatronics birds, plants and statues singing a shrill Pacific Island tribute. You'll want to strangle the little buggers before it's over.

Where to eat
At some point you'll want to eat. Our advice is don't. Despite improvements, the Magic Kingdom offers resoundingly mediocre fare. If feasible, grab snacks from street vendors. There are fresh fruit stands as well as the mysterious smoked turkey legs. These caveman-sized appendages are sold throughout the park for $4.25. Where do they come from? Who knows. We've never seen a turkey with legs so large. They're tasty, but a bitch to eat standing up.

If you must eat a full meal in the Kingdom, try **El Pirata y el Perico** (Adventureland), **Liberty Tree Tavern** (Liberty Square) or the **Crystal Palace** (Main Street, USA). If you're in the mood for a show, have a sandwich at the **Diamond Horseshoe Saloon Revue**. Better yet, hop a monorail to the Contemporary or Grand Floridian resorts and have a real meal (*see below* Disney restaurants). Should you crave sugar, the Kingdom's best snack is the ice-cream sandwich at the **Main Street Bake Shop**: two rich cookies of your choice with a slab of vanilla ice-cream in between. It's big enough to split and at only $2.65, a rare Disney bargain.

DISNEY-MGM STUDIOS
I-4, exit 25B/bus 50, then Disney transport. **Open** 9am-9pm daily. **Admission** one-day $41 adults; $33 children. Disney-MGM Studios boasts the same studio backlot motif as Universal Studios, but feels a bit more tame (not surprising for a company still uncomfortable with its production of R-rated movies). It's nearly the same size as the Magic Kingdom and organised in a similar circular fashion, with Hollywood Boulevard serving as Main Street. A confusing layout hides large areas of the park behind walls or buildings, which makes navigation a bitch and convinces first-timers that the park is much larger. If you time it right, a visit should take less than a full day.

Six-year-olds will probably enjoy this park more than older siblings as there are several kiddie-oriented live shows based on Disney animated features. As with Universal, there is an annoying tendency to lazily regurgitate a film's plot or characters in attraction format. It's completely pointless but popular with yokels who don't want to think much while being entertained ('We've seen this already? Good.'). The best attractions usually create new content for familiar characters.

What to see
Without a doubt, **The Twilight Zone Tower of Terror** wins Best of Park honours. Visitors start with a video visit from Rod Serling, then get strapped into a elevator car with about 20 other people. The car moves through spooky holographic displays and suddenly, in pitch blackness, rushes up to an opening window 13 stories above the park. After a brief pause, it's freefall time. The elevator plummets, shoots up and drops again. Notice how your behind floats above the seat during the drops; only the steel bar across your legs holds you to the chair. It's an amazing ride and over much

too quickly. Another must-see is **Jim Henson's Muppet Vision 3D**, a hilarious 3-D film with live puppets in the theatre and plenty of audience gags. As always, the Muppets are funny, rude and original: kids and adults will enjoy it. And watch out for the fake flower on the lapel gag: those 3-D glasses won't protect you.

Although Disney-MGM Studios doesn't do much film production work, it does have a functioning animation studio which stars in **The Magic of Disney Animation**. This tour starts with a museum of animation cells from Disney's latest epic followed by a funny film explaining the animation process (with Robin Williams and Walter Cronkite). Visitors then tour the workspace of animators, followed by a talk/demonstration from a Disney animator. Though long, this is one of the park's best and most intelligent attractions.

Star Tours recycles *Star Wars* footage and plot, but that's forgivable since the action is intense and the presentation very well done. Motion-simulator fans will love it but those with a weak stomach should pass. The **Studios Backlot Tour** is interesting for **Catastrophe Canyon**, where that popular theme park refrain 'Oh-nooo! Something's gone wrong!' is heard again. The tram gets stuck in the middle of a simulated earthquake with explosions and rock slides all around. The more interesting segment comes immediately after, as the tram goes behind the set to expose the machinery necessary for this illusion.

Of the live shows, **Voyage of the Little Mermaid, Beauty and the Beast Stage Show** and **The Hunchback of Notre Dame – A Musical Adventure** are essential if your kids own any of the related merchandise. Luckily, they're also excellent. The same can't be said for the dumb, obnoxiously loud **Indiana Jones Epic Stunt Spectacular**. Actors pretend to shoot stunt sequences lifted from the film, a director pretends to give directions and the audience pretends to care. It would be better if they explained how the real film was shot instead of turning it into a floorshow. At the **Monster Sound Show**, four audience members try to add live sound effects to a short film starring Martin Short and Chevy Chase. Try to stand at the front of the queue outside and volunteer. Then, don't make any attempt to synch your sounds to the film, just bash away gleefully. You'll get big laughs during playback. As you leave, be sure to have a go on the Theremin – a musical instrument that responds to movement – built into the TV set.

The absolute nadir of Disney-MGM Studios is **The Great Movie Ride**, a deathly dull sled tour through cinematic history. The Sigourney Weaver figure looks like a life-size Barbie that's been hit with a blowtorch. (Disney employees jokingly refer to this as 'The Ride', since it's neither great nor much related to the movies.)

Where to eat

When it comes to eats, Disney-MGM Studios rules over the Magic Kingdom. The elegant **Hollywood Brown Derby** is heartily recommended. Awash with glorious 1930s art deco interiors, it's the perfect place for a Cobb salad, a fancy dinner or a few cocktails (this is the popular spot for Disney employee office functions). The **Sci-Fi Dine-In Theater** offers sandwiches, burgers and desserts with a drive-in movie twist. Each booth is the interior of a classic car and faces a screen upon which cheesy monster movies are projected; it's very popular, so book in advance. Also worth visiting are **Mama Melrose's Ristorante Italiano** and the **50's Prime Time Café**. If you want to keep moving, there are decent snack bars throughout the park.

EPCOT

I-4, exit 26B/bus 50, then Disney transport. **Open** 9am-8pm daily. **Admission** one-day $41 adults; $33 children.

To Walt Disney's mind, Epcot stood for 'Experimental Prototype Community of Tomorrow': a futurist living situation where new technologies and concepts would be roadtested by residents for use in real-world communities. The living community portion of that project got bumped to Celebration, Disney's first residential community (*see box page 256*). Epcot evolved into a never-ending World's Fair, showcasing high-tech visions in Future World and the

Messin' about on the river.

cultures of 11 countries in World Showcase. Future World and World Showcase are a mighty odd pairing and suggest Epcot is really two unrelated parks linked by a figure-eight layout. World Showcase occupies the top circle furthest from the main gate and surrounds most of World Showcase Lagoon. Future World, dominated by the giant dome known as Spaceship Earth, inhabits the bottom circle. They're separated by bridges and water and the only similarity is an appeal to audiences more interested in learning than thrills. Though very young visitors might get bored, Epcot is a treat for those not seeking mindless diversion. Many rate it as Walt Disney World's best major park. A complete visit involves lots of walking and takes at least one very long day or (preferably) two days. A big negative in Epcot is the blatant use of corporate sponsorships. There's a company name attached to virtually every square inch of Future World. With all the advertising shoved down your throat, you'll wonder why an admission fee was necessary.

What to see
Future World
Visitors entering Epcot though the main gate come face to face with the 180ft high dome Spaceship Earth. The queue under it leads to a sled ride through the dome themed on the history of communication (the queue moves fast, as do most in Epcot). The exhibits are interesting, but the sled system is in dire need of an overhaul – it audibly creaks and wheezes as it strains to pull its load to the top of the dome.

The rest of Future World consists of nine pavilions, each with a different assortment of corporate-sponsored treats. The one truly kicking attraction is Honey, I Shrunk the Audience, a 3-D film starring Rick Moranis. The audience is 'shrunk' to the size of a bread box and threatened by snakes, mice and babies. Great special effects will send you leaping from your seat (this film really belongs at Disney-MGM Studios). Wonders of Life is the most interesting pavilion, featuring health and sports areas as well as cool shows. Cranium Command is a very funny look at the workings of a 12-year-old boy's brain (minus heavy metal, masturbation and *Playboy*). The Making of Me, a film hosted by Martin Short, is a graphic explanation of where babies come from (kids pay very close attention). Body Wars is another motion-simulator ride, this time through the human body. Thankfully short, it is marred by murky footage: it looks like you're cruising through a milkshake.

The Living Seas pavilion features a 6 million-gallon salt water aquarium with over 5,000 sea creatures of 65 different species. Visitors to Sea Base Alpha explore this spectacular undersea world by walking through and under it. Certified divers can sign up for a 30-minute swim through the aquarium, for about $150 (book on 1-407 939 8687).

The two Innoventions pavilions house dozens of high-tech companies striving for positive PR by offering live demonstrations of their products, ranging from home insulation to virtual reality skiing – anyone who's been to a high-tech trade show will recognise the scene. Quality varies widely. There are many hand-on showcases to occupy the Nintendo-trained hands of seven year olds, who won't care in the slightest about the corporate sponsorships.

World Showcase
This is strangely enjoyable, especially if you hit the area in late afternoon or evening. Each 'country' features distinctive national architecture, an attraction, restaurants, retail and craft shops and entertainment in the form of street performers. The performers are loads of fun and you should catch as many as possible; it's like browsing town squares across the planet except that no one's asking for spare change. World Showcase countries serve national beers to go (Harp and Bass in the UK area), so it's quite relaxing to get a pint, watch a streetshow, then stroll to the next country for a new beverage and new entertainment.

Of the attractions, Norway's Maelstrom, a lurching sled ride in a Viking boat, is the most fun (and the most like a regular theme park ride). The Circle-Vision 360 films O Canada! and Wonders of China are huge and impressive and a great way to cool off in air-conditioned splendour. The American Adventure is sugar-coated, patriotic nonsense depicting 'America's incredible struggles and triumphs'.

Once you've made the loop, sampled the beers and seen the street performers, find a nice patch of lawn or a café seat near to World Showcase Lagoon and watch IllumiNations 25 at 9pm. It combines fireworks, lasers, lights and dance music from around the world in an extravaganza over the lake. Yeah, it's tacky and outlandish, but it's fun on a warm night, especially with kids nearby.

Where to eat
Epcot's restaurant list crushes other Disney parks, so plan on at least one meal here. In Future World, Pure & Simple is the choice for a light healthy lunch, Garden Grill for family-style dining and Coral Reef for seafood served a few feet from the wall-sized aquarium of The Living Seas. In the World Showcase, almost every national restaurant is excellent, even the UK's Rose & Crown Pub and Dining Room (a shock to many Americans who assume all Brit food is fried crap). Favourite spots include Germany's Biergarten, Morocco's Restaurant Marrakesh, France's Chefs de France, Japan's Teppanyaki Dining Rooms and Mexico's San Angel Inn. Reservations are required for most, but one place that's usually less than packed is Norway's tasty Restaurant Akershus. Some folks may be skittish about the joys of herring served 10 ways, but don't let that stop you – it's strongly recommended.

Smaller parks

It gets hot in Central Florida, so it doesn't take a rocket scientist to decipher the allure of water parks. Disney has tried three times – Blizzard Beach, Typhoon Lagoon, River Country – to put its signature on a water park in an obvious attempt to compete with the standalone Wet 'n Wild park. Disney's parks are excellent for younger kids, have some good rides and certainly win for scenery, but in the category of thrills and lots of them, Wet 'n Wild is still the clear winner.

BLIZZARD BEACH
I-4, exit 25B/bus 50, then Disney transport. Open 10am-7pm daily. Admission one-day $26 adults; $21 children.
This is Disney's stand-out water park. According to Disney's own 'legend', a freak snowstorm once encouraged Disney to build a ski resort. As the snow melted, Disney was left with a mountain of slush, so it transformed the joint into a water park, retaining the chair lift, bobsled run, slalom courses and toboggan slides. Here, Disney hits peak thrill levels with excellent rides such as Runoff Rapids, Teamboat Springs, Downhill Double Dipper, Snow Stormers and Slush Gusher. At the pinnacle is Summit Plummet, billed as the 'world's tallest freefall body slide'. Riders feel like they're falling off a building. It's direct competition to Wet 'n Wild's Der Stuka.

Blizzard Beach's biggest problem is its popularity: admission is often halted by 11am due to crowds and queues don't move fast, especially compared to Wet 'n Wild. Part of this is down to Disney's safety fetish, which slows the pace, and part to ride capacity (there's only one slide at Summit Plummet while Der Stuka has two).

Typhoon Lagoon
I-4, exit 26B/bus 50, then Disney transport. Open 10am-7pm daily. Admission one-day $26 adults; $21 children.
Disney's mid-tier water park, a lushly landscaped retreat

that's supposedly the remains of Placid Palms Resort after 'a furious storm' (Disney is incapable of creating a park without a plotline). To remind visitors of the terrible storm, the shrimp boat Miss Tilly is impaled high above the park atop Mount Mayday – it's the kind of beyond-belief sight that makes even the jaded appreciate Disney's magic. The waterslides here are mild and best suited for pre-teens and their parents. However, there are two attractions not to be missed. The **Typhoon Lagoon Surf Pool** generates four-foot waves with an ominous 'thwomp' followed by screams from hundreds of swimmers as a wall of water rolls towards them. Body surfing is not only possible, it's encouraged. At the **Shark Reef**, swimmers don snorkel gear and float through a 362,000-gallon salt water tank fitted out like a shipwreck and teeming with schools of fish (including sharks and sting rays). It has a bad rep for long queues but don't let that stop you; go in the afternoon when queues are shorter and stay

to the far right of the tank, near the wall, to maximise your swim time. When you're done, do it again. We watched a father and son swim the Shark Reef five times in a row and both proclaimed it one of their best Disney experiences.

River Country

I-4, exit 25B/bus 50, then Disney transport. **Open** 10am-7pm daily. **Admission** one-day $17 adults; $13 children.
The smallest and oldest Disney water park. A glorified swimming hole on the edge of Bay Lake, it's a great, shady spot to take small children. They love the rope swings and slides and will probably exhaust themselves before noon. There's also a wonderful (and free) petting zoo near River Country's entrance. Bring some quarters to buy goat feed or take a pony ride ($2). If the cost of River Country or the thought of screaming kids doesn't excite you, turn left near the River Country gate and head to Fort Wilderness beach. There are no ropes, swings, slides or screaming kids – and it's free. Get a tan and enjoy the day.

Discovery Island

I-4, exit 25B/bus 50, then Disney transport. **Open** 10am-6pm daily (last boat leaves 4.45pm). **Admission** one-day $13 adults; $7 children.
Across Bay lake from River Country is Discovery Island, an 11-acre zoological sanctuary specialising in endangered and disabled animals, where over 100 species roam free. There's a huge walk-through aviary that serves as a breeding colony for birds, schedules shows on reptiles, birds and Florida wildlife and runs a half-day exploration programme for kids in the summer. The park is surprisingly low-key, which makes it a pleasant stop. Look for special River Country-Discovery Island combo tickets ($21 adults; $15 children) and make a day of the area. Discovery Island is reached by boat, from the pier at Fort Wilderness beach and other Magic Kingdom area resorts.

Pleasure Island

I-4, exit 26B/bus 50, then Disney transport. **Open** 7pm-2am daily. **Admission** one-day $19 adults.
Disney suits are nothing if not observant. When they saw adults leaving for a night of dancing and bar-hopping in Downtown Orlando, they created Pleasure Island. For one cover charge, this complex offers seven clubs and three outdoor stages of entertainment until 2am. As an added treat, every night is New Year's Eve, complete with countdown and fireworks display at midnight. On crowded evenings, the party spills onto the street and the sloshed crowd dances to hits spun by Pleasure Island's own DJ. This is where Pleasure Island excels: security maintains a watchful eye, but basically stays out of the way – in marked contrast to the Orlando police, who act as if they have a mandate to hassle Downtown clubgoers the moment they step onto the street. The Pleasure Island clubs are part of Downtown, and through 1997 and '98 will be joined there by an expanded 24-screen cinema complex, a branch of the House of Blues, a Wolfgang Puck café, a restaurant/nightclub from Gloria Estefan and her husband and a Cirque du Soleil theatre.

The clubs

Adventurers Club: An eccentric space featuring character sketches and improvisational comedy in its five rooms.
Rock N Roll Beach Club: A dance/rock venue with live bands and a DJ. On a good night, it's primarily a meat market for the under-25 set (exposed navels on the women and baseball hats on half of the guys). 'Dressed-up' here means a pressed T-shirt.
Comedy Warehouse: Offers the improv talents of the Who What and Warehouse Players and occasional touring headliners (expect an extra charge for the big names). You can't pop in and out of this club, you have to stay for a show. Seating is tight, especially later in the evening.
8Trax: The happy sound of 1970s dance music is spun here (all together now: 'Y-M-C-A!'). The floor is usually packed

Celebration

You loved Walt Disney World so much that you never want to leave. Well, now you don't have to. Disney has built its own planned community, Celebration, billed as 'An American Town', and is inviting up to 8,000 people to live there.

Don't expect to see Mickey and his pals strolling past the white picket fences or enjoying an ice-cream cone at the sweet shop in cosy downtown. Rather, the whole place is a kind of cartoon of small-town USA (though the curved row of Georgian townhouses across from the school scream London's Regent Street). But, compared with suburbia's typical sprawling development of cookie-cutter homes, Celebration's village greens, garages behind the houses and inviting front porches win hands down for enlightened planning. There are even apartments above the shops and restaurants downtown. Noted architects lent a hand, such as Philip Johnson (who designed the town hall) and Michael Graves (the post office).

Visitors are welcome to shop and eat downtown (there is a great art deco-style cinema) as well as drive the streets. The Celebration Preview Center has all the information you need to scoop up a home for anywhere from just under $200,000 to a million bucks. The staff are all smiles, speak in upbeat but measured tones and pepper their sentences with a slew of buzzwords such as 'community', 'safety' and 'wellbeing'. Prepare for an apple-pie high.

To reach Celebration, take I-4 to US 192 (exit 25A) and go a quarter of a mile east to Celebration Avenue (the second traffic light). Turn right and follow the road into town. More information on 1-407 566 4663.

and the bartender sometimes blows fire. This is probably the most fun club on Pleasure Island.

Mannequins Dance Palace: A huge techno/house dance hall (21s and over only) with rotating floor and state-of-the-art sound and lighting. Very hip, even with locals. Disney resort guests sometimes stumble in and appear baffled by the noise and attitude. The DJs seem to be hooked on oppressive, drum machine music.

Neon Armadillo Music Saloon: Straight-up country music bar offering line dancing lessons on Sundays, 7-8.15pm.

Pleasure Island Jazz Company: An excellent room that attracts a more sedate, sit-down crowd. Besides drinks, it offers appetisers, desserts and a nice US wine list.

Other attractions

Disney's BoardWalk Resort

I-4, exit 26B/bus 50, then Disney transport.
Walt Disney World's smallest hotel has a 1930s-style boardwalk along half of Crescent Lake. Most popular in the evening, the boardwalk has street performers and carnival-style amusements as well as several bars (including a microbrewery) and an excellent restaurant, **Spoodles**. At the far end lurks the hidden jewel of Disney, the **Atlantic Dance Hall**, a picture-perfect recreation of an art deco ballroom complete with snappy bartenders, fancy drinks and an authentic swing band. Disney hasn't figured how to market this, so it's rarely crowded. Music fans must visit.

Disney Village Marketplace

I-4, exit 26B/bus 50, then Disney transport. **Open** 9.30am-11pm daily.
Disney's attempt at a Florida-style outdoor mall is surprisingly dull, probably due to a lack of nationally known retailers (surprise – a gargantuan Disney Store anchors this mall). The location alongside Buena Vista Lagoon makes for pleasant strolling and visitors can rent boats by the half-hour at **Cap'n Jack's Marina** (1-407 828 2204). But if you want real shopping, head to the Florida Mall or I-Drive outlet malls (*see page 251*). The Village Marketplace is redeemed by restaurants. For the kids, there's **Chef Mickey's Village Restaurant**; the food is bland, but Chef Mickey greets guests during dinner. A little higher up the taste scale is **Cap'n Jack's Oyster Bar**, offering solid fish dishes in a comfortable setting. The **Rainforest Café** is a combination retail shop and theme eatery complete with a rumbling volcano that belches smoke regularly (don't worry, it's outside). The menu is diverse and the dining room dense with jungle foliage. The food gets mixed reviews, but the place is newish, so expect improvements.

Richard Petty Driving Experience

I-4, exit 25-B/bus 50. **Open** 8am-6pm daily.
Reservations essential call 1-407 939 0130.
If you feel the need for speed, investigate this stock car racing course located just beyond the Magic Kingdom parking gates. There are three options: ride as a passenger with a professional driver for three laps ($99), take a three-hour course and drive for eight laps ($399) or try the 'Experience of a Lifetime', an all-day affair where you'll drive three 10-lap sessions ($1,299). All prices are without tax.

Disney hotels

Two things to remember about Disney digs: quality and service are always high, and so is the price. Staying at Disney hotels gives you perks such as early admission to parks, priority tee times, free parking and a Disney 'credit card' so you don't have to carry money. But, frankly, there are hotels as nice or nicer off Disney property for less money. Prices quoted are per night (single or double) and should be viewed as a guide because rates change constantly. To book, call the **Disney Reservations Centre** on 1-407 934 7639.

At the top end, Disney has the elegantly conceived **Grand Floridian Beach Resort** ($265-$470), which is nestled on the Seven Seas Lagoon and just a monorail stop from the Magic Kingdom. Quieter rooms face the lagoon rather than the pool. Visting celebrities often check in here. Nearer to Epcot is the **Yacht Club Resort** ($225-$405), featuring an 1870s New England theme shared with its less fancy neighbour, the **Beach Club Resort** ($205-$305). The recently renovated **Contemporary Resort** ($195-$290) is popular with families and has a 15-storey atrium with the monorail running through the middle. Disney's best restaurant, the California Grill (*see below*), offering one of the best while-you-eat views in the park, is upstairs and the lobby café is a great spot for breakfast.

In the mid-range, Disney offers tasteful choices such as **Port Orleans Resort**, **Dixie Landings Resort**, the huge **Caribbean Beach Resort** (all $95-$129) and the **Wilderness Lodge** ($159-$215). Families might like the roomy digs at the **Old Key West Resort** ($265-$290 for a one-bedroom home), or if Epcot gave you a taste for learning, the **Disney Institute**. The Institute offers classes and lectures in all kinds of subjects for people who don't want to switch off their brains just because they're on holiday, as well as nicely priced resort bungalows ($195-$230 for up to five people) and fancier digs that sleep up to eight. Institute classes cost extra; there's a fax-back service on 1-407 566 4701 for more information.

To capture the low-end who book at Kissimmee's main gate hotels, Disney recently introduced the **All-Star Music Resort** and the **All-Star Sports Resort** (both $69-$79). The Sports Resort is the louder of the two and tends to have more kids. Campfire fans should look into **Fort Wilderness** campsites where you can rent ground to pitch a tent ($35-$44), space for your camper ($43-$58) or one of Disney's Wilderness Home trailers ($185-$215).

Disney restaurants

If the Magic Kingdom's prehistoric turkey legs didn't fill you up, Walt Disney World has a galaxy of restaurants outside the parks. As with the hotels, nothing comes cheap. To make a reservation, call **Disney Central** (1-407 934 7639).

At the top of the heap is the excellent **California Grill**, located atop the Contemporary Resort. It's expensive and crowded (with locals aznd tourists), but the food is great and the view even better – if possible, catch the Magic Kingdom's Fantasy in the Sky fireworks from here. Another top-notch haunt is **Victoria & Albert's** at the Grand Floridian, a small, fixed-price spot featuring two waiters, Victoria and Albert. Also at the Grand Floridian, **Narcoossee** fills the needs of red-meat eaters and seafood fans.

Sushi lovers should high-tail it to the large, upscale Swan hotel and dig in at **Kimonos**. If you're looking for something a bit more European, the Swan also houses **Palio**, an excellent Italian eatery where visitors can watch the chefs work in the open kitchen. Chinese food fans should head next door to the Dolphin hotel and enjoy **Sum Chows**. If you're near the Beach Club Resort, the **Cape May Café** serves a tasty clam bake along with its usual buffet, and **Ariel's** is the top spot with its seafood-heavy menu. If you're planning to stroll the boardwalk on Crescent Lake, book a table at **Spoodles**, which has won raves for its Mediterranean-style pasta.

Visitors planning a night at Pleasure Island should consider starting with a meal next door. Just beyond Pleasure Island's west gate is **Planet Hollywood**, the world-famous, over-priced burger joint financed by movie stars jealous of the Hard Rock Café's success. You like movie memorabilia? You like lines that rival Space Mountain? Then Planet Hollywood is for you (the food is OK, but the queues are a killer). Beyond Pleasure Island's east gate are several good restaurants, including **Fulton's Crab House**, **Portobello Yacht Club** (seafood, pasta and pizza) and **Enzo's** (top-notch Italian food).

The Gulf Coast

Edged by silver sand and studded with cities of character, the Gulf Coast is where the smart holiday money goes.

St Petersburg & Clearwater

The cities of St Petersburg and Clearwater sit on the Pinellas peninsula, divided from the mainland – and the city of Tampa – by Tampa Bay. For years, St Petersburg has tried to change its image as 'heaven's waiting room', a retirement haven filled with green benches so that the large senior citizen population could rest their aching feet every few yards. In fact, it is a lovely city, named by a Russian immigrant who founded a railway and pined for his home city. Most of its neighbourhoods are safe (though you should avoid the area immediately south of the huge, domed baseball stadium, Tropicana Field), and it offers a respectable amount of culture to balance the appeal it has long held because of its climate and beaches.

This is the city where the evening newspaper had a long-standing offer of free copies if the sun didn't shine; it had to hand out an average of just over four a year. They don't call this section of Florida 'the Sun Coast' without reason.

The low-rise city centre is an attractive amalgam of businesses, restaurants and museums. **The Salvador Dali Museum** (1000 Third Street S; 1-813 823 3767) holds the world's most comprehensive collection of the Spanish artist's work. The Pier (at the east end of Second Avenue NE; 1-813 821 6164), a widely recognised landmark, is an inverted pyramid that houses an information centre, an aquarium, shops and restaurants. A small kiosk sells fish to visitors, and large numbers of lazy but wily pelicans sit opportunistically on the railings to beg.

Nearby, the **St Petersburg Museum of History** (335 Second Avenue NE; 1-813 894 1052), showcases the city's claim to fame as the home of the world's first commercial air service, established in 1914 when seaplanes regularly flew the 21 miles across the bay to Tampa. Don't miss **Haslam's Book Store** (2025 Central Avenue; 1-813 822 8616), which has a national reputation as the best and largest independently owned bookstore in the south-eastern US.

Clearwater, the other large city that sprawls across the peninsula, north of St Petersburg, is a pretty nondescript collection of businesses and retirement communities, most notable for being the world headquarters of the Church of Scientology. You'll recognise Scientologists in

their new raspberry, taupe, lavender and olive uniforms, a slightly different design and colour scheme for each of the church's seven divisions – so John Travolta and Tom Cruise stand out when they're in town. Clearwater's broad, sandy shore attracts hundred of thousands of visitors. In March, during Spring Break, US college students descend in droves on the beaches, making them even more crowded than usual.

North of Clearwater sits the pretty little Scottish haven of **Dunedin**, whose founders reassigned the original Gaelic name for Edinburgh. Ten miles north of Dunedin lies Florida's version of Greece, **Tarpon Springs**. To reach it, take US 19 or, for a better local flavour, US 19A. Walk the narrow, bumpy streets and you'll notice that only the tourists speak anything other than Greek. On 6 January each year the town gives itself over to the Greek Orthodox Epiphany Celebration, with a street procession to Spring Bayou from the Church of St Nicholas, a replica of St Sophia in Istanbul. The town was famous as a sponge centre until red tide algae destroyed most of the sponge beds in the 1940s. The industry is still important, however, as is apparent from a visit to the **Sponge Exchange** (735 Dodecanese Boulevard; 1-813 934 9262). This open-air complex of sponge shops, boutiques and restaurants sits just across from the main sponge dock along the Anclote River, where sponge boats still tie up each afternoon. Staff at the nearby **Coral Sea Aquarium** (850 Dodecanese Boulevard; 1-813 938 5378) feed moray eels and demonstrate the workings of a coral reef. Tarpon Springs' restaurants are very popular. Don't leave without ordering a Greek salad at **Louis Pappas'** riverside restaurant (10 Dodecanese Boulevard; 1-813 937 5101). **Paul's Shrimp House** (530 Athens Street; 1-813 937 1239), **Mykonos** (628 Dodecanese Boulevard; 1-813 934 4306) and **Mama Maria's** (521 Athens Street; 1-813 938 5475) also have menus that evoke the Dodecanese.

The best – and easiest – place from which to start a beach-athon down the Gulf Coast is **Clearwater Beach**. The central area by the pier is usually crowded and noisy; further north, near Bay Esplanade Avenue, is where local residents head for peace and quiet. Drive south along the coast road, Gulf Boulevard, to **Sand Key Park** for easy parking and serene, palm-studded surroundings. The beach is just to your right as you drive south through Indian Rocks Beach, Indian Shores, Redington Shores, North Redington Beach, Redington Beach and Madeira Beach. There are free parking areas at infrequent intervals. **Treasure Island**, further south still, has one of the broadest beaches along the Gulf Coast, very good for walking. The deep sand comes to a temporary end at **St Pete Beach**, but you can pick it up again at **Fort DeSoto Park**, off the tip of the peninsula (*see also box* **Best beaches bets**).

Getting there

By car: To St Petersburg from Orlando (just over 100 miles), take I-4, then I-275. From Miami (270 miles), take I-75 up the west coast, then I-275 across Tampa Bay. For downtown, take exits I-375 or I-175. Beach exits are marked from I-275.
By air: International and domestic airlines fly into Tampa International Airport (*see below* **Tampa**). St Petersburg-Clearwater International Airport is used chiefly by charters.
By train: One Amtrak (1-800 872 7245) train from Miami to Tampa continues on (by bus) to St Petersburg. A single fare is $68, return $76-$136; journey time seven hours.
By bus: Three Greyhound (1-800 231 2222) buses run daily from Miami ($34.50/$57; seven hours). Six buses go daily from Orlando ($14/$25; three and a half hours).

Where to stay

If you can afford it, stay at either of two outstanding resorts on the western side of Tampa Bay. The **Renaissance Vinoy Resort** (501 Fifth Avenue NE, St Petersburg, FL 33701; 1-813 894 1000), on the bay in downtown St Petersburg, has been recently restored to its 1925 opulence. The **Don Cesar Beach Resort and Spa** (3400 Gulf Boulevard, St Pete Beach, FL 33706; 1-813 360 1881) is a pink palace built on the white sand shore of the Gulf of Mexico. The resident psychic will read your tarot cards by the pool. Good resorts, hotels and motels of all descriptions line Gulf Boulevard from Clearwater to St Pete Beach.

Where to eat

Restaurants line Fourth Street N in St Petersburg, on the eastern edge of the city. Eating places range from elegant to barely utilitarian along Gulf Boulevard through the beach towns.

Tourist information

St Petersburg/Clearwater Area Convention & Visitors Bureau
14450 46th Street N, suite 108, Clearwater, FL 34622 (1-800 345-6710/1-813 464 7200). **Open** 8.30am-5pm Mon-Fri.
Offers a useful accommodation-finding service.

Tampa

Only a supremely confident group of officials would festoon the roads leading into their city with signs reading 'America's Next Great City', but that's Tampa in the 1990s. The slogan is good for business. Tampa is more a working city than a tourist town, and continually ranks high among the best places to live in the US.

Among the first visitors was Spanish conquistador Hernando DeSoto, who found Indians living in a village they called 'Tanpa', meaning 'sticks of fire'. Its name misspelt on maps, for 200 years 'Tampa' remained much as it had been before the Spanish arrived. In 1883, entrepreneur Henry Plant extended his pioneering railway to Tampa, then started a steamship line from Tampa to Key West and Havana. Already growing as an economic centre, the city's future was assured.

The heart of Tampa remains where it was when DeSoto arrived. It's largely a business district, but take time to look inside the **Tampa Theatre** (711 N Franklin Street; 1-813 274 8981), a delightfully restored movie palace built in 1926. Not far off is the **Tampa Museum of Art** (600 N Ashley Drive; 1-813 274 8130), which has a well-regarded collection of European and South American antiquities.

Just across the Hillsborough River is the **Tampa Bay Hotel**, built in 1891, beneath whose silver, onion-shaped minarets and turrets US hero and later president Teddy Roosevelt stayed while whipping his Rough Riders cavalry into shape for the foray into Cuba in 1898 during the Spanish-American War. It is now the home of the University of Tampa, but the **Henry B Plant Museum** (401 W Kennedy Boulevard; 1-813 254 1891) exhibits opulent furnishings and art from the original hotel.

From the **Garrison Seaport Center**, just east of downtown, cruise ships depart for Mexico, New Orleans and destinations in the Caribbean. The landslide attraction here is **The Florida Aquarium** (701 Channelside Drive; 1-813 273 4020), resembling a giant, pastel-coloured, glass mollusk, which holds a respectable collection of Florida aquatic and bird life. Just north-east of downtown is **Ybor City** (*see box*).

Further north is **Busch Gardens** (between Busch Boulevard & McKinley Drive; 1-813 987 5082), a unique, multi-themed, 300-acre park, has a huge collection of African animals, shows and high-tech thrill rides and is one of the city's chief attractions. Less than a mile north is **Adventure Island** (1001 McKinley Drive; 1-813 987 5600), which offers 36 acres of water thrill rides. Nearby is the **Museum of Science and Industry** (4801 E Fowler Avenue; 1-813 987 6100), the most comprehensive museum of its kind in the south-eastern US, which contains the only IMAX movie theatre on the Gulf Coast. The manatee hospital at **Lowry Park Zoo** (7530 N Boulevard; 1-813 932 0245) houses these lumbering sea cows and tends to injured creatures. If time permits, a slow drive along **Bayshore Boulevard**, which has the world's longest unbroken stretch of pavement – 6.5 miles – will give you a sense of the best of Tampa. You can stare at the homes of some of the city's rich and famous while watching the beautiful people jog next to Hillsborough Bay. Turn north on

Ybor City

Ybor City, Tampa's miniature version of New Orleans' French Quarter, grew from a puff of Cuban cigar smoke. It's the kind of place that takes pride in such an origin, particularly in today's anti-smoking era. There isn't a wilder place on the Gulf Coast.

In Ybor (pronounced 'E-bor'), which lies just north-east of downtown Tampa, inhibitions disappear, gluttonous appetites are sated and, especially during 'Guavaween', the annual Hallowe'en street celebration, social codes evaporate. Gay men dressed as condoms parade along the old brick streets and young women flash their breasts from wrought-iron balconies while the disapproving older set sit under metal street lamps, shake their heads and knock back too many Cuba Libres. Most days, life in Ybor is more sedate, but the music, dance and nightclubs hum year-round. Named after Don Vincente Martinez Ybor, the founder of the Ybor City Cigar Factory, which in 1886 was the largest in the world, Ybor drew Cubans, Spaniards, Italians, Germans and Jews, all dependent on the hand-rolled cigar industry. This unlikely cultural mix worked. Factories proliferated, Cuban revolutionary José Martí stopped by weekly to raise funds and Teddy Roosevelt's Rough Riders trained on Ybor's fields before dashing off to Cuba to challenge Spain by charging up San Juan Hill.

In the prosperous 1920s, the only tri-lingual (Spanish, Italian and English) newspaper in the US began publication here; it's still on the street every week. But Ybor's mainstay was the hand-rolled cigar, and in the 1930s cigar-rolling machines brought the Great Depression brought ruin and poverty to Tampa's Latin Quarter. But the good times are back. A few workers in small factories still hand-roll cigars. The world's largest Spanish restaurant, the city-block sized **Columbia** (2117 E Seventh Avenue; 1-813 248 4961), which hasn't missed a meal since 1905, features nightly flamenco dancing, and Don Vincente's brick factory serves as a boutique and restaurant centre.

The **Ybor City Chamber of Commerce** (1800 E Ninth Avenue, Tampa, FL 33605; 1-813 248 3712) arranges free ninety-minute walking tours, but you don't need a guide to stroll along **Seventh Avenue**, through the gargoyle shops, clothing boutiques, tattoo parlours, antique shops, art galleries, Haitian art displays and souvenir shops offering a hint of French Quarter voodoo. Hot jazz seeps into **Ybor Square** from

the **Jazz Cellar** (1311 E Ninth Avenue; 1-813 248 1862). You may not be able to hail the indifferent waiting staff at **The Blues Ship** (1910 E Seventh Avenue; 1-813 248 6097), but the music is mesmerising. **Carmine's** (1802 E Seventh Avenue; 1-813 248 3834) has acclaimed food, cigar-tastings and a dress code (forget denim; sew a collar on your shirt), while **Frankie's Patio Bar & Grill** (1920 E Seventh Avenue; 1-813 248 3337), upscale but casual, has three bars and bands playing modern rock and blues. Some food critics say the best food, if you like it New Orleans-style, is at the **Café Creole** (1330 E Ninth Avenue; 1-813 247 6283).

The Masquerade (1503 E Seventh Avenue; 1-813 247 3319) draws the most outrageous stage acts. Bands such as Genitorturers play alternative music and perform onstage nipple and genital piercings. The **Cherokee Club** (1330 E Ninth Avenue; 1-813 247 9966) is a former bordello which now keeps the mood as mellow as its jazz.

Ybor City is all about having a good time, but at night, when the bands start playing and the crowds start gathering, the pickpockets and car thieves start operating. So imagine you're actually in the French Quarter in New Orleans, and act accordingly.

Rome Avenue to find the heart of **Hyde Park**, an upper-crust shopping and eating area in one of the city's most affluent old residential districts.

Getting there

By car: From Orlando, take I-4 and I-275 to downtown Tampa (68 miles). From Miami, take I-75 to Brandon, then the Crosstown Expressway (75¢ toll) into Tampa (294 miles).
By air: Most domestic airlines fly into Tampa International Airport. British Airways flies non-stop from Gatwick.
By train: Amtrak (1-800 872 7245) has two trains daily from New York and points along the eastern seaboard. One train runs daily from Miami ($62 one way, $60-$124 return; journey time about five and a half hours), and one from Orlando ($22 one way; $30-$44 return, about two hours).
By bus: Six or seven Greyhound (1-800 231 2222) buses run daily from both Miami ($32/$53; 5½ to 9 hours) and Orlando ($14/$25; 2½-3 hours).

Where to stay

Pricey, but excellent, is the **Hyatt Regency Westshore Hotel** (6200 Courtney Campbell Causeway, Tampa, FL 33607; 1-813 874 1234, built next to a small conservation area right on Tampa Bay. Otherwise, there are rows of good hotels on West Shore Boulevard, near the airport. Busch Boulevard and other streets near Busch Gardens are thick with respectable motels.

Where to eat

Dress formally for **Armani's**, the city's most romantic restaurant, atop the Hyatt Regency Westshore , overlooking sparkling Tampa Bay. The more famous **Bern's Steak House** (1208 South Howard Avenue; 1-813 251 2421), claims the longest wine list in the world. Less expensive is **The Castaway** (7720 Courtney Campbell Causeway; 1-813 281 0770), on Tampa Bay.

Tourist information

Tampa/Hillsborough Convention & Visitors Association
400 North Tampa Street, Suite 1010, Tampa, FL 33602 (1-800 448 2672/1-813 223 2752). **Open** 9am-5pm Mon-Sat.

South to Naples

Head south from St Petersburg/Tampa on I-275 and you'll get a stunning view of the Florida landscape that stretches south to the Everglades from the spectacular four-mile long **Sunshine Skyway Bridge** ($1 toll). From the top of the bridge's arc, 192ft above the mouth of Tampa Bay, the evergreen flatland of palm scrub, mangroves and pine trees is outlined by white sand.

With few breaks, beaches run the entire distance (about 160 miles) to Marco Island, just south of the upscale city of Naples. At the southern end of the 12-mile bridge/causeway that crosses Tampa Bay lies **Bradenton**. Take the Tamiami Trail (US 41) south into town, then turn west onto Manatee Avenue to the ankle-deep sand of the pretty and uncrowded beaches of **Anna Maria Key** and **Longboat Key**.

Alternatively, stay on I-275 until it connects with I-75 south, then leave at exit 43 (US 301). You'll find bargains just east of the exit, at the **Gulf Coast Factory Shops** (1-941 723 1150) in Ellenton. There is a useful tourist information centre to the right of the exit. Further on the right is

The **Sunshine Skyway Bridge** stretches for four miles across Tampa Bay.

Best beach bets

From Tarpon Springs to Marco Island, Florida's Gulf of Mexico coastline is one long, sandy beach, save only where several miles of thick mangrove stands touch the sea. While some are broader than others (Treasure Island, near St Petersburg, has some of the widest), and the sand seems whiter and just a little deeper from Captiva Island south, there are no poor choices. But lets ask Dr Beach. Professor Stephen Leatherman of the University of Maryland, a coastal geologist, annually ranks the top 20 beaches in the United States. His taste leans towards uncrowded beaches where the swimming is pleasurable, where there are palm trees, exotic birds and peace and quiet, and where you are not too remote from creature comforts.

Five Gulf Coast beaches are in Dr Beach's Top 20: **Caladesi Island** (limited access by boat from Honeymoon Island in Dunedin), uncrowded, wide, white sand, some shells; **Fort De Soto Park** beach (at the southern tip of the Pinellas peninsula), coarse, shelly sand, but watch out for sand spurs; **Sand Key Park** (just south of Clearwater Beach), a municipal beach that looks like a resort's palm-studded park; **Delnor-Wiggins Pass State Park** (on Immolakee Road, off Highway 41 near Bonita Beach), a mile-long stretch of deep sand with mini-dunes and sea oats where the Cocohatchee River empties into the Gulf; and **Clam Pass Recreation Area** (near the Registry Hotel in the northern part of Naples). Open to the public but hidden behind vegetation, the beach is reached by a tram that follows a boardwalk over a tidal bay and through mangroves. For walking, Dr Beach recommends **Crescent Beach** on Siesta Key, near Sarasota, and for romantics, the long, deep sugar-sand beach on Captiva Island. Another noteworthy stop is **Boca Grande Beach Park** at the south end of Gasparilla Island (off State Route 771), which has shade trees, smooth sand and seclusion.

---

the **Gamble Plantation State Historic Site** (3708 Patten Avenue; 1-941 723 4536), Florida's premier pre-Civil War mansion. An interesting half-day may be spent on **Egmont Key**, a historic island in the mouth of Tampa Bay. Dolphins often accompany the Miss Cortez excursion boat to the island (Cortez Fleet, 4330 127th Street W, Cortez, FL 34215; 1-941 794 1223).

Gulf of Mexico Drive, the main drag through the outlying islands, leads south to **Sarasota** and **St Armands Key**, best known for the 100 upscale shops of St Armands Circle (1-941 388 1554). On the mainland, just north on the Tamiami Trail (US 41), visit the ornate home of circus magnate John Ringling and the circus and art museums here (5401 Bay Shore Road, Sarasota; 1-941 359 5700). On the way south on US 41, stop at the **Marie Selby Botanical Gardens** (811 South Palm Avenue, Sarasota; 1-941 366 5731), with its banyan tree grove, bamboo stands, bromeliads and orchid displays. The Tamiami Trail leads south to **Venice**, an island city crisscrossed with canals and studded with Italianate buildings. If you have a week to spare and a yen for some peace, install yourself at nearby **Palm Island Resort** off Cape Haze (7092 Placida Road, Cape Haze; 1-941 697 4800), a place at one with nature (strictly no cars allowed). The beach and Gulf are only steps from your room, and tortoises and exotic birds wander about at will. Man is a careful intruder.

Fort Myers, on the south bank of the Caloosahatchee River, is a city of towering royal palms and the former winter homes of two well-known Americans, the prolific inventor Thomas Edison and his close friend, automobile manufacturer Henry Ford (visitors' centre at 2350 McGregor Boulevard; 1-941 334 3614). Most travellers head to the beaches on Sanibel and Captiva Islands (*see below*) or **Fort Myers Beach** on Estero Island. In Fort Myers Beach, stay on the island road until Bonita Beach Road takes you back to US 41. It's then only 16 miles to **Naples**, the most expensive city on Florida's Gulf Coast. It has 41 miles of public beach, but is best known as the west coast version of Palm Beach. Trendy boutiques, gourmet restaurants and ritzy shops add to the glitter along its very own Fifth Avenue. This is a first-class place to swim, play golf, shop, collect shells and enjoy luxurious accommodations. Just bring money.

Marco Island, the northernmost of Florida's Ten Thousand Islands, lies 20 miles south. Like Naples, it is expensive, but the lodgings, restaurants and beach facilities are first-class.

Getting there

By car: From Tampa or St Petersburg, take I-275 south across Tampa Bay. To begin the scenic route, take the first exit after the bridge (US 19) to US 41 (Tamiami Trail). Take I-75 for a fast, direct trip to Naples (about 3½ hours).

By air: From Orlando, Miami and Tampa, several airlines fly to both Sarasota-Bradenton International Airport and Southwest Florida International Airport, which serves Fort Myers and Naples.

By bus: From Tampa and St Petersburg, Greyhound runs

six buses a day south through Bradenton, Sarasota and Fort Myers ($16 one way/$30-$32 return; three hours. Four continue to Naples (same prices; 4½ hours. No train services run to these destinations.

Where to stay

US 41 and the beach roads are lined with places to stay, from pricey resorts in Sarasota and Naples to cheaper motels in the smaller towns.

Where to eat

Along I-75, stop at one of the three **Cracker Barrel** restaurants, or try any of the hundreds of eating places along the beach roads or US 41.

Tourist information

Bradenton & Gulf Island Beaches Convention & Visitors Bureau

1 Haven Boulevard, Palmetto, FL 34221 (1-800 462 6283/1-941 729 9177). **Open** 8am-5pm Mon-Fri.

Sarasota Convention & Visitors Bureau

655 N Tamiami Trail, Sarasota, FL 34236 (1-800 522 9799). **Open** 9am-5pm Mon-Sat.

Lee Island Coast Visitor & Convention Bureau

2180 W First Street, Suite 100, Fort Myers, FL 33901 (1-800 733 7935). **Open** 8am-5pm Mon-Fri.

Sanibel & Captiva Islands

On boomerang-shaped Sanibel Island and its northern extension, Captiva Island, that old 'life is a beach' cliché comes true – life is indeed a 20-mile beach here. Gulf breezes blow ashore, sugary sand spills through your toes, perfectly intact shells lie waiting for collectors to find them and the native wildlife pays little attention to the carefully controlled human invasion. Consider those who have found inspiration here: the flier Charles and his writer-wife Anne Morrow Lindbergh on Captiva Island, US poet Edna St Vincent Millay on Sanibel and conservationist Jay N 'Ding' Darling on both islands.

Move slowly on Captiva Drive through an arching evergreen tunnel of Australian pines, walk the length of Bowmans Beach or cycle through lanes of brilliant tropical flowers and you'll understand why this is a year-round mecca for affluent pleasure-seekers. After crossing San Carlos Bay on the Sanibel Causeway ($3 toll), turn left at the four-way stop to the **Sanibel Lighthouse** and the beach. Parking is allowed only in designated areas, pre-paid at 75¢ an hour. Drive along East, Middle and West Gulf Drive past the resorts and inns. Along Periwinkle Way are shops and shopping centres. **Periwinkle Place** (2075 Periwinkle Way) has a particularly wide-ranging collection of shops, boutiques and restaurants. For a visual treat, step inside **Paradise of Sanibel**, a clothing shop that puts you smack in the middle of a jungle. Two miles west is Sanibel's own

jungle, the **JN 'Ding' Darling National Wildlife Refuge** (1 Wildlife Drive, off Sanibel-Captiva Road; 1-941 472 1100), with 5,000 acres of alligators, manatees, butterflies, bobcats, gopher tortoises, tricolored herons and roseate spoonbills, among hundreds of other species. The bridge at Blind Pass leads to Captiva's one road, with two public beach accesses.

Getting there

By car: From Orlando, take I-4 to I-75 south (175 miles). From Tampa, take I-75 south (145 miles); from Miami, I-75 west (158 miles). Near Fort Myers, take exit 21 (Daniels Parkway) west to Summerlin Road and the Sanibel Causeway.
By air: Most major airlines serve Southwest Florida International Airport in Fort Myers, 30 miles (45 minutes) from the causeway.
By bus: Greyhound (1-800 231 2222) buses arrive in Fort Myers from Orlando (five a day, one-way $31, return $62; journey time six to seven hours), Tampa (six a day, $16/$30-$32; three hours) and Miami (five a day, $18/$35; 4½ hours).
By train: One train a day runs from Miami (only) to Fort Myers ($81/$88-$162; 5½ hours).

Where to stay

Casa Ybel (2255 West Gulf Drive, Sanibel Island, FL 33957; 1-941 472 3145) is Sanibel's most luxurious resort. **South Seas Resorts** (5400 Captiva Road, Captiva Island, FL 33924; 1-800 227 8482/1-941 472 5111) has five impressive properties, including the South Seas Plantation on the northern half of Captiva Island, a former key lime and coconut plantation. You could also try the **Sundial Beach Resort** (1541 Middle Gulf Drive, Sanibel, FL 33957; 1-800 237 4184/1-941 472 4151); the European-style inn **Song of the Sea** (863 East Gulf Drive, Sanibel, FL 33957; 1-800 231 1045/1-941 472 2220); or the Key West-style **Seaside Inn** (541 East Gulf Drive, Sanibel, FL 33957; 1- 800 831 7384; 1-941 472 1400), all on Sanibel's south beach.

Where to eat

Your life won't be complete without a meal at **The Bubble Room** (15001 Captiva Drive; 1-941 472 5558) on Captiva Island, where the décor is eclectic, tables are glass-topped display cases housing old toys and theatrical memorabilia and the seafood and ample desserts are to die for. No reservations, but worth the long wait. Beautiful **Portofino's** (937 East Gulf Drive; 1-941 472 0494) is elegant Italian from its bruschetta al pomodoro to its rollatine de vitello (veal medallions). For Sanibel seafood, try **The Jacaranda** (1223 Periwinkle Way; 1-941 472 1771), and for creative dinner buffets, **Chadwick's** (at South Seas Plantation, Captiva Island; 1-941 472-5111). At lunch, try the lighter fare at **Sanibel Island Chowder Co** in Periwinkle Place Shopping Center (2075 Periwinkle Way; 1-941 472 2525).

Tourist information

Sanibel Captiva Islands Chamber of Commerce

1159 Causeway Road, Sanibel, Fl 33957 (1-941 472 1080/fax 1-941 472 1070). **Open** 9am-7pm Mon-Sat; 10am-5pm Sun.

Lee Island Coast Visitor & Convention Bureau

2180 W First Street, Suite 100, Fort Myers, FL 33901 (1-800 733 7935). **Open** 8am-5pm Mon-Fri.

Shell collecting

The Gulf Coast is a shell collector's heaven, and Sanibel Island calls itself the 'Shelling Capital of the Western Hemisphere', a title well earned. Amateur and professional shellers explain that Sanibel's east-west orientation, lack of offshore reefs and the sea's sandy bottom allow Sanibel's beaches to snare intact shells from everywhere in the Caribbean and South Atlantic – coquinas, olives, cones, lightning whelks, worms, tulips, cockles, eight-inch horseconches (the largest found in Florida) and 300 other varieties. The shell-collecting position is so common here that islanders gave it a name: 'Sanibel Stoop'.

Head for **Bowmans Beach**, about halfway across Sanibel Island, or stoop along the beaches on the bay near the ends of **Dixie Beach Road** or **Bailey Road**. Just after low tide, the sand south of the mainland causeway is worth exploring. Access is easy for everyone here, so the earliest shellers get the spoils of the night. **Fort Myers Beach** on Estero Island, south of where the beach crowds collect near the San Carlos Boulevard bridge, and **Bonita Beach** on Little Hickory Island further south, can also yield exciting discoveries.

While they're not all created equal, most beaches along the Gulf Coast offer shells for the picking. Of course, the best shelling is in places without easy access. If you're determined, hire a boat or take a shelling charter (try Captain Jim Burnsed at 'Tween Waters Marina on the north end of Sanibel Island; 1-941 472 1779) and do the stoop on **La Costa Island** (between North Captiva and Boca Grande); **Big Hickory Island**, a favourite with local shellers; **Caladesi Island** (north-west of Clearwater); or **Keewaydin Island** (south of Naples).

Professional shellers look for intact live specimens of wentletraps or lace murex, among others, but there is a legal limit of two per person per species. As cleaning live shells is a smelly, messy business, it's best for tourists to collect those already abandoned by their inhabitants, or look out for shark's teeth. There's a huge variety, ranging in size from prehistoric eighth-of-an-inch black triangles to rare three-inch white teeth that have been recently shed. (There are no toothless sharks; they lose teeth regularly and grow new, sharper ones). Venice, south of Sarasota, is said to be the world's capital of shark tooth collecting. You can rent what are jokingly called 'Florida snow shovels' – sifters designed to help separate sharks' teeth from Venice Beach sand.

Bookshops, gift shops and shell shops everywhere along the Gulf Coast sell shell guides. You can also buy ready-gathered shells at numerous shops all the way down the coast. One of the best is **Sanibel Sea Shell Industries** (905 Fitzhugh Street, Sanibel; 1-941 472 1603). And if these gifts from the sea fascinate you, don't miss the impressive collection at **Bailey-Matthews Shell Museum** (3075 Sanibel-Captiva Road, Sanibel; 1-941 395 2233), the only museum in North America devoted to shells of the world.

Cuba

Miami's unofficial alter ego, Cuba is becoming a desirable travel destination, despite the US embargo and its antiquated state.

Cuba's relationship with Miami is a long and complex one (*see chapters* **History** & **Latin Miami**), resulting in a two-way cultural exchange that even the US embargo has failed to suppress. But though the two are spiritually close – and indeed physically close, with Cuba a mere 180 miles away – direct travel between the two is almost impossible, unless you are a journalist, academic or visiting relations in Cuba. Miamians do visit, however, travelling most commonly via Mexico or the Bahamas. Non US citizens also have to travel by a roundabout route: you can't buy a ticket to Cuba with a US stopover. For routes, *see below* **Getting there**.

Tucked under the US's armpit, 90 miles from Key West, the biggest of the Caribbean islands is the size of England. Cuba is a rum-soaked country of cigars, rhythm and beauty, where Communism, Catholicism and voodoo coexist. Since the 1959 revolution this has been Communism in the sunshine, but now it's lived without nuclear weapons, Soviet friends, money or trade with the US. Life may begin at 40, but it also begins to show. Castro's Cuba, whose politics and economy have been moulded by the man, is suffering severe shortages and rationing under the deepening US embargo, as well as sheer physical deterioration. Officially there's full employment but this seems to include begging, so take a supply of chewing-gum, pens, or soap – valuable currency.

It's now pitching hard for tourist dollars, and having some success – it's currently a buzz destination. But tourism is far from institutionalised: expect low-key tourist facilities. If you're a vegetarian, learn to eat meat, particularly pigs and chickens. But don't come for the food. The hit-and-miss standards usually miss, even in the best hotels. Be prepared to survive on drink. The locals probably run their cars on the cheapest rum ('aguardiente'), there are real Cuba Libres and good local beer, and the non-alcoholic sugar cane juice ('guarapo') is welcome in the heat. Get a cheap hit (around $1.50) from a devilishly refreshing 'moji-to' (rum, sugar, crushed mint, ice and sparkling water). Sink a couple of these and your salsa will improve immediately. It's mysterious that with all the fruit grown on the island you'll rarely see any, or be offered its juice.

The choice of take-home goodies is dire. Cigars, of course, are everywhere. Dodgy men lurk around the tourist haunts and offer 15 for $10. Be warned. These are the unofficial, low-quality variety that the government will confiscate if they find them in your luggage – officially you're only allowed to export good-quality cigars such as Cohibas, and a limited amount of those. You'll see gaudy naive art, but maracas and 'claves' (rhythm sticks) make better and cheap mementos (around $1). Street markets sell dubious quality tapes and CDs. Seek out 'Hasta Siempre', Carlos Puebla's songs of the revolution – celebratory, plaintive and rhythmic stuff. Che Guevara T-shirts for $6-$10 always go down well back home. (The Jim Morrison look-alike also looms large on billboards, Big Brother-like, extolling the virtues of hard work and revolutionary zeal; the revolutionary martyr whose personality keeps the regime alive – even though he was Argentinian and died in 1967).

There are two seasons here – wet and dry. Both are hot and neither is really that much wetter or drier than the other. Officially the wettest and warmest months are from May to October. Expect year-round temperatures of between 26-32°C.

Havana

If any one part of Havana typifies Cuba, it's the sweeping curve of the **Malecon** – a wide deserted promenade. On one side is an endless arc of beautiful but decaying colonnaded buildings, on the other the sea lapping against low walls where lovers sit to cradle each other and yet more shady characters lurk offering whatever you might want. (Watch the film *Strawberry and Chocolate* for a taste of the scene.)

Havana is a place to absorb life and atmosphere – a glorious, shabby and lively city unlike any other. Cars don't constipate the streets (but there are plenty of 1950s Buicks, Chevrolets and Dodges), there are few shops and locals queue at those that do exist, often for hours. Don't expect bars and restaurants on every street. The sounds of son, salsa and lambada creep out of doorways and along the pavements. Music and sex are the only things that aren't rationed. Wander round just for the hell of it, exploring the grid of streets lined with magnificent buildings. The rewards are great – invitingly down-at-heel back streets and squares of faded elegance (such as the **Plaza de Armas**) dappled with Caribbean sunlight. There's no glitz

here – it's real and it's falling down. Stroll along **Calle Obispo** with its old drugstores and evening promenaders or laze in the Parque Central. **Calle Oficios**, where scribes used to write wills and love letters for the early settlers, is a heady place.

Where to stay

Choose a hotel in Habana Vieja, the old town. The **Inglaterra** (Prado 416; 7 33 8593), with its colonial architecture, interior patio and rooftop bar is expensive but superb (around $100 for a double room) and the **Sevilla** (Trocadero 55; 7 33 8566) is attractive and in the thick of Havana life. If you're here for a while and don't mind a taxi or bus from the newer and more modern hotels springing up in the Vedado district, try the **Melia Cohiba** (Avenue Passeo; 7 33 3636). But nothing can match the **Nacional Hotel** (between Calles O and 21; 7 33 3564/3569) – a gem, with prices to match ($180 double), where rooms and the gardens overlook the ocean. It's straight out of Graham Greene – the Mafia used to meet here, and some say still do.

For a night out that's 'in your face', **Club Tropicana** is the place (Calle 72 at 41, Marianao; 7 27 0110). Half-naked men and women demonstrate 101 ways to wear large feathers, gyrating under bright lights to distorted music.

Where to eat, drink & hang out

There are several Hemingway haunts. A must is **El Floridita** restaurant (Calle Obispo 557; 7 63 1060/1063), where the daiquiri was invented and Hemingway, never a man to be seen sipping tea from bone china, drank them like they were about to be rationed. Or hang out in **La Bodequita** de Medio (Calle Empedrado 207; 7 62 4498) with a mojito. A short taxi ride or a number 58 bus ride six miles east is the village of Cojimar, where **Las Terrazas** (Calle Real y Candelaria; 7 65 3471) provides a breezy bar and eatery with good if expensive food. Huge windows overlook the sleepy port where the man moored his boat for deep sea fishing and wrote *The Old Man and the Sea*.

If you want to mix with the people, don't hang out in hotel bars – Cubans aren't allowed there. Go to the Old Town and explore the area round **Plaza de Armas** and the **Plaza del Catedral**, or have a coffee on the shaded bar terrace of the **El Patio Colonial**, near the spectacular cathedral.

Or simply join the throng for Mass on Sunday mornings. If you have a couple of hours to spare, queue under the trees at the **Coppelia** ice-cream parlour (Avenida 23 and Calle L). This is a meeting place for Cubans (particularly young, although it's illegal to be openly homosexual here) and the ice-cream's actually very good. But the best way to chill out with the locals is to catch a ferry to the **San Carlos de la Cabana** fort, where you'll find a number of bars where you can sip rum and watch the sunset.

When you're leaving Havana's airport it's worth checking in early. A bamboo hut at one end of the departure area offers cheap mojitos and live samba. Buy some 'claves' and maracas from the shop and play along. It's the best send off you could have – you may even hope your flight is delayed.

Beyond Havana

Use Havana as a base to explore **Pinar Del Rio** and the **Vinales Valley**, 110 miles to the west. In Pinar city there's the ubiquitous Coppelia ice-cream parlour but not much else. North of Pinar at **Cayajabos** is Hotel Moka, a lush ecological oasis with pool and air-conditioned rooms. **Vinales** town is a sleepy, laid-back place with an abundance of verandahs and rocking chairs. Hotel Los Jazmines, three miles south, has amazing views over the valley. A couple of miles up the road to Minos de Matahambre follow signs to the huge 'Prehistoric Mural' rock painting – painted in around 1960. But the simple food at the restaurant is worth a trip – if you don't mind sharing a communal meal with coachloads of Spanish and Italian tourists. The draw is tasty suckling pig marinated for days in orange juice and herbs before roasting in brick ovens, served with moros and christianos (rice and beans) and local beer. The surrounding countryside should not be missed. Head four miles north of Vinales on the road to Puerta Esperanza for the **Cueva del Indio** – dark caves through the mountains which can be explored by small boat.

Take the Via Blanca 60 miles east of Havana to **Matanzas**. This is Cuba's Venice, with several rivers, lots of bridges and a few grand buildings – but there the similarity ends, though exploration, as with other Cuban cities, does bring rewards. Buses from Havana are crowded and take hours. Another 25 miles on and you're at **Varadero**. Here a long white-sand peninsula is lined with modern international hotels and offers all the usual hedonistic pleasures for the beach bum. The best thing is its proximity to Havana. The beaches are beautiful and the sea is warm, but you could be on any beach almost anywhere in the world, and only the Cubans who work in the package hol hotels and bars are allowed here.

Trinidad is a 'pinch me I must be dreaming' UNESCO World Heritage site six hours by car from Havana. There is not a single concession to tourism, although it's on the up-and-up with major renovation underway. There are cobbled streets and beautiful buildings, few tourist hotels, no billboards and hardly any cars – the locals get around in horse-drawn carts. Almost all the buildings are one storey, so life really is lived at street level. Soak up the rum and the laid-back atmosphere in the shaded courtyard of La Canchanchara tavern (Martinez Villena; 419 4345). There are museums devoted to local archaeology and architecture, but best of all is the beautiful Museu Romantico, with interior patio, gorgeous furniture, marble floors and lovely views from its balcony. Eight miles away are the ugly tourist beach hotels: Hotel Ancon (Playa Ancon; 419 4011) a Soviet-style block, and the even plug-uglier Hotel Horizontes Costasur (419 2524), surrounded by acres of flat salt marshes and miles of beachcombing territory. The food is mostly buffet-style mediocrity (better than most in Cuba, though), discos throb into the next day and cabaret includes synchronised swimming to distorted US pop songs. But the best reason to stay is the short trip into Trinidad. Get out to the **Valley of the Sugar Mills**, too, and up into the cool of the **Escambray mountains**.

Cienfuegos has animated streetlife and markets selling parts from disposable lighters and other junk in abundance. A visit to the mock-Moorish Palacio de Valle restaurant (Punta Gorda; 432 9605) is like eating in Spain's Alhambra Palace. The lobster's wonderful, if expensive, and Carmen Miranda's mother plays the piano and blows kisses to male customers. Or simply sip Cuban coffee under one of the rooftop pagodas. The nearby Hotel Jagua (1 Punta Gorda, Calle 37; 432 3021) has a terrace overlooking the bay.

Cuba's central lands are flat and frankly boring. The **Sierra Meastra**, the highest and most spectacular mountains, are at the far east, as is **Guantanamo**, where a US Naval base bides its time uncomfortably until its lease runs out in 2033. **Santiago de Cuba** has an international airport and a very different atmosphere to other Cuban cities. It feels Caribbean and cosmopolitan. Coffee is grown in the hills and life is lived at a faster pace than elsewhere.

Getting there

There's no need to pre-book accommodation. As long as you've got a passport and a tourist card you can simply turn up. Cuban consulate offices, airlines, travel agents and tour operators will supply the card, which permits a stay of up to 30 days. (US citizens can only get a card outside the US, usually at the staging post on their journey.) International flights from all over the world arrive at Havana (Jose Marti Airport) and Varadero in the west, and Santiago de Cuba, Holguin and Camaguey in the east. **Cubana**, the national airline (0171 734 1165 in London, [53] 7 33 4949 in Cuba), runs scheduled flights from most European countries, including three weekly scheduled flights from London Gatwick to Havana. There are also Cubana flights from many of the Caribbean islands.

Officially there are no direct air or sea routes from the US for tourists. Some US citizens, such as journalists and researchers, can get permission to fly direct to Cuba from Miami, but flights are expensive, are not announced at the airport, and spookily don't appear on the departures board. If you can't get on one of these you'll have to go to a third country and fly into Cuba from there. The Bahamas, Mexico (Cancun) and Jamaica are the preferred en-routes from Miami (**Bahamasair** 1-800 222 4262; **Mexicana Airlines** 1-800 531 7921; **Air Jamaica** 1-800 523 5585); fly there, then transfer to a Cubana flight (daily from Cancun, twice a week from Kingston and charter only from Nassau, bookable through **Havanatur**, *see below* **Getting Around**). You will need the appropriate entry documents for the interim country.

Charters will take you from the UK direct to Varadero and other airports in the east of the island. Look around for the increasing number of companies offering sun and sand package deals and charter flights from around the world.

Getting around

The half-hour trip from Jose Marti airport to central Havana is best tackled by taxi – around $18. In a country where there is a shortage of transport and fuel to make it move, getting around isn't simple. Hitch-hiking is a way of life for Cubans and is the best way to meet them. You'll have to queue, maybe for hours, to squeeze onto one of the infrequent local buses. Long-haul coaches are busy and often booked up weeks in advance – especially at weekends. There's even a waiting list. And 'camels' – huge people carriers pulled by trucks – criss-cross the island carrying up to 300 in a sweaty crush. Hire cars, taxis, organised coach trips and domestic flights are the most reliable transport. They're more expensive but worth it if you have limited time. Many of the main hotels will help with arrangements.

For car hire contact **Havanautos** (505 Calle 36, Havana; 7 24 2369). Excursions and tours can be arranged through **Cubatur** (La Rampa, Calle 23, Havana; 7 32 4521) and **Rumbos** (60 Esquina a M, El Vedado, Plaza, Havana; 7 66 2113), both government organisations which own and run most of the tourist hotels, restaurants and bars. **Havanatur** tend to look after those on packages (17 Calle 2, Miramar, Havana; 7 22 8273).

Money & safety

Credit cards and travellers cheques (in US dollars) are useful, although US citizens may find their credit companies getting shirty when they find out where they've been spending their money. American Express travellers cheques should be OK, but don't risk any other US brands. US dollars are the accepted currency.

Any Cuban goods you bring back into the US may be confiscated by customs, including cigars. No inoculations are necessary and healthcare for visitors and Cubans is excellent, though not free, so insurance is a must. You'll be pestered, particularly by children, but safe – crime isn't a big issue. Just stay alert and don't wave around wads of cash.

If you're phoning from abroad just dial the appropriate exit code, then 53 for Cuba, followed by the area code and then the local number. Area codes for the main places are: Havana – 7; Cienfuegos – 432; Trinidad – 419; Santiago de Cuba – 226; Vinales – 8. We have included these in the numbers given, but if you're dialling from within the area you can drop the prefix. Note that though we have checked all numbers given, they are subject to frequent change.

Further Reading

Fiction

Various *Naked Came the Manatee*
A chain story co-written by 13 *Miami Herald* writers about the discovery of the head of Fidel Castro.

Russell Banks
Continental Drift
Showdown on a street in Little Haiti as the American Dream implodes.

Christine Bell
The Perez Family
Mariel refugees use their considerable talents to get a sweet immigration deal. Made into a film.

Edna Buchanan *Miami, it's Murder* and others
The strong woman protagonist is a news reporter investigating bizarre and dangerous crimes.

Ernest Hemingway
To Have and Have Not
Hemingway is virtually Key West's mascot, but *To Have and Have Not* is the only book set here.

Carl Hiaasen Various
All *Herald* columnist Hiaasen's crime novels are set in Florida, and all are sharp-edged, satirical and deliriously off-the-wall. Since he deals with local themes (theme parks in *Native Tongue*, hurricanes in *Stormy Weather* and the sex and sugar industries in *Strip Tease*), Hiaasen is as good a holiday primer as a whole shelf of non-fiction.

Marjorie Kinnan Rawlings *The Yearling*
1938's Pulitzer Prize winner documents the human story of a boy growing up in Central Florida.

Elmore Leonard Various
Not all Leonard's books are set in South Florida. Those that are include *Stick*; *La Brava*; *Gold Coast*; *Maximum Bob* and (part of) *Get Shorty*.

Peter Matthiessen *Killing Mister Watson*

The settlement of the Everglades, and how it sowed the seeds for some of South Florida's current problems.

Thomas McGuane
Ninety-Two in the Shade
Cult favourite about the quest for self-discovery of an aspiring Key West fishing guide.

John Sayles *Los Gusanos*
The film director's take on Cuban Miami.

Charles Willeford
Miami Blues
The film is better known, but the book is better, as are the others in the series, which follows Miami cop Hoke Mosely through his caseload. Very funny.

Non-fiction

Susan Weiss, ed *Miami Bibliography*
A good beginner's research guide. Published by the Historical Association of Southern Florida.

TD Allman *Miami City of the Future*
It was a contemporary classic, but things change fast here, so the social commentary now feels dated.

Barbara Beer Capitman *Deco Delights*
A photo-tour of Miami Beach's deco buildings, by the woman who played a major role in ensuring their survival.

Edna Buchanan *The Corpse had a Familiar Face*
The Pulitzer prize-winning *Miami Herald* journalist's in-your-face account of her years covering one of the world's edgiest crime beats.

David Leon Chandler *Henry Flagler*
The lowdown on the 'Robber Baron' who was largely responsible for establishing Miami's infrastructure.

Joan Didion *Miami*
Compelling impressions of the meltdown pot.

Michael Gannon *The New History of Florida*
History divided according to theme.

Howard Kleinberg *Miami Beach: A History*

Stuart B McIver *Dreamer, Schemers & Scallawags: The Florida Chronicles*
The underground history of Florida's mobsters, gamblers and risk-takers.

Gary Monroe *Life in South Beach*
Black and white photographs of pre-renaissance South Beach.

Ralph Middleton Munroe & Vincent Gilpin
The Commodore's Story: The Early Days on Biscayne Bay
Settlement memoirs from the Coconut Grove pioneer, chronicling Miami's hard early days.

Miami, USA *Helen Muir*
Updated historical classic.

Arva Moore Parks *Miami, The Magic City*
The official history of the city, with many pictures.

David Rieff *Going to Miami: Exiles, Tourists and Refugees in the New America*
Losing its power to shock a decade on from publication, but still a controversial vision of Miami alienated from the US.

Rolf Shields *Bought and Sold*
A no-gloss history of Miami.

Marjory Stoneman Douglas *The Everglades: River of Grass*
A personal testament to the vulnerable beauty of the Everglades that kick-started the conservation programme in the 1940s. An environmental classic.

Alexander Stuart
Life on Mars
Moving, observant and funny essays on the heart and souls of Florida, from the renowned British writer. A must-read.

Advertisers' Index

Please refer to the relevant sections for
addresses/telephone numbers

Index

Section sponsored by
AT&T

Maps

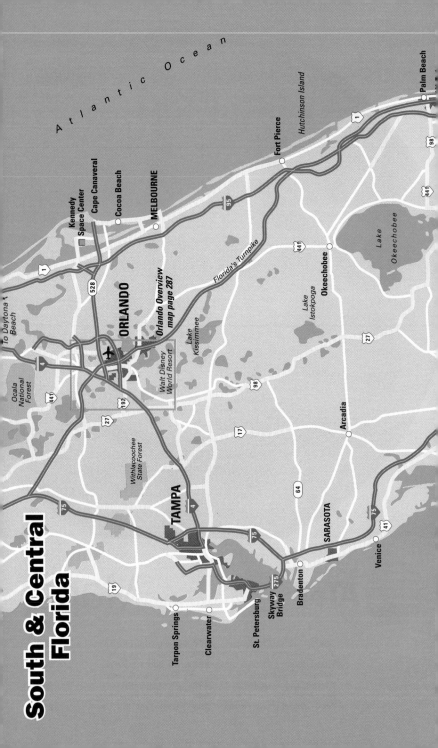

South & Central Florida

Atlantic Ocean

To Daytona Beach

Ocala National Forest

Withlacoochee State Forest

Walt Disney World Resort

ORLANDO

Orlando Overview map page 287

Kennedy Space Center

Cape Canaveral

Cocoa Beach

MELBOURNE

Fort Pierce

Hutchinson Island

Palm Beach

Lake Okeechobee

Okeechobee

Lake Istokpoga

Lake Kissimmee

Florida's Turnpike

Arcadia

TAMPA

SARASOTA

Bradenton

Venice

Skyway Bridge

St. Petersburg

Clearwater

Tarpon Springs

95

1

98

441

527

528

192

27

19

75

4

17

98

64

75

41

275

441

1

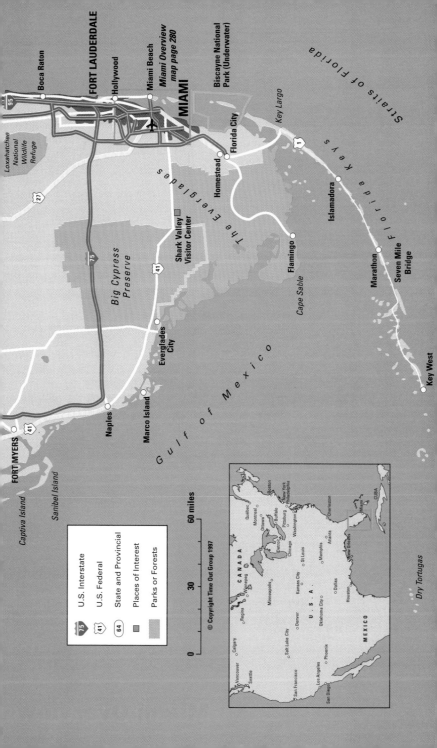

Miami Overview

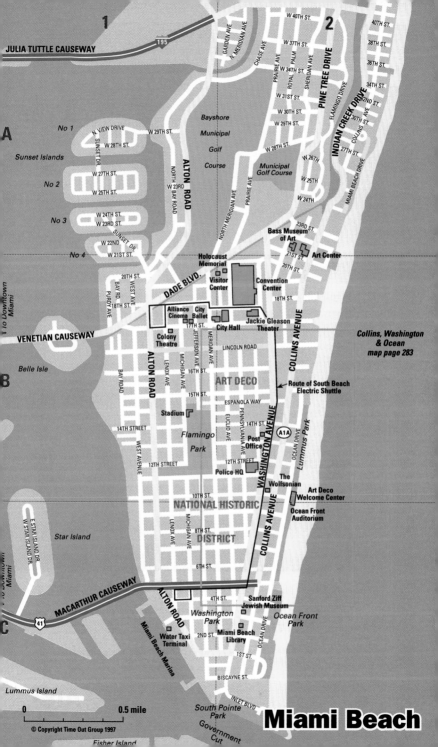

Miami Beach

1

JULIA TUTTLE CAUSEWAY

195

No 1

Sunset Islands

No 2

No 3

No 4

N. VIEW DRIVE

W 29TH ST.

W 28TH ST.

SUNSET DR.

W 27TH ST.

W 25TH ST.

W 24TH ST.

W 23RD ST.

W 22ND ST.

W 21ST ST.

SUNSET DR.

NORTH BAY ROAD

ALTON ROAD

Bayshore
Municipal
Golf
Course

2

GARDEN AVE

N MERIDIAN AVE

W 40TH ST.

W 37TH ST.

CHASE AVE

PRAIRIE AVE

ROYAL PALM AVE

SHERIDAN AVE

W 34TH ST.

W 31ST ST.

W 30TH ST.

W 29TH ST.

PINE TREE DRIVE

FLAMINGO DRIVE

INDIAN CREEK DRIVE

40TH ST.

38TH ST.

36TH ST.

34TH ST.

32ND ST.

30TH ST.

27TH ST.

COLLINS AVE

MIAMI BEACH DRIVE

A

Municipal

Golf Course

W 28TH ST.

W 26TH

W 25TH

W 24TH

NORTH MERIDIAN AVE

PRAIRIE AVE

23RD ST.

Bass Museum
of Art

21ST ST.

20TH ST.

Art Center

VENETIAN CAUSEWAY

Belle Isle

B

To Downtown
Miami

BAY RD.
WEST AVE.

20TH ST.

PURDY AVE

18TH ST.

DADE BLVD.

Holocaust
Memorial

Visitor
Center

Convention
Center

18TH ST.

Alliance
Cinema

City
Ballet

City Hall

Jackie Gleason
Theater

JEFFERSON AVE.

MERIDIAN AVE.

Colony
Theatre

17TH ST.

Lincoln Road

LENOX AVE.

MICHIGAN AVE.

ALTON ROAD

16TH ST.

BAY ROAD

ART DECO

15TH ST.

ESPANOLA WAY

Stadium

14TH STREET

WEST AVENUE

Flamingo

Park

12TH STREET

PENNSYLVANIA AVE

EUCLID AVE.

14TH ST.

Post
Office

12TH STREET

Police HQ

COLLINS AVENUE

WASHINGTON AVENUE

OCEAN DRIVE

A1A

Lummus Park

Route of South Beach
Electric Shuttle

*Collins, Washington
& Ocean
map page 283*

C

To Downtown
Miami

E STAR ISLAND DR.
W STAR ISLAND DR.

Star Island

NATIONAL HISTORIC

DISTRICT

MICHIGAN AVE.

LENOX AVE.

10TH ST.

8TH ST.

6TH ST.

The
Wolfsonian

Art Deco
Welcome Center

Ocean Front
Auditorium

COLLINS AVENUE

MACARTHUR CAUSEWAY

41

ALTON ROAD

Water Taxi
Terminal

Miami Beach Marina

4TH ST.

Washington
Park

2ND ST.

Miami Beach
Library

1ST ST.

Sanford Ziff
Jewish Museum

Ocean Front
Park

OCEAN DRIVE

BISCAYNE ST.

Lummus Island

0   0.5 mile

© Copyright Time Out Group 1997

INLET BLVD.

South Pointe
Park

Government
Cut

Fisher Island

How to get from Peoria to Pretoria.

©1997

AND **1 800 CALL ATT**® GETS YOU FROM
THE U.S. TO THE WORLD.

It's all within your reach.

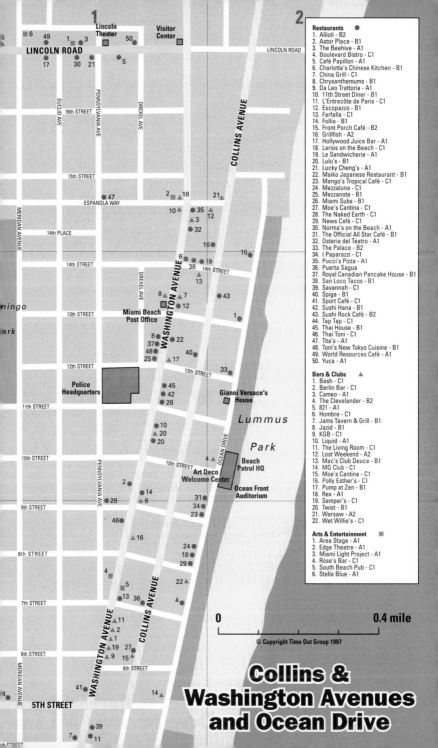

© Copyright Time Out Group 1997

Downtown Miami

Restaurants ●
1. Big Fish - C1
2. Capital Grille - C2
3. East Coast Fisheries - B1
4. Fishbone Grill - C1
5. The Fish Market - A2
6. Greenwich Village - C1
7. Hard Rock Café - B2
8. Los Ranchos - B2
9. Porcao - C2
10. Tobacco Road - C1

Accommodation ●
1. Everglades Hotel - B2
2. Hotel Intercontinental - C2

Arts & Entertainment ■
1. 3rd Street Black Box - B2
2. Gusman Center - B2
3. Metro-Dade Cultural Center
   (Historical Museum of Southern
   Florida, Miami Art Museum,
   Metro-Dade Public Library) - B1
4. Miami Arena - B1
5. Miami-Dade Community
   College Centre Gallery - B2

To Miami International Airport

NE 1ST AVE
E 1ST COURT

Omni International

VENETIAN CAUSEWAY

NE 15TH STREET

NE 14TH TERRACE

Miami Herald Building

NE 14TH STREET

MACARTHUR CAUSEWAY

NE 13TH STREET

41

395

BISCAYNE BOULEVARD

Bicentennial

N. MIAMI AVENUE

NE 11TH STREET

NE 2ND AVE

NE 9TH STREET

Park

NE 7TH STREET

Bay of Miami

NW 2ND AVE
NW 1ST AVE

Overtown

Miami Arena

Greyhound Terminal

NW7TH STREET

Post Office

Freedom Tower

NW 5TH STREET

State Plaza

NE 5TH STREET

Edcom

Bayside Market Place

HMS Bounty Exhibit

I-95

NW 3RD STREET

Courthouse

American Express

College

Bayside Amphitheater

Lummus Park

Government Center

NE 3RD STREET

Miami Dade Community College

1

7

Metro-Dade Cultural Center

NW 1ST STREET

1st Street

Bayfront

W. FLAGLER ST.

Metromover

Park

SW 1ST ST.

Miami Ave

E. FLAGLER ST.

World Trade Center

SE 1ST ST.

Bayfront Park

SW 2ND AVE

Fort Dallas Park

SE 2ND ST.

Nationsbank Building

World Trade Center

2

NORTH RIVER DR

SW 3RD STREET

Convention Center /Knight Center

SE 4TH ST

Brickell Key

95

Metrorail

SW 2ND AVE

SE 5TH STREET

Brickell Park

4
10
1

SE 6TH STREET

S. MIAMI AVENUE

SW 6TH ST.

BRICKELL AVENUE

SW 7TH ST.

SE 7TH ST.

Convention & Visitors Bureau

SW8TH ST.

SE 8TH ST.

0   0.8 mile

SW 1ST AVE

BRICKELL PLAZA

9

SW 10TH STREET

Brickell

6

SE 10TH ST.

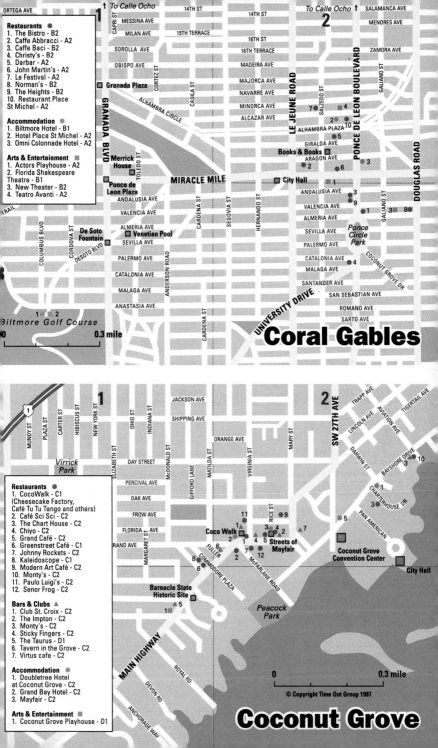

Coral Gables

ORTEGA AVE

1

To Calle Ocho
14TH ST — 14TH ST

CAPRI ST

MESSINA AVE

MILAN AVE

15TH TERRACE

SOROLLA AVE

16TH ST

16TH TERRACE

OBISPO AVE

MADEIRA AVE

Restaurants ●
1. The Bistro - B2
2. Caffe Abbracci - A2
3. Caffe Baci - A2
4. Christy's - B2
5. Darbar - A2
6. John Martin's - A2
7. Le Festival - A2
8. Norman's - B2
9. The Heights - B2
10. Restaurant Place
St Michel - A2

Accommodation ●
1. Biltmore Hotel - B1
2. Hotel Place St Michel - A2
3. Omni Colonnade Hotel - A2

Arts & Entertainment ■
1. Actors Playhouse - A2
2. Florida Shakespeare
Theatre - B1
3. New Theater - B2
4. Teatro Avanti - A2

2

To Calle Ocho

SALAMANCA AVE

MENORES AVE

ZAMORA AVE

MAJORCA AVE

NAVARRE AVE

MINORCA AVE

ALCAZAR AVE

LE JEUNE ROAD

PONCE DE LEON BOULEVARD

GALIANO ST

ALHAMBRA PLAZA

7   SALZEDO ST   4

2   10

5

GIRALDA AVE

Books & Books ■

ARAGON AVE   6   3

ANDALUSIA AVE   3

VALENCIA AVE   9

ALMERIA AVE   1

SEVILLA AVE   Ponce   3
Circle
PALERMO AVE   Park

GALIANO ST

1   8

DOUGLAS ROAD

CATALONIA AVE   4

MALAGA AVE

SANTANDER AVE

COCONUT GROVE DR

SAN SEBASTIAN AVE

ROMANO AVE

SARTO AVE

GRANADA BLVD

CAPRI ST

CORTEZ ST

CASILA ST

ALHAMBRA CIRCLE

Granada Plaza ■

Merrick
House ■

Ponce
de Leon Plaza ■

TOLEDO ST

MIRACLE MILE

City Hall ■

ANDALUSIA AVE

CARDENA ST

SEGOVIA ST

HERNANDO ST

TRAIL

COLUMBUS BLVD

CORDOVA ST

DESOTO BLVD

De Soto
Fountain ●

Venetian Pool ■

ANDALUSIA AVE

VALENCIA AVE

ALMERIA AVE

SEVILLA AVE

PALERMO AVE

CATALONIA AVE

MALAGA AVE

ANASTASIA AVE

ANDERSON ROAD

1   2

Biltmore Golf Course

0   0.3 mile

CARDENA ST

UNIVERSITY DRIVE

Coral Gables

Coconut Grove

1

1

MUNDY ST

PLAZA ST

CARTER ST

HIBISCUS ST

NEW YORK ST

OHIO ST

INDIANA ST

JACKSON AVE

SHIPPING AVE

2

SW 27TH AVE

2

TRAPP AVE

TIGERTAIL AVE

LINCOLN AVE

AVIATION AVE

Virrick
Park

ELIZABETH ST

DAY STREET

McDONALD ST

MATILDA ST

VIRGINIA ST

ORANGE AVE

MARY ST

DARWIN ST

BAYSHORE DRIVE

3   10

PERCIVAL AVE

CHARTERHOUSE DR

1

PAN AMERICAN

Restaurants ●
1. CocoWalk - C1
(Cheesecake Factory,
Café Tu Tu Tango and others)
2. Café Sci Sci - C2
3. The Chart House - C2
4. Chiyo - C2
5. Grand Café - C2
6. Greenstreet Café - C1
7. Johnny Rockets - C2
8. Kaleidoscope - C1
9. Modern Art Café - C2
10. Monty's - C2
11. Paulo Luigi's - C2
12. Senor Frog - C2

Bars & Clubs ▲
1. Club St. Croix - C2
2. The Impton - C2
3. Monty's - C2
4. Sticky Fingers - C2
5. The Taurus - D1
6. Tavern in the Grove - C2
7. Virtus cafe - C2

Accommodation ●
1. Doubletree Hotel
at Coconut Grove - C2
2. Grand Bay Hotel - C2
3. Mayfair - C2

Arts & Entertainment ■
1. Coconut Grove Playhouse - D1

OAK AVE

FROW AVE

FLORIDA AVE

RAND AVE

GIFFORD LANE

MARGARET ST

3   5

COMMODORE PLAZA

FULLER

11

Coco Walk ▲

RICE ST   9

3   4   2   7

2   1

6   1   5   Streets of
Mayfair

2   12

McFARLANE ROAD

8

6

Barnacle State
Historic Site ■

1   5

Peacock
Park

MAIN HIGHWAY

ROYAL RD

DEVON RD

ANCHORAGE WAY

5

Coconut Grove
Convention Center ■

City Hall ■

0   0.3 mile

© Copyright Time Out Group 1997

Coconut Grove

Miami Street Index

Please note that numbered streets and avenues are not listed in this index. For an explanation of how Miami's grid system works, *see* page 52 **Orientation**.

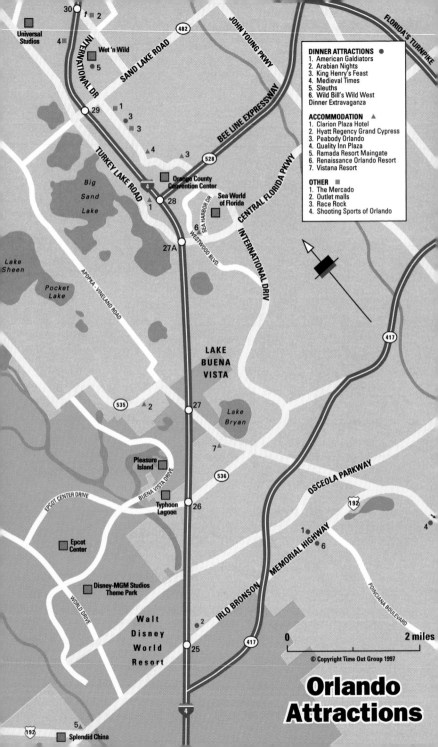

Orlando
Attractions

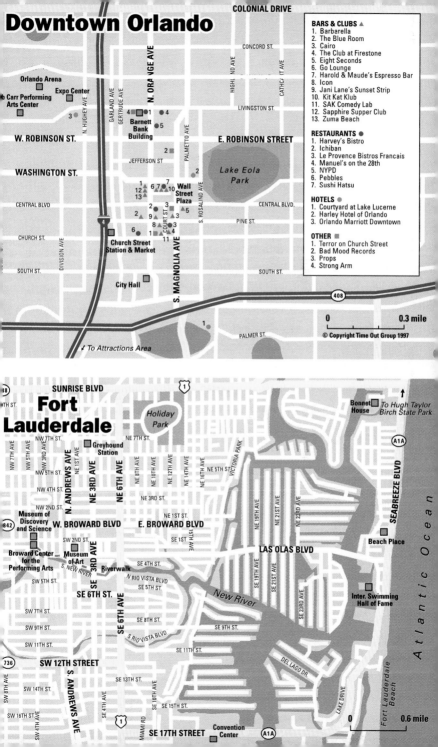

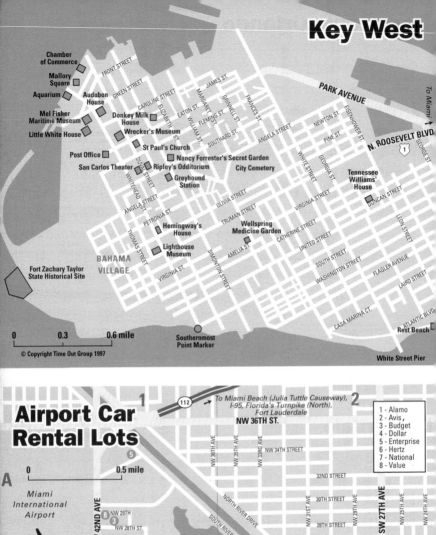

Key West

Chamber of Commerce

Mallory Square

Aquarium

Audubon House

Mel Fisher Maritime Museum

Donkey Milk House

Little White House

Wrecker's Museum

Post Office

St Paul's Church

San Carlos Theater

Nancy Forrester's Secret Garden

Ripley's Odditorium

City Cemetery

Greyhound Station

Tennessee Williams' House

Hemingway's House

Wellspring Medicine Garden

Lighthouse Museum

BAHAMA VILLAGE

Fort Zachary Taylor State Historical Site

FRONT STREET

GREEN STREET

CAROLINE STREET

EATON ST.

FLEMING ST.

SOUTHARD ST.

ANGELA STREET

JAMES ST.

MARGARET ST.

GRINNELL ST.

FRANCES ST.

NEWTON ST.

PINE ST.

PARK AVENUE

EISENHOWER ST.

N. ROOSEVELT BLVD

To Miami

GEORGE ST.

WHITE STREET

GEORGIA ST.

VIRGINIA STREET

DUNCAN STREET

LEON STREET

CATHERINE STREET

UNITED STREET

SOUTH STREET

WASHINGTON STREET

FLAGLER AVENUE

LAIRD STREET

ATLANTIC BLVD

ELIZABETH ST.

WILLIAM ST.

DUVAL STREET

WHITEHEAD STREET

ANGELA ST.

PETRONIA ST.

THOMAS STREET

OLIVIA STREET

TRUMAN AVENUE

AMELIA ST.

SIMONTON STREET

VIRGINIA ST.

CASA MARINA CT.

Rest Beach

Southernmost Point Marker

White Street Pier

0   0.3   0.6 mile

© Copyright Time Out Group 1997

Airport Car Rental Lots

To Miami Beach (Julia Tuttle Causeway), I-95, Florida's Turnpike (North), Fort Lauderdale

112

NW 36TH ST.

1 - Alamo
2 - Avis
3 - Budget
4 - Dollar
5 - Enterprise
6 - Hertz
7 - National
8 - Value

Miami International Airport

0   0.5 mile

A

NW 34TH STREET

32ND STREET

30TH STREET

28TH STREET

26TH STREET

24TH STREET

NORTH RIVER DRIVE

SOUTH RIVER DRIVE

NW 42ND AVE

NW 38TH AVE

NW 35TH AVE

NW 33RD AVE

NW 31ST AVE

NW 29TH AVE

SW 27TH AVE

NW 25TH AVE

NW 24TH AVE

24TH COURT

8 NW 29TH

3 NW 28TH ST.

NW 27TH ST.

NW 26TH ST.

NW 25TH ST.

2

NW 24TH ST.

38TH CT.

NW 37TH AVE

24TH ROAD

7

1

NW 22ND ST.

NW 21ST ST.

6

Sheraton Hotel

NW 20TH ST.

NW 20TH S

NW 19TH ST.

B

NW 35TH AVE

NW 34TH AVE

NW 18TH ST.

NW 17TH ST.

NW 16TH ST.

NW 32ND AVE

NW 30TH AVE

NW TAMIAMI CANAL DR

42ND COURT

4

To Coral Gables, US 1

836

To Florida's Turnpike (South), Key West

Marriot Hotel

To Downtown Miami, Miami Beach (Venetian Causeway), South Beach (MacArthur Causeway)